Children, Teachers and Schools in the History of British Columbia

Edited by

Jean Barman,
Neil Sutherland
J. Donald Wilson

Detselig Enterprises Ltd.
Calgary, Alberta, Canada

Children, Teachers and Schools in the History of British Columbia

© Detselig Enterprises Ltd., 1995

Canadian Cataloguing in Publication Data

Children, teachers and schools in the history of British Columbia

Includes bibliographical references.
ISBN 1-55059-103-7

1. Education--British Columbia--History. I. Barman, Jean,
   1939- II. Sutherland, Neil, 1931- III. Wilson, J. Donald.
   LA418.B7C54 1995   370'.9711   C95-910318-X

Publisher's Data
Detselig Enterprises Ltd.
210, 1220 Kensington Road, N.W.
Calgary, Alberta T2N 3P5

*Detselig Enterprises Ltd. appreciates the financial support for our 1995
publishing program provided by the Department of Canadian Heritage,
Canada Council and the Alberta Foundation for the Arts, a beneficiary of
the Lottery Fund of the Government of Alberta.*

Front cover painting: Maple Bay, Vancouver Island, B.C., by noted B.C. artist E.J.
Hughes. Thank you to Pat Salmon and E.J. Hughes for permission to use this painting and to the Dominion Gallery of Montreal.

Back cover: South Cedar School in the 1880s. South Cedar was in the countryside behind Maple Bay. BCARS F-4280.

Cover design by Bill Matheson

Printed in Canada   ISBN 1-55059-103-7   SAN 115-0324

*To our fellow historians of education
John Calam and Jorgen Dahlie.*

Permissions

Permissions have been granted for the following: chapter 1 is reprinted from Nancy M. Sheenan, J. Donald Wilson and David C. Jones, eds., *Schools in the West* (Calgary: Detselig Enterprises Ltd., 1986); chapter 2 reprinted from J.A. Mangan, ed., *Making Imperial Mentalities: Socialization and British Imperialism* (Manchester: Manchester University Press, 1990); chapter 4 adapted from *History of Education Review* 15, 2 (1986); chapter 5 adapted from R.A.J. McDonald and Jean Barman, eds., *Vancouver Past: Essays in Social History* (Vancouver: University of British Columbia Press, 1986); chapter 6 adapted from *Histoire sociale/Social History* 24 (November 1991); chapter 11 adapted from *BC Studies* 79 (Autumn 1988); chapter 14 reprinted from Alison Prentice and Marjorie Theobald, eds., *Women Who Taught: Perspectives on the History of Women and Teaching* (Toronto: University of Toronto Press, 1991); chapter 15 reprinted from *Journal of Education for Teaching* 20 (January 1994); chapter 16 reprinted from Rebecca Priegert Coulter and Ivor F. Goodson, eds., *Rethinking Vocationalism: whose work/life is it?* (Toronto: Our Schools/Our Selves, 1993); chapter 17 adapted from Jean Barman, Yvonne Hébert and Don McCaskill, eds., *Indian Education in Canada*, vol. 1: *The Legacy* (Vancouver: UBC Press, 1986); chapter 18 adapted from J. Donald Wilson and David C. Jones, ed., *Schooling and Society in 20th Century British Columbia* (Calgary: Detselig Enterprises, 1980); chapter 19 adapted from *Historical Studies in Education* 4 (1992); chapter 20 adapted from *Canadian Journal of Education* 16, 1 (1991); and chapter 21 adapted from *Policy Explorations* 3, 1 (Winter 1988).

Table of Contents

Introduction *9*

Beginnings

1 The Emergence of Educational Structures in Nineteenth-Century
   British Columbia, *Jean Barman* *15*

Part 1. Childhood and Pupilhood

2 White Supremacy and the Rhetoric of Educational Indoctrination:
   a Canadian case study, *Timothy J. Stanley* *39*

3 Schooled for Inequality: The Education of British Columbia
   Aboriginal Children, *Jean Barman* *57*

4 "Everyone seemed happy in those days": The Culture of Childhood
   in Vancouver Between the 1920s and the 1960s, *Neil Sutherland* . . .   *81*

5 The Triumph of "Formalism": Elementary Schooling in Vancouver
   from the 1920s to the 1960s, *Neil Sutherland* *101*

6 "I can't recall when I didn't help": The Working Lives of Pioneering
   Children in Twentieth-Century British Columbia, *Neil Sutherland* . . .   *125*

7 "New Canadians" or "Slaves of Satan"? The Law and the Education
   of Doukhobor Children, 1911- 1935, *John P.S. McLaren* *147*

8 "The war was a very vivid part of my life": the Second World War and
   the Lives of British Columbian Children, *Emilie L. Montgomery* *161*

9 Reflections on a Century of Canadian Childhood, *Neil Sutherland* . . .   *175*

Part 2. Becoming and Being a Teacher

10 British Columbia's Pioneer Teachers, *Jean Barman* *189*

11 "May the Lord have Mercy on You": The Rural School Problem in
    British Columbia in the 1920s, *J. Donald Wilson and Paul J. Stortz* . .   *209*

12 "Mrs. Gibson looked as if she was ready for the end of term": The
    Professional Trials and Tribulations of Rural Teachers in British
    Columbia's Okanagan Valley in the 1920s, *Penelope Stephenson* . . .   *235*

13 The Diary of Mary Williams: A Cameo of Rural Schooling in
    British Columbia, 1922-1924, *Thomas Fleming and Carolyn Smyly* . .   *259*

14 "I am ready to be of assistance when I can": Lottie Bowron and
Rural Women Teachers in British Columbia, *J. Donald Wilson* *285*

15 From Normal School to the University to the College of Teachers:
Teacher education in British Columbia in the Twentieth Century,
Nancy M. Sheehan and J. Donald Wilson *307*

Part 3. Organizing and Reorganizing Schools

16 Reflections on the Role of the School in the Transition to Work
in British Columbia Resource Towns, *Jean Barman* *323*

17 Separate and Unequal: Indian and White Girls at All Hallows
School, 1884-1920, *Jean Barman* *337*

18 Growing up British in British Columbia: The Vernon Preparatory School,
1914-1946, *Jean Barman* *359*

19 "Due to their keeness": The Education of Japanese Canadian Children
in the British Columbia Interior Housing Settlements during World
War Two, *Patricia E. Roy* *375*

20 Deprivatizing Private Education: The British Columbia Experience,
Jean Barman *393*

21 Royal Commission Retrospective, *Jean Barman and Neil Sutherland* . . *411*

About the Authors

JEAN BARMAN is a Professor in the Department of Educational Studies at the University of British Columbia. She is the author of the prize-winning *The West Beyond the West: A History of British Columbia* (1991) and co-editor of *First Nations Education in Canada: The Circle Unfolds* (1995). She is currently exploring the history of British Columbia in the late nineteenth century with particular interest in early settler families of mixed Aboriginal and non-Aboriginal descent, and in teachers and teaching.

THOMAS FLEMING is a Professor of Education at the University of Victoria. His most recent publication is *Review and Commentary on Schooling in Canada 1993: A Report to the UNESCO Office for Latin America and the Caribbean*. He is currently researching the history of school leadership, psychological testing, and school radio in British Columbia.

JOHN McLAREN is Landsdowne Professor of Law at the University of Victoria. He has recently co-edited two books, namely *Law for the Elephant, Law for the Beaver: Essays in the Legal History of the North American West* (1992) and *Essays in the History of Canadian Law*, vol. 6, *British Columbia and the Yukon* (1995). His areas of research interest include the history of race, ethnicity and the law in Canada, and the history of vice law and its enforcement in Canada.

EMILIE L. MONTGOMERY holds a M.A. from the University of British Columbia. Her thesis was entitled "'The War Was a Very Vivid Part of my Life': British Columbia School Children and the Second World War." At present, she is working full time raising her two young children and hopes to pursue a Ph.D. in the future.

PATRICIA E. ROY is a Professor of History at the University of Victoria. She is the author of *A White Man's Province* (1989), *Vancouver: An Illustrated History* (1980), and co-author of *Mutual Hostages: Canadian and Japanese during the Second World War* (1990). She is currently working on volume 2 of *A White Man's Province* and on the political history of B.C.

NANCY M. SHEEHAN is Dean of Education at the University of British Columbia. She has published widely in the area of women and reform, curriculum history, teacher education, and sexism in education. She is the co-editor of *Schools in the West: Essays in Canadian Educational History* (1986). Her research interests include the role of voluntary associations in curriculum change, and the history of women and education in Canada.

CAROLYN SMYLY is a private researcher who writes about various aspects of British Columbia's social and educational history. She lives in Victoria.

TIMOTHY J. STANLEY is a sessional lecturer in the History Department at the University of British Columbia. He uses Chinese and English language sources to examine racist state formation in turn-of-the-century British Columbia. His work has appeared in J.A. Mangan (ed.), *Making Imperial Mentalities: The British Empire and Socialization* (1990), *Historical Studies in Education,* vol. 2, no. 2 (1990), and the *Dictionary of Canadian Biography.* He is currently completing a book manuscript entitled "'White Canada' Revisited: Racism, 'the Chinese' and the Making of British Columbia Society."

PENELOPE STEPHENSON holds a M.A. in History of Education from the University of British Columbia. She is working on a book based upon her M.A. thesis entitled "Portrait in the First Person: Rural Teachers and Teaching in British Columbia's Okanagan Valley in the 1920s." She is currently teaching English as a Second Language to high school students in Toronto.

NEIL SUTHERLAND is a graduate of the University of British Columbia and the University of Minnesota. His special field of interest is the history of childhood. He teaches at the University of British Columbia and has served as a visiting professor at the University of Washington, Stirling University in Scotland, and Monash University in Australia.

PAUL J. STORTZ holds a M.A. in history of education from the University of British Columbia. His thesis was entitled "The Rural School Problem in British Columbia in the 1920s." He has co-authored articles on that subject in *BC Studies* 79 (1988) and in *Histoire sociale/Social History* 26 (1993). He is currently pursuing his Ph.D. in Higher Education at the Ontario Institute for Studies in Education where he is editor of the *Ontario Journal of Higher Education.* His doctoral thesis concerns the professoriate, research, and teaching at the University of Toronto during the Second World War.

J. DONALD WILSON is a Professor of the History of Education at the University of British Columbia. He has published widely in the area of Canadian educational history and educational policy and Canadian ethnic history especially as it relates to the Finns. He has edited or co-edited nine books including *Schools in the West: Essays in Canadian Educational History* (1986) and *Quality in Canandian Public Education: A Critical Assessment* (1988). His current interest concerns the history of racism and multiculturalism in Canada.

Introduction

We were all children once. And almost all of us, when we were children, went to school. And we had our favorite teachers.

This collection of essays is about the children we once were, the teachers we might have had, and the schools we attended, especially if we grew up in British Columbia. It is also about the children, teachers, and schools of our parents', grandparents' and great-grandparents' time. Wherever they grew up, they would likely have shared some of the experiences of their British Columbia counterparts.

Children, Teachers and Schools in the History of British Columbia offers a variety of perspectives on British Columbians' shared past. Common themes link the essays, some of which are original to the volume, others which have been published elsewhere. Children's lives are far richer than what goes on in schools. Teachers make a difference. The schools attended by British Columbia children have in the past, just as they do today, come in many different forms and kinds. The essays in *Children, Teachers and Schools* give us an opportunity to recall the child we once were, the teachers we had, and the schools we attended in the context of other children, teachers, and schools in British Columbia.

Children, Teachers and Schools is not just a book for British Columbians. Its three sections – Childhood and Pupilhood, Becoming and Being a Teacher, and Organizing and Reorganizing Schools – speak to a common experience that has reached across the Western world over the past century and a half. Many of the themes explored in the essays are central to the history of childhood and education in Canada and beyond, while others point up differences that have sometimes separated provinces and regions. Among the topics examined in *Children, Teachers and Schools* that resonate for much of Canada are the everyday life of children and teachers, the difficulties of providing schooling across vast geographical spaces, the special circumstances of rural life, differing treatment of children not regarded as part of mainstream society or who do not so consider themselves, the influence of war on children's lives, and the professionalization of teachers.

Children, Teachers and Schools opens with the creation of the first schools in British Columbia almost 150 years ago. The British North America Act of 1867 made education in Canada a provincial responsibility and, as demonstrated in "Beginnings," British Columbians accepted the challenge. Within a year of British Columbia entering the Canadian Confederation in 1871, legislation mandating common schools was enacted and a diverse group of men and women, described in "Pioneer Teachers," were at work. The educational system became increasingly complex to meet the needs of a growing province, yet remained remarkably stable over time. "Royal Commission Retrospective" reviews public schooling in British Columbia from the perspective of the special commissions that have from time to time been established to assess changing conditions. "From Normal School to the University" examines the process of becoming and being a teacher. "Reflections on a Century" looks at both continuity and change in children's lives.

Children's experiences of schooling have differed across British Columbia depending on a range of factors. One of the most critical has been race. "White Supremacy" analyzes the situation for Chinese and other non-White immigrant children. "Schooled for Inequality" and "Separate and Unequal" probe the special circumstances of Aboriginal children whose schooling was made a federal responsibility under the British North America Act. "'New Canadians' or 'Slaves of Satan'?" focuses on Doukhobor children and families who wanted, not equitable schools, but rather no public schools at all. Class and status have set some children apart, and "Growing Up British" and "Separate and Unequal" evoke daily life at two private schools catering to families self-selected out of the public system.

Childhood and pupilhood in British Columbia have also been shaped by geography. British Columbia is an extremely large and diverse province, which early on became divided between a fairly densely populated and increasingly urban southwest tip and a largely rural and sometimes very isolated rest of the province. Public schools were, and continue to be, administered out of the provincial capital of Victoria on southern Vancouver Island, whose location has virtually ensured that an urban ethos would permeate the educational system. "'Everybody seemed happy'" and "The Triumph of Formalism" recover the voices of urban children both in and out of school. The differences that long existed between urban and rural British Columbia come through even more clearly on comparison with the rural settings described in "'I can't recall'" and "'May the Lord Have Mercy,'" and the resource towns discussed in "Reflections on the Role." Geography was as important for teachers as for children, as emphasized in "'Mrs. Gibson,'" "The Diary of Mary Williams" and "'I am ready.'" These three essays, as well as "Pioneer Teachers," also highlight the ways in which gender set female teachers apart from their male counterparts.

Larger events have sometimes had dramatic consequences for children, teachers, and schools. The Second World War altered the lives of all British Columbia children, as described in "'The war was a very vivid part.'" The war was far more traumatic for children of Japanese ancestry forcibly evacuated from the Canadian west coast with their families, as examined in "'Due to their keenness.'"

Children, teachers, and schools continue to interact with the larger society that is British Columbia and Canada. "Royal Commission Retrospective" brings public schools up to the present day. "Deprivatizing" does the same for private alternatives. "From Normal School to the University" examines the current circumstances of teachers, and "Reflections" very appropriately returns us full circle to childhood and pupilhood.

Children, Teachers and Schools in the History of British Columbia joins a small number of monographs on the history of education and childhood in British Columbia. The two pioneer works on the history of schooling are F. Henry Johnson's *A History of Public Education in British Columbia* (Vancouver: UBC Publications Centre, 1964) and his *John Jessop: Goldseeker and Educator* (Vancouver: Mitchell

Press, 1971). J. Donald Wilson and David C. Jones have co-edited a volume of essays entitled *Schooling and Society in 20th Century British Columbia* (Calgary: Detselig, 1980). Rural schools are evoked in *Floating Schools and Frozen Inkwells: The One-Room Schools of British Columbia* (Madeira Park: Harbour, 1985), by Joan Adams and Becky Thomas, and in Alex Lord's *British Columbia: Recollections of a Rural School Inspector, 1915-36* (Vancouver: UBC Press, 1991), edited by John Calam. Mary Ashworth has written *The Forces Which Shaped Them: A History of Education of Minority Group Children in British Columbia* (Vancouver: New Star, 1979). The two principal volumes on private schooling in British Columbia are Sister Mary Margaret Down, *A Century of Service: A History of the Sisters of Saint Ann and Their Contribution to Education in British Columbia, the Yukon and Alaska* (Victoria: Sisters of Saint Ann, 1966), and Jean Barman, *Growing Up British in British Columbia: Boys in Private School* (Vancouver: UBC Press, 1984). *Annotated Bibliography of Educational History in British Columbia* (Victoria: Royal British Columbia Museum, 1992), compiled by Valerie Giles, is a useful guide to journal articles and theses, as well as monographs.

We especially want to thank the students in our various classes at UBC, both on campus and at Castlegar, for their assistance and patience in assessing essays for possible inclusion in this volume. We have taken their comments seriously, and hope that they and their successors are pleased with the results.

Jean Barman
Neil Sutherland
J. Donald Wilson

Vancouver, B.C.
April 1995

Beginnings

1

The Emergence of Educational Structures in Nineteenth-Century British Columbia

Jean Barman

During the third of a century between 1849 and 1886 the geographical area we know as British Columbia was transformed from an isolated British colony to a Canadian province directly linked by rail with the rest of the country. Educational structures similarly altered from a simplistic approximation of the British class-based denominational model to a free non-sectarian system similar to that desired, if not always in place for religious and political reasons, elsewhere across North America.

The alteration in educational structures is most readily explained in terms of the larger political shift: British Columbia became a Canadian province; therefore, its educational structures should as a matter of course come to resemble those already in place elsewhere in Canada.[1] Closer assessment of events suggests that such an explanation is simplistic, overemphasizing the influence of external forces on the province's development. Until the completion of the railroad, British Columbia remained geographically separated from the rest of the Dominion. Even when ideas came from elsewhere, they were worked through and very possibly modified to accommodate social and economic priorities in British Columbia.

Such was the case with education. Institutions were not imposed by a minority group within British Columbia; nor were those already in place elsewhere merely reproduced. Rather, educational structures emerged out of the needs of families living in British Columbia for schools that were universally accessible by virtue of being non-sectarian and free of cost. While this growing consensus of opinion was usefully informed by events elsewhere, in particular the geographical areas from which settlers came, it rapidly acquired its own impetus and direction in response to conditions within British Columbia.

Three stages leading to the consensus realization can be distinguished. The first years of white settlement, from 1849 to the early 1860s, witnessed the transfer of structures approximating English practice with their clear class and religious divisions between schools. Dissatisfaction with fee-based denominational education developed during the decade prior to entry into Confederation in 1871. While led primarily by settlers from within British North America and opposed most fervently by British Anglicans, the emerging consensus soon became more broadly based, resulting in new forms of schooling being enacted into law first on Vancouver Island in 1865 and then by the new province's Legislative Assembly. The third period, 1872 to 1886, saw the consensus implemented. Not only were its central premises firmly entrenched, but attempts by the major denominational groups to secure special treatment were repulsed. As well, the role to be accorded non-public schools was defined. The consequence was an educational consensus so well-suited to the particular conditions of British Columbia that it would endure virtually unaltered for almost a century.

I

White settlement on the southern tip of Vancouver Island was initiated by the decision of the Hudson's Bay fur trading company to move its western North American headquarters northward from the Oregon territory, as a consequence of the 1846 boundary settlement between the United States and Britain. The handful of Englishmen and Scots in charge of the new British colony at Victoria quite naturally continued familiar patterns of behavior, living so far as possible as if in Britain itself. To quote a contemporary, a "fairly rigid class structure" quickly developed, with clear social divisions existing between the Company's officers and "servants," as well as among the handful of settlers who came to work Company farms.[2] Schools were expected to reinforce these divisions.

In the new colony as in England, education was perceived as having two prime functions: preparation to maintain existing place within the social order, and inculcation of denominational religious beliefs. Children from poor families were best prepared to accept their own inevitably inferior position by being given only rudimentary literacy training. Conversely, children in families of high status had to be extensively educated were they to take their expected positions at the forefront of their generation. In England opportunities for poor children were limited to denominational charity schools of great simplicity, while families able to afford the fees could choose between local grammar schools and a variety of private-venture schools, generally under the oversight of clergymen of the state Church of England, or Anglican church.[3]

The Hudson's Bay Company traditionally delegated responsibility for the education of officers' children to its chaplain. Thus, the Rev. Robert Staines, an Anglican cleric who arrived from England in 1849, was to receive £200, or $1 000, a year for serving as Company chaplain, and another $1 700 for maintaining a fee-based boarding school with both beginning and advanced studies.[4] The education of "the children of the labouring and poorer classes" was a different matter. Governor James Douglas, who soon had charge of both Company and colony, proposed in late 1851 that they be provided with "one or two elementary schools" run by individuals "of strictly religious principles" and offering "a good sound English education and nothing more."[5] A young laborer who had acted as school master during the outward voyage of a group of settlers was hired to open a modest day school in Victoria for the sons of the "Company's labouring servants," with students supplying their own books and stationery, as well as contributing a $5 annual fee to supplement the teacher's salary. In 1853 a similar school was opened at Nanaimo, about 110 kilometres north of Victoria, for the children of English miners working Company coal deposits, and a third district school began a year later at the Company's agricultural settlement of Craigflower west of Victoria.[6] When a new Hudson's Bay chaplain, the Rev. Edward Cridge, arrived in 1855 he was, like his predecessor, expected to "take charge of a Boarding School of a superior class," and very soon was also given oversight of the three district schools, then enrolling about eighty pupils.[7] In addition, for Hudson's Bay servants who were French-Canadian, an alternative existed from time to time when a visiting Catholic priest would offer their children lessons. At least two private-venture girls' schools also operated, perhaps briefly.[8]

In 1858 the tranquility of this isolated British outpost of perhaps 500 non-Aboriginal people was shattered by the discovery of gold on the adjacent mainland.[9] The news having reached California just as its gold rush was in decline, the port of Victoria was inundated over the next several years with miners and entrepreneurs moving north from San Francisco as well as by adventurers from Britain and British North America. In 1858 alone some 25 000 individuals passed through Victoria on their way to the gold fields. By the end of the year the city's stable White population had reached 3 000.[10] The British Crown moved quickly to assert administrative control. Hudson's Bay oversight of the mainland was terminated and a new Colony of British Columbia was created on August 2, 1858. The Company's grant of Vancouver Island was not renewed at its expiry on May 30, 1859, and that area also passed under direct administration of the Colonial office.

The immediate effect of the gold rush on education was to extend fee-based denominational structures. The Catholic church moved most quickly. A girls' school was begun in June 1858 by the young, dynamic Quebec order of the Sisters of St. Ann, invited to the west coast by the local bishop. Its first prospectus stated boldly that "difference of religion is no obstacle to admission," and early students included not only "English, American and German" boarders with parents in the gold fields but various "girls of Victoria's upper social class."[11] Of fifty-nine boarders who enrolled during the first nine months of 1860, twenty-two had typically Jewish surnames, the majority giving their home address as "California."[12] By 1861 nearly a hundred girls were in attendance, day students assessed $35 to $60 a year in fees. Catholic boys' education fared less well: the apparent inability of the French Oblates, who dominated missionary activity, to teach in English meant that most efforts were somewhat sporadic until 1863 when Irish Oblates arrived.[13]

The Church of England was not about to be left behind. No sooner had an Anglican bishop to the two British colonies arrived in early 1860 than he was denouncing "the zealous Church of Rome," so "forward in the matter of education." Bishop George Hills reported home: "Boys of the upper class go at present to the Roman Catholic Bishop's school. . . . The case is therefore urgent." Similarly, "the whole question of Female agency in the mission is most important, in order to prevent the sapping of the very lifeblood of the future population with unsound religion and infidelity."[14] The Anglican church therefore acted quickly both to maintain religious control over the district schools and to establish fee-based schools on a par with its Catholic competition.

While three district schools continued under the supervision of the Rev. Cridge, with their operating subsidy now provided by the government, Bishop Hills personally ensured that they adhered to Anglican doctrine. For example, a farmer" who protested he "did not wish his children to be taught such trash as the Catechism" was given no alternative but to withdraw them. Use of school buildings was denied such groups as the Quakers and Jews "on the grounds that we never allow our educational or religious buildings to be used for any religious objects not in connection with the Ch[urch] of England." At the same time, these schools remained, to quote the bishop, "old fashioned & inferior"; the Rev. Cridge termed them "in an imperfect and elementary state."[15] Pupils came and went with great rapidity: during the first half of 1861, for instance, the three schools enrolled 111 students, of which forty-two had arrived during the time period and thirty-six departed.[16] Despite population growth, additional district schools were opened very slowly, one at Cedar Hill just north of Victoria in 1863 and another a year later at a small settlement in the Cowichan Valley between Victoria and Namaimo. Little incentive existed to improve or expand these schools, for they were, to quote a contemporary description of Vancouver Island, "designed for families unequal to the expense of a first-class education."[17] As Bishop Hills noted in his diary, he and the colonies' governor agreed that such "schools were only for charity children."[18]

The Anglican church focused its attention on establishing new schools "for the better classes." Collegiate School for Boys opened on May 28, 1860, and a female complement in September of the same year. Intended "for girls of the middle & upper sort," Angela College offered "careful religious training, in combination with a solid English education, and the usual accomplishments," including "music, singing, drawing, French, Italian, German & Spanish." Collegiate School was, according to its original prospectus, unique "along the shores of the Pacific." "Conducted on the principles of a superior English Grammar School" and intended "to fit the rising generation, as well for commercial and professional pursuits, as for the Universities," the school offered subjects ranging from classics and modern languages to advanced mathematics and architecture. As assessed by an English visitor of 1861, "boys receive a first class education, second only to that of our highest Public Schools."[19]

Although day student fees at the two Anglican schools ranged from $60 to $120 a year, they had immediate appeal. As one original Collegiate student, son of a Hudson's Bay surgeon, recalled, "All boys whose parents could afford it were immediately sent on the opening of the institution."[20] Among the school's first pupils were also a number of Jewish boys, sons of local businessmen, attracted by the assistant head's teaching of the "Holy Scriptures in Hebrew."[21] In similar fashion, Angela College served "the young ladies of the colony – those requiring the best education."[22] Some four dozen boys and half as many girls were enrolled by the end of 1860, the lesser appeal of Angela College probably due to the competition of St. Ann's Academy and of several private venture schools for girls. About four years later, an educational census was taken of Vancouver Island: of 500 children in school only a quarter were attending the subsidized district schools, the remainder preferring in roughly equal proportions Anglican, Catholic and private-venture alternatives.[23]

II

Even as fee-based denominational structures of education were seemingly being entrenched on colonial Vancouver Island, opposition was emerging. Centred among arrivals from within British North America, it reflected larger discontents. The historian Allan Smith has argued that by this date Ontarians already possessed a "sense of community and self-consciousness" which came "increasingly to encompass all of British North America in their vision of the national future."[24] Many Ontarians and Maritimers of relatively modest background had come to the west coast with the gold rush, only to discover in this far corner of British North America a self-contained and self-confident social order centred around the original Hudson's Bay families, which they could neither penetrate nor, indeed, provoke into confrontation. However much Amor De Cosmos, the Nova Scotian who established the *Colonist* newspaper in Victoria in December 1858, railed against the Island's monopolistic "Family-Company-Compact," he and his Canadian compatriots remained outsiders, even as newcomers from Britain were being absorbed into the established social life and coopted into administrative positions.[25]

Social and religious tensions intertwined. The Church of England had over the last two centuries become a bastion of the privileged due to the disaffection of large numbers of the lower-middle and working classes to the Non-Conformist denominations of Presbyterianism, Congregationalism and Methodism. The Anglican church's base of support was similar in British North America, where it was also identified with the dominant socio-administrative structures. Newcomers from Ontario and the Maritimes belonging for the most part to Non-Conformist, or Evangelical Protestant, denominations almost all favored greater state intervention in education to create structures intended to be in common for all the children in a community.[26] Across the United States and British North America, their contemporaries had repeatedly initiated "common" schooling along the frontier.[27] Such activity was consonant with their beliefs for, unlike the Anglicans and Catholics who considered good works and sacramental worship concomitants of salvation, Evangelical Protestants believed salvation possible only through personal conversion. Consequently, less need existed for children to be educated into ritual than for them to grow up adhering to basic Christian morality.

At first advocates of common schooling in British Columbia played within the rules established by the dominant society and created their own fee-based common schools. In August 1861, John Jessop, a Methodist school master from Ontario, opened co-educational Central School with yearly fees of about $30 to $35.[28] "Conducted exclusively on non-sectarian principles" and based "on the admirable system of Canada West [Ontario]," Central School aimed, according to its founder, at "placing the common school system here on a satisfactory basis."[29] The next spring a school run as "the Common Schools of Canada are conducted" was begun at the mainland capital of New Westminster by a missionary sent west by the Canadian Presbyterian church.[30] The schools' limitations soon became evident. For them to be truly "common" to all children necessitated the financial support of government, preferably at levels obviating fees. The New Westminster school early sought a government subsidy, and on its receipt was reorganized as a district school, still charging relatively high fees of $30 and then $18 a year.[31] As such, it continued through the 1860s, complemented in that small mainland community of several hundred White residents by fleeting private ventures, two abortive efforts of the Anglican Church, and small Catholic schools established by the Sisters of St. Ann and the Oblates.[32] By mid-decade small government-subsidized schools were also in operation at nearby Sapperton and in the more distant communities of Langley, Douglas, Lillooet and Yale.[33]

Victoria's first "common" school survived about three years as a private venture. Early enrolments reached some hundred pupils for reasons found reprehensible by Bishop Hills. The private and district schools under Anglican supervision had resisted pressure by White American Southerners settled in Victoria to exclude the offspring of "colored" families also arrived from the United States. Jessop however agreed, and enrolments boomed. Buoyed by success, he began major physical expansion, a project which, given the school's low fees, became financially disastrous once enrolments stagnated, probably due to the general economic decline which set in as the gold rush ran its course. The school closed in March 1864.[34]

The demise of Jessop's Central School coalesced a consensus of public opinion that was by now expanding beyond its Evangelical Protestant North American origins to include numerous individuals of other backgrounds, both North Americans and Britons, who either out of principle or because of their limited financial means did not support the colony's class-based denominational system of education. The proportion of total population such individuals comprised is impossible to determine. Perhaps 7 500 Whites resided on Vancouver Island in 1864, over half in Victoria.[35] Neither is the proportion of those non-British in background known, although in 1865 a British naval officer did report that half of the two colonies' 14 000 White residents were "foreign."[36] Due to a gender imbalance in the non-Native population, the proportion of families with children was considerably less than would normally be the case: shortly after Central School's closure, the Rev. Cridge had found 500 children in schools across Vancouver Island, 400 of them in Victoria.[37] Other children received no formal education. In Victoria alone, fifty to a hundred were, according to contemporary accounts, "running through the streets . . . acquiring street education that will prepare many of them in after years for every description of crime and depravity."[38]

The concern felt by Victoria residents for the education of their children amidst growing economic recession was evident at a public meeting called shortly after Central School's closure in March 1864. Fully 500 residents, with "every element in the community pretty thoroughly represented," turned out to "demand the establishment of a free Common School in a central position, efficiently conducted, open to all classes of the community and non-sectarian in the strictest sense of the term." Some 500 signatures had been collected on a petition calling on the Island's Legislative Assembly to act. At the meeting only Collegiate School's principal and the Rev. Cridge dared defend the existing situation. Both were immediately denounced, the Rev. Cridge for having as head of the district schools "done nothing toward promoting education" but "come forward now and oppose the movement." One parent reminded him caustically that "the District School is as full as it can hold." Another related how, to quote the *Colonist*, "he had a large family, and that if he sent them to the Collegiate School, it would cost him from $900 to $1 500 for the same education which in Canada was free."[39]

Speakers at the meeting were especially dissatisfied with the hold exercised by denominational schools in a city as cosmopolitan as Victoria had become since the gold rush. One father stated that, although he "was a member of the Church of England, and was strongly in favour of bible teaching, . . . in a mixed community like this, where Jew, Turk, Roman Catholic and every other denomination was represented, a school system must be totally devoid of any religious teaching." Another parent added "that for his part he would wish to see denominational schools in every part of the colony and government aid extended to them all, but we must do here what can be done; in the present state of the colony an entirely non-sectarian system of education was necessary."

The next year witnessed vigorous debate both in and out of the Legislative Assembly over what, according to the *Colonist*, had become "the two great principles – free schools and the non-sectarian system of education."[40] The debate's religious component was summed up by a Non-Conformist English minister:

> The clergy of the English Church have been loud in agitation for the introduction of the Bible in the proposed Common Schools; but the bulk of the inhabitants are unwilling to accede to that arrangement in consequence of the mixed character of the community. There are individuals of every race, and members of every religious persuasion in the colonies; and it is maintained; as in Canada and the United States – that it would be unjust to Jews, Catholics, Buddhists, and Mohammedans, to adopt exclusively the text-books of any one religion.[41]

Consensus on the denominational issue was difficult to attain, its adherents assuming that, "as an integral portion of the English state, we, a small and remote colony," must adopt the structures in place in the mother country: "Since Vancouver [Island] and [British] Columbia are British colonies, let them be truly British in all their institutions; and perchance we shall enjoy domestic happiness and general prosperity."[42] Opponents countered that "the instruction of youth in new countries is valued much [more] highly than it is in Great Britain," where overall educational levels were relatively low.[43] In that case, so responded a proponent, properly complete the denominational system now partially in place:

> In this city there are already schools for the children of Catholics and Episcopalians [i.e., Anglicans]. There is now an excellent opportunity for one of the other [Evangelical Protestant] denominations to secure one in which, most probably by

the admission of the bible, they could all unite; the Jews from their wealth and numbers would hardly be behind as regards a schoolhouse for their children. With these four schools, established by and the property of the separate parties, let the government give to each such a portion of the grant to which, from the number of their scholars, they are entitled.[44]

Probably decisive in tipping the balance was Arthur Kennedy, the colony's new British governor who within days of his arrival in late March 1864 had made clear to an Anglican delegation headed by the Rev. Cridge that he preferred to replace the district schools under the cleric's control with "a non-sectarian system" which "included Roman Catholic and all denominations." "Don't you think that in a country like this, where men are thrown much together, it would be better that they should be educated together?"[45]

The public debate over free schools rapidly became the more critical of the two, centred as it was on the key issue of what should be the nature of society in the British colony. The proponents of continued student fees argued for the maintenance of the same clearly-defined class divisions as existed in the mother country, while those favoring free schools stressed their important role in bringing together all classes within the community in a single institution, as was occurring in the "Canadian schools."[46] As the *Colonist* pointed out, so long as fees existed, whether or not disallowable on grounds of inability to pay, they "brought in those invidious distinctions between the rich and the poor, so inimical to the growth of independence, and so detestable in a young community like our own."[47]

By October 1864, when a "Free Schools bill" was introduced into the Vancouver Island Legislative Assembly, its members were publicly agreed "to legislate for the majority of people."[48] The chairman of the committee which brought in the bill was Dr. Israel Wood Powell, an Ontario physician and Anglican, who summed up popular opinion in his formal proposal "that there should be established in this colony a system of free schools, conducted by thoroughly competent trained teachers, wherein the intellectual, physical and moral training would be such as to make the schools attractive *to all classes of the people*." It therefore followed logically, so continued Dr. Powell, "that in a community such as this, where religious opinions are so diversified, and where the benefits of a well-devised educational system should be extended to all, the reading of the bible or the inculcation of religious dogmas in free schools would be inadvisable."[49] In the Assembly debate, Dr. Powell vigorously defended use of the word "free" in the wording of the bill as standing "in contradistinction to charity schools," such as existed in England. "The object of the committee was to establish schools free to all, and where the system of education under thoroughly trained teachers would be such as to attract all, both rich and poor." Nonetheless, he soon suffered a tactical defeat when a bare majority in the Assembly decided, apparently in the interests of discretion, to substitute "common" for "free."[50]

This concession on form probably helped unite Assembly members when the bill, passed by them, came under attack from the Legislative Council. Unlike the Assembly which was elected, the second legislative body was appointed by the governor and tended to reflect his position which, while favoring non-sectarianism, did not extend to free schools. The bill was returned, amended so as to give the General Board of Education in charge of implementation "power to regulate the amount of School fees payable for Educational purposes in any Common School so, however, that the same do not exceed fifty centimes per month for each scholar." The Assembly was outraged at the action of Council members: "They had murdered the bill." Sent back unchanged, the bill was again amended by the Council, and again the Assembly rejected this challenge to "the very principle of the bill which had been distinctly enunciated as a free school measure." An Assembly member had no hesitation in attributing class motives to the Council:

> The fifty cents a month would at the best bring in but a paltry revenue, while on the other hand the discretionary powers of remitting fees would tend to make distinctions of the most invidious character among the pupils, sapping the foundation of the children's independence.[51]

This time the Council acquiesced, and the bill became law as "An Act respecting Common Schools."[52]

The triumph was short-lived. Even as non-sectarian free schools under direct government control were opening – most notably a revived Central School under Jessop enrolling over 200 pupils – opposition was strengthened by both the poor state of the economy and the appointment of a forceful new governor even more committed than his predecessor to fee-based education. To save money, the two colonies of Vancouver Island and British Columbia were amalgamated in 1866 as the Colony of British Columbia under a single legislative body, a Legislative Council half or more of whose members were appointed by the governor and therefore amenable to his will. Within days of the union having received royal assent on August 6, Vancouver Island's General Board of Education was notified by the government that no expenditures, including teacher salaries, would be guaranteed "beyond the 31 of August, instant." Frederick Seymour, the new governor appointed to the united colony, concurred, since "the whole system of the public schools required reforming."[53] He soon elaborated his position, referring to himself in the third person:

> He thinks that any man who respects himself would not desire to have his children instructed without some pecuniary sacrifice on his part . . . else it may happen that the promising mechanic may be marred, and the country overburdened with half-educated politicians or needy hangers-on of the Government.

Unnecessary education, likely if it be free, would only result in individuals unhappy with their destined place in the social order. "The system he would desire to see," while containing "a public school open to all denominations" teaching "children to read, write and go through the simpler forms of arithmetic" at a fee of perhaps $6 a year, would encompass "Denominational Schools, also, to which the Government contributed, but in a moderate degree." Under such a plan, it would probably be the case, so argued the governor, that the "Denominational Schools, though more expensive to the parents, absorbed the greater number of children."[54]

The governor's public position on education gave new heart to the powerful supporters of a class-based denominational system of schooling. As a student at

Collegiate School recollected, his classmates in these years were the sons of "the very earliest pioneers of our beloved city of Victoria and the Pacific Coast," including leading Hudson's Bay families.[55] Angela College was headed by a sister of the Attorney General and then by the sister of a leading Hudson's Bay official, both from Britain.[56] While families of comparable social status resident outside Victoria could not maintain educational exclusivity as easily, opportunities did from time to time arise. The Anglican rector in Nanaimo reported in 1868: "The mornings I devote to teaching my own boys, and those of the better class of parishioners who are not satisfied with the associations and the *non-religious* education of the public school."[57] Not surprisingly, when the governor's appointed Executive Council was asked its views on the educational situation in 1867, members responded that the state's role should be limited to establishing "a cheap general common school of an elementary description in each Town or district where at least a certain limited average number of pupils can attend winter and summer, on the plan of so much per head." Denominational schools also ought to be supported, if "at a much lower rate per head," so that their clientele "who contribute their full quota to the taxes and revenue but who consciously object to what they consider 'godless' Schools will derive some benefit." "On no account should absolutely Free schools be supported."[58]

Although outmanoeuvered politically, the consensus in favor of free, non-denominational schooling remained intact, as was indicated by a public meeting called in Victoria in August 1867 to endorse the General Board of Education's declaration to the governor "that the system of free education established in Vancouver Island is in accordance with the wishes of the community." Whereas at mid-decade, prior to the passage of the Common Schools Act, just a quarter of the Island's 500 pupils had been attending subsidized schools, now fully half of the 800 children receiving a formal education were in free schools. After Dr. Powell, chairman of Vancouver Island's General Board, reviewed its troubled history, considerable discussion ensued. Aware both of "the present financial embarrassments of the Colony" and of the board's inability "to re-open the schools owing to a want of funds," participants debated at some length whether or not a fee ought temporarily to be charged. The position of the great majority was reiterated by a Methodist missionary from Ontario:

> The age of exclusiveness was passing away, and if Britain expected to continue great she must make every effort to educate the young or she would go behind. We are here to found a new State, and it was the interest of every State to educate its children. It was not alone the interests of parents – it was the interest, the *duty*, of the State to furnish free education. [prolonged applause] . . . Let this meeting speak out loudly and unhesitatingly in support of Free Schools and in denunciation of the system attempted to be enforced by the Government.

Other participants were more succinct, one merely pointing out that among parents "there were a good many here who could not pay. Adopt the fee system and you send half the children into the streets to become worse than Siwashes [Chinook term for Indians]." The only declared supporters of denominational schools were "two Catholic gentlemen," and the meeting virtually unanimously supported the Vancouver Island board's actions.[59]

This consensus of popular opinion gained new adherents from both Vancouver Island and the mainland as a consequence of the unworkability of new, more stringent school legislation enacted in early 1869. During the debate in the Legislative Council, the free-schools principle had received primary attention. Opponents argued, much as did members of the Executive Council, that,

> The system of free education was most vicious; it was burdensome to those who contributed to denominational schools, who did not desire free school education, and it destroyed that stimulus to exertion which would exist were the scholar required to pay something towards the cost of education.[60]

Among the supporters of school fees was John Robson, an Ontario Presbyterian who since 1861 had edited the New Westminster *British Columbian* newspaper. While Robson had repeatedly editorialized that schools should be "free from sectarian domination and exclusiveness" and "placed within the reach of all," he had never favored their being free of cost to pupils.[61] Now he asserted:

> To throw free education open to everyone was a serious principle, it caused people to forget the advantages that were bestowed on them and rendered the parents careless as to the attendance of the children at school. There could be no doubt that making the parents pay one-half the cost of educating their children was the true principle.

Outnumbered in the Council, the proponents of free schools still pressed their case. The bill, they argued, proposed that "certain of the people were supposed to be worthy of charity, and thus class was set against class." As a model for British Columbia to follow, "it would be better to be taught by Canada or the United States, where education was understood to be the right of all and not that of a class." One of the most vocal defenders of free schools was J.S. Helmcken, an English physician brought out by the Hudson's Bay Company who had married Governor Douglas' eldest daughter. Dr. Helmcken pointed out that, particularly in rural districts where families "were struggling to get their farms into a state of cultivation," teachers would simply not be paid under the proposed system by which the government would provide half their salaries, but only after the remainder had been collected in the locality, "whether by voluntary subscriptions, Tuition fees, or General Rate."[62] In the end the bill passed with little real opposition, due both to the Legislative Council's composition and to members' primary concern during this period with the even more divisive issue of whether or not the colony should join the new Canadian Confederation.[63]

Implementation of the 1869 act proved as difficult as its detractors had forecast. While at least twenty localities scrambled to meet its rigorous demands, most soon found themselves in an intolerable situation, even after levying student fees of $6 to $18 a year, in addition to taxes. Reporting to the governor in early 1871, the Inspector General of Schools appointed under the act, who had been its principal supporter in the Council, acknowledged that only fifteen schools were managing to operate and that the equipment in all but one was "of the scantiest description" with many buildings "small and inconvenient." Local school boards were simply unable or unwilling to enforce collection of school taxes. The situation would improve only when the government took a bigger role by levying and collecting the necessary taxes, possibly with an exemption "made in favour of those who support private or denominational schools" which were "certified to be efficient by the Inspector approved by the government."[64]

III

British Columbia entered Confederation later in 1871, by which time the deteriorating educational and economic situation of the last half-dozen years had amply reconfirmed the need for free non-denominational schooling. The opposition had been discredited: according to the *Colonist*, in the election for the first provincial legislature, "no candidate, be his private opinions what they might, volunteered to say a word against this form of education." "No measure was more distinctly or more unanimously demanded."[65] Almost immediately, without disagreement on principle, the Assembly passed a bill "for the establishment, maintenance, and management of Public Schools throughout the Province of British Columbia," whose provisions were based both on the 1865 act and on systems being put in place in Ontario and across the United States. The critical issue of finance was resolved by the annual allotment out of general revenue of a specified sum "for Public School purposes," the amount accorded the first year being virtually triple that allowed just a year previous. The act dealt explicitly with the denominational issue: "All Public Schools established under the principles of this Act, shall be conducted upon strictly non-sectarian principles."[66]

The non-sectarian provision, reflecting the social and economic conditions of British Columbia, distinguished this act from recent legislation elsewhere in Canada and in England. The English Education Act of 1870, while establishing non-denominational state board schools, also recognized existing church schools as a fundamental part of the subsidized state system of elementary education.[67] Similarly, the British North America Act had safeguarded "any Right or Privilege with respect to Denominational Schools which any Class of Persons have by Law in the Province at the Union."[68]

As a consequence, separate Catholic schools officially recognized in Ontario or elsewhere at Confederation had been brought under their provincial systems. The case for recognition had been made several times in colonial British Columbia: Governor Seymour had been in favor, as had members of his Executive and Legislative Councils as well as the Inspector General of Schools in 1871. During the debate on the 1869 bill, one of several proponents of financial support for the colony's denominational schools had even cited the situation "in Canada" to make his case. About the same time, the religious orders operating Catholic schools had petitioned the Legislative Assembly for financial assistance.[69] All these moves had either been rejected or simply not acted upon, and the British Columbia legislation therefore did not even mention, much less take responsibility for, denominational or other non-public schools.

British Columbia's educational consensus did not immediately become, to quote the *Colonist*, "acceptable to all and good enough for all."[70] First, each of the principal religious groups in the province – Anglican, Catholic and Evangelical Protestant – had to be rebuffed in their efforts to secure special treatment. The Anglican attempt to coopt educational structures may have existed primarily in the perceptions of others, reflecting larger distrusts. Union with Canada had been purely economic, the new province emerging from negotiations with debts paid and the promise of a transcontinental railroad. As the last colonial governor had reported home, "the most prominent Agitators for Confederation are a small knot of Canadians."[71] The Anglican bishop still considered, for instance, that since "the great heart of the people beats with that of England so fervently," the preferred course would have been "the closer union and protection of the mother country."[72] At the same time, many Canadians viewed Confederation as both a vindication of their discontents and the guarantee of a new, more acceptable status deemed theirs by right in a geographical entity now itself Canadian. Any suggestion of opposition became a deliberate affront, as witnessed by a letter in the *Colonist* of April 1872 from "Citizen" concerning a rumor that the Anglican rector in Nanaimo, a community characterized by a contemporary as having "a divided line betwixt the aristocracy and the democracy," might open a parish school:

> Now to establish a denominational school in such a community is nothing more than to keep up caste distinctions in a country where "Jack is as good as his master" – where we are supposed to ignore the old fogy teaching of the old country where children are taught to regard the squire and the parson with dreadful and deferential awe.[73]

Confrontation occurred almost immediately after the education bill's passage. Lieutenant-Governor Joseph Trutch, despite having been appointed for his acceptability to both Britons and Canadians, requested reconsideration of the act by the Assembly after receiving a petition from sixty-eight Victoria residents opposed to a clause prohibiting appointment of a clergyman as Superintendent of Education.[74] The *Colonist* was furious: given "the present condition and circumstances of the Province," such an appointment, especially if it went to an Anglican cleric, would be met "with distrust and disappointment."[75] The Assembly was equally incensed, and the bill was returned unaltered for the lieutenant-governor's signature. Less than two weeks later, the *Colonist* again charged interference. Certain individuals were refusing to sit on the provincial Board of Education, "thus seeking to block the wheels of the new School Act." The newspaper stated that the government had "confined the invitations chiefly to those who are in reality at heart enemies of the system," men it termed "Canada haters."

The spate of letters which followed made clear the antagonism existing between Evangelical Protestant Canadians and the Anglican Britons. Among the most vocal was "Non-Conformist," who wrote that of the first six men invited on to the board, five were Anglicans, of whom "four are unbelievers in the free, nonsectarian system." Anglicans totalled less than a third of the province's population, "but I suppose the Cabinet being formed exclusively of members of the Anglican Church, it is considered proper that the Board of Education should be composed of similar material."[76] While the appointment shortly thereafter of longstanding common schools proponent John Jessop as Superintendent of Education diffused suspicions, tensions did not completely disappear, as evidenced by an attack a few years later on the board's class assumptions:

> Having arrived here with the prejudices against popular education of England of twenty years ago, they have retained their opinions and are at present only tolerant of the system of public education established here because of political pressure.

The writer further charged that board members were "of too high a social rank to condescend to have their children taught with Tom, Dick and Harry" but rather educate "their children in private schools."[77]

Such a course became increasingly less feasible, for Anglican education was in decline, and with it disappeared what supporters of the province's educational consensus perceived to be a major threat. The Anglican church's difficulties were largely self-induced; for over two decades after Confederation, the church in British Columbia remained under the direct oversight of the Archbishopric of Canterbury, through which came personnel, finance and direction.[78] Thus, attitudes formed when the province was still a British colony received constant reinforcement. The church continued to believe that British Columbia was a class-based society, and that parishioners gave the same priority as at home to the maintenance of social distinctions through education. In 1878, for instance, the Englishwoman heading Angela College opened a separate "subsidiary" for "girls of poor parents" so as "to give a religious training to all classes" while still reserving the school itself for "girls of the upper and middle classes."[79] When a founding bishop was appointed to the new mainland Diocese of New Westminster created in 1879, one of his first acts was to set up local church schools. That conditions in British Columbia might differ from those of Britain had not even crossed his mind: months "before I ever set foot in the country I occupied myself in laying plans for the education of both boys and girls."[80]

So far as the Church of England in British Columbia was concerned, common education was to be disparaged. As late as 1891, Bishop Hills was condemning the public system, noting that its "depressing and atheistical character" would certainly result "in criminality increasing by leaps and bounds."[81] The lack of fees at the public secondary level caused special alarm: "the lesson of the dignity of labor" would be taught the poor "not by Free High Schools, full of Latin and Greek and the Higher mathematics and Dancing and Deportment, but by Free Industrial and Technical Schools, which will turn out clever mechanics and artisans and agriculturalists, and good wives."[82] Education's function was to ensure the maintenance of class distinctions from generation to generation.

In reality, important socio-economic differences had separated Britain and British Columbia since the 1860s. As reports to the church's London headquarters acknowledged, "there are no wealthy people in British Columbia belonging to the Church," "no resident proprietors with means and leisure at their disposal."[83] The experience of the Bishop of New Westminster pointed up the harsh reality. Having expended even his private income on the diocese's church schools, he was especially "disappointed at finding Church children sent indiscriminately to Roman and to free schools, while our own are left to languish for want of support."[84] Soon his schools had to be closed for lack of pupils. While Victoria did contain numerous established families still favoring class-based denominational education, even this support gradually dissipated, due in part to a theological dispute erupting in 1874 between Bishop Hills and the Rev. Cridge. The city's longtime cleric promptly established the Reformed Episcopal Church, taking with him many Hudson's Bay families and the staff of Angela College.[85] His subsequent creation of competing church schools diminished the prestige of all the institutions, and enrolments fell. In 1880 Angela College became a private venture to be closed in the next economic recession. Collegiate shut its doors in 1885.[86] Long before then, most Anglicans had reconciled themselves to the province's public system.

Interior of Craigflower School, near Victoria, in the mid-1880s.
(British Columbia Archives and Records Service [BCARS])

Acceptance of the province's educational consensus by Catholics, whose theological commitment to denominational education was even greater than that of Anglicans, also took time. Their desire for tacit recognition and financial support similar to that given Catholic schools in Ontario came to a head in 1876 over a proposal in the provincial Assembly to levy a $3 annual school tax on all adult males, the cost of education having up to this time come out of general revenue. Although the measure was directed against the province's growing Chinese population – "the present tax would really be a saving to the white population of some $17,000, which sum would now be paid by Chinamen" – it was Catholics who protested. A petition signed by sixty-four Catholic residents of Victoria, including the bishop, argued that

Catholics should be exempted since "your Petitioners cannot in conscience send their children to the so-called unsectarian schools, wherever they have schools of their own." The *Colonist* opposed the Catholic initiative as threatening once again to "draw the lines of sectarianism." As participants in the Assembly debate pointed out, "there are other denominations besides the Catholics that objected to secular education." "If the Catholics were to be excepted, the Jews and in fact every other sect would claim the same privilege." The bill passed unaltered, and Catholics thereafter turned their principal attention to the maintenance of their own private institutions.[87]

And, unlike Anglican church schools, Catholic institutions remained strong, continuing to service the 15 to 19 percent of the White population of that faith. Impressive new physical structures existed in Victoria and New Westminster. In 1873 the Oblates began a boarding school in the Cariboo offering a "Thorough English and Commercial Education." Three years later, the Sisters of St. Ann joined them. A girls' school opened in Nanaimo in 1877. In 1880 the two orders jointly established a school in the interior settlement of Kamloops in anticipation of the transcontinental railroad, with additional schools being established as settlement warranted.[88]

Neither were all Evangelical Protestants wholly satisfied with the province's educational consensus, and they attempted co-option through redefining the concept of "non-sectarianism" in the Public Schools Act more closely toward their particular religious tenets. In spring 1876, a Presbyterian minister was appointed principal of the new Victoria High School, the first public secondary institution in the province. Although Alexander Nicholson renounced his ordination before taking up the post, trouble erupted.[89] A letter from "Father" in a local newspaper shortly after the school opened comprised a single sentence:

> Will you inform me why the Master of the High School (in contravention of the Public School Act) is allowed to perform the duties of Minister in one of our churches and also religious services at the school supposed to be non-sectarian?[90]

The subsequent outrage showed that public sensibilities were offended. Both Victoria newspapers argued that such a practice would favor Protestants over Catholic, "Israelite," or "Spiritualist." "In the general rivalry of the sects for their share of the material patronage, the Free School system would soon receive its death-blow." While maintaining he had spoken in church as a layman, Nicholson was forced to resign the principalship to defend his position that "a simple non-sectarian prayer to God" be allowed in the schools.[91] Shortly thereafter school exercises were officially "limited to the Lord's Prayer and Ten Commandments, and it is optional with the various Trustee Boards whether the same shall be used or not."[92]

Even as these efforts by the major religious groups to secure special treatment were being repulsed, Jessop and his successors as superintendent of education were implementing an educational system which would endure virtually unaltered for a century. As the biographer of Jessop has noted, he was indefatigable in establishing free non-sectarian common schooling across British Columbia.[93] By the time of his forced departure from office for political reasons in August 1878, the young province of 10 to 15 000 Whites possessed fifty-one common schools as well as the high school in Victoria, together enrolling 2 200 students.[94] At the railroad's arrival eight years later, eighty-three existed, including three high schools, with enrolment at 4 500.[95]

By then, the role to be accorded non-public education within the consensus was also defined. The Catholic issue had reaffirmed the intention of the 1872 legislation not to provide financial support to denominational schools, a demand which lost much of its force once the Anglican schools with their more politically powerful supporters collapsed. Jessop had made clear that private schools would remain unsupervised. His annual reports virtually ignored these institutions which had earlier so bedevilled him. Only once, writing in 1877 about conditions in New Westminster, did he reveal any lingering antipathy: "There are several denominational and private schools in this city competing for pupils with the public school, notwithstanding which, the latter is decidedly gaining in attendance and the confidence of parents."[96] After 1883 for virtually a century, the annual reports did not even acknowledge, much less attempt to monitor, non-public schools.[97]

In 1886 British Columbia began a fundamental transformation as the long-promised transcontinental railroad finally arrived, and the province was for the first time directly linked to the rest of the nation of which it had thus far been a part primarily on paper. In the case of education, however, this change was not critical, for the consensus which had first coalesced during the mid-1860s favoring free non-denominational education was firmly in place. Not until the late 1970s, when private schools would be accorded official recognition and financial support, was there fundamental alteration of the system which had emerged in response to social and economic conditions in British Columbia from 1849 to 1886.

Notes

1. For this perspective, see F. Henry Johnson, "The Ryersonian Influence on the Public Schools System of British Columbia.," *BC Studies* 10 (Summer 1971): 26-34.

2. John Sebastian Helmcken, *The Reminiscences of Doctor John Sebastian Helmcken*, Dorothy Blakey Smith, ed. (Vancouver: University of British Columbia [hereafter UBC] Press, 1975), 114-16, 293.

3. On England, see Brian Simon, *The Two Nations & the Educational Structure, 1780-1870*, v. 1 in his *Studies in the History of Education* (London: Lawrence & Wishart, 1981), esp. 277-367. On British Columbia, see Donald L. MacLaurin, "Education before the Gold Rush," *British Columbia Historical Quarterly* [hereafter *BCHQ*] 2 (1938): 247-53; and his "The History of Education in the Crown Colonies of Vancouver Island and British Columbia and in the Province of British Columbia" (Ph.D. thesis, University of Washington, 1936). Examination in the British Columbia Archives and Record Service [hereafter BCARS] of MacLaurin's primary manuscript sources confirms his research on colonial British Columbia to have been exhaustive, inclusive and exact. Therefore, sources are cited from MacLaurin to facilitate access by other researchers.

4. Recollection of Roderick Finlayson, quoted in Alexander Begg, *History of British Columbia From Its Earliest Discovery to the Present Time* (Toronto: Ryerson Press, 1894, reprinted 1972), 212. See also C. Hollis Slater, "Rev. Robert John Staines," *BCHQ* 14 (1950): 187-240. On education provided by the Hudson's Bay Company at Fort Vancouver, see G. Hollis Slater, "New Light on Herbert Beaver," *BCHQ* 6 (1942): 13-29; and Juliet Pollard, "Growing Up Metis: Fur Traders' Children in the Pacific Northwest," in J. Donald Wilson, ed., *An Imperfect Past: Education and Society in Canadian History* (Vancouver: Centre for the Study of Curriculum and Instruction, UBC, 1984), 120-40.

5. James Douglas to Archibald Barclay, Hudson's Bay governor, 8 Oct. 1851, in Douglas' letter book, BCARS, quoted in MacLaurin, "History of Education," 12-13.

6. See MacLaurin, "History of Education," 13-20.

7. "Memorandum of Salary Allowances for a Clergyman for Vancouver's Island," BCARS, quoted in MacLaurin, "History of Education," 12-13; and "Minutes of the Council of Vancouver Island," quoted on 22-23. The minutes have been published in *Journals of the Colonial Legislatures of the Colonies of Vancouver Island and British Columbia, 1851-1871*, 5 vols., James E. Hendrickson, ed., (Victoria: Provincial Archives of British Columbia, 1980). For this reference, see v. 1, 16-17. See also J. Forsyth, "Early colonial Schools on Vancouver Island" parts I-III, *Times* (Victoria), Mar. 1922, located in Vertical Files, BCARS. The evidence suggests that, while Mrs. Cridge ran a school for girls, a complement for boys was never opened.

8. See MacLaurin, "History of Education," 12-14, 24 and 26.

9. G.P.V. and Helen B. Akrigg, *British Columbia Chronicle, 1847-1871* (Vancouver: Discovery Press, 1977), 59; and W. Kaye Lamb, "The Census of Vancouver Island, 1855," *BCHQ* 4 (1940): 51-58.

10. *Times* (London), 19 January 1859.

11. Reprinted in *Colonist* (Victoria), 21 April 1908; see also Sister Mary Margaret Down, *A Century of Service, 1858-1958: A History of the Sisters of Saint Ann and Their Contribution to Education in British Columbia, the Yukon and Alaska* (Victoria: Sisters of Saint Ann, 1966), 28-41.

12. "St. Ann's Convent, Register, Victoria, B.C.," in Vertical Files, BCARS. For one Jewish girl's account of her experience, see *A Chaplet of Years: St. Ann's Academy* (Victoria: *Colonist*, 1918), 29-35.

13. Kay Cronin, *Cross in the Wilderness* (Vancouver: Mitchell Press, 1960), 99-101, 53 and 134. See also Down, *A Century of Service*, 23-27, 42-45; and *Colonist*, 1 Sept. 1863; 3 Nov. 1863; and 3 May 1925.

14. Anglican Church, Columbia Mission, *Special Fund Obtained During a Ten Months' Appeal by the Bishop of Columbia* (London: R. Clay, 1860), x; and Angl. Ch., Columbia Mission, *Occasional Paper*, June 1860, 14-16. See also Frank A. Peake, *The Anglican Church in British Columbia* (Vancouver: Mitchell Press, 1959); and Rev. George Hills, Bishop of Columbia, Diary, 1860-69, excepting 1867-68; typescript copy in British Columbia Provincial Synod Archives, Anglican Church of Canada, Vancouver School of Theology, UBC, esp. entries for 3 Sept. 1860, and 7 Nov. 1861.

15. Hills, Diary, 25 Apr. 1861. Report of Rev. Cridge to Colonial Secretary on Colonial Schools, 27 Aug. 1861, BCARS, reprinted in MacLaurin, "History of Education," 38; and *Colonist*, 11 Apr. 1864. See also Hills, Diary, 30 Jan. 1860, 20 Aug. 1860, and 10 Sept. 1860. On fees, see 10 Mar. 1863.

16. 1861 report, reprinted in MacLaurin, "History of Education," 37.

17. Matthew MacFie, *Vancouver Island and British Columbia* (London: Longman, Green, 1865), 84.

18. Hills, Diary, 10 Mar. 1863; see also 8 Mar. 1861.

19. Ang. Ch., Dioc. of Col., *Annual Report* 1860: 85 and 95; *B.C. Directory,* 1863: 134 and 138-39; *Colonist,* 22 and 24 May, 7 and 10 July, and 25 Dec. 1860; Hills, Diary, 29 Sept. 1860, and 19 Jan. 1863; and Dorothy Blakey Smith, ed., *Lady Franklin Visits the Pacific Northwest* (Victoria: Provincial Archives of British Columbia, 1974), 16 and 36.

20. *Colonist,* 26 April 1925; see also 6 Apr. 1919.

21. Ang. Ch., Dioc. of Col., *Annual Report,* 1860: 84, and *Colonist,* 26 Apr. 1925.

22. Smith, *Franklin,* 16.

23. Undated report from Rev. Cridge for 1864 or 1865, BCARS, reprinted in MacLaurin, "History of Education," 41-43, and in F. Henry Johnson, *A History of Public Education in British Columbia* (Vancouver: Publications Centre, UBC, 1964), 29-30. One report puts the number of private venture schools in Victoria in 1863-64 at eighteen. *Colonist,* 2 May 1876.

24. Allan Smith, "Old Ontario and the Emergence of a National Frame of Mind," in F.H. Armstrong, H.A. Stevenson and J.D. Wilson, eds., *Aspects of Nineteenth Century Ontario* (Toronto: University of Toronto Press in association with the University of Western Ontario, 1974), 197 and 209.

25. Margaret Ross, "Amor de Cosmos, a British Columbia Reformer" (M.A. thesis, UBC, 1931), offers a vigorous defence of De Cosmos' position. See also James Gordon Reid, "John Robson and the *The British Columbian,*" (M.A. thesis, UBC, 1950); and F. Henry Johnson, *John Jessop: Goldseeker and Educator* (Vancouver: Mitchell Press, 1971), 31; Helmcken, *Reminiscences,* 174-78; and Hills, Diary, 9 Jan. 1860. Despite the *Colonist's* visibly pro-Canadian sympathies, even after De Cosmos' departure as editor in 1863, it is an invaluable source of contemporary information concerning events in early British Columbia. As well, its editorials provide a useful guide to Canadian attitudes toward particular issues.

26. See MacFie, *Vancouver Island,* 83; and Alexander Rattray, *Vancouver Island and British Columbia* (London: Smith, Elder, & Co., 1862), 171.

27. See, for instance, David Tyack, "The Kingdom of God and the Common School: Protestant Ministers and the Educational Awakening in the West," *Harvard Educational Review* 36 (1966): 447-69; and Timothy L. Smith, "Protestant Schooling and American Nationality, 1800-1850," *The Journal of American History* 53 (1967): 679-95. On Canada, see Neil McDonald and Alf Chaiton, eds., *Egerton Ryerson and His Times* (Toronto: Macmillan, 1978), and Alison Prentice, *The School Promoters: Education and Social Class in Mid-Nineteenth Century Upper Canada,* (Toronto: McClelland and Stewart, 1977).

28. *Colonist,* 10 Jan. 1863, and 19 Oct. 1864.

29. John Jessop to E. Ryerson, Victoria, 16 Aug. 1861, quoted in Johnson, *Jessop,* 38; see also 36-43 and *B.C. Directory,* 1863: 137.

30. Margaret Lillooet McDonald, "New Westminster, 1859-1871" (M.A. thesis, UBC 1947), 356-58.

31. *Ibid.,* 358-59; and *Columbian* (New Westminster), 2 Sept. 1864, quoted in Reid, 116.

32. McDonald, "New Westminster," 353-67; Anl. Ch., Dioc. Col., *Annual Report,* 1870, 16; Down, *A Century of Service,* 62; and *Columbian,* 18 Jan. 1926, and 19 June 1965. On population, see McDonald, "New Westminster," 69-70; Margaret A. Ormsby, *British Columbia: A History* (Toronto: Macmillan, 1958), 201 and 209; and Akrigg, *Chronicle,* 200.

33. See MacLaurin, "History of Education," 60-61.

34. Hills, Diary, 27 Mar., 20 Apr., and 13 June 1862; 18 Mar. 1860; 18 Feb. and 21 Mar. 1861; and 20 Jan. 1862; *Colonist,* 10 Jan. 1863, and 22 Mar. 1864; and Angl. Ch., Dioc. Col., *Annual Report,* 1861: 26, and 1863: 10. On the Catholic attitude to race, see Down, *A Century of Service,* 48-50. On the various schools' positions on race, see also Smith, *Franklin,* 10.

35. See Hubert Howe Brancroft, *History of British Columbia* (San Francisco: History Co., 1887), 592, who probably based his estimate on contemporaries' recollections. Population figures for the early 1860s are sparse. One estimate puts Victoria's White population in February 1861 at 2 500, another that of 1862 at 5 to 6 000. See I.J. Benjamin, *Three Years in America 1859-1862*, vol. 2 (Philadelphia: Jewish Publication Society, 1956), 142; and R. Byron Johnson, *Very Far West Indeed: A Few Rough Experiences on the North-West Pacific Coast*, 5th ed. (London: Sampson, Low, Marston, Low & Searle, 1873), 34. A letter in the *Colonist* on 4 April 1864 gave the city's population as 7 000. See also Ormsby, *British Columbia*, 169, 209 and 239. As well as Whites and Indians, the city and colony contained numerous adult Chinese males and a handful of Black families.

36. Rear-Admiral the Hon. Joseph Denman to the Secretary of the Admiralty, Esquimalt, 3 June 1865. Public Records Office, ADM 1/5924, cited in Akrigg, *Chronicle*, 319-20. Benjamin stated that Victoria contained about 100 Jews in 1861. In his general research on Jewish life in British Columbia, Cyril Edil Leonoff evidently encountered no information on early Jewish education. See his *Pioneers, Pedlars, and Prayer Shawls: The Jewish Communities in British Columbia and the Yukon* (Victoria: Sono Nis, 1978).

37. 1864/65 report, quoted in MacLaurin, "History of Education," 41-43. Cridge's list did not include Central School but referred to a small successor school founded under Presbyterian auspices in April 1864. See *Colonist*, 6 Apr. 1864. The male/female ratio in both an 1868 Victoria area census and an 1870 Vancouver Island census was approximately 3:2. *Colonist*, 6 Oct. 1868, and H.L. Langevin, *Report* (Ottawa: I.B. Taylor 1872), 152, also reproduced in Akrigg, *Chronicle*, 404.

38. *Colonist*, 4 Apr. 1864.

39. *Ibid.*, 11 and 12 Apr. 1864. For evidence of this meeting's direct effect on subsequent legislation, see 13 Dec. 1908.

40. *Ibid.*, 23 May 1865.

41. MacFie, *Vancouver Island*, 84.

42. *Colonist*, 21 Oct. 1864, and 9 May 1864.

43. *Ibid.*, 14 and 21 Oct., and 13 Apr. 1864.

44. *Ibid.*, 19 Apr. 1864.

45. *Ibid.*, 4 Apr. 1864. On the various deputations soliciting the new governor's favor, see 27 and 31 March and 1 Apr. 1864. For evidence of the Rev. Cridge's continuing authority, see 9 Apr. 1864. On Kennedy, see Cecil Gilliland, "The Early Life and Early Governorships of Sir Arthur Edward Kennedy" (M.A. Thesis, UBC, 1951); and Robert L. Smith, "The Kennedy Interlude, 1864-66," *BC Studies* 47 (Autumn 1981): 66-78. Gilliland suggests that Kennedy was early influenced by Utilitarianism in his view that sate-supported schools should be non-denominational, but offers no evidence dating prior to Kennedy's arrival on Vancouver Island to back up his assertion. See pp. 19-20 and 382-83.

46. *Colonist*, 19 Oct. 1864. By contrast, American precedent was very seldom cited in discussions.

47. *Ibid.*, 13 Apr. 1865.

48. For the chronology of this and a previous bill introduced in the 1864 session, see *Journals*, v. 3, 591-92.

49. *Colonist*, 8 and 12 Oct. 1864. On Dr. Powell, see B.A. McKelvie, "Lieutenant-Colonel Israel Wood Powell, M.D., C.M.," *BCHQ* 11 (1947): 33-54. Italics in original.

50. *Colonist*, 19 and 26 Oct. 1865. On the bill's progress through the Assembly, see *Journals*, v. 3., 201-02, 204-06, 208-10, 213, 229, 238-41 and 243-45.

51. *Colonist*, 26 Oct. 1864, and 17 Mar. and 13, 21 and 27 Apr. 1865. On the disagreement between the two bodies, see *Journals*, v. 3., 289, 294, 298, 304-06, 308 311, 368; and v. 1., 289-90, 292-93, 301-03, and 307-08.

52. Reprinted in MacLaurin, "History of Education," 44-46. No evidence was encountered explaining the Council's reversal. On the two bodies' authority, see "The Constitutional Development of Vancouver Island," *Journals*, v. 1., xxvi-vlviii.

53. See MacLaurin, "History of Education," 51-52 and 63-90; and Johnson, *Jessop*, 53-61.

54. Speech of 24 Jan. 1867, reprinted in *Journals*, v. 5, 43-44, and in MacLaurin, "History of Education," 65-68; and comment of 19 Apr. 1867, quoted on p. 74. On Seymour's upper-class background and career, see Margaret A. Ormsby, "Frederick Seymour, The Forgotten Governor," *BC Studies* 22 (Summer 1974): 3-25.

55. *Times*, 30 Jan. 1939. See *Colonist*, 21 Aug. 1949, on students attending Angela College. See Angl. Chl, Dioc. Col., *Annual Reports*, and Hills, Diary, for development of the two schools.

56. Angl. Ch., Dioc. Col., *Annual Report*, 1869: 76; Harriet Susan Sampson, "My Father, Joseph Despard Pemberton: 1821-1893," *BCHQ* 8 (1944): 121-22; and *Colonist*, 21 Aug. 1949.

57. Angl. Ch., Dioc. Col., *Annual Report*, 1868: 85. Italics in original.

58. Views of members of Executive Council, 12-18 Apr. 1867, BCARS; reprinted in MacLaurin, "History of Education," 71-74.

59. *Colonist*, 12 Aug. 1867; and Arthur Harvey, *A Statistical Account of British Columbia* (Ottawa: G.E. Desbarats, 1867), 24, which states that in 1867, 404 students were enrolled in the ten Vancouver Island common schools, with another 419 spread between the two Anglican and two Catholic schools and eight private ventures, all in Victoria. Harvey also observed that mainland facilities were sparse.

60. *Colonist*, 5 Feb. 1869.

61. *Columbian*, 18 July 1861, and 16 Dec. 1866, quoted in Reid, "John Robson," 114. See also 27 Feb. 1862, and 6, 13 and 23 Apr. 1864, cited on pp. 114-15.

62. Since mid-decade the White population had apparently declined by almost half to about 8 500. See Langevin, *Report*, 152. Harvey, *Statistical Account*, 9, put the population of Vancouver Island in 1867 at about 5 to 7 000 Whites, Chinese and Blacks, that of the mainland at perhaps 10 000. He also noted that the latter was "very fluctuating," with many miners leaving each winter for Vancouver Island or California. On the other hand, settlers were "steadily increasing in number."

63. "An Ordinance to establish Public Schools throughout the Colony of British Columbia," reprinted in MacLaurin, "History of Education," 93-98. On the debate, see *Journals*, v. 5, 198, 210, 217, 221, 223, and 233-34; and *Colonist*, 5, 8-9, 11-12 and 17-18 Feb. 1869.

64. See MacLaurin, "History of Education," 103-27.

65. *Colonist*, 23 Apr. and 5 May 1872.

66. "An Act Respecting Public Schools," 11 Apr. 1872, reprinted in British Columbia, Superintendent of Education, *Annual Report*, 1875, Appendix A. On passage, see *Colonist*, 12, 14, 20 Mar. and 7, 9, 11 and 12 Apr.1872.

67. See Simon, *Two Nations*, 365; also 337-67.

68. See J. Donald Wilson, "Education in Upper Canada: Sixty Years of Change," and "The Ryerson Years in Canada West," in J. Donald Wilson, Robert M. Stamp and Louis-Philippe Audet, eds., *Canadian Education: A History* (Scarborough: Prentice-Hall, 1970), 190-240.

69. Executive Council session of 27 Feb. 1869, in *Journals*, v. 4, 115.

70. *Colonist*, 5 May 1872.

71. Anthony Musgrave to Earl Granville, 30 Oct. 1869, quoted in Ormsby, *British Columbia*, 242.

72. Angl. Ch., Dioc. Col., *Annual Report*, 1868: 102. Bishop Hills was in England on leave 1869-71 and so came back to a *fait accompli*.

73. *Colonist*, 13 Apr. 1872, and 29 Apr. 1867.

74. *Ibid.*, 7 Apr. 1872. See Ormsby, *British Columbia*, 252, on Trutch's appointment; and Hills,

Diary, 5 Dec. 1884, on Trutch's attitude to Canadians.

75. *Colonist*, 9 Apr. 1872; see also 11 and 12 Apr. 1872.

76. *Ibid.*, 23 and 24 Apr. 1872; see also 25 and 26 Apr. 1872.

77. *Ibid.*, 7 May 1876; see also 9 May 1876.

78. The Anglican Church in Canada amalgamated in 1893. Walter N. Sage, "The Early Days of the Church of England on the Pacific Slope, 1579-1879," *Journal of the Canadian Church Historical Society* 2 (1953): 1-17; Peake, "The Anglican Church"; and Angl. Ch., Dioc. Col., *Annual Report*, 1883: 37-38. On Bishop Hills' opposition to the consolidation of the church in Canada, see Hills, Diary, 25 June 1891; on Canadian indifference to the church in British Columbia, see 10 Nov. 1892.

79. Angl. Ch., Dioc. Col., *Annual Report*, 1878: 18; see also 1871: 72, and 1872: 8.

80. Rev. Robert H. Gowen, *Church Work in British Columbia, Being a Memoir of the Episcopate of Acton Windeyer Sillitoe, D.D., D.C.L., First Bishop of New Westminster* (London: Longmans, Green, and Col, 1899), 71, 77 and 93; *The Churchman's Gazette and New Westminster Diocesan Chronicle*, 1883: 283; Angl. Ch., Diocese of New Westminster, *Quarterly Paper* 1 (1884): 10-12, and 2 (1884): 8-10 and 29-35.

81. Angl. Ch., Dioc. Col., *Annual Report*, 1891: 33-34.

82. *Churchman's Gazette*, 1891: 823; see also Angl. Ch., Dioc. N.W., Synod, *Address*, 1899: 6-10; and *Churchman's Gazette*, 1886: 298; 1887: 397 and 406-07.

83. Angl. Ch., Dioc. Col., *Annual Report*, 1868: 9; 1874: 29; 1876: 13; and 1884/85: 7.

84. Gowen, *Church Work*, 137-39; and Angl. Ch., Dioc. N.W., *Quarterly Paper*, no. 6 (1885): 12-13. See also 4 (1885): 13-14, 7 (1886): 11-13; and *Churchman's Gazette*, 1883-1888.

85. *Colonist*, 30 Dec. 1874; *Guide to the Province of British Columbia for 1877-78* (Victoria: T.N. Hibben & Co., 1877), 270; and Hills, Diary, 1874-1875, esp. 1 and 4 Nov. 1874. See also 3 and 6 Jan. 1877 and 19 Dec. 1877.

86. Angl. Ch., Dioc. Col., *Report*, 1881: 15 and 30; 1883: 17; 1885: 12; 1886: 10; 1887: 1-11 and 18; 1889: 18; and 1895: 15. See also *Colonist*, 31 Aug. 1892; 29 Aug. 1893; and 21 Aug. 1949; and *Victoria Illustrated* (Victoria: Ellis & Co., 1891), 26-27.

87. *Colonist*, 28 Apr. 1876; see also 29-30 Apr. and 2-3 May 1876.

88. See Edith Down, *St. Ann's: Mid Twin Rivers and Hills, 1880-1980* (Kamloops: Sisters of St. Ann, Victoria, 1980); Down, *A Century of Service*, 66, 68-69, 74-79, 82-87 and 92-96; Cronin, *Cross in the Wilderness*, 108-120, 134 and 136; *Colonist*, 21 Nov. 1879, 25 Aug. 1901, 28 Aug. 1907, 21 Apr. 1908, 19 Apr., 3 May and 9 Aug. 1925, 27 Aug. 1930, 14 Apr. 1940, 3 Nov. 1960, and 9 May 1976; *Province* (Vancouver), 28 May 1938, and 1 June 1968; *Columbian*, 18 Jan. 1926; *Nanaimo Daily Press*, 15 Mar. 1962; *Cowichan Leader*, 26 Oct. 1939; and *Kamloops Daily Sentinel*, 4 Feb. 1967.

89. On the passage of the new act, see *Colonist*, 4, 6 and 11-13 May 1876.

90. *Daily Standard* (Victoria), 7 Sept. 1876. See also *Colonist*, 8 and 22 Aug. and 15 Sept. 1876.

91. *Colonist*, 6, 7, 9, 15 and 16 Sept. 1876; and *Daily Standard*, 2, 5-8, 11 and 12 Sept. 1876.

92. British Columbia, Superintendent of Education, *Annual Report*, 1876: Appendix B.

93. See Johnson, *Jessop*.

94. British Columbia, Superintendent of Education, *Annual Report*, 1878: 179. The first national census to include British Columbia, taken in 1881, put the White population at 19 448. *Census of Canada*, 1881, v. 1, 298-99 and 394-95.

95. British Columbia, Superintendent of Education, *Annual Report*, 1886: 135.

96. *Ibid.*, 1877: 20.

97. *Ibid.*, 1876: 91; see also 1872: 31; 1874: 7; and 1883: 92, for the last mention. For more detail on the history of private education, see chapter 18 in this book.

Childhood and Pupilhood

Part 1

2

White Supremacy and the Rhetoric of Educational Indoctrination: A Canadian Case Study

Timothy J. Stanley

By 1925, British Columbia (B.C.), Canada's westernmost province, had been made into a White supremacist society. In this society, an individual's "race"[1] defined his or her political and civil rights and potential areas of economic activity and circumscribed such day-to-day matters as place of residence. First Nations people (North American "Indians") and Asians, unlike Whites, were politically disenfranchised, barred from certain occupations and free associations, confronted by legalized discrimination and subjected to random violence.[2] In short it was "A White Man's Province" which defined non-White peoples as intrinsically alien.

This society, however, did not come into existence overnight. It was constructed through political and ideological definitions which claimed that Whites properly "belonged" in British Columbia and First Nations people and Asians did not.[3] Definitions of this kind were evident shortly after the province's entry into the Canadian confederation in 1871, when First Nations people and Asians were disenfranchised. At the time, First Nations people were the overwhelming majority of the population, and the Chinese were one-sixth of the remaining population.[4]

State-controlled schooling was integral to the construction of supremacist hegemony in B.C. As state schooling became a mass phenomenon,[5] the school came to be one of the chief vehicles for indoctrinating the population of the province in supremacist ideology. School textbooks were particularly important in transmitting a nexus of ideas about patriotism, citizenship and "character" which made supremacist notions virtually impossible to challenge. Above all textbooks fostered "an ideology of difference" which legitimated the White occupation of the province as both natural and morally necessary, at the same time that it rendered First Nations people and Asians as "Other," as "that which Europeans were not,"[6] as morally depraved and illegitimate in their presence.

Imperialism was at the centre of this process of indoctrination. Canada in 1885 was an integral, although self-governing, part of the British Empire. Imperialism, and Canada's role in it, was at the heart of discussions among the country's leading intellectuals,[7] many of whom argued that Canada had its own imperial mission: expansion into, and the European settlement of, the West where a new and better British nation could be built.[8] Canada's own westward expansion was in this sense part of the New Imperialism which led the Western powers to scramble to divide up the remaining autonomous areas of the world.[9]

✳   Imperialism and racism went hand in hand. Imperial expansion required the subjugation of the peoples already inhabiting the land. In Canada, expansion was not a peaceful process, but was carried out by the same means employed in other parts of the British Empire: troops, gunboats, police, government agents, civilian traders and missionaries.[10] As in other parts of the British Empire, "opening up" areas for European settlement was achieved at tremendous cost to aboriginal peoples.[11] And, once territories were "opened up," efforts were made to ensure that non-Europeans were kept out of the now "unoccupied" lands. In the British Empire these efforts were often directed against Asians. The Asiatic Exclusionists of South Africa, Australia, New Zealand and Canada were well aware of, and often consciously copied, each others policies.[12]

As the infrastructure of western expansion, the Canadian Pacific Railroad (CPR), neared completion during the 1880s, racism intensified for both the First Nations people and the Asians of British Columbia. In 1885, new federal franchise legislation reaffirmed the disenfranchisement of both groups.[13] Increasingly, First Nations were subjected to the federal system of control, established under the Indian Act, involving "wardship," Indian agents, reservations and regulations. In 1884, for example, Parliament barred West Coast groups from practising the Potlatch, ceremonies central to traditional government and economy. As the nineteenth century drew to a close, where First Nations people had earlier played important roles in the White economy, they were often marginalised.[14] The mid-1880s also saw an intensification of anti-Chinese racism. Large number of Chinese laborers, brought into B.C. to build the CPR line, immediately found themselves to be the objects of exclusionist pressure. In 1885, at a time when certain Europeans were given free land to encourage their immigration to Canada, the Chinese became the only group to be subjected to an immigration head tax.[15] In subsequent years, a series of provincial and municipal policies effectively barred the Chinese from working on Crown contracts or for certain corporations, and from practising professions such as law, pharmacy and teaching. Various practices ghettoised Chinese workers into low-paying, labor-intensive sectors of the economy, segregated them in Chinatowns and deprived them of family life. These measures culminated in 1923 with the enactment of the Chinese Immigration Act which effectively excluded Chinese from immigrating to Canada.[16]

By 1925, as mentioned above, British Columbia had become a White supremacist society. "Race" concepts were fixed and used to justify differential political and social treatment of Whites, Asians and First Nations people. Institutional and social segregation on the basis of "race" ensured that members of these groups normally did not interact with each other at the level of day-to-day existence and that supremacist notions went largely unchallenged.

By helping to "organize"[17] British Columbia society on the basis of "race," and by indoctrinating students in supremacist ideology, schooling played an important role in promoting White domination in B.C. The schools' roles of organization and indoctrination were inseparable. By segregating students according to "race," schools insulated White students from the common humanity of non-Whites, thus facilitating their indoctrination in the ideologies of dominance: imperialism and racism. Meanwhile, racist notions of innate differences among Whites, Asians and First Nations people justified school segregation.

First Nations and White children normally attended completely different school systems. Under the division of powers established by the British North America Act of 1867, education was a provincial responsibility, while the federal government assumed "wardship" over and responsibility for Indians, including their education. This division of responsibilities was continued under the Terms of Union through which British Columbia entered confederation in 1871. Consequently when the public school system of British Columbia was formally established the following year, First Nations people were excluded. A separate federally funded and controlled system of missionary-run schools for First Nations children was established in B.C. as elsewhere in Canada. These schools were often established away from urban areas. Thus First Nations people would have been rendered invisible as far as most White children were concerned.[18]

Asians for their part were usually segregated within the provincial school system. For example, after 1900 when Chinese students began to enter the provincial school system in significant numbers, school boards in Vancouver, Victoria, and other centres, segregated them in "special" classes and "special" schools for at least part of their education. This segregation continued until after the Second World War. Visibly setting Asian children apart from White children helped to define them as self-evidently aberrant from the norm of White society.[19]

The ideological role of schooling was evident in the textbooks used in B.C. schools. The late nineteenth and early twentieth centuries were eras in which textbooks were in practice the curriculum and in which school readers, geographies and histories were intended to transmit what one contemporary observer referred to as "the dominant ideas of the people at the time that they were written."[20] Readers, for example, the most important textbooks, were intended to "excite the interest, improve the taste, develope [sic] the judgment, and ennoble the ideals of the pupils."[21] Through a variety of contents – fairy stories, adventure fiction, morality and historical tales, heroic and nature poetry, and excerpts from the great works of English literature – readers sought to describe and explain the world. In the process of describing the world, readers simplified and abstracted it. They presented the world not so much as it actually was, but rather as it was "represented" to be in Western, and especially British, elite culture.[22] In later years, as the curriculum diversified, other texts joined this function.

One of the central facts of the world as represented to B.C. students by their textbooks was imperialism: the Western European and increasingly American domination of the world.[23] The textbooks used in B.C. between 1885 and 1925 never questioned this domination. Instead they reproduced and propagated a world-view based on an "ideology of difference" which legitimated it.

Textbooks were able to play this ideological role because their carefully controlled contents presented a world-view that was consistent with elite opinion.[24] The extent of ideological agreement about textbooks in B.C. was demonstrated on one occasion when a textbook which did not completely support conventional interpretations was banned in the province for presenting a supposedly subversive perspective.[25]

From the inception of the British Columbia school system, control over textbooks was one of its chief forms of bureaucratic regulation. Teachers in B.C. were required to use only certain "prescribed" texts. As in other parts of English Canada, "School inspection and examinations were directly linked to textbooks. Inspectors policed their use and based their judgments of school achievement upon pupil knowledge of their contents."[26] Periodically lists of these textbooks were revised and published in official documents.[27]

The official weight placed on textbooks suggests that teaching rarely deviated from them. Classroom teaching often involved little more than having students read, memorize and recite passages from the prescribed text. This emphasis was apparent in the high-school entrance examinations. For example, the 1904 Canadian history exam gave students seventy-five minutes to answer seven questions. Typical of the questions was one requiring students to write a paragraph describing "North American Indians, telling the names of the tribes, where they lived, their physical characteristics and manner of life."[28] Unless students memorized sections of the authorized textbook which dealt directly with the examination content, it is difficult to imagine that they could have satisfactorily completed such an exam in so short a time.

Starting in 1908, students were given most elementary textbooks, and some high-school texts, by the Free Text Book Branch of the Department of Education. This distribution ensured the mass distribution of "school knowledge" as 10 000 or more copies of a reader and 5 000 copies of a history might be given away each year.[29] Textbooks were thus able broadly to disseminate imperialist and racist ideology in B.C.

The textbooks themselves were remarkably stable in their contents, at least as far as their imperialist and racist themes were concerned.[30] First, through patriotic themes, they described the British Empire as a moral enterprise to the benefit of subject peoples and linked Canada and British Columbia to this enterprise. Second, an imperialist ethic constructed around the notion of "character" transformed B.C. classrooms into imperial outposts and allowed students personally to become part of, and share in the responsibility for, this imperial mission.[31] Third, by explaining the Empire as the product of genetically based moral superiority, they presented subject peoples as morally deficient Others. Finally, textbooks fixed these notions of difference into a scientifically proscribed division of humanity in a hierarchy of "race."

In his 1893 geography primer, *Round the Empire*, George R. Parkin wrote that he hoped his "little volume" would assist teachers "in building up British patriotism on that basis of wider knowledge which is necessitated by the wonderful facts of our national growth."[32] To Parkin and many of his contemporaries, "patriotism" and support for imperialism were synonymous.[33] Between 1885 and 1925 textbooks presented B.C. students with Parkin's "wider knowledge" in order to instil patriotic feelings. The "wonderful facts" of "national growth," that is, of Britain's imperialist expansion, linked B.C. classrooms to the Empire. Historical, geographic and civic knowledge described Canada as an integral and important part of the Empire and made the Empire into a terrain for the imaginations of B.C. students.

Textbooks often linked Canada and the Empire directly through their physical organization. Typical was a reader in the W.J. Gage and Company's *Canadian Readers* series of the 1880s and 1890s which contained "Canadian" items such as a letter form a "friend" in Ottawa, the poems "Our Canadian Home" and "The Maple Leaf Forever." Also included were British stories such as one on the Duke of Wellington and an imperial epic about a boy who chose certain death by staying at his father's side during a colonial war in Africa.[34] Even after the First World War, the *Canadian Readers* (1922) series included Canadian and British contents. For example, the Fifth Reader began with "Rule, Britannia" but also contained "A Canadian Boat-Song."[35]

Textbooks not only physically linked Britain and Canada: they did not differentiate between Canadian nationalism and British imperialism. For one thing, even the language used in Canadian texts to describe the Empire was inclusive. For example, William Francis Collier's *History of the British Empire*, one of the history texts authorized for use in B.C. before 1900, referred to "Our Indian Empire,"[36] while an early twentieth-century elementary-level Canadian history spoke of "the common burden" resulting from the Boer War.[37] A 1921 high-school text, written by the chairman of the History Department at the University of Toronto, identified the Canadian troops wounded and killed during the First World War as "only part of the vast cost to the British Empire for its share of the victory."[38]

Discussions of citizenship made clear that students were citizens both of Canada and of the Empire. A contribution to Gage's Fourth Reader during the 1880s argued that the relatively new Dominion of Canada had only one respectable option open to it, "to seek, in the consolidation of the empire, a common imperial citizenship, with common responsibilities and a common heritage."[39] The theme that Canadians and British Columbians shared in "a common imperial citizenship" was returned to repeatedly in subsequent years. Even W.L. Grant's *History of Canada*, the history text which was banned in B.C. shortly after its introduction in 1920 for being "anti-British" and "pro-German,"[40] pointed out that "every Canadian is at once a citizen of a municipality, of a province, of a Dominion, and of an Empire," and concluded by urging students to love their municipality, province and dominion:

And beyond even Canada we must love the worldwide Empire of whose people an English poet has said:

> We sailed wherever ship could sail,
> We founded many a mighty state,
> Pray God our greatness may not fail
> Through craven fear of being great![41]

Thus throughout the period under consideration, the textbooks used in B.C. represented Canada and Canadian identity as inseparable from Britain and the Empire.

In order to instil patriotic feelings for the Empire, British Columbia textbooks portrayed imperialism as a fundamentally moral enterprise. Britain, itself, was made into the guardian of civilization and virtue. W. J. Robertson's turn-of-the-century elementary text, *Public School History of England and Canada*, made this characterization explicit. After noting the vastness and diversity of the Empire, Robertson concluded his discussion of English history by pointing out,

> But better than all, England's influence for truth, justice, and righteousness, is greater than ever. She still leads all peoples in the struggle against vice, ignorance and tyranny. Her shores are still a safe refuge for the oppressed of all nations, and from her the patriots of all lands derive hope and encouragement.[42]

Potential moral dilemmas associated with imperialism were rationalized on the ground that British rule was more just and better for subject peoples than any other system of rule could ever be. This rationalization was especially evident in discussions of British rule in India. For example, the post-First World War *History of England for Public Schools* noted, "But it is well for India that she is under British rule. Without the firm control of a guiding power, she would be torn by internal strife and exposed to the greed and trickery of powerful neighbors."[43] Readers were told that only one-seventh of the Empire's population was "of British blood" and that,

> Unless this fact is grasped clearly, it is impossible to appreciate the wonderful work being done in controlling and civilizing the millions of subject peoples, comprising hundreds of races, each with its own language, customs, and religion. Rarely, if ever, does Britain find it necessary to resort to force in governing her subject peoples. Even their prejudices are respected; their religion, their social customs, and local laws are seldom interfered with, unless for the purpose of preventing crime or abolishing brutal customs.[44]

Thus the Empire was the best possible form of government as its was really a moral crusade bringing civilization and enlightenment to millions.

According to textbooks' rendering of the world, the Canadian federal government was the direct heir of this benign imperial tradition. For example, Canada's treatment of its aboriginal peoples was categorized as "honest and generous."[45] Texts praised the Royal Proclamation of 1763, which recognized aboriginal title to the land and called for the negotiation of treaties or purchases of land prior to European settlement, as the basis of good government in Canada. Textbooks claimed that the Royal Proclamation "has ever since been followed,"[46] even though in British Columbia and much of northern Canada aboriginal title had yet to be recognized through treaty or purchase. The Riel Rebellion of 1885, which was put down through military action, was explained as a temporary aberration due to the unjustified fear of the Metis that their lands would be taken away from them. "There were also complaints of ill treatment and neglect of duty by dominion officers in the North-West, and the petitions of the half-breeds and Indians did not receive prompt attention from the proper authorities," a 1902 history text admitted, but these problems were put to rest as "an inquiry was made into the grievances of the Indians and half-breeds, and many of the causes of complaint removed."[47]   *proven false now*

British rule in British Columbia similarly was characterized as just and far-seeing. Pre-war texts claimed that the benefits of "British justice" were extended to British Columbia during the 1857 gold rush,[48] while the "wisdom" of British rule was identified as beginning much earlier with the fur trader who "year after year occupied the outposts of civilization, surrounded by savages . . ."[49] and whose "skill in the management of the native races did much to save Canada from the horrors of Indian warfare, and made it possible for the more capable among the Indians to share in the occupations and adopt the pursuits of White men."[50] Still other textbooks presented the process of "civilizing" the B.C. Indians as ongoing. British Columbia texts assured students that the Indians of the province were in the process of transformation from "savages." Maria Lawson and Rosalie Watson Young provided an extended discussion on the "lonely" work of missionaries among First Nations people in their elementary textbook, *A History and Geography of British Columbia* (1913). They noted that "it is felt that more lasting and better work can be done with the children than the adults," and provided sketches labelled "Indian boy, civilised" and "Indian girl, civilised" to demonstrate the lasting results.[51]

Imperialism and its ethos permeated B.C. textbooks between 1885 and 1925. British imperialism was described as morally uplifting and Canada represented as an essential participant in the imperial mission. The British Columbia school curriculum, however, not only depicted the British Empire as a moral enterprise, it was also intended to instil in students a morality built around imperialism, mobilize students behind this enterprise and <u>enable them personally to participate in it.</u>] *how?*

"Patriotism," "citizenship" and "morality" were inexorably linked in the worldview presented in B.C. textbooks. Central to the textbook construction of the nexus of patriotism, citizenship and morality was the notion of "character." "Character" was in fact a metaphor[52] through which the individual stood for the group, and the group could be reduced to an individual. Thus textbooks explained British imperialism by presenting stories about imperialists which were not so much celebrations of their conquests and deeds as they were about their supposedly superior characters. An example was the story "Fidelity" about the son of Sir Henry Havelock, who later won the Victoria Cross in India.[53] Other stories emphasized the virtues of military heroes like Nelson,[54] historical characters such as Oliver Cromwell[55] or the blind courage of The Charge of the Light Brigade.[56] Indeed readers are remarkably stable in their contents throughout this era as certain "tried and true" stories were repeated in different series and editions.[57] History was also seen as the basis for instilling notions of character. As one school inspector noted:

> This subject gives the teacher great opportunities of inculcating true patriotism and citizenship by means of the illustrations of those virtues found in the lives of the great and good men of the nation. From it also an ambition to imitate noble actions and be faithful in the performance of duty may be inspired in the scholars, and all the principles of true morality be brought to their notice in the most forcible manner.[58]

"Character" was also a gendered concept, often meaning "manliness."[59] That it was modelled upon male upper-class ideals is apparent in the readers, whose contents overwhelmingly consisted of stories about upper-class men. But girls were also expected to exhibit "character" as the few stories about women made clear. Thus readers perennially included stories about British heroines such as Florence Nightingale[60] and (after the First World War) Edith Cavell[61] and Canadian heroines Madelaine de Vercheres[62] and Laura Secord.[63]

Above all, "character" linked individual student behavior and feeling to the Empire. This link was made explicit in Lord Rosebery's 1893 foreword to Parkin's *Round the Empire* in comments which were later reprinted in a geography text used during the 1900s.[64] Rosebery told students,

> A collection of states spread over every region of the earth, but owning one head and one flag, is even more important as an influence than as an Empire. . . . With the Empire statesmen are mainly concerned; in the influence every individual can and must have a part. Influence is based on character; and it is on the character of each child that grows into manhood within British limits that the future of our Empire rests.[65]

By exhibiting character in their daily lives, students could play a role in maintaining the "influence" that was the glue of the Empire. Rosebery made clear that this "character" involved selfless devotion, "work, sacrifice and intelligence." These were the same kinds of virtues modelled by readers and other textbooks. Even tolerance was transformed into an imperial virtue by the first B.C. civics text, which identified "a certain imperial feeling" as part of "The Duties of the Citizen." Since "[t]he British Empire is so vast that it contains within itself nations of all languages and all religions," *Canadian Civics* suggested, "respect and toleration for the opinions of others" was essential so that "our brother nations may all have an ardent loyalty, whatever may be their creed, race or tongue."[66]

Through their emphasis on "character," textbooks linked individual students and the Empire. Unless they wished to be accused of undermining the Empire, students had to be virtuous. Since, as has been described earlier, textbook knowledge represented Canada as an integral part of the Empire and the Empire as necessarily good, questioning one's personal responsibility for maintaining the imperial system would have required challenging the self-evident truth of the textbooks. Questioning the legitimacy of the Empire itself would probably have been seen as the ultimate demonstration of "bad character."

If the superior "character" of the British explained their control of the largest empire in history, it followed that the objects of imperial rule – subject people, and the groups to which they belonged – must have had "characters" which were inherently deficient in important ways. In other words, part and parcel of the instillation of imperialist sentiment amongst B.C. students and in the transformation of their classrooms into outposts of Empire was a simultaneous process of "othering."[67] Renderings of this kind were apparent in the treatment Asians and aboriginal peoples received in the textbooks used in B.C.

Textbooks consistently described Asians as the opposites of Whites. Even before most of the restrictive measures against Asians were imposed, Gage's *Canadian Readers* were fostering notions of intrinsic Asian difference. This was evident in the extracts from Montgomery's *A Voyage Round the World* published in the Fifth Reader. It described "Tokio," [sic.] the capital of Japan, as "a veritable human ant-hill," while China was "the land of oddities and contrarities" where:

> Everything seems to be the exact opposite of what we have in this country. In China, the old men fly kites, and the boys look on; people whiten their shoes with chalk, instead of blacking them; white is the colour worn in mourning; the Chinaman mounts his horse from the right, instead of the left side; the place of honor is the left; when he enters a room he takes off, not his hat, but his shoes; and when he meets a friend he shakes hands with himself, and works his own hands up and down like a pump. Men carry fans, and women smoke; men wear their hair as long as it will grow, women carefully put their hair up. The spoken language of China is never written, and the written language is never spoken. A Chinese begins to read a book from the end; and he does not read across the page, but up and down. The wealthy classes have a soup made of bird's nests. Wheelbarrows have sails; the ships have no keels; the roses have no perfume; and the workmen have no Sunday.[68]

This description of the Chinese as the antithesis of the Western norm is an example of the way in which Victorian travel literature promoted notions of innate differences between people. Like travellers' representations of African societies, this description, while appearing to be an objective account of Chinese customs, was in fact creating "a stable form of 'othering.'" Through renderings of this kind, the Chinese were "homogenised into a collective 'they,' which is distilled even further into an iconic 'he' (the standardized adult male specimen)." Even the tense of this description is important as it made people such as the Chinese "the subject of verbs in a timeless present tense, which characterises anything 'he' is or does, not as a particular historical event but as an instance of pregiven custom."[69]

The "othering" of the Chinese remained remarkably consistent throughout this period. The 1922 Canadian Readers Series also had stories contrasting the Chinese with the unspoken norm of White society. For example, the Third Reader in the 1922 series contained a story of "a funny little boy named Ning-Ting." Ning-Ting was also an abstraction removed from history. He was described as "a Chinese boy and does not wear his hair all cropped short as you do. But it is shaved off his head, all but a little piece at the back, and that is plaited into a 'pig-tail,'" despite the fact that the wearing of pig-tails, a symbol of Chinese subjugation under the Manchu, had ended with the 1911 Nationalist Revolution which overthrew the Manchu regime. Again the Chinese were contrasted to the unspoken Western norm as the reader was told that unlike "boys here," Ning-Ting wore "queer, tiny shoes, turned up at the toes," and ate "his supper of rice, not with a spoon, but with two little sticks made of bone, called 'chop-sticks.'" Even Chinese names were fictionalized, as "Ning-Ting" had a cousin "Foo-Choo" and an uncle "Pon-ge-wan-ge."[70]

In British Columbia, the Chinese were not simply the inhabitants of an exotic and distant land, but a major and visible proportion of the population. Textbooks encour-

CHARACTERISTICS OF THE RACES OF MANKIND.[1]

	ETHIOPIAN.	MONGOLIAN.	AMERICAN.	CAUCASIAN.
Former home.	Africa, south of Sahara; Madagascar; Australasia (for example, Philippine Negritos).	Probably highlands of Tibet.	New World.	North Africa.
Present accession.	Africa; United States; West Indies; Nicaragua; Guiana; Brazil.	China; Indo-China; North Asia; Korea; Japan; Malaysia; Turkestan; Asia Minor; Russia (Baltic); Balkan Peninsula; Hungary.	Most are now found in Mexico, Central America, South America, and western United States.	All of Europe; India; northern, central, and western Asia; America; South Africa; Australasia; New Zealand; in fact, over almost all the world.
Physical characteristics.	Long, narrow head; jaws projecting; nose broad, flat; thick lips, rolled outward; large, round, black eyes; deep brown color; black, woolly hair; coarse black hair; scanty beard; height above average.	Broad, round head; moderately projecting jaws; small, concave nose; thin lips; small, oblique, black eyes; color yellowish, pale, and even white; long, coarse black hair; no beard; height below the average.	Head both long and round; slightly projecting, massive jaws; aquiline nose small, black eyes; color coppery, shading to yellowish or brown; hair long, coarse, black; scanty beard; height variable.	Two types: (1) fair; head long; moderately large, blue or gray eyes; long flaxen, brown, or red hair; height above the average: (2) dark; head long in south, round in north; large black eyes; hair wavy, curly, brown or black; in both types jaws small, nose large, straight, or aquiline.
Mental characteristics.	Unintellectual; unprogressive; no science or letters; few arts beyond agriculture and simple weaving, pottery making, etc.; religion very crude, including witchcraft, nature worship, and human sacrifice.	Sullen; sluggish; industrious in temperate zone, elsewhere indolent; arts and letters moderately developed; science slightly; their culture not of modern kind. In religion some are pagans, but most are Buddhists and Mohammedans.	Stern; moody; not emotional; vary from savagery to barbarism; slight knowledge of arts, for example, agriculture, pottery, etc. Highest had rude knowledge of letters and some simple science. Religion a superstition, with nature worship and human sacrifice.	Fair type solid and even stolid; dark type fiery and fickle. Both active and enterprising. Science, letters, and art highly developed. Religion varies from belief in one God to belief in several; includes Christianity, Judaism, Mohammedanism, Brahminism.
Numbers.	Africa 150,000,000 Madagascar 8,000,000 America 20,000,000 Australasia 2,000,000 Total 175,000,000	China, 360,000,000 Japan and Korea, 55,000,000 Indo-China, Malaysia,[2] 85,000,000 Rest of Asia, 80,000,000 Miscellaneous, 4,000,000 Total, 540,000,000	Full blood 9,900,000 Half-breeds 12,270,000 Total 22,170,000 Most in Mexico (6,765,000); Brazil, 4,900,000); 250,000 in United States.	Europe 355,000,000 Asia 290,000,000 Africa 115,000,000 Australasia 15,000,000 5,000,000 Total 770,000,000

1 Based on table in Mill's *International Geography*.
2 The brown race (Fig. 545), often recognized as a fifth division of the human race, is here included among the Mongolian.

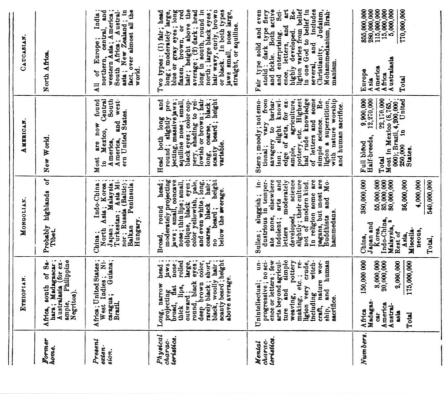

The "races of mankind" as shown in a high school geography text used in B.C. schools from 1905 to 1920.

aged students to consider the Chinese people in their midst. For example, a 1909 geography text stated:

> Most boys and girls, or at least those who live in a city, have seen the Chinaman who keeps a laundry. You will generally see him with his hair plaited into a queue at the back of his head, wearing a blouse and strange-looking thick soled shoes. You can easily see that he is not a native of this country. He does not speak our language. The color of his skin is different from ours. He has no family, no wife, no children.[71]

Again here the Chinese were abstracted into an "iconic *he*" whose customs and appearance were different and who was self-evidently "not a native of this country." Even the use of the epithet "Chinamen" suggested intrinsic alienness. This term, when applied to the Chinese in Canada, identified them as the "men" who belonged in "China."[72]

First Nations people were similarly defined as Other. For example, history textbooks consistently depicted them as "wild," "savage," "cruel" and "uncivilised." The description of Indian "character and habits" in W.H.P. Clement's *The History of Canada* (1895), the winner of a Dominion Education Association contest for a Canadian history text, was typical:

> Master of woodcraft, he was seen at his best when hunting. Upon the warpath he was cruel, tomahawking, scalping and torturing with fiendish ingenuity. A stoic fortitude when himself tortured was about his only heroic quality. In his own village among his own clansmen he spent his time in gambling, story-telling, or taking part in some rude feast. In his domestic life the Indian was not without virtues, and his squaw and papooses were treated with a somewhat rough and careless kindness. To his tribe he was usually faithful, though to his enemies false and crafty. Indian religion was purest superstition . . . .[73]

Once again this kind of description reduced entire peoples to a single "iconic *he*" Unlike the Chinese Other, this Indian Other was described in the past tense. This reflected and would have reinforced the notion that Indians were no longer actors in Canadian society and that they were at best a "vanishing race."[74]

The creation of racial Others did not end with the textbooks' representation of the non-White peoples of British Columbia. From 1900 on, B.C. textbooks fixed notions of character and of the Otherness of non-Whites into "objective" and supposedly morally neutral concepts of "race." In fact, such "race-thinking,"[75] most evident in geography texts, hid the socially constructed nature of "race" and would have lent the authority of science to the differential treatment of Whites, First Nations people and Asians.

The Dominion School Geography, an elementary textbook authorized for use in B.C. between 1911 and 1923, was typical. It began to "lay the foundation for an intelligent study of the continents as places where men live and work" with a consideration of "The Principles of Geography."[76] The principles involved the "objective" description of such matters as the shape of the Earth and its rotation around the sun, and basic geology.[77] Included among these principles was a description of the people of the world. "The White Race" was described as "the most active, enterprising, and intelligent race in the world."[78] Thus Whites were established as the positive norm against which the other "races" could be evaluated. Asians evidently were the opposite of this norm as students were told that "The Yellow Race" included "some of the most backward tribes of the world and, as a rule, are not progressive."[79] Africans and aboriginal peoples in the Americas were described as in need of the paternal guidance of Whites as "The Red Race" was "but little civilised, although a few are beginning to develop industries, such as basketry, pottery, and a little farming," [80] while "The Black Race" was described as "somewhat indolent, like other peoples whose homes are in tropical countries. They are often impulsive in their actions, but they are faithful and affectionate to any one for whom they care."[81]

The most detailed presentation of race concepts was in the high-school geography used between 1900 and 1920. *New Physical Geography* described many of the same "Principles" as the *Dominion School Geography* only in much more detail. Its chapter on "Man and Nature" included a table on "Races of Mankind" which divided up humanity under headings such as "Former home," "Present extension," "Physical characteristics," "Mental characteristics" and "Numbers." The "Mental characteristics" of each "race" made explicit the arrangement of people in a hierarchy of inferiority and superiority. The "Ethiopian" race was described as "unintellectual; unprogressive; no science or letters; few arts beyond agriculture . . .; religion very crude." The "Mongolian" as "Sullen; sluggish; industrious in temperate zone, elsewhere indolent; arts and letters moderately developed, science slightly; their culture not of the modern kind." The "American" race was described as "Stern; moody; not emotional; vary from savagery to barbarism . . . Religion a superstition." By contrast the "Caucasian" race was "Fair type solid and even stolid; dark type fiery and fickle. Both active and enterprising. Science, letters, and art highly developed."[82] The page across from the table presented stereotypical sketches of "the standardised adult male specimen"[83] of each "race" which would have further reinforced the notion that this was a description of objective reality.[84]

By imbuing racial concepts with the authority of science, these texts would have made it as difficult for B.C. students to question the idea of innate differences between Whites, Indians and Chinese as it would have been for them to question that the earth revolved around the sun or that Victoria was the provincial capital.

From the above it is apparent that schooling was an integral element in British Columbia's White supremacist society. Schooling and school textbooks indoctrinated young people in imperial racist ideology, linked notions of difference and notions of character, justified and glorified Western domination and control over the world, and dressed up these notions in a scientific and supposedly objective description of the world. Racism as ideology and organization was so integrated in the forms and content of schooling that it would have been almost impossible to question it, or to conceive of British Columbia as anything other than "the White man's country."

This is not to say that this ideology was universally accepted by all young people or uncritically presented by all teachers. Forcing students to memorize and regurgitate passages of texts does not guarantee agreement or understanding, and children when left to their own devices are quite capable of circumventing adult conventions. Many a teacher has also been in the position of disagreeing with the prescribed textbook's view of the world. Certainly Asians and First Nations people themselves, in challenging racist policies and practices, often resisted being "othered" and took steps to confront Whites with their shared humanity. As Brian Simon has observed, even the most carefully thought-out educational policies often have "unintended consequences."[85]

However, there is considerable evidence that the White people of British Columbia, by and large, bought the ideas of innate difference, "race" and imperial superiority. This is readily apparent in the case of the White working class and Asians. During the same era in which the industrial workers of B.C. established a tradition of labor militancy,[86] they also proved to be among the strongest supporters of Asiatic exclusionism, to the point where they organized their own unions on the basis of "race." Indeed, it has been convincingly argued that they did not see Chinese, and other minority workers, as their fellow workers at all.[87] Support among workers for supremacist ideology was evident in 1902 when the Victoria Trades and Labour Council initiated a call for the segregation of the Chinese students attending Victoria School Board schools. It was evident in 1907 when all fifty-eight of the City of Vancouver's White-only trade unions endorsed a rally called by the Asiatic Exclusion League and continued their support for the League even after the rally ended in major anti-Asian rioting. Again in 1914 White working-class organizations were in the forefront of opposition to the unsuccessful challenge of Canadian immigration regulations by Indian nationalists on the chartered Japanese vessel, the *Komagata Maru*. Thirty years later, acceptance of racist ideology was such that few British Columbians questioned the forced resettlement and internment of over 20 000 Japanese Canadians, many of them Canadian-born, during the Second World War.

While it may be too much to suggest that schools alone were responsible for indoctrinating the population of B.C. in White supremacist concepts, it was in school that many of those who believed that B.C. was and should be the White man's province were first indoctrinated, and systematically so, in racist ideology. It is certainly evident that by 1925 schooling was part of the "organization of an entire texture of life according to an ideology."[88] Racism in B.C. was not an aberration. It was a sustained reality, part of the air that people breathed.

Notes

For invaluable assistance in the preparation of this paper I would like to thank Frances Boyle, J. Donald Wilson, Vincent D'Oyley, Theresa Richardson, Bill Maciejko, Madeleine MacIvor and Michael Jennings for their comments on various drafts of the paper.

1. Throughout this paper the term "race" is used to refer to a socially constructed division of the human species, and should not be construed as having any "objective" biological meaning. See, for example, Ashley Montagu, ed., *The Concept of Race* (London, Free Press of Glencoe, 1964). "Racism" should be taken to mean not only prejudice or hostile attitudes, but "part of the method by which societies, under certain conditions, are structured." See Marion

O'Callaghan, "Introductory Notes," *Sociological Theories: Race and Colonialism* (Paris: UNESCO, 1980), 35.

2. For discussions of White attitudes towards Asians, see W. Peter Ward, *White Canada Forever: Popular Attitudes and Public Policy Towards Orientals in British Columbia* (Montreal: McGill-Queen's University Press, 1978); Patricia E. Roy, "British Columbia's fear of Asians, 1900-1950," *Histoire Sociale/Social History*, Vol. 13, 1980, 161-72; Terrance Craig, *Racial Attitudes in English Canadian Fiction*, Waterloo (Ontario: Wilfrid Laurier University Press, 1987); and Patricia Roy, *A White Man's Province: British Columbia Politicians and Chinese and Japanese Immigrants, 1858-1914* (Vancouver: UBC Press, 1989). Two major histories on the Chinese in Canada are Anthony B. Chan, *Gold Mountain: the Chinese in the New World* (Vancouver: New Star Books, 1983), and Edgar Wickberg, ed., *From China to Canada: A History of the Chinese Communities in Canada* (Toronto: McLelland & Stewart, 1982). Similar histories of the Japanese community remain to be done, but important works focusing on the Second World War era are Ken Adachi, *The Enemy that Never Was: A History of the Japanese Canadians* (Toronto: McLelland & Stewart, 1976) and Ann Gomer Sunahara, *The Politics of Racism: The Uprooting of the Japanese Canadians During the Second World War* (Toronto: J. Lorimer, 1981). Comparable historical studies of the First Nations people in B.C. have also not as yet been done with the exception of Robin Fisher, *Contact and Conflict: Indian-European Relations in British Columbia, 1774-1890* (Vancouver: UBC Press, 1977), which remains the major work on the nineteenth century. More recent works dealing with racism and the role of the state are Kay Anderson, "'East' as 'West': place, state and the institutionalization of myth in Vancouver's Chinatown, 1880-1980" (PhD thesis, UBC, 1987); Duncan Dunae Thomson, "A history of the Okanagan: Indian and whites in the settlement era, 1860-1920" (PhD thesis, UBC, 1985); and Gillian Creese, "Working-class politics, racism and sexism; the making of a politically divided working class in Vancouver, 1900-1939" (PhD thesis, Carleton University, 1986).

3. A similar process of definition took place on the Canadian prairies; see Bill Maciejko, "Ukrainians and prairie school reform, 1896-1921: ethnic and domestic ideologies in Canadian state formation," *Canadian Ethnic Studies/Etudes ethniques au Canada* XXII, no. 2 (1990): 19-40.

4. For population figures, see Ward, *White Canada Forever*, 170-1.

5. Timothy A. Dunn, "The rise of mass public schooling in British Columbia, 1900-1929," in J. Donald Wilson and David C. Jones, eds., *Schooling and Society in Twentieth Century British Columbia* (Calgary: Detselig Enterprises Ltd., 1980), 23-51.

6. For discussions of the creation of notions of the "Other" and ideologies of difference, see Edward W. Said, *Orientalism* (New York: Vintage Books, 1978). See also Henry Louis Gates Jr., ed., *"Race," Writing and Difference*, special issue of *Critical Inquiry*, vol. 12, No. 1 (Autumn 1985), esp. Edward W. Said, "An ideology of difference," 38-58.

7. Carl Berger, *The Sense of Power: Studies in the Ideas of Canadian Imperialism* (Toronto: University of Toronto Press, 1970). See also Douglas Cole, "Canada's 'nationalistic' imperialists," *Revue d'études canadiennes/Journal of Canadian Studies* vol. 5, (1970), 44-9; and "The problem of 'nationalism' and 'imperialism' in British settlement colonies," *Journal of British Studies*, vol. 10 (1971), 160-82.

8. Doug Owram, *Promise of Eden: The Canadian Expansionist Movement and the Idea of the West, 1856-1900* (Toronto: University of Toronto Press, 1980), esp. 125-48.

9. On the importance of the New Imperialism in Canada, see Robert Craig Brown and Ramsay Cook, *Canada, 1896-1921: A Nation Transformed* Toronto, McLelland & Stewart, 1974, p. 27. See also Robert J.D. Page, "Canada and the imperial idea in the Boer War years," *Journal of Canadian Studies*, vol. 5 (197), 33-49; and Robert M. Stamp, "Empire Day in the schools

of Ontario: the training of young imperialists," Alf Chaiton and Neil McDonald, eds., *Canadian Schools and Canadian Identity* (Toronto: Gage, 1977), 100-15.

10. Fisher, *Contact and Conflict;* John L. Tobias, "Canada's subjugation of the Plains Cree, 1879-1885" *Canadian Historical Review,* 64 (1983): 519-48; Barry Gough, *Gunboat Frontier: British Maritime Authority and Northwest Coast Indians, 1846-90* (Vancouver: UBC Press, 1984). See also Robin Fisher, "The impact of European settlement on the indigenous peoples of Australia, New Zealand, and British Columbia," *Canadian Ethnic Studies,* vol. 12 (1980), 1-14.

11. The native population of British Columbia declined from more than an estimated 80 000 in 1835 at the beginning of contact with European settlement to less than 23 000 in 1929. Wilson Duff, *The Indian History of British Columbia, vol. 1: The Impact of the White Man* (Victoria: British Columbia Provincial Museum, 1964), 39, 45.

12. Robert A. Huttenback, "No strangers within the gates: attitudes and policies towards the non-white residents of the British Empire of settlement," *Journal of Imperial and Commonwealth History,* 1 (1973), 271-302, or Robert A. Huttenback, "The British Empire as a 'white man's country': racial attitudes and immigration legislation in the colonies of settlement," *Journal of British Studies* 13 (1973), 108-37.

13. "An Act respecting the electoral franchise," Statutes of Canada, 48-9, (Victoria, 1885), 40: 19-53.

14. Fisher, *Contact and Conflict,* 175-211. For a local study of the institutional containment of native aspirations and the progressive marginalization of aboriginal peoples, see Thomson, "History of the Okanagan."

15. Initially set at $50, by 1903 this tax was raised to $500.

16. See Wickberg, *From China to Canada,* 42-72, 118 ff.; Chan, *Gold Mountain,* 74-85, for discussions of various discriminatory measures. For a discussion of the role of racism in shaping Vancouver's Chinatown, see Anderson, "'East' as 'West,'" and on the ways in which "race" and gender create a differentiated laborr market, see Gillian Creese, "Exclusion or solidarity? Vancouver workers confront the 'oriental problem,'" *BC Studies,* 80 (Winter 1988-9), 24-49.

17. The term "organize" is used here in the same sense that Hannah Arendt, when discussing totalitarian regimes, refers to "[the] organisation of an entire texture of life according to an ideology . . ." See Hannah Arendt, *The Origins of Totalitarianism,* new edition with added prefaces (San Diego, New York and London: Harvest/HBJ, 1951, 1979). She observes that "in Nazi Germany, questioning the validity of racism and anti-semitism when nothing mattered but race origin, when a career depended upon an 'Aryan' physiognomy (Himmler used to select the applicants for the SS from photographs) and the amount of food upon the number of one's Jewish grandparents, was like questioning the existence of the world" (363). Arendt maintained that imperialism was an earlier, albeit less ruthless, form of totalitarianism.

18. Mary Ashworth, *The Forces Which Shaped Them: A History of the Education of Minority Group Children in British Columbia* (Vancouver: New Star Books, 1979); E. Brian Titley, "Indian industrial schools in Western Canada," in Nancy M. Sheehan, J. Donald Wilson and David C. Jones, eds., *Schools in the West: Essays in Canadian Educational History,* (Calgary: Detselig Enterprises Ltd., 1986), 133-53; and Celia Haig-Brown, *Resistance and Renewal: Surviving the Indian Residential School,* (Vancouver: Tillicum Library, 1988).

19. David Chuen-Yan Lai, "The issue of discrimination in education in Victoria, 1901-1923," *Canadian Ethnic Studies,* 19 (1987), 47-67. See also Ashworth, *The Forces Which Shaped Them,* 54-80; and Roy, *A White Man's Province,* 24-7.

20. E.T. White, *Public School Textbooks in Ontario* (London, Ontario: Chas. Chapman Co., 1922), 14. Although completely concerned with Ontario, this remains a valuable resource on textbooks, their selection and reception. White describes a number of instances in which texts

were banned or rewritten because they presented controversial opinions.

21. *New Canadian Readers, 20th Century Edition, Third Reader* [henceforth *New Cdn Third Reader*] (Toronto: Gage, 1900), v.

22. For a discussion of the way in which the world was "represented" to Europeans, see Said, *Orientalism*, 21-3.

23. Other facts included gender and class constructions.

24. Jean Anyon, "Ideology and United States history textbooks," *Harvard Educational Review* 49 (1979): 361-86. Canadian textbook authors included such establishment figures as the noted scientist and Principal of McGill University, Sir William Dawson, the long-time chairman of the Department of History at the University of Toronto, George M. Wrong, and the Rhodes Trust administrator, George Parkin.

25. W. L. *Grant's History of Canada* (Montreal: William Heinemann & Renouf Publishing Co., 1916). See Charles W. Humphries, "The banning of a book in British Columbia," *BC Studies* 1 (Winter 1968-9): 1-12.

26. George Tomkins, *A Common Countenance: Stability and Change in the Canadian Curriculum* (Scarborough, Ontario: Prentice-Hall Canada, 1986), 237.

27. Between 1872 and 1892, these lists were published as part of the Annual Reports of the Superintendent of Education. See British Columbia, Department of Education, *Annual Reports* [hereafter *AR*], Victoria, 1872-92. Between 1893 and 1916, these lists were published periodically in the Department of Education publications, *Manual of the School Law and School Regulations of British Columbia*, with minor changes reported in the *Annual Reports*. After 1919, the Curriculum Branch of the Department of Education published detailed descriptions of the increasingly complex and diversified curriculum, variously titled *Course of Studies*, *Programme of Studies* and *Curriculum Guide*.

28. *AR*, 1904: A, cxiv.

29. See the reports of the Free Textbook Branch in the *ARs*. In 1916, for example, over 10 000 copies of the Beginners Reader, 9 000 of the First Reader, and 10 000 of the Second Reader, along with over 6 000 copies of the Canadian history text were distributed. See *AR*, 1917: A, 85.

30. For a discussion of how textbooks "shift" in their contents during this era, see Harro Van Brummelen, "Shifting perspectives: early British Columbia textbooks from 1872 to 1925," in Sheehan, Wilson and Jones, *Schools in the West*, 12-28. Reprinted from *BC Studies* 60 (Winter 1984-5: 3-27.

31. H. John Field had identified "character" as the "shared supposition" of late Victorian imperialism, the device that linked the individual and the Empire, mobilized the elite round the Empire and enabled the indoctrination of the masses in the imperial idea. "Its usages transmitted a sense of shared intellectual currency; as though, when 'character' came up, everyone knew without further explanation what was being discussed and could in fact even anticipate the ensuing conclusion." See H. John Field, *Toward a Programme of Imperial Life: The British Empire at the Turn of the Century* (Westport: Greenwood Press, 1982), 231-2.

32. George R. Parkin, *Round the Empire* (London, Paris, and Melbourne: Cassell & Co., 1893), xii. This text, written for British elementary schools, was used as a teacher's reference between 1893 and 1906.

33. Hugh Cunningham, "The language of patriotism, 1750-1914," *History Workshop: A Journal of Socialist Historians*, No. 12 (Autumn 1981): 8-33.

34. See *Cdn Readers, Book III* (Toronto: Gage, 1881), 162-6, 170-8, 182-6, 187-8, 193-8, 199-204. See also *Cdn Readers, Book IV* (Toronto: Gage, 1883), 198-201, 226-32, 257-74; *Cdn Readers, Book V* (Toronto: Gage, 1883), 50-5 ff.

35. *Cdn Readers, Book V* (Toronto: Gage/T. Nelson & Sons, 1922).

36. William Francis Collier, *History of the British Empire*, Canadian Series of School Books (Toronto: Canada Publishing Co., 1876), 320.

37. W.J. Robertson's *Public School History of England and Canada, British Columbia Edition* (Toronto: Copp Clark Co., 1902), 192. This text is an adaptation for senior elementary schools of the *High School History of England and Canada* (Toronto: Copp Clark Co., 1891) which was revised for Canadian schools by Robertson from Arabella B. Buckley's (Mrs. Fisher) *History of England (High School History*, p. [5].) The *High School History* also included a section, "History of Canada," written by Robertson. The B.C. edition of the *Public School History* included an appendix, "The History of British Columbia," written by R.E. Gosnell.

38. George M. Wrong, *History of Canada* (Toronto: Ryerson Press, 1921), 353.

39. *Cdn Readers, Bk IV* (1883), 168-73.

40. Humphries, "Banning of a book," 1-12.

41. Grant, *History of Canada*, 377, 378. For similar sentiments, see Clement, *The History of Canada*, 340; Maria Lawson, *History of Canada for Use in Public Schools* (Toronto: Gage, 1906), 265; and I. Gammell, *History of Canada* (Toronto: Gage, 1921), 255. This latter text was originally authorized in 1912.

42. *Public School History*, 1902, 195.

43. *History of England for Public Schools* (Toronto: Macmillan Co. of Canada, 1923), 301.

44. *History of England for Public Schools*, 297.

45. Gammell, *History of Canada*, 108.

46. Clement, *History of Canada*, 95.

47. Robertson, *Public School History*, 275, 276.

48. Maria Lawson and Rosalind Watson Young, *A History and Geography of British Columbia* (Toronto: Educational Book Co., 1913), 54; Gammell, *History of Canada*, 30.

49. Lawson and Young, *British Columbia*, 41.

50. *Ibid.*, 36. This page contains an illustration of an "Indian raid" which indicates the extent to which aboriginal peoples have been fictionalized. A group of white men with revolvers are shown holding off a much larger group of knife-wielding, Afro-haired blacks.

51. *Ibid.*, 70, 67, 72.

52. Nancy L. Stepan, "Race and gender: the role of analogy in science," *Isis* 77 (1986), 261-77.

53. *New Cdn Third Reader* (1900), 180-2.

54. *Ibid.*, 23-8; *Cdn Readers, Book III* (Toronto, Gage/T. Nelson & Sons, 1922), 137-41.

55. Nathaniel Hawthorne, "Oliver Cromwell and Charles I," *The British Columbia Readers, Fourth Reader* (Toronto: Gage, 1916), 20-8. [henceforth *BC Fourth Reader*].

56. *Cdn Readers, Bk V* (1922), 36-9.

57. For example, the *Cdn Reader, Book III* (1881), and the *New Cdn Third Reader* (1900), had sixteen stories in common. The *New Canadian Reader, 20th Century Edition, Fourth Reader* (Toronto: Gage, 1900), and the *BC Fourth Reader* (1916), had identical contents, although different pagination, except for five stories. Many of the same contents reappeared in the 1922 *Cdn Readers, Bk III* which again emphasized character models.

58. William Burns in *Annual Report* (1895), 217.

59. I am indebted to Jane Gaskell for bringing this point to my attention.

60. *New Cdn Third Reader* (1900), 111-14; *Cdn Readers, Bk III* (1922), 67-72.

61. *Cdn Readers, Bk IV* (1922), 251-4.

62. *Cdn Readers, Bk IV* (1883), 226-32.

63. *BC Fourth*, 251-6; *Cdn Readers, Bk V* (1922), 167-9.

64. *New Canadian Geography*, (Toronto: Gage, 1899), 209.

65. Lord Rosebery in Parkin, *Round the Empire*, p. v.

66. R.S. Jenkins, *Canadian Civics* (Toronto: Copp Clark Co., 1918), 167-8. This was used as a teachers' reference and high school text between 1916 and 1925.

67. For a discussion of the ways in which the people of the Middle East have been represented as the opposite of Europeans, see Said, *Orientalism*, 39 ff.

68. *Cdn Readers, Bk V* (1883), 244-6.

69. Mary Louise Pratt, "Scratches on the face of the country; or what Mr. Barrow saw in the land of the Bushmen," *Critical Inquiry* 12 (1985): 120.

70. *Cdn Readers, Bk III* (1922), 25-6.

71. *Our Home and Its Surroundings: A First Book of Modern Geography* (Toronto: Morang Educational Co., 1909), 91-2.

72. The epithet "Chinaman" is an example of an imposed ethnic category. During this era, most Chinese in British Columbia were from the area of South China surrounding Guangzhou. Their collective political term for themselves before 1911 would have been Qingren or "people of Qing," while popularly they referred to themselves as "Tangren" or "people of Tang." This is the name that survives to this day, Vancouver's "Chinatown" being known as "Tangren Qu" or "Tang People's Quarter."

73. Clement, *History of Canada* (1895), 12-13. Indians are described in almost exactly the same terms by Gammell, *History of Canada* (1921), 22-3.

74. The notion of the Indians as "a vanishing race" was popular in B.C. at the turn of the century. This was evident in the memoirs of D.W. Higgins, *The Passing of a Race* (Toronto: W. Briggs, 1905).

75. Hannah Arendt, "Race-thinking before racism," *Review of Politics* 6 (1944): 36-73.

76. *Dominion School Geography* (Toronto: Educational Book Co., 1910), ii.

77. *Ibid.*, 7-59.

78. *Ibid.*, 60.

79. *Ibid.*

80. *Ibid.*, 61.

81. *Ibid.*

82. "Characteristics of the races of mankind" in Ralph S. Tarr, *New Physical Geography* (New York: Macmillan, 1910), 385.

83. Pratt, "Scratches on the face of the country," 120.

84. The sketches included a representative of the "Malay race" and a caption noted that some classifications include "five races" thus creating the illusion that the number of "races" was an objective issue.

85. Brian Simon, "Can education change society?", J. Donald Wilson, ed., *An Imperfect Past: Education and Society in Canadian History* (Vancouver: Centre for the Study of Curriculum and Instruction, UBC, 1984), 30-47.

86. Paul Phillips, *No Power Greater: A Century of Labour in British Columbia* (Vancouver: Boag Foundation, 1967); A. Ross McCormack, *Reformers, Rebels and Revolutionaries: The Western Canadian Radical Movement, 1899-1919* (Toronto: University of Toronto Press, 1977); and Barbara Latham and Roberta Pazdro, eds., *Not Just Pin Money: Selected Essays on the History of Women's Work in British Columbia* (Victoria: Camosun College, 1984).

87. See Creese, "Exclusion or solidarity?", 24-51; W. Peter Ward, "Class and race in the social structure of British Columbia, 1870-1939," *BC Studies* 45 (Spring 1980): 17-36; and Rennie Warburton, "Race and class in British Columbia: comment," *BC Studies* 49 (Spring 1981), 79-85.

88. Arendt, *Totalitarianism*, 363.

3

Schooled For Inequality:
The Education Of British Columbia Aboriginal Children

Jean Barman[1]

The residential school has become a metaphor for the history of Aboriginal education in British Columbia, as in Canada more generally. Any discussion of the broader topic must begin with, and centre on, the residential school, for its existence both curtailed and set the agenda for other educational options. Recent critics of residential schools have very persuasively drawn attention to a range of unacceptable practices from prohibitions on speaking Aboriginal languages to incidents of physical and sexual abuse, and to their consequences for the quality of Aboriginal life in Canada into the late twentieth century.[2] "Subjugation has taken its toll on our cultures. Indigenous peoples have the highest rates of impoverishment, incarceration, suicide and alcoholism in Canada. Much of this can be traced back to the abuse received at the residential schools."[3]

Residential schools' stark legacy assumes an element of tragedy when set in context. The schools' origins in the late nineteenth century lay in a federal policy premised on Aboriginal peoples' assimilation into mainstream Canadian society. "The Indian problem exists owing to the fact that the Indian is untrained to take his place in the world. Once teach him to do this, and the solution is had."[4] By taking children away from the old ways and "civilizing" them into European ways, so the argument ran, "the Indian problem" would have been solved in a single generation.[5] The initial goal of the residential school – and of its less favored counterpart, the federal day school – was the absolute opposite of what occurred. Instead of becoming agents of assimilation, they served, so students' recollections attest, as vehicles for marginalizing generations of young men and woman both from the Canadian mainstream and from home environments.[6]

The purpose of this essay is not to assess the rightness or wrongness of the federal goal of assimilation, but rather to examine why that policy's principal vehicle, the residential school, became such a dismal failure with far reaching consequences for the history of Aboriginal education. The reasons for the failure had to do less with the actions of individual teachers or administrators than with a federal policy that legitimized and even compelled children to be schooled, not for assimilation but for inequality. While teachers and administrators of good will were able to ameliorate the worst aspects of the system for their pupils, all of the individual good will in the world could not have rescued a system that was fundamentally flawed.

The inequality inherent in federal schools for Aboriginal children rests in four complementary attributes of the system as devised and overseen by the federal Department of Indian Affairs. The first was an assumption of the sameness of Aboriginal peoples across Canada. Differences existing between tribes, bands and individuals played no role in a federal policy which viewed Aboriginal peoples solely as a singular "object" to be acted upon. In British Columbia some Aboriginal families were already sending their children to public school when federal policy intervened in the late nineteenth century to declare the residential school, and its lesser complement the day school, their sole educational options. Secondly, despite a parallel curriculum between federal schools and the provincial schools that educated other Canadian children, Aboriginal children were allotted less time in the classroom than were their non-Aboriginal counterparts. The difference was particularly marked in the residential schools that formed the system's showplaces. Thirdly, through the mid-twentieth century the instruction of Aboriginal children occurred within the much older Western tradition of voluntarism as opposed to the growing professionalism of public-school teachers across Canada. Aboriginal schooling was carried on with few exceptions by Christian missionaries primarily concerned with saving souls, only secondarily with literacy education. Fourth, federal funding of schools for Aboriginal children quickly fell below provincial funding levels for public schools. However fine a school's intentions, they became unrealizable. For these four reasons, as well as others, generations of British Columbia Aboriginal children were, effectively if not always deliberately, schooled for inequality.

Assumption Of Aboriginal Peoples' Sameness

When British Columbia joined Confederation, it became subject to the provisions of the British North America Act which made Aboriginal peoples "wards" of the federal government, eligible for federally sponsored schooling, health care and other services on their agreeing to treaties that surrendered traditional lands for much smaller reserves. The policy combined economics with racism. At the time the Canadian Confederation was created in 1867, Aboriginal peoples still occupied much of the land on which newcomers hoped to settle. The rhetoric of the day, premised in biological determinism, assumed that persons who were non-White were inferior by virtue of their race alone and so incapable of using the land to best advantage or otherwise determining their own destiny.[7] The British North America Act was consistent with this thinking. It made no attempt to distinguish Aboriginal peoples in all of their diversity and individuality, but simply reduced them to a single dependent status.

Schooling was initially viewed as something of a panacea by the new Department of Indian Affairs [DIA] encharged with overseeing all aspects of federal policy. Using reasoning very similar to that gaining force in the United States, policy makers looked to Aboriginal peoples' civilization "so as to cause them to reside in towns, or, in the case of farmers, in settlements of white people, and thus become amalgamated with the general community."[8] The residential school became viewed as the best means to achieve that goal, by separating the young from their families and thereby from the old ways.

> The Indian youth, to enable him to cope successfully with his brother of white origin, must be dissociated from the prejudicial influences by which he is surrounded on the reserve of his band. And the necessity for the establishment more generally of institutions, whereat Indian children, besides being instructed in the usual branches of education, will be lodged, fed, clothed, kept separate from home influences, taught trades and instructed in agriculture, is becoming every year more apparent.[9]

Two types of residential schools came into being in Canada, boarding schools for younger children and industrial schools for their older siblings. Not only did the latter put greater emphasis on occupational training, but they tended to be larger and located further away from pupils' home reserves.[10] Over time the distinction broke down between the two types of schools, and they all became known as residential schools. Day schools were perceived as less acceptable than either boarding or industrial schools, to be established only where circumstances did not permit their preferred counterparts.

For Aboriginal peoples in British Columbia, the consequences of federal policy favoring residential schools were particularly poignant, for it removed an educational option already in place that might have given the children rough equality with their contemporaries across the young province. For more than a decade British Columbia Aboriginal children had been finding their way into provincial public schools alongside their neighbours and, to some extent, gaining acceptance there. Another narrative might well be constructed today about British Columbia Aboriginal peoples had not federal policy intervened.

Part of the explanation for this situation lies in demographics and part in Aboriginal peoples' circumstances of everyday life. At the time British Columbia entered Confederation in 1871, Aboriginal peoples still formed the overwhelming proportion of the population. They totalled some 25 000 or more as compared to about 1 500 Chinese, almost all of them adult males, some 500 Blacks, and approximately 8 500 Europeans.[11] In many outlying settlements Aboriginal children were necessary to secure the minimum enrolment necessary for a public school's establishment and survival.

British Columbia Aboriginal peoples were among the world's most distinctive. Linguistic divisions were complex, economies self-sufficient, and cultures more developed, in many respects, than in any other part of the continent north of Mexico.[12] Generational continuity was assured through ongoing, lifelong education premised on the young modelling their behavior upon their elders. There was, moreover, a long tradition of economic and social interaction with Europeans, initially in the fur trade and then during the gold rush beginning in 1858. The continued availability of such traditional staples as salmon, cedar and game animals meant that British Columbia Aboriginal peoples never experienced the wrenching despair and utter dependency that befell their prairie counterparts. As the Department of Indian Affairs phrased it with particular reference to British Columbia, "The Indians have been from the earliest times self-supporting, and the advent of white population, which in the west caused the complete disappearance of the buffalo, did not occasion any serious change in their source of food-supply."[13] Long after British Columbia entered Confederation in 1871, contemporaries continued to distinguish the province's Aboriginal population from those elsewhere in North America. A guide to prospective settlers asserted: "The intending settler may depend on finding the Indians peaceable, intelligent, eager to learn and industrious to a degree unknown elsewhere among the aborigines of America."[14] More than one settler was struck by how "the Indians differ *toto caelo* from the North West plains Indians. They are very well off."[15]

The published annual reports of the Department of Indian Affairs repeatedly lauded British Columbia's Aboriginal peoples. 1874: "The intelligence of the Indians of that province gives encouragement to the expectation that with liberal encouragement the Indians, who form so large a proportion of the population, may, as they are not deficient in enterprise, be transformed into valuable members of the community."[16] 1880: "The Indians of British Columbia exhibit more enterprise than those of any other Province in the Dominion."[17] 1890: "The Indians of this Province, with but few exceptions, pursued their wanted course of manly independence, intelligent enterprise, and unflagging industry during the past year."[18] 1902: "Taking them altogether, the British Columbia Indians are remarkably industrious, enterprising, self-reliance, honest, sober and law-abiding. They are good neighbours, and friendly with the whites and with each other."[19]

Perhaps then, it is not surprising that as public schools became established across the far-flung province in the 1870s and 1880s, Aboriginal children were often among the first pupils to enrol alongside their settler neighbors. The Superintendent of Education received numerous letters from teachers and others enquiring about provincial policy toward "Indian children of school age in the immediate vicinity whose parents express a willingness to send to School."[20] "There are a few bright-looking native children here. Would it be all right if I get them to attend the school?"[21] "There are numbers of Indian children that for whom no provision in the way of education has hitherto been made."[22] "There are three Indian children that wish to attend the school when it is established."[23]

The Superintendent of Education was consistently supportive. "You are doing perfectly right in admitting Indian children so long as they are not taken [by force] & conduct themselves properly. . . . If they are troublesome or dirty the trustees must prohibit their attendance – Personally I am glad to hear of their attendance wherever circumstances will admit of it."[24] The Superintendent responded in 1886 to a query by some "parents of white children" about Indian children's attendance: "There is no authority given in the School Act to refuse them admittance. Since the inception of the present School system they have been admitted on an equality with other pupils."[25]

Aboriginal children's attendance was for the most part accepted without question, as a matter of course, perhaps because they were often not that different in actions and even appearance from their non-Aboriginal contemporaries. Some teachers encouraged Aboriginal children into their schools. One young woman wrote the Superintendent about a young Aboriginal boy who "sent another boy to me to get a book as he wanted to learn to read. . . . I told him if he was so anxious to learn he could come to school as long as he behaved properly. He has come ever since and is acquitting himself creditably both to himself and me."[26] This teacher may have started a trend. "Since then another Indian boy has come to me wanting to come. I permitted him to do so on the same conditions."[27] Another teacher wrote with particular reference to the Aboriginal children in her classroom: "I love the children, black and white, are the same to me. I am an impartial Teacher. Act conscientiously and as long as I am able to impart instruction to them they shall all have it in equality."[28]

Aboriginal families in British Columbia demonstrated a resourcefulness that would have served them well had not a federal education policy assuming their sameness across Canada intervened. Although only a handful of treaties were ever made in British Columbia, similar federal services were gradually provided there as well. And despite the repeated statements in the annual reports of the Department of Indian Affairs lauding the distinctiveness of British Columbia Aboriginal people, they were treated no differently than their counterparts across Canada.

As the number of federal schools grew, it became increasingly difficult for Aboriginal children to attend their local school. The shift began in about 1888. A teacher noted concerning an "application to admit an Indian as a pupil" that the Trustees "are of the opinion that the Dominion Government undertakes to provide for the educational interests of the Indians," to which the Superintendent responded:

> Although Indian children are considered to be wards of the Dominion Government, yet it has not been the custom to refuse them admittance to Public Schools whose attendance is not over large. Of course they are required to comply with the Rules and Regulations as to cleanliness, supplying themselves with books etc. In all cases refer such matters to the Board of Trustees.[29]

The Superintendent was less sanguine a year later, considering that "Indian children are wards of the Dominion Government, and are not presumed to be entitled to attend the Public Schools of the Province."[30]

Yet so many Aboriginal children continued to attend British Columbia public schools that in the fall of 1891 the Superintendent of Education somewhat relented, stating in a circular that "the matter of attendance of Indian children is left entirely in the hands of the [local] Board of Trustees."[31] Responses from individual teachers and boards of trustees almost all supported Aboriginal children's continued presence. A teacher wrote that they were "quiet, tidy and much more devoted to study than the average child,"[32] another that "the rate-payers seem to be of the opinion that it is of advantage to the community if the young Indians who reside here was [sic] educated."[33] The secretary of a school board reported that "the present Trustees all think the privilege of getting a better education should not be denied them especially as their parents seem grateful for it."[34] Two years later, in the fall of 1893, the Superintendent ruled that, "if a single parent objects to the attendance of Indian pupils, they cannot be permitted to attend,"[35] to which one trustee responded indignantly that "it is desirable that in every locality the relations between Indians & settlers should be friendly but this ruling is not likely to secure it."[36]

While some Aboriginal children continued to attend individual public schools up to the time of the First World War and a few thereafter, they were the exceptions rather than the rule. Growing numbers of settlers meant that Aboriginal pupils were no longer essential to most schools' survival, schools received no funding for Aboriginal pupils, and federal policy discouraged their attendance. The moment of opportunity had passed. By 1900 British Columbia possessed 14 residential and 28 day schools, enrolling 675 and 893 pupils respectively.[37] Two decades later totals had risen to 1 115 children in 17 residential schools and 1 197 in 46 day schools, by 1940 to 2 035 children in 15 residential schools and 2 025 in 65 day schools.

Into the mid-twentieth century federal policy toward Aboriginal peoples, adults as well as children, refused to acknowledge their distinctiveness within geographical areas or as individuals. They were treated as a single category to be dealt with as expeditiously and economically as possible. The initiative demonstrated by British Columbia Aboriginal peoples, in political and economic matters as well as schooling, only served to label them as nuisances for refusing to conform into dependency.[38]

Time In The Classroom

Logically, the shift of British Columbia Aboriginal children from provincial to federal schools should not have made any difference to them academically, for in 1895 the newly established School Branch of the Department of Indian Affairs laid down a uniform curriculum little different in form from its provincial counterparts. Aboriginal pupils were to move between six "standards" or grades centred around readers similar to those being used in provincial systems.[39] Instruction was to be offered in writing, arithmetic, English, geography, ethics, history, vocal music, calisthenics and religion. It was anticipated that "the work done and results obtained [would] equal those of the common-schools of the rural districts."[40]

The new curriculum would have boded well for the proclaimed federal goal of Aboriginal peoples' assimilation had not children been expected somehow to get through it in less time each day than was allotted their counterparts in provincial schools. While some flexibility existed in day schools which were never that closely monitored by federal authorities, in residential schools only half of each day was usually spent in the classroom. Sometimes this occurred in segments. At one school, the hours of instruction ran 9-11:30 and 2-3 p.m.[41] Regardless of format, the total was two to four hours per day compared with the five hours or longer that other Canadian children spent on the prescribed curriculum.

The reports on individual schools included in the annual reports of the Department of Indian Affairs often implied longer hours of instruction, but accounts from individual schools almost always reveal a shorter time period. Personal testimonies are damning. "We went to school in the mornings about ten o'clock. I would stay there till dinner time. Twelve o'clock."[42] "We spent very little time in the classroom.

We were in the classroom from nine o'clock in the morning until noon. Another shift [of children] came into the classroom at one o'clock in the afternoon and stayed until three."[43] At a third, "We knew we had to do our chores, such as sweeping the dormitory, cleaning the washrooms, in the morning, and go to school half a day. We had our chores to do in the afternoon."[44] This pupil's daily round grew more onerous as he got older: "Our job was getting tougher. We went to school for half a day. One month you worked in the mornings and the next month you worked in the afternoons. We never went to school full-time until the last year, in grade eight."[45] In his discussion of the academic subjects taught in British Columbia Catholic residential schools, oblate historian Thomas Lascelles concluded:

> Usually they occupied the students several hours a day, the remainder being devoted to training in practical skills such as farming, shoemaking and housekeeping, an arrangement which was not abandoned until the 1940s or 1950s when pupils began to spend full time on academic subjects, and to follow Provincial curricula more closely.[46]

Shorter time periods for classroom instruction existed despite many children's being forced to study in a second language. As part of their becoming "civilized," federal policy asserted that Aboriginal children be "taught in the English language exclusively."[47] The languages that most boys and girls brought with them to school were almost always prohibited, even for private conversations between pupils. "Native languages were forbidden. English was the only allowable language."[48] "What I could never understand, we weren't allowed to speak our language. If we were heard speaking Shuswap, we were punished. We were made to write on the board one hundred times, 'I will not speak Indian any more.'"[49] "In my first meeting with the brother, he showed me a long black leather strap and told me, through my interpreter, 'If you are ever caught speaking Indian this is what you will get across your hands.'"[50]

The logic behind the limited time allotted to the formal curriculum was obvious to policy makers. While it was important that Aboriginal children be made literate in English, it was even more critical that they acquire the practical skills permitting their entry into mainstream society, but only at its very lowest rungs. Although assimilation was a desirable goal, its achievement should not challenge the status quo. During the second half of each school day boys learned how to do farm chores or some low-status trade such as shoemaking, girls to perform household tasks ranging from potato peeling to dusting to needlework. As a pamphlet widely distributed by the Methodist church put the case in 1906:

> The girl who has learned only the rudiments of reading, writing and ciphering, and knows also how to make and mend her clothing, wash and iron, make a good loaf of bread, cook a good dinner, keep her house neat and clean, will be worth vastly more as mistress of a log cabin than one who had given years of study to the ornamental branches alone. . . . The Indian must be educated along industrial lines. It should be along the line of the physical rather than the mental.[51]

However much federal rhetoric might have maintained the illusion of assimilation, the Department of Indian Affairs was assuring failure in terms of Aboriginal pupils competing socially or intellectually with their White neighbours. Whereas most pupils in provincial schools reached the upper elementary grades by the end of the First World War, the overwhelming majority of Aboriginal children never got beyond grades 1 or 2. Up to 1920 four out of every five Aboriginal boys and girls attending a federal school across Canada were only enrolled in grades 1, 2 or 3. This did not mean that they had been in the school so short a time period, but more likely that they were simply kept in the lower grades year after year for convenience's sake or because the level of instruction was so poor. "We only had two hours of classes when I went to residential school. We worked . . . you had to get out as soon as you're sixteen. I didn't get much education, very little education."[52]

Aboriginal pupils were in any case long prohibited by law from going beyond the elementary grades. "There was a rule at that time that Indians could not go past Grade 8. I do not recall many boys staying around long enough to protest the education that was being denied us."[53] "We had to stay in school until we were eighteen years of age to go as high as grade eight. And then no high school after."[54] Through the middle of the twentieth century the proportion of Aboriginal children in school across Canada who were in grades 1-3 stagnated at two-thirds or more. In sharp contrast the percentage of their counterparts in provincial schools who were enrolled in grades 1-3 fell by mid-century to just over a third, indicating that almost all non-Aboriginal children were by then completing the elementary grades. Similarly, whereas the proportion of children of the dominant society reaching grade 7 or higher grew from less than one fifth in 1920 to about one third by 1950, the percentage of Aboriginal children to reach grade 7 moved up from none in 1920 to 3 per cent a decade later and then to just 10 per cent by mid-century.[55] Father Lascelles summed up the situation in his observation that, "The half-day academic program in effect until the middle of this century ensured that the children did not receive an education on a par with that given in the public schools."[56] Even then, a boy at school during the mid-1950s recalled that "Classes were from nine in the morning until three in the afternoon, but many times we were taken from class to work outside."[57]

Teachers And Teaching

The third attribute of federal policy ensuring that Aboriginal children were schooled for inequality grew out of the remarkable symbiosis in purpose that developed between the federal government and the various religious denominations across Canada. Unlike the American education policy where missionaries were subordinated to the federal government, in Canada they were left in charge. The major churches had already carved Canada up into spheres of influence for the purposes of Aboriginal conversion and they eagerly accepted the new challenge, subsidized by a federal per-pupil grant to exisiting schools and sometimes also by funding to build needed new ones. The Department of Indian Affairs restricted itself to general oversight which included annual reporting by each school and periodic visits by local officials, known as Indian agents.

While the Canadian policy was justified as suitably acknowledging a schooling system already underway, it was also an economy move alleviating the federal government from having to create and maintain its own institutions. "The department has fully recognized its inability to conduct such institutions as economically as can be done by denominations, and consequently it has endeavoured to have their management placed in the hands of the respective churches."[58] A student has recalled, "One day Sister Catherine told us in the classroom, 'We work so hard for you, we don't get any pay at all for looking after you Indians.'"[59]

By leaving schools' ongoing operation to missionary groups, the federal government relieved itself of direct responsibility for the provision, payment or supervision of teaching staffs. In residential schools teachers were most often missionaries principally motivated by commitment to Aboriginal peoples' conversion. "We had prayers ten, twenty times a day and when we weren't praying, we were changing clothes for prayers. We prayed when we got up, we prayed before breakfast and after breakfast, and we prayed when we got to the classroom and when we were in the classroom, I lost count of how many times a day we prayed."[60] One pupil shrewdly observed: "Mr. Hall wasn't paid to teach us, I don't think. I think he was just paid as a minister."[61] At their best teachers possessed, as one federal official phrased it, "infinite patience and tact, although without scholarly attainments."[62]

The situation was comparable between residential and day schools.[63] Although individual teachers were sometimes sympathetic to pupils' plight and so remembered by them, they were with rare exceptions untrained. A group of local parents informed the Department of Indian Affairs in 1936 that "The Indians of our Band are quite willing and anxious to do their part in educating their children, but we are asking the Department to give us a capable Instructor who will take a deeper interest in the progress of our children."[64] Having considered the request, DIA concluded, "While he is not a trained teacher, and the children do not make the same progress as they might with a modern highly trained instructor, he is rendering good service to the Department in a variety of ways."[65]

The contemporary literature is replete with observations attesting to the poor quality of teaching. A pupil of the 1920s has mused, "it is said by many that the teachers are not really teachers at all. They are not trained as the teachers are in the [local public] school."[66] Conversely, a sister teaching at the same school recalled being informed by the federal inspector of Indian schools that, "There is no training for your situation anyway, just for public schools."[67] An anonymous comment in DIA's internal files dated 1932 acknowledged that teaching positions are sometimes "merely posts provided for persons for whom billets had to be found."[68] The next decade the refrain was the same, that teachers "were often unqualified to teach. They used to just send old missionaries to the village to try and do the best they could."[69] The situation continued largely unchanged into the mid-twentieth century in sharp contrast to the growing professionalism distinguishing teachers and teaching in the dominant society.

Where individuals' religious commitment conflicted with their role as a teacher, the former usually triumphed. A local Indian agent observed in 1912 that "there is a disposition to devote too much time to imparting religious instruction to the children as compared with the imparting of secular knowledge, which is perhaps not unnatural when the teachers are employed and selected by the various churches."[70] The pupil-teacher relationship outside of the classroom was often determined more by religious than by didactic considerations. "If you passed them [the nuns] in the hall or anywhere, you're to stop and bow your head. They were really up on the pedestal. . . . They sure put themselves somewhere where you couldn't touch them. You couldn't reach them and you had to bow to them . . . it made me to a certain extent very bitter by the time I left school."[71] Language sometimes compounded difficulties. Whereas Aboriginal children were expected, once in school, totally to abandon their Aboriginal tongue in favor of English, their teachers did not necessarily know the English language sufficiently well to speak it, much less teach it to others. "But them French teachers you know they don't really pronounce their sounds right. There was only Sister Patricia who was Irish."[72] The Department of Indian Affairs acknowledged a possible conflict in its observation that "the dual system of control between the department on the one hand and the church on the other, each with their different ideals, the one requiring a secular education, and the other looking more to the spiritual instruction of the children, is almost somewhat anomalous."

Underfunding

The fourth and perhaps most fundamental reason why Aboriginal children were schooled for inequality lay in schools' low levels of federal financial support. Even taking into account the largely volunteer labor available as a consequence of schools' missionary ties, they were underfunded when compared with provincial institutions or even with the bare basics of survival. The per-pupil subsidy provided by the federal government assumed that much of the teaching would be volunteer, but even then it was inadequate to provide a minimum standard of everyday life, much less material conditions conducive to learning. The men and women who ran the schools were expected to scramble for donations simply to survive. Father Lascelles has made an important link: "Crucial to the determined efforts [of Catholic residential schools to secure better qualified teachers], however, were dollars; dollars which were few and far between."[74]

The published reports of the Department of Indian Affairs were very open in acknowledging the inadequacy of funding of residential schools, as in 1896: "The denominations interested in the last-named, owing to the smallness of the annual per capita grant, are forced to meet any shortage of the Government grant by contributions from outside sources."[75] A decade later the annual report stated bluntly that residential schools across the country were "all largely supplemented by the missionary societies."[76] Father Lascelles concluded that between 1915 and about 1950, "funding for the education of Indian children by the Department [of Indian Affairs] remained at a relative standstill."[77]

The half-day program adopted in most residential schools became little more than pupils' undertaking of the manual labor necessary for institutions' survival. From the early years, federal officials aspired to schools "becoming self-supporting" through pupils raising crops, making clothes and generally doing "outside work."[78]

> The longer half of our day was spent in what the brothers called 'industrial training.' Industrial training consisted of doing all the kinds of manual labour that are commonly done around a farm, except that we did not have the use of the equipment that even an Indian farmer of those days would have been using.[79]

The need for manual labor cut across the sexes, and many "an Indian girl washed, cooked, cleaned, and mended her way through residential school." "We had to patch. We had to patch the boys' clothes. We had to wash and iron Mondays and Tuesdays. We had to patch and keep on patching till Saturday." "We made all of the dresses and uniforms worn in the school, and socks, drawers, chemises, and aprons." The situation was, in this woman's view, even more detrimental for her male counterparts:

> The bigger ones spent almost no time in class. Instead, they were cutting down trees and pulling up stumps, or else they were up before daylight feeding the horses and milking the cows. Long after he left Lejac [residential school] one boy said, 'I'm just a human bulldozer!'[82]

"I was up at five-thirty every morning either to serve as an alter boy for Mass or to work on the farm, milking cows, working in the garden, and so forth."[83]

From the perspective of some pupils, poor or too little food caused most distress. "Hunger is both the first and last thing I can remember about that school. I was hungry from the day I went into the school until they took me to the hospital two and a half years later. Not just me. Every Indian pupil smelled of hunger."[84] Particularly difficult for pupils was their being expected to eat the barest of fare day after day while subjected to the smells and even the sight of schools' staffs dining far more sumptuously:

> After Mass we put our smocks over our uniforms and line up for breakfast in the hall outside the dining room. We can talk then because Sister goes for breakfast in the Sisters' dining room. They get bacon or ham, eggs, toast and juice. We can see when they open the door and go in for breakfast. We get gooey mush with powder milk and brown sugar.[85]

"The food given to us daily was not of the best. I am saying the food for the staff was of better quality and more palatably prepared."[86]

> At school it was porridge, porridge, porridge, and if it wasn't that, it was boiled barley or beans, and thick slices of bread spread with lard. Weeks went by without a taste of meat or fish. . . . A few times I would catch the smell of roasting meat coming from the nuns' dining room, and I couldn't help myself – I would follow that smell to the very door. Apart from the summers, I believe I was hungry for all seven of the years I was at school . . . we were on rations more suited to a concentration camp![87]

The comparison was not inapt: according to the wife of the commander of a First World War camp for German prisoners of war, they were provided only with "cheap" food, the allocation for food being limited to "approximately seventeen cents per person per day," or just over $50 a year.[88]

The actual situation on the ground was that many Aboriginal children fared less well than did prisoners of war. Up to 1910 boarding schools received from the federal government a grant of $60 a year per qualifying pupil, which was intended to cover all costs, not just food. Industrial schools received double that amount or even a bit more, but the consequence for all residential schools was what one administrator termed "frugal maintenance."[89] Moreover, because most schools, as part of their religious commitment to service, accepted additional children to the total allotted them by the Department of Indian Affairs, federal funds were usually stretched over a larger pupil body than intended. Federal day schools in British Columbia received an annual federal grant of $12 per pupil. The paucity of the amount becomes evident on comparison to neighboring British Columbia public schools, whose budgets rose from an average of $15 per pupil at the turn of the century to double the amount by 1908.[90]

From 1900 to 1908 some industrial and boarding schools' statements of income and expenditure were published in DIA's annual reports. They make clear the extent to which schools struggled to make ends meet. Including donations, the annual income per pupil at the three British Columbia boarding schools whose financial statements were published for 1900 averaged $94. Of this total, $41 comprised the government subsidy, which in theory was $60 per pupil but in practice much less due to the schools' greater enrolments than allotted by DIA. The remaining $53 of income per pupil consisted of donations, contributed primarily to further the schools' religious purposes. Housekeeping expenses alone, principally food, exceeded total federal funding at $44 per child. Physical upkeep of facilities added another $16 per pupil. Salaries for the minority of staff who received wages totalled $28 per pupil, and miscellaneous expenses ranging from school books to clothing $9 per pupil.[91] Financial statements were published for 1908 for seven British Columbia boarding schools. Their average income per pupil was $87, of which $46 comprised the federal subsidy and $41 donations. Out of necessity, housekeeping expenses including food had fallen to an average of $38 per pupil. Physical upkeep was $13, salaries $21 and miscellaneous expenses $13.[92]

The parsimony of federal funding is particularly evident when comparison is made to private schools for children of the dominant society. At the only British Columbia boarding school enrolling both Aboriginal and White female boarders, the latter's families were charged $160 a year in 1900.[93] At the turn of the century even a relatively modest private day school had fees of $50 a year, roughly the amount on which the federal government expected Aboriginal boarders to survive.[94]

Federal subsidies for Aboriginal pupils were revised upward in 1910, but not to adequate levels. Moreover, "increased financial assistance" came at the cost of "greater demands" in the standard of buildings, care and administration. For instance, the per pupil subsidy for boarding schools was doubled from $60 to $125, but only after schools met rigorous new requirements demanding more space per pupil, better physical facilities and far higher health and sanitation standards, no easy matter given that capital costs for upgrading were not integral to the revised policy.[95] By comparison, in 1912 an elite private school for White boys charged $470 a year for boarders, $150 for day pupils.[96]

Day school grants were raised in 1910 to $17 per child, but by then the comparable allocation per pupil in the British Columbia provincial system had reached $34.[97] As the reports of Indian agents repeatedly emphasized, teachers' salaries were a central issue for day schools often compelled to hire from outside of religious orders. "Complaint is continually made of the small amount allowed for a teacher. The teachers of the public schools receive at least $80 per month, with a long summer vacation, and have fewer scholars than the teachers of Indian day schools."[98] Another Indian agent noted that "the churches do not pay an adequate salary and trained teachers prefer to go to white schools, where social surroundings are always preferable to the isolated location among the Indians."[99]

Within a few short years, federal schools in British Columbia, and across Canada, were in even worse financial straits. A school inspector on the prairies reported in 1915 concerning residential schools:

> Although the per capita grant given by the department was increased about four years ago, the religious bodies, under whose auspices these schools are operated, find the grant to be inadequate to meet the advanced cost of foodstuffs daily in use in these schools. Moreover, contributions toward the support of such institutions are said to have been diminished, owing chiefly to the financial stringency caused by the war in Europe.[100]

Contributing to a deteriorating situation was some missionaries' growing interest in conversion of Asians, viewed as more tractable and perhaps more glamorous than Aboriginal peoples.[101] To some extent Aboriginal schools ended up with the leftovers, missionaries lacking the zeal and determination to put themselves in the front line of Christianity's advance.

Federal stinginess was not lost on contemporaries. The respected anthropologist Diamond Jenness undertook considerable personal observation across Canada during the 1920s prior to writing his landmark description of the country's Aboriginal peoples. While damning the quality of teaching in many schools as "exceedingly poor," he was very concerned that missionaries not be blamed since "they lacked the resources and the staffs to provide a proper education. . . . It was not the missions that shirked their responsibility, but the federal government, and behind that government the people of Canada."[102] Yet, as late as 1947, even as a Joint Parliamentary Committee was finally being established to probe Aboriginal affairs, the federal government was spending $45 a year per Aboriginal pupil in a federal day school compared with about $200 that the British Columbia government allocated per pupil in a public school.[103] As Father Lascelles insightfully concluded, "Financial problems were one of the major handicaps the schools laboured under for more than half a century."[104]

The Aboriginal Response And Changing Times

Perhaps the most fundamental critique of federal policy was its deluding of Aboriginal peoples. Certainly, not all parents sought formal schooling for their offspring. Concerning "a large no. of children of the pure Siwash [Chinook word for Indian] persuasion between the ages of 5 and 16 in the district," an early British Columbia public teacher reported that "it will be a difficult matter to get them to attend school as their respected progenitors believe them to be as well off without book learning as with it."[105] Many an Indian agent reported that "parents see in education the downfall of all their most cherished customs."[106]

Yet many more families accepted at face value what they were given every reason to believe was, despite its obvious tradeoffs, a genuine opportunity for their children. Aboriginal parents in British Columbia sent their children, first to public schools and then to federal schools, as one former pupil put it, "to learn White people's ways."[107] A woman born in 1931 remembered her mother's words: "'You're going to have to learn to read and write because when you grow up you're going to have to get a job.'"[108] Other times it was fathers who made their children aware of changing times. "'It's going to get crowded in the valley in a few years,' he said, '. . . you kids want to get yourselves an education. Get a job. That way you'll be okay.'"[109] The deception wrought on Aboriginal parents was deliberate. Pupils were repeatedly admonished against giving their families details of what went on in school and in some cases prohibited from doing so. As late as the 1950s, letters were routinely censored. "Sister Theo checks our letters home. We're not allowed to say anything about the school. I might get the strap, or worse."[110]

British Columbia families became frustrated as they realized that their children were being treated unfairly. The refrain was the same regardless of geographical area or particular circumstances. "Children are not taught enough."[111] "They just get nicely started – they just get their eyes opened the same as young birds and then they are turned out to fly. They don't get enough education for a livelihood nor are they taught a trade of any kind."[112] "The boys are not learning how to hunt and trap and set a net for fish. . . . They are supposed to go to Lejac to be educated, but they are not in the classrooms. They are in the fields or the barns, and the girls are too much in the sewing room or the kitchen."[113] "We all apply to have school at our own place. . . . Please look into matter soon as possible. We feed our children at home then."[114]

Not only were such voices unheard by federal policy makers, but individual parents faced tremendous obstacles when they sought to intervene in their children's best interests. Two examples from Vancouver Island are indicative. "I wanted my boys to go to high school, so I went to see the Indian agent, M.S. Todd, and told him so. He said to me, 'Nothing doing!' I asked him, 'Isn't it for everybody?' and he answered me, 'Not for you people.'"[115] A second father was forced to desperate measures so that his children "would be able to go to school a full term."

The school at Village Island was run by the Indian Department and we used to have that schoolteacher for three months a year. . . . I went over to the Indian Office at Alert Bay and pleaded with the Indian agent to keep her on for another couple months. He told me that he had no authority to pay her for another month and that they had spent all that was allowed. So I went to the school teacher and asked if she would accept $50 to stay for another month. . . . So the next month Simon Beans paid her $50 to stay for another month. That's how hard it was.[116]

Parents who resisted federal schools altogether in favor of the local public school rarely succeeded. One exception was a North Vancouver parent who, having spent a decade in residential school, was determined that his children would not do so. Given that this was at the beginning of the Second World War, it may be that the system was beginning to crack, alternatively that this father was particularly determined:

We didn't want to send them to no boarding school because I was working and we wanted them at home. We had quite a time to have them accepted into the public school. We finally got them admitted. Priscilla and Barbara were the first Indian children to be accepted into the public school. . . . I had to struggle with Indian Affairs, the North Vancouver School Board, the West Vancouver School Board to get my children in school. I had to pay their tuition fee myself for two years to have my children go to the public school. I paid five dollars a month per child.[117]

It was not just adults but also children who became actors. In some cases pupils through their own efforts mitigated the schools' worst characteristics not just for themselves but for their fellow pupils. As one of them recalled about his time at residential school:

Sometimes we used to help the ones who needed it. I always had that in my mind because I was brought up by my people, the teaching I got was to always try to help the other person. . . . I used to take the lower class out who were having problems, go for a walk. . . . I taught them about nature, making a bow and arrow, little canoes, to get their minds off problems.[118]

More often, pupils simply refused to cooperate as they realized that residential school was not what it purported to be. "The boys often rebelled and I didn't blame them. They were supposed to be in Lejac to get educated, but instead they were unpaid laborers, living on poor food and no more freedom than if they were prisoners in a jail."[119] Pupils protested treatment deemed unfair and discriminatory and, in cases of desperation, they ran away. "I ran away from the bus that was going to take me back to school and I hid in the bush until the priests and the police officers stopped looking for me."[120] "Some were successful and managed to reach their parents' traplines, but more often, they were caught by the Mounties, brought back and whipped."[121] Sociologist Celia Haig-Brown has argued that resistance was integral to everyday life in residential school.[122]

Over time Aboriginal peoples did effect change, but extraordinarily slowly. Unlike the United States where federal policy began to encourage children into public schools during the interwar years, in Canada the symbiosis between state and church was too comfortable to be altered until it became absolutely impossible to ignore changing times.[123] Only after the Second World War did increased awareness of Aboriginal peoples lead to the creation of a Select Joint Committee of the Senate and

House of Commons, which in 1951 called for Aboriginal peoples' integration into the Canadian mainstream. Although Aboriginal education was still under federal jurisdiction, Aboriginal children were encouraged to attend provincial schools or a private school run by one of the religious denominations that had previously operated federal residential and day schools. Funding still came from the federal government, through tuition agreements negotiated with provincial governments or religious denominations. Early integration during the 1950s was often top down, Aboriginal children attending a local public school for grades beyond those available in an existing federal school. "Dorothy goes to classes at St. Mark's now, the Catholic high school in town. All the pupils in grade ten, eleven and twelve do. Father Pitt drives them in a yellow school bus every day."[124] Integration sometimes led to new forms of discrimination. "We still had to wear the residential school clothes and this made an obvious distinction between us and the other students who would taunt us."[125] For individual Aboriginal children integration sometimes existed more in theory than in practice. "It was difficult going to [public] school, a lot of ideas and attitudes haven't changed much. Segregation is happening, not visibly but in the classes." At this school Aboriginal children were seated separately in the classroom, and it remained very much a "white man's school."[126] Other children continued to attend federal schools not that much changed from previous decades. "We had a school that taught Grades One to Seven, with teachers hired by the Department of Indian Affairs. Some of them were good, but others were young and didn't give a hell. The villagers, the chief, and the councillors had no say in the qualifications or lack of them in the teachers who were hired – we just took what we could get."[127] By 1970 three quarters of the 13 000 Aboriginal pupils of British Columbia were attending integrated institutions.

About the same time, in 1969, Prime Minister Pierre Elliott Trudeau issued a white paper, or policy document, calling for total Aboriginal integration into his "just society." He proposed to repeal the Indian Act and abolish Aboriginal peoples' special status in Canada. The Aboriginal response was overwhelmingly negative, a decade and more of growing awareness having awoken pride in heritage and culture. The white paper was withdrawn in favor of Aboriginal self-determination looking toward Aboriginal control over their own affairs. Band-operated schools, whose numbers have steadily increased across Canada, were intended to encourage pride in Aboriginal languages and cultures alongside the necessary skills to participate in mainstream society.

The official shift in Aboriginal education policy did not effect change immediately. As one band leader recalled about the 1970s: "We had to fight for every dollar and every bit of independence we could get for the education of our children. A policy of delay, delay, delay, delay, was practised and is still practised."[128] The schooling of Aboriginal children remains a federal responsibility overseen by the Department of Indian Affairs, but tuition agreements with provinces, churches and bands means that children in British Columbia, like their counterparts across Canada, no longer have a single educational option. Aboriginal children living on a reserve often attend a school operated by the local band, especially at the lower grade levels. Older children usually go by bus to the nearest public or Catholic parochial high school. Other families living on a reserve may have chosen to send their children from kindergarten on to a nearby public or parochial school. Most Aboriginal children living in urban settings now attend school alongside their non-Aboriginal contemporaries almost as a matter of course. Children in some urban areas also have alternative Aboriginal-oriented facilities available to them. These shifts, as important as they are, only go part way. A paucity of Aboriginal teachers, inadequate support for teaching Aboriginal languages, and lack of appropriate Aboriginal content in textbooks and in the classroom are only some of the difficulties yet to be resolved for the education of British Columbia Aboriginal children to become truly equal to that of all other British Columbia children.[129]

The Legacy

Although the residential school has disappeared from the Canadian educational landscape, its legacy endures. Federal policy resulted in practices whose consequences are still being lived across British Columbia and in the rest of Canada:

> If I had to pick one area where the federal government, through the Department of Indian Affairs, inflicted the most harm on my people, it would have to be in the field of education.... At the beginning of the white man's rule, Aboriginal people were confined to reserves, most of them far away from schools. When the government was finally forced to do something about the lack of educational facilities, the solution was a partnership between church and state to set up residential schools. Children were removed from their communities and placed in an alien environment that almost destroyed their culture and their language; we call it cultural genocide.[130]

The personal accounts used to ground this essay have ranged through time and across British Columbia, but they have all told a similar story.

Half or fewer British Columbia Aboriginal children of past generations actually attended residential school, but numbers were sufficient for family life to deteriorate. A pupil has recalled her "inability to show love to my mom, brothers, and sisters."[131] Students of different sexes were almost always separated in residential school, and siblings in the same school often could not even speak to each other for months and years on end. "I never did get to know my brothers. We were kept away from each other for too long. To this day I don't know much about my brothers. I just know that they are my brothers."[132] "After a year spent learning to see and hear only what the priests and brothers wanted you to see and hear, even the people we loved came to look ugly."[133] "Some of the most damaging things that resulted from my experiences at residential school was lack of nurturing as well as being denied learning parenting skills."[134] The next generation reaped the consequences:

> Although my older brother and I didn't attend residential school, we didn't really escape it either as it visited us every day of our childhood through the replaying over and over of our parents' childhood trauma and grief which they never had the opportunity to resolve in their lifetimes ... I grieve for the gentle man in my father who was never allowed to grow, and I grieve for my mother who never had the

loving relationships she deserved, nor the opportunity to be the mother I knew she could have been.[135]

Languages became a casualty. A father who spoke six languages in his job as a court interpreter deliberately refrained from teaching his children.

> He speaks lots of Indian languages, but he won't teach us. Mom won't either. She says the nuns and priests will strap us. . . . The nuns strapped her all the time for speaking Indian, because she couldn't speak English. She said just when the welts on her hands and arms healed, she got it again. That's why she didn't want us to learn Indian.[136]

The practice was widespread. "Because my parents also attended residential school they didn't see the value in teaching us our language. The Indian Agent told them not to speak to their children in Haida because it would not help them in school."[137] "It didn't matter that Carrier was the only language we knew – we were told not to use it and, if we did, wham! right now. I think now that it was the worst thing that happened to us."[138]

The self-fulfilling prophecy inherent in racism came to fruition as Aboriginal peoples deemed to be inferior were schooled for inequality and thereby largely did end up at the bottom ranks of Canadian society. "The residential school (not just the one I went to – they were the common form of Indian education all across Canada) was the perfect system for instilling a strong sense of inferiority."[139] The reasons are not difficult to fathom:

> For many of us our most vulnerable and impressionable years, our childhood years, were spent at the residential school where we had always been treated like dirt and made to believe that we weren't as good as other people. . . . I find it hard to believe that these schools claim to have groomed children for success when we were not allowed to be normal children . . . the constant message [was] that because you are Native you are part of a weak, defective race, unworthy of a distinguished place in society. That is the reason you have to be looked after. . . . That to me is not training for success, it is training for self-destruction.[140]

"I was frustrated about how we were treated, humiliated, and degraded, so I drank and took drugs to numb the frustrations of how my life had turned out."[140] And,

> A lot of us left residential school as mixed-up human beings, not able to cope with family or life. Many of us came out with a huge inferiority complex realizing something was missing, but not knowing what it was. Many searched for love and support in the wrong way. Girls became promiscuous, thinking this was the only way they could feel close to another person. Never having learned to cope with the outside world, many turned to drinking and became alcoholics.[142]

For almost a century the federal government in Canada sought to control the lives and souls of Aboriginal peoples. Outwardly espousing assimilation through education, the federal government neither took the leadership nor provided the financial resources to achieve any other goal than the self-affirming prophecy inherent in racist rhetoric. Religious denominations may have acted from the highest of motives, in their view, but lives were destroyed nonetheless. The logic behind the concept of the residential school was muddled at its best, duplicitous at its worst. The system's attributes made possible no other goal than Aboriginal peoples' absolute marginalization from Canadian life – a goal that schools achieved with remarkable success.

Unable to consider Aboriginal peoples as differing between time and place or capable of exercising control over their daily lives, federal policy deliberately bypassed the opportunity to integrate Aboriginal peoples into the larger society at their own pace, a process which had begun at least in a small way in late nineteenth-century British Columbia. The Department of Indian Affairs may have saved a few dollars in the short run, but the cost was generations of diminished and even wasted lives. The past cannot be undone, but it can be better understood. Only then can the cycle of the residential school, and its dominance of Aboriginal educational history, be broken. "The silent suffering has to end. It is time for the healing to start and the only way that will happen is if we acknowledge the past, face it, understand it, deal with it, and make sure that nothing like that ever happens again."[143]

Notes

1. Funding was provided by the Social Sciences and Humanities Research Council of Canada made possible research on which this essay draws. I am grateful to SSHRCC and to Donna Penney, Clint Evans, Dana Whyte, Valerie Giles and Roger Wiebe for their research assistance. Sections of this essay draw on Jean Barman, Yvonne Hébert and Don McCaskill, ed., *Indian Education in Canada*, vol. 1: *The Legacy* (Vancouver: UBC Press, 1986); and Jean Barman, *The West beyond the West: A History of British Columbia* (Toronto: University of Toronto Press, 1991).

2. See, for example, *Breaking the Silence: An Interpretive Study of Residential School Impact and Healing as Illustrated by the Stories of First Nations Individuals* (Ottawa: Assembly of First Nations, 1994); Linda Jaine, ed., *Residential Schools: The Stolen Years* (Saskatoon: Extension University Press, University of Saskatchewan, 1993); Maddie Harper, *"Mushhole": Memories of a Residential School* (Toronto: Sister Vision Press, 1993); Jo-ann Archibald, "Resistance to an unremitting process: Racism, curriculum and education in Western Canada," in J.A. Mangan, ed., *The Imperial Curriculum: Racial images and education in the British Colonial experience* (London: Routledge, 1993), 93-107 and 223-7; Isabelle Knockwood with Gillian Thomas, *Out of the Depths: The Experience of Mi'kmaw Children at the Indian Residential School at Shubenacadie, Nova Scotia* (Lockeport, N.S.: Roseway, 1992); Marilyn Millward, "Clean Behind the Ears? Micmac Parents, Micmac Children, and the Shubenacadie Residential School," *New Maritimes* (March/April 1992): 6-15; Shirley Sterling, *My Name is Seepeetza* (Vancouver: Douglas & McIntyre, 1992); Linda R. Bull, "Indian Residential Schooling: The Native Perspective," *Canadian Journal of Native Education* 18 (supplement 1991): 1-64; N. Rosalyn Ing, "The Effects of Residential Schools on Native Child-Rearing Practices," *Canadian Journal of Native Education* 18 (Supplement 1991): 65-118; Jo-Anne Fiske, "Gender and the Paradox of Residential Education in Carrier Society," in Jane Gaskell and Arlene McLaren, ed., *Women and Education*, 2nd ed. (Calgary: Detselig, 1991), 131-46; Basil H. Johnston, *Indian School Days* (Toronto: Key Porter, 1988); and Celia Haig-Brown, *Resistance and Renewal: Surviving the Indian Residential School* (Vancouver: Tillicum Library, 1988). For a generally positive perspective, see Thomas A. Lascelles, *Roman Catholic Residential Schools in British Columbia* (Vancouver: Order of OMI in BC, 1990).

3. Jaine, ed., *Residential Schools*, x.

4. Department of Indian Affairs [DIA], *Annual Report* [AR], 1895, xxi.

5. DIA, *AR*, 1895, xxi.

6. Personal testimony is used not to set apart individuals or schools but rather to demonstrate how federal policy constructed Aboriginal pupils' experience of education regardless of individual or institution. At the same time, it is important to note that the recollections of residential school used here, all of which are in the public domain, do refer to a variety of schools: All Hallows (Clara Clare), Christie (Francis Charlie), Kamloops (George Manuel, Shirley Sterling), Lejac (Lizette Hall, Mary John), Port Alberni (Vera Manuel, Charlie Thompson), St. Eugene's at Cranbrook (Troy Hunter), St. George's at Lytton (Simon Baker), St. Joseph's at Williams Lake (Bev Sellars, Augusta Tappage), St. Marys Mission (Mary Englund), St. Michael's at Alert Bay (Mabel James, Clayton Mack), St. Paul's at North Vancouver (Lois Guss) and Edmonton (Rosa Bell, Art Collison, sent from Haida Gwaii/Queen Charlotte Islands). Testimonies not otherwise footnoted are in Jaine, ed., *Residential Schools.*

7. For elaboration, see for Canada Daniel Francis, *The Imaginary Indian: The Image of the Indian in Canadian Culture* (Vancouver: Arsenal Pulp Press, 1992); and Robin Fisher, chapter entitled "The Image of the Indian" in his *Contact and Conflict: Indian-European Relations in British Columbia, 1774-1890* (Vancouver: UBC Press, 1977 and 1992); and for the United States Robert F. Berkhofer Jr., "White Conceptions of Indians," in Wilcomb E. Washburn, ed., *History of Indian-White Relations*, vol. 4 of *Handbook of North American Indians* (Washington: Smithsonian Institution, 1988), 522-47, which summarizes Berkhofer, *The White Man's Indian: Images of the American Indian from Columbus to the Present* (New York: Knopf, 1978).

8. DIA, *AR*, 1887, lxxx.

9. DIA, *AR*, 1880, 8.

10. On the industrial school, see E. Brian Titley, "Indian Industrial Schools in Western Canada," in Nancy M. Sheehan, J. Donald Wilson and David C. Jones, ed., *Schools in the West: Essays in Canadian Educational History* (Calgary: Detselig, 1986), 133-53.

11. See Table 5 in Barman, *West beyond the West*, 363.

12. For detail, see Barman, *West beyond the West*, 13-17.

13. DIA, *AR*, 1910, 327.

14. *The West Shore*, September 1884, 275, cited in Patricia E. Roy, "*The West Shore*'s View of British Columbia, 1884," *Journal of the West* 22: 4 (October 1984): 28.

15. Charles Mair to George Denison, Okanagan Mission, 5 December 1892, Mair Correspondence in possession of Duane Thomson and used with his permission. Emphasis in original.

16. DIA, *AR*, 1874, 37.

17. DIA, *AR*, 1880, 3.

18. DIA, *AR*, 1890, xxx.

19. DIA, *AR*, 1902, 283.

20 Alex Deans? to John Jessop, Superintendent of Education, Langley, 26 June 1876, in British Columbia Superintendent of Education [hereafter BCSE], Inward Correspondence [IC], British Columbia Archives and Records Service [BCARS], GR 1445.

21. Walter Hunter, teacher at Lillooet, to S.D. Pope, Superintendent of Education, Lillooet, 7 August 1886, in BCSE, IC.

22. Petition from a group of parents at Port Essington to S.D. Pope, Port Essington, 27 August 1888, in BCSE, IC.

23. O.N. Hughett, Secretary of Genoa Trustees Board, to S.D. Pope, Genoa, 21 September 1891, in BCSE, IC.

24. John Jessop to J[ane] E. Trenaman, Victoria, 30 October 1876, in BCSE, Outward

Corresponence [OC], BCARS, GR 450.

25. James Malpass, Secretary of North Cedar Trustee Board, to S.D. Pope, North Cedar, 17 May 1886, BCSE, IC; and S.D. Pope to James Malpass, Victoria, 20 May 1886, in BCSE, OC.

26. J[ane] E. Trenaman, teacher at Hope, to John Jessop, Hope, 25 October 1876, in BCSE, IC.

27. Trenaman to Jessop, 25 October 1876.

28. Mrs. [Catherine] Cordiner, teacher at Granville, to John Jessop, Granville, 16 September 1875, in BCSE, IC.

29. S. Shepherd, teacher at Yale, to S.D. Pope, Yale, 12 December 1888, in BCSE, IC; and S.D. Pope to S. Shepherd, Victoria, 15 December 1888, in BCSE, OC.

30. S.D. Pope to George Hopkins, Victoria, 29 July 1889, in BCSE, OC.

31. S.D. Pope to Samuel Cutler, Victoria, 1 August 1893, in BCSE, OC. The circular's date is inferred from M.E. Sheirs, teacher at Port Kells, to S.D. Pope, Port Kells, 13 October 1891, in BCSE, IC.

32. M.E. Sheirs, teacher at Port Kells, to S.D. Pope, Port Kells, 13 October 1891, in BCSE, IC.

33. William McAdam, teacher at Port Hammond, to S.D. Pope, Port Hammond, 2 November 1891, in BCSE, IC.

34. Samuel Cutler, Secretary of Sooke Trustees, to S.D. Pope, Sooke, 31 October 1892, in BCSE, IC.

35. S.D. Pope to H[arriet] Young, teacher at Pavillion, Victoria, 27 March 1894, in BCSE, OC.

36. Samuel Cutler, Secretary of Sooke Trustees, to S.D. Pope, Sooke, 8 November 1893, in BCSE, IC.

37. For historical statistics on B.C., see Lascelles, *Roman Catholic Residential Schools*, 95-8.

38. This argument grounds Paul Tennant, *Aboriginal Peoples and Politics: The Indian Land Question in British Columbia, 1849-1989* (Vancouver: UBC Press, 1990).

39. Reproduced in DIA, *AR*, 1895, 348-51; also DIA, *AR*, 1894, xxi.

40. DIA, *AR*, 1896, xxxvii.

41. Jacqueline Gresko, "Creating Little Dominions Within the Dominion: Early Catholic Indian Schools in Saskatchewan and British Columbia," in Barman, Hébert and McCaskill, *Indian Education*, v. 1, 96.

42. Jean E. Speare, ed., *The Days of Augusta* (Vancouver: J.J. Douglas, 1973), 18.

43. George Manuel and Michael Poslums, *The Fourth World: An Indian Reality* (Toronto: Collier Macmillan Canada, 1974), 64. According to Celia Haig-Brown's portrait of the same school, "no child attended school for longer than two hours a day." Haig-Brown, *Resistance and Renewal*, 61.

44. Verna J. Kirkness, ed., *Khot-La-Cha: The Autobiography of Chief Simon Baker* (Vancouver: Douglas & McIntyre, 1994), 30-1.

45. Kirkness, ed., *Khot-La-Cha*, 29.

46. Lascelles, *Roman Catholic Residential Schools*, 30.

47. DIA, *AR*, 1895, xxiii.

48. Lizette Hall, *The Carrier, My People* (Fort St. James: n.p., 1992), 81.

49. Speare, *Days of Augusta*, 7.

50. Manuel and Poslums, *Fourth World*, 64.

51. Thompson Ferrier, *Indian Education in the Northwest* (Toronto: Department of Missionary Literature of the Methodist Church, Canada, c1906), 17 and 25. The Methodist Church was parroting federal rhetoric; see, for instance, DIA, *AR*, 1888, x, and 1897, 60.

52. Francis Charlie, quoted in Lascelles, *Roman Catholic Residential Schools*, 44.

53. Manuel and Poslums, *Fourth World*, 66.

54. Hall, *Carrier*, 81.
55. Data on Indian pupils taken from "School Statements" in DIA, *Annual Reports*; on pupils in provincial schools from *Annual Survey of Education* (Ottawa: Dominion Bureau of Statistics), renamed *Elementary and Secondary Education in Canada*.
56. Lascelles, *Roman Catholic Residential Schools*, 83.
57. Bridget Moran, *Justa: A First Nations Leader* (Vancouver: Arsenal Pulp Press, 1994), 51.
58. DIA, *AR*, 1896, xxxviii.
59. Hall, *Carrier*, 81.
60. Moran, *Justa*, 57.
61. Clellan S. Ford, *Smoke from their Fires: The Life of a Kwakiutl Chief* (New Haven: Yale University Press, 1941), 100.
62. Correspondence concerning Lejac School, 1910, cited in Jo-Anne Fiske, "Life at Lejac," in Thomas Thorner, ed., *Sa Ts'e: Historical Perspectives on Northern British Columbia* (Prince George: College of New Caledonia Press, 1989), 243.
63. The yearly reports submitted by individual day schools and extracted in DIA's *Annual Reports* often include information on teachers. See, for example 1910, 328-41.
64. Letter from Chehalis band following meeting of 5 March 1936, cited in Archibald, "Resistance" 101.
65. Inspector's response to letter from Chehalis band following meeting of 5 March 1936, cited in Archibald, "Resistance" 101.
66. Bridget Moran, *Stoney Creek Woman: The Story of Mary John* (Vancouver: Tillicum, 1988), 53-4.
67. Quoted in Fiske, "Life at Lejac," 244.
68. Notation dated 1932, cited in Norma Sluman and Jean Goodwill, *John Tootoosis: A Biography of a Cree Leader* (Ottawa: Golden Dog Press, 1982), 157.
69. James P. Spradley, *Guests Never Leave Hungry: The Autobiography of James Sewid, a Kwakiutl Indian* (New Haven: Yale University Press, 1969), 191.
70. DIA, *AR*, 1912, 399.
71. Mary Englund, quoted in Margaret Whitehead, *Now You Are My Brother: Missionaries in British Columbia, Sound Heritage series* no. 34 (Victoria: Provincial Archives of British Columbia, 1981), 64.
72. David Johnson, quoted in Whitehead, *Now You Are My Brother*, 50.
73. DIA, *AR*, 1911, 374.
74. Lascelles, *Roman Catholic Residential Schools*, 42.
75. DIA, *AR*, 1896, xxxvii.
76. DIA, *AR*, 1906, 251.
77. Lascelles, *Roman Catholic Residential Schools*, 42.
78. DIA, *AR*, 1891, xiii.
79. Manuel and Poslums, *Fourth World*, 64.
80. Marjorie Mitchell and Anna Franklin, "When You Don't Know the Language, Listen to the Silence: An Historical Overview of Native Indian Women in BC," in Barbara K. Latham and Roberta J. Pazdro, eds., *Not Just Pin Money: Selected Essays On The History Of Women's Work In British Columbia* (Victoria: Camosun College, 1984), 24
81. Speare, *Days of Augusta*, 18.
82. Moran, *Stoney Creek Woman*, 44-5.
83. Moran, *Justa*, 51.

84. Manuel and Poslums, *Fourth World*, 65.

85. Sterling, *My Name is Seepeetza*, 24.

86. Hall, *Carrier*, 83.

87. Moran, *Stoney Creek Woman*, 39.

88. Gwen Cash, *Off the Record: The Personal Reminiscences of Canada's First Woman Reporter* (Langley: Stagecoach, 1977), 23.

89. *All Hallows in the West* [school magazine of All Hallows School, Yale, British Columbia, 6, no. 8 (Ascension 1906): 538.

90. Comparisons were made for the school years 1899/1900 and 1907/08. The two years compare Aboriginal and rural public schools operating in close geographical proximity, in the case of 1899-1900 Alberni, Alert Bay, Comox, Quamichan, Saanich and Somenos, in 1907/08 Alert Bay, Bella Coola, Clayoquot, Hazelton, Lytton, Telegraph Creek and Uculelet. Comparative data extracted from British Columbia, Department of Education, *Annual Report*, Tables A and D, and DIA, *AR*, "School Statement.'

91. DIA, *AR*, 1899/1900, pt. 2, 14-15, financial statements for All Hallows, Port Simpson and St. Mary's boarding schools.

92. DIA, *AR*, 1907/08, pt. 2, 21-4, financial statements for Ahousat, Alberni, All Hallows, Port Simpson, St. Mary's, Sechelt and Squamish boarding schools.

93. Calculated from financial statements in *All Hallows in the West*.

94. Advertisement in *News-Advertiser* (Vancouver), 10 August, 1902.

95. DIA, *AR*, 1911, xxvi and 294-5.

96. University School, *Prospectus*, 1912, in St. Michaels-University School Archives, Victoria.

97. Because no breakdown of financial support for individual Indian day schools is included following the 1910 revision, mean support per pupil across British Columbia is compared with mean cost in rural public schools operating in geographical proximity to an Indian day school, being in this case Alert Bay, Bella Coola, Clayoquot, Hazelton, Lytton, Masset, Similkameen, Telegraph Creek and Uclelet. Comparable data is extracted from British Columbia, Department of Education, *Annual Report*, Tables A and D.

98. DIA, *AR*, 1912, 408. For another example, see DIA, *AR*, 1911, 378.

99. DIA, *AR*, 1912, 399.

100. DIA, *AR*, 1915, 238.

101. This point is made in John Webster Grant, *Moon of Wintertime: Missionaries and the Indians of Canada in Encounter since 1534* (Toronto: University of Toronto Press, 1984), 191.

102. Diamond Jenness, "Canada's Indians Yesterday. What of Today?" *Canadian Journal of Economic and Political Science* 20, no. 1 (February 1954), reprinted in A.L Getty and Antoine S. Lussier, eds., *As Long as the Sun Shines and Water Flows: A Reader in Canadian Native Studies* (Vancouver: UBC Press, 1983), 162.

103. Data comes from DIA, *Annual Reports*.

104. Lascelles, *Roman Catholic Residential Schools*, 83.

105. Thomas Leduc, teacher at Lillooet, to John Jessop, Lillooet, 8 January 1876, in BCSE, IC.

106. DIA, *AR*, 1888, 104.

107. Clara Clare, cited in Jean Barman, "Separate and Unequal: Indian and White Girls at All Hallows School, 1884-1920," in Barman, Hébert and McCaskill, *Indian Education*, v. 1, 112.

108. Ruth Cook, quoted in Dorothy Haegert, *Children of the First People* (Vancouver: Tillicum, 1983), 21.

109. Sterling, *My Name is Seepeetza*, 125.

110. *Ibid.*, 12.

111. DIA, *AR*, 1911, 381.

112. William Sepass, Sto:lo Chief, testifying before Royal Commission on Indian Affairs reporting in 1916, cited in Archibald, "Resistance," 100.

113. Moran, *Stoney Creek Woman*, 53.

114. Stoney Creek Council to DIA, 1917, cited in Fiske, "Life at Lejac," 240.

115. Harry Assu with Joy Inglis, *Assu of Cape Mudge: Recollections of a Coastal Indian Chief* (Vancouver: UBC Press, 1989), 95-6.

116. Spradley, *Guests Never Leave Hungry*, 125-6.

117. Kirkness, ed., *Khot-La-Cha*, 73.

118. *Ibid.*, 31.

119. Moran, *Stoney Creek Woman*, 44.

120. Moran, *Justa*, 10.

121. Moran, *Stoney Creek Woman*, 44.

122. Haig-Brown, *Resistance and Renewal.*

123. See Margaret Connell Szasz and Carmelia Ryan, "American Indian Education," in Wilcomb E. Washburn, ed., *History of Indian-White Relations*, vol. 4 of *Handbook of North American Indians* (Washington: Smithsonian Institution, 1988), 284-301; Irving G. Hendrick, "The Federal Campaign for the Admission of Indian Children into Public Schools, 1890-1934," *American Indian Culture and Research Journal* 5 (1981): 13-32; Margaret Connell Szasz, *Education and the American Indian: The Road to Self-Determination Since 1928* (Albuquerque: University of New Mexico Press, 1977); and Guy B. Senese, *Self-Determination and the Social Education of Native Americans* (New York: Praeger, 1991).

124. Sterling, *My Name is Seepeetza*, 41.

125. Art Collison, "Healing Myself Through Our Haida Traditional Customs," in Jaine, ed., *Residential Schools*, 38.

126. Sharon McIvor Grismer, quoted in Niehaus, Valerie, "Mrs. Sharon McIvor Grismer," *Nicola Valley Historical Quarterly* 1: 4 (October 1978): 7.

127. Moran, *Justa*, 103, referring to 1971.

128. Moran, *Justa*, 156.

129. This assessment is necessarily simplistic; on the complexities see Archibald, "Resistance," 93-107 and 223-7; and the essays in Marie Battiste and Jean Barman, eds., *First Nations Education in Canada: The Circle Unfolds* (Vancouver: UBC Press, 1995).

130. Moran, *Justa*, 155-6.

131. Rosa Bell, "Journeys," in Jaine, ed., *Residential Schools*, 13.

132. Bell, "Journeys," 10.

133. Manuel and Poslums, *Fourth World*, 67.

134. Charlie Thompson, "The First Day," in Jaine, ed., *Residential Schools*, 129.

135. Vera Manuel, "The Abyss," in Jaine, ed., *Residential Schools,* 115.

136. Sterling, *My Name is Seepeetza*, 36, 67 and 89.

137. Bell, "Journeys," 10.

138. Moran, *Justa*, 55.

139. Manuel and Poslums, *Fourth World*, 67.

140. Bev Sellers, "Against All Odds," in Jaine, ed., *Residential Schools*, 131.

141. Collison, "Healing Myself," 39.

142. Lois Guss, "Residential School Survivor," in Jaine, ed., *Residential Schools*, 92.

143. Sellers, "Against All Odds," 129.

4

"Everyone seemed happy in those days": The Culture of Childhood in Vancouver Between the 1920s and the 1960s[1]

Neil Sutherland

Consider the playground of a Vancouver school as it was on a dry October morning sometime between the 1920's and the 1960's.[2] In the few minutes before the bell rang for the first time, it became a noisy scene that could be heard for a couple of blocks in all directions.[3] Most boys in the upper grades had assembled on the boys' field. Some raced continually after the soccer ball, trying, as they said, to get a "kick in." Sometimes a group of the older boys tried to keep the ball to themselves, passing it within a fairly tight circle. A single mistake put it back into play for all. Other boys lounged in clumps. If the ball came arching down their way, these clumps dissolved as the boys raced for the ball. The lucky victor booted it as hard as he could across the field and another clump dissolved after it. On the girls' playground, many youngsters bounced lacrosse balls, and one could hear, amongst other chants, "One, two, three, alary." Others skipped, some on their own with short ropes, more in groups. In the latter arrangement, two girls twirled a longer rope, while the rest of the group lined up to take turns skipping over it. While younger girls employed relatively simple routines and rhymes, older, and more adept, girls followed elaborate sequences, some of which involved two or even more girls skipping at the same time. Those who faltered went to the end of the line. On the smaller playgrounds younger children played tag and other chasing games.

Many children stood in pairs, some girls holding hands, or in small groups talking to each other. Other pairs or small groups promenaded the schoolyard so that they would be seen and would know what was going on everywhere. Except for the boldest of the grade 7s and 8s, these pairs and small groups were composed of children of one sex only, and most children of each sex were separated either by rule or by custom on the schoolgrounds. Some groups talked loudly, argued, laughed and the boys particularly but also some of the girls, hit, pushed, and shoved each other playfully and sometimes not so playfully, and wrestled in "play" fights. Others talked quietly, exchanging gossip and telling jokes. ("Did you hear 'The Great Gildersleeve' last night?" "Old Bell is wearing a new sweater today;" "Why did the little moron . . .?") A few children, usually at the edge of the playground, stood alone looking on.

"Duty" teachers on their patrols and those others who surveyed the scene from the staffroom window saw a boisterous, noisy world, but also one that they were sure they controlled. The bell symbolized their authority, and the response it brought from the children demonstrated its strength. Parents, neighbors who heard it from afar, and others passing were also aware of this lively gathering, but viewed it as one in which children had moved easily from the control of their families into the control of the school. On the other hand, to the children on the playground the scene displayed, as it would again during recess, just before the afternoon bell, and right after school, the culture of childhood in one of its most rigid and complete forms. This culture governed what went on there in front of teachers and parents. It controlled who played in which games and who did not play at all. It gathered together the smaller groups, and it pushed to the side of the playground those who observed the world from there.

The culture of childhood was not confined to the school playground. To a quite remarkable degree it structured the lives of children throughout their waking hours and may have affected their dreams as well. It exerted its influence within the homes of the most strong-minded of parents. It controlled some behavior in the classrooms of even the most tyrannical of teachers. Outside of home and school, it affected relationships between the young even when they were right under the eyes or ears of adults with authority over them. As they moved away from these arenas, children also moved more deeply into a world in which they had to come to terms with a culture passed on directly from one generation of children to the next. As they had already learned in their families, they discovered that the power of some over others also governed their relations with their peers; they found the third locus of power in their lives. "When we start school," wrote Charles Dougan, "the lessons we are taught in the classroom pale in comparison to the lessons learned when we are immersed in the school yard society. . . . One better be quick to understand that 'might is right.'"[4] In these instances, however, children learned that power could be relative as well as absolute; that as they were subject to those older, bigger, stronger or more confident than themselves, so they could dominate those younger, smaller, weaker, or less confident than themselves.

In this chapter I will first explain what I mean by the culture of childhood. Next, I will outline my approach to this culture as it manifested itself in Vancouver between the end of the First World War and the 1960s. I will examine the various groups that made up the culture, and then describe how children played their part in the culture of childhood. Finally, I will discuss what I have discovered about the workings of the culture; how children found their place in it, and how they felt about it.

What do I mean by the "culture of childhood?" Most of the institutions in which children spent their lives – family, congregation, voluntary association, school, truant home, industrial school and so on – had as a principal goal the socializing of the young into the whole cluster of ways of living that characterized the larger cultures of which they were a part. At the same time, however, children had to learn to be children, to become members of both the almost timeless world of childhood and their own brief generation within it.[5] At its simplest level, this meant learning to do certain things. Learning to skip, for example, involved mastering a complex system of rhymes and physical activities. But learning to skip also involved learning to behave in appropriate ways with other girls. In learning how to behave towards each other, children absorbed the knowledge, customs, expectations, beliefs, norms, values and social roles that governed relationships between them. They absorbed the multitude of unwritten rules that regulated social behavior. Sometimes this learning harmonized with what adults wanted of their children; sometimes it appeared irrelevent to adults, and sometimes it ran contrary to their wishes. Indeed, most points of great tension between adults and children had their roots in the competing requirements of childhood and adult cultures.

How can one study the culture of childhood? While my text and endnotes will reveal an eclectic use of the psychological, sociological, and even psychoanalytic literature on children, my approach to the culture of childhood will be largely descriptive. This approach is in line with my view that what historians of childhood at this stage in the development of the field can best do, is to construct natural histories of childhood in different places and at different times. My description is primarily rooted in the recollections of adults who were children in these years. Most of them spent some or all of their childhood in Vancouver. One group grew up in predominantly working-class neighborhoods and the other in predominantly middle-class ones. Within each of these groups, I have examined a set of overlapping memories from a single neighborhood.

While social class affected many aspects of childhood, it was not particularly important in forming childhood culture. Further, while parents often employed class distinctions in their efforts to control the lives of their youngsters they made at least equal use of ethnicity, religious denomination, and social status. Indeed, interviews and other sources emphasize how common certain broad sorts of childhoods were to all neighborhoods.[6] Each community possessed its isolated or almost isolated children, its diffident observers, its gregarious and popular youngsters, and some of those truly self-possessed individuals. The last group moved easily between taking part in the whole range of their group's activities and such solitary pursuits as caring for pets, reading, playing musical instruments, model building, or playing on their own with blocks, dolls, doll houses, model soldiers, model airplanes, and trains, or sorted through their collections of movie magazines, pop bottle caps, street car transfers, cigarette and bubble gum cards, or other "collectibles."

One can visualize the geography of the culture of childhood as a personal landscape made up of concentric circles with the child's family at the centre and the whole community encompassed by the outer ring. Children entered the culture of childhood when they first established a relationship with another child or group of children. Most infants made their first connections with siblings, with cousins, or with the children of friends or neighbors met while parents took part in adult activities to which their children accompanied them. As children moved outside of their households, they met the boys and girls who lived nearby. As they grew older, and extended their range, children began to associate more extensively with their peer group; those who were relatively close in age to one another and who came together because of schooling, or activities sponsored by the congregation, and for neighborhood play. In the next outward ring, and much more important than the psychological and sociological literature makes clear, was the whole youthful population of the neighborhood; at one end those just emerging from infancy and at the other adolescents on the verge of adulthood.

Children found their place in the culture of childhood as they interacted with friends, with peers and with all the other young people of their neighborhoods. To most children, the role of "friend" and of "best friend" was the most important of these relationships. Two friends who, however temporarily, had woven their lives together – talking, playing, walking, laughing, giggling, arguing, fighting, holding hands in school lines, attending the Saturday matinee, window shopping, buying penny candy together – formed the smallest component of the culture of childhood. ("I always had a good friend"; "We were friends for sixteen years.") According to the *Gage Dictionary of Canadian English*, the most common use of the term "friend" is a "person who knows and likes another." Children grew into and within their friendships in this sense of the term; the older they were the more they expected from a friendship. Young children became friends because they lived close to each other and shared activities ("X and I were together all the time. She lived just down the street.")

Older children became or remained friends because, as well as activities, they came to share values, and the same attitudes towards the way in which their world worked. Best friends were usually, although not always, of the same sex.[7] In the upper intermediate and senior elementary grades, children may have added to their friendships a certain intimacy, a degree of sharing, and a level of feeling that, in its most complete form, might be as Harry Stack Sullivan argued, "something very like full-blown psychiatrically defined love."[8] (As one man said, "Best friends are fantastic because you share so much with them that you can't share with anyone else, even your parents.") Some research in social psychology suggests that girls may enter into this level of friendship more often than boys.[9] Friends spent as much time together as possible. If they could, they walked to school together, and played together at recess and noon hour. Friends read together, or played cards or other games, or talked about parents, sibling, friends, teachers, wishes, hopes for the future and so on. ("We spent long periods of time lying and talking.")

Most children also forged a membership for themselves in what social scientists call the peer group. A child's peer group was made up of those youngsters of roughly the same status and stage of development with whom he or she talked, played, argued, fought, or otherwise interacted on a reasonably regular basis.[10] ("We had friends that did things together but no hoodlum gangs.") As did friends, the peer group helped youngsters develop a sense of belonging, and provided a common view as to how its members should look, think, and behave towards each other and other children. Generally, a hierarchy developed within a peer group with a few children at the core providing leadership and a fluctuating group following along.[11] For young children, the peer group of the neighborhood might be very different from that of the classroom or schoolground. As children got older, and extended their boundaries, peer groups began to blend together but only rarely did they merge. As children got older, as well, the peer group became a stronger and stronger influence on them or, perhaps more accurately, they acquired enough sense of autonomy and even physical independence that they were able to adopt some peer norms or practices even when these conflicted with those of parents or teachers. For this reason both parents and teachers tended to distrust the peer group.

Vancouver children swimming at English Bay in the 1920s
(Vancouver Public Library, [VPL] 5456.)

Most children also interacted with the other young people of their neighborhood. If youthful culture could no longer be characterized by the "promiscuity of ages" that Joseph Kett ascribed to the pre-industrial world, intermixture had not declined to the extent that research based on age-graded classroom groupings has suggested.[12] At the broadest level, children merely knew who all the other children were in their neighborhood. From neighborhood young people, children picked out those whom they admired from a distance or even emulated in clothing or behavior. They also sorted out those whom they avoided; the cruel, the vicious, the bullies, those likely to tease or torment them. Generally, they kept away from the handicapped. Sometimes they avoided those of other religious denominations, ethnic groups or races.

The culture of childhood and its norms even affected the relationship between siblings. Those who told tales on each other also quickly learned that such behavior violated the norms that governed the relationships between children. ("My brother called for father; it was unfair.") Possibly these norms were less effectively enforced between siblings than they were in the wider community – things had a way of slipping out at home – but they were surprisingly strong and especially so when they involved one sibling's knowing about another's visiting a forbidden place or conducting a forbidden practice. A younger child might be aware of an older sister's habit of shoplifting, or a brother's cigarette smoking, know that both were wrong, both were against family rules, and yet not report either.

Parents and guardians controlled the extent to which children participated in the lives of other children. A few parents prevented their children from playing with any but siblings – if they had any – and thus often restricted their youngsters to the role of onlookers or solitary independent players, or perhaps playing parallel to children outside the home or yard. However, when members of an extended family lived fairly close to each other, and visited regularly, then cousins and various other youthful relatives played an important role in incorporating children into the childish culture. ("I had twenty-four first cousins on Dad's side. We had huge family gatherings.") For the children of those families who built much of their lives around the activities of their congregation or ethnic group, then the youngsters they met in those settings also served a similar role. ("I saw a lot of X because his parents were involved in our church.") Thus some youngsters regularly entered into a number of distinct settings, all of which helped to socialize them to the norms of the culture of childhood. Indeed, for many children these three physically separate worlds of neighborhood, extended family and congregation continued to exist throughout the whole of their childhoods.

Even after their children started school, most parents continued to exert a very considerable measure of control over their children's social relations. At one extreme, certain parents continued to keep their children away from other youngsters for most or all of the time. Some parents decided on this course as a matter of principle: they feared the physical effects or the social consequences of relationships with other children. Other parents took this route out of necessity; they needed the time of their children for a whole range of domestic activities, and a steady round of chores characterized all the time they were not at school. Some parents organized their children into studies of various kinds – singing, dancing, elocution, a second language, piano or other musical instrument – so that lessons and practices took up much or most non-school time. And at the other extreme, certain parents let – or pushed – their children out of the home at an early age and left them to fend more or less for themselves. Again, parents took this step for a variety of reasons. Some single parents went out to work and could not afford much or any child-minding. Other parents, emotionally disturbed, abused, abandoned, alcoholic or otherwise cast down by their lives, seemed to have lost the capacity or perhaps the energy to care. Some parents, and especially those with large families, encouraged their children to assume responsibility for themselves from a very early age onward. A few parents so lost control over their youngsters that the latter ignored wishes or demands that went contrary to their own.

Those parents who did permit their youngsters to spend a reasonable amount of time with their peers set all sorts of boundaries to this play. As parents set boundaries, however, so children tested them. Even the most timid and most rigidly controlled youngsters at some time or another ventured to forbidden places and attempted forbidden practices. Children were most likely to test their boundaries when there was conflict between family and youthful norms and values. Nearly every child, for example, experimented with smoking. Probably fewer children attempted shoplifting than smoking, but soft drinks, penny candies, fruit, and later, makeup, presented strong temptations, and undoubtedly justified the watchful eye that shopkeepers kept on this merchandise. Children sometimes felt guilty when discussion or play with friends or peers became overtly sexual. Nonetheless, the play began with pre-school children trading "peeks" and apparently continued right through elementary school. ("Two girls tried to take me home to be the 'doctor.'") I must not, however, overemphasize the conflict between children's norms or behaviors and those of adults, for research elsewhere suggests that, most of the time, parental and peer influences were surprisingly congruent.[13]

In the context, then, of youthful desires and adult constraints, let us examine the relationships between children and their culture. Our direct access to the lives of preschool children is very limited and that which we have is unreliable. Most adult memories of childhood begin with certain unique events that took place between their third and fourth birthdays. ("My earliest recollection . . . was a very traumatic stay in St. Vincent's Hospital at the ripe old age of three, for a tonsillectomy";[14] "I remember the other children in our block had a pin fair, and we played games"; "I remember my first day at dancing class when I was about three." A few people can give connected accounts of certain regular aspects of their lives from about the same age. "We had our weekly bath on Saturday and put on our clean clothes on Sunday.") Both sorts of memories, however, raise questions about what is truly recalled and what is the product of absorbing family lore, and following family practices over the years. Moreover, many of the most important early events in human lives – learning to walk, learning to control bladder and bowels, learning to talk, developing complex emotional relationships with parents, siblings and other relatives, learning to express (or suppress) a wide range of emotions, learning some things about being a boy or being a girl, learning to play relatively complicated physical and mental games, beginning to display qualities that will structure personalities and life-long characteristics, and learning to make connections with other children – take place before the years of either unique or systematic recall. What follows, therefore, must be seen in this broader context.

Since, until well into the 1950s, Vancouver possessed few nursery schools or kindergartens, most children entered the world of other children as it existed immmediately around their own homes or in the homes in which they received day care.[15] Although parents and guardians controlled the extent to which children participated in the lives of other children, most parents permitted their children to play with the youngsters of the very immediate neighborhood. Thus propinquity provided one's earliest companions: "All my friends were from the immediate vicinity." Children played inside their own homes, in the hallways outside their apartments, or on the covered, shared porches of Vancouver's characteristic wooden tenements (called "cabins"). They played in their own yards and some parents did not permit them farther than this until they started school. ("I was not allowed to play outside our yard, and inside it only with certain other children.") More played in other yards as well, on the sidewalk, the street in front of their homes or the back alley behind them, and those vards a few doors away in either direction. ("I was sent out to play in the back alley. It was my main area of play as a smaller child.") Some ventured to nearby vacant lots. Puddles and the damp earth, or sand that accompanied rain fascinated them. The more fortunate or well-to-do rode tricycles, or pulled wagons, or laid out roadways for small cars in sandboxes or on patches of dirt. Many children played with homemade or self-made toys: washed out tin cans, block of wood, old pots or pans, pieces of metal items and so on. They used rocks or sticks to lay out floor plans for homes, and in these settings practised parental or other roles with each other, or with dolls. Sometimes they picked flowers for their playhouse or mother.

In their play they began to acquire some of the secret knowledge of childhood, such as the truth about Santa Claus, which they did not tell their parents that they had learned. Here they also began to learn the separate language of childhood, to understand that certain things could be said only with one's own sex, and never in front of adults, to master a more complex set of "we's" and "they's" than those of the family, and to comprehend the basic rules of the childhood culture. Thus, preschool children had to shift their play space if it conflicted with the needs of older youngsters. In their preschool play, some children acquired those whom they described as friends. They also recognized some on whose behavior they modelled their own, and some whom they disliked. Adults remember both those whom they liked and those whom they disliked but have little recollection as to why they felt the wav they did. Clearly, both friends and enemies came from those who lived close by. If we can be guided by the psychological literature, then these feelings were less a matter of personality than they were of behavior; aggressive children, who pushed their way into the play of others, were generally disliked by other children.[16]

Although parents and teachers viewed children's trips to and from school as a means to an end, many children looked upon them as separate, special elements of the day. ("Half the fun of school was the walk to and fro, having a friend, going home for lunch, and admiring the flowers in people's gardens.") As youngsters left their own home and yard or apartment block they also moved towards the edge of the circle of family authority. They knew that the school's effort to control the territory between home and school was mostly directed at regulating conduct, and especially conduct that could put children into danger, or bring the school itself into disrepute.[17] Those who felt particularly hemmed in by the constraints of family and school took special delight in these periods of freedom and stretched them out as long as they could. For some this was not very far. One child who had to leave just in time for school, come home for lunch and right after school reported that she "always had a good time" on the playground, "with lots of friends," that "her playground was recess."

Parental concerns, school regulations, personal habits, and attitudes towards, and place in, a group governed how children made this trip. Many children began to gather with their own group while on their way to school. ("I would leave about twenty to nine and jaunty off to school. I would meet my friends at the corner or they would come and yell for me.") Although in the era before telephones became universal, boys practised this mode of, literally, calling on their friends more often than girls did, many of both sexes stood in the lane behind the house or on the sidewalk in front calling out the name of the friend inside. ("Everyone I palled around with went over and called on each other: 'Hey, X!'") Since many parents objected to this practice – "Why doesn't he just come up and knock on the door?" – some collected their friends more decorously by waiting quietly outside at some previously agreed upon time or, indeed, by knocking quietly on the back door. Sometimes children travelled alone, more often in pairs, and sometimes in a large group.

If time were pressing, or the playground activity of particular interest to the children, they walked, sometimes roller skated or, in the upper grades, cycled fairly quickly to school. ("We were always there by 8:30.") On cold days those inadequately clothed or from cold homes left early and moved quickly to get to a place that was warm. At other times, children followed a regular route in a leisurely way along certain streets, down back lanes, and through vacant lots and bits of "bush." Certain dogs could be provoked into fits of furious barking. Children examined the changing characteristics of creek beds and ditches. After a rain, they stomped in puddles, built dams and bridges or tried to catch tadpoles. They broke ice wherever they found it. In the spring, they looked for salmonberries and in the fall they picked overhanging apples in the back lanes. In the marble season they played "chase." They admired houses and gardens and observed changes in the neighborhood. Some children carefully picked their routes to avoid things that frightened them. Some houses had fierce dogs, or quarantine signs, and others had owners or tenants of whom the children had real or imagined reasons to be afraid. They avoided routes on which they might meet children whom they feared or disliked. Most walked with members of their own sex.

Most children arrived at school in time to join the scene that I described in the opening paragraphs of this chapter. From afar, all the movement that characterized the playground appeared kaleidoscopic but in fact much of what went on was highly structured. While most children preferred to play outside in all seasons and most sorts of weather, seasons and weather did govern what they played. In large schools, each level – primary (grades 1 to 3), intermediate (grades 4 to 6) and senior (grades 7 and 8) – had a core group who dominated the activity that the season dictated. They also controlled the best bit of the playground that custom assigned to children in that grade or level. A large number of children played the same game close by. A small group of youngsters played, or watched, from the edge. ("We spent a lot of time observing ... and talking about people.") If there was a "special" class of some sort in the school, its pupils were generally ignored by the "regular" pupils. ("They didn't talk clearly or walk right; they didn't socialize with us"; "one boy with c.p. talked funny and other kids did not want to talk with him.")

Both boys and girls played many of the traditional games of childhood.[18] Girls played singing games. They skipped in a variety of games – "Dutch," "Double Dutch" and so on – of increasing complexity. They bounced balls – "there were lots of games with lacrosse balls" – on the sidewalk or against the wall of the school. They played with jacks and balls together. ("I loved jacks.") They played hopscotch "with favourite things sewn together." They played house and "Initials." Boys played "conkers" with horse chestnuts "to see who was the king of the chestnut bashers." They played with marbles or "alleys" (such as "steelies" and "cobs") in such games as "round pot," "square pot," "odd or even," "poison," stink," or with marble boards. They played with milk bottle tops, using their "stickers" to increase their supply. They chased and shot at each other with finger-guns, while making appropriate noises in their throats. In the school basement particularly, they played a game called, variously "ship ahoy," "ships and sailors coming in," or "piling on." They played handball, murderball, "two finger whacking, tagball, and pie." Both boys and girls employed traditional starting rhymes and chants: "On your marks"; "Liar, liar"; "Cry baby"; "You're getting warm"; "Sticks and stones."

Both boys and girls occasionally promenaded the schoolground to see what was going on, or to spot a particular member of the opposite sex. Younger children of both sexes played hide and seek. Both boys and girls stood in pairs or small groups talking, sharing the secret knowledge of childhood, telling jokes and sometimes "dirty" stories. (X: "Do you want to hear a dirty story?" Y: "Yes." X: "A white horse fell into a mud puddle.") More boys than girls played adaptations of adult games. Thus the school taught children to play soccer, softball and basketball. On their own, boys played soccer without any of the inhibiting rules of adults; there were, for example, no "off sides" in their play. ("Soccer was our game!") Both boys and girls played, separately if there were enough of each sex, otherwise together, a transformed softball game called "scrub," which may also have been an adult game but one which children learned from each other. ("I loved baseball and enjoyed it best if boys and girls played it together.") Both boys and girls played tag ball, dodge ball, andy-andy-eye-over, and "single basket." On wet days in the separate basements, both boys and girls played a version of tag sometimes called "British bulldog."

The ringing of the school bell dissolved all the elaborate arrangements of the playground but they quickly reformed at recess and lunch hour. The trip home after school was the reverse of that to school in the morning. Many children had to hurry home to be under the eye of a parent, to babysit or undertake other family chores, to attend to lessons of various kinds, or to practise. Others could make a more leisurely progression, replicating the morning's activities. Those who could afford it bought broken cookies from Dad's or Baders, or day-old, or "sinker" doughnuts.

Playground relationships and mores spilled over into the classroom. In contrast to their lively manifestation outside, however, inside they had to be conducted with considerable subtlety. Some girls had their hair dipped in inkwells. Those whom the children taunted, bullied or picked on continued to be treated in this way. Pupil monitors gave them the oldest textbooks, or "accidentally" knocked things off their desks as they went by. Bigger boys stepped on the feet of smaller ones. Victimized children were extremely reluctant to inform on those plaguing them. Except under the most severe interrogation, the code that forbade tattling held sway in the classroom as strongly as it did on the playground and in the wider community. Perhaps to retaliate, certain children developed careers as informers but suffered the penalty of being despised by their peers and not really liked by the teachers with whom they tried to ingratiate themselves.

Neighborhoods displayed an even greater diversity of characteristics in the culture of childhood than schoolgrounds. Nevertheless, my interviews revealed some central features. As they did on the schoolground, children projected a kaleidoscopic image of movement and sound that only partly concealed the fairly rigid structure that actually governed their relationships. Personal and family characteristics did much to determine what role children played in their culture. The neighborhood provided more scope for parents and children to differ over boundaries of place, time and friendship. In it, as well, most children found a wider opportunity to explore forbidden places, to spend time with forbidden people and to partake of forbidden pastimes.

Most children played with other children as much and as often as they could. They played after school ("I came home from school and put on my play clothes"), in the evening when the days lengthened, on the weekend and over the summer vacation. As on the schoolground, what they did followed a seasonal cycle. On the other hand, neighborhood play lacked the rigid sexual and age constraints of that on the school-ground. Without the press of time and a large crowd of children, neighborhood play was also less frantic, less intense than that of the schoolyard.[19] Nonetheless, children played many of the games of the schoolground – house, skipping, ball bouncing, marbles, scrub, tag, hide and seek, and the like – in their yards, on the sidewalks, in the streets, on vacant lots and playgrounds as well. ("I spent my youth in Balaclava Park!")

Youngsters also played such non-schoolyard games as cowboys, peggy, kick-the-can, and run-sheep-run. In the 1920s, some boys and girls still rolled hoops, but that longstanding youthful diversion faded away in later years. ("I never had a hoop, but had a buggy wheel and a long stick.") They played with such homemade or "boughten" toys as dolls (each of which had a name), scooters (homemade ones were made out of a piece of two-by-four, an old roller skate, and an apple box), wagons, baby buggies and roller skates. Sometimes, they "put on plays for our elders, with a blanket strung up for a curtain."[20] They rode their much-coveted bicycles, which they were not usually given or permitted until the upper elementary or even the junior high grades. ("I rode my V-handled bike to school; they were a big thing then"; "I delivered groceries on my balloon-tired bike.") Older boys played street hockey, sometimes on roller skates, and often with homemade equipment. In the fall, they played in the leaves and collected chestnuts. When it snowed, they made snowmen, snow forts and threw snowballs. In the summer, they followed the ice-wagons to collect chippings. Those who lived near the sea, the river or a stream, fished for trout, salmon, cod and crabs. In all but the worst weather, boys and girls played in playhouses, "caves," or forts in basements, under porches or in trees or in vacant lots in the "bush."[21] ("I spent a lot of time building forts"; "We spent a lot of time playing in the woods.") The bush

"Each year saw the arrival at the school grounds of the salesmen/demonstrators of yoyos, bolos, or other patented toys." Yo-yo experts demonstrate their tricks to Vancouver children in the 1930s. (VPL, 11793)

also provided a location for discussion and exploration of bodily functions – such as urinating and wind-breaking contests – and for exploratory sexual play.

Even such a solitary activity as reading had a social dimension. Children read the same books as their friends, and they went to the public library together to borrow books. People described the pleasures they found during childhood in reading and sharing Nancy Drew, the Bobbsey Twins, the Henty books, the Anne books, the Boy's and Girl's Own Annual, Chums, and even Books of Knowledge. ("In grade six X and I set to read every Tom Swift book.") Mordecai Richler has argued that, for his generation, there was nothing quite like comic books."[22] While many of my interviewees have mentioned comic books – "We traded comics; it was a big activity" – none has confessed to a real fascination with them.

Although newspapers and radio reached out to children in a variety of ways, Canadian children of these years clearly valued motion pictures above all other forms of popular culture. The stories themselves, and the movie stars, captured a central place in the imagination of some children. ("I was fascinated by the movies.") While children clearly enjoyed the features, the serials – ("The serial I recall was Jack Mandy and the Indians are coming") – they also enjoyed movie-going, and most especially Saturday matinees, as a social experience. The "good day was Saturday" recalled one person, because of the matinee. On Saturday afternoon two friends each got ten cents; "we went to the Fraser Theatre for five cents and bought five cents worth of candy to take to the movie."

In the 1920s matinees generally showed adult features – accompanied by raucous piano music – together with various short subjects. Thus on Saturday, 21 November 1925, between 2 and 5 p.m. children attending the Kitsilano Theatre paid ten cents to see *The Iron Horse* ("a drama of love and adventure during civilization's march towards the West") together with "Fables, Topics, and Fox News." A decade later, the Kitsilano showed Joe E. Brown in *Bright Lights*, offered *Little Big Shot* as its second feature, and showed a chapter in the serial *Tarzan*. Those children who attended the same theatre on Saturday, 24 November 1945, saw Betty Grable and Dick Haymes in *Diamond Horseshoe* (in color) together with *Charlie Chan in The Scarlet Clue*, a chapter from a serial and a cartoon. By November 1955, Famous Players apparently no longer had a Kitsilano Theatre but, on the other side of the city, at its Grandview Theatre, from 1 p.m. onward children could see John Wayne and Lana Turner in *The Sea Chase*, Fred MacMurray and Barbara Stanwyck in *The Moonlighter*, and view no less than four cartoons. By now, however, the price had risen to fifteen cents.[23]

If over these years the fare changed – silent films accompanied by piano music gave way to the "talkies," color replaced black and white in the major films, and the technology of cartoons improved greatly – the children's response to the Saturday matinee did not. In an atmosphere of what one described as "disorganized bedlam," "they stamped their feet, went on an endless procession to the bathroom," hissed scenes they didn't like, "threw stuff over the edge of the balcony and at each other," and otherwise "did all the things you couldn't do at school." Movies sometimes frightened their youthful audiences, and might even bring on nightmares. However, most children learned to know what to expect, looking forward, as one explained, to "the safe but delicious terror" brought on by certain movies. Sometimes they employed such mechanisms as closing, or partly closing, their eyes, covering their ears, or putting their heads down during the parts they both did and did not want to watch. Occasionally, events from the wider world displayed in newsreels penetrated children's consciousness. Thus scenes of Nazi concentration and death camps, and of released prisoners-of-war who had been captured by the Japanese, affected some youngsters in 1945.

Girls and boys looked at films in different ways, and movies thus added another dimension to emerging gender identities. Boys identified themselves with the leading male characters, especially when they were involved in vigorous activities: fighting, shooting, riding horses, and so on. When the male lead turned to romance, boys jeered. In their fantasies, boys saw themselves in the hero's role as he dealt with villain. A man declared that, after "action" movies, "I deliberately walked on the "tough" side of the street, hoping a sailor would try to jump me, and I would beat him up." Girls identified with female leads in a more romantic way. They enjoyed the tender moments between romantic leads, and studied the clothing of attractive women. They disliked the noise made by boys during "love" scenes and tried to hush them. In their fantasies, girls saw themselves in a romantic relationship with the male lead. Since movies were then both less violent and less sexually explicit than later became the case, these daydreams neither led to an explicit understanding of the grim realities of death nor, in male-female relationships, beyond dreams of hand-holding, gentle kissing, and so on. Children then could still retain a child's view of the world.

The social value of the motion picture continued into the next week. One man explained "You were nothing in school if you didn't know what happened in the serial the Saturday before," and a woman noted we "would get together and retell the movie with much arguing over the sequence of events." In the case of a particularly good movie, a number of women reported, they "would spend the whole week reconstructing it with an effort to get the dialogue correct and facial expressions described accurately."

Not all children went to the Saturday matinee. Some stayed away through choice; they found the noise and the press of so many children confined in a small space, uncomfortable or even frightening. As already noted, some families took up all of their youngsters' non-school time with family chores. Other families objected to movies on religious, moral or safety grounds, and forbade their children to attend them. ("I was embarrassed to say I didn't go to the movies.") As they got older some of these children ignored or defied the parental ban. Some children were unable to scrape up the necessary admission and so attended only irregularly. Many older children worked on Saturdays. Whether they attended or not, however, most children made it their business to have at least a rough idea of what was going on in the world of the feature film, the cartoons and the weekly serials.

Together with their relationships with their parents and with the school, children believed that their place in the culture of childhood was one of the most important elements of their lives. ("I was more afraid of kid . . . than of adults.") It governed how they experienced their childhoods, how they felt about themselves and their families, and how they came to see their place in the world. As they moved from one neighborhood to another, they left one cultural edifice behind to enter into another, just as complex in the new environment. ("My mother was a mover. I had to make new friends each time. I hated it.") Though some hoped that moving might raise their status and others feared it might lower it, most who moved seemed to end up in a place similar to the one they had left behind. Children remained in the culture of childhood until they were almost adults. Indeed, for some the effects and memories of their place in that culture would affect their relationships with certain people over the whole of their lives.

Children, of course, varied greatly in the intensity of their introspection regarding their status in the youthful culture. Some children entered the culture of childhood mostly for positive reasons, because they found great pleasure there. One recalls the "feeling of warmth. It was more like a family." Some entered it for negative reasons, because it kept them away from chores, from child-minding, or unpleasant parents. Some children moved into it, and through it, in an almost automatic way, absorbing its norms, obeying its codes and generally participating unselfconsciously in it. More moved through the culture with a certain caution, especially when they decided to extend their personal boundaries, or when they moved from one neighborhood to another. Some retreated from it into private worlds of their imaginations. A few children saw the territory as being almost analogous to a war zone that held innumerable threats and dangers they had to circumvent as best they could. ("My strongest memory is of running to and from school; to school in the morning, home at lunch time, to school at the last minute in the afternoon; running home after school. . . . Recalling school, I'm overwhelmed again by a childhood sense of inadequacy.")

How did children establish positions for themselves in the complex social structures of schoolyard and neighborhood? They did so, apparently, through the interaction of such personal qualities as their physical attributes, their personal characteristics, their possessions, and the way in which they took part in the process of creating and sharing group behaviors and group values. Group standards applied to such matters as speech, clothing and, especially, the way in which children behaved towards each other. First, children evaluated themselves and other children according to such attributes as their age, their size and physical maturity in relation to their age, their strength, their physical dexterity, the shape of their bodies, their facial features, the sound of their voices, and their possession of birth marks, hairlips, buckteeth or other disfigurements. ("Smaller kids had to show that they were tougher"; "They tended to think of me as more mature because I was bigger"; "I was still short"; "I was a skinny kid"; "From grade four onward I was the 'baby' to everyone, and written off in a number of ways. It didn't bother me.") Next, children measured themselves and other children on the basis of their temperament, their courage, their intelligence, and the sense of the freedom of choice that they projected. (As a result of some school successes, "I saw myself in a different light, and saw myself as seen differently by the other kids.") They were acutely conscious of each other's sense of self, especially as they revealed this quality in their attitudes to, and behavior towards their peers, and the weak and the strong in their midst. How, for example, did they respond to teasing or bullying? How did they treat parents, teachers and other adults with authority over them? They noted how newcomers behaved: did they avoid any social contact, did they initiate themselves gradually and cooperatively into the group, were they willing to assume appropriate roles, did they try to threaten, insult or fight their way into it?

Children placed enormous importance on how their own and their family's possessions compared to those of friends, peers and neighborhood acquaintances. ("It was socially important to have the best [hop scotch] tassles, the neatest hop scotch squares.") Children felt their status was threatened by a family or home that did not conform, sometimes in even minor ways, to the supposed norms of the neighborhood, by the habits of parents, or by the absence of one of them, by their lack of the customary quantity and quality of clothes, toys and other personal possessions, by the size of their bedrooms if they had one, and whether or not they had to share it or even a bed with siblings, and so on. One boy recalls that he was "never one to take kids to my house" because his mother worked and he was "embarrassed that his was not a normal situation." Another "became embarrassed because his father was a janitor." A third "never took people home because there might be a fight on." On the other hand, and despite these strong feelings, my investigation of family life at this time shows that, while children who spent truly miserable childhoods may have done so more commonly in families that, whatever their class or status, did not conform to neighborhood norms, there seems to be no close correlation between the two.

Children could do little to change the ways in which their personal characteristics and family possessions contributed to their status with their friends and peers. Short children could not make themselves taller, and those with hand-me-down clothing could not buy a new wardrobe. However, as they talked, played, argued and fought together, all could join in creating and sharing the cluster of behaviors and values that governed their relationships with each other. Friends and peers influenced one another's behavior through a combination of modelling, discussing and reinforcing. Older children, and those with the most prestige, set group standards and, through their behavior, they demonstrated them to the rest. Sometimes ethnic, class or behavioral differences led to the emergence of more than one group or gang in a neighborhood. Then the core members of each would model the standards to which other members or aspiring members followed as they tried to find their place in the group, and to behave appropriately and play correctly. All had to learn, for example, to avoid behavior that might draw the attention or the intervention of parents, teachers or other adults. While group membership was relatively open at the bottom, only the right combination of qualities – in an as yet incompletely understood process – made one a leader.

Children most clearly demonstrated the dynamics of their relationships when they differed with each other. While the community of children was perhaps more stable than the constant noise and movement suggested, four sorts of activities led to arguments and sometimes to minor or major incidents of violence. In a general context in which youngsters believed that games should be played properly and that the code of conduct be followed meticulously, children of roughly equal status vigorously debated exactly what the rule or code was and how it should be interpreted in individual circumstances. In fact, from the children's point-of-view, the code already existed; indeed, in their minds it possessed the characteristics traditionally ascribed to natural law. Through this discourse the older children taught the rules to the younger, and established their application to particular situations in the way in which adults applied case law. Children settled these sorts of differences relatively quickly. After a certain amount of shouting and arguing they either came to a consensus or the minority noisily withdrew from the game or discussion which immediately resumed.

Bullying, vicious, and seriously disturbed children posed more serious challenges to playground and neighborhood harmony. Even though they rarely followed through on their most severe threats, such children were a source of disquiet, fear, and sometimes even dread on the part of smaller or more peaceable youngsters. ("I was attacked without provocation by aggressive kids"; "I stayed as far as possible from those capable of dismembering animals. I didn't hang around with kids like that";

"The tough kids would use their boots to hack at ankles, to kick in the rear, and to hack shins"). These subjects felt particularly vulnerable when their tormentors were also able to stimulate other children to join in their taunts or physical threats or even assaults.

Some differences between children arose from conflicts over status. While the particular status arrangements of a schoolyard or neighborhood remained stable over long periods of time, a number of events could disturb it. Probably most important were changes in physical or other characteristics that occurred as children moved through the various stages of their development. When one combines these with the grade structure in school, and the crowded nature of schoolyards, then the evidence suggests three points of increased tension amongst children. Even though beginners came lowest in the school's status hierarchy, they had to work out their own status relationships. Similarly, when children moved into either the intermediate or the senior grades, some, and especially those whose relative size or self-concept changed, made an effort to change their relative positions in the group. Pupils moving in and pupils moving out could also raise tension, especially if those moving vacated or expected to assume a high status position.

At a very early age children began to learn how they differed from each other on racial, ethnic, class or religious grounds. In each neighborhood and on each school-ground a tacit truce generally characterized the relationships between self-classified different groups of children. Sometimes, children of different groups played together. Sometimes children of a particular group came to "own" a part of the playground or neighborhood and the rest generally respected it or tolerated their possession of it. Nevertheless, children could and did draw attention to these differences and most often did so in a negative way. Most children, for example, employed fairly regularly the racial, ethnic and other slurs they picked up from their parents and from their own culture. If a particular group denigrated elsewhere in the city happened to have a substantial minority or even a majority in the class or school, then prudence some-times reduced the use of the slur on that particular group, but had no effect on those used against others. Indeed, each group seemed to use all the slurs except the one that referred to themselves. Sometimes, even, children physically attacked those whom they disdained. ("We'd pass Catholic kids and fight them.")

Children settled most of their differences verbally. In their arguments they employed such weapons as scorn and merciless teasing. They probed for failures in skill, school mastery and other weaknesses ("You failed!"), mocked those who had physical defects ("Four-eyes"; "gimpy"), taunted those who differed in some way from the norm ("Buckle shoes"; "You are a 'bloody Englishman'") and tried to bring those who wept easily to tears. ("A couple of kids were school martyrs. Pupils could do what they liked with them. . . . Teachers had contempt for them as well.") If not close friends, then those of relatively equal status often developed severe rivalries and were particularly harsh on each other. Those who were younger, smaller or of inferior status found themselves particularly vulnerable to the whole range of childish

sanctions. Older and bigger youngsters employed peremptory instruction with younger and smaller peers, and sometimes reinforced their demands with threats.

If a dispute moved beyond verbal exchanges into what was called a "mad" fight,
then most commonly children pushed or shoved each other or attempted to twist their
opponent's arms or to trip them. Since most children tried to avoid them, only rarely
did differences lead to a full-fledged fight. ("I had a hard time in fighting. I was easily
intimidated and ran home and felt embarrassed about it.") Girls fought less often than
boys. As a fight began, children shouted "Fight, fight," and a crowd quickly gathered.
Fights generally comprised a combination of boxing and wrestling ("I got him in a
scissor grip.") Although children generally considered kicking, hair pulling, biting,
or using weapons such as sticks unfair practices, outraged opponents would occasionally indulge in one or more of them. ("There were certain rules upon which we
were beaten up, or beat each other up: (a) You didn't hit when someone was down;
(b) You didn't kick ever.") Fights ended when the victor held the vanquished flat on
the ground, when parents or others interevened to break it up, or when a teacher
arrived to take the opponents to the "office."

If it is a truism that childhood is one of life's happiest times, it is also a truism that
children do not really appreciate this fact. ("It was the best time in my life but I didn't
realize it.") Since they are adults, most of my interviewees see their own childhoods
from both perspectives. In a general sense many of them, although by no means all,
look back on their childhood as a time of considerable happiness and joy. ("I had a
very pleasant childhood. We were not as afflicted by the Depression as most
families"; "I had an enjoyable childhood, an active one, without many fears"; "I have
nice memories of a great childhood"; "Everyone seemed happy in those days.") Even
those whose childhoods were marred by extreme poverty, parental severity, or acute
family disharmony, found some moments in which they took delight in themselves
and their lives. Nevertheless, many people had unhappy childhoods, and it is difficult
to find out about them. ("My life was not happy, generally, either at home or at
school"; "I was very unhappy at home.") One soon reaches the limits of oral and
written personal evidence on the matter. From court reports and the evidence stored
by social agencies in case files one sometimes receives a glimpse of the exterior
dimensions of such childhoods – thus we learn, for example, that a child hanged
himself in grade 9. Nonetheless, the interiors of these childhoods are opaque. Bullies
have forgotten or suppressed their memories of what they did. I have not talked to
those who dismembered animals or, if I have, they have not told me about the habit,
or why they did it, or what they felt about it.

My interviews, however, do indicate that family conditions were at the root of
most really unhappy childhoods. Some such children received solace through their
association with their friends and peers. Indeed, Harry Stack Sullivan argued that
through a close relation with a "chum" some "influences of vicious family life may
be attenuated or corrected."[24] ("Some kids really liked school because it was the only
place they had an out from wonky homes.") Be that as it may, other children did not
make close friends or fit in well with their peers; the community mirrored the

emptiness, the rejection and sometimes the abuse that characterized their home lives. We can easily sympathize with them in their envy of those who could honestly say: "This is the best time of your life," or, as someone whose family spent much of the Depression on relief said, "It was a great time to be in this neighborhood and a great neighborhood to be in."

Notes

*This is a revised version of an article that appeared in *History of Education Review*, 15, 37-51. Reprinted with permission.

1. This chapter is built mostly out of the memories of many anonymous interviewees. Readers will soon discover my enormous debt to them which I gratefully acknowledge. I discuss the historiographic and methodological matters related to using oral evidence in Neil Sutherland, "When You Listen to the Winds of Childhood, How Much Can You Believe?" *Curriculum Inquiry* 22,3 (Fall 1992): 235-56. Both the chapter and the article are a product of the Canadian Childhood History Project to which the Social Sciences and Humanities Research Council of Canada and the University of British Columbia gave generous support.

2. See Barry Glassner, "Kid Society," *Urban Education* 11 (1976-77): 5-21 for a description of a school ground culture in the United States.

3. Naomi Miller once visited a school in Saskatoon. Of this visit she wrote: "There were over a hundred students playing in the schoolyard, but there was no roar. Some were swinging and sliding on slides, some were skipping, some playing catch or football. The only sounds were the slap, slap, slap of skipping ropes, or the thud of a football being kicked with different degrees of strength. The children were happy, even laughing without a sound. It was an amazing silence that I observed at the School for the Deaf." Letter to the writer, 23 May 1989.

4. Charles A. Dougan, *My Daughter's Request: Spotlight on the Yesterday of Country Folk* (Duncan, BC: Alexo Enterprises, 1991), 12.

5. From the point-of-view of the transmission of the folk lore of childhood, Edith Fowke notes that there is a complete turnover of children about every five years. Edith Fowke, *Sally Go Round the Sun: 300 Songs, Rhymes and Games of Canadian Children* (Toronto: McClelland and Stewart, 1969), 6.

6. In a study that uses very different sorts of evidence, Jean Barman has also concluded that there was a considerable degree of social consensus between Vancouver neighborhoods. Jean Barman, "Neighbourhood and Community in Interwar Vancouver: Residential Differentiation and Civic Voting Behaviour," *BC Studies* 69 (Spring, 1986): 97-141.

7. Willard W. Hartup, "Peer Interaction and Social Organization," in P.H. Mussen, ed., Carmichael's *Manual of Child Psychology* vol. 2 (New York: Wiley, 1970), 392-3; see also Lilian B. Rubin, *Just Friends: the role of friendship in our lives* (New York: Harper & Row, 1985), especially ch. 9.

8. Harry Stack Sullivan, *The Interpersonal Theory of Psychiatry* (New York: Norton, 1953), 245.

9. Willard W. Hartup, "Children and their friends," in Harry McGurk, ed., *Issues in Child Development* (London: Methuen, 1978), 157-8; D. Eder and M. Hallinan, "Sex Differences in Children's Friendships," *American Sociological Review* 43 (1978): 273-350; Rubin, *Just Friends*, ch. 4.

10. This definition is looser than that employed by psychologists. David R.Shaffer, for example, says that "The 'peer group' consists mainly of same-sex playmates of different ages. Indeed, developmentalists define peers as 'those who interact at similar levels of behavioural

complexity' because only a small percentage of the child's associates are actual age mates." Shaffer, *Developmental Psychology: Theory, Research, and Applications* (Monterey: Brooks/Cole, 1985), 688.

11. See Hartup, "Peer Interaction," 369-73.

12. Joseph Kett, "The History of Age Grouping in America," in Arlene Skolnick, ed., *Rethinking Childhood: Perspectives on Development and Society* (Boston: Little, Brown, 1976), 216; see also Melvin Konner, "Relations Among Infants and Juveniles in Comparative Perspective," in Michael Lewis and Leonard A. Rosenblum, eds., *Friendship and Peer Relations* (New York: John Wiley & Sons, 1975), 123.

13. See Hartup, "Peer Interaction," 429-36.

14. Frances Woodward, "Childhood Memories of the Coast," *Vancouver Historical Society Newsletter*, April 1975, n.p.

15. A survey conducted in 1948 concluded that only about five percent of the preschool population of British Columbia attended any kindergarten or other preschool group. E.J.M. Church, "An Evauation of Preschool Institutions in Canada," *Canadian Education* 5 (June, 1950): 20; see also Gillian M. Weiss, "The Development of Public School Kindergartens in British Columbia," (M.A. thesis, UBC, 1979), 135.

16. Hartup, "Peer Interaction," 392-3.

17. See, for example, Section 3.04, "Rules of the Council of Public Instruction," *Manual of the School Law* (Victoria: Queen's Printer, 1958), 114.

18. Edith Fowke has made invaluable collections of the games and pastimes of Canadian children. See her *Sally Go Round the Sun* and *Red Rover, Red Rover, Children's Games Played in Canada* (Toronto: Doubleday, 1988).

19. Opie and Opie also noticed that neighborhood play in Britain was less aggressive than that of the schoolyard. See Iona and Peter Opie, *Children's Games in Street and Playground* (Oxford: Clarendon Press, 1969), 13.

20. Woodward, "Childhood Memories."

21. For a discussion of "bush" in Vancouver see James M. Sandison, "City Bush," *Vancouver Historical Society, Newsletter* 13 (February, 1974), n.p.; and Rolf Knight, *Along the No. 20 Line: Reminiscences of the Vancouver Waterfront* (Vancouver: New Star Books, 1980), 60-66.

22. Mordecai Richler, "The Great Comic Book Heroes," in *Hunting Tigers Under Glass: Essays and Reports* (London: Panther Books, 1971), 78-89.

23. *Vancouver Province*, 20 November 1925, p. 10; 22 November 1935, p. 12; 23 November 1945, p.8; 25 November 1955, p.14.

24. Sullivan, *Interpersonal Theory*, ch. 16.

5

The Triumph of "Formalism": Elementary Schooling in Vancouver from the 1920s to the 1960s*[1]

Neil Sutherland

In *Survey of the School System*, published in 1925, J. H. Putman and G. M. Weir blamed the "state of intellectual torpor" that they found, "markedly evident" in British Columbia education on the "formal discipline theory of studies current almost everywhere throughout the Province." Advocates of this theory believed that education consisted of training such "faculties" of the mind as memory and reasoning because such training generalized itself. Through studying algebra and formal grammar, for example, one trained the reasoning faculty and came to be able to apply this talent to actual situations throughout life. Putman and Weir also discovered that lay people in British Columbia "who regard education chiefly as learning out of a book" shared the formal doctrine with professionals. If a teacher, so parents believed, "drills incessantly on the formal parts of grammar and arithmetic or the facts of history and geography, he is . . . a good teacher."[2]

A major strain in the history of Canadian education during the first half of the twentieth century was the effort made by educational theorists and school officials to overcome the popularity of formalism. Hilda Neatby examined the results of these efforts as they manifested themselves in the curricula of the 1950s. Her survey of these materials indicated that the reformers had apparently triumphed and that the new fare, in contrast to the old, provided "so little for the mind."[3] However, when one looks behind the curricula at what actually went on in classrooms, one finds that formalism in anglophone Canadian education was as strong in the 1950s as it had been in the 1920s. In fact, most of the improvements of the Froebelians, the "new" educators, and the Canadian "progressives" – a transformed curriculum, improved teacher education, more thorough inspection and supervision, and the like – had worked to refine and strengthen traditional modes of teaching and learning. Nevertheless, Professor Neatby accurately characterized Canadian education not only as it was in the 1950s, but as it had been over the whole of the twentieth century: it did not and had never done much to train the minds it served.

To substantiate this argument I will employ elementary schooling in Vancouver – including South Vancouver and Point Grey – as a case study.[4] I will begin by looking carefully at schooling as it appeared to the pupils. To do so I will describe an elementary school that I have assembled mostly out of the memories of some who attended school in Vancouver between the end of the First World War and the end of the 1950s. There I will follow the pupils through their day, their week and their school year, describing what they learned and how their teachers taught it. Next, I will explain how the school ensured its "peace, order and good government." Finally, I will survey certain structural features of this school and its social context that, in my view, made formalism inevitable.

I

To children just starting out, schooling was only one segment of lives that were already engaged in a round of activities associated with families, friends and congregations, and with playmates of yard, street and playground. While this new segment of the circle loomed large in the minds of all children, it was only one part of it. For families who centered their lives around a religious or ethnic organization, then the congregation, or a congregation-like association, impinged on the school as well; pupils tended to find their first school friends and playmates among those already well known to them through those activities, such as Sunday school. While very few have forgotten the very first day of school — "I could smell how clean my clothes were that day" — many of those interviewed had much sharper recollections of events that happened outside school than they do of early days or even of any days inside school. One person's only memory of his first two years of school, for example, is of the big bully of the grade 1 class: "I was petrified of him."

Most children starting school had been initiated into its ways long before they arrived for their first day. Parents, brothers and sisters, playmates and older children all helped to craft in the preschool child expectations of a traditional sort of schooling. The characteristics of the teaching staff, the rituals of discipline and the content of the curriculum were part of the lore of childhood. On a bright summer day a brother, sister or an older playmate had taken the prospective beginner to the schoolyard. Together they had climbed the fire escape to peer into the shadowed classrooms; the neophyte heard exaggerated tales of "rubber nose," or "weasel mouth," or "Dynamite D," or "the strap," or "Mr. Robb," who cast so all-pervasive an aura over the school of which he was the principal that in the minds of some pupils he and his school almost merged together as one being. Some children — the less sceptical, the less realistic, the more gullible, perhaps — were afraid to start school and often remained intermittently frightened by it throughout the whole of their school careers. They knew about events which gave a grim touch of reality to the apocryphal lore: of W from down the lane being strapped for throwing a spitball, of X's rash brought on by fear of physical education classes, of Y's stomach cramps before each weekly spelling test, of Z's outburst of tears when a page of her exercise book had been ripped out by her teacher. They expected such things to happen to them too. Some feared other children. Those whose families moved occasionally or frequently had to go through the ritual of "starting to school" a number of times. Some children recall feeling "inferior" and "insecure" or even frightened after each move. Others felt only lightly touched by changing schools. One boy remembers a moment of concern at recess on the first day at a new school — his third — when one big boy said to another, about him, "Do you think you can take him?" but it was all talk that quickly faded away.

Most beginners were only partly taken in by ritual tales of "horrors" ahead; they recalled the carefree departures of friends and neighbors to school as recently as the previous June and themselves set off in the same way; typically, children were "very excited about school." Most departed for their first day with their mothers. Some insisted that their mothers accompany them for the first few days and, very occasionally, the first few weeks. Some, even among those who were really keen to go to school, cried when their mothers left them on the first day. Most quickly overcame their initial shyness. And, however they came and whatever their expectations of how the school would be ordered, most beginners shared one very clear idea of what they would do in school. They were going to learn to read. After a half century many can recall stories such as "Chicken Little," and even phrases and sentences such as "Pretty pink ice cream from a pretty pink glass," "Cut, cut, said the King," "I am a boy. My name is Jerry," and "See Spot Run," which were among the first that they decoded.[5]

Despite problems posed by periods of rapid growth, Vancouver generally provided substantial concrete and brick schools for its pupils. Well maintained, most stood out as the most impressive buildings in their neighborhoods. The front of each school presented its best side to the community; the building was set back behind low fences which protected lawns and shrubs. Since most had above ground basements, those using the main entrance of the school – forbidden to pupils – climbed a set of wide granite steps and entered on one side of a double door. Most schools had a boys' entrance and a girls' entrance, generally at ground level. Behind the school lay the main playing field. Since intensive use made grass impossible, this part of the playground was usually covered with packed earth and gravel, which meant that those who fell on the playing field often tore their skin or pitted their knees.

Most children arrived at school well before the bell. On all but the worst days they played outside. On very wet or very cold days they would gather in the basement play areas of those schools which had such facilities. Since basements were usually dark, noisy and unventilated, children tended to avoid them if they could. If the school was a large one, the children would play in sharply segregated areas of the playground; the older boys monopolized the largest field, the older girls and the primary children played in their smaller areas. The duty teacher circulated from field to field, sometimes carrying the brass bell by its clapper. If she taught one of the primary grades she might have a small chain of girls attached to each hand.

Although the children were socially more or less integrated in their play, even on the playground they displayed characteristics that showed some of the sharp differences amongst them. To eyes accustomed to the present rich range of pupil garb, hairstyles, and so on, all pupils in this earlier era would appear very drab indeed. Even in the middling levels of society, children bathed less frequently than they do today. More children then than now did not bathe at all. Children had fewer clothes and changed them far less frequently. Some boys wore heavy boots, often with metal plates around the toes and with "blakeys" on toes and heels. Despite the admonitions of teachers and nurses, many wore only cheap "runners" in the summer and when it was dry, and "gumboots" when it was wet or snowy. A few wore runners whatever the weather. Some were unkempt and even dirty, while others wore clean but threadbare clothes. One of the latter recalls always having "hand-me-down clothes" and boots that at first were too big, for a time just right, and then, "for another interminable while, they were too small."

Grade 6 pupils in a middle-class Vancouver neighborhood, 1960.
(Courtesy of Kathleen Greenwood Mukai, far left, front row.)

At about five to nine, those schools equipped with bell towers or electric bells sounded a warning ring. In other schools a senior pupil or a teacher circulated throught the corridors and on the grounds ringing the brass hand bell. At the bell, monitors collected the sports equipment. The children moved rapidly to the inside or outside assembly point for their classes. There they lined up in pairs; girls in front, boys behind. The younger children held hands with their partners. Many of the girls moved to an already-reserved place in the line. Since the front was a much coveted position, those who wanted it reserved it by placing coats, lunch bags or other possessions there, or even lined up well ahead of the bell to ensure their prime positions. At the bell, the boys raced up and tussled either for first position behind the girls or for the very last position in the lines. The principal, vice-principal or the duty teacher appeared and stared – or roared – the children into silence. He or she then signalled the classes one by one to march into their classrooms. The classes passed more or less silently down corridors, some of which had a line painted down the middle. Teachers stood vigilantly by the doors of their rooms. After the children entered their rooms they placed their coats and lunches in the right place – some classes had dark, high-ceilinged cloakrooms which were often the scene of semi-silent scuffling, shin-hacking, and the like – and then moved to their desks. Those with problems in hearing or seeing – again more then than now – sat at the very front of the room. In the 1920s some teachers arranged their pupils according to their academic rank in the class, a practice which had disappeared by the 1950s.

The children entered classrooms that were, by today's standards, somewhat dark and gloomy. Incandescent bulbs, usually encased in milky glass globes, hung from the ceilings. The left-hand side of the room was covered by windows which could be opened and closed. In all but the new schools of the 1950s, freshly washed black slate blackboards covered two or even three of the other sides of the room. On one panel of the blackboards the teacher or some favored pupils had gently tapped chalk brushes on onionskin stencils to etch out a ghostly scene appropriate to the season – autumn leaves, or Santa Claus, or valentines and coloured it with soft coloured chalk. Another panel displayed the list of classroom monitors, whose tasks included cleaning blackboards and chalk brushes (never on the side of the school), operating the pencil sharpener, filling ink wells from copper containers or glass bottles with delicate glass stems, watering plants, and so on. Beneath the monitors came the "detention" list which, first thing in the morning, held only the names of those miscreants who had collected more of these punishments than they had yet been able to serve. Other lists showed those receiving milk, those who had bought war savings stamps, or other unofficial records. The timetable, in later years by law posted in a prominent position in the classroom, dictated the regular pattern of the events of the day and of the week.

The morning's seat work covered much of the rest of the blackboard. In the upper grades this was sometimes concealed by a rolled-down map or maps; sometimes one of the world, British Empire in red, or Canada surrounded by Neilson's chocolate bars. Above the front blackboard hung a portrait of King George V and Queen Mary or, later, King George VI and Queen Elizabeth or later still, Queen Elizabeth II. From 1927 onward children gazed at a sepia reproduction of Rex Wood's lifeless copy of Robert Harris' "Fathers of Confederation," which the Canadian Club had presented to schools in celebration of the fiftieth anniversary of Confederation. In 1940 it was joined, courtesy of the Kiwanis Club, by a colored picture of the Union Jack, beneath which appeared the words:

> "One Life One Fleet
> One Flag One Throne"
> Tennyson[6]

In some classrooms these pictures were flanked by such scenes of British prowess as the capture of Quebec, the Battle of Trafalgar and the signing of the Magna Carta. Above other boards hung model alphabets, health posters, or murals created by the pupils. Some open shelves holding atlases and class-set textbooks sat under the windows or in a corner beside the teacher's desk.

The floors were either oiled wood or brown "battleship" linoleum. Individual desks were generally screwed onto wooden runners. The seat in front of the front desks held texts and marked and unmarked exercise books. A metal ink well or glass ink bottle sat in a hole that had been bored into the top of the right hand corner of the slightly sloping desk. A pencil trough crossed the top of it. Below lay a shelf for storing pencil boxes, crayons, textbooks and scribblers. On the days when the windows could not be opened the characteristic classroom odor was particularly strong: on the one hand, plasticine, sour paste, pencil shavings, orange peels in the waste baskets, chalk dust, oiled floors and dust bane; on the other stale bodies and sweaty feet, occasionally enriched by "fluffs." Characteristic sounds complemented these smells: steam radiators clanked, "blakeyed" toes and heels clattered down the aisles, chalk screeched on the blackboard, and bells divided the day into its segments.

Each teacher began the day by calling the roll. The children responded, "Present, Miss X," or "Here, Mr. Y." In the 1920s and 1930s some teachers preceded roll call with a scriptural reading or Biblical story and a prayer. From 1944 onward, teachers read, without introduction or comment, a prescribed selection from the King James version of the Bible and then the children recited "The Lord's Prayer" in unison.[7] Next, teachers conducted the daily health inspection; they looked for nits, clean hands, clean nails, clean faces, combed hair and possession of a handkerchief. Once a week they collected the milk money and, during the war, quarters for war-savings stamps. They gave iodine tablets to those who had paid a dime for a year's supply. Pupils who aspired to be nurses "would count out the tablets with a tongue depressor onto a tray and then carry them around the room, pushing out each kid's with the depressor.[8] Monitors gave out new pen nibs to those who needed them, from which children had to suck the thin coating of wax off before they would hold ink. As these routines came to an end, the children took out their texts and exercise books (almost universally called "scribblers") for the first lesson. Most scribblers had solid-colored covers made of heavier, shiny paper and pupils were expected to provide one for each subject. In some primary classes pupils used exercise books made of newsprint, on which the children could only use pencils, which tore easily and which were hard to erase.

Whether pupils attended elementary school cheerfully, apprehensively or in a state of fear, the curriculum, the teaching methods and the pattern of school discipline combined to press them into a single mode of learning. Even those who then enjoyed it now recall a system that put its rigor into rote learning of the times tables, the spelling words, the "Lady of the Lake," the capes and bays, "the twelve adverbial modifiers of place, or reason, of time . . . " and the Kings and Queens. It was a system based on teachers talking and pupils listening, a system that discouraged independent thought, a system that provided no opportunity to be creative, a system that blamed rather than praised, a system that made no direct or purposeful effort to build a sense of self-worth.

Teachers taught groups of children rather than individual youngsters. Except for classes in which there was more than one grade and for the teaching of reading in the lower grades, the whole class usually constituted a single group. Primary reading groups went, in turn, to the front of the room where they sat on little chairs or on the floor in a semicircle in front of their teacher. After the teacher conducted a "phonics" drill, she introduced and drilled the new words. Then, in what was often the highlight of the day, the children each read a short segment of the day's story. "I enjoyed it when it was my turn to read," recalls one; another explains that the dull repetition didn't matter at all because "learning to read was such a fabulous thing." While one reading group was at the front with the teacher, the other two or three did seat work at their desks. (One page of an unlined scribbler, completed in 1933, shows, in its owner's printing, "the cat sits on the rug," "the rug is by the fire the fire is warm," followed by a colored drawing of a cat, a fire and a rug.) Some primary classes had library corners or "interest centres" or sand tables to which the children who had finished their seat work could go. Others had a dress-up box or store where children quietly practised using money made from cardboard circles or milk bottle tops.

Although the tone varied a great deal from room to room, the methods of teaching the whole class were remarkably consistent from teacher to teacher and subject to subject. Teachers began each lesson by reviewing what they had taught in the previous one. Often they worked – or had a pupil come up and work – an example on the blackboard. Then they went over, item by item, the exercise that was to have given practice in what had been taught. In arithmetic, language, spelling and grammar classes a number of girls and boys would move up to the blackboard to work a question from the exercise or spell one or more words from the week's list. The rest of the class was supposed to watch for mistakes. Teachers would move along the board, releasing those who had the correct answer or taking those in error through the question again. In reading lessons teachers reviewed by correcting questions, always answered in sentences ("that were never to start with 'Because,' or 'And' or 'But'"), that tested pupils' comprehension of the story, or had pupils read aloud dictionary definitions of the "new" words that they had copied into their scribblers. In arithmetic, teachers conducted individual or group drills of the number facts or the times tables ("What a proud thing it was" to come first in an arithmetic race.) In history, geography and home economics classes pupils raised their hands to answer questions based on yesterday's "notes," or identified the places pointed to on a wall map, or passed exercise books forward or back for classmates for marking to ensure that the correct word had been placed in a "blank" in a paragraph, copied from the blackboard, that had summarized a section of the textbook.

When teachers decided that most of the class were ready for the next segment of the subject, they instructed the pupils to put down their pens, pencils and rulers, place their hands on their desks or behind their backs and "sit up straight and face the front." With all eyes thus on the blackboard, teachers then demonstrated, sometimes through question-and-answer, the letter for handwriting, the syllables in, or the pronunciation of, the new spelling words, or took the pupils a further step in the language, arithmetic or grammar sequence. Again, some pupils would move eagerly and more would move reluctantly to work examples on the blackboard, or teachers would lead the class in chanting a "drill" of the spelling, or the times tables, or the number facts, or the capitals of the provinces. In reading, history, geography and science lessons, the pupils often read, in sequence, from textbooks. Some teachers conducted this reading in a regular and predictable pattern, up one row and down the next. Others, to keep the pupils alert, "called out our names at random and we would respond immediately." In some classes, children were allowed to volunteer to read. Those who read well read long bits and those who read badly short ones. ("I could read with 'expression,' but sometimes would say the wrong word, and would be embarrassed.") Some teachers passed over the really poor readers altogether or had them read while the class did seat work. Teachers broke into the sequence to read themselves, to thrust a question at wandering minds or to explicate some point in the text. Most pupils found these sessions boring. Wool-gathering was common. Those who read well had long since read ahead and mastered the content. Those who did not worried only about getting through their own portion. Some doubted that the period would ever come to an end.

Teachers occasionally varied this routine in science classes by performing experiments for their pupils. In a format that was "progressive" in form rather than content, they laid out what they were doing step by step on the blackboard according to a precisely prescribed sequence that called for tackling a "problem" through a sequence that led from a "plan" through "apparatus and materials method," "observations," to a "conclusion," the last sometimes written out even before the experiment was begun.[9] Demonstrations also characterized the introduction of something new in manual arts, manual training and home economics.

Teachers closed the oral part of lessons with an explanation of the seat work which was to follow. In the upper grades, teachers often assigned exercises laid out in the prescribed texts to be completed in the lined exercise books. Admonished to "keep between the lines," pupils wrote a couple of rows of "ovals," and other practice elements in writing, some rows of the letter in capital and then lower case form, and a list of words in which the letter appeared. In the rooms of teachers who were writing "purists," pupils had to use H.B. MacLean's "whole arm" or "muscular movement" method of handwriting.[10] They wrote a sentence to illustrate each of the spelling words or "syllabicated" the list. They worked many arithmetic questions that employed the new skill or wrote out and "diagrammed" sentences in ways that showed understanding of the newest wrinkle in usage or parsing form. They wrote out dictated drills in arithmetic and spelling. They wrote friendly letters, business letters and thank you notes. They wrote short essays ("Study pages 94, 95, 96, 97, 98 and the first paragraph on page 99 and write . . . a full account of Edward the III's reign . . .").

Much seat work consisted of copying notes from the blackboard. In the upper grades these notes were characterized by systems of headings, sub-headings, sub-subheadings and the like. Those whose older brothers or sisters had preceded them in the classroom soon discovered that some teachers used the same notes year after year. Often these notes were so copious – "reams and reams" of them covering board after board – that pupils groaned inwardly and sometimes outwardly at the sight of them, and even the recollection of them can still create a sinking feeling in some stomachs. One teacher "covered the blackboard with notes and that's how we learned English." Teachers often left blanks in the notes that pupils were to fill in by referring to the textbook. The straight pens with steel nibs that had to be dipped frequently in the ink well and which often blotted added a further arduous dimension to the task, especially for those whose motor coordination was not very good, who were left-handed, or whose teachers insisted on "muscular movement." Occasionally pupils did history or geography "projects" on such topics as "British Columbia," or totem poles, or logging, or "our new allies, the Russians." Some recall that they occasionally made models, such as a fort in history class, using plasticine and card paper. Most recall that they made butter in grade 1 or 2. ("We each took a turn shaking.")

Pupils freed themselves from the bonds of this routine as best as they could. Some learned to talk to neighbors in such a way that they were rarely seen or heard, or to throw balls or wads of paper when the teacher was not looking. Some "mastered the skill of copying . . . without ever needing to comprehend" and were thus able "to dream outdoor matters while rarely missing a word." Others travelled to the pencil sharpener as frequently as they felt they could get away with the practice. This activity was especially popular in classrooms where the sharpener was on the bookcase under a window; then one "could have a look out of the window."

"Some pupils would move eagerly and more would move reluctantly to work examples on the blackboard." (Courtesy of Vancouver School Board)

While the pupils worked, some teachers moved about the room correcting questions, checking on the neatness of the work and adding to explanations. In primary classes they awarded gold, blue and red stars or colored stickers to those whose work reached a high standard. Other teachers increased the store of notes on the blackboard, erasing and adding new material to one panel after the other in what in many rooms became an endless sequence. Still others sat at or on their desks or watched the children from a favorite standing place by the window. All regularly surveyed the class to ensure that heads were down, that no whispered conversations took place and that no notes were passed. They acknowledged the hands that were raised, answered questions or permitted pupils to go to the pencil sharpener or the lavatory, one child at a time. As the period drew to a close, teachers summarized the main points that they had tried to make in the lesson. They reminded the pupils of what was to be finished before the next period, they assigned even more material for homework or they dispatched monitors to collect exercise books for marking.

Music, art, industrial arts, home economics and physical education had welcome or unwelcome characteristics that made them somewhat different from the other subjects. First, children generally found their classes in these subjects somewhat livelier than the others. Second, they often brought their competence to the classroom rather than learning it there. Finally, their competence, or lack of it, often made the children look upon them as either high or low points in the weekly routine. Aside from a small amount of what was called "music appreciation" – that is, listening to a classical piece played by teacher or pupils or on a recording or school broadcast – most school music consisted of singing. Classes began with vocal exercises using the tonic sol fah scale, often displayed on such commercially produced cards as "Curwen's Modulator." Taking their cue from the piano or tuning fork, the children moved first up the scale – "doh, ray, me, fah, soh, lah, te, doh" – and then down it again. In many classrooms pupils then sang such "ridiculous songs" as "Hearts of Oak" and "Early One Morning" from Sir Ernest MacMillan's inaccurately titled *A Canadian Song Book*.[11] Some teachers could make this bill-of-fare enjoyable. "We had a good music program, with lots of British songs," one person recalls. Another remembers that her music teacher made it "so enjoyable we really wanted to sing for him." In many schools teachers sorted out the best singers to prepare for the annual music festival. Many who took part in the festival remember it as one of the really great days in the school year; we "got at a minimum a complete day off!" Others, especially self-styled "crows," did not enjoy music very much but only really disliked it when they were asked to sing alone.

In physical education teachers concentrated on those who already could perform well. If the facilities were available and their parents had provided the strip, pupils changed into white shirts, blue shorts for boys, tunics and bloomers for girls, and running shoes. The class would line up in rows or teams and the teacher would take them through such exercises as touching toes or astride jumping of the sort originally laid out in the Strathcona Trust *Syllabus*.[12] Next, the teacher would take the class through some activities that practised skills related to whatever sport was emphasized at the moment. In softball season, for example, pupils tossed balls back and forth and practised batting and bunting, and teachers batted "grounders" out to be retrieved. The period then culminated in the playing of one or more games of softball. In some classes teams would be picked to last over the season; in others the best players were picked as captains each day and, as captains selected their teams, children received a finely honed demonstration of exactly how their peers evaluated their competence.

Those who were picked towards the end still recall the selfcontempt this system engendered. Sometimes, however, even the incompetent were lucky. One less-than-athletic student still has a "vivid recollection of when I was on third base and just reached out and caught the ball; what a fabulous feeling it was, just to catch a ball."

Since the subject had neither a text nor a festival to ensure consistency, art programs in these years differed more than most subjects from teacher to teacher and from school to school. Recollections of art in the primary grades focus on craft activities, especially those involving making such things as woven place mats, bookmarks and pen wipers out of burlap. Intermediate grade pupils also sewed burlap, measured, folded and pasted cardboard and sometimes made things out of soft wood. Children also sketched still lifes, copied drawings illustrating perspective, made designs that "always involved a ruler" and did a variety of paintings. Tasks tended to be specific; there was "no free-lancing at all." Some had art teachers who made the subject really exciting for the pupils; we did "all kinds of sketching, watercolours, poster paint[ing]; we put up big displays at one end of the school ground on sports day for our parents to see the work."

Most former pupils recall their home economics and manual training classes with pleasure. While they may not always have enjoyed these subjects, only really nasty teachers could make them actively dislike them. Those who had some practical bent often looked on them as the high point of the week and remain grateful for what they were taught. ("She was fussy, and taught me to be fussy.") Girls who had already learned some cooking or sewing at home sometimes became impatient at the slow pace of their classes, but they also enjoyed the annual tea or "parade of fashion" at which they showed off their skills to their mothers. In industrial arts, one less-than-handy lad remembers that "you got to make the occasional simple object that had a use. . . . So we did pencil boxes, simple stands for mom's flower pots, some sort of wall bracket, etc. I remember spending five or six months alone remaking the lid to my pencil box until I managed one that fit snugly. Meanwhile more adept pupils finished small end tables in time for Mother's Day."

Beginning in the mid-1920s, Vancouver made traditional practices more efficient by "platooning" some of its schools.[13] In platooned, or "departmentalized," schools pupils moved from room to room, some of which had special equipment, to visit specialist teachers. Platooning also had its special set of routines. On the bell, or in those rooms in which the teacher regularly said, "The bell is for me, not for you," on his or her signal, the pupils would gather up their materials. The children then lined up in pairs to move from room to room. Although officially forbidden to talk in the corridors, most pupils looked upon moves as pleasant breaks in the day. However, those moving to the rooms of the vicious fretted at what was ahead and those leaving them were sometimes giddy with relief at having survived another day in their presence.

Friday brought some variation in school routines. Pupils did the final draft of the week's writing exercise in their "compendiums." In spelling and other subjects the teacher dictated the weekly test, which the children wrote out on thin strips of foolscap. Some teachers then "read out the results of these weekly and other tests so all would know who came first and last." The tests might be followed by spelling bees or games such as arithmetic baseball. For some children Friday afternoon brought a relaxation in the rigidity of the week's work. Teachers read stories or perhaps a chapter from a novel by Walter Scott or Charles Dickens – sessions recalled with special warmth. In many schools pupil officers conducted the weekly meeting of the junior Red Cross.[14] In others older pupils dispersed to a range of "clubs" for the last period of the day.

Many schools also marked the end of the week with a school assembly. After the pupils had filed in, the principal or music teacher led the school in "O Canada." Two or three classes then presented items that they had prepared: a song that they would later sing in the music festival, a play taken from a reader or some acrobatics learned in physical education. Sometimes assembly programs drew attention to talented individuals who would play or sing a classical piece or perform a dance. Classes which had had the best turnout of parents at the last Parent-Teacher Association received a banner. During the Second World War the principal or a visitor would honor the classes which had bought the most war-savings stamps or collected the most metal or paper for the regular salvage drives. In some schools the pupils would all join together to sing a hymn, a patriotic song, a Christmas carol or a round such as "Row, row, row." In nearly every school the penultimate item on the program was the principal's message: he – or, in a very few schools, she – usually addressed some problem of school or community governance.[15] The principal explained that some pupils were "hanging around" too long after school, or that there was too much talking in the halls, or that there was too much fighting to and from schools, or that the police were about to crack down on those who rode their bicycles on the sidewalk or who had not renewed their bicycle licences. Finally the children all stood to sing "God Save the King" (later, "Queen") and then marched back to their classrooms.

Some events broke irregularly into class and school routines. Pupils enjoyed those occasions when the teacher wandered or was drawn from the subject into discussion. "The room hushed" because pupils did not want to break the thread. Some teachers told war stories or recounted personal adventures. Others talked about their families; one told "about all the people in her family who had TB, and how terrible it was." During outbreaks of such infectious diseases as measles, chicken pox, mumps and scarlet fever, or during the seasonal visit of lice, the school nurse would inspect each of the pupils. Sometimes the teacher, principal or nurse would warn children about men hanging around the school grounds, admonishing them to go directly home after school and not talk to any strangers on the way. At other times individual children would be called out of class to visit the nurse, the school doctor or the school dentist or to attend a toxoid or vaccination clinic. Pupils particularly welcomed fire drills. They enjoyed not only the events themselves but also preparing for the music festival, for the Christmas concert, for maypole dancing on May Day, for a tea or fashion show in home economics, for a production of a play or operetta and for sports day.

Those who attended one elementary school in the 1930s remember the delight they took in their production of "The Mikado."

Occasionally events outside of the school impinged on what went on in it. Influenza closed schools for some weeks in 1918, and a fuel shortage did so in 1943. Schools made much of such royal visits as that of the Prince of Wales in 1919, the visit George VI and Queen Elizabeth in 1939, and of Princess Elizabeth and the Duke of Edinburgh in the 1950s. During the Second World War pupils knitted for the Red Cross and bought war-savings stamps. In some schools that early casualty among the elements of the "new" education, the school garden, reappeared for a time as the "victory garden." "We planted things that grew quickly"; pupils were supposed to persuade their parents to plant such gardens at home. Some school gardens had short-term and long-term effects. "I persuaded my parents to plant potatoes in our yard; to this day my hobby is vegetable gardening." On a more serious and more frightening note, pupils practised what they would do in an air raid; in one school they went to the school basement, in another they filed out into the playground, where "the principal blew a whistle and we would all fall down." In another the principal gave a vivid description of just how bombers would destroy Vancouver in air raids. In a fourth the janitor added to the fear occasioned by a Japanese submarine shelling the lighthouse at Estevan Point, in June 1942, by telling the children it was "the beginning of the end."[16]

II

The ways in which pupils and teachers behaved toward each other were what bound them and the curriculum together to make a school. Thus recollections of what was taught, how it was taught and who taught it lead naturally into an elaboration of what is implicit therein about how elementary schools controlled their pupils and how the pupils responded to that control. First, an overall observation. Discussions of "fair" and "unfair," usually initiated by interviewees, often burned through with an intensity that belied the fact that the events discussed took place not the day before but sometimes four or more decades ago. One teacher "was very annoyed and took four of us into the cloakroom where she used the ruler on our knuckles. It was grossly unfair: she had watched a note go through the four people before she intervened." Another marked a set of tests without noting anything on the papers, returned them to the children to mark their own, asked the youngsters to call out their marks and then excoriated those who had yielded to the temptation to pad. Another, who believes that corporal punishment is a "beneficial" device and that schools would be better places if strapping were restored, "to this very day feels wrongly punished" on two out of the three occasions he was strapped. In this context one must note that children of these years seem to have been predisposed to accept the consequences of just about any code of conduct so long as the school administered it fairly.

People's recollections of their teachers divide them into four rough categories. They gave – and as adults generally continue to give – their highest rating to those teachers who emphasized the fundamentals, who drilled frequently and tested often, who concentrated on having their pupils learn those things that both community and educational tradition told them were the "core" curriculum. These teachers knew their business and they taught this curriculum thoroughly and systematically. "Good" teachers also taught this curriculum in a particular way. They had dominant, overpowering personalities. They conveyed a sense that what they did, and what they wanted their pupils to do, was of immense importance. They sometimes yelled at their pupils. They ran "no nonsense" classrooms in which routines were all-pervasive and cast in a code that itemized many "thou shalt nots." Some pupils also knew that these were good teachers because "you KNEW you'd learned a thing. The evidence was there because you could REPEAT the learning accurately – even years later." Good teachers, however, were also fair teachers. They dispensed their rebukes and punishments rarely, in an even-handed way and in strict accordance with the rules. It was appropriate, it was fair, for these teachers to give special attention to the best pupils – to those who learned the rote packages, obeyed the rules meticulously and did everything neatly – so long as these children did not receive blatant favoritism. Good teachers did not pick on children unfairly. In this regard, pupils believed it was "fair" for teachers to ride herd on those who did not do their homework or who were often unruly, and even on those who were not very bright, so long as the teachers did so without malice and so long as the breach in the rules was evident to all.

A much larger group of teachers were "nice." Such teachers are remembered less sharply, less vividly than the others; recollections of them tend to be enveloped in a pleasant haze. One was "always warm and friendly"; another was a "lovely person, an excellent teacher"; a third was "a very quiet man; we kids thought he was really nice"; a fourth was "a very kind man, the first one who really challenged us . . . he made you think about things." Such people apparently taught well and easily; they mothered or fathered their charges without all the elaborate apparatus that characterized the classroom of the "best" teachers. They did, however, use a pedagogy almost identical to that of their more overbearing colleagues. Although few people remember them in this way, I hypothesize that they were probably as effective in carrying out the bread-and-butter tasks of teaching as were their more famous and martinet-like colleagues. (One former pupil, however, argues that, in contrast to the efforts of the "good" teacher, what the "nice" teacher taught didn't seem to have the same mental precision or self-evident value and worthiness as the product of the "good" teacher's teaching.)

If the above are memory's satisfactory elementary teachers, two other sorts also stand out. One was made up of teachers and principals who were mean, nasty, sarcastic, cruel or even vicious. They constantly put their pupils down. One recalls a teacher who called her, alternatively, "Dummy" and "Fatty"; and another who described her classmate as a "filthy little pig" because she ate garlic. There was also Miss W, who "smiled when you stumbled, and then waited for the moment to pin the truth on you," Miss X who announced that she was "sick and tired of calling out 'foreign' names," Miss Y who mocked those who stuttered until they cried. On the really dark side there were, as well, the principal who fondled girls and the school physician who sexually assaulted some of the boys. Such teachers usually employed a pedagogy that was not very different from other teachers. They differed from their colleagues mostly in that, instead of being respected or liked by their pupils, they were feared and hated. Only in retrospect did these people achieve a dubious sort of merit; some former pupils gradually came to look upon the fact that they had "survived" these teachers as evidence that they had in their classes taken a major step towards adulthood.

Finally, pupils looked on a few teachers with contempt. These unfortunates displayed their ineffectiveness or their incompetence in a variety of ways. They could not explain things clearly. The oral parts of their lessons rambled, their notes were incoherent. They could not keep order; they sometimes broke down and wept. While most disappeared in a year or less, a few persisted to become almost legendary objects to be scorned by class after class of pupils. Whether they stayed or left, they received no compassion or mercy from either pupils or parents.

Two main themes characterized overall school discipline in this era. The first and dominant mode was that imposed by the school. It displayed itself in a continuum that at one end had the presence, the personality, the aura of the teachers and the principal and at the other, the strap and expulsion. School staffs held back the latent barbarism they perceived in the children with an increasingly severe range of sanctions that began with displeasure and ended with corporal punishment. Teachers and parents justified this range of measures by appealing to a very long-standing tradition – to the proverbial "Spare the rod and spoil the child." The second mode saw some schools introducing a range of practices through which the children were to learn what was sometimes called democratic self-control. Through a system of monitors, the older and abler in fact enlisted with teachers and principals in the task of teaching and maintaining appropriate standards, especially among the younger children." Thus democratic self-control was tightly circumscribed by traditional disciplinary means which were brought in these years to a peak of effective performance.

The presence of the seasoned teacher was clearly the first line of defence against barbarism. Teachers had presence; pupils and their parents expected them to possess it. Teachers with this quality said, "Do this," and the children did it. All but ineffectual teachers exerted their personalities with more or less intensity on their pupils and expected, and received, a reasonably automatic compliance with their directions. Even those who created a loving atmosphere in their classrooms did so in this broader context. The woman who now recalls, "I knew who the teacher was and did as I was told," speaks for her classmates as well as herself. Presence surely came with experience, but neophytes set out, self-consciously, to acquire it. Eighteen- and nineteen-year-olds stare at us from Normal School annuals of these years with an intensity that makes them look older, more severe, and altogether more formidable than the twenty-two or twenty-three-year-old beginning teachers of the 1980s and 1990s.[17]

Teachers backed up their demands that pupils meet certain standards of behavior and work habits with an armory of sanctions. They gave children "the ray." They gave them the cutting edge of their tongues; they spoke sharply, they made nasty and sometimes sarcastic remarks, they spoke more and more softly, coldly, ominously; they shouted and even raged against their charges. ("She really lambested us; she had a short fuse"; "I recall his scarlet face and his ferocious temper.") Many maintained full control solely through verbal means. Others made children sit or stand in a corner, or even on the floor under the sand-table; they kept children in at recess, at lunch hour and after school. One person recalls being kept in after school, asking to leave the room, being refused, and then wetting his pants. "I stayed away for three days." Teachers made pupils sit up straight, motionless, with hands behind their backs, for periods of time up to half an hour. They forced chewers to put their gum on the ends of their noses or behind their ears. They gave extra work of an excruciatingly boring and valueless sort, such as eight or nine digit long division questions and their proofs, the writing of lines – some wrote such things as "I will not chew gum," or "Silence is golden," 500 to 1000 times, the copying of pages out of textbooks or dictionaries, and the memorization of poems and assigned those classroom and school chores not popular with "monitors" such as picking up paper and other garbage in the school and on its grounds. They sent miscreants to school detention halls, where the duty teacher or vice-principal presided, often with great severity of tone. Some teachers and schools kept elaborate systems of "demerit" records, through which offending pupils progressed through an increasingly severe range of sanctions. Fewer schools and teachers employed the opposite of this system by giving out merit points for good behavior and providing minor rewards – such as being dismissed first – to those pupils or rows of pupils which collected the most points.

Teachers and principals kept corporal punishment as their ultimate sanction short of expulsion. Classroom teachers often employed less formal – and unlawful – sorts of physical punishment. Former pupils recall teachers who spanked youngsters on the bottom or slapped them on the hands or about the shoulders and, occasionally, on the face. Other teachers pinched the upper arm or the earlobe or hit victims on the top of the head with tightened knuckles. Still others used pointers, rulers, chalk brushes, gym shoes or other bits of school equipment to hit children on their bottoms, hands, knuckles, shoulders, elbows – especially on the "funnybone" – and, rarely, heads. A somewhat fondly remembered grade 1 teacher, who enrolled forty-six pupils in the year, "stepped on their toes as she hit them with a ruler." A few, carried by temper almost beyond control, sometimes dragged children from their desks to shake them, to bang them against walls or even to manhandle them out of the classroom. Unlike the cold formality that so often characterized corporal punishment by a principal, classroom teachers sometimes struck out in a high pitch of unleashed emotion. A few teachers tried to be light-hearted, even affectionate, in their physical punishment. On these occasions the ritualized rules of the "game," especially as it was played between boys and male teachers and in such all-boy classes as those in physical education or industrial arts, required that the victim accept, however reluctantly, that their physical punishment was part of a game.

For really serious violations of class or school codes, children were sent to or summoned by the school principal. Pupils found these interviews with the principal to be extremely stressful occasions; some were tongue-tied into silence. Being strapped was not an inevitable product of a trip to the "office," but it happened often enough for youngsters to be extremely wary of visiting there. Once a principal decided to strap a boy or, more rarely, a girl, he followed a routine – almost a ritual – laid down by the department of education.[18] The principal summoned a witness, explained the crime and punishment to the latter, positioned the subject carefully, administered the strokes and counted them out in a firm voice, and then recorded the event in a special book. Some principals removed their jackets and hung them up on a coat hanger. Others emphasized the formality of the occasion by buttoning their jackets. If there was more than one victim, those waiting their turn either watched or listened from just outside the door. The worst thing was when friends were there "because then you couldn't cry." One person, recalling his first four on each hand, says, "I couldn't understand the pain, it was so intense." Since principals used these events as much to deter as to punish, they often permitted the sounds to carry their warning through the school; the appearance back in the classroom of a red-eyed and red-handed victim quickly reinforced the message. A few even prolonged the misery by administering punishment over more than one session or by announcing it and then postponing its administration to noon hour or after school, or even to another day.

Although girls sometimes received corporal punishment of the informal classroom sort, they rarely took part in the ritual in the office. When one looks at this difference between the sexes more systematically, however, one sees that it appears to be the product of two sorts of influences. On the one hand, teachers seem to have demanded more docile conduct from girls than they did from boys. On the other, children themselves structured much of the different ways that boys and girls behaved. Most beginners of both sexes probably came to school disposed to conduct themselves appropriately. However, as they got to know other children, as they formed same-sex friendships, groups and gangs, as they integrated themselves into the playground pecking order (the "culture" of childhood), the sexes came to have different norms as to how they should behave toward each other and toward the school. These norms seem to have almost completely governed what happened to children between their homes and their classrooms. Further, they seem to have had more influence even inside classrooms than many teachers were aware.[19]

If parents and teachers often justified stern discipline and corporal punishment by appealing to proverbial wisdom, their approach was also deeply rooted in fear. On the one hand, they feared that without severe sanctions, family, classroom, school and society would quickly descend into disorder and even barbarism; on the other hand they feared for the future of the unchastened. Many still believed that the "old Adam" was very close to the surface in boys and especially in early adolescence. In the eight-grade elementary school some teachers in the upper couple of grades seem to have seen a barely suppressed violence in some of the boys; in responding to it savagely they perhaps transformed their own fears into realities. In turn, these violent episodes communicated such beliefs and fear to the younger pupils and gave them notions of a sort of behavior that one day they might well perform. The school's informal communication system passed down and exaggerated stories of epic disciplinary events in the upper grades. These tales seem to have kept certain youngsters in a state of anticipatory tension over much of their school days "feeling that the certainty of it occurring to you was not only high, but preordained." Many now recall the paradox in this system; it terrified the good children who only very occasionally got caught up in its machinery but gave those who were often punished and who "could take it" an heroic status among their peers. X, for example, was one of those boys "who was strapped two or three times a year." One day he kicked a football at a school window; "it took him three kicks to get it through the window. He just stayed there until the teacher came and took him away" for the usual punishment.

Learning to survive was thus an important part of the hidden curriculum of the school. Its pupils had first of all to learn how to deal with their fears: their fear of the other children in their own class, their fear of the bigger children who might harass them to and from school or on the playground, their special fear of "tough" boys and girls, their fear of teachers and the principal, their fear of the strap. Most children obviously learned to manage, or at least to live with, their fears. It is important to note that those whom I interviewed reported that, overall, they enjoyed much of their school experience. ("I sure enjoyed my days at school, even if I wasn't good at it.") A few were less fortunate. What was school really like for those who decline to talk about it because they still do not want to conjure up memories they say are really unpleasant?

III

According to Putman and Weir, the alternative to formal discipline was "the project method." They pointed out that it was pedagogically sound to select "big projects of study as cores of interest, from which the child's investigations radiate in [as] many directions as the spokes from a wheel." Thus older youngsters might investigate "the various factors that have built up the Okanagan fruit industry and describe the industry as it is now carried on" or younger children "might spend a whole term on a study of what the people of Vancouver eat and wear and where their food and clothing came from."[20]

Since Putman and Weir's recommendations were very much in the mainstream of then-current educational theory, British Columbia gradually put many of them into effect. In a series of what were really administrative reforms, the province standardized the curriculum and the time allotments for each subject, adopted the notion of the junior high school, eliminated high school entrance examinations, tightened standards for admission to the Normal schools and promoted school consolidations. After the Liberals won the provincial election of 1933, Weir became Minister of Education. In 1935 he embarked on a major revision of the curriculum. By 1937 his department produced a new course of study which was over 1 600 pages long. In the words of one of its chief architects, H. B. King, the philosophy characterizing this new curriculum "may be briefly expressed as the promotion of individual growth and social adjustment through purposeful activity."[21] The philosophy of the new education – now generally called progressive education – thus lay at the heart of the new program. Nonetheless, if my interviewees are to be believed, then all of the changes that took place in education outside of the classroom had very little effect on what went on behind its doors. The "good" teacher who "drills incessantly" kept Vancouver elementary schools in a torpid formal state for at least three decades after Putman and Weir made their report.

Why Canadian education had become formal lies outside of the scope of this paper.[22] What is of interest here is why formalism persisted and even extended its sway in Vancouver – and elsewhere in Canada – despite the fact that most theorists attacked it so vigorously and, indeed, its opponents had come to dominate the provincial department of education and the upper levels of the Vancouver school system.[23] A good part of the answer to this question lies within the school system itself. To introduce integrated learning of the sort and on the scale envisioned by Putman, Weir and King, schools must have appropriately educated and trained teachers and appropriately-sized classes. In these years Vancouver met neither condition.

To organize "big projects of study" in such a way that the children's "investigations" led to intellectual growth placed two demands on teachers. First, they themselves must have received the sort of education that showed them the connections between the different branches of knowledge; and second, they must have had the sort of professional training that taught them to structure activities through which children could come to see the connections. In fact, however the vast majority of Vancouver's elementary teachers had only high school level academic training. Few if any Vancouver or other Canadian high schools, whose classroom life Robert Stamp has characterized as "circumscribed by a prescribed curriculum of traditional subjects, authorized textbooks, deductive reading, and external examinations," taught even their best students a modicum of the sort of independent thought that is a prime product of a liberal education.[24] "I didn't think a thought in the whole of school," recalls one student with an excellent academic record; "I just regurgitated."

In addition to their junior or senior "Matric," elementary teachers had one year of Normal school which they may have taken in two or three segments spread over a number of years or, after 1922, in a single nine-month term.[25] The first task of the Normal school was to ensure that its students knew what they were going to teach; that their spelling, handwriting, grammar, arithmetic skills, and so on, were up to the grade 8 level. Its next task was to initiate its students in practices that would enable them to teach these subjects first in a multi-graded rural classroom and then in a graded consolidated or urban school. Thus training for much of the new as well as the traditional education was limited and perfunctory.[26]

In their practice teaching and in their early years in the profession these young people naturally modelled themselves on the best practitioners who had taught them and on the best they saw in their schools; they became proficient at their craft by doing it in the way it had been done to them. Most modelled themselves on those teachers, described above, who emphasized the fundamentals and rigorous discipline in equal measure. Most forged themselves in the crucible of the one-roomed rural school. Hard work, dedication and concern for their pupils clearly characterized most of the products of such training and early experience. Although many undoubtedly had the ability, very few had the training to introduce their pupils to the joys of intellectual activity of any sort, let alone those which were supposed to emerge from projects. Indeed, as the traditional system became more efficient, more systematic and more effective, it simply co-opted the elements of the new education as it ignored its goals. Further, most teachers conveyed to children, to colleagues and to parents the sense that there was in each subject only one right way of doing things.

Even if some teachers had somehow acquired a theoretically sound and practical approach to progressive learning or other new ways of organizing classroom activities, they would have found enormous difficulty in putting them into practice. In addition to the almost insuperable problems posed by trying to function independently in a system that pressed pupils, teachers and principals into the formal mode, the very size of classes made other forms of teaching and learning virtually impossible. In classes that averaged for most of these years about forty pupils and could range up to the mid-50s, teachers could not get to know their charges as individuals. Class size forced them to teach to the whole class, to let the good look after themselves and to let the weakest fall by the wayside. Their responsibility for so many children probably also forced all but the ablest teachers to take a stance in their classrooms that emphasized children's weaknesses and propensity to err, to capitalize on their vulnerability, and to keep an extremely wary lookout for bad behavior. In these circumstances, when some teachers introduced "projects" or "activity units" into their classrooms they did so merely as an occasional change of pace in such subjects as social studies, science or art. Like their other colleagues, they continued to teach factual material, tested their pupils' memories and evaluated their work habits; what they did is best epitomized in their answer to a question common in classroom discourse until relatively recently: "Yes, neatness does count."

And neatness also "counted" in the community as a whole. Pupils, parents and employers in Vancouver continued to believe that education was "learning out of a book." Parents of all social classes shared in this common viewpoint as to the nature and value of elementary schooling. They knew what children should learn, they knew how teachers should teach it, and they knew how principals and teachers should maintain order. Indeed, because parents and employers lacked the daily empirical testing of their expectations against the real world of the classroom, they often held the most rigid of formalistic expectations of what school should be like.

That working-class parents apparently held the same views on elementary education as did their middle-class counterparts may, at least initially, seem somewhat surprising. While my interviews revealed considerable differences among aspects of the non-school lives of Vancouver children from one neighborhood to another, recollections of schooling, were surprisingly similar. Thus Vancouver schools sorted children within schools rather than between schools.[27] As we have seen, they continually told those who were not as able as their peers that they were not going to climb very far up the educational ladder. Nonetheless, formal schooling of the sort offered in Vancouver schools met, in a rough and ready way, somewhat different class needs. At the political level, organized labor in the city supported free public education, and working-class people ran for, and were elected to, the school boards.[28] At the personal level, in a city composed of people born elsewhere, parents took seriously their role as educational strategists for their children. In this role most parents insisted that their children at least get their "entrance" – still in common parlance long after the high school admission examinations had been abolished – as their basic educational credential. For those who left school at the end of grade 8 or over the next couple of years, "entrance" certified that they had well and truly mastered the three "R's."[29] For those who aspired to the wide range of occupations and other levels of training for which matriculation was necessary, entrance admitted them to the high school.

IV

On 5 September 1934 the teachers of Charles Dickens School assembled for their first staff meeting of the school year. The principal, J. Dunbar, introduced the exchange teacher from Ontario, outlined the procedure for getting new sand for sand tables, discussed how a teachers' badminton club could function and explained how to get boots, shoes and school supplies for desperately needy children. He also reminded the teachers about such policies as those regarding substitutes, posting their names on the doors of their classrooms, keeping their class registers and turning in their previews to him every week. A quarter of a century later the staff of Queen Elizabeth School gathered, on 6 September 1960, for their first staff meeting. The principal, I. D. Boyd, introduced the five new teachers and the new nurse, explained that French would be taught to grades 5 and 6, and asked that all teachers attend the first meeting of the Parent Teachers Association. He also reminded the teachers about such policies as those regarding substitutes, signing in in the morning, keeping their daybooks and seating plans up-to-date and preparing previews for each two-and-one-half monthly period in the school year. These staff meeting minutes both clearly display a similar administrative underpinning for formal learning. Visits to classrooms in both schools would have revealed that nearly all teachers believed in, and followed, traditional practices. Further, their stance received strong support from the provincial Royal Commission on Education, the Chant Commission, that in its 1960 *Report* endorsed a traditional view of education.

Over the 1960s and 1970s, however, pupils, parents, teachers and employers abandoned the long-lived consensus on elementary education.[30] Some began to take seriously the child-centred rhetoric of contemporary child-rearing and educational literature and to insist that it be employed in the schools. Elementary teachers gradually became well enough educated that they could structure the learning in their classrooms in the context of new theories about learning and teaching. Classes became smaller. Decades of changes in curricula and teaching practices would transform elementary schooling in Vancouver. No particular pedegogy predominated in the way that formalism did in its heyday. Certainly some formal practices persisted, and some schools both within and without the public system tried to operate as if nothing had been learned about the process of schooling since the nineteenth century. In this view they had the support of some parents. Nonetheless, if formalism did not entirely disappear over these years, after the mid-1960s, one could no longer use the term to characterize elementary schooling in the city.

Notes

*This is a revised version on an article that appeared in *BC Studies*, 69-70 (Spring-Summer 1986), 175-210. Reprinted with permission.

1. This chapter is built mostly out of the memories of many anonymous interviewees. Readers will soon discover my enormous debt to them. I discuss the historiographic and methodological matters related to the use of oral evidence in Neil Sutherland, "When You Listen to the Winds of Childhood, How Much Can you Believe?", *Curriculum Inquiry* 22: 3 (Fall 1992): 235-56. Both are a product of the Canadian Childhood History Project to which the Social Sciences and Humanities Research Council of Canada and the University of British Columbia gave generous support.

2. British Columbia, Department of Education, *Survey of the School System*, by J. H. Putman and G. M. Weir (Victoria: King's Printer, 1925), 118-21.

3. Hilda Neatby, *So Little for the Mind* (Toronto: Clarke, Irwin, 1953).

4. In 1929 the municipalities of Vancouver, South Vancouver and Point Grey were amalgamated. In 1923 British Columbia extended the regular elementary school program from seven years to eight. In the late 1920s school districts began to introduce junior high schools for grades 7, 8 and 9. The depression, however, severely retarded their growth. On the other hand, declining secondary enrollment provided more space for them after 1938. In 1945-46, 54 percent of grade 7 and 8 pupils in Vancouver attended elementary schools, 30 percent junior high schools and 16 percent junior-senior high schools. Vancouver School Board, *Report* (1948), 93; British Columbia, Department of Education, *Report* (1945-46), MM 173-75.

5. "Chicken Little" appeared in *The Canadian Readers: Book One A Primer and First Reader* (Toronto: Macmillan, 1922), 74-80. I have not been able to find out from which books the first two sentences came, but the person who recollected the third is recalling an early story in the reader by Henrietta Roy, Elsie Roy, P. H. Sheffield and Grace Bollert, *Highroads to Reading: Jerry and Jane: The Primer* (Toronto: Ryerson and Macmillan, 1932). British Columbia began replacing the "Canadian Readers" with the "Highroads Readers" in the mid-1930s. British Columbia, Department of Education, *Report* (1934-35): S64-65. "Spot" was a pet in the famous American "Dick and Jane" series of primary readers, introduced in Canada after the Second World War. The three "pre-primers" in the series were William S. Gray, Dorothy Baruch and Elizabeth Montgomery, *We Look and See* (Toronto: Gage, n.d.); Gray, et al., *We Work and Play*, and Gray, et al., *We Come and Go*. The primer was, of course, Gray and Mary Hill Arbuthnot, *Fun With Dick and Jane* (Toronto: Gage, n.d.).

6. The wording is taken from a copy now in the possession of Jean Barman. See also Vancouver School Board, *Report* (1940), 55.

7. See British Columbia, Department of Education, *Report* (1943-44), B30; British Columbia, *Statutes* (1944), c. 45.

8. In 1930, 3.9 percent of Vancouver pupils had goiter. By 1936 this had declined to 1.1 percent. Vancouver School Board, *Report* (1937), 31-32.

9. See George H. Limpus and John W. B. Shore, *Elementary General Science* (Toronto: Macmillan, 1935), 11-12.

10. H. B. MacLean, *The MacLean Method of Writing: Teachers' Complete Manual: A Complete Course of Instruction in the Technique and Pedagogy of the MacLean Method of Writing for Teachers of Elementary Schools, Junior and Senior High Schools, Commercial Schools, and Normal Schools* (Vancouver: Clarke & Stuart, 1921). The note at the foot of the title page of the 31st edition says that it is authorized for use in British Columbia, Quebec, Nova Scotia, Prince Edward Island, New Brunswick and Newfoundland.

11. Sir Ernest MacMillan, ed., *A Canadian Song Book* (Toronto: Dent, 1937). The first edition of this text appeared in 1928.

12. Strathcona Trust, *Syllabus of Physical Exercises for Schools* (Toronto: Executive Council, Strathcona Trust, 1911). This was the first edition of the Canadian version of this British manual. In the 1960s Lorne Brown recalled that he had been taught at the Vancouver Normal School in the 1920s to take his pupils through a calisthenics sequence which he had memorized as IT AB LAB: I – for introductory activity; T – for trunk exercise; A – for arm exercises; B – for balance activity; L – for lateral trunk exercise; A – for activity; usually a form of relay; B – for breathing. Lorne E. Brown, "Personal Reflections – Physical Education in B.C. . . . 1927 to 1967," unpublished paper, n.d. (1967?).

13. Lord Tennyson School pioneered platooning in 1924. By 1938 all elementary schools employed some form of specialist teaching. Vancouver School Board, *Report* (1925), 11-12; *ibid.*, 1937-38, pp. 64-65. The origins of platooning are described in Raymond E. Callahan, *Education and the Cult of Efficiency: A Study of the Social Forces That Have Shaped the Administration of the Public Schools* (Chicago: University of Chicago Press, 1962), 128-36.

14. A "demonstration" Junior Red Cross meeting conducted by a class at Tecumseh School in May 1936 is described in "Practical Citizenship," *B.C. Teacher* (June 1936): 17-19. By 1945-46, 253 Vancouver elementary classes had junior Red Cross branches. British Columbia, Department of Education, *Report* (1945-46), MM 77.

15. In the 1920s one woman in Vancouver, one woman in Point Grey and nine women in South Vancouver held school principalships for one or more years. By the school year 1930-31 only one woman – a former South Vancouver principal – still held the role. After Miss E. M. Dickson retired in 1934, all forty-nine Vancouver elementary schools had male principals. British Columbia, Department of Education, *Report* (1935-36), H165-H182.

16. The minutes of a staff meeting held at Charles Dickens School on 5 October 1942, note "Re Air Raids (1st) If there is time – Send class home. (2nd) If there is only a little time, send pupils to the basement. (3rd) If there is no time, pupils and teachers under their desks. N.B. If you hear any anti-air craft fire, there is no time to go home."

17. John Calam drew my attention to what old annuals and class photographs tell us about the determined maturity of beginning teachers of earlier eras. Perhaps this characteristic reinforced the view of pupils that all their teachers "were as old as the hills." One, recalling a teacher of the 1930s who "wore her hair in a bun and had dark clothes," was really surprised when she read that this teacher had just retired.

18. Corporal punishment was rooted in the Canadian Criminal Code. Statutes, precedents and reported cases are discussed in Peter Frank Bargen, *The Legal Status of the Canadian Public School Pupil* (Toronto: Macmillan, 1961), 125-33; see also *Manual of the School Law and School Regulations of the Province of British Columbia* (Victoria: King's Printer, 1944), 127-28.

19. See "Everyone Seemed Happy" (ch. 4).

20. *Survey of the School System*, 118-21.

21. British Columbia, Department of Education, *Report* (1939-40), B32. For the Putman-Weir report and its results, see F. Henry Johnson, *A History of Public Education in British Columbia* (Vancouver: University of British Columbia, 1964), ch. 7, 8 and 12 and Jean Mann, "G. M. Weir and H. B. King: Progressive Education or Education for the Progressive State?", in J. Donald Wilson and David C. Jones, eds., *Schooling and Society in Twentieth Century British Columbia* (Calgary: Detselig, 1980), ch.4.

22. For a comprehensive analysis of this question, see George S. Tomkins, *A Common Countenance: Stability and Change in the Canadian Curriculum* (Toronto: Prentice-Hall, 1986).

23. Robert Patterson clearly shows that the Vancouver experience was representative of the situation in other parts of Canada. See his "The Canadian Response to Progressive Education" and "The Implementation of Progressive Education in Canada, 1930-1945" in Kach, et al, *Essays on Canadian Education* (Calgary: Detselig, 1986), ch. 4-5.

24. Robert M. Stamp, "Canadian High Schools in the 1920's and 1930's: The Social Challenge to the Academic Tradition," Canadian Historical Association, *Historical Papers* (1978), 92.

25. Johnson, *Public Education in British Columbia*, 86, 210; for an analysis and an evaluation of the Normal schools, see John Calam, "Teaching the Teachers: Establishment and Early Years of the B.C. Provincial Normal Schools," *BC Studies* 61 (Spring 1984), 30-63. The education of elementary teachers in British Columbia did not move to the university until 1956. Even then, for many years students on the Bachelor of education program could receive a teaching certificate after two years, the equivalent of senior matriculation and a year at the Normal schools.

26. See Irene Howard, "First Memories of Vancouver," Vancouver Historical Society, *Newsletter* 13 (October 1973), for a brief account of Normal schooling from a student's perspective.

27. This statement is supported both by my interviews and by an examination of such data as class size and teacher qualification for selected schools from different neighborhoods in the city.

28. Jean Barman, "Neighbourhood and Community in Interwar Vancouver: Residential Differentiation and Civic Voting Behaviour," *BC Studies* 69 (Spring, 1986): 97-141.

29. Between the 1920s and the 1950s Vancouver children significantly increased the number of years they spent in school. While exact retention rates are extremely difficult to compute, enrollment and related data provide a clear indication of trends. Of the cohort born in 1918, about one-third stayed in school to enrol in grade 11: of the cohort born in 1928, over 40 percent did so; and of the cohort born in 1938 over 60 percent did so. These percentages are provincial ones, but other compilations suggest that Vancouver youngsters stayed in school for slightly longer periods of time than did those for the province as a whole. British Columbia, *Report of the Royal Commission on Education* (Victoria: n.pub., 1960), 43-49.

30. See "Royal Commission Retrospective"(ch. 21).

6

"I can't recall when I didn't help" :
the Working Lives of the Children of Modern Pioneers[*][1]

Neil Sutherland

From the time the apothecary Louis Hebert, his wife Marie Rollet, and their three children began to cultivate land in New France until the present day, children have played a central role in pioneering in Canada.[2] This chapter describes how, over the years after the Great War, work permeated the lives of children growing up in Evelyn, a pioneering community in the Bulkley Valley of British Columbia. It shows how families tried to integrate new notions with traditional practices. It begins by outlining the daily round of chores, it moves on to discuss "the greater circle of the seasons's tasks," and then considers two sorts of work – house and barn building and land clearing – that were so central to pioneering. The chapter concludes with general observations on the role of work in the lives of the rural young, including its place in the development of their adult identities.

As what follows clearly demonstrates, the differences between a pioneering and a long-settled agricultural community is mostly a matter of degree, rather than kind. Indeed, there were broad continuities across most Canadian childhoods of the time, whatever their individual settings. Nonetheless, a community in the throes of creating itself reveals with particular clarity the tensions between the demands placed on children by their families on the one hand and an increasingly intrusive state on the other.

Although childhood in newly-settled areas in the twentieth century closely resembled pioneer childhood in earlier eras, the years between the end of the First World War and the end of the 1950s had characteristics that made the period unique. Arduous, endless, and generally mindless work remained a central element in the lives of all pioneering children. Like predecessor generations, they treaded, as Robert Collins put it, "two endless wheels of labour . . . one within the other: a daily round of chores spinning inside the greater circle of seasons' tasks."[3] A transforming society added to these customary burdens. On the one hand, urban popularizers of new notions of childhood and of child health, welfare, and education endeavored to bring children in the remotest areas under the sway of their ideas. School teachers and inspectors, outpost nurses, public health nurses, travelling physicians and dentists, mothers' allowance investigators, and missionaries brought the new ideas and practices, and some of the apparatus of the fast-emerging modern state, to pioneering areas. In particular, the state incorporated nearly all school-aged children into the laddered school system. It, rather than parents, now held the major responsibility for when and how children would learn their literary and cultural tradition. Much more schooling and school work had to be fitted into the "two endless wheels of labour."

On the other hand, twentieth-century pioneers interested themselves in the effects that social, medical, technological and scientific changes might bring to their lives. They came out of a motorized community and expected its roads and railroads to follow them.[5] They also expected eventually to employ mechanized farm and other equipment, and to own automobiles. Since they were always short of cash, and with the demands of farm and family competing for their meagre supply of it, pioneering families were extremely sceptical of anything they regarded as a "frill." As one woman explained, "We didn't have the cash to buy these things [such as a new coat for school] . . . because every time there was cash in our family there was a threshing machine to buy. . . . Always on a ranch it's . . . machinery and equipment." Nonetheless, and to cite but two examples, most settlers wanted the benefits of recent advances in medicine and an up-to-date education for their families.

Women demonstrated their commitment to modern medicine for themselves and their families by their enthusiasm to bear their babies in hospitals. From the late nineteenth century, social reformers and medical practitioners campaigned to reduce extremely high rates of infant and maternal mortality. Pregnant women were exhorted to bear their infants in hospitals rather than at home. Although the shift from home to hospital was eventually accompanied by decline in maternal mortality, historians do not agree as to whether these events were causally linked.[6] Interviews and other data show, however, that most rural and pioneer women welcomed the shift to the hospital.[7] Before the railroad was completed, one woman from Evelyn "walked forty miles to the hospital . . . where her first child was born." Later, and despite the presence of a trained midwife in their midst (the "lady who helped when babies were born" as one child thought of her at the time), many Evelyn women chose to go to the hospital in Smithers. One woman, who had an exciting race with time getting to Smithers for the birth of one child, for the next went early to Smithers and "stayed with a friend . . . for three whole weeks before the baby decided to come."[8] Some children continued to be born at home, even after the Smithers hospital opened. One man reported that he had been "born in the farmhouse. No midwife was present. Since my father had been an amateur vet he may have helped."

Most Evelyn parents wanted a modern education for their children. After initiating formal schooling in a private home, the community soon built a log schoolhouse.[9] In Canada in the half century before the First World War, state and community together had lengthened the school year, increased the number of years children spent there, and given a more urban cast to standardized curricula. In consequence, twentieth century rural schools such as Evelyn's were less able than their nineteenth century predecessors to fit themselves tightly into local mores and work patterns.[10] In the not so distant past, rural school trustees set the dates for opening and closing schools so that they accorded with the rhythms of community life. By the 1920s, Evelyn's schools opened and closed on province-wide dates set by the department of education in far-away Victoria.[11] Fewer families followed the time-honored rural practice of sending their children to school only at those times when they were not needed at home. As passing the high school entrance examinations became the goal for city children, so it did for many of their rural counterparts. Eight whole years of ten months attendance became the norm to which the community, children, and many parents aspired. Attendance records provide some objective evidence of what Evelyn parents and children accomplished in this regard. In 1921-22, the average daily attendance in graded elementary schools in British Columbia was 87 per cent, by 1931-32, it was 90 per cent, and in 1941-42, it was 89 per cent. Average daily attendance of all pupils in British Columbia first exceeded 90 per cent in 1939-40. By that time Evelyn School had *exceeded* that figure in thirteen of its first eighteen years.[12]

For Evelyn families that needed children's work, the new educational norm added a sometimes enormous burden to them. Some families came closer to meeting the goal than did others. As one man reported, "some kids couldn't attend school regularly; they had to stay at home for work." This was especially so at seedtime and at harvest. "I did not attend school during threshing time," explained one woman. Although the man quoted above, the son of a particularly demanding father, did not complete his entrance, he nonetheless spent much of each of eight years at school. Another youngster, whose day started at 6 a.m. and who sometimes did not complete his chores until 9 p.m., "studied to 12 at night." In his last year, in the entrance class, he had a "teacher who was determined I would not fail [the entrance examinations]" so she had him "at school at 8:30 until 4:30." He "would have continued" beyond grade 8 if there had been school buses into Smithers, thereby precluding the necessity of boarding away from home. Other Evelyn youngsters did go on to complete their high school. Coming as they did somewhat later in the settling process, some younger children had more time than their older siblings to attend school regularly.

Pioneering families possessed an "ideal" division of labor that was very similar to those of their urban and long-settled rural counterparts. The work of pioneering families differed from both mostly in the much greater demands that it placed on all members of the family. Mothers' work centered on the household. Fathers' work centered on the land. Mothers' and fathers' duties met in the farmyard.[13] As one person recalled, barnyard chores were "middle ground, fair for either boys or girls to do." Since pioneer families always had more to do than time to complete it, their children assumed major responsibilities very early in their lives; in the words of one: "I can't recall when I didn't help." In normal circumstances, daughters helped with their mothers' duties and sons helped with their fathers'. Boys who were called upon to do "inside" chores did so because, as one man explained, "my mother had no daughters." However, when it came to "outside" chores, there was, as one woman explained, "no such thing as boys' work; as soon as you could walk you worked." In concurring with this view, one man also revealed the fairly common male attitude that the "real" work of farming lay in the male domain. There was, he reported, "no sex difference in chores" and his sisters could "handle chores like a man." At those times when fathers worked away at such tasks as tie hacking and hauling, the rest of the family had to assume an extra share of the burden.

Children and adults started early on their daily rounds, including the ubiquitous chores, all made more arduous by the primitive settings in which they were done. As one woman put it, "lots of things had to be done every day, and they had to be done at a certain time." First, someone lit the kitchen stove and other fires, sometimes using curls of wood or a shaved stick – "paper was precious" – to ignite the kindling. "My father got up first," reported one woman, "lit the kitchen stove, and stirred up the heater," while another told that her mother "was up first and lit the fire." Soon, the whole family was up, the younger children to dress by the fire, the older ones, after having something hot to drink or eat, on their way to the first of the morning's chores. "We would have coffee with father," noted one man, "and then went to the barn to milk the cows, to feed the calves, to feed the pigs." One lad, whose family homesteaded near Powell River at this time, "had to milk 8 head morning and night." A woman had "fond memories of mornings with cattle bawling and horses whinneying." Until she was herself old enough to help with the milking, she "threw hay down from the hay barn."

Meanwhile, mothers and other youthful helpers worked inside. They tended the youngest children. They emptied the contents of chamber pots into the "honey pail" to dispose of in the privy. They prepared a hot breakfast, usually a porridge made from grain grown on the farm, together with bacon, eggs, toast or pancakes. Mothers or children made lunches for those going to school and packed them in each child's lard, toffee, or Rogers syrup pail. "After breakfast we rushed to school," explained one man, and another noted that he was "up no later than 6 a.m. and started to school just after 8." A third man noted that "we always liked to go to school, in the sense that it was a relief from . . . farming."

In addition to their school work, pupils attending Evelyn School also had a round of chores to do there. In winter, after a walk of from about a kilometre to over four kilometres, sometimes through deep snow, the children were cold when they arrived. As soon as he arrived one of the older boys lighted the "drum-type stove in which the logs were loaded from the front." He and the other boys chopped the wood, brought it in from the woodshed, and kept the fire going. Children took "turns bringing milk, cocoa and sugar. The first thing you'd do is make a big kettle of hot chocolate. Everybody would have a drink." Both men and women recalled going, usually in pairs, with a pail to get water from glacier-fed Toboggan Creek, which was a quarter of a mile away. Since it was "a good big creek," children had to be careful, especially in the winter when the boys "used an old axe" to cut holes in the ice. They often came back, as one man reported, "with icicles on my pants." The older children also took weekly turns as school janitor, sweeping it out, cleaning the wash basin, washing blackboards, and cleaning brushes. Eventually the school board paid one boy to light the fire and another to fetch the water. Towards the end of the summer, and at other times in the year as well, children helped their mothers as they gave the school a thorough cleaning, and their fathers as they brought in or supplemented the winter's wood supply and undertook necessary repairs to the school, barn, woodshed, privies and fences.

Children hurried home from school; as one put it, "work was there waiting for us." Probably the most important tasks were caring for animals of which "choring with cattle" took the greatest amount of time. Except in the winter, cows remained outside, sometimes in pastures but more often "roamed free" as widely as they liked. Children hunted out the cattle to bring them home to the night pasture or barn. Fortunate youngsters would "go on horses for them, sometimes [as many as] four miles." Others, who put in "hours of walking" as they brought home the cows, would "love to have had a pony." Once the cows were in the night pasture or barn, in some families "Mom and the kids did the milking," while in others fathers took charge. Some families were "before supper milkers," while others were "after supper milkers." Children eagerly acquired the skill and the woman who reported that she "learned to milk at six years of age" was not unusual. However, she, like a male contemporary, also soon "wished I hadn't started it because it became a regular chore!"

After the morning or evening milking, mothers and children ran much of the day's milk through the cream separator. One woman explained that, when she was small, "it took two children to turn the handle." After each use the separator had to be taken apart and thoroughly washed with water as hot as the hands could bear it and then reassembled. Since no soap could be used, separators had a characteristic odor that people can still summon up in their minds. Children then feed the skim milk to chickens, calves and pigs, and helped to make butter with the hand churn and then "to mould it on the wooden 'butter table.'" As Ferne Nelson recalled of churning: "The action of the heavy handle made my little arms ache, and it seemed as though the cream would never turn to butter."[14]

In winter, cattle also had to be fed and watered. Families grew much of their turnip crop for cattle feed. While families eventually came to own a turnip pulper, in the early days parents and children chopped them up by hand. One man reported that "I didn't do a very good job; [the too-large pieces] got stuck in the cattle's throats." As another man reported, this could "kill the cow because cows don't chew, they just swallow." On some farms, children took the cattle from the barn to drink at spot in a creek where holes had been cut in the ice for them, and on others they filled drinking troughs. "In the very coldest weather," one woman explained, "the water had to be slightly warmed by pouring in a kettle of boiling water into each troughful, or the milk production went down." Cleaning the barn was also a major daily chore to which both boys and girls were assigned. One man reported that "I escaped the mundane jobs of milking cows by offering to do the 'dunging out,' the 'mucking out' that had to be done on a daily basis."

Evelyn farms also kept horses, pigs, and chickens, all of which required daily care. In addition to her daily milking and wood carrying, one woman "fed the chickens, looked after the young chicks, gathered the eggs and cleaned out the chicken houses. . . . Dad killed the roosters, mother scalded them, and the kids plucked them." Another, in a family that kept about 100 chickens, recalls "gathering the eggs, cleaning them for the store, and cleaning the hen house." She may, like other children, have candled the eggs as well. In another family, the daughter whose job it was to look after the chickens selected the older one destined for the supper table, "got the axe, put it on the chopping block, cut its head off, got the hot water, [and took] the feathers off, but Mom would clean it." This woman also had the job of finding the barn cats' litters, "just leave one and the rest I had to drown . . . to make sure we weren't over-run with cats."

Girls and boys also had regular meal-time duties. Before supper, they filled coal oil lamps and lanterns, cleaned their chimneys, and trimmed their wicks. Helping prepare supper often took one to the root cellar or root house. As one woman explained, "you had to put on . . . your boots and your heavy clothes because usually in the winter time that was quite a chore to go to the root house and make sure you got everything. . . . Usually you had to light a lantern to take with you . . . because you couldn't leave the door open for light. . . . [You would get] three or four days' supply" at one time. Another woman noted that "the fruit and vegetables in the cellar had to be picked over carefully," and "any that had started to rot had to be culled out." One woman "had to do the vegetables for supper, then all the dishes after the meal." Mothers seem rarely to have delegated much actual cooking to their youngsters. As one woman explained, her mother would not let her bake because the mother had "lived through the hard times" and thus was "afraid I would waste." When the mother baked "she would use her fingers to scrape out the bowl so there would be nothing left to lick, . . . not a thing!" A man remembers that "my brother and I took turns washing and drying dishes every night. We did that for years." In another, perhaps more representative family, however, neither father nor brother "ever did dishes, or even put the dirty ones in the sink." Elizabeth Varley, whose family pioneered in the Kitimat Valley, explained that dishwashing was the worst chore "because of insufficient water" and the fact that, in order not to scratch it, the "enamel porridge pot . . . had to be scraped with a wooden chip from the woodshed."[15]

Most Evelyn pioneers built their homes close to creeks from which they took most of their water. Some also had a "rain barrel" in which they collected rain water for "washing hair and white clothes." Others "melted snow for washing; . . . it took more and more buckets of snow." A few had the pump for their well right inside the house beside the sink. Most families used buckets to bring their water to the house. Once at the house, children would "bail water into the reservoir on the stove, or stored it in pails in the kitchen." In many families for youngsters "carrying water from the creek was an endless chore, winter and summer." One "household used four buckets every day . . . [and] the butter called for an extra couple of buckets." Dave McIntosh, who worked on his uncle's New Brunswick farm, explained that "carrying water from the well was a sort of test of growing manhood. The object was to carry two pails from well to house or barn [about forty metres] without once putting them down to rest."[16]

Where the creek was far away, parents or children hitched horses to stone boats or wagons and went there to fill wooden barrels, milk cans or drums. On nice days children found this to be an agreeable task; it was certainly more pleasant than weeding the kitchen garden or hilling potatoes. In winter, however, it could be one of the most unpleasant chores a child had to do. "We went to the creek with a stone boat, pulled by a horse, with a barrel on it. We [then] chopped a hole in the ice," recalled one woman. Children then used numb hands to fill the buckets they used to pour near-freezing water into the barrel. Their mittens got wet and froze, and they often accidentally splashed water over themselves. The canvas tops and the ropes used to tie them over barrels to prevent splashing became rigid with ice. Any water that slopped over the edge froze on the side of the barrel, on the stone boat, and on clothes. When he was a boy on an Alberta ranch, H. "Dude" Lavington was "cutting water holes half a mile or so from the house one day when it was around 30°C below. On the last water hole my axe got away from me . . . I reached to make a grab for the disappearing handle and slipped into the water hole. . . . Panic struck me. I was sure I would freeze to death before I could get home. . . . In no time my pants, boots, and socks were frozen solid and my legs and feet just like encased in splints." When Lavington made it home he was surprised "to find out that I was warm as toast and even sweating from all the effort and panic!"[17]

In her recollections, Bulkley Valley pioneer Nan Bourgon explained that "Everything was brown – soil, house, kids, farmers."[18] One woman's story nicely emphasizes this point. "My Dad was clearing land," she recalled, "and I was supposed to take a message to him . . . I could see my Dad walking and a black bear was walking with him on its hind legs." In fact, it was not a bear but another man "who was so black from clearing land doing it by hand." A constant battle with the "brown" and the "black" formed a central characteristic of pioneer women's work. In this, as in all else, children found they had a major role to play. Much of the battle took place inside the house, in the early years especially in a house often unevenly floored with planks or even poles. Fathers and children brought dirt in on their shoes and clothes, with the never-ending supply of wood and kindling for the stoves and, during dry, dusty periods, it blew in through doors and windows. Stove ash added to accumulations.

Of all the tasks connected with keeping things clean doing the washing was clearly the most onerous. Since hauling water was so difficult, one family built a wash house right on their creek: "it was cold in winter." At one home, about a hundred feet from the creek, the large washing was done "in a large tub on top of a huge block of wood" which sat outside on the back porch. A woman reported that, "if a neighbour was sick, my mother [would come] home with a big sheet full of wash. We'd light a fire by the creek rather than carrying [the water]." In another family, one of the boys helped with the water; "the night before I had to make sure that there was enough water to do the washing." After the clothes were boiled, "they were washed on scrub boards" and then wrung out "with a hand-turned wringer." Most people "hung out washing all year round." In winter they "brought in frozen articles as needed." For clothes and other things that needed ironing, mothers and daughters used "sad" or flat irons.

Some families were, as one woman put it, "haphazard about caring for themselves and hygiene." Such families caused distress to some of their neighbors. As members of the first generation acutely aware of the role of germs ("microbes") in spreading disease, to some mothers "dirt . . . was often synonymous with disease and infection" and they labored hard to keep it at bay. What one must marvel at is not the shabbiness and sometimes even dirtiness of those children and adults who sometimes offended insensitive teachers, public health nurses, and other outside observers, but that so many children, at the cost of tremendous labor on their part and that of their mothers, went to school and community events relatively clean and tidy and remained remarkably healthy.

After children completed all of their post-supper chores, they sometimes had school work to finish. As one woman remembered it she had homework only "occasionally"; it was not a "ritual that you had to do a certain amount when you got home." A man recalls having to do "lots of memorizing," while another did "no homework – never!" On days when they had none, or completed it quickly, young-sters might read, or be read to, sing, play or listen to a parent play a musical instrument, or play cards or other games. In later years they might gather round a battery radio to listen to such distant stations as KPO, San Francisco, or to "Mr. Good Evening" who read the news from CKWX in Vancouver. On evenings and weekends, girls also began to learn how to mend, darn, sew, knit and embroider. One woman, for example, had "knitted myself a sweater by the time I was twelve." Since early rising also mandated an early bed time, this relaxing time was not as long as most youngsters would have liked. Children generally slept in unheated rooms in their uninsulated, drafty houses. As one person reported, "there was frost around the edges of the floor in the house" and another explained that, in her bedroom, sometimes there was "snow on the windowsills inside." In consequence, going to bed in the winter time involved certain routines. One woman recalled that she wore "long johns, pyjamas, her housecoat, a nightcap, and took a hot water bottle with her." In another home, the kids "all moved down [from upstairs] to the living room beside the heater" when it got really cold. Cold bedrooms and outdoor privies, in turn, led to constipa-tion, the consequent pain, and then one of the popular treatments.[19]

The many chores relating to the wood supply fitted into both daily and seasonal rounds and describing them makes an appropriate transition between the two. To pioneer children, their family's need for wood seemed insatiable. As one man put it, "it seemed like there was no end to getting wood." People often started out with only a single stove. As families and houses grew larger, they also added to the number of their stoves and heaters. Some homes had "air tight" heaters which "took a whole block of wood" and kept the house "warm all night." The Bourgon house in Hubert, a few kilometres south east of Evelyn, eventually had seven stoves.[20] Since "green" wood was difficult to light, produced a low level of heat and copious amounts of smoke as it burned, and built up heavy deposits in stove pipes and chimneys (which brought on dangerous and frightening chimney fires), most families organized themselves so that they always had a plentiful supply of dry, well-seasoned firewood.

Therefore, on the short days in the midst of winter, before the sap started to run and the ground was frozen hard, they cut enough trees to provide firewood for the whole of the next year. "On weekends," reported one man, he and his father "went to the woodlot. We cut the wood and, with horses and sleighs, would haul it in."

Next, in the wood area near the house, they cut the logs into stove-length rounds. In some families, fathers and sons placed it on the saw horse and "bucked it by hand with a cross cut saw." In families in which the father worked away from home, or where there were no boys of an appropriate age, mothers and daughters undertook this task. One woman recalled being "on one end of a cross-cut saw with one of my brothers on the other." Some families cut up their wood on a "motorized" cross-cut saw, or more commonly, with an unprotected circular saw mounted on a frame and driven by a gasoline engine. Victor Carl Friesen vividly described this dangerous work. "My brother, or sometimes my mother, dragged the logs to the saw. At the saw stood my father, who repeatedly pushed each log into the whining blade . . . I stood right next to the open blade and grasped the end of the log . . . and followed it through its journey into the biting blade until it was severed. Then I threw the piece of wood over my shoulder."[21] After it was sawed off, each round had to be split, a process most easily done while the wood was still "green."

Many families tried to get ahead in their wood splitting over the summer months. They created enormous piles of chopped wood outside, and then stacked it in sheds so they had a good supply on hand for the winter, and especially in case of heavy storms, serious illness, or other emergencies. As one woman explained, the children in her family "had to spend a half hour each day stacking up the cut wood in the shed so that it would dry for the winter." Other families cut their wood over the winter. A man recalled that he and his father each spent an hour a day splitting wood: "Sometimes on the weekends we might get a little ahead." One woman remembered that, by the time she was six, she was splitting wood and kindling. Since in even the warmest months families needed to use their stoves for cooking, for preserving, and heating water, wood and kindling chopping and carrying had to be done over the whole year: "We packed wood in every day," reported one man, and a woman recalled that "one night I went to bed without cutting the kindling. My father rooted me out at midnight to do it."

Evelyn farms grew various combinations and proportions of hay, oats, wheat, barley, turnips and potatoes as their principal crops. Some kept sheep as well as the ubiquitous cattle. In addition, families – usually mothers – planted "kitchen gardens" in which they grew radishes, lettuce, beets, cabbages, cauliflower, carrots, peas, spinach, beans, rhubarb, parsnips ("I hated parsnips!") and other vegetables and some small fruits for their own use. (The climate of the Bulkley Valley was too severe for fruit trees.) Both the major crops and the kitchen garden involved children in a succession of tasks that began early in the spring and only came to a halt in the late fall. Before the ground thawed, families hauled loads of manure from beside the barn and scattered it over the fields. Spring in Evelyn was often accompanied by flooding, or the threat of flooding, as melt water rushed down the hillsides over the still-frozen ground. As soon as the ground thawed and dried out, the family prepared it for planting. Although no Evelyn woman told of learning to plough, those who grew up elsewhere did. Annie Donald, oldest of seven girls and the "boy" of a family pioneering in Alberta was, at age eleven, "taken out of school and became the full-time 'hired hand'" who drove "a team of oxen which in turn pulled the plough and other farm implements."[22]

In Evelyn, after fathers and older sons completed the ploughing, all the children helped with the further preparation of the soil. As one woman explained, for her "there was always disking and harrowing . . . [and she] used to harness and unharness the [part Percheron] horses by the time I was twelve." Children also helped get the kitchen garden ready, by digging, raking and planting the seeds, the latter often done on or near the 24th of May school holiday. One family put in "a large garden; one acre of potatoes, one-half acre of small vegetables – it seemed like more than that – and one half acre of turnips." Another planted "at least three acres of potatoes" and a third had "a large vegetable garden of almost an acre." After the sheep were shorn in the spring, children helped to wash, card, and spin the wool.

Of all the chores they had to do children remember weeding with the most distaste. It was, recalled one man, "a wearisome sort of thing." Another remembered that "we had a vegetable garden. I had to weed and thin the bastards." "I'll never forget the long rows of turnips I had to weed," noted one woman, "it seemed like there was no end to them." Some farmers with large crops employed a horse-drawn cultivator to weed between the rows, but in many families, and especially in the early years, such work was usually done with a hoe. Boys and girls also would "crawl on hands and knees pulling weeds out of the garden." Weeding also seemed never-ending: "everything that grows is more weeding than gardening," as one person lamented. During and after rainfall damp soil clung to boots, building up into large clumps on the soles. These clumps made walking even more difficult and uncomfortable but were hard to dislodge and grew again almost immediately. Weeding went on over the late spring and summer, which were also the seasons of black flies and mosquitoes. As one woman explained, "holidays were from school only; that is when parents got the most out of you." After one woman had her tonsils out, she was absolutely delighted to hear the doctor instruct her father that "I wasn't to pull weeds. I remember it very clearly. I wasn't to work in dirt!" In addition to the weeding of vegetable gardens and root crops children also cleared grain fields of such noxious weeds as wild oats and stinkweed.[23] In one family, the father "made each child responsible for a certain area. Dad checked it at night." Once a year, families dug new holes for their privies and filled in the old one.

If children remember weeding as their most distasteful chore, they fondly recall berry-picking as their most-liked spring and summer activity. As one man explained, "I liked . . . picking huckleberries up on the hillsides . . . there were kind of endless dreamy days like that, and you had bright, sunny weather." Another recalled that "In the spring time for greens you gathered nettles, pigweed . . . and dandelions for salads." A woman explained that to pick wild strawberries in June, "was a thrill . . .

We would take a lunch . . . we were picking them for Mom to make jam with; that was a serious business." A man explained that "children picked wild strawberries, raspberries, low-bush blueberries, and huckleberries. Sometimes we would take two or three hours to walk to a site for picking." His mother "put them up in jars; if it was a good year, we often had berries for dinner." While picking berries children had to keep a wary eye out for bears, especially those with cubs. Children called out to each other regularly, or shook "a tin with stones in it to keep animals away."

Evelyn residents began harvesting in the summer and it continued until late into the fall. Especially in the early days, harvesting was very labor intensive. Long hours of sunlight made hay ready for cutting by mid to late July. At haying time, reported one woman, "it was always hot." While families might scythe hard-to-reach patches – "I used a scythe a little bit for hay among the trees" – they customarily employed a horse-drawn mower to cut the hay. With a wary eye on the lookout for rain, families then left their cut hay laying in its swaths to dry. As soon as it was dry, families used either long-handled or horse-drawn rakes to collect it together and then their hands or pitchforks to put into haystacks. From there it was pitched onto horse-drawn hay ricks to be carried to sheds, barns or large outdoor stacks. Mothers and children took part in all phases of this work. As one woman reported: "Haying was a . . . family job. Dad did the mowing and I [and the other children] stooked and cocked it." Another woman reported that, at age twelve, she ran both mower and hay rake, and drove the hay ricks. Older children pitched hay onto the wagons, while the younger ones rode on the wagons, stamping the hay down. "At about [age] nine or ten, Dad had me on the hay rig," reported one man, while a woman recalled that she didn't like "tramping the loads; . . . it was hot, dusty work." When the rick reached the barn, in one family, an eight-year-old girl drove the horse-drawn "fork" that lifted the hay off the rick and unloaded it in the hayloft. Adults and older children did the very heavy work of distributing the hay and children then "tramped the loft" to level it out.

Grain – oats, wheat, and barley – were harvested later on in the year. Fathers or older children drove the three- or four-horse binders, which cut and bound the grain into bundles. The rest of the family would follow behind and stook (sometimes "shock") the grain, that is, stack the bundles upright, leaning in towards each other. As one person explained, "we made a field of these [stooks] because if it rained it ran off and did not rot the grain." Since threshing called for considerable heavy labor, parents employed only their older children directly in the operation. "As soon as I was old enough, twelve or thirteen," reported one woman, "I joined the team of threshers." Younger children, as another woman explained, helped "mother feed the hungry workers and to carry drinks out to the fields." When threshing was done early in the season, two or three teams pulling wagons with racks on them took stooks from the fields directly to the threshing machine. Two "field pitchers" pitched stooks onto the rack while the driver loaded them, heads in, butts out. After the driver had taken a full load to the machine he or she helped the "spike pitcher" spike them onto the belt and into the machine. Twelve-year-olds could load, drive, and help off-pitch the stooks. If the threshing machine was not to come until late in the season, or even after the first snow, then families worked together well beforehand to bring stooks to a central point and stack them. Stooks were pitched from the wagon to the stack builder who placed them heads in, butts out to keep them dry. Although throwing up stooks was too heavy for most girls and younger boys, they could load and drive the wagons. When the threshing machine arrived, two pitchers on the stack threw the stooks onto the belt. Grain came out of the machine via a spout into sacks or a bin. Again, only older children could help with these tasks and were often kept out of school to do so.

In the Bulkley Valley "potato picking" and "turnip picking" were the last major harvesting operations of the year. Children helped with all phases of this work. "We had a large potato field," one woman recalls. "We did the potato picking in the fall. I would come home from school and change. We would load sacks onto the stone boat and ride it home to the root cellar." Another woman explained that "potatoes [were] . . . always picked in October . . . and it was so cold. I can remember crying at the cold, . . . picking them." Floyd Frank, whose family pioneered in the Skeena Valley at about the same time as Evelyn was settled, explained that the potatoes he picked "were lying on the top of the ground" and were "picked into half-bushel baskets, thirty pounds capacity, and dumped into gunny sacks that held three to four baskets."[24] Often children rewarded themselves by turning one of the largest turnips into a Halloween jack-o'-lantern.

In addition to mothers' already onerous round of daily and weekly tasks of child-minding, cooking, cleaning, washing, ironing, mending, tending the kitchen garden, and the like, summer and fall brought the added burden of preparing, preserving, and storing as much food as possible for long months of winter and early spring. In the summer, children helped clear out and clean the root cellar to make it ready for the new crop. Then, over the late summer and fall, fathers and children placed cabbages, potatoes, turnips, carrots, and other root vegetables directly on to storage racks in the cellar. Together with the wild berries, mothers canned (in glass sealers) such vegetables as cauliflower, peas and beans. If chickens, pigs, or cows were slaughtered over the summer, then the meat had to be preserved by pickling, smoking, or canning. "We would," one man reported, "kill one pig for ourselves and the rest were sold. . . . All the meat was canned; jars and jars of canned meat." His "mother did all the canning and, since she had no daughter, I helped with whatever was necessary." A woman recalled "slaughtering time . . . and then the meat was hung . . . and then brought into the house, and cut up, and canned." Both remembered that, if the weather were cold enough, some meat was allowed to freeze untreated. As one man reported, "we would eat a milk cow in the fall if Dad didn't get a moose; . . . [we] had to wait until it was cold . . . to kill a moose or other animals." Over the summer, a woman reported, native people from their nearby village of Moricetown, "came with horses and wagons to sell salmon, big beautiful salmon . . . and Mom would can it . . . [which was] lots of work . . . [since it] had to be cooked on the wood stove and the house would be hot." Another woman explained that their "ham was smoked and cured . . . in a little smoke house . . . [which] need some special kind of bark . . . and a salt mixture ('Habicure') you rubbed into it."

Evelyn and other pioneers had to integrate their daily, weekly, and seasonal rounds into the on-going process of settling in. Settling in initially involved creating at least basic shelter for families and animals.[25] Families often spent the first summer and sometimes longer periods on or near the new site living in a tent, shed, or abandoned cabin. While her father built their house, one woman explained, he lived in a tent on the site while the family lived in a vacant cabin, "five miles away through the bush. . . . We would take a lunch down and watch as he used horses, and a block and tackle to build. . . . It had to be built before cold came." The first home was usually a small log cabin, chinked with clay or moss, and roofed with poles covered with canvas, sod, shakes, or corrugated iron. At first, these cabins contained only a single room, with sometimes a sleeping loft at one end and perhaps a lean-to on the side. Hard-packed dirt, poles, or rough planks served as the floor. If a family had animals, then it would also have to construct a barn before the first winter.

Those with a little capital as well as their labor to invest in their homes built a permanent home right from the start, or after only a brief stay in the cabin which could then be converted to other uses. Others, whose time was completely absorbed by the need to clear, or to work elsewhere, lived in their gradually-extending initial home for many years. Some families thus spent most of their child-rearing years in the cabin with only the youngest children spending some of their youth in the second, "permanent" home. Nan Capewell married Joe Bourgon in June 1915, and moved into a little house with a lean-to kitchen on their partially cleared farm. Only after very considerable family stress – Nan left Joe for a time – and the birth of their first child did they move into their permanent home in the spring of 1917.[26]

"School holidays! No one asked where you were going for holidays. You knew you were going to do your part to help clear the land during Easter Holidays," wrote one Evelyn pioneer, one of those whose "family was starting out from scratch." For most, "trying to make a farm" in a heavily-wooded area was a long process and some were still doing it when they died or sold their farms. As with their other work, children, as one man put it, "began [helping] earlier than I can remember." They helped cut down and cut up the trees, pile them and their branches on the fire, pull the stumps or gather up the pieces after they were blown with stumping powder. As one woman explained, "if they blew stumps they . . . would blow three at a time . . . and you would count so long and wait for the bang . . . a boom you would hear for miles and . . . feel it too." She would then "pick up sticks for hours." One boy "got a wagon as a toy but used it to pick roots." Further west, near Terrace, Floyd Frank's father had a team of horses "which we used, along with pulley blocks and cable, to clear out the stumps. My brother Ivan and I, before we were teenagers, were experts at handling cables and blocks."[28] Root-picking and rock-picking went on for years, with children spending hours and hours collecting them, especially during ploughing season. Lena Capling of Evelyn recalled "picking rocks from the fields" and putting them into a stone boat drawn by a "huge ox."[29] Cyril Shelford, pioneering further east near Ootsa Lake, wrote that both his father's and his uncle's ranches were "infested with rocks" which he and his brothers had to help clear, despite the fact that they "did everything possible to avoid picking them."[30] As one man summarized the experience of clearing and preparing the land, "each year the fields got a little bigger and each year the boys got a little bigger." They cleared "a couple of acres a year" and by the time of his father's death had cleared 125 acres.

Evelyn School closed in June 1946. War-time and post-war prosperity enabled British Columbians to look to the future with a sense of hope that had not character-ized them since the end of the 1920s. Rural school consolidation, long advocated but only very partially implemented, became a post-war goal and a province-wide plan for it was laid out in the Cameron Report.[31] Consequently, in September 1946, Evelyn children travelled by taxi to school in Smithers. They continued to do their allotted share of the daily, weekly, and seasonal routines on farms, most of which still lacked such amenities as running water, electrical power, and tractors. "We got our first tractor in 1950," reported one man and another noted that "we got our first electricity in '57." Many families continued to add to the store of cleared land. Nonetheless, the closing of the Evelyn School can be said to mark the end of the initial phase in the history of the district. The "pioneer fringe" had passed beyond post-war Evelyn and the Bulkley Valley as a whole, leaving behind a relatively prosperous agricultural and lumbering region with well-established patterns of seasonal work.[32] If the workload of Evelyn's post-war youngsters remained similar to that of earlier years, for most of them there was little of the sense of desperate ugency that had character-ized the lives of their predecessors.

Noting this major event in the history of the community also provides a convenient opportunity to make some general comments on Evelyn as a case study; on why pioneering children worked, and continued to work, as they did; on the practical dimensions of education in Evelyn and similar communities; on the differing effects of their work on the development of gender identity amongst girls and boys; and, very briefly, on the overall quality of life in a pioneering community.

At this point I must emphasize that my description of pioneering childhoods at Evelyn is a case study. Evelyn did not exemplify all aspects of pioneering childhoods in Canada during these years. A different landscape, different crops, a harsher or milder climate; each might structure children's tasks in ways that were somewhat unlike those followed in Evelyn. Thus, some Peace River pioneers did not have to clear their land but all were farther from markets for their products than those in the Bulkley Valley. Despite accounts of childhood illnesses and accidents, the Bulkley Valley seems to have been a reasonably healthy place to bring up children. Its rates of infant and childhood mortality seem to have been lower than those which Cynthia Comacchio Abeele discovered for "Outpost" Ontario at the same time.[33] Nonetheless, pioneering children anywhere else in Canada in these years would have had in common with their Evelyn contemporaries a heavy load of work, would have taken a major share in what Elizabeth Varley, a pioneer child in the Kitimat area, called "the rush to get things done."[34] Descriptions of pioneer life in the Peace River district, for example, contain many Evelyn-like accounts, such as that of Stanley (Punch) Landry, of youthful work. "When I was nine and my brother Waldo ten," Landry wrote, "I remember helping thresh oat bundles with Tremblay's machine when it came to our area. . . . It was operated with 12 horses and, to save power, had a feed table and a straw conveyor . . . Waldo and I were band cutters even though we had to stand on boxes to reach the bundles."[35]

Even as a case study, this description of Evelyn is incomplete. This account is built almost entirely on the recollections of those who went on to live reasonably successful lives. Families that failed usually moved out of the district. We heard a few stories of siblings and neighbors who encountered problems and difficulties in their lives but have no sense as to whether these were in some way rooted in their childhoods or were the product of later events. Except for the casual and very occasional observations of neighbors or teachers, rural and pioneer children with ephemeral or permanent "problems" do not appear in records in the way in which some of their urban counterparts did. Thus, in "the winter," Nan Bourgon wrote, "I would see some of the children coming to our Hubert school so poorly clothed that it worried me. I always begged shoes and warm clothes from my friends in town for them."[36]

Through a short vignette from elsewhere, however, we can glimpse two children in homely situations that were not altogether uncommon in pioneering areas. In the Peace River district, Monica Storrs took an interest in "Gladys, a girl I am rather sorry for. She is about sixteen, and is a 'hired girl' at the store, i.e., general slavey to the storekeeper's wife. She has no mother and her father has just gone to prison for distilling moonshine, liquor. . . . The poor girl is terribly shy now, and I think feels a sort of outcast." Gladys' brother, Hughie, was twelve "and he is the most delightful little boy in the school; desperately eager, full of fun and completely unselfcon-scious." A year later, Storrs wanted to recruit Hughie to attend a summer camp. Hughie now lived "as chore boy with some people who are very kind to him but alas, said they were too busy and could not spare him. Poor Hughie said nothing at all through the conversation but stood at the door and stared and stared at us. He was the life and soul of the camp last year. But of course there was nothing for it but to say, 'Better luck next year Hughie,' to which cheap comfort he made no reply but only went on staring till we had gone."[37]

In a companion paper, I explained that urban children worked as hard as they did both because they had to and because they wanted to.[38] If not altogether impossible, then creating a farm out of the "bush" would have been an extremely difficult enterprise without the free, and generally freely-given, labor of children. Isaiah Bowman's research showed that, on the land, boys and girls were useful at eight and ten years and by sixteen they could take the place of men and women.[39] In Evelyn, children of both sexes seemed to be more than "useful" at eight and, depending on their pattern of growth, capable of working as adults when they reached school-leaving age or very soon thereafter. What also comes through very clearly in their accounts of their childhoods is how proud they all were of what they had been able to do, that as girls and boys they had done "a man's work." As one woman put it,

"You did [any job] if you could possibly do it." One man was even more explicit, explaining that of "any physical work . . . as soon as you were able, you did it. . . . It was partly that I liked doing it, I liked this responsibility, those chores." Elizabeth Varley "was proud, too, to be doing adult work with the adults, and felt very grown-up," despite the fact that her mother said she "would ruin my hands, make them coarse and rough."[40] Nevertheless, a few of my informants conveyed the sense that parents, and especially fathers, aspired to more than they had or could reasonably acquire through their own efforts and that of their children. Such families pushed their children into more work than they really had time to do, and more than could be fairly asked for in the circumstances. One man noted that although "he never stayed out of school for farm chores," certain other Evelyn children were sometimes kept out of school and "worked like a bugger" by their fathers.[41]

Implicit in this account of children's work is a strong sense of the family's central role in the education of Evelyn's youngsters, including helping them to decide what they would do when they they grew up. Parents encouraged some, and especially daughters, to use the school to provide an opportunity so that they need not settle on, or drift into a life in the local community. Accordingly, for those Evelyn children who went on to secondary education and then to trade, semi-professional and professional training, the school assumed a major role in their vocational education. Nonetheless, for those entering such practical or semi-practical fields as nursing or the mechanical trades, their home training also provided them with a substantial base in practical experience onto which their later theoretical learning could be built. The student nurse who had helped butcher the family pigs had a head start in anatomical studies (and the control of squeamishness) over most of her urban counterparts. For those Evelyn young people who embarked on careers as farmers, loggers and the wives of farmers and loggers, their childhood and youths had provided them with most of the practical knowledge they would need in their working lives. Both girls and boys could use and repair tools and machinery. Both could care for livestock. Both knew the seasonal routines of planting and harvesting. Both could do most of the domestic chores involved in running a household. Both knew the local vagaries of weather and climate and how to incorporate this knowledge into their seasonal planning. In short, both possessed the full complement of what they needed to know to succeed, even to thrive, in a rural environment.

When the pioneering generation of children came to marry, they could base their family economy on a farm or ranch. Especially after 1939 and in an economic climate of fairly continuous development, wives could manage much of the farm work. Meanwhile, their husbands could work away seasonally at land clearing, logging, saw milling, rough carpentry, laboring on construction sites and on road building and other related jobs with an almost equal ease. As the seasons and the economic climate changed, such men moved with deceptive ease from one job to another. Sometimes they worked for themselves, sometimes they hired others to help them, and some-times they worked as part of someone else's small crew. Occasionally they found work in large, fully-regulated concerns, although this sort of monotonous employment was not their first choice. Serving their own needs as well as those of a capitalist society, many such families did and do reasonably well, shrewdly customing a good standard of living out of their land, their wide range of abilities and their mastery of the informal economy.[42] In roughly analagous situations, other families, less skilled or, perhaps, less adept at the ways of the world, lived or live sometimes despairing lives just above or even below subsistence.

Whatever their eventual fate, Evelyn and other pioneering and rural youngsters had acquired their substantial fund of practical knowledge and skills in time-honored ways. They observed their parents and siblings, they mimicked their activities or they were shown how to do them, or to share in them, and soon grew into full responsibility for them. As Elizabeth Varley put it, "We were like all primitive people and those in frontier places, learning almost everything by working with our parents."[43] After describing how she had helped with the birth of a calf – "I was asked to put my smaller hand in to pull the foot forward and the calf was born instantly" – one woman expressed amazement "at what six year olds can learn." Andy Russell elaborated: "We learned by watching, helping, and doing. We found out that there is a skill in about everything . . . even using a spade or a pitchfork."[44] Such practical learning could, of course, be dangerous. H.A. (Bud) Cole recalled, for example, that when he was less than five he all but cut one finger off "while trying to chop kindling."[45] In this regard we must note that my informants reported remarkably few youthful injuries. They also explained that, while certainly not fool-proof, farm machines of the era were much simpler and less dangerous than their modern counterparts.

If pioneering in Evelyn was a way of life that employed girls and boys almost interchangeably as workers, it was also a way of life that encouraged both sexes to see themselves as growing into sex roles characteristic of the late nineteenth and early twentieth centuries. As one man accurately observed, Evelyn "was a chauvanistic society." It was also a paternalistic one. In childhood, Evelyn girls and boys mostly had their mothers and fathers to model appropriate forms of adulthood for them, including the core sense of what it was to be a woman or a man, and one version of the relationship between men and women. If they looked beyond the confines of their own nuclear family, they could see in the lives of their relatives and neighbors only mildly different arrangements of family relationships. If they looked more widely in the community, they could see the different sorts of life possibilities portrayed by such locally visible occupations as store-keeping, teaching, nursing, medicine, preaching, agriculturalist, and some of the railway trades. Ferne Nelson, who grew up on a prairie homestead, vividly described the "Rawleigh lady" [sic] who "had a husband and a houseful of kids at home . . . [who] spent her days bumping over rutted roads, making a living. An early independent business woman."[46] Nonetheless, and in their childhood years especially, they absorbed most of what they learned on these matters from their own families. In them they saw the very considerable range of overlapping skills that each parent possessed, the tremendous amount of work that each put into the family enterprise, and what each felt about the experience. In one family, for example, the daughter recalled that "Dad was happy: he was working towards his dream. Mother not so much . . . it was a full day's work just to cope with the family's needs."[47]

"Most [Evelyn] youngsters found release from their work in family and community activities, in school, and in the culture of childhood." Here they "dress up" for a mock wedding. (Courtesy of Mollie Ralston, fourth from right)

Children also saw the distribution of power in the family. In some, fathers exercised an almost Biblical domination over their families. In most others, while each parent exercised it in his or her own sphere of the families' activities, fathers exerted a sometimes residual but nonetheless final overall authority. These fathers held the final authority in matters of discipline and usually administered the still widely-prevalent corporal punishment. Within the framework set by the seasons they made the decisions and allocated the tasks, and whether or not sowing or harvest took precedence over schooling. They decided whether new machinery was more essential to family welfare than new clothes or further schooling. They conducted most of the families' dealings with the outside world, making most of the trips into town. Finally, and beyond the range of a book about childhood, it was against fathers that many of the youngsters, and especially the boys, came in their adolescence to rebel.

Most pioneering boys and girls thus observed male behavior models who, though they were by no means sole "breadwinners" of the sort then becoming common in urban society, were clearly heads of their families in the broadest sense of that term. For most boys, therefore, there was an easy continuity between their practical education and their developing identities as males of their time and place. As they acquired "male" skills through their chores, boys also learned to value such supposedly male characteristics as bodily strength, stamina, stoicism in the face of pain, an aggressive sense of self, and the vulgarity that permeates all-male environments. Evelyn boys, for example, absorbed some of this last quality as they told dirty stories to each other or conducted urinating contests behind the school privy. After school consolidation, however, Evelyn boys in the early grades found that their clothes, haircuts, lack of experience of such village phenomena as running water subjected them to teasing. In high school, however, "things turned around" and their status in the male hierarchy rose sharply. As one man explained, "farm kids were stronger, could win at arm wrestling and the like. . . . Later, we could get jobs, we knew how to work hard, we had the skills and could go to work right away." After their first day of part-time work away from the farm in the 1930s, "cutting logs and hauling them out of the bush," Mary Cook's three school-aged brothers talked "as if they couldn't wait to get back into the bush next Saturday. They talked about being men, doing men's work and how the other workers treated them just like the rest of the crew."[48]

On the other hand, Evelyn children saw women who, although they worked at least as hard as men, generally played a distinctly secondary role in the management of the family enterprise. For most girls, who possessed virtually the same range of skills as boys, and some of the other "male" characteristics as well, there was discontinuity between their practical education and experience and their developing identities as females. The local cultural ethos valued and reinforced paternalistic patterns that called girls to a sense of nurturing and sustaining womanhood. No matter how severe the weather they wore girls' clothes to school and usually when they worked outside as well. Their mothers modelled appropriately female roles for them (they always addressed each other as "Mrs."). Their parents and teachers instructed them in sexually appropriate ways of behaving, peers influenced them at school and in the neighborhood, and books, newspapers, Sunday School papers, magazines, and other printed material expounded traditional modes of female behavior. A few who were pioneering children told of mothers who regretted where their lives had led them. In these cases, however, the fault was usually seen as a failure to choose a spouse wisely rather than being rooted in the structure of the traditional family situation itself. Capable as they clearly were, none of the Evelyn girls seem to have aspired to be farmers, rather than farmers' wives. (However one woman recalled that "when war broke out in '39 I thought what I could do would be to run a farm if necessary.") Those who moved off the farm entered such "women's" occupation as waitressing, nursing or teaching.

By concentrating as it does on the work of children this chapter may suggest a somewhat bleaker picture of pioneering childhood than was actually the case. Although one of the earliest children in the Evelyn area recalled that "there was no time for childhood," most youngsters found release from their work in family and community activities, in school, and in the culture of childhood. Most families read books (some from the circulating library to which they subscribed) and newspapers, taking an interest in public affairs. They made occasional visits to Smithers to shop and to visit. They celebrated birthdays and Christmas. They came together for church services in the school, and then in the community hall that they had banded together to build. The United Church minister from Smithers, for example, "came to the school house every other Sunday" and some children regularly attended services. Families gathered for dances, the school Christmas concert, the school closing activities, and community picnics. Expecially with those teachers whom they liked, some children found pleasure in the generally informal and relaxed atmosphere of the Evelyn School. While one man felt "school was something you had to do, and worse than working by far" another "looked forward to going to school because it got you out of the boredom of being at home."

Evelyn children also shared in the "culture of childhood," (see chapter 4). They walked to school together, they played together there before school, at recess, and over the lunch hour. Except at peak times in the seasonal round they found time to roam the countryside. As they did so they fished and hunted. They went horse-back riding, sledding, skiing, hiking, and skating. Sometimes they made pocket money through cutting wood for sale, doing the school chores, by collecting bottles, by trapping, or by shooting crows and other creatures on which the province paid a bounty. When she was about ten years old Elizabeth Varley took complete charge of a flock of chickens and the next year of one of ducks. With her profits from the sale of the former she bought her "most precious possession," a .22 Winchester rifle.[49] As Evelyn became more established, it also entered into more organized sports. "When all the chores were done we played ball . . . once a week there were community ball games." Although work continued to form a major dimension of the lives of Evelyn youngsters, it no longer was as all-pervasive as it had been in the earlier years.

Notes

*This is a revised version of an article that appeared in *Histoire sociale – Social History*, XXIV, 48 (novembre-November 1991): 263-288. Reprinted with permission.

1. This chapter is built mostly out of the memories of many anonymous interviewees. Readers will soon discover my enormous debt to them which I gratefully acknowledge. I discuss the historiographic and methodological matters related to using oral evidence in Neil Sutherland, "When You Listen to the Winds of Childhood, How Much Can You Believe?" *Curriculum Inquiry* 22:3 (Fall 1992): 235-56. Both the chapters and the article are a product of the Canadian Childhood History Project to which the Social Sciences and Humanities Research Council of Canada and the University of British Columbia gave generous support.

2. For a charming but unsentimental account of pioneering in the 1970s, written from a child's point-of-view, see Ann Blades, *Mary of Mile 18* (Montreal: Tundra Books, 1971).

3. Robert Collins, *Butter Down the Well: Reflections of a Canadian Childhood* (Saskatoon: Western Producer Prairie Books, 1980), 171.

4. See Monica Storrs, *God's Galloping Girl* (Vancouver, University of British Columbia Press [UBC], 1979); Neil Sutherland, "Social Policy, 'Deviant' Children, and the Public Health Apparatus in British Columbia Between the Wars," *Journal of Educational Thought* 14

(August 1980): 80-91; and John Calam, ed., *Alex Lord's British Columbia: Recollections of a Rural School Inspector, 1915-1936* (Vancouver: UBC Press, 1991).

5. See Isaiah Bowman, *The Pioneer Fringe*, (New York: American Geographical Society, 1931).

6. Norah Lewis, "Reducing Maternal Mortality in British Columbia: An Educational Process," in B.K. Latham and R.J. Pazdro, eds., *Not Just Pin Money* (Victoria: Camosun College, 1984), 337-55; Veronica Strong-Boag and Kathryn McPherson, "The Confinement of Women: Childbirth and Hospitalization in Vancouver, 1919-1939," *BC Studies* 69-70 (Spring-Summer 1986): 142-174. See also Cynthia Comacchio Abeele, "'The Mothers of the Land Must Suffer': Child and Maternal Welfare in Rural and Outpost Ontario, 1918-1940," *Ontario History*, LXXX (September 1988): 183-205.

7. Lewis, "Reducing Maternal Mortality."

8. "Mrs. Jim Owens Reminisces," *Bulkley Valley Stories, Collected From Old Timers Who Remember* (n.pl.: The Heritage Club, n.d.), 145-6.

9. While the Evelyn school displayed some of the difficulties discussed in chapter 11, it was never an example of "a pedagogical charnel house" of the sort noted in John H. Thompson with Allen Seager, *Canada 1922-1939: Decades of Discord*, (Toronto: McClelland and Stewart, 1985), 156; see also Paul James Stortz, "The Rural School Problem in British Columbia in the 1920s," (M.A. thesis, UBC, 1988), especially Part II, "The Schools in the British Columbia North Central Interior: Terrace to Vanderhood."

10. Ian E. Davey, "The Rhythm of Work and the Rhythm of School," in *Egerton Ryerson and His Times*, edited by Neil McDonald and Alf Chaiton (Toronto: MacMillan, 1978), 221-253.

11. Although the calendar limits of the school year were laid out in British Columbia as early as 1882-83, rural school districts only gradually fell in line with provincial requirements. School attendance records suggest that nearly all districts had come to comply by the 1920s. British Columbia, Department of Education, *Report* (1882-83), 99; ibid., 1920-21, 76-99.

12. British Columbia, Department of Education, *Report* (1921-22 to 1944-45), passim.

13. Although interviewees variously reported that "Scandinavian women didn't do that sort of thing [outdoor farm work]" nor did Ukrainian women, apparently such restraints did not apply to their daughters. See also Sharon D. Stone, "Emelia's Story: A Ukrainian Grandmother," *Canadian Woman Studies/Les Cahiers de la Femme* 7, 4 (Winter 1986): 10.

14. Ferne Nelson, *Barefoot on the Prairie: Memories of life on a prairie homestead* (Saskatoon: Western Producer Prairie Books, 1989), 14.

15. Elizabeth Anderson Varley, *Kitimat My Valley* (Terrace: Northern Times Press, 1981), 111.

16. Dave McIntosh, *The Seasons of My Youth*, (Toronto: General Publishing, 1984), 52.

17. H. "Dude" Lavington, *The Nine Lives of a Cowboy* (Victoria: Sono Nis, 1982), 22.

18. Nan Bourgon, *Rubber Boots for Dancing and Other Memories of Pioneer Life in Bulkley Valley*, Marjorie Rosberg, ed., (Smithers: Tona and Janet Hetherington, 1979), 9.

19. See Norah L. Lewis, "Goose Grease and Turpentine: Mother Treats the Family's Illnesses," *Prairie Forum* 15 (Spring 1990): 67-84.

20. Bourgon, *Rubber Boots*, 113.

21. Victor Carl Friesen, "Sawing the Winter's Fuel," *Bank of British Columbia's Pioneer News* (August/September 1988), 10. See also Anna Friesen and Victor Carl Friesen, *The Mulberry Tree* (n.pl.: Queenston House, 1985) for a fine account of Mennonites pioneering in Saskatchewan.

22. "Resident of the Month – Mrs. Annie Donald," Evergreen House, [Lions Gate Hospital, North Vancouver, B.C.], *Residents' Newsbulletin* (September 1988): 2.

23. Clearing fields of noxious weeks displayed prudent farming practice and respect for the law which compelled that they be controlled. See "Noxious Weeds Act," *R.S.B.C.* 1924, c. 272.

For wild oats and stinkweed as examples thereof, see Canada, Department of Agriculture, *Farm Weeds in Canada* (Ottawa: King's Printer, 1923), 28, plate 3 and 80, plate 27. Both of these references were shown me by the daughter of an Evelyn farmer.

24. Floyd Frank, *My Valley's Yesteryears* (Victoria: Orca,1991), 77.

25. The urban centre tried to exert its influence even on the design of "outpost" houses. See, for example, Canada, Department of Health, *Beginning a Home in Canada*, and *How to Build the Canadian House*, No. 7 and No. 8 in the "Little Blue Books Home Series" written by Helen McMurchy, Chief of the Division of Child Welfare.

26. Bourgon, *Rubber Boots*, 49-68.

27. Beryl Jones, "The MacMillans Settle at Evelyn," *Bulkley Valley Stories*, 155.

28. Frank, *My Valley's Yesteryears*, 44.

29. Mrs. Jim Capling as told to Marjorie Rosberg, "A Long Time Ago," *Bulkley Valley Stories*, 140.

30. Arthur Shelford and Cyril Shelford, *We Pioneered* (Victoria: Orca Books, 1988), 10.

31. Maxwell A. Cameron, *Report of the Royal Commission of Inquiry into Educational Finance* (Victoria: King's Printer, 1945.) See "Royal Commission Retrospective" (ch. 21).

32. Post-1945 economic development of the Bulkley Valley is described in British Columbia, Department of Lands and Forests, *The Prince Rupert-Smithers Bulletin Area: Bulletin Area No. 8* (Victoria: Queen's Printer, 1959).

33. Abeele, "'The Mothers of the Land Must Suffer.'"

34. Varley, *Kitimat*, 47.

35. Lillian York, ed., *Lure of the South Peace: Tales of the Early Pioneers to 1945* (n.pl.: South Peace Historical Book, 1981), 180.

36. Bourgon, *Rubber Boots*, 97.

37. Storrs, *God's Galloping Girl*, 93, 95, 215.

38. Neil Sutherland, "'We always had things to do': the Paid and Unpaid Work of Anglophone Children Between the 1920s and the 1960s," *Labour/Le Travail* 25 (Spring 1990): 105-41.

39. Bowman, *The Pioneer Fringe*, 5.

40. Varley, *Kitimat*, 75.

41. Martha Ostenso's *Wild Geese* (Toronto: McClelland and Stewart, 1961), first published in 1925, gives us a clear view of the role of children in families where the father's desire for land goes beyond the more customary need to use it to provide for his family and for his old age. As I understand the Evelyn experience, no father there employed the brutalized tyranny Ostenso's lightly fictional Caleb Gare exerted over his wife and children.

42. In turn they are part of what H. Craig Davis and Thomas A. Hutton call the "ROP" (Rest of Province) economy in British Columbia which they separate out from the "metropolitan" one. "The Two Economies of British Columbia," *BC Studies* 82 (Summer 1989): 3-15.

43. Varley, *Kitimat*, 71.

44. Andy Russell, *Memoirs of a Mountain Man* (Toronto: Macmillan, 1984), 18.

45. Marilyn Wheeler, *The Robson Valley Story*, (n.pl.: McBride Robson Valley Story Group, 1979), 199.

46. Nelson, *Barefoot on the Prairie*, 27-9.

47. Capling, "A Long Time Ago," 141.

48. Mary Cook, *One for Sorrow, Two for Joy* (Ottawa: Denaau, 1984), 121-3.

49. Varley, *Kitimat*, 175-7.

7

"New Canadians" or *"Slaves of Satan"?*
The Law and the Education of Doukhobor Children, 1911-1935

John P.S. McLaren

It is not difficult to find in the historiography of Canadian education instances of the invocation of law to support policies which have had as their objective the compliance of deviant populations or ethnic or religious minorities with mainline "Canadian values." The deployment of law to produce social or cultural homogeneity is evident in the establishment of Upper Canada's public school system in the 1840s;[1] in the progressive denial or erosion of French language education in Manitoba, Ontario and New Brunswick;[2] the Indian residential school system;[3] the attempts to force public education on communalist Christians, such as the Strict Mennonites and Hutterites;[4] and the coercion of Jehovah's Witness children into religious and patriotic exercises.[5] It is also clear that the targets of such strategies have not been reticent about resisting them, whether it be through legal challenge, civil disobedience, non-cooperation, or, in rare instances, violence. Of all of these records of conflict none matches that of the Doukhobors with the government and the "British" population of British Columbia in terms of both durability and visceral quality.

Fundamental differences existed between many Doukhobors and the non-Doukhobor community over the value and utility of education, as a formal, institutional process. To the majority of the Doukhobor community in B.C. in the early days of their settlement, formal education under the control of the state was both unnecessary and dangerous. The knowledge and skills of life, as well as religious precept, were learnt within the family and village community.[6] State run education was threatening because of its capacity to subvert Community beliefs, values and practices, to undermine the respect of young members of the Community for their elders and ultimately to lure them away from family and village into the temptations and hazards of the world outside. As Doukhobor representatives observed in their response to William Blakemore's 1912 Royal Commission Inquiry into the Community, state education prepared children for war and led inexorably to the exploitation of others.[7] Not even the prospect of higher education impressed them. University graduates were described as "crack brained people" who "swallow down all the national peoples power and the capital" while others are left to starve.[8]

Within the non-Doukhobor community formal education lay at the heart of attempts by both state and community to engender pride in anglo-Canadian achievement, and to build a nation with the capacity to meet the challenges of an increasingly complex society and dynamic economy.[9] As the Putman-Weir schools survey of 1925 put it:

> The development of a united and intelligent Canadian citizenship actuated by the highest British ideals of justice, tolerance, and fair play should be accepted without question as a fundamental aim of the provincial school system. Such an aim has stood the test of time and its application in the daily lives of British peoples has enhanced the good name of the British Empire. The moral and patriotic aim . . . is both cultural and practical, traditional and modern, the keynote of past national progress and the foundation for future advancement.[10]

Two general comments are in order on the history of Doukhobor education between 1911 and 1935 and its legal resonances, which help to explain the tensions between the Community and the state. First, periods of conflict were interspersed with periods of calm. These cycles reflected on the one hand disturbance and anxiety within the Doukhobor community over external pressures for its conformity in matters of education, and on the other accommodation between the group and the state, where a degree of compromise was possible, or seemed strategically advisable. Both the theory and practice of leadership among the Doukhobors ascribed great, even semi-divine, authority to the leader. However, because the leader had to rely on charisma to impress the faithful and so to maintain credibility and power, Community sentiment had in certain circumstances to be respected and taken into account.[11] When the leader and Community were at one, or he had been able to use his persuasive powers to good effect, concerted cooperative action was possible. At times, however, when the Community was split or the leader had failed to get his way, then there was a tendency on the part of the leadership to steer clear of decisive action, and sometimes to backtrack. If incautious decisions which offended the Community, or part of it were made, then factionalism could easily take hold. These facts of Doukhobor life were incomprehensible and a matter of great frustration to politicians and bureaucrats from the dominant society who did not understand (and often did not want to) the cultural dynamics at play. The puzzlement and negative reaction was not assisted by the fact that the Doukhobor leaders invariably did not deal directly with government, but through intermediaries, adding to the opportunities for misunderstanding.

Secondly, the application of the law in the matter of school attendance and truancy during this period was marked by the progressive turning of the legal ratchet by the government to induce compliance. At times this was to involve individually or in combination the Department of Education, the Premier's Office, the Attorney General's Department, the Office of the Provincial Secretary and the British Columbia Provincial Police. The legal strategies attempted moved quickly from the imposition of individual to that of collective responsibility, and ultimately to the more dramatic and invasive expedient of using child custody procedures to resocialize some Doukhobor children.

The conflict over education in British Columbia was originally secondary to a dispute relating to vital statistics legislation. At the encouragement of Peter Verigin, the Lordly, the first Doukhobor leader in Canada, Doukhobor families had enrolled their children in a government-built school at Grand Forks, and another had been built by the Community at Brilliant.[12] However, when the British Columbia Provincial Police, acting on instructions from Victoria, arrested and charged four Doukhobor men in 1911 for failure to register a death, the Community's reaction, with Verigin's approval, was to withdraw their children from school.[13] Despite the recommendations of William Blakemore in his 1912 Royal Commission Report on the Doukhobors that accommodation be made with the Community as a means of securing their observance of both vital statistics and school attendance laws,[14] the Conservative government of Richard McBride proved to be more interested in listening to local criticism of the Community and calls for more vigorous enforcement of the law from the non-Doukhobor population in the Kootenays.[15]

Difficulties with enforcing these laws against people living in communal circumstances, identified in a report by A.V. Pineo, a solicitor for the Attorney General's Department, led the government to enact special legislation.[16] The object of the *Community Regulation Act* of 1914 was to impose communal responsibility for breaches of school attendance, vital statistics and public health legislation, and to authorize the execution of judgement for unpaid fines against community property.[17] The legislation was not immediately used because of doubts about its validity. Moreover, before it could be tested the Attorney General, William Bowser, and Peter Verigin reached a compromise on the education issue. By this accord Doukhobor children would attend school, but would be exempt from religious observance and the military drill in place at many schools with the support of the Strathcona Trust.[18] Both men, it seems, saw benefits in mutual resolution of the truancy problem, while the country was at war.[19]

During the period from 1915 to 1922 tension between the Doukhobors and the B.C. government over education diminished as enrolments increased and new schools were built and occupied.[20] Although school attendance from the Community was not universal, it steadily grew under the benign coaxing of A.E. Miller, the School Inspector with responsibility for the Kootenays. Miller rejected coercion of Doukhobor parents as likely to be counterproductive.[21]

By 1922 trouble on the education front was brewing again. The problems flowed in large part from the resolve of John Oliver's Liberal government to enforce school attendance in Doukhobor villages.[22] Where individual students were absent this was to be achieved by charging the parents under the *Schools Act*, and, if necessary, executing judgement against community property under the *Community Regulation Act*.[23] The latter was by then clearly applicable as the Community had been incorporated in 1917. Where the problems of attendance were more generic, and school enrolments fell below what the authorities considered a reasonable level, the strategy was to reduce or remove grants to school boards and charge the educational costs directly against the local community. Amendments to the *Schools Act* in 1920, designed to put pressure on the Doukhobors to comply with the law, vested the necessary power in a Council of Public Instruction (the cabinet).[24]

The legislative initiatives and subsequent actions of the Oliver government were part of a conscious policy of "Canadianization" which was being argued by many educationalists at this time. One of the leading proponents of this view was James T.M. Anderson who as School Inspector for the Yorkton area of Saskatchewan had authored an influential book on the subject in 1918.[25] This work strongly advocated the public education of the young of non-English speaking immigrants as the way to achieve a virtuous, monolingual, homogeneous Canadian society and polity.[26] A disciple of Anderson was E.G. Daniels, who replaced A.E. Miller in 1922 as the School Inspector for the Kootenay region. His arrival coincided with a general growth of dissatisfaction within the Doukhobor community at its apparently tenuous economic position and the perceived hostility of both the government and its non-Doukhobor neighbors towards it.[27] In the educational context this was manifest in increasing truancy and refusal by the Community to countenance a new school building.[28] None of this was to deter Daniels. With gusto and a firm belief in the rectitude of what he was doing, he proceeded to have charges laid by the Grand Forks School Board against Doukhobor parents who were unwilling to send their children to school in that town.[29] The Board was particularly compliant because it had been advised by Victoria that enrolment in the mixed enrolment school had dropped below what was considered reasonable, and it stood to lose its grant under the amended provisions of the *Schools Act*.[30]

Events took an ominous turn when subsequent prosecutions by the Department of Education were followed by a succession of school burnings by zealots in the Community. Nine schools were torched between 1923 and 1925.[31] Verigin the Lordly who seems to have supported the withdrawal of children from school in the first place condemned the incendiarism in communicating with government, but felt powerless to deal with the perpetrators within the Community. In a letter in April, 1924 he made his feelings known to Premier Oliver, and sought the cooperation of the government and police in calling the anarchistic "Nudes," as he described the zealots, to account.[32]

After Verigin's death in an explosion on October 29, 1924 on the Kettle Valley Railway, Victoria turned up the heat on school attendance, supposing the Community to be in a demoralized state and thus vulnerable and malleable.[33] After a major raid on April 9, 1925 coordinated by Inspector Dunwoodie of the British Columbia Provincial Police and School Inspector P.H. Sheffield to seize community property in lieu of unpaid fines imposed for breaches of the *Schools Act*,[34] the climate suddenly changed. The children returned to classrooms, and plans to rebuild the destroyed schools went ahead.[35] It is not clear whether the government's "mailed fist" approach had prevailed for the moment, or the Community had relented pending the arrival of their new leader from the Soviet Union – Peter Petrovich Verigin, the "Purger," as he described himself. The latter had let it be known by letter to the Community that he favored compliance with the education laws.[36]

On his arrival in North America in September, 1927 Verigin the Younger indicated that he was interested in an accommodation with the state on schooling. In a judicious response to a reporter's question he stated:

Yes we will take everything of value which Canada has to offer, but we will not give up our Doukhobor souls. We will educate our children in the English schools, and we will also set up our own Russian schools and libraries.[37]

These views, when they were repeated in the Kootenays and began to permeate the consciousness of the Doukhobor community in B.C. were to lead to dissension in the ranks. The zealots, now clearly recognizable as the Sons of Freedom, began engaging in civil disobedience, whether in protest at Verigin's policy of appeasement, or, because they attributed an inverted meaning to what he said.[38] During 1928 and early 1929 they began marching, stripping and, on occasion, disrupting schools.[39] This was all in the cause of condemning what one of their leaders, Peter Maloff, described as a system which was turning Doukhobor children into "slaves of Satan."[40] School enrolments dramatically declined as both zealot and sympathetic or anxious Community parents removed their children from school.

During 1929 school burnings broke out again. In mid-August a group of 109 protestors sought to march on Nelson. They stripped when the police and Verigin sought to dissuade them.[41] All were arrested, charged with public nudity and sentenced to six months in jail. At this point a change occurred in the government's strategy on Doukhobor education. In dealing with the eight children arrested along with their parents outside Nelson Victoria decided to invoke the *Infants Act* in order to make them wards of the province.[42] Under that statute the Superintendent of Neglected Children was empowered "to apprehend, without warrant, any child apparently under the age of eighteen years . . . [with] no parent capable and willing to exercise proper parental control over the child."[43] Superintendent Thomas Menzies, in a statement to the hearing on wardship conducted by Magistrate Cartmel in Nelson, indicated that the purpose of invoking this provision was to ensure the proper care of the children and their education in Canadian values.[44] The children would be returned to their parents on their release from jail, or at such time as they were adjudged competent to give them the appropriate care and guidance. It was no coincidence that in the recently elected Tory government of Simon Fraser Tolmie, the Attorney General R.G. "Harry" Pooley announced contemporaneously that the Tolmie government intended getting tough with the Doukhobors. It proposed, he said, "to sequestrate a number of their younger children by proper court action under the Neglected Children's Act and place them under such bodies as Children's Aid societies for education." If the Doukhobors behaved themselves, Pooley stated, they would get their children back, if not, "they will lose more children until we have them all under training in institutions."[45]

This limited experiment was not a success. Some of the children turned out to be above school age and, in the mind of the Attorney General, not ripe for resocialization. The target of any future initiatives, he asserted, should be "young children, and those whose education can be attended to."[46] Furthermore, the children refused to cooperate and twice ran away. After the seven girls were transferred to Provincial Industrial Home and the one boy to the Industrial School in Vancouver, they were sent back to their parents, as soon as the latter were released.[47]

The resentment of both parents and children easily fed into the Freedomite martyr myth, and together with action by Verigin to move them off community land as criminals was to lead to further acts of defiance. Victoria, for its part, saw no connection between unrest among the Sons of Freedom and its policies. From the viewpoint of the Tolmie government the "Doukhobor problem" stemmed from their adherence to autocratic and irresponsible leadership, and their communal mode of living. The conclusion was that action was required to rid the country of Verigin who was believed to be both the *eminence grise* behind the zealots and a dangerous Bolshevik, and at the same time to bring the Sons of Freedom to heel.

Five Freedomite Wards of the Province, September, 1929.
(BCARS, ba47198)

The abortive attempts to deport Peter Verigin II have been chronicled elsewhere.[48] The plan, for that is what it was, to deal with the Sons of Freedom, was worked out in Victoria, and facilitated by Ottawa.[49] The dominion government of R.B. Bennett, elected in 1930, bowed to pressure from the B.C. authorities and amended the *Criminal Code* in 1931 to provide for the detention of Freedomite protesters for longer periods. Public nudity was converted into an indictable offence with a maximum sentence of three years in jail.[50] On the assumption that the Sons of Freedom would continue protesting in the nude, Victoria now had the capacity to get them out of the way, while they worked on their children and resocialized them.

The opportunity to test the plan presented itself during May and June, 1932. A series of nude protests took place in the Kootenays, in large part in reaction at

Verigin's continued rejection of them.[51] Close to 600 men and women were arrested, charged with and convicted of public nudity and uniformly sentenced to three years in jail. They were taken off to a special penal facility on Piers Island at the north end of the Saanich peninsula.[52]

The 365 children who had been apprehended along with their parents were divided up between orphanages, foster homes and the industrial home and school to be cared for and educated for the three years the parents were expected to be inside jail.[53] Unlike the earlier experiment, however, the children were not adjudged wards of the province. Through agreement between William Manson, the Superintendent of Welfare, his deputy, Laura Holland and Attorney General Pooley it was decided to treat the children as "destitutes."[54] Under the law and child welfare practice this classification which was typically appealed to "when a parent or guardian, though competent, was unable to provide for the child over a temporary period, often as a result of illness or during confinement of the mother" could be made without a court appearance or order.[55] However, the status, unlike that of wardship, preserved the rights of parents to custody and guardianship and required parental consent to decisions on the child's welfare. The motives of the authorities in adopting this strategy almost certainly reflected a concern to avoid public scrutiny which a court application would have engendered and possible political challenge in society at large, as well as a calculation that any dispensing with legal scruple would escape attention. The Department of Child Welfare did indeed ignore legal requirements by placing some of the children in care over the objections of their parents. The advice of the Attorney General was that parental refusal could be safely ignored. To the extent that legal and welfare authorities proceeded without parental consent, Victoria was acting beyond its powers and in a thoroughly illegal manner.[56] Felicitously for it, the gamble paid off as there were no legal challenges to its actions.

Although the younger children in the orphanages and fosterage seem to have fared reasonably well in trying circumstances and some apparently took to conventional public schooling,[57] the older boys and girls consigned to the industrial home and school were effectively "warehoused." In these establishments there were discipline problems. Moreover, when a Royal Commission investigated the Industrial School for Boys in 1933-34 it found scattered instances of unreasonably harsh and even cruel mistreatment of Doukhobor inmates.[58]

The effectiveness of this second experiment in resocialization was not tested to the full. It was aborted in mid-stream because of pressure on the Tolmie government to cut welfare spending, and, more particularly, because of criticism from MLAs and others in the non-Doukhobor community that much more money was being spent on Sons of Freedom children "in care" than on the children of welfare families.[59] When figures were bandied around which purported to show a disparity of more than $15 a month, Victoria began to lose its nerve and cast around for a way out.[60] Interest expressed by both Community and Independent Doukhobors in fostering the children was fastened upon by the government as providing the solution to their dilemma.[61] By mid-1933 the children had been returned to Doukhobor communities from the lower mainland and Victoria.[62] At that point the Department of Child Welfare washed its hands of them, taking no further financial responsibility for their care, or running any sort of systematic check on how they were being treated.[63]

The result of being moved from pillar to post in this way was to create further confusion in the minds of the children.[64] Some were placed with Doukhobor families with different values and beliefs from those of their parents. Some were used as an additional source of labor by people struggling through the Depression. The bruised psyches which were the result of the insensitive treatment the children had received from the authorities were compounded by the early release of their parents in late 1934 and early 1935.[65] This group of people was extremely embittered, a state of mind which all too easily rubbed off on their children. In the case of some of these young people the mental scars of those years forcibly separated from their parents were not to heal, with the result that they grew into a new generation dedicated to further "dark work" – burning, bombing and other acts of depredation – through the 1950s and into the 1960s.[66]

In its own way the government of British Columbia was to learn a lesson from the fiasco of this early attempt at enforced resocialization. When the Social Credit government of W.A.C. Bennett determined in 1954 to solve the Sons of Freedom problem once and for all by removing children from Freedomite families, it was careful to establish a special facility at New Denver exclusive to the children, and to treat the initiative as an educational one using the experience and skills of teachers, rather than those of child welfare professionals.[67]

In contention in this long-running dispute were two diametrically opposed views of the state, that of the Doukhobors which was highly critical and anarchic, and that of the dominant society which was accepting and instrumentalist. The gap between the two sides was exacerbated by the intense racism which was present in the non-Doukhobor community in British Columbia and well represented among its political leaders.[68] In the case of the dominant community in the Kootenays this racist consciousness manifest itself in the practice of many people describing themselves as "white."[69] By the early 1930s the Doukhobors were clearly targeted as a group to be denied their communal heritage and assimilated, forcibly if necessary.

The unfamiliar, impenetrable and sometimes unstable nature of leadership in the ethnic/religious group was another negative factor at work. It made for difficulties of communication and understanding by educational authorities, already suspicious of groups averse to public education. In the process considerable frustration was generated among both politicians and bureaucrats. Relations were also strained by the extreme rhetoric employed by both sides. Among non-Doukhobors, including politicians, there was a tendency towards hyperbole in demonstrating how alien and problematic these people were, and to label all Doukhobors indiscriminately as perverse, deviant and immoral. The public communications of the community Doukhobors were often hard-hitting, and not shy about rehearsing the deceit of the Canadian state in dealing with them and their history of persecution.[71] Those of the Sons of Freedom which embodied both highly chauvinistic statements of the faith and radical left-wing political sentiment were invariably extreme.[72] These manifestos were particularly hard for non-Doukhobors to stomach, and undoubtedly led to the conclusion in certain circles that they were deranged.

There is no doubt that the British Columbian politicians and bureaucrats viewed this exercise increasingly as one of social control. Indeed, they were very explicit about the need to educate Doukhobor children in Canadian values and the superiority of its institutions if these immigrants were ever to be assimilated satisfactorily. It was, moreover, the agents of the state – Pineo the government lawyer; Daniels the school inspector; Menzies, Manson and Holland the social work bureaucrats – who were the originators of the various legal and administrative strategies deployed. That the experiments were not only less than successful, but in many respects counter-productive, reflects a naivety among those experts and their political masters about the state of education and social work in that era and what they could jointly achieve in the way of resocialization.[73] It also betrayed an ignorance of the phenomenon of resistance in subject groups in general, and its strength among a people who had through their history been outsiders, persecuted for their beliefs and practices and so ill-disposed to the exercise of dominion over them.

Could the Doukhobor education issue have been played to another, less acrimonious, script? Although the British Columbian educational system was highly centralized, compared with those in some other provinces, it did not prevent cultural or religious groups who so desired establishing and operating their own schools, as long as they continued to pay taxes to support the public school system.[74] Given the resistance of a significant part of the Doukhobor community to formal education, it is unlikely that the Community would have readily taken this sort of initiative, unless satisfied that the function of the education was to bolster and not subvert the language, traditions, practices and beliefs of its members.

Despite the centralized nature of administration and curriculum in the province's public school system, it is not impossible that some accommodation could have been made. Blakemore had recommended this in terms of both teacher selection for and the teaching of Russian in Doukhobor schools.[75] Even the system itself, as the Bowser-Verigin accord shows, was prepared to make concessions, in that instance on religious observance and military drill. As is evident in the rather different record of Doukhobor education in Saskatchewan, it was possible over a period of time to coax both community Doukhobor and even zealot parents into sending their children to public school.[76] This was undoubtedly made simpler by a history of greater local autonomy in educational administration in that province. However, it also reflected a more tolerant and patient attitude on the part of educational administrators in working towards greater school attendance, and on the part of those charged with enforcing the general law where Doukhobors were charged with offences designed to protest education policy, for example public nudity.[77] Police officers, prosecutors and magistrates all showed commendable restraint by not attributing the crimes to the Community in general, and in discriminating in terms of charges and sentences, where the zealots were arrested and prosecuted. This was especially true, between

1929 and 1934, when Saskatchewan's administration was in the hands of the government of James Anderson, the former educationalist. Like his counterpart in Victoria, he was committed to crushing communalism among the Doukhobors and getting rid of Verigin.[78] His government also introduced a nativist amendment to provincial schools legislation to divest Doukhobor and other non-English-speaking school trustees of their positions, and talked of holding the Community liable for the activities of the zealots.[79] These strategies were respectively scotched by the bureaucrats charged with educational administration, and by more general criticism in the province of the validity and utility of such extreme expedients.

In British Columbia neither those in politics nor in the bureaucracy were willing to stand up to racist sentiment in the non-Doukhobor community. Nor do they seem to have been enthusiastic in learning about Doukhobor history and understanding the political and social dynamics at work in the Community. The very few voices of reason, like that of A.E. Miller, were effectively voices crying in the wilderness. Only in the last generation, as the effects of later dispersal and assimilation were felt and the non-Doukhobor population began to develop greater sensitivity to civil liberties, becoming more accepting of cultural and ethnic diversity, were serious accommodations made with the Doukhobors over education and other contentious issues with the state.

The result of this sad story has not been the crushing of the culture but a great deal of social dysfunction and individual and group unhappiness. As with other oppressed ethnic groups there has developed a resolve to recapture and share the values and traditions which were formerly so despised on the outside and obsessively shielded on the inside. However, as the most recent dispute in the West Kootenays between Victoria and a segment of the Freedomites over land occupancy and taxation shows, the ghosts of past intransigence and misunderstanding live on.[80]

Notes

* My thanks are due to Tom Christenson, Tom Fleming, Hamar Foster, Catherine Parker, Kathleen Pickard and Donald Wilson for their advice and comments at various stages of preparing this chapter.

1. N. McDonald and A. Chaiton ed., *Egerton Ryerson and his Times* (Toronto: Macmillan of Canada, 1977); H. Graff, "'Pauperism, Misery and Vice': Illiteracy and Criminality in the Nineteenth Century," *Journal of Social History* 11 (1977), 245.

2. Douglas Schmeiser, *Civil Liberties in Canada* (Oxford: Oxford University Press, 1964), 125-95.

3. J.R. Miller, *Skyscrapers Hide the Heavens: A History of Indian-White Relations in Canada* (Toronto: University of Toronto Press, 1989), 97-115, 130-32, 189-207; C. Haig-Brown, *Resistance and Renewal: Surviving the Indian Residential School* (Vancouver: Tillacum Library, 1988).

4. William Janzen, *Limits on Liberty: The Experience of Mennonite, Hutterite and Doukhobor Communities in Canada* (Toronto: University of Toronto Press, 1990), 88-115, 142-161.

5. William Kaplan, *The State and Salvation: The Jehovah's Witnesses and Their Fights for Civil Rights* (Toronto: University of Toronto Press, 1990), 88-115, 142-161.

6. Mary Ashworth, *The Forces Which Shaped Them* (Vancouver: New Star Books, 1979), 136-42.

7. William Blakemore, *Report of the Royal Commission on Matters Relating to the Doukhobor Sect in the Province of British Columbia*, B.C. Sessional papers, 1913, T58.

8. *Ibid.*

9. Neil Sutherland, *Children in English Canadian Society: Framing the Twentieth Century Consensus* (Toronto: University of Toronto Press, 1976), 155-241; Timothy A. Dunn, "The Rise of Mass Schooling in British Columbia, 1900-1929" and Jean Mann, "G.M. Weir and H.B. King: Progressive Education or Education for the Progressive State" in J.D. Wilson and D.C. Jones eds., *Schooling and Society in Twentieth Century British Columbia* (Calgary: Detselig Enterprises, 1980), ch. 1 and 4.

10. J.H. Putman and G.M. Weir, *Survey of the School System* (Victoria, B.C.: King's Printer, 1925), 38.

11. Max Weber, *Economy and Society; An Outline of Interpretive Sociology*, vol. 1 (New York: Bedminster Press, 1968), 215-6.

12. George Woodcock and Ivan Avakumovic, *The Doukhobors* (Toronto: McClelland & Stewart, 1977), 245.

13. British Columbia Archives and Record Service (hereafter BCARS), GR 1323, Attorney General's Correspondence, Microfilm B2086, File 4488-16-12, letter Chief Constable J.A. Dinsmore, BCPP, Grand Forks to Deputy Attorney General, J.P. McLeod, 13 July 1912.

14. Blakemore, T66.

15. See e.g. the resolution from the Grand Forks Conservative Association sent by Donald McCallum, President to Attorney General William Bowser, 7 May 1913 – BCARS, GR 1323, Microfilm B2077, File 7021-1-12, 98. The direction from the Premier to the Attorney General to get tough is at *ibid.*, 105, letter McBride to Bowser, 26 May 1913.

16. See BCARS, GR 1323, Microfilm B2094, File 7547-7-13, for the report by A.V. Pineo to Bowser, 8 November 1913.

17. *Act to make Provision for the Welfare and Protection of Women and Children Living under Communal Conditions,* S.B.C. 1914, c.11. The long title of the act shrouds its real purpose which was to threaten and, if necessary, impose collective responsibility on the Community.

18. Ewart Reid, *The Doukhobors in Canada* (M.A. Thesis, McGill University, 1932), 118. On the Strathcona Trust and its funding of military exercises at schools in B.C., see "Public Schools Reports for 1909-1910," British Columbia, *Sessional Papers,* 1911, no. 39, A58.

19. Reid, *ibid.*, 118, suggests that Verigin was anxious not to provide an excuse for the government of Canada to conscript Doukhobors. Bowser seems to have been motivated by a desire to resolve this irritant while World War I was being waged.

20. Woodcock and Avakumovic, *The Doukhobors*, 251.

21. Janzen, *Limits of Liberty*, 129.

22. On the government's purpose, see report of speech by J.D. Maclean, Minister of Education, *Victoria Daily Colonist*, 26 March, 1920, pp. 6, 9.

23. The process of using both pieces of legislation to enforce the provisions of the *Schools Act* on truancy is set out in a memorandum from Attorney General Alexander Manson to Premier Oliver, 12 March 1925 – BCARS, Oliver Papers, vol. 246, File 13.

24. *Public Schools Amendment Act*, S.B.C. 1920, c. 82, s.22 (inserting s. 115A into the existing Act), further amended and consolidated, S.B.C. 1922, c. 64, s. 129.

25. J.T.M Anderson, *The Education of the New Canadian: A Treatise on Canada's Greatest Education Problem* (London: J.M. Dent & Sons, 1918).

26. *Ibid.*, 7-10.

27. Woodcock and Avakumovic, *The Doukhobors*, 254-5.

28. BCARS, GR 441, Premier Oliver Papers, vol. 246, File 13, Resume of File re: Doukhobors, 8.

29. BCARS, GR 441, Premier Oliver Papers, Vol. 231, File 13, Hon. Dr. MacLean's File, 1.

30. *Ibid.*

31. BCARS, GR 441, vol. 246, File 13, Resume of File on the Doukhobors, 6.

32. BCARS, GR 441, vol. 239, letter Peter Verigin to Premier John Oliver, 25 April 1924.

33. Woodcock and Avakumovic, *The Doukhobors*, 256. There is evidence too that the government was under continuing local pressure in the Kootenays to get tough with the Doukhobors – see BCARS, GR 441, Oliver Papers, vol. 239, File 13, letter from Secretary-Treasurer, Creston Liberal Association to Oliver, 27 October 1924. This communication described the Doukhobors as "a detriment to this country, similar to the Japanese in California" who need "a strong hand" as the only thing they are capable of appreciating.

34. Woodcock and Avakumovic, *The Doukhobors*, 256-7.

35. Koozma Tarasoff, *Plakun Trava – The Doukhobors* (Grand Forks, B.C.: Mir Publishing Society, 1982), 257.

36. Koozma Tarasoff, *In Search of Brotherhood: The History of the Doukhobors,* vol. 2 (Vancouver: mimeographed, 1963), 527, quoting from a letter from Vereshagin and Plotnikoff, Emissaries from the Christian Community of Universal Brotherhood to Verigin in the Soviet Union, in P. Maloff, *Dukhobortsy: Ikh Istoria, Zihn i Bonba*, 33.

37. Quoted in Ashworth, *The Forces*, 146-7.

38. Shortly after his arrival in Brilliant, B.C. Verigin had flattered the Sons of Freedom, describing them as the "ringing bells of Doukhoborism." Their response was to read into his pronouncements the opposite intention to the one expressed, so that accommodation with the state on education really meant resistance. This inversion of meaning is what Woodcock and Avakumovic, 12, 291, have described as the "upside-down" theory of discipleship. On the emergence of this radical wing of Doukhoborism, see J. Colin Yerbury, "The 'Sons of Freedom' Doukhobors and the Canadian State,'" *Canadian Ethnic Studies* (1984): **16, 45.**

39. Ashworth, *The Forces*, 147.

40. *Vancouver Daily Province*, 3 May 1928.

41. Ashworth, *The Forces*, 147-8.

42. *Infants Act,* R.S.B.C. 1924, c. 112.

43. *Ibid.*, s. 56(j).

44. BCARS, GR 2817, Provincial Secretary's Papers, Box 1, File 1, transcript of hearing under the *Infants Act* before J. Cartmel, Magistrate, County of Kootenay, Nelson, 6 September 1929, 4. The story of this experiment is related in some detail in Ronald Hooper, *Custodial Care of Doukhobor Children in British Columbia 1929 to 1933* (M.A. Thesis, Social Work, University of British Columbia, 1947), 23-31.

45. *Victoria Times*, 31 August 1929.

46. BCARS, GR 2817, Box 1, File 1, memorandum Pooley to Menzies, 24 September 1929.

47. In December Superintendent Menzies wrote to P.H. Sheffield, Inspector of Schools for Nelson indicating that the government had concluded that sending the children to the industrial home or school was the only way to deal with children at an age where it was doubtful that they were reeducable – BCARS, GR 2817, Box 1, File 1, 4 December 1929.

48. On this part of the strategy, see John McLaren, "Wrestling Spirits: The Strange Case of Peter Verigin" (to be published in *Canadian Ethnic Studies*, 1995).

49. As early as September, 1929 Attorney General Pooley had been advocating that "the ringleaders" should be convicted of "rioting charges" and sent to D'Arcy Island off Victoria – see BCARS, GR 441, Tolmie Papers, vol. 283, File 4, telegram Pooley to Premier Simon Fraser Tolmie (in Toronto), 8 September 1929.

50. *Criminal Code Amendment Act*, S.C. 1931, c. 28, s. 2.

51. Woodcock and Avakumovic, *The Doukhobors*, 298.

52. Records relating to the planning and implementation of this carceral experiment are in National Archives of Canada (NAC), RG 73, Penitentiary Service Files, vols. 43-5, 131.

53. Hooper, *Custodial Care*, 40-2.

54. *Ibid.*, 37.

55. *Ibid.*, 37-38.

56. *Ibid.*, 38.

57. This was certainly the view of the care-givers. See e.g. BCARS, GR 2817, Provincial Secretary's Papers, Box 1, File 17, letters Zelda Collins, Manager, Children's Aid Society, Vancouver to Laura Holland, 25 September 1932.

58. BCARS, GR 1424, Boys Industrial School Inquiry, Box 1, File 7, Minutes of Evidence, 749-52, 715-6.

59. Hooper, *Custodial Care*, 98-9.

60. MLA Tom Uphill was reported in the *Vancouver Sun*, 23 March 1933, p. 16 as complaining that the government was spending infinitely more on a handful of lawbreaking zealots "than it did to feed British Columbia's jobless army."

61. Hooper, *Custodial Care*, 99.

62. This was the result of a letter from Superintendent of Welfare William Manson to his deputy, Laura Holland, 1 March 1933 – BCARS, GR 2817, Box 1, File 5. Again, some of the children were moved without the consent of their parents.

63. BCARS, GR 2817, Box 1, File 9, memo Holland to Dr. G.F. Davidson, Superintendent of Welfare, 8 March 1935.

64. Ashworth, *The Forces*, 153.

65. Hooper, *Custodial Care*, 105-6.

66. Woodcock and Avakumovic, *The Doukhobors*, 318-9.

67. Margaret Hill, "The Detention of Freedomite Children, 1953-59" (1986), *Canadian Ethnic Studies*. 18, 46, 50-4.

68. On racism in B.C. which was directed against Asians, see Patricia Roy, *A Whiteman's Province: British Columbia's Politicians and Chinese and Japanese Immigrants 1854-1914* (Vancouver: UBC Press, 1989); Peter Ward, *White Canada Forever: Popular Attitudes and Public Policy Towards Orientals in British Columbia* 2nd. ed. (Montreal and Kingston: McGill-Queen's Press, 1990); Hugh Johnston, *The Voyage of the Komagatu Maru: The Sikh Challenge to Canada's Colour Bar* (Vancouver: UBC Press, 1989).

69. Woodcock and Avakumovic, *The Doukhobors*, 244.

70. See note 33.

71. See e.g. BCARS, GR 441, Oliver Papers, Vol. 246, File 13, letter W. Sherstibitoff, Director, Christian Community of Universal Brotherhood (CCUB) to Premier Oliver, 16 April 1925.

72. See the example mentioned in Woodcock and Avakumovic, *The Doukhobors*, 313-4.

73. On the lack of self-evaluation in the social and educational services at both a political and professional level in Canada during this period, see Sutherland, *Children in English Canada*, 228-33.

74. Putman and Weir, 38. As this study noted, apart from the schools for Indian children run by Ottawa, there were private Roman Catholic schools in large urban centres, and in one or two locations, schools run by Asian groups. Ironically, given the pressure to force compliance of the Doukhobors, the Oriental schools were established because of local antipathy to the enrolment of Asian children in existing public schools – a sentiment quietly condoned by Victoria.

75. Blakemore, *Report of the Royal Commission*, T66.

76. John Lyons, "The (Almost) Quiet Evolution: Doukhobor Schooling in Saskatchewan," *Canadian Ethnic Studies* (1976): *8, 23.*

77. *Ibid.*, 27-31.

78. *Ibid.*, 31-4.

79. *Ibid.*, 33.

80. *Castlegar Sun*, 24 August 1994.

8

"The war was a very vivid part of my life":
the Second World War and the Lives of British Columbian Children.

Emilie L. Montgomery

The Second World War played a major part in the lives of British Columbia's children. They were affected by the war's events, by the changes, fears and excitements that war brought. They learned about the war's events from newsreels and from movies. They cheered as their favorite actors fought the hated Nazis and Japanese on the movie screen. They followed the news on the radio and in the newspapers. They studied the war in their classrooms and pledged their allegiance to Britain and to the King. Many children drilled in their school's cadet corps in physical training for the service. They made extra money working, after school and on weekends, in shipyards and factories and contributed to the war effort by purchasing war savings stamps. They also raised funds, collected bottles, cans, foil, fat and bones and they worked tirelessly for the Canadian Junior Red Cross. They experienced rationing, air raids and blackout. They listened to talk of invasion and tried to understand why their Japanese Canadian friends had been taken away.

The account that follows is based on the recollections of men and women who spent their childhood years in British Columbia during the Second World War. When I interviewed them they discussed the upheaval and change the war brought to their lives. They remembered those six years as a chaotic time full of fears and hopes, patriotism and blind racism, victory as well as tragedy. Consequently, to some, the war was an exciting and fascinating time to grow up. One man remembered the war as "being a terribly interesting time to live. The types of weapons and guns and as a kid being interested in all these sorts of fascinating things, war weapons, airplanes and all that." Another disclosed: "it was a very vivid part of my life, to me it was the war to end all wars, not World War I."[1]

The war for Canada began 10 September 1939, and interviewees had a variety of individual memories about the beginning of the war. One woman described the anxiety at home: "I knew the adults were tense and I could feel that. The night that war was declared, everyone was talking in hushed voices." Invasions were recalled by many as signifying the beginning of war. "We had relatives in Budapest and Czechoslovakia and there was terrible fear when Germany invaded Poland . . . the Germans were so close our relatives were terrified," recalled one woman. Another interviewee described "coming home at lunch hour and hearing the news about the Japanese invasion of China. . . . " Now that the Second World War had started it became a dominant topic of conversation in many homes. One man recalled, "there would be political discussion over the dinner table and I'd sit and listen to that." In another home a woman's "brother was very interested in the war. He and my mother used to talk about it all the time. I can remember listening in . . . "

In some homes the war was discussed in a less than straightforward manner. Parents felt it was better to shelter their children from any upsetting news. With his father stationed in England, one man reflected "My mother never seemed to be concerned . . .we never thought of it from the point of view that his plane might be attacked." He concluded that he was "really pretty sheltered. . . . A lot of my knowledge of the war came after the war." Many parents, like his, did not want their children to worry. "I was never really interested in it. To me it was more a problem for adults to solve . . . at home the war was something our parents would take care of." Said another, "It was an adult topic of conversation." To a number of children the war in Europe and the Orient seemed to be too far away to be real. "It was a romantic feeling about the war, it was so distant, so far away" recounted one man. Another man "would define the war as being romantic, unreal, full of expectations, everyone with positive views." One woman recalled, "For a young girl in those days it was a romantic period. Bands played, and young men marched." One interviewee attributed this idealism to her age: "I think when you are that young you can be frivolous about those kinds of things."

Much of the romantic feeling stemmed from the media's attempts to maintain public morale. Much of what they saw, heard and read was carefully censored as morale had to be maintained for six long years. One woman related: "There was a patriotism that was never generated again, not in Canada." This patriotism upheld the notion that the war "was always for the right cause, we were doing the right thing." Children had only to glance at a newspaper, walk into a movie theatre, or turn on a radio to learn news of the war. "Once the war was on we read the paper every day," recalled one. Another explained that "the war became real for us when we read about people being killed." "Hitler was spoken of as a mad man or evil," stated another, "we saw, in the news, his atrocities and it was the same with the Japanese, their prisoner of war camps were horrible and we saw this too."

"We learned about the war in the movies," declared one interviewee, "movies were the main source of entertainment. We went to the movies all the time." Children watched and learned about the war from the newsreels, movies and National Film Board productions. One interviewee recalled "crying buckets of tears over *Mrs. Miniver*." Another described the newsreels: "virtually all actual footage, scenes of battles, air raids . . . searchlights, bombs falling." One woman remarked that "it was probably the newsreels that caused my terrifying nightmare that the Germans were going to kill us all." The National Film Board of Canada produced documentaries and newsreels on the war. One interviewee remembered the *Canada Carries On* series, it was like a newsreel but it showed the Canadian reserves training, and army bases in Canada." The films conveyed a message that war is exciting, dramatic and only for the courageous.

If there was a radio in their homes or classrooms, the children of British Columbia could listen and learn about the war. To most families radio had become a habit and an obsession. "I remember the radio playing all the time," said one interviewee. Another stated: "We listened to the radio every evening. I can remember being shushed every night at 7 o'clock. The news was taken very seriously in our house." Another recounted, "We'd have the volume right to the top, if we even sneezed we'd get yelled at!" Children who had radio in their classroom could listen to wartime issues in a school broadcasting program produced by the Canadian Broadcasting Corporation. The program included such shows as "The Child in Wartime" and "The Child and His War Service" as well as short news broadcasts designed for young listeners. One woman remembered her teacher "used to bring the radio into our classroom . . . we would listen to the news and to Hitler." One man recalled that as the war dragged on "what was once cheers for victory and songs on the radio turned to very very sober reflections and the hope, the anticipation of any good news." Radio brought the war into their daily lives.

The massive amount of wartime propaganda generated by the media served to generate fear. During family discussions many adults expressed their fears about the war and these fears were passed on to their children. One man remembered listening in and he "got the impression from overhearing the adults conversations that they were quite scared." Another explained: "My parents felt very threatened by the war because they had three boys." Another interviewee remembered his "mother very nervous, concerned about it. . . . As a kid I had this great imagination that anything might happen." The war became a very frightening thing to one woman who remembered listening to adults say that "Hitler was going to invade the rest of the world, that Hitler and his war machine was coming closer. There was terrible fear in these people." She remembered a nightmare that sent her "running, screaming and sobbing into the living room, 'I'm so scared of Hitler' . . . I believed that Hitler was going to come and kill mommy and my sisters and Ginger and the cat and the chickens, everything."

Particular, significant events also made the war a very real and frightening experience to many of British Columbia's children. A number of people from British Columbia were on board the *Athenia* and the event was well publicized and talked about. "It was September 4th, 1939 . . . we sat in my parents living room," explained one man, "and we listened to the news. . . . The announcer said that the steam ship *Athenia* had been sunk by German submarines off the coast of England." One woman recalled "when the *Athenia* sank that was a more important event than the war itself. One of the girls from St. Mary's church was on it when it went down." Another fellow nearly lost his classmates, the Kitsilano Band, "that really brought it home to us all. That this war could effect us in Canada, that it was real." The attack on Dieppe was also remembered by some. "I remember . . . listening to the radio for news on Dieppe. . . . It was a great loss and we talked about it . . . for weeks afterwards." One woman said "I never thought of Canadians being at war until all the news of Dieppe."

The war in the Pacific seemed particularly close to home. Many remembered a sequence of events and the escalating fear of invasion that they caused. In December 1941, the Japanese forces bombed Pearl Harbor. In March 1942, Japanese Canadians were forcibly evacuated from the west coast. Early in June 1942, two Aleutian islands were seized and Japanese troops appeared to be advancing on the Alaskan mainland. On 7 June 1942, an American freighter was torpedoed at the mouth of Juan de Fuca Strait. On 20 June a Japanese submarine shelled the lighthouse and radio station at Estevan Point on Vancouver Island. One interviewee stated: "I remember the day Pearl Harbor was bombed quite clearly, we listened to the broadcast on the radio, and we thought it was all over, that the Japanese would invade Canada next." Another said: "I remember Pearl Harbor. Invasion was the big thing, and incendiary bombing. Those were the things we worried about." One man recalled that "they were scared that there would be an invasion . . . the Japanese were in Pearl Harbor which didn't seem so far away from Vancouver or Victoria. We moved to Banff in 1942. A lot of people we knew went to Banff because of the perceived military threat to the coast of B.C."

The internment of Japanese Canadians exacerbated these fears. In 1942 the Government of Canada created the British Columbia Security Commission to evacuate more than 21 000 Japanese Canadians from their homes and means of livelihood. Among those evacuated were approximately 4 000 children of elementary school age. "We felt danger from Japan once we'd seen the removal of the Japanese," stated one interviewee as he recalled the internment of the Japanese Canadians, "there were two Japanese families in the community and both of them just disappeared." One man recounted a memorable school day, "an assembly was called at school. The R.C.M.P. came in and took out all the Japanese kids." He specifically recalled "a Japanese fellow in our class . . . was taken away. . . . We talked about it amongst ourselves. We thought it was quite cruel." A woman also remembered one school day "the police came to school and took the Japanese girls out of the school." Another fellow in Kitsilano high school reported "I had a friend at school . . . his family moved to Kaslo. [Neither] I, nor my family understood the implications. Why should this happen to them?" One interviewee recalled, as a teen, visiting the internment camp at Hastings Park: "They had strung barb wire up around the top of the wire fence . . . the Japanese would come over and spit on us. We never understood." It was a second visit that helped him understand: "They were as frightened as we were. . . . I remember going in after they had gone . . . and I saw the mess, it was pretty bad, yes, living conditions were bad, they were in stalls . . . ."

The shelling of the light house on Point Estevan on Vancouver Island shocked British Columbians and augmented their fear of invasion. One man stated, "we were always afraid of a Japanese invasion. When Point Estevan was shelled by the Japanese sub, we thought for sure we had been invaded." "Everyone became very frightened that we were going to be invaded by the Japanese," stated another. He also remembered that invasion was taken very seriously in his home. "People were almost paranoid of being invaded . . . my parents wanted to move to Kelowna . . . ." One woman recalled a visit by the minister: "He stated that if the Japanese came over here he would kill himself and his children before he let their filthy hands touch them." Other children were not as afraid, some even thought it was an exciting adventure. One woman remembered that at her school the nearby woods was the agreed meeting place in case of an invasion. "I suppose that we were to hide there in case of an invasion . . . every plane that flew over, we went ran out to the woods. . . . It was fun for kids . . . I learned to smoke in the air raid shelter . . . smoking in these dried out bushes, we didn't need the help of the Japanese to start a fire!"

Children adopted the prejudices of their parents and other adults and expressed them in words and actions. One man explained "there were terms used about them. I remember 'Fifth Column' and 'Quisling.' These were names you called someone who was a spy or a traitor or a collaborator. That's what they were regarded as."

"I certainly grew up with a dislike for Germans," one woman disclosed. Another woman remembered the media made "the Germans into such terrible people. I guess they were terrible then. . . ." One woman revealed "my father dropped our last name because it was of German background." Many children listened as the media and adults referred to the "yellow peril" as the enemy and as spies. One man explained "there was a lot of prejudice in Vancouver . . . the Japanese were the slant-eyed, yellow peril. They were really dreadful, they butchered babies and raped people." I remember the Japanese were more our enemy than the Germans," stated one woman. Another remembered "being scared to death by the wartime anti-Japanese hysteria." One interviewee explained, "whenever we saw Japanese on the streetcars we would look away."

Racist attitudes, comprehended or not, were often expressed through play. Children, mostly boys, played war in the play grounds. One man recalled, "We were playing 'Cowboys and Indians' at the time and just changed to 'Soldiers and War.' Another interviewee had a similar memory: "It was like 'Cops and Robbers' but 'British and Germans.'" He described the games as "pretty elaborate. . . . We would round up prisoners and we played in a field that was riddled with trenches. We dug trenches like crazy, or we'd use branches and boughs to build booby traps." One man remembered his games included racial insults "we used to play 'Kill the Krauts or Japs'. . . . You were the bad guy if you were the Kraut or Jap." Another man played war games: "The Japanese or the Germans were the enemy and someone always had to be the other side. With me it was usually the Japanese were the bad guys." 'War' was also a game for some girls as well. One woman remembered "playing Battleships at school." Another recalled: "We played war a lot on the island [Vancouver] . . . . We split into teams and would try to get into enemy territory . . . . We would crawl on our stomachs."

One man portrayed the war games very perceptively: "It was like playing authority. What amazes me now were the fascist overtones . . . we used to call the guy at the top of the hierarchy 'the fuhrer'. . . ." He explained that the games included "fascist terminology . . . systems of control, neatness, order, obedience . . . I think we used to give the Hitler salutes. The implication of an elite group that enforced authority on others, the words and actions signifying it were around us."

Children discussed the wars events, and developed opinions about the war in their classrooms. British patriotism was evident in schools. "You have to realize you were still a British colony with strong ties to Britain" explained one interviewee. Another stated: "We were British subjects, you had that mind set in that you were part of England's population, part of the British army, all huddled together under the crown." These patriotic feelings made it difficult for teachers to remain objective about the war. "Our teachers had only one point of view," recalled one woman, "they saw nothing else . . . Hitler had to be stopped." Another remembered learning racist values from "our teachers [who] were all afraid and frightened of the Japanese." One man described "drawing a swastika on a note book, my teacher saw it and dramatically tore it to pieces." While another remembered his "teacher trying to get us to read the English translation of *Mien Kampf*." Some teachers went to the extreme of unnecessarily scaring their students; "My teacher . . . told us that if Hitler was to bomb Vancouver he would use Quilchena school as a bullseye, it was on the top of a hill and therefore a focal point; he really scared the kids and we believed him about the bombing."

War also changed the curriculum of British Columbia's schools. The Social Studies program was altered to include, amongst other things, the causes and events of the war. One interviewee shared a Social Studies project that involved clipping "a map from the newspaper which would show the battle positions . . . ." Another recalled "marking the German advance into the Soviet Union." One man described the importance of war in his senior year Social Studies class. "Social Studies was the only time we could talk about the war. The entire back wall of the classroom was covered with maps on the war. There were different sections on the back wall: Progress of War; Devastation of the War; Reasons for the War."

Other subjects also felt the effects of the war. The Department of Education made cadet training compulsory in all public high schools. Thus children in high school learned squad drill and rifle shooting as well as skills in throwing hand grenades. We were "playing at recognizing the war" confided one interviewee. Another remembered being "given these wooden rifles and we paraded around twice a week." For another it was more realistic: "We were given old World War I guns, the recoil was so violent we had to stuff sweaters to pad our shoulders." "We were like toy soldiers" declared one fellow about the cadet corps, "children trying to act like grown men."

The Physical Education curriculum had expanded to incorporate the community-based Provincial Recreation (Pro Rec) program. In Pro Rec classes older children learned military marching and practised First Aid and Air Raid Precaution drills, as well as war-time nutrition, home nursing and women's industrial lifting. The Pro Rec program encouraged boys to build up muscles in preparation for recruitment. It also encouraged girls to knit and sew clothing for the air raid victims of London. Both boys and girls developed their skills in squad drill and rifle shooting. Members also enjoyed socializing with troops stationed in their districts at fund-raising events.

Concert parties and dances were held to raise money for Victory Bond drives, the Air Supremacy drive, the Lord Mayor's Fund and the Queen's Canadian Fund for air raid victims.

War also brought small changes in the harmony of daily life that created a feeling of uncertainty and novelty. The guns installed around and the war ships in the harbor, air raid drills, blackouts and ration books brought the war into children's lives and made it a more definite and vivid experience. One man remembered "Certain areas were suddenly out of bounds . . . this was when they built the reinforcements at Stanley Park and Wreck Beach . . . and the guns at Point Atkinson." For youthful entertainment, he also recalled, "We used to go down to English Bay and watch them lob shells into the water." Another man described "a great place to play . . . where the old Expo ['86] site is. It's hard to believe that they were launching ships down in that area during the war." One fellow remembered: "the *Queen Mary* was in English Bay and everyone went down to see it. It was painted grey and I couldn't believe the size of it. It had come to pick up about 10 000 troops. It was this totally grey monstrous thing!"

Air raid drills, blackouts and ration books added to the tension. "We had an assembly at school that morning," recounted one former student, "some man in a uniform, I'm not sure if he was military or police, explained to us about the blackouts, about bombers flying overhead and air raids, general security." Another explained, "We had oil lamps, extra food and blankets . . . in case of attack." One man described the air raid drills at his school: "We went to the basement of the school, it was sort of fun but serious too. Another interviewee remembered, "There were air raid drills at school, we would get under our desks." An interviewee from Trail recalled the Air Raid Precaution shacks in her community: "They kept gas masks and things in them. So if something did happen you were prepared." Many children practised with the use of respirators. One man described his experience with a gas mask: "I do remember being given a gas mask at school . . . putting them on, and it was very hard to breathe. We kept them in a khaki box with a handle." One woman remembered "carrying my gas mask during these drills." Another enjoyed "handing out . . . gas masks, for practice drills if we were ever attacked. . . . For us it was fun in a way, something more social to do than school work." "Sirens still bother me," one woman explained, "my stomach tightens even now when I hear sirens. The school siren especially made my stomach turn."

All interviewees remembered blackouts. To some it was an unnerving event, while other children accepted it as a part of life in wartime. "I can remember the blackouts, that was when we were expecting the Japanese to attack any time." "The Air Raid Police [Air Raid Precaution] would come around and check for any light showing in your windows." One interviewee explained: "We were having Japanese scares. When the alarm went off we had to cover our windows. . . . The lights on cars were to be blacked out, the street lights went out." Another revealed that "we had to black out the windows. Everyone became frightened that we were going to be invaded by the Japanese." Another described the "weird, strange environment" and the belief that "it was a real threat." Another remembered, "When they declared a blackout everyone would rush outside to see what it was like with no lights on. We would go up to the bend on Alma road . . . there was a nice view from up there."

The first ration books came out in September 1942. During various phases of the war sugar, meat, tea and coffee, gasoline and liquor were rationed. "My mother went out right away," claimed one interviewee, "and bought 100 pounds of sugar, a great big bag of sugar." Another described her duty of dividing the precious commodity with her siblings. "I took three glass jars and painted our names on them with nail polish. We divided the sugar into three and that was what we had for the week." There was a certain amount of excitement if something was in stock. "There were days when we heard the candy was in," recounted one man, "you ran to the store, because it didn't last long." One woman related, "When we heard a shipment of nylons were coming in we'd send someone down to line up for us."

Important things in a child's life were hard to find during the war years. "You certainly couldn't buy toys or any of those things in the stores," declared one man, "It was hard to buy anything. My bike was third hand . . . they did away with lead toy soldiers." Another interviewee reported, "I couldn't get new ice skates. My mother traded her liquor coupons for my skates." One fellow remembered such American publications as "the *Big Little* books . . . we couldn't get access to these any more." Another recalled a British children's magazine: "*Chips and Crackers*, you couldn't get it any more once the war started." One interviewee remembered taking full advantage of the rationing, "a couple of us sold our roller skates to our school principal. . . . I guess he had kids and you couldn't get skates. . . . So my friend and I became war profiteers, we brought in our old skates which were rusty as all get out!" Another concluded that during the war "you just did without and that was the sacrifice you made."

Much of the aura of excitement that surrounded the war years in British Columbia came from the growing number of people volunteering their energies for the war effort. Children watched as their parents and others became involved in new activities to win the war on the home front. "My mother was involved, she used to dish out ration books" one interviewee explained. Life at home was altered for another because her "mother worked at the United Services centre, she was always bringing home service men, boys really, from Australia and Yorkshire." She remembered "Wally from the Air Force, he stayed with us and then he was killed over Burma . . . Stanley, who loved music. . . . There was quite a steady flow of people, quite a socialization, meeting people from all over the Commonwealth." One fellow recalled that his "father served in a paramilitary outfit, a group called the Frontiersmen . . . [he] also joined the Reserves during the war. . . . It's hard to imagine him now packing a rifle dressed in his full army gear." One woman recalled with pride, "My mother trained in first aid . . . also drills and parade. She wore a blue outfit with silver buttons . . . and she learned how to repair a car." One woman claimed that she grew up wearing "big bandages that my mother learned how to make for the Red Cross." To another, "The war had a greater impact on me because my family members were all involved in some way, father was 'playing soldier' with the reserves, mother worked for the Red Cross. . . . I remember father started a Victory Garden, that's what he called it."

As part of their "Air Raid Precaution" program, school children learned how to put on a gas mask. (Vancouver Archives, 586-1228)

There were numerous other war work activities that children were involved in. They raised hundreds of thousands of dollars for the war effort in a variety of ways. Children bought war savings stamps, became Junior Red Cross members and salvaged scraps for the war effort. One interviewee recalled "At school we bought War Savings Certificates, they were twenty five cents each, and we had to buy one stamp a week, until we had a five dollar book." "We had to buy one a week, you always did," explained another. Yet another remembered: "War was a big thing in my family. I was encouraged to give money . . . to give to the war effort." In turn parents were exhorted to buy Victory Bonds. One interviewee recounted an exciting day when he was "walking home from school and the bombers flying overhead and the doors open up and tons of literature comes out advertising Victory Bonds." Another recalled a "Dutch resistance fighter addressing the whole of the school, describing how he killed a German, this was during one of the war bond drives."

Working for the Red Cross, school children were called Juniors and were identified by their red cross pin, memorized their motto; "I serve" and read the *Canadian Red Cross Junior* magazine. "The lady would come in from the Red Cross and give us a pep talk," declared one interviewee, "every week she would tell us what was needed, what we should be knitting." Another recalled "Red Cross meetings on Wednesday afternoons . . . we would knit most of the time." One fellow assumed that "the government never gave anyone any socks . . . you knitted balaclavas and mitts with no fingers." Juniors did more than knit; "we did *Alice in Wonderland* to raise money for the war" one interviewee stated. "We used to sort rivets," another said. While another Junior "would pile into a truck and go around to collect for the salvage drives." One Junior remembered, "I rolled bandages for the Red Cross and packed boxes to go overseas."

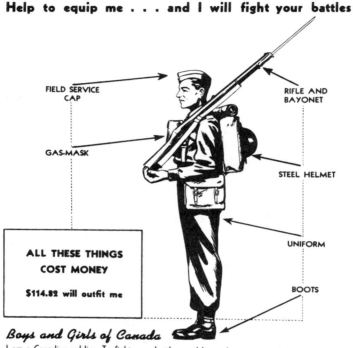

Help to equip me . . . and I will fight your battles

FIELD SERVICE CAP

RIFLE AND BAYONET

GAS-MASK

STEEL HELMET

UNIFORM

ALL THESE THINGS

COST MONEY

$114.82 will outfit me

BOOTS

Boys and Girls of Canada

I am a Canadian soldier. To fight your battles, and keep the war away from your homes, I need all the equipment shown on this page, and many other things.

It costs $5.47 to keep me in reserve in Canada for one day.
It costs $8.22 to keep me in action overseas for one day.

This war must be won, but it will cost a lot of money. Every time you buy a War Savings Stamp, you are helping a little. Every time you buy a War Savings Certificate, you are helping a great deal. Keep up the good work; we're counting on you to back us up.

The back of a folder into which children stuck their 25 cents war savings stamps. When they had $4 worth, they could exchange them for a War Savings Certificate that would be worth $5 after the war. (Courtesy of Jacqueline Gresko)

It was not enough for school children to purchase war savings stamps and work tirelessly for the Junior Red Cross; they poured their energies into countless other fund-raising activities and projects for the war effort. School children rummaged around in basements, garages and attics as they participated in salvage drives. One man recalled that "for the war effort I collected aluminum toothpaste tubes and cigarette foils." Another told that her mother "kept a can on the back of her stove, she saved all the grease, which we collected to make munitions." In some schools clothing was collected for Victory Bundles for Britain. One woman confessed that she "found the worst pair of socks, because I didn't want to give them my good socks!" Some children planted Victory gardens. One man remembered that he "had a Victory garden and I got marks for it so I planted things that grew quickly: radishes and onions." Others sent packages of food and necessities overseas. One woman recounted, "I was very tiny but I remember helping my mother put together packages. . . . We would hide money in the cocoa tin."

Paying jobs became more plentiful and men, women and children made money working for the war effort. For the first time in many years prosperity became the norm for many. People who had lacked employment and money through the depression embraced the war and the jobs it provided. One fellow recalled that "the one good thing about the war is we're getting jobs. People were building ships right here in Vancouver. There were defense efforts, particularly on the coast. . . . For the first time in quite a while there was prosperity." Another explained that: "People had money in their pockets once again. Those not in uniforms had jobs. . . . The war effort brought a crazy kind of prosperity." Yet another described the atmosphere: "It was a prosperous time but it was very turbulent too." Some children's lives were effected in a personal manner. One man described the lack of parental discipline once his mother started working: "I wasn't allowed to go to these movies but my mother had a job for the federal government." He also explained that most children "always went home for lunch, certainly I didn't" and that "mother was never there after school, to her it was a great boon and it freed me from parental supervision!" Going home for lunch to an empty home was remembered by another: "My mother worked in a smelter . . . so I was virtually on my own once the war started. I thought I'd never open another can of Campbell's soup."

As the labor shortage intensified, governments began to ease legislative restriction on child labor.[3] One man remembered, "A lot of kids left school to work in the ship yards . . ." Some tried to balance both school and work. One man explained that the late shift in the shipyard was interfering with his school work until "I moved to the machine shop . . . and worked after school four hours a day, which was better, I stopped falling asleep in class all the time." Another recalled his brother "working one summer in a munitions plant, at age sixteen." One man described the abundance of jobs: "Kids could get jobs easily. It was not very difficult to get an after school job, the war made it easy in that sense."

The war became a reality to many children the day their father, their brother or someone they knew enlisted. Wartime propaganda presented service in the Canadian forces as a way to earn money and an education while helping our allies to victory. One woman recalled that the war "didn't seem relevant then, until my brother joined the air force." Some children feared for their loved ones. One woman described her "strongest memory of the war was when my brother joined the Air Force . . . we were excited but afraid for him." Another remembered the war as being very stressful as she "knew her brother would eventually go to war. I was terrified that something would happen to [him]." Another remembered his parent's fear as he had one brother in the Air Force, "[and] my oldest brother was in the Navy. . . . My parents made me promise I wouldn't join up." To some the service was remembered as a beneficial experience. One woman declared that for her brother who "hated school, he really loathed it. He probably would have dropped out . . . it really was the war that saved him." For others life in the service was not a positive experience. One man's brother "was an Air Force pilot, an instructor . . . " he ended up a nervous wreck; he flew sixty missions in Mosquitoes and he flew on D-Day." One man remembered a first-hand account from a friend who "came back early . . . and he told me he was glad to be back."

Children corresponded with their relatives and learned about the war and life in the service through these letters. Secrecy was important and any information about the war's events was carefully censored from, among other things, family letters. It was not uncommon for children to excitedly open a letter only to find that it "looked as if someone had been playing paper dolls," declared one man. One woman clearly recalled her relatives in Europe would write "in very general terms about the war. They would be reprimanded for giving any details . . . they censored everything." Another woman received "quite a few letters" from her brother and "they were censored, they would actually cut bits out of the letter before we got it." Even so, censored letters were well received. "Happy Birthday" one serviceman wrote home. It was a "secret signal, it meant he was coming home" one woman explained. Another declared that while the war was on "we were always anxious for any news from the old country." Another talked of her brother: "When he did go to war I wrote him one air letter a day."

Visiting on leave, or home from the war, service men and women shared their war stories with young and captivated listeners. One fellow remembered his "cousin in the U.S. Marines . . . we would see him occasionally. His stories were always very good." "We always had people over, officers over to the house," recalled another. One interviewee described his meeting "whole troops of airmen with accents you could cut with a knife." Cross-cultural meetings were remembered by one who met "men from New Zealand, Australia, Englishmen, all over really." Another told of "a baby-sitter, her boyfriend was an American sailor who came to visit. He'd tell us things, he'd be back on leave and spin yarns for us, we kids loved it." One person remembered listening to his mother's friend "a major from a prison camp . . . he would tell us of the Germans who had tried to escape." A woman's brother-in-law returned from the war and told her of men in a prisoner of war camp who "were walking skeletons, it was the most horrible thing he had seen in the war."

Many interviewees had decided that they would join the services for a variety of personal reasons. Some were tired of school, they lied about their age and joined up early. A woman remembered that the boys who "signed up before they finished school . . . weren't very good students to begin with." Another recalled that "one of our neighbour friends basically dropped out of school and joined the Navy." One fellow claimed, "They lied about their age," and described his senior high class "decreasing in numbers as the boys signed up." Some interviewees remembered the excitement of volunteering. "The tone of discussing the need for servicemen was one of excitement," explained one man, "join up and learn a new trade, have new experiences, all very positive." Another recalled, "There was no conscription when war broke out, but we were certainly encouraged to join." Some children were quite taken with the image of those in the service. One woman "wanted to go into the forces and wear the uniform. I remember the women in uniform, they looked very nice. I was quite interested in the army. . . ." Another explained that her "best friend and I both wanted to be WRENs [Women's Royal Canadian Naval Service]. Their uniform was better than the others . . . ." One fellow was much more pragmatic: "I was going to get forty-eight dollars a month and, of course, all the food you could eat."

With the war came the inevitability of death. Many children experienced the tragic loss of a friend or a family member because of the war. To some the war became tangible when people that they knew were killed. A woman explained that it "greatly affected us, to know someone who had died." Another declared that "it wasn't until a few of the boys we knew were killed that we really began to take it seriously." "A friend's brother was killed," explained one woman, "I remember taking it more seriously then." One woman, in grade 9 when the war began, recalled "the first death, a boy from school who had been a rear gunner." One interviewee "had a friend . . . an evacuee, when she was old enough she went back to England to enlist, but a torpedo hit the ship and she never made it." One woman remembered "a boy from our school was shot down in his plane and we really were shocked and very upset about it." Remembering his sister's boyfriend, one interviewee explained, "Melvin was killed so early in the war, it was a terrible loss and I suppose it really sobered us all up." He also told about the older boys he watched play basketball. They went to war and one "was shot down over Singapore" and the other "died in an army battle over in France. That really had an impact on m[e] . . . ." So much of an impact that he decided "to pursue University rather than signing up." When the numbers of casualties began to increase, so did concern for those overseas. A woman recalled the anxiety after her brother joined up. "We used to watch for the telegraph boy, when we saw him it was usually bad news . . . I remember being upset that my brother was away . . . always watching for the telegraph boy."

The deaths of relatives was extremely difficult for children and other family members to endure. As one woman maintained: "For the people who lost sons, they were the ones really affected." Remembering his community, one man stated: "The neighbourhood was drastically touched. A lot of families lost their sons." Children who lost a sibling realized that their parents would never recover. One interviewee revealed that her brother "was taken prisoner in Holland. He was shot for trying to escape." She remembered that her "mother took to her bed and died four years later." Recounting his brother's death, one interviewee declared: "In 1943 my brother was killed. . . . It was very sad when my brother died. . . . My mother and father were never the same after that. None of us were. They never got over it, especially my mother." As more people were reported dead what was once one man realized that "we were the privileged ones who stayed behind."

When, after six long years the end of the war finally came, many British Columbians joined in the celebrations. Both VE [Victory in Europe] Day and VJ [Victory over Japan] Day were very distinct days in most interviewee's minds. One man described VE Day: "We dropped everything and rushed out onto the street, it was total massive excitement, arms waving, people screaming and shouting, shaking hands, very exciting day and it went on all night. One woman recalled "VJ Day in the summer . . . the cars on the road were honking, and the drivers were shouting." One interviewee remembered the mood at her school: "Everyone was very excited. A lot of kids played hookey that day . . . everyone was celebrating." Another declared: "I remember VE Day because they gave us the day off at school and all the kids were excited about that." Most remembered the end of the war as a happy time. One man remarked that "it seemed like we were entering a new and wonderful world where all our problems would be solved." Another interviewee was relieved that "the war was over . . . on my eighteenth birthday, to the day. Otherwise I would have joined up . . . it was over, the pressure was off."

To other children the end of the war was not a victory but a time of devastation. One interviewee stated: "I do remember the reports of the atom bomb attacks on Hiroshima and Nagasaki. . . . An enormous amount of destruction . . . ." Another recalled the day "the bomb was dropped. We knew it would all be over soon. . . ." Recounted on interviewee, "I remember the two bombs being dropped." She described the reaction: "Everyone talked about these bombs. Some people said it was the beginning of the end. They would quote passages from the bible and say it was all over, the end of the world."

Clearly the Second World War affected children of British Columbia, having an impact on their daily lives that many still remember years later. "The war did touch all the families in my school. The neighborhood was drastically touched." Children tried to comprehend adults fear, and pains, they tried to understand a world of killing and chaos. The war infiltrated their daily lives in ways we may consider small and insignificant, but those changes would alter their childhoods. Of all the recollections and memories that were shared about growing up during a world war one aspect was clear. The lives of British Columbia's children "were terribly dislocated" during war time. "It was quite a time to live."

Notes

1. This chapter is built out of the memories of anonymous interviewees. Readers will discover my enormous debt to them.

2. British Columbia Security Commission, Government of Dominion of Canada Department of Labour, *Removal of Japanese form Protected Areas* (Vancouver: British Columbia Security Commission, 1942), 2.

3. Neil Sutherland, "'We Always Had Things to Do': The Paid and Unpaid Work of Anglophone Children Between the 1920s and the 1960s," *Labour/Le Travail* 25 (Spring 1990): 135.

9

Reflections on a Century of Canadian Childhood

Neil Sutherland

I recently completed the second of two books that deal with aspects of childhood in English Canada over the century from the 1870s to the 1960s. In the first, the formation of public policy is very much in the foreground, with the actual experiences of children serving mostly as illustrations of either needs or of experimental remedies.[1] In the second, children are very much in the foreground, with public policy towards children as a backdrop.[2] These two books, together with some less formal research on the period since the 1950s, have prompted me to describe on the continuities and changes in childhood in English Canada – and thus in British Columbia – over the span of about 120 years, from the 1870s to the 1990s.

There is a bittersweet quality to nearly all recollections of childhood. If it is a truism that childhood is one of life's happiest times, it is also a truism that children do not really appreciate this. As one of those I interviewed for the second volume put it, childhood "was the best time in my life but I didn't realize it." Since they are adults, most of those interviewed saw their own childhoods from both perspectives. In a general sense many of them, although by no means all, looked back on their childhood as times of considerable happiness and joy. People variously reported: "I had a very pleasant childhood. We were not as afflicted by the depression as most families;" and, "I had an enjoyable childhood, an active one, without many fears;" and, "I have nice memories of a great childhood;" and, "The days weren't long enough because we had so much fun" and, "Everyone seemed happy in those days."

Some people reported, however, that: "My life was not happy, generally, either at home or at school" or, "I was very unhappy at home." When the woman whose farmer father worked his children very hard reported that he had told her that "we were among the luckiest. . . . We never have to worry," there was more than just a touch of irony in her voice. On the other hand, I couldn't detect any irony in the voice of the woman who told me that the work-centred childhood experience of pioneering children "was good for us," or another with the same background who explained that "as children we had a good life." One can sympathize with those who envy others who honestly said, "This is the best time of your life"; or even the man whose working-class family spent much of the depression on relief but nevertheless claimed: "It was a great time to be in this neighborhood and a great neighborhood to be in."

But these are judgments in retrospect. At the time, children take the circumstances of their lives as givens: "We didn't know any different," as one explained. Or, as they came to know of other ways of life, they also concluded that their own circumstances were apparently immutable. In their powerlessness like children everywhere, English Canadian children over all these years had to take life as it came. If nearly all had some moments of love, of delight, of physical and mental exuberance, of great joy, they also had periods of acute boredom, of weariness, of despair, of hatred, and of anger. Only from the context provided by adulthood can they now compare their own experience with that of people who grew up in different families, or in different environments, or at different times; only now can they come to more or less objective judgments or summative evaluations of their childhoods.

What can one say, then, about continuity and change in childhood in English Canada? People's opinions on the topic – often firmly held and vigorously expressed – are to some degree influenced by where they were in their own life course. Not surprisingly, for many, the times of their our own childhoods were perhaps the *best* times to have been a child in Canada. The elderly tend to put a rosy glow not only over their own childhoods, but also sometimes an even rosier one on those of their parents and grandparents. For them, the expression "the good old days" conveys no irony. The middle-aged, with children of their own, are generally committed to the notion of "progress" that permeates our society. Their children will, or should, have the "better life" that flows from a combination of their good parenting and of "progress." Although many young adults are now deeply concerned about their own future, they too are committed to crafting a better future for their children. (We are always environmentalist when talking about our own youngsters!)

Not altogether consistently but probably not surprisingly, some people in each of these groups also employ another framework for commenting on childhood. Yes, by and large, their childhoods were better in many, mostly material and physical, ways than those of their parents. On the other hand, they see present cohorts of the young (but generally not their own children) evidencing Canada's supposed social, moral, intellectual decline.

This generally negative assessment of the present situation finds widespread support. Liberal societies are generally environmentalist in behavior if not always in belief. In consequence, much of a century or more of rhetoric surrounding childhood and public services for children has cast what currently prevails as in a critical or nearly critical condition in need of considerable reformation. Thus the children of today (whenever the "day") are "spoiled rotten." From the time in the nineteenth century that schooling became primarily a state responsibility right up to the present, the supposed failure of schools to teach the "basics" has been a perennial theme of popular discourse. The "lax" treatment of youthful offenders has been an issue for at least the same length of time.[3] Public investigations, such as those conducted by royal commissions, and professional and academic research directed at social situations, are also, at least implicitly, conducted within an alarmist framework. One is not therefore surprised to find that such investigations tend to confirm popular suppositions regarding the "decline" of the family, of the quality of education, and of other dimensions of childhood. This stance contrasts sharply with that of most front-line workers in the professions that help children, who often see themselves doing a better, more professional, job than their predecessors.

In the 1960s, and in a climate of increasing social concern if not yet one of crisis, Canadians held the first and second Canadian Conference on Children, the first Canadian Conference on the Family, and established the Vanier Institute of the Family. The research for my second volume was partially funded by the Social Sciences and Humanities Reseach Council of Canada out of its "strategic grants" programme in the area of the family and the socialization of children. This programme, initiated in the late 1970s, grew out of the Council's belief that, while the "quality of relationships within the family has a profound effect on the quality of our daily living," there were "indications that in recent years the stability of the family has deteriorated considerably with the increased incidence of divorce, adolescent pregnancies and family violence."[4]

In response to popular opinion and conventional wisdom one can, of course, apply certain objective measures to childhood over time. Public health, bacteriology, and medicare have improved enormously both the life chances and long-term physical well-being of infants and children. Cholera infantum, diphtheria, poliomyolitis, tuberculosis, measles, mumps, scarlet fever, and other illnesses rarely exact their traditional toll of youthful lives or of life-long affliction. That often-used index of a nation's social health, the rate of infant mortality, has in Canada declined from over 150 per 1 000 live births at the turn of the century to less than eight, one of the lowest in the world.[5] At a more mundane level, children suffer far fewer of the earaches, toothaches, and other causes of pain that made many childhoods miserable.

Smaller families and a higher standard of living have substantially increased the amount of family resources, both physical and emotional, that can be devoted to each child. Thus most Canadian children today live in warmer, more comfortable homes (and, much more often than predecessors, they have their own beds and even their own bedrooms), they have money to spend as they like, and are better fed and better clothed than youngsters of any earlier generation. The community makes extensive provision for their recreation and entertainment. And, despite certain arguments to the contrary, smaller classes and better educated teachers ensure that most children are better, and certainly more humanely, schooled.[6] (Those who "believe" in corporal punishment, however, point to its decline in families, and its demise in schools, as a symptom of social decay). Indeed, in the era since the Second World War we have perhaps gone some way towards "sacralizing" childhood, to employ Viviana Zelizer's vivid term for the process. By this she means that as, the economic value of children to their families declined, their emotional value increased.[7]

On the other hand, improvements in the condition of children are not distributed evenly across Canadian society. The greatest have been made in child health, the least in child and family welfare. These unevenly-distributed outcomes are a direct reflection of the amount of resources we have invested in each area. Even in the area of child health, while infant mortality has declined, this decline has not been the same for all groups. In the 1980s, for example, the infant mortality rate of the "most poor" in British Columbia was twice that of the "least poor," and that of the aboriginal population four times that of the most favored group.[8] Within the public system, the rewards of schooling still vary according to the class, sex, and ethnic group to which children belong.[9] Further, upper middle class parents can give their youngsters the added edge that comes from attending publicly-supported elitist private schools established to attract their patronage.[10]

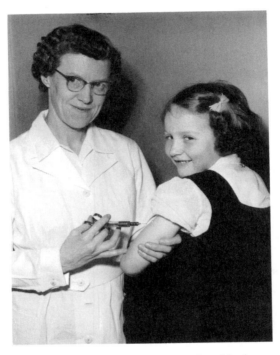

As soon as a polio vaccine was perfected in the 1950s, health authorities rushed to give it to children. (VPL, 79463)

As the stories told below vividly illustrate, poor children continue to live different lives than those who are not. Many of them are still ill-housed, ill-clothed, and often hungry. Indeed, the Canadian Institute of Child Health argues that the proportion of children living in poverty has been increasing in the last couple of decades. The Vancouver children recently interviewed by Sheila Baxter for her book *A Child Is Not a Toy* (the title in the words of an eleven-year-old girl), for example, tell the almost timeless story of what children feel about living in poverty.[12] In describing a sketch he made of a kitchen, twelve-year-old Chris told Baxter that it showed "when my mom didn't have money and we couldn't afford to buy food.... There was hardly any clothes to wear . . . I felt so sad and embarrassed when I went to school. I was afraid that kids would make fun of me. My mom was full of stress, she would sometimes cry at night thinking about the rent.... At night I would cry as well because I would be hungry...."[13]

Juanita and Billy are two "healthy-looking and well-adjusted" native Indian youngsters. They get good grades in school. They and their single parent mother, Freida, lived on welfare until she completed a manpower training programme and became employed. During their two years on welfare, the family were "binners" who searched back lane garbage bins and dumpsters with their mother for pop bottles and cans. They used the money to buy food. They also searched the dumpsters behind discount and second-hand stores. As Frieda reported, "That's where we got our kids' clothes. . . . If you find something that will fit a neighbour's child, you take that, too." Of the experience, eight-year old Billy remarked, "I don't feel bad about it, because we needed the money." Ten-year old Juanita added: " I'd rather eat than starve, even if I have to do that (binning). The welfare cheque isn't enough for three people to survive." Now their mother has an adequate income, the family doesn't go binning any more. As Juanita explains, "I leave it for the kids who really need it."[14]

Other aspects of childhood remain as they were. Most children grow up in families in which some form of the modern patriarchal order is the norm.[15] Throughout their childhood girls and boys continue to absorb traditional notions about gender identity and gender roles. "When I was 12 or 13," reported one woman, "I noticed that men and boys had life-long wishes and dreams. Girls' wishes and dreams ended with 'and they lived happily ever after.'" Nonetheless, the ideology of domesticity did change over time. Although most continued to grow up believing that family responsibilites would be the first charge on a woman's life, they also learned that this responsibility could be combined with part- or full-time work outside the home. Recently, and generally not until late adolescence or early adulthood, some women and fewer men are now beginning to question what until then they accepted as a "given" of social life; appropriate gender relationships seem always a matter of re-learning rather than initial learning.

Many children still live in emotionally cold, even abusive families. Even if families employ psychological rather than physical means of control, the former can be applied as with as much severity as the latter. If the incidence of the physical and sexual abuse of children has not increased, it also seems not to have declined very much. In *Children in English-Canadian Society,* I argued that the supposed increase in juvenile crime at the end of the nineteenth century was mostly a product of middle-class members of society establishing new standards of public order for themselves and then imposing these standards on everyone. In the same way we have now, and certainly not before time, come to circumscribe much more tightly certain kinds of physical and sexual behavior and to label them as abusive.

Many children in need of foster and or other sorts of care live lives only superficially different from those of their predecessors. Welfare and other agencies who try to help such youngsters find the structures and relationships that characterize a good child-rearing environment generally lack the resources to do so; case loads are large, neglected children often more difficult than others to rear, and foster parents minimally trained and rewarded. A few youngsters who leave or are taken from their families find satisfactory placements, but many do not. Others take to the streets.

There they seem to be as vulnerable as were the nineteenth century "waifs and strays" who attracted the attention of the child savers of that time. Now, as then, few such children find themselves in the sort of happy foster family that was Anne Shirley's.

Two examples put a human face to these conclusions. "Harry," "Alice," and "Joan," came into care in the late 1930s when, after several years of marital disagreement, their parents separated. The Vancouver Children's Aid Society placed them all in a home "where the foster father was a very kindly man, interested in his home and very fond of children." There "Joan, the younger sister, was very well liked . . . in spite of her bed wetting habits." Alice, also a bed wetter, "was considered to be 'cheeky' and disobedient, and the foster mother felt she could not keep her." In any case, illness in the foster family intervened and all three children had to move. When it was unable to place all three together, the C.A.S. separated Harry from his sisters. Over the next few years the children went through no less than five more placements. In their next home, the girls "seemed to get along quite well" but had to move when the foster parents left British Columbia. Their "enuretic difficulties" led to further moves and, in the seventh home, the social worker reported "enuresis still persists." The foster mother in this particular placement found "Alice a very sweet child who likes to help about the house" but "Joan's problems are increasing. She lies, steals food and is very high strung." Meanwhile, Harry also moved through a series of foster homes. In the fourth, the foster father had "fallen for the child" and everyone "loved him and they wished to keep him." Unfortunately, the foster father died suddenly and Harry moved on to another "superior" foster home. There, although he seemed to settle in well, he had to move again when it appeared the foster mother was developing tuberculosis. In this next home Harry, now six, began to wet the bed, much to the annoyance of the foster father. Eventually, Harry himself "asked to be taken away." In his next home he continued to wet his bed but was "loved by both foster parents" and said himself that he "wishes to marry" his new foster mother. Since the oldest of these three children was only about twelve when this record of their lives was compiled, none of them may have been in their final placement.[16]

Richard Wolfe was born in 1974. When he was four years old, his father deserted his mother and her three boys. Her task of child-rearing was exacerbated by the fact that they lived on welfare, and that she had a drinking problem. Wolfe was first arrested, for breaking and entering, when he was eight. By the time he was ten he was living on the streets and had been arrested more than twenty times before he was twelve. After each arrest, "Wolfe was simply escorted back to his mother by police officers . . . [who] could do nothing because the Young Offenders Act precludes anyone from under 12 from being arrested." In the years since he turned twelve, and was subject to jail, Wolfe has been out of institutions, mostly the Manitoba Youth Centre, for a total of only nine months, seven of which were after one of his eight escapes from the Centre.[17]

Throughout history one of the unchanging characteristics of being a child is a sense of powerlessness. Even those who were lovingly cared for occasionally felt imprisoned, bound by conditions over which they had no control, subject to the arbitrary authority of parents, teachers, and other adults often unwilling to explain or even to listen. Indeed, an all-enfolding love can sometimes form a prison. Children felt powerless in such minor matters as how they could employ their spare time to such major ones as being separated from their family and being placed in care. Such freedom that they did have was in the gift of adults, and could be withdrawn as easily as it was granted. In one perhaps extreme example, a woman I interviewed explained that the only part of her day that she could organize herself, that she could carve out for herself from the scripts of family and school, was the school's recess interval; every other minute was organized by mother or teacher.

In this context, consider the story of "Joan." Born illegitimately in British Columbia in the early 1940s, Joan lived until she was five with her maternal grandparents and their young children. According to a social worker, this "close family" then got into "very desperate straits." One upshot of their desperation was that they decided, or more likely were forced to decide, to give Joan up when she was five years old. The C.A.S. placed Joan with a foster family with whom she stayed until she was an adult. Her case file reported, "Joan had been prepared somewhat for placement, and on the drive to the foster home the worker tried to explain placement further and why she was in care." However, she "seemed quite confused . . . [and] asked numerous questions . . . was very quiet and did not smile or laugh. . . ." Years later, as an adult, Joan wrote "I remember asking why I had to leave and these were the words spoken, 'There are too many in the family now, and one has to leave, and you being the youngest are chosen.' That is stamped on my mind forever! How cruel and absurd!" Throughout her years with her foster family Joan persisted in wondering about herself, "but when I would even mention the subject [her foster parents] would freeze up, like everything in my past was a bad sin and should not be revealed to me." Although now happily married "deep down I have this awful pain. The pain of not knowing who, what or where I am."[18]

Most feelings of youthful powerlessness and the fears it often engendered were rooted in family and community circumstances. Our century, however, has been a century of war, and rumors of war, and these also impinged on many children. Those with relatives in the armed services helplessly feared and sometimes grieved. The German Pacific fleet frightened many in British Columbia early in the First World War, and Pearl Harbor and the shelling of Estevan did so in the Second. From the 1950s onward, the Cold War was never far from the minds of young people. "In Junior high school during the early 80s," wrote Airdrie Hislop, "my English teacher gave us the bleak task of writing about what we would do in the 15 minutes preceding the arrival of a barrage of Soviet nuclear warheads. I sat in front of my Keytab notebook for what seemed like hours – I was paralysed with fear."[19]

If some changes over a century or more clearly fit onto a "good" list or a "bad" list, other data requires more complex interpretation. The fact that, after decreasing for thirty or more years, the proportion of lone-parent families in Canada has returned to that prevailing in the depression is one example of complexity.[20] While some children of these families have perhaps been deprived of the benefits of being raised by both a mother and father, others have escaped from harmful situations that some of their predecessors may have had to endure in the era when some unhappy parents came or stayed together for "the sake of the children," or because the mother and children had nowhere else to go. Until recently, this latter situation was very common and certainly persists to a considerable degree.

A similar complexity surrounds the fact that in many families both parents work away from the home. If in some, especially middle class families, it is a matter of choice, in many working class ones it is clearly a matter of economic necessity. While the former usually have the means to make good alternative arrangements for their children, the latter often lack the means to do so, and the state has made only a grudging and minimal effort to assist them.[21] And, whatever the form of family in which they live, children themselves have no say in the making of it, or of its social and economic circumstances.

Perhaps even more complex is the matter of the moral education of children. According to the traditional formula and practice, moral education began in the home. Good behavior was seen to be rooted in religious beliefs. Parents instructed children in behaviors and beliefs that were often an inextricable mix of morality on the one hand and politeness and even gentility on the other. The parents of those I interviewed for my second volume laid out the ways in which they expected their children to behave. They "made it clear that parents were the authority at home and teachers at school." Thus, "you obeyed your parents"; you "did as you were told"; you didn't talk back ("we would be given a smack for talking back"); "you solved problems on your own"; you understood that "children should be seen and not heard"; you didn't "listen to adult conversation"; you "stayed out of the way when there were visitors"; you "didn't swear" or smoke ("no profanity and no smoking tolerated"); you "always washed your hands before touching a book"; you didn't lie; and you were "good losers and good sports" (because "Father would not tolerate cheaters"). Her parents (and many others), one woman stated, were strict "about manners, like chewing gum and vocabulary . . . 'a lady doesn't say that.'" Another was told, "Don't chew gum in public, don't run in the house, don't say 'what?' or 'huh!'" and, a man explained, "Mom insisted I tip my lid to ladies." Other family requirements, such as individual or family prayers, learning the Commandments or other codes of belief and practice, asking the forgiveness of parents or siblings for transgressions, and so on, were more explicitly religious and moral.

Both congregation and school extended and systematized what parents had initiated. All denominations gave religious and moral instruction to youngsters, most beginning it at a very young age. In the early years of elementary schooling what was right and wrong continued to mix moral and genteel behaviors. Separate and parochial schools systematically inculcated the moral code and set of beliefs of a very conservative Catholicism. Public schools were generally conducted in the context of a non-denominational Protestantism. There, while the difference between right and wrong were taught and appropriate behaviors enforced, religious and moral instruction displayed more variety than that in parochial schools.

Although the range of religious belief and practice in Canada has greatly expanded, many children still receive in their families and relogous institutions instruction in religiously-based moral and behavioral codes. Those who attend public schools are still expected to behave in accordance with traditional strictures in favor of honesty, kindness, politeness and generosity, and against lying, stealing, cheating, tattling, and so on. Far less often, however, are schoolchildren taught a religious basis for their behavior towards others. Secondary classes, especially those in the humanities, often focus on value questions, usually with at least an implicit commitment to a search for shared, although not necessarily religiously-based values.[22] The surveys conducted by Reginald W. Bibby and Donald C. Posterski show that adolecents who received formal religious training are more likely to affirm such values as honesty, forgiveness, and generosity than those who do not. Bibby and Posterski also point out, however, that affirmation does not necessarily translate into practice.[23]

Whether these changes in the moral education and beliefs amongst young people are evidence of a social decline is not nearly as clear, however, as some of the rhetoric surrounding the topic may suggest. On the one hand, the history of social behavior clearly shows that traditional moral inculcation may have been superficially understood and observed, and only sometimes transformed into practice. How effective, for example, were such common practice exercises or punishments as writing such lines as, "It is never too late to do good" or "Honesty is the best policy" sometimes hundreds of times? On the other, in times when social convention does not demand even superficial commitment to traditional beliefs, or even to social civility, those who do subscribe to them are perhaps more likely to put them into practice. Is ours really a less civil society than it was in the depression, in juvenile unrest at the end of the Second World War, in the turbulent late 1960s and 1970s? Are our present concerns merely the latest manifestation of the usual uneasiness that age customairly displays towards the manners and morals of youth? Our uncertainty in these matters argues that the subject is one needing both more thought and more investigation.

For most young people, the end of childhood no longer means entering the world of work and relative independence, but that of adolescence and its culture. As well as the expansion of life choices it provides, the gradual lengthening of the number of years children spent in school has given some youngsters longer periods away from such tight bonds as those imposed by abusive, tyrannical or emotionally over-possessive parents. (The current fad for home schooling – turning the family into a form of "total" institution – gives rise to the concerns that characterize all such arrangements.) Children fostered for the work they could do benefitted from a tightening of school attendance regulations. On the other hand, those of thirteen or fourteen whose entry into full-time work in earlier eras might have meant they became fairly independent now find themselves dependent through and even beyond adolescence, or even as runaways in the culture of the street. Thus a longer period of dependency may have benefitted many but not all young people.

When one moves away from these more-or-less objective criteria to more subjective ones the question as to whether the lives of children have improved, declined, or remained unchanged becomes even more difficult to resolve. In the mid-1980s, about one-quarter of grade 4 children responding to a survey reported that "most of the time" they couldn't sleep worrying about things, or had trouble making decisions, forty percent did not have confidence in themselves, and half of them felt they did not make friends easily or did not feel good about the way they looked.[24] Surely these sorts of anxieties were felt by many in each cohort of children over the years, but perhaps media and other aspects of contemporary culture have exacerbated them. Nonetheless, when one tries to compare the totality of one childhood with others at different times, one faces an insuperable task. Novelist Gabrielle Roy once posed the question: "Is it possible," she asked, "to record in a book the spellbinding powers of childhood, which can put the whole world inside the tiniest locket of happiness?"[25] At whatever period they lived, some children found innumerable "lockets of happiness" in their lives. And, at whatever period they lived, others found few. Whether they did so depended, of course, on how they were treated at home, at school, and by their peers, and perhaps even on their temperament.

Of these variables, the home was and is the most important. My interviews demonstrated with particular clarity that family conditions were the foundation of most happy and unhappy childhoods. Some children in unhappy family circumstances, however, received solace through their association with their friends and peers.[26] If the content of the discourse of the culture of childhood has changed over time – some traditional activities such as skipping and marbles have faded in importance – it remains second only to the family in crafting the emotional dimensions of growing up. School could also provide a refuge. As one person explained, "Some kids really liked school because it was the only place they had an out from wonky homes." Other children did not do well in school, did not make close friends, or fit in well with their peers; for them, the community mirrored the emptiness, the rejection, and sometimes the abuse that characterized their lives at home.

Children saw, and see, their own situation mostly as it relates to that of others in their local cohort. Although the children of welfare families are today perhaps more colorfully dressed than even their middle class counterparts of a generation or so ago, it does not mean that they feel any less about the inadequacy of their clothing, say, than did the child of the 1930s who went to school in runners but without socks. In April 1989, fourteen-year-old Steven told the Surrey, B.C. Child Poverty Forum that "I cannot afford all the designer clothes that are worn by my fellow classmates. We shop at Value Village and those clothes are used and sometimes stained and ripped, and that makes me feel like dirt."[27]

I will conclude by emphasizing another truism; that we can only live our own lives in our own times. Nonetheless, it seems clear that happiness or unhappiness in childhood is only very lightly connected to the era in which it is lived. *Growing Up* shows both happy and unhappy childhoods. They were not unique to the years described: the years before the Great War and the years after television also had, and have, many examples of both. To emphasize the point, let me conclude with two vignettes.

Writing of a moment in his life in the 1970s, when the whole panalopy of the welfare state was in place, Richard Cardinal noted, although

> I was not considered an outcast this year . . . I was halfway through the school year when a Social Worker came to our home and I was to be moved and asked me how soon I would be ready . . . and I answered, one week. I should have answered never. When I would move alone, Charlie and Linda [his brother and sister] would stay.

> I had four hours before I would leave my family and friends behind and since Linda and Charlie were at school, I went into the bedroom and dug out my old harmonica and . . . sat on the fence and began to play real slow and sad like the occasion, but before halfway through the song my lower lip began to quiver and I know I was going to cry and I was glad so I didn't even try to stop myself.[28]

Cardinal had been taken into care as a toddler and, when he committed suicide at age seventeen in 1984, he was living in his twenty-eighth placement or institution.

In 1897-98, thirteen-year-old Christina Young kept a diary. This document, written long before modern developments began to affect the children of rural families, surely displays a girl as happy (and sometimes as sad) as any girl was before, during, or after that year. On 4 October 1897, Christina wrote:

> This has been a good, good day, and I expect when we are old ladies, and our bodies have grown too feeble to move around much on the earth . . . and we wander back in our spirits to these days when we were thirteen and will find amoung them beautful days, and we'll live it all over again.[29]

Children in English-Canadian Society described the origins and development of the child-centred agenda of earlier reformers. While we may now think some elements, but by no means all, of their programme naive, surely their goal was not "to ensure for every child a fair chance to attain self-reliant and self-respecting citizenship."[30] All children still need to live in circumstances that enable them to grow and flourish in self-reliance and self-respect. For them to do so may not solve all our social problems, but might sharply reduce those rooted in childhood.

If we do take the challenge of crafting a better life for all children, we can also learn from a century or more of experience. Substantial investments in child health have brought substantial social rewards. Mediocre investments in child and family welfare have brought mostly superficial changes in the treatment of the most vulnerable of the next generation. At the beginning of this century, the Swedish social activist Ellen Keys made a widely-read appeal that the twentieth century should be "the century of the child."[31] Even though we failed to meet this goal in this century, perhaps we should try again in the twenty-first?

Notes

1. *Children in English-Canadian Society: Framing the Twentieth Century Consensus* (Toronto: University of Toronto Press, 1976).
2. *Growing Up: Childhood in English Canada From the Great War To the Age of Television* (Toronto: University of Toronto Press, 1995).

3. Research by criminologist Peter Carrington suggests that youthful crime in Canada is at about the same level as it was in 1984 before the much-maligned Young Offenders Act was proclaimed. *Vancouver Sun*, 10 May 1994, A4.

4. *The Family and the Socialization of Children: Report of the October 1979 Workshop directed by David Radcliffe . . . [at] the University of Western Ontario*, (Ottawa: Social Sciences and Humanities Reseach Council of Canada, 1980), 1.

5. Canadian Institute of Child Health, *The Health of Canada's Children: A CICH Profile* (Ottawa: The Institute, 1989), ch. 2.

6. For a vigorous articulation of this point, see William A. Hynes, "Lies, Damned Lies and Statistics," *Our Schools/ Our Selves* 33 (February 1994): 93-103; "A Good Idea and its Enemies: Part 2: The Best Kept Secrets of North American Education," *ibid.* (July 1994), 95-107.

7. Viviana A. Zelizer, *Pricing the Priceless Child: The Changing Social Value of Children* (New York: Basic Books, 1985), 11. In my view, the change has much been more one of degree than of kind. In the past, most families viewed their children as affective as well as economic assets. On the other hand, children still play a major if not necessarily monetary role in their family's economy. They are also seen as a bulwark against neglect, loneliness, and hardship in old age.

8. British Columbia, *A Report on the Health of British Columbians: Provincial Health Officer's Annual Report*, 26.

9. Bruce Curtis, D.W. Livingstone and Harry Smaller, *Stacking the Deck: The Streaming of Working-Class Kids in Ontario Schools* (Toronto: Our Schools/Our Selves Educational Foundation 1992).

10. While I generally agree with Jean Barman's argument, in "Deprivatizing Private Education" (ch. 20), that the public funds provided independent schools in British Columbia have to some extent "deprivatized" many of them, the elitist schools in their ranks have changed very little. Indeed, one could argue that public assistance has enabled such schools to increase the social if not intellectual distance between them and public schools.

11. *Health of Canada's Children*, ch. 6.

12. Sheila Baxter, *A Child Is Not a Toy: Voices of Children in Poverty* (Vancouver: New Star, 1993), especially "Interviews With Children," 42-77.

13. *Ibid.*, 48.

14. *Vancouver Sun*, 7 May 1994, B 12.

15. In nineteenth century working-class families, wives and children who worked for wages outside the home often had greater control over their lives than their absolute legal dependence might suggest. In turn, the "family wage," in which husbands and fathers were the sole supporters of their families, and which became increasing prevalent from the late nineteenth century until the 1960s, may actually have increased paternal authority. The complexities of family dynamics, however, suggest that one should generalize on this topic with great caution. For the nineteenth century working-class family, see Bettina Bradbury, *Working Families: Age, Gender, and Daily Survival in Industrializing Montreal* (Toronto: McClelland and Stewart, 1993).

16. The children's names are pseudonyms. I have not seen the confidential files in their cases. They are, however, extensively cited in Vivian Mauretta Ellis, "Multiple Placement of Foster Children: a Preliminary Study of Causes and Effects, Based on a Sample of Fifty Foster Children in Vancouver," unpublished M.S.W. thesis, University of British Colubia, 1949, 35, 62-5.

17. *Winnipeg Free Press*, 30 September 1994, B1.

18. "Joan" is a pseudonymn. I have not seen the confidential files on her case. They are, however, extensively cited in Katherine Rider, "Interviews with Former Wards," (Vancouver: Children's Aid Society of Vancouver, 1974). Fortunately, the C.A.S. eventually enabled Joan to be happily reunited with her extended family.

19. *Vancouver Sun*, 9 April 1994, D20.

20. Canada, Statistics Canada, 1981 Census, *Canada's Lone Parent Families* (Ottawa: Ministry of Supply and Services, 1984), Table 1.

21. See Alvin Finkel, "'Even the little children cooperated': Family Strategies, Childcare Discourse, and Social Welfare Debates 1945-1975," an unpublished paper presented to the Canadian Historical Association, Calgary, June 1994.

22. See, however, Donald J. Weeren, *Educating Religiously in the Multi-Faith School* (Calgary: Detselig, 1986) for some Canadian examples of efforts to add an explicitly religious dimension to such courses.

23. Reginald W. Bibby and Donald C. Posterski, *Teen Trends: A Nation in Motion* (Toronto: Stoddart, 1992), ch. 7. See also Reginald W. Bibby and Donald C. Posterski, *The Emerging Generation: An Inside Look at Canada's Teenagers* (Toronto: Irwin, 1985). Some related American literature is more alarmist. See, for example, Ken Magrid and Carole A. McKelvey, *High Risk: Children Without a Conscience* (New York: Bantam, 1988).

24. A.J.C. King, A.S. Robertson, and W.K Warren, *Canada health Attitudes and Behaviours Survey – 9, 12 and 15 year olds, 1984-85*, (Kingston, Social Program Evauation Group, Queen's University, and Health and Welfare Canada, 1985), quoted in *Health of Canada's Children*, 64.

25. Gabrielle Roy, *The Fragile Lights of Earth: Articles and Memoires 1942-1970*, Alan Brown, trans., (Toronto: McClelland and Stewart, 1982), 149.

26. Harry Stack Sullivan argued that through a close relation with a "chum" some "influences of vicious family life may be attenuated or corrected." Sullivan, *The Interpersonal Theory of Psychiatry* (New York: Norton, 1953), ch. 16.

27. *A Child is Not a Toy*, 73.

28. Richard S. Cardinal, "I Was a Victim of Child Neglect," *Edmonton Journal*, 4 August 1984; reprinted as "Alone and Very Scared" in *Native American Testimony: A Chronicle of Indian-White Relations From Prophecy to the Present, 1492-1992*, ed. Peter Nabokov (Harmondsworth: Penguin 1991), 413-18. I am grateful to Rebecca Priegert Coulter for drawing this diary to my attention.

29. Mary McKenzie, *When I Was Thirteen*, (Aylmer, Ontario: Aylmer Express, 1979), 112. Mary McKenzie was the pseudonym Christina Young employed when she first published her diary some twenty years after writing it. She was the fifth of nine children of an Ontario farm family of very modest means.

30. The words are those of pioneer child saver J.J. Kelso, quoted in *Children in English-Canadian Society*, 17.

31. Ellen Keys, *Century of the Child* (New York: Putnam, 1909).

Becoming and Being a Teacher
Part 2

10

British Columbia's Pioneer Teachers

Jean Barman[1]

British Columbia's pioneer teachers were unique in Canada. In 1872, less than a year after British Columbia entered the Canadian Confederation, legislation was passed authorizing the establishment of schools wherever a dozen or so children could be brought together. Not until 1901 was provision made to train the men and women who were expected to teach them.[2] Unlike the rest of Canada, all that was required to become a teacher in British Columbia was to pass a knowledge-based examination held annually in the provincial capital of Victoria and later also in the interior community of Kamloops. The standard was roughly equivalent to high school graduation. A mark as low as 30 percent gained a Third Class Grade B certificate good for a year, a better performance a longer-term credential and a university degree a First Class Grade A certificate valid for life. In special circumstances it was even possible to teach on a temporary certificate issued prior to taking the examination.

British Columbia's pioneer teachers were essentially self-selected. As William Burns, principal of the province's first teacher training college, or normal school, established in 1901, pointed out: "There was no requirement of actual experience in the school-room or of ability to teach."[3] Moreover, since teachers long remained in short supply, it was usually possible to obtain employment, if not in the city then certainly on the settlement frontier, if not at the start of the school year then a bit later as incumbents departed for one reason or the other. Men and women who became teachers were motivated primarily by their own needs and desires rather responding to any criteria set by the larger society or by the occupation itself.

This essay explores the motivations of British Columbia's pioneer teachers.[4] It seeks to understand why men and women chose to become teachers. Certainly, the three decades, 1872-1901, were in no way static. When British Columbia entered Confederation it was a small and fragile entity, containing about 10 000 settlers alongside 25 000 or more Aboriginal people.[5] Just eighteen teachers were needed to staff the province's fledging public schools at the beginning of the 1872 school year.[6] Only with the completion of the Canadian Pacific Railway in the mid-1880s did the settler population surpass the Aboriginal population. In the fall of 1886 the number of public school teachers reached a hundred. By 1901 the non-Aboriginal population had risen to 150 000 and the number of employed teachers grown to almost 600. Between 1872 and 1901 approximately 1 500 men and women taught in British Columbia's public schools.

As a first step in understanding teachers' motivations, the careers of all 1 500 individuals were retrieved from the Department of Education's *Annual Reports*. The manuscript censuses of 1881, 1891 and 1901 added basic demographic data for many of these men and women. The assistance of descendants has made it possible to recover fairly complete stories for about a hundred teachers, or one in fifteen.[7] For a handful, teachers' own voices have survived in the form of diaries, memoirs or correspondence. The individual teachers profiled in this essay may or may not be representative of the larger group. No evidence suggests that they were exceptional. In any event, the biographical vignettes reconstructed here provide a useful starting point for reflecting on teacher motivation.[8]

Without question, British Columbia's pioneer teachers were *not* professionals in the sense of "adhering to certain norms of conduct and belief and [being] guided by specialized knowledge in their decisions."[9] Not only did they lack distinctive training, but few of them demonstrated long-term, or even short-term, commitment to the occupation.[10] To the extent that greater commitment, if not professionalism, developed among individual teachers, it sometimes resulted from occupational longevity. Since the expectation, although not necessarily the reality, of longevity was principally associated with men teachers, due in part to general prescriptions against the paid employment of married women, such professionalism as did emerge became equated with maleness.[11]

Both men and women took up teaching for reasons that were principally short term and utilitarian. Teaching appealed precisely because it did *not* require any period of professional preparation or long-term commitment, be it (1) young women just out of school, (2) women forced to fend for themselves, (3) men in need of ready cash, (4) young people determined to get ahead, or even (5) experienced teachers.

Young Women Just Out Of School

A very considerable proportion of British Columbia's teachers over the three decades, 1872-1901, were young women just out of school. The province's first high school opened in Victoria in 1876, followed by others in New Westminster in 1884, Nanaimo in 1886 and Vancouver in 1890. The mere fact of high-school attendance presumed an interest in one of the traditional professions – law, medicine or the church – or in teaching. Since the first two required further specialized training, unavailable in British Columbia except possibly through apprenticeship, and the church was even more gender exclusive than were law and medicine, teaching became per force viewed as the logical goal for most of the young women who persevered through high school. This assumption was even legitimized through females being able to take the teacher's examination and go to work at age sixteen, whereas males had to wait to age eighteen to do so. As one daughter put the case concerning her mother, "in those days if you were good enough in school you became a teacher."[12]

The Mebius and Sylvester sisters were typical. Charles Mebius had come to the United States from Germany as a boy. He made his way west in the California gold rush of 1848 and then worked for the fur trading Hudson's Bay Company as a cooper, or barrel maker, at Fort Simpson on the north coast and at Fort Victoria. By the time of his marriage to a young Irish girl, Jeannette Martin, in 1864 he had established himself in Victoria as a cooper. After Jeannette's father was lost at sea, her mother had earned a living teaching in a village school in Ireland, and Jeannette had come out to Vancouver Island as governess to a minister's family.

So it is not surprising that two of the four Mebius daughters turned to teaching. As put by one of their daughters, "teaching has been a family tradition." Lucy Mebius was just seventeen when she got her first job, at Nanaimo in 1884. Despite such harsh realities as seventy pupils enrolled in an early class, she would remain a teacher there for over forty years, until her death in 1925. In 1889 Lucy was joined in the occupation by her younger sister Jeannette, then also seventeen and fresh from winning the Governor General's Medal for top academic performance at Victoria high school. Despite the accomplishment, higher education was out of the question, given that the province possessed neither a normal school nor a university. So Jeannette, perhaps a bit reluctantly, followed her older sister's lead. Jeannette, described by her niece as "tall and blondish, kind and fun loving," would remain restless. She moved between half a dozen schools on Vancouver Island until her marriage over a decade later to a man she met while teaching at Beaver Creek near Alberni.[13]

The Sylvester sisters' background was similar. Their father had come to the Pacific Northwest six years after Charles Mebius, exemplifying Vancouver Island's transition from a fur trading outpost to a gold rush colony. Frank Sylvester, acting as agent for a brother-in-law in San Francisco, was the first recorded Jewish arrival in Victoria among the thousands of newcomers in the heady summer months of 1858. Within a year his small Victoria store had failed, and he set out for the gold fields. Frank returned no richer to the British colony's capital city, where he worked as an accountant for a Jewish auctioneer who had arrived in 1862 with his family via the gold fields of Australia and California. Frank courted the auctioneer's pretty young daughter Cecilia for several years until they finally wed in 1869 when she was twenty-one.

Frank and Cecilia Sylvester became the parents of five girls and three boys, all of whom were encouraged to obtain as good an education as had each of their parents. Frank Sylvester had reputedly won the first prize for literature given in the New York City schools before setting out with his sisters overland by stage to California. Cecilia had by chance followed the headmistress of her private French-language school in San Francisco, Madame Pettibeau, north to Victoria, where she simply re-enrolled in her new school. According to the eldest Sylvester daughter, Elizabeth, the eight Sylvester children were expected to make good use of their schooling and go "to work as soon as they were able." Educated along with her sisters at the best Victoria private school of the day, Catholic St. Ann's Academy, Elizabeth began teaching in 1886 at age seventeen. After a brief stint in the Cowichan Valley, she worked in

Victoria until her marriage at age thirty-four. Only at the age of twenty-three-years-old did Louisa Sylvester follow her older sister into teaching. She first moved on an annual basis or even more frequently from one small frontier school to another — Ducks, Grand Prairie, Galiano Island, Round Prairie, Lumby, Metchosin and so on — but on her sister's marriage took over her job in Victoria, which she held until her retirement.[14]

About the time that the Mebius and Sylvester sisters were becoming teachers, British Columbia was undergoing a demographic transformation. The completion of the transcontinental railroad brought a shift in teachers' origins. Previously most teachers, if not born in British Columbia itself, came either from Britain or from the Maritimes whose poor economy encouraged the westward migration of the most ambitious of the younger generation. The proportion of British Columbia teachers born in Ontario had originally been under one in ten, but by 1891 it mushroomed to over a third, and another sizable proportion came from the United States. While young men arriving with their families often assisted their fathers in homesteading or setting up a business, many young women just out of school turned to teaching, particularly on finding out that it required no specialized training as was probably the case whence they came.

Typical were Jane Higginson, Carrie Ogle and Phoebe McInnes. Jane's grandfather had emigrated from Ireland to an Ontario farm in 1819, whence his ninth and youngest son was drawn westward on the completion of the CPR. Once Charles Higginson found the land he wanted at Sardis in the Fraser Valley, he brought out his family composed of three sons and nine-year-old daughter Jane. The children went to the school at nearby Chilliwack of which Jane's father soon became a trustee. There Jane studied for the provincial teacher's examination, which she proudly took in the summer of 1898 at age 16 and shortly thereafter received her Second Class Grade B certificate in the mail. Perhaps through her father's influence or perhaps simply because the local population was growing rapidly and Chilliwack school in need of additional teachers, Jane Higginson was soon employed as a teacher at the very same school where she had been a pupil. She married in 1904.[15]

In 1892 Carrie Ogle's family moved north from Nebraska to take over the general store and then the post office at Sardis, but fifteen-year-old Carrie was left behind with her older sister to finish school. As indicated by a graduation program still proudly retained by her daughter, Carrie completed high school in Beatrice, Nebraska, in May 1893 with honors in Latin before following her family to the Fraser Valley. Within the year she had passed the teacher's examination and was working at nearby Dewdney. Asked why Carrie had chosen that route, her daughter responded, "In those days if you were good enough in school you became a teacher." Adventurous if diminutive at 4'10" and 90 pounds, Carrie taught at Burton on Arrow Lake and then at Hat Creek in the southern interior where she later recalled "thrashing" an ill-behaved young man two feet taller than herself. Four years later her mother's illness forced Carrie to return home to help out in the family store. What Carrie Ogle's daughter remembers as a "love of teaching" probably was responsible for her continuing to renew her teaching certificate until she married a recent English immigrant in 1901.[16]

In similar fashion, Phoebe McInnes came with an extended family clan from Ontario to Langley in the Fraser Valley. Although fortunate enough to get a job at the local school which her father had helped to build, Phoebe indicated through the diary she kept during her third year of teaching, 1901, that her interests lay elsewhere. Despite, or perhaps because of, an affirmation that "this diary is supposed to contain all the events which have any bearing on my life," it mentioned her days spent in the classroom only in reference to a trustee's "deep regrets at the low attendance," the annual spring "Public Exam" and such observations as "getting pretty tired teaching" and "Just 4 more weeks of school!" Phoebe was far more interested in going "for a spin on my wheel after school" or going "to Blaine on my wheel," buying "a sailor & veil" in Vancouver or a "foulard dress" in Blaine, and playing "Courtship and Marriage a silly game." Her principal worry was she might end up an "old maid," hardly likely given her very active social life. Indeed, Phoebe McInnes quit teaching the next year at the age of twenty-three and soon married.[17]

Women Forced To Fend For Themselves

However much teachers like Phoebe McInnes might have enjoyed the perks of a bicycle and ready cash to spend on themselves, they did not absolutely have to work for a living, as did some of their female contemporaries. In a largely male world of paid employment the occupation of teaching, together with nursing and office work, were among their most attractive options. Again, teaching's immediacy of access enhanced its appeal.

Janet Wilson, orphaned in Ontario at age thirteen, was educated in a Catholic convent and at the Toronto normal school. Janet decided in 1888, aged twenty-one, to join her brothers already gone west and so simply answered a newspaper ad for a teaching position at Hope. She soon found herself being met off the transcontinental train at Yale by two Indian guides who put both her and all her worldly goods in their canoe and headed down the mighty Fraser River to Hope. Janet revelled in frontier conditions, learned to ride horseback and soon gave up boarding, which was the general rule for female teachers, to set up house on her own. She taught three years in Hope before heading for Vancouver where her brothers had settled and where she become, according to her daughter, "the first female ever to work on the C.P. Telegraph office on Hastings Street." It was there that Janet Wilson met her future husband, a Morse code operator.[18]

The two oldest of the five Robertson sisters, from Sidney on Vancouver Island, turned to teaching while "still teenagers themselves" in order to support their younger siblings on their parents' death within a short time of each other in 1894. Maude took the teacher's examination that very summer, Jessie two years later. Although the family was not Catholic, the two youngest sisters, Gertrude and Ethel aged three and five, were sent to board at St. Ann's Academy in Victoria. According to a daughter, they "hated every minute of it" and eventually ran away to Maude and Jessie, who then cared for the two youngsters. Two other Robertson sisters, Ethel and Janet, also became teachers.

Between them the Robertson sisters taught in a host of small one-room schools on Vancouver Island and in the Kootenays and central interior, becoming known for their adventuresome spirit. Ethel Robertson later recalled how, "A year after the turn of the century, I went to the Education Office in Victoria to see if there were any vacant schools." From a choice of two, she accepted Athelmere. "Now, how do I reach Athelmere. The only information I received was 'go to Golden,' then I went to the C.P.R. office, received the same information. 'Go to Golden.' So I went to Golden." At the local hotel she was informed that there were two ways to get to Athelmere, by stage or by boat. "I was anxious to start school the following Monday so decided to take the boat." This meant leaving 1 a.m. on Friday on a small sternwheeler whose "captain and crew were not anxious to have lady passengers on board but they kindly fitted up a bed on the dining room table" which Ethel then had to leave at 4 a.m. so the crew could have breakfast. The sternwheeler reached Athelmere on Sunday afternoon. "Quite a few to meet the boat or maybe to see the School Marm." Ethel soon discovered that her "School was the community hall and after a dance the wooden desks would slide on the waxed floor."

Sisters Gertrude, Maude, Ethel, Jessie and Janet Robertson, of whom all but Gertrude became teachers.

Whereas Ethel Robertson had only a handful of pupils at Athelmere, her sister Jessie would tell stories, possibly with a touch of exaggeration, of teaching seventy children in a one-room school at Matsqui, many of them recent Norwegian immigrants speaking no English. Jessie is remembered in family lore for having ridden eight kilometres each way each day by bicycle from Nanaimo to teach at Departure Bay and for playing saxophone for the dances held in the local school house. Even after Jessie married, she retained her commitment to teaching and, while living in Williams Lake with her gold commissioner husband, both ran a kindergarten and gave piano lessons. As summed up by a grandson, the Robertson sisters "were real pioneers in the opening up of some very remote parts of the province."[19]

Other women, such as Dora Fowler and Carolina McLellan, opted for teaching over less agreeable alternatives. Dora Fowler's mother died when she was two and by the time she was twelve the Fowlers had moved from Ontario to a remote area of Manitoba and her stepmother expected Dora, to quote her daughter, "to do a large share of the work." Dora escaped to a married sister in Brandon and then to a brother in Winnipeg where she obtained a teacher's certificate. Dora taught in several small prairie schools, but again her family put pressure on her, this time to marry a courting Presbyterian minister. To quote her daughter, Dora, at age twenty-five, "was by now, they considered, practically an old maid." So Dora escaped west to British Columbia and taught in the last years of the century at Tobacco Plain and Elko before marrying a man of her own choosing and settling down in nearby Fernie.[20]

Not unlike Dora Fowler, Carolina McLellan followed a widowed father and his family west from Ontario and, on finding herself keeping house for two brothers farming in North Dakota, "decided teaching would be easier," to quote her daughter. Even though Carolina had only a grade 8 education, she passed the British Columbia teacher's examination and in 1891 got a job in Surrey. By this time her father and family were living at Blaine and, according to a daughter, "each morning she would walk across the border the 2 ½ miles to the school." Carolina's diary has survived and, unlike that of Phoebe McInnes, reveals a strong interest not only in her pupils but in the methodology of teaching, as attested by such entries as "Pronounce before spelling" and "When a mistake is made stop right there until that is corrected if nothing else is done." Other entries reflected the contemporary emphasis on order: "Stand straight"; "March to seats"; "Stand when answering a question." Discipline was a priority for Carolina. When "Fred laughed immoderately," he had his seat changed. Two days later, "Wilbert caused a little trouble wrestling with F. [Fred] and S. and I kept him in." And so on. "Mary Thrift pricked Gustave with a pin and had to stand in the corner." Over time Carolina gained confidence: "I'm learning when to smile in the schoolroom without damaging my dignity." Carolina McLellan's teaching career ended with her marriage in 1897 at age twenty-seven.[21]

In British Columbia as elsewhere, married women were seldom deemed suitable to be in the classroom. The exceptions arose either out of trustees' desperation to secure a teacher or the equal desperation of married women in need of paid employment. Fanny Nias Richards and Clara Smith Starret faced comparable situations, the first because she had lost a husband, the second because she left one.

Fanny Nias was the daughter of a well-connected Englishman who had edited one of San Francisco's first newspapers during the California gold rush and then come north in 1858 to begin one of Vancouver Island's earliest newspapers, the *Victoria Gazette*. Fanny married at seventeen but a year later, in 1871, she found herself widowed and pregnant. Her father having also fallen on hard times, Fanny Richards decided to get a teacher's certificate in order to support herself and her infant son. In 1873 she became the second teacher at Hastings Mill, a logging settlement that would a dozen years later become the city of Vancouver. First boarding just outside of the mill gates and then living with her son in a cottage behind the school, she struck up an acquaintance with a young accountant and engineer serving as a trustee to the Moodyville school located on the north side of Burrard Inlet. According to his biographer, Ben Springer "made a point of discussing educational matters with the attractive young widow as often as possible." Remarried in 1874 in what was the first recorded wedding in nearby Granville, the elegant Fanny Springer went on to "set the social tone for the Inlet" into the next century.[22]

Clara Smith Starret had two teaching careers, one before and one after marriage. "Nurtured in a cultivated atmosphere," to quote her granddaughter, Clara Smith went to high school in New Westminster and then followed in her mother's footsteps to become a teacher. Just sixteen, she taught briefly at Hope before marrying there in 1885 "in the face of her parents' objections." Her husband of over twice her age was a true frontier adventurer, and the Starrets had four children before, to quote a son, he "lost his job as road superintendent and had to eke out a living as a stump rancher." Life was hard, and the growing friction between the Starrets was visible to their son.

> She was a very determined person, rather strong-willed, and so was my father. He should have got married before thirty instead of after. . . . The ranch didn't pay off, either, just the same as any other stump ranch, and my mother needed money to buy new shoes and clothing and one thing and another. She objected to getting them on credit; she didn't want to wear the storekeeper's clothes, she explained to me. . . . So she thought she'd better go back to school teaching. . . . So my mother gathered up the rest of us and took us to Victoria, left us with her people and started teaching.

In 1899 Clara Smith Starret got a job at Bella Coola on a hastily arranged temporary certificate, possibly given to her as a married woman because of her willingness to work in that very remote coastal settlement of recent Norwegian immigrants. Clara would teach at a number of similarly isolated locations, including a stint at Metlakatla Indian school, before embarking on yet another challenge. In 1909, using money saved up from teaching, she joined with a son to open a fur trading post on Babine Lake beyond Hazelton. Only on her husband's death in 1923 did Clara return to the Fraser Valley. For Clara Starret, as for Fanny Richards and other women, teaching provided a critical lifeline even after marriage.[23]

Men In Need Of Ready Cash

Teaching's immediate utility for desperate married women like Fanny Richards and Clara Starret was not that different from the instrumental role that the occupation played for young, middle-aged and even elderly men in need of ready cash. For John McMillan teaching proved time and again to be a lifesaver. One of ten children of a New Brunswick farm family, he had gone straight from high school into teacher training, but rather than get a job he had in 1877 matriculated at the University of New Brunswick. His parents wanted him to become a minister, so after receiving his B.A. in classical languages, he had gone off to the University of Edinburgh to study theology. Home on holiday, John botched his parents' plans by courting a young woman against their wishes. Likely in need of money to marry, he went west to Manitoba in 1883 where he acquired a Manitoba teacher's certificate and may have taught briefly before returning home to obtain a New Brunswick teacher's certificate and to marry. About 1890 John followed his father-in-law west to Vancouver, where he turned once again to teaching as, to quote his son, "just a case of survival" in order to support a growing family that would eventually total nine children. John McMillan's university degree meant that he qualified for a First Class Grade A certificate, and this undoubtedly gave him a boost, as did four years' teaching experience, to secure a first job at the Vancouver East Public School instead of at one of the many one-room schools dotted around the province. In 1894 John decided to quit teaching to open a small grocery store on East Hastings. Bad economic times soon forced him back into the classroom, but this time the best he could do was Gibsons on Howe Sound. Pleasure over being able to "shoot a deer in the backyard and get a salmon in the bay in a few minutes" was offset by having to leave all his family except for two older sons back in Vancouver. In one of his letters home he waxed philosophical to his wife: "I would like to have a place where I might be more helpful at the house, but I suppose we must be patient. I feel that this is not the ideal home, still it is not as bad as it might be." Two years later John was rewarded with a teaching job at Moodyville in North Vancouver.

The economics of survival as opposed to any sense of longterm commitment may have repeatedly put John McMillan back into the classroom, but he was nonetheless committed to the enterprise and used his academic training to best advantage. At the annual meeting of the Mainland Teachers' Institute held in Vancouver in January 1894, he gave the opening reading. His surviving notes on "the propriety of giving systematic instruction in Temperance," a topic of considerable interest during these years, make a systematic and persuasive argument for teaching "the chemical constituents of and properties of alcohol and its injurious influences upon the functional organs of the body" as part of the existing school subjects of Chemistry and of Physiology and Hygiene.

> By educationalists it is understood to be the duty of every instructor of youth not only to cultivate in them the powers of language, memory, attention, imagination and reason; but also, so far as possible, to call into action the moral power, to train the feelings, to exercise the sentiments and emotions. The sentiments require to be cultivated until they form habits. . . . Intellectual knowledge in respect to alcohol is a necessary accompaniment to the habit of temperance.

John McMillan died accidentally in 1905.[24]

For Raffles Purdy, teaching was a necessary backdrop to the freedom in lifestyle that he primarily sought. One of ten children of an English stone carver, "he couldn't," according to his daughter, "see himself chipping away at a bit of stone or wood, so took up teaching." He got a job in London, but was so captivated by signs "advising people to 'Come to the new Land, just tickle the soil with the spade and it smiles with the harvest'" that he gave it up at age twenty-one to emigrate with his sister and family to Nebraska. The first year lived up to expectations with "potatoes as big as a man's head," but the second year there was "a terrible plague of locusts, 7 miles wide, which ate everything green in sight." So they decided to try British Columbia, and in San Francisco purchased a sailing sloop and headed up the coast with "all their worldly goods" including five children. Like so many arrivals during these years, what Raffles

198 Becoming and Being a Teacher

Purdy and his relatives sought was land of their own, and they found it in the summer of 1884 on Saltspring Island. Soon the local trustees were pursuing Raffles to teach, since they had "such trouble keeping lady teachers, as they were in great demand by the single men." He agreed to take on the school at Vesuvius for "$50 a month, which he thought at the time was a handsome salary," while also preempting 125 acres across the bay for fifty cents an acre, clearing the land on weekends and planting an orchard. Yet Raffles Purdy is remembered on Saltspring as "a highly certified teacher and an outstanding man." "He instructed eight grades and, if a youth had the potential and inclination, Mr. Purdy would educate him through to university entrance." Raffles continued his dual occupations for a dozen years until he was able to pursue his first love of farming full-time. This he did in solitary fashion for a decade and a half until he and his sister went back to England for a visit, where he met a woman that he married at age fifty.[25]

The experience of Alexander Shaw was particularly quixotic. Born in Scotland in 1833, he had been forced to go to work as a shepherd at age fourteen to support a widowed mother. In 1870 he emigrated to Ontario with his wife and family, in part to give his children a better education than he himself had been able to obtain. In the mid-1880s Alexander Shaw, his pregnant wife and eight children joined the westward movement to British Columbia. By then fifty years old, Alexander worked briefly as a telegraph operator at Yale before taking up farming on Gabriola Island only to find the local school closed for lack of a teacher. So he took matters in his own hands. Finding out that no formal training was necessary to become a teacher, Alexander wrote off to Victoria for the necessary high school texts, studied in the evenings and the next summer rowed off to Victoria to take the qualifying examination. Reopening the Gabriola school in 1881, Alexander quickly discovered the advantages of having a cash income and so the next year took along two of his grown sons, and they too passed the teacher's examination. Whereas Alexander Junior would only teach a year on Gabriola before going on to other things, John Shaw taught in Nanaimo for over two decades. For his part Alexander Senior soon became bored with a settled existence and headed off on another adventure, using his savings from teaching to begin a company to provide electricity to Nanaimo. On the company's insolvency, Alexander Senior once again took the teacher's examination. This time he combined teaching, at first just outside of Nanaimo and then at Beaver Creek near Alberni, with being a farmer, local postmaster and lay preacher. When numbers at Beaver Creek fell below the minimum to keep the school open, Alexander Senior simply persuaded some of his grandchildren to come live with him. Only deafness at age seventy-five finally forced Alexander Shaw Senior out of the classroom.[26]

Young People Determined To Get Ahead

Other men and women consciously and deliberately used teaching as a stepping stone toward what they really wanted out of life. To the reasonably well educated young person desirous to build up the necessary capital to get ahead, teaching's immediacy of access and assurance of a cash income made it particularly attractive.

George Dockrill taught first in Ontario and then in New Westminster in the late 1880s before entering Dalhousie Law School.[27] Arthur Proctor farmed part time while teaching at Alberni, also in the late 1880s, so as to save up even faster to become a medical doctor.[28] Arthur Currie, frustrated in studying law or medicine by his father's death, trained in Ontario as a teacher and taught during the 1890s at Sidney and Victoria before switching to real estate and in the First World War achieving military prominence.[29] John Tolmie went in the mid-1890s from a first job at BC Sugar's factory in Vancouver to the relatively greater comfort of teaching school at Steveston, nearby Mud Bay and Salmon Arm in order to finance medical school.[30] Garfield King taught at Lac La Hache, Langley Prairie, Fort Langley and Victoria late in the century prior to becoming a leading Vancouver lawyer.[31] Harvey Watson, enticed from the outskirts of Toronto to the Okanagan Valley by an elder brother already in the classroom, similarly used the occupation as a stepping stone, in his case to become first a newspaper editor during the Kootenays mining boom and then a successful real estate agent in the Collingwood area of Vancouver. Older brother Fred soon also quit the classroom to return to Ontario, since, as Harvey's daughter put it, teaching was "just a young man's world at that time."[32]

The view of teaching as a young person's game was also held by the Bannerman and Goostrey bothers. The Bannermans had on their father's death in Ontario in 1884, to quote a granddaughter, "headed off to the 'golden west' to seek their fortunes." The "fortunes" that William aged twenty-eight, Alexander aged twenty-six and John aged twenty, found in British Columbia came via the classroom. William had attended normal school and already taught several years in Ontario. He worked half a year at Cedar Hill and three years at Barkerville in order to save the necessary funds to attend Princeton Theological Seminary preparatory to a career first as a Presbyterian missionary in Gabon and Sitka and then as a clergyman in the United States. His long-term intent to use teaching in instrumental fashion is suggested in the observation in his obituary that "in early life he consecrated himself to the service of Christ and the Church."

The younger Bannerman brothers followed suit, both becoming teachers on temporary certificates almost as soon as they arrived in British Columbia and eventually abandoning the occupation. Alexander taught on Mayne Island and at Colwood and Craigflower, where he married a local girl who just a few years earlier had been a pupil at the school. The newlyweds lived in the teacherage on the second floor of Craigflower School, and it was there that their first child was born. Alexander had always considered teaching to be "a stop-gap," and about this time decided that he had to get on in the world, and went to work for a Victoria grocer before opening up his own business. The youngest of the Bannerman brothers, John, may have been the most restless. He taught at Metchosin, Colwood and Enderby before going to work on a survey party and then as a teamster and horse breeder during the Kootenays mining boom of the late 1890s. Still seeking his "fortune," in 1905 John and his growing family moved to Hornby Island to farm and to horse log, five years later they moved to Denman and on to Comox and then Abbotsford. Later he ran "a little country grocery store" just north of Bellingham.[33]

The father of the Goostrey brothers was drawn north to British Columbia from Nebraska in the late 1880s by the promise, in the words of a granddaughter, of a "good supply of cheap land" for his four sons. "Sadly none of them shared his ambition." After a brief venture into agriculture the eldest James taught at Langley Prairie, where a younger brother was among his first pupils. In the meantime James' brother George, who had made an attempt at farming near Ladner, was kicked in the knee by a horse. After two out of three doctors advised removing his leg simply because he had a stiff knee, George decided to ignore their advice and become a doctor himself. According to his daughter, to do so "he had to earn some money and so he got into teaching." Even though he clearly perceived his job in the little log school at South Aldergrove as a short-term venture, George enjoyed the challenge, writing to a brother in 1899: "Well I am training the young minds to study; have about twenty pupils and like it very much. Of course it is hard work (brain work I mean)." George Goostrey attended medical school in San Francisco and became a family doctor in the Grandview area of Vancouver. What we do not know is whether or not George's older brother might have persevered as a teacher, for John Goostrey died of tuberculosis in 1901, contacted from a local farm family with whom he boarded after getting tired of "batching."[34]

For the young person determined to get ahead, considerable perseverance was sometimes necessary. John Duncan MacLean, born in 1873 the son of a Prince Edward Island farmer, had his hopes of advanced education dashed by his father's demand that he assist the family economy by teaching school. At age nineteen, John left home, working his way west by teaching on the prairies. He sought his fortune in Vancouver, but was soon back in the classroom. After a dozen years teaching at Mount Lehman and Mission, John joined the Kootenays mining rush of the late 1890s, but financial difficulties again forced him to take a teaching job. As he later wrote, "Rossland was the centre of big activity and the home of some very fine people, but school teaching in a mining town in those days was not particularly lucrative." So, "I decided to make the plunge" to become a doctor. As soon as finances permitted, he enrolled at McGill University. John Duncan MacLean returned to the Kootenays to practice until his election as an MLA, whence he would become Minister of Education and then premier on the death of John Oliver in 1927.[35]

It was not young men alone who used teaching to get ahead in life. Margaret Burns, the only daughter alongside eight sons of a provincial school inspector, was determined from a young age to achieve the medical career which her father felt he had been denied by family circumstance and fate. Margaret taught during the 1890s at Wellington and Rossland and then in Vancouver, but only in order to gather together the finance to study medicine in Los Angeles and then practice in Ogden, Utah.[36]

Comparable in their determination to succeed were Thomas and Belle Wilson, a married couple who taught across the British Columbia interior during the 1890s – North Thompson, Ferguson, Trout Lake and so on. At the same time the Wilsons were using home study and practical courses in the summer holidays at Portland Medical College to earn their separate medical degrees. First practicing medicine and running a drug store at Port Essington on the remote north coast, in 1909 Thomas and Belle Wilson moved to the Mount Pleasant area of Vancouver. There they had a joint medical practice in the Lee building on the corner of Main and Broadway while also raising two sons to become doctors, a daughter a nurse. The Wilsons' experience confirms the observation of a longtime British Columbia teacher that during this early time period, "teaching was often used as a stepping stone to other professions."[37]

Experienced Teachers

As the above vignettes indicate, numerous men and women came to British Columbia with teaching credentials and in some cases considerable experience. The examples of Ivar Fougner and William Burns demonstrate that such experience did not necessarily equate to commitment to teaching as a profession. Ivar Fougner had already graduated from a Minnesota normal school and taught two years before heading west in 1894 with a party of fellow Norwegian immigrants to establish the colony of Bella Coola. Although he taught there off and on until appointed Indian Agent in 1909, his diary reveals ongoing ambivalence toward the occupation. On his first day of teaching in a tent, he only observed, "Same as usual, nothing new about the business." As time passed he was penning such comments as "Finished my school yesterday; that made me feel exceedingly happy yesterday afternoon – rather too much so," and "Sometimes I feel painfully for some other kind of work."[38]

William Burns arrived in British Columbia as a middle-aged man firmly ensconced as a career teacher, but he was possibly no more committed than Ivar Fougner to teaching as a profession. Burns had wanted to become a medical doctor but his father, who ran an English private school, determined that young William would follow his footsteps, a course made inevitable when his father's health began to deteriorate and he had to take over the school. As William Burns later wrote, "It has ever been a matter of regret that I did not attend the University but my father ever forbade me to leave, I was too useful and he would not spend any money on my education." Eventually William emigrated to Ontario, by this time possessed of a wife and seven children. He continued to teach, but was determined to get the further education denied him in England. At about age forty-five he obtained his bachelor's degree from Queen's University through taking examinations over a five-year period while being excused from attending classes. This was followed in 1891 by the offer of an inspectorship in British Columbia.

> During the next 5 years I wandered on duty over the whole of the inhabited part of B.C. gaining considerable experience, notoriety and geographical knowledge. In 1897, the government considered it advisable to divide the Province into 4 Inspectorates on account of the increasing number of schools and I was sent to No. 4 Inspectorate, with headquarters at Nelson, Kootenay. My district covered 11 000 square miles, so that to visit the schools, there was constant travelling.

William Burns' travels convinced him of "the absolute necessity for a Normal School for training our teachers," and when an institution was finally established he played a part.

> In January, 1901, the Government opened a Normal School in Vancouver and Insp. Wilson was appointed Principal. In three weeks he had to resign and I was summoned from Revelstoke to come to Vancouver and take charge for 6 months until a principal could be appointed in July, 1901, and I retained this position until 1st of September, 1920, when after a severe illness I resigned, receiving the superannuation to which I was entitled for services.

While William Burns made teaching his career, retiring only at age seventy-seven, throughout his life he likely viewed teaching as a lesser goal: only one of his nine children, Margaret, followed his lead and then only in order to secure the finance necessary to pursue the medical career denied her father. As William Burns summed up at the end of his memoir, "I was compelled by force of circumstances to 'teach.'"[39]

Certainly, not all long-time teachers were as ambivalent toward the occupation as Ivar Fougner and William Burns may have been. Alfred Henry Poltair Matthew and Ellen Lawson exhibited lifetimes of commitment, if not also professionalism. Coming to Ontario from England as a small boy, Alfred worked for his father in construction. According to his granddaughter, "he had to do his studies for his teacher's certificate alone at night by candle-light as his father wanted him to be a carpenter." By 1891 married with two daughters, he answered "the call of opportunity in the West" and for over two decades taught across the Fraser Valley. Then, "at the persuasion of his wife, who was ill and tired of moving around," he gave up teaching for a bookkeeping job, nonetheless "he always had a book in his hand or pocket, and taught students in his home as hobby classes." "If he could get a group together to study with him no subject was neglected."[40]

The Lawson sisters came out to British Columbia from Prince Edward Island in 1890 when their father became editor of the Victoria *Colonist* newspaper. He had started out as a "teacher in a backwoods school" and clearly considered it an acceptable occupation. Maria had already taught in Prince Edward Island for two decades and continued to do so – at Rocky Point outside of Victoria, Nanaimo and Victoria – until her talent at writing made it possible for her to work full-time as a journalist. Following in her father's footsteps, she was employed from 1910 to 1922 at the *Colonist* as women's editor and editor of the weekend children's page. While Maria Lawson's younger sister Fanny only taught briefly on Pender Island before she married a local man, Ellen became a career teacher in Victoria, to be remembered by a six-year-old at the end of the First World War as having always "sat or stood ram-road straight in a suit-coat above a long skirt below which high-laced leather foot-wear disappeared somewhere up the calf." "Her hair was always piled high on the top of her head and her pince-nez spectacles were supported by a little chain." "Miss Lawson was the epitome of the Victorian-Edwardian governess spinster." Ellen Lawson was truly committed to teaching as a career. Indeed, according to a niece: "Aunt Nell was a very determined woman. The school board didn't superannuate her until age seventy. She clearly thought she should go on teaching. So she went to bed and wouldn't get out."[41]

Reflections

The contribution of British Columbia's pioneer teachers is undisputed. Without formal teacher training except for what they brought with them from elsewhere, they educated thousands of young British Columbians to levels probably not that different from what was achieved elsewhere in North America. In doing so they demonstrated remarkable resourcefulness and responsiveness to often difficult circumstances. British Columbia's pioneer teachers were tough men and women willing to accept a challenge and make a go of it. Men like Alexander Shaw and William Burns and women like Janet Wilson, Ethel Robertson, Dora Fowler and Clara Starret were true pioneers. Limited commitment to the occupation over the long term probably did not much diminish the commitment that they demonstrated in the short run toward their charges in the classroom. Some, like Jessie Robertson and Alfred Matthew, retained that commitment to teaching long after they left the classroom. British Columbia's pioneer teachers like John McMillan and Raffles Purdy used the system to their own advantage but also to the advantage of their pupils.

A number of the men and women whose stories have been recounted here, and many others, did make the occupation their life's work. Lucy Mebius taught for over forty years in Nanaimo, Louisa Sylvester taught an equal length of time in a variety of frontier schools that might have deterred any young woman. Even some of those women who married had very long careers before so doing. Jeannette Mebius taught for over a decade, Elizabeth Sylvester for almost two decades. Other men and women gave up teaching only reluctantly. Carrie Ogle did so in order to assume family responsibilities when her mother became ill, Alfred Matthew to appease an ailing wife. Indeed, the latter's attitude toward teaching was probably more professional than many of these who remained longer at the job. Men as disparate in background as Ivar Fougner and William Burns shared an ambivalence toward teaching that had little to do with the number of years spent in the occupation. Neither Carolina McLellan nor Phoebe McInnes stayed that long as teachers, yet the former's diary entries demonstrate both concern and commitment to her responsibilities as a teacher whereas the latter's entries make a different statement.

Many men and women used teaching as a stop gap or as a source of ready cash to support a preferred lifestyle. If few were as explicit as Phoebe McInnes in her diary, these individuals nonetheless reveal through their relatively short duration in the occupation some sense of its utility. This was particularly the case for young men possessed of far more life options than had their female contemporaries. John McMillan and Raffles Purdy may or may not have been good teachers, but they were not professionals since for them the occupation remained a means rather than an end in itself. The reasons for this lack of commitment went beyond the individuals themselves. Even where men like John Duncan MacLean repeatedly gave teaching an opportunity to prove itself, the occupation could not satisfy male aspirations. As one close observer has summed up, "While I suppose there were many personal reasons for young men abandoning teaching I suppose the over-riding ones would be the very modest salaries paid and limited opportunities in one-room ungraded schools located in isolated communities."[42] Although the extent to which training in a normal school could overcome these fundamental constraints of frontier society is questionable, at the least the training made the more committed aware of the cluster of attitudes, dispositions and skills expected of them that would over time turn an occupation into a profession.

Vancouver's first high school teachers: George Robinson, James Shaw, John Kerr, Joseph Henry and Alexander Robinson. (from **The First Fifty Years: Vancouver High Schools 1890-1940***, Vancouver, 1940)*

Even before the establishment of a normal school, other factors were dramatically altering the character of teaching. As a consequence of rapid population growth, important differences were emerging across British Columbia, both between schools and between teachers. On the one hand were the small one-room schools on the settlement frontier, most of which would continue relatively unchanged until school consolidation after the Second World War. In sharp contrast were the new brick structures appearing in urban areas. The exemplar was Vancouver, whose very rapid growth following the CPR's completion brought a spate of construction. A new brick central school opened in January 1890, replacing an earlier wooden building. The same year Vancouver acquired a high school in temporary quarters, its first class containing a number of older students probably returning to school with very specific career plans in mind. Indeed, fully thirteen of the sixteen girls in this first class would become teachers, as did one of the eight boys, a reality which again underlines the far wider range of career opportunities available to educated young men as opposed to their female counterparts.[43] Three years later, in 1893, a separate high school building, yet another imposing brick edifice, was constructed in Vancouver.

Paralleling the striking physical differences developing between rural and urban schools were the distinctions emerging between kinds of teachers. The mass of British Columbia teachers were becoming female, as exemplified by the first Vancouver high school class. Juxtaposed were the growing numbers of university graduates who were coming to dominate the most prestigious and highest paying jobs. The shift is exemplified by the five teachers in the Vancouver high school from 1893 to 1899. All men, four of them held bachelor's degrees from Dalhousie, the fifth a degree from Toronto, and one of the five also possessed master's degrees from both Harvard and McGill.[44] By the end of the century the harsh reality was that the young girl just out of school with a teaching certificate fresh in her hand almost inevitably ended up in a one-room frontier school whereas male teachers, especially if they possessed an academic degree, dominated urban schools, particularly their top positions. Even before the province's first normal school opened its doors, the relative freedom of entry into the occupation and even in job selection that characterized British Columbia's pioneer teachers had largely disappeared in favor of an increasingly bureaucratic, credentialized and sex-differentiated occupation on its way to becoming a profession.[45]

Notes

1. Research was supported by the Social Sciences and Humanities Research Council of Canada. This essay is only possible because of the many individuals who shared stories and other information with me, some of whose names are included below. I thank you all.

2. Facilities for training teachers existed elsewhere in Canada and in other countries. See, for instance, Noelene Kyle, "'Can You Do as You're Told?': The Nineteenth Century Preparation of a Female Teacher in England and Austrialia," *Comparative Education Review* 36, 4 (1992): 467-86; and Alison Prentice, "'Friendly Atoms in Chemistry': Women and Men at Normal School in Mid-Nineteenth Century Toronto," in David Keane and Colin Read, eds., *Old Ontario: Essays in Honor of J.M.S. Careless* (Toronto: Dundern, 1990).

3. William Burns, "The Necessity of Teacher Training," *Queen's Quarterly* 17 (October 1909), 114.

4. Teacher motivation has been examined principally from the perspective of women who long formed the bulk of the occupation. Alison Prentice and Marjorie R. Theobald, ed., *Women who taught: Perspectives on the History of Women and Teaching* (Toronto: University of Toronto Press, 1991), especially Prentice and Theobald, "The Historiography of Women Teachers: A Retrospect," 3-33, provides a good overview of recent scholarship. Canadian studies include chapters 11-14. Paul Stortz and J. Donald Wilson, "Education on the Frontier: Schools, Teachers and Community Influence in North-Central British Columbia," *Histoire sociale/Social History* 26 (1993): 265-90; Janet Guildford, "'Separate Spheres': The Feminization of Public School Teaching in Nova Scotia, 1838-1880," *Acadiensis* 22, 1 (1992), 44 - 64; Jean Barman, "Birds of Passage or Early Professionals? Teachers in Nineteenth-century British Columbia," *Historical Studies in Education* 2, 1 (Spring 1990): 17-36. Marta Danylewycz and Alison Prentice, "Teachers' Work: Changing Patterns and Perceptions in the Emerging School Systems of Nineteenth and Early Twentieth Century Central Canada," *Labour/ Le travail* 17 (1986): 59-80; John Abbott, "Accomplishing 'a Man's Task': Rural Women Teachers, Male Culture, and the School Inspectorate in Turn-of-the-Century Ontario," *Ontario History* 78, 4 (1986): 313-30; Marta Danylewycz and Prentice, "Teachers, Gender, and Bureaucratizing School Systems in Nineteenth Century Montreal and Toronto," *History of Education Quarterly* 24 (Spring 1984); Danylewycz, Beth Light and Prentice, "The Evolution of the Sexual Division of Labour in Teaching: A Nineteenth-Century Ontario and

Quebec Case Study," *Histoire sociale/Social History* 16, 31 (1983): 81-109; and Alison Prentice, "The Feminization of Teaching," in Susan Mann Trofimenkoff and Prentice, eds., *The Neglected Majority: Essays in Canadian Women's History* (Toronto: McClelland and Stewart, 1977), 49-65.

5. On the history of British Columbia generally, see Jean Barman, *The West beyond the West: A History of British Columbia* (Toronto: University of Toronto Press, 1991).

6. Data taken from Department of Education, *Annual Reports*, elaborated in Jean Barman, "Birds of Passage.

7. Letters to the editor were sent to approximately a hundred local newspapers across British Columbia, the geographical diversity of replies suggesting that most were printed.

8. Where pieces of information acquired from descendants can be checked in other sources such as newspaper clippings, the Department of Education's *Annual Reports* or the British Columbia manuscript censuses, they are remarkably consistent, suggesting little family mythmaking about pioneering parents' and grandparents' lives.

9. John I. Goodlad, "Connecting the Present to the Past," in Goodlad, Roger Soder and Kenneth A. Sirotnik, eds., *Places Where Teachers Are Taught* (San Francisco: Jossey-Bass, 1990), 32.

10. R.D. Gidney and W.P.J. Millar, *Professional Gentlemen: The Professions in Nineteenth-Century Ontario* (Toronto: University of Toronto Press for the Government of Ontario, Ontario Historical Studies Series, 1994), 241, makes the same point for male teachers in late nineteenth-century Ontario. Particularly useful for thinking about teacher professionalization are Donald Warren, ed., *American Teachers: Histories of a Profession at Work* (New York: Macmillan for the American Educational Association, 1989); Jurgen Herbst, *And Sadly Teach: Teacher Education and Professionalization in American Culture* (Madison: University of Wisconsin Press, 1989); and Paul H. Mattingly, *The Classless Profession: American Schoolmen in the Nineteenth Century* (New York: New York University Press, 1975). Insightful on teacher professionalism in British Columbia are Charles S. Ungerleider, "Power, Politics, and the Professionalization of Teachers in British Columbia," in Lorna Erwin and David MacLennan, eds., *Sociology of Education in Canada: Critical Perspectives on Theory, Research & Practice* (Toronto: Copp Clark Longman, 1994), 370-79; and Rennie Warburton, "The Class Relations of Public Schoolteachers in British Columbia," in Warburton and David Coburn, eds., *Workers, Capital and the State in British Columbia: Selected Papers* (Vancouver: UBC Press, 1988), 240-62.

11. Gidney and Millar argue persuasively that in nineteenth-century Ontario professionalism was perceived as a male prerogative. Thus, "when male teachers spoke of the nature of their profession, women were either dismissed as transitory or were invisible. . . . Their social ambitions could not help but be diminished and their claims to be professional men rendered ambiguous when they had to participate in an occupation filled with women, and women as well qualified, and as competent as themselves." Gidney and Millar, *Professional Gentlemen*, 239. Gidney and Millar also point to Ontario teachers' lack of "control over their conditions of work" (236-7) and the increasingly mass character of schooling as "reasons internal to the occupation itself" (247) mitigating against it becoming a profession.

12. Conversation with Gwen Morrice concerning Carrie Elizabeth Ogle, 8 March 1988.

13. Sketch constructed from letters and enclosures from Beatrice Cooke, 2 February and 28 April 1988; typescript memorandum by Mrs. Cooke, 15 June 1965, in Vertical Files in British Columbia Archives and Records Service [BCARS]; *Memories Never Lost: Stories of the Pioneer Women of the Cowichan Valley and a Brief History of the Valley 1850 - 1920* (Altona: D.W. Friesen, 1986), 191-92; and biographical dictionary of fur trade employees created by Bruce Watson, used with his permission. All of the biographical vignettes also incorporate relevant information from the Department of Education's *Annual Reports* and the British Columbia manuscript censuses for 1881, 1891 and 1901.

14. Letters and enclosures from Joan Modrall, 4 and 17 February 1988; and Cyril Edel Leonoff, *Pioneers, Pedlars, and Prayer Shawls: The Jewish Communities in British Columbia and the Yukon* (Victoria: Sono Nis, 1978), 15-18.

15. Letters and enclosures from Edith Barr, 15 February and 25 April 1988, including typescript entitled "The Sardis Higginsons."

16. Conversation with Gwen Morrice, 8 March 1988; letter and enclosures from Gwen Morrice, 15 March 1988; and Cecil C. Coutts, *Cancelled With Pride: A History of Chilliwack Area Post Offices, 1865-1993* (n.p., 1993), 78-81.

17. Letter from Lynne Guinet, 31 January 1988; conversation with Lynne Guinet, 13 February 1988; letter from Allan Guinet, 2 February 1988; and "Diary of Phoebe A. Fulton – 1901" in possession of the family.

18. Letters and enclosure from Janet Pedersen, 7 March and 5 May 1988.

19. Letters from John M. Yorston, 2 February and 30 March 1988; letters and enclosures from Don Yorston, 9 May 1988; letters and enclosures from Joan Kelly, 20 and 30 April 1988; phone conversation with Jessie Hunter, 2 June 1988; and memoir of Ethel Robertson in possession of the Yorston family.

20. Letters and enclosures from Edna E. Wallace, 1 February and 9 March 1988.

21. Letter and typescript diary from Lil McIntosh, 3 March 1988. See chapter 13 for the teaching career of Carolina Mclellan's daughter Mary Williams.

22. Letter from Douglas Harker, 30 January 1988; and Douglas Harker, unpublished Miller-Springer typescript manuscript, esp. pp. 37-38, 61, 84 and 113 - 15.

23. Letter from Ruth Barnett, 4 March 1988; and Imbert Orchard, *Martin: The Story of a Young Fur Trader. Sound Heritage* series 30 (Victoria: Provincial Archives of British Columbia, 1981), esp. 12, 14, 24-5 and 31.

24. Conversation with Robert McMillan, 23 February 1988; and letter, with enclosure of correspondence and other papers of John McMillan, from Mary Gardner, 15 February 1988.

25. Letters from Mary Inglin, 10 February and 8 April 1988; Bea Hamilton, *Salt Spring Island* (Vancouver: Mitchell Press, 1960), 96-8; and Richard Mouat Toynbee, *Snapshots of Early Salt Spring Island* (Ganges: Mouat's trading Co., 1978), 60.

26. Letter and enclosures from Margaret Nicholls, February 1988; June Lewis-Harrison, *The People of Gabriola* (Gabriola: Friesen, 1982); and *Alberni Valley Times*, 10 January 1968.

27. Conversation with T.J. Trapp, 29 February 1988; genealogy and undated clippings from Mr. Trapp; and Kathleen Bourne Elliot, "Sunnyside Our Heritage – Our Love," typescript, June 1965.

28. Letter from Margaret Nicholls, 19 February 1988.

29. Letter from Ernest Harris, 22 February 1988; and A.M.J. Hyatt, *General Sir Arthur Currie: A Military Biography* (Toronto: University of Toronto Press, 1987), 5-7.

30. Conversation with John Tolmie, 28 January 1988.

31. Letter and enclosures from Don Munro, 15 February 1988.

32. Conversation with Nora Burrows, 19 February 1988; and letter from Ernest Harris, 22 February 1988.

33. Letters from Gladys M. Smith, 14 February and 6 March 1988; and Gladys M. Smith, "The Teaching Bannermans" typescript.

34. Letter and enclosures from Alex Goostrey, 4 April 1988; conversation with Katie May Goostrey Martin, 18 April 1988; and letters and photos in possession of family members.

35. Letter from Ernest Harris, 22 February 1988; and S.W. Jackman, *Portraits of the Premiers* (Sidney: Gray's Publishing, 1969), 199-205.

36. Letters from Dr. Robert E. Burns, 30 January and 20 February 1988. including typescript entitled "The Burns Relationships by William Burns."

37. Letters from Ernest Harris, 5 and 22 February 1988.

38. Conversation with Milo Fougner, 23 February 1988; Ivar Fougner, "Diary, 30 Dec 1889" and "Diary April 8, 1892 – Dec 30 1915," typescript of original in BCARS.

39. Letters from Dr. Robert E. Burns, 30 January and 20 February 1988, including typescripts entitled "William Burns" and "The Burns Relationships by William Burns."

40. Letters from Velma Bernice Ramsey, 4 and 20 February 1988.

41. Letter from Albert Charles Young, 29 January 1888; letter from Jean Norris, 13 March 1988; conversation with Mary Norris, 12 April 1988; information from Linda Hale; and Elizabeth Forbes, *Wild Roses at Their Feet: Pioneer Women of Vancouver Island* (Victoria: British Columbia Centennial '71 Committee, 1971), 58-9.

42. Letter from Ernest Harris, 22 February 1988.

43. *The First Fifty Years: Vancouver High Schools 1890 - 1940* (Vancouver, 1940), 23.

44. George Robinson (Dalhousie), James Shaw (Dalhousie, Harvard, McGill), John Kerr (Toronto), Joseph Henry (Dalhousie) and Alexander Robinson (Dalhousie). Data from *First Fifty Years*, 26 - 28.

45. See chapter 15.

11

"May the Lord Have Mercy on You":
The Rural School Problem in British Columbia in the 1920s

J. Donald Wilson and Paul J. Stortz

In September 1919 John Gibbard, fresh out of Vancouver Normal School, took up his first teaching post in a one-room school in Steelhead, a logging community thirteen kilometres north of Mission in the Fraser Valley. Arriving to inspect the school, he opened the desk drawer to find a note from his predecessor whose salutation began: "May the Lord have mercy on you."[1] Gibbard and hundreds of other British Columbia rural teachers in the 1920s would come to understand during their tenure the full meaning of this cryptic greeting. The purpose of this study is to try to convey some sense of the life of a teacher in remote corners of the province in the 1920s and the nature of rural teaching conditions. Second, it discusses in some detail the various solutions to the rural school problem as well as other educational reforms proposed by educational bureaucrats in the Department of Education. The essay attempts, therefore, to be both descriptive of a situation not much studied and analytical in a way that might contribute to a better understanding of the province's educational history in the twentieth century.[2]

I

In the aftermath of World War I the rural schools of British Columbia did not escape the scrutiny of the educational bureaucracy in the provincial capital of Victoria.[3] For the time, education occupied a relatively favored status in comparison with other social services provided by the state. By 1920 British Columbians had benefited from the existence of a state-run public school system for almost half a century. The attention accorded rural schools came within the framework of an intensely introspective post-war society dominated by progressive thought embodied in the "New Education" movement.[4] Every structural and philosophical assumption underlying the school system was called into question, and the rural school was given special consideration as a unique form of education separate from municipal (small town or village) and urban schools. Its educational and social functions made its reform a distinct problem, and this concern was evident in both the inspectors' annual reports and the survey of provincial education undertaken by John Harold Putman and George Weir in 1924.

Earlier, around 1910, the New Education movement (later referred to as progressive education) had been very much preoccupied with the need for schools in rural areas to promote rural regeneration, but as a result of economic realities (rural poverty and urban industrialization) and demography (rural depopulation) the movement entered into a second phase characterized by vocational training in urban schools. The third phase, starting in the 1920s, blurred urban and rural differences as education moved towards a distinctly practical curriculum geared towards the talents of the individual child. Progressivism formed the basic theme with the belief that each student was capable of certain predictable achievements and should be taught appropriately. Hence the growing reliance on intelligence tests.

In the face of increased urbanization and industrialization, many provincial administrators in education voiced concern over the preservation of what they perceived as superior rural values. To many Department of Education officials, the rural schools were the last bastion where the values of a pure and uncontaminated society could be taught. The efficiency of the rural schools, therefore, became a pressing subject. A.R. Lord of the Kelowna inspectorate only slightly exaggerated when he noted in 1920 that "the rural-school problem is the most serious question confronting educational administration in this province."[5] The combination, to quote another source, of "improper and useless buildings, inefficient apparatus and incompetent teachers or officials" created a situation where "there are in the aggregate hundreds of children . . . attending schools who as result of distance, weather, outside work, physical defect, are receiving the merest scraps of education."[6]

Throughout the 1920s, approximately 20 percent of all pupils in British Columbia attended small rural schools, both rural and assisted, as they were designated. The rural school was typically one-room, was geographically isolated, had a small and sometimes fluctuating pupil attendance, and experienced a rapid turnover of teaching personnel. Two administrative statuses existed: rural and assisted schools. Rural status implied a school that was neither urban or consolidated, and as a result was without the benefit of centralized municipal administration or finance. Still, the rural school on the average was more prosperous than the assisted school, which was so impoverished that the teacher's salary for school equipment and supplies were underwritten entirely by the provincial government. Provision of the schoolroom or building was the responsibility of the parents and other interested persons. A monthly enrolment of at least ten and an average daily attendance of not less that eight was essential to avoid closure.[7] In 1926 the assisted schools outnumbered the rural schools by three to one. Of the 574 one-roomed schools in the province, 88 percent were classified as assisted, while the remaining 12 percent were rural.[8] Conversely, out of a total of 521 assisted schools, 504 were one-room while just 70 of the 150 rural schools were one-room.

Most assisted school districts had a local assessment to supplement the provincial grant, and the voluntary labor of the community constructed and maintained the school. In such cases a property tax was levied on the residents according to the school's particular needs, subject to the approval of the Provincial Assessor.[9] The level of local support differed from community to community. Between 1918 and 1930 in the Bulkley and Nechako valleys in north-central B.C., a typical rural district, the average contribution paid by those communities with tax assessments was only $221.57 with a recorded low of $13.10 in Fort Fraser in 1919 and a high of $1 239.07 paid by the residents of Quick in 1922. Incidentally, the average operating budget, including the teacher's salary, for all the one-room schools in this particular region was $1 179.49.[10]

No more apt description of the variety of B.C. rural schools is likely to be found than in the following from the Putman-Weir Report (1925):

> Many are in remote and lonely places beside a lake, under a towering mountain capped with snow, or on an arid plateau where all vegetation is brown and dusty. Some are on beautiful but lonely islands in the Pacific, where the settler is part farmer, part fisherman and part lumberman. Some are on steep mountain sides in "Company Towns" where tall chimneys of pulp mill or smelter form the center of a busy industrial life. Some are close to the water on an arm of the sea, which is an outlet of a salmon river and the site of a canning factory and some stand on ground over coal mines. Some have ideal surroundings, but the school buildings themselves are primitive and very small. Many are built of logs. Some are not larger than 15 by 18 feet with a ceiling just above your head. Some have attractive grounds, some have bare and unattractive yards, and some area built on rocks. Some of these buildings are tidy and clean inside and some sadly in need of paint, whitewash and soap.[11]

One scholar of Canadian school architecture has concluded that B.C.'s assisted schools were "probably, by 1930, inferior to similar schools in the other western provinces."[12]

Among the many problems associated with the rural school, the progressive-minded educators of the era were most often concerned with the academic retardation of the students. The school inspectors and the commissioners of the Putman-Weir Report discovered that rural, and especially assisted school students were less "intelligent" than their urban counterparts according to the proper grade levels determined by standardized tests. Leslie J. Bruce, inspector of a large coastal district on the mainland, observed that "the standing and progress of people in upgraded rural schools was usually far below that of pupils in the other schools of the district."[13] The Putman-Weir Survey contained elaborate retardation statistics which showed that the average number of months a pupil was behind his/her course work in relation to age was 22.7 in assisted schools (almost two years!) as opposed to 15.7 and 8.07 in elementary rural and city schools respectively. Also fully half, 53.7 percent of pupils, in assisted schools were overage in respect to their proper grade.[14] For an educational system that was intended to be cost-effective, scientifically run and generally efficient, these statistics were unsettling indeed.

The blame for the rural school problem was placed squarely on the teacher. In both the Department of Education's annual reports (henceforth AR) and the Putman-Weir Survey, the amount of attention given rural school teachers was as much a testimony to their importance as it was a condemnation of their pedagogical effectiveness. The rural schoolteacher was easy to isolate because she – it was most often a woman[15] – was the manager of the schoolhouse. In her capacity as manager, she played many roles. She was a role model for the students, usually the caretaker of the facility, ideally a leader in the community where she was expected to help formulate school and community policy, and also the local representative of the Department of Education between the inspector's annual or biennial visits. Most important, she was the educator expected to create a stimulating atmosphere conducive to maximum learning. She was solely responsible for the standard of the schooling each student received.

Schools and teachers were extremely important socializing agents in the remote areas of the province. Such districts often lacked the amenities of urban life including Boy Scouts, Girl Guides, C.G.I.T. (Canadian Girls in Training) and other church-based clubs, as well as the recreational centres and organized playgrounds that by the 1920s were becoming quite the rage in urban areas. In rural B.C. the school was one of the few public gathering places specifically designed to educate and socialize children. Although it was imperative to keep up friendly relations with the local school board if her classroom authority was not to be interfered with, the school was ultimately the teacher's domain. Like its Ontario prototype, the local school board was composed of three trustees elected by the local ratepayers and exercised considerable authority over the day-to-day operation of the school within the general guidelines established by the department. The local school board hired the teacher, set the teacher's salary and controlled the expenditure of funds for the daily operation of the school.

Was the Department of Education's blame on the teacher for the rural school problem well placed? Both the Survey and the AR drew attention to the teacher's lack of qualifications and preparation to work in remote areas, but evidence suggests that the problem was far more complex. The teacher's age, gender and marital status were important determinants of her effectiveness, as were the economic and social conditions of each particular community on school efficiency. The reformers and inspectors failed to realize that not even the best-trained teacher had much chance of success against the restlessness of rural youth and the impoverishment and transiency of local communities.

The rural school problem becomes clearer by examining the solutions proposed in the AR and the Survey together with two sets of teacher-completed questionnaires known as the Teachers' Bureau Records (henceforth TBR).[16] The Teachers' Bureau was set up by the Department of Education in 1920 and placed in charge of the Department's Registrar, J.L. Watson. Its main responsibility was to act as sort of a teachers' exchange, providing names of suitable candidates to rural school boards anxious to hire teachers as well as acquainting teachers with rural school vacancies. In the school year 1922-23, notices of approximately 300 vacancies were received, over 200 of which were filled by teachers selected by the Bureau at the request of the school boards.[17] Because the information in the questionnaires is so detailed – salary, boarding costs, condition of school, living conditions, relations with board and parents, etc. – they throw a great deal of light on the rural teachers' impressions of their "lot" and the exigencies of their job. The existing TBR straddle the appearance of the Survey in 1925. About 700 questionnaires are available in the PABC in each of the two years 1923 and 1928. This allows for some comparisons of the 1923 set with the conditions of the rural schools detailed in the Survey while the TBR completed in 1928 help form conclusions as to whether any changes occured in conditions as a result of the recommendations proposed by the Survey.

Trout Lake District School: "Many [rural] schools are in the remote and lonely places beside a lake, under a towering mountain capped with snow." Putman Weir Report, 1925. (BCARS B-1521)

The teachers' responses to their physical and teaching environment varied greatly. Some complained about everything down to the mosquitoes in the summer. Some responded rather unenthusiastically with a singular adjective – the weather, pupils, parents, trustees, salary, school and school grounds were all "fair" – while others appeared elated over their teaching prospects and the natural beauty of their surroundings. A number criticized their situation in some detail. At Burgoyne Bay on the west coast of Saltspring Island, "many of the residents," the teacher complained, "have the attitude that 'what was good for them 40 years ago is good enough for the children of today.'" At the fish cannery in Kildonan, west of Port Alberni on Vancouver Island, Abigail Nicholson found the community rather rowdy. Her problem was exacerbated by the fact that she resided in a small room (8' by 19') backing onto the school. Since the school was used for many community functions, such as church services and dances, she found she often had to put up with "many disagreeable annoyances."

> At present, I have to eat, sleep, cook, dry clothes, etc. in just this little room, which is by no means healthy, not very much sunlight as it is behind school, also noisy dances which are frequently held, school room is outrageously abused. Men smoke and throw matches, partly used cigarettes, cigars on floor, desk, blackboard ledges. As the room is low shaped thus, it takes a long time to air it out and after a Saturday night's diversion, the pupils and myself have to endure the impure air most of the next week, in spite of me having the door and windows open during the weekend.[18]

To be sure, each school and teacher were different and the accuracy of the reports, taken individually, is impossible to verify. While many teachers enjoyed their rural experiences and some actually married local men and women and settled down in the community, most spent a short time there, a year or two at most. Often born and bred in urban British Columbia, they had little opportunity to acquire a genuine "feel" for the community or its inhabitants. Their intention was to complete their tour of duty and move on to the next, superior posting, or in some cases, to marriage and family. Their impressions of local life then may well have been quite superficial. On the other hand, the TBR do provide a legitimate perspective from a participant viewpoint and, when used together with the inspectors' reports summarized in the AR and with the observations of the education experts, Putman and Weir, provide quite a fascinating tripartite view of a similar set of circumstances. All told, it seems reasonable to suppose that the impressions recorded by the teachers were for the most part sincere and reflected the actual situation at least as the teacher perceived it.

The other major sources, the AR and the Putman-Weir Survey, diverged widely from each other. In sharp contrast to the Survey, the AR gave favorable descriptions of the rural schools and teachers (and for that matter of the entire educational system). This discrepancy can be partially explained, however, by understanding the purposes of these two sources. The Survey was commissioned by the Department of Education as a comprehensive stock-taking of the entire educational system. Its function was to recommend necessary changes to make the system as efficient as possible. The Survey's job was to be critical: "It is the intention of the Survey to point out defects, with a view to their betterment or elimination, [rather] than to praise the qualities of the many able teachers found in the schools in the Province."[19] The Survey examined in detail the nature of each problem and offered specific solutions.

A closer look at the authors of the Survey, however, reveals important biases that may have distorted their portrait of the rural school. Dr. J. Harold Putman and Dr. George Weir entered the educational scene in British Columbia with national reputations. Both had earned doctorates in education and were actively involved in educational research and administration. Putman came from Ottawa, where he was chief inspector of schools, and Weir, a professor of education at the University of British Columbia, from Saskatchewan, where he had been principal of the Saskatoon Normal School. Their removal from the administrative machinery of the Department of Education in Victoria permitted them to distance themselves from the province's educational bureaucracy. In brief, their comments placed neither their survey nor their jobs in jeopardy; their pens were free to commend or condemn. But the Survey's authors were not unbiased. Putman and Weir were liberal and progressive, and the Survey was deeply influenced by their philosophic outlook. Whatever did not fit into their idea of progressive pedagogy was censored.[20] During the commissioner's whirlwind fact-finding tour of the province in 1924-25, the public became aware from the various public meetings held that the commissioners had "embarked on the task with preconceived notions and not with an open mind."[21] The ultimate result was an administrative report disproportionately negative in relation to the real situation.

While the Survey was hampered by ideological biases, the AR suffered from political and administrative connections. The inspectors whose evaluations formed the basis of the AR were expected to report annually on the general state of affairs, both good and bad, in each district by describing the conditions and problems of local schools. However, as part of the bureaucracy, they were tied intimately to the Department of Education and their views were valued highly in teaching circles. Thus, their negative comments were more likely to be damaging to colleagues with whom they were in constant contact. For example, normal school staffs often included ex-inspectors; as a result, any condemnation of the quality of the rural and assisted school teachers could be seen as an indirect criticism of members and friends of their own profession.[22] Over the years a close network evolved among B.C. school inspectors, all but one of whom between 1888 and 1958 were men.[23] They not only sensed where their loyalties lay; they also realized their own advance up the bureaucratic ladder from their current middle management status constituted a sort of *cursus honorum*. Loyalty to those around and above you plus a modicum of merit usually found its reward.[24]

So while the AR described, the Survey explained, and in this way the Survey appeared far more critical than the AR. The difference was in emphasis, not content. Both sources studied the same thing, problems associated with the rural school, but with different intentions and levels of analysis. Thus taken together with the TBR, we have a second and third perspective on the rural school.

II

Both the Survey and the AR identified the teacher as the basic reason for the problem of the rural school, and in particular they blamed pupil retardation on archaic teaching practices. Isolated from the New Education and unwilling to update her education through summer school,[25] the rural teacher "lost (her) studious habits" and fell "into the rut of old fogeyism, routine and drudgery."[26] She sustained "formalism" – an undue stress on drill, memorization, and routine – which was especially condemned by the Survey as the nemesis of modern progressive education. Instead of leading active discussions with the pupils based on a curriculum designed for practical purposes (e.g. bookkeeping rather than mathematics), the teacher's schoolhouse pedagogy was characterized by oppressive discipline and rote learning. H.H. Mackenzie of the Vancouver Inspectorate No. 4 noted the results of this inflexible form of instruction:

> There is still in the majority of our schools too much "textbook teaching" and too little oral and mental work. In rural schools generally . . . about 90 percent of all recognized talking is done by the teacher. Under such conditions it is futile to expect any real development of language-power on the part of the pupils.[27]

Along with suspect pedagogy, the problem of teacher transiency also had deleterious effects on school efficiency. According to the Survey, the most frequent changes of teachers were in the rural and assisted schools.[28] The situation was graphically described by Inspector H.H. Mackenzie with a colorful Gaelic reference bespeaking his ethnic background:

> To [rural and assisted school districts] young inexperienced teachers still come as members of a sort of migratory species: their movements not quite synchronizing with those of Nature's creatures, however, for in soft September days they come and in balmy June they flit away. And there is sadness in their passing, for in these lonely glens the soughing of the wind in the pines, the murmuring of the mountain streams seem to unite in the ancient lament, "Ch till shinne tuille" – "we return no more."[29]

The inspectors frequently lamented the unfortunate effects of teacher transiency on school efficiency. A.F. Matthews of the Kamloops inspectorate observed that "in those schools where the teachers have remained on for two or more years the work has invariably been of higher quality and the progress much more marked than in the schools where a new teacher has been engaged each year."[30] Inspector G.H. Gower of Prince George reported in 1922 that "the most important problem that faces the rural district is how to retain the services of a competent teacher . . . the great majority of those teachers who are qualified do not remain sufficiently long in the schools to make a definite impression on the children."[31]

The Survey and AR attributed the phenomenon of teacher transiency to the rural teacher's below-average salary. There was virtual unanimity among inspectors in favor of increasing the salary of rural and assisted teachers.[32] An exception was A.R. Lord, who noted in 1921 that "the salary paid by most of the [rural] schools has been at least $1,200 per annum, yet teachers remain no longer than when the remuneration was much less – a clear indication that the appeal of the graded school does not lie solely in dollars and cents."[33] Actually Lord's figure was too high; nor did he mention the fact that the assisted schoolteacher was still paid on the average of $300 less than her urban counterpart, not to mention her urban-male counterpart.[34] In 1923, 496 out of 689 teachers (or 70.5 percent) reported in the TBR that they were making under $1 100 per annum. Most of the remainder made under $1 250. In 1928, 545 out of 739 teachers (or 73.7 percent) reported salaries under $1 100 per annum. Most of the others by then made under $1 200, indicating some slippage in salary payments.

Despite the salary issue, most inspectors directed their energies towards recommending improvement in rural teachers' education. They believed that teacher transiency as well as the prevalence of traditional pedagogical styles were directly related to a lack of professional training. Inspector G.H. Gower of the Prince George district wrote that,

> A number of the schools in these northern parts are handicapped year after year by the employment of unskilled, temporary certificated teachers, who have little knowledge of our courses, standards and methods. Inability to organize the work of their classrooms constitutes the chief criticism of the teachers in the one-room schools of this inspectorate.[35]

The inspector's concern was only marginally supported by statistics. For example, in 1925, the average rural and assisted schoolteacher was less educated than the urban teacher; only 4 percent of them as opposed to 10 percent of the teachers in the city held a teaching degree from a university, and 23 percent versus 33 percent had a first-class teaching certificate. The matter of experience was a more telling statistic: the rural and assisted schoolteacher was much less experienced. The total teaching experience of city elementary school teachers was twice as great as that of the rural teachers: 7.9 years as opposed to 3.1 years. In addition, 48 percent of the rural and assisted school teachers had less than three years' teaching experience compared to 16 percent of urban teachers.[36]

The reformers strove to remedy the lack of education and experience through the creation of "rural-minded" teachers.[37] The Survey recommended that the normal school instructors should improve their own professional training as well as rectify the oppressive relationship between the domineering older male instructor and the younger female student teacher. Instructors were overwhelmingly male and over forty-five; student teachers predominantly female and under twenty. Also rural-oriented subjects could be added to the curriculum, particularly training in rural sociology and administration, educational theory, philosophy, psychology and history, in addition to tests and measurements. These courses would increase the teacher's understanding of her duties and situation in the rural school.[38]

The Survey strongly suggested the implementation of practice teaching in isolated schools. Teacher discontent and subsequent migration would no longer be problems if the properly trained teacher knew exactly what to expect in a rural school. Thus the Survey called for the development of a system of reports of each remote community in relation to educational, social, economic and geographical conditions, and especially teacher accommodation. These reports would be distributed to potential candidates for rural school teaching, and in this way would temper teacher expectations of comfortable conditions in such employment. The wildest hope of the administrators was for the training of a legion of the "strongest" teachers,[39] rural-mined and well-versed in progressive technique and philosophy, intent on delivering the highest standards of education possible to isolated children. The Survey seemed to have prudently taken to heart the theme encapsulated in Norman Fergus Black's comparison in an article on rural schools in the *B.C. Teacher* in 1924: "Teaching in an urban graded school and teaching in an ungraded rural school have about as much in common as the grocery business and the hardware trade."[40]

School at Carlin, December 1913. "The majority of the children are Finns, very nice children willing to learn and help in any way." (BCARS, D-3246)

A better-trained teacher was considered a panacea to the rural school problem. This was only part of the solution, however, as the reformers failed to take into account both market forces and the teacher demographics. To a great extent, market forces determined teacher turnover in the school as teachers tended to migrate from the remote areas if jobs were available in the town or city. In general, the rural school was considered by the young and inexperienced teacher as a training ground,[41] by the older and more experienced teacher merely as a temporary setback, by the "birds of passage" as a "stepping stone" to another profession,[42] and by others as a place to get away from to improve their lives and career chances elsewhere. Most favored urban locations if not by birth and upbringing, then by aspiration, given their time in normal school and exposure to urban amenities.

Does the teacher's demographic profile explain teacher discontent and transiency? Whatever the case, the rural teacher was most likely to be young, female and unmarried. In 1925, out of 903 rural and assisted school teachers, 79 percent were female, 91 percent were unmarried and their average age was 23.6 years. By 1930 the proportion of women teachers rose to 83.5 percent and those who were single climbed to 92.5 percent.[43] The combination of youth and gender caught the attention of many inspectors and eventually led to the appointment in 1928 of a Rural Teachers' Welfare Officer, whose sole responsibility was to minister to female teachers in difficult, out-of-the-way postings.[44] The notion that the rural areas were too rugged and wild for the delicate sensibilities of the young female permeated teacher correspondence with the educational authorities in Victoria. Overall there was a sense, as the sociologist Mary O'Brien has noted in another connection, that "a young woman living alone, protected by neither father nor husband but only by her rather feeble morality, was worrisome."[45] It has been said that the rural teacher was mindful of three things: her clothing, her money, and her reputation. The anxiety about "children" away from home, especially "girls" has been pointed up by the historian John Calam. In recounting the pre-World War I campaign for establishing a normal school in Victoria, Calam underlined the public concern among Victoria's citizenry about having to send aspiring teachers from Vancouver Island to Vancouver for their training. "Children" would be "separated from home influence at a most critical time in their lives," warned the *Victoria Times*, and girls, if not boys, made vulnerable to certain dangers "out among strangers." The reference to "girls" and "boys" and anxiety over "children" away from home goes to the root of the problem of rural school teachers in remote environs since the same "boys" and "girls" within a year found themselves in a world of men and women, often far from the protection of home.[46]

Schools located near mines, logging camps, and railway construction sites were "dangerous" for young female teachers. The male teacher at Stevenson Creek south of Princeton warned: "This would be a dangerous district to send a young girl to as there are many lone prospectors passing to and fro."[47] Lexie McLeod, who taught in Lower Nicola in 1921, remembered that the only single non-Indian male in the area automatically "thought that I should be his girl," and it was a frightening experience indeed when "Alf" entered her room uninvited one night looking for romance.[48] Mildred McQuillan, who taught in Fort Fraser west of Vanderhoof in 1927, noticed a preponderance of "poor niggers," who, after traveling miles to ask for her consideration, were subsequently turned down. The closest she came to a romantic evening was at a monthly dance where she danced with the only man in the hall to whom she was attracted, but was reluctant to become intimate with him for fear of the rumors that would start in the community.[49] Miss Edna May Hicks, who taught in Olsen Valley near Powell River in 1926, remembered well "the shock when a young teacher in a remote spot in Northern B.C. was murdered by a sad young man she encouraged then rejected. . . ."[50]

Living arrangements were very important for rural teachers since where and how they lived intimately affected both their work and their private lives. Problems with boarding arrangements and the lack of facilities for "batching" were often very stressful for the unmarried teacher and were a perennial problem for most teachers. "Batching" held numerous difficulties for young, green female teachers living away from home for the first time. At Shutty Bench, a farming community on Kootenay Lake, Kathleen Murphy rode horseback to school six kilometres each day from the village of Kaslo, where she had a home of her own. By contrast, on the province's west coast near Bella Bella, Annie Haughton rowed every morning to her school on Hunter Island, an Icelandic settlement. On Thetis Island, one of the Gulf Islands, "nobody will board the teacher. I have just been out of my shack and have got another till the end of June." Five years later in 1928 the new teacher complained: "One must 'batch.' Nearest home to school 1-1/2 miles. Can rent for winter but not during summer months. Very hard to find a house at any time." At Soda Creek north of Williams Lake, C. Bertrand lamented, "I am at present living in the government jail with borrowed furniture."[51]

At least this jail was a solid structure. The alternative of boarding presented no end of worries, especially for the new teacher who often found herself greeted at the train station or steamship dock by at least two trustees each of whom wanted to board her. Her cash income, translated into boarding costs, was the prize. Typical of the competition was the story told of the Cawston teacher (south Okanagan) who was expected to arrive by the Great Northern Railway from Princeton. Arrangements had been made for her to board at a certain home, but the other family that wanted her journeyed to Hedley by car, took her off the train and drove her to their home where she stayed.[52] At Stuart River, fifty kilometres from Vanderhoof:

> There is a great deal of jealousy and quarreling over where the teacher boards. This spirit is carried on by the parents towards the teacher, and some of the pupils carry this attitude into class with them, making this a very difficult and unpleasant district to be in.[53]

In the 1920s boarding costs averaged about $35 per month or about one-third of the teacher's monthly salary. In the 1923 TBR, four out of five teachers (446 out of 574 reporting) estimated boarding costs in the range of $30 to $40 per month in their community. In 1928, 520 out of 624 (or 83.2 percent) reported boarding costs in the same range.

Just as the teacher's living conditions were often problematic, so was the school building itself. Since the building was a community responsibility, its condition tended to reflect the economic situation of the locality. The cost for the construction of assisted schools was underwritten by the government once the building was erected. Thus the state of the school often reflected the level of community prosperity.

The Putman-Weir Survey pointed to the wide discrepancies in the socio-economic conditions in remote areas of the province by arguing that "while urban British Columbia has long since emerged from the pioneer stage of its social evolution, the same cannot be said of the many remote areas of the province where primitive conditions still prevail."[54] Owing to the poverty of the community, the school itself was often inadequate. School was held in such places as a parents' house, village store, church, social hall, tent, lighthouse, shack, or log cabin. Some rural schools were modern, built with lumber, but frequently even these were too small to house the pupils adequately. Running water, electricity and toilets were rarely to be found in the school. The Survey observed that:

> One would not expect to find other than modest school buildings in the assisted areas. The type of building varies from district to district, depending upon the degree of interest manifested by the citizens in their schools and on the wealth of these communities. Some buildings are neat and comfortable. Others are scarcely habitable. In certain cases dilapidated log structures, with numerous defects in heating, lighting and ventilation are used for school purposes. The water supply is usually inadequate, while the privies are often found in filthy condition. Especially is this the case in the more remote schools. The school sites, generally unfenced, have a most picturesque natural setting. . . . In fact, every prospect (except the building and privies) pleases until, on entering the schoolhouse, the visitor's aesthetic sense receives a violent shock.[55]

The inspectors' reports assessed the general condition of some schools, from the extreme of "dangerous and unsanitary firetraps" to the severe lack of equipment and supplies.[56] Indeed, the most common complaints in the TBR dealt with the school size, lack of lighting, ventilation, conveniences, and supplies,[57] but education officials were hard-pressed to find a remedy for the situation. The Survey conceded that:

> Many handicaps, both economic and social, incident to rural life, will necessarily be experienced in the remote areas . . . for a considerable number of years. The conditions of pioneer life in many of these areas are still in existence and cannot be entirely overcome by any government.[58]

But how could the teachers influence school efficiency if the community was insolvent? Dorothy A. Clarke wrote from North Dawson Creek that "the settlers are very poor and they find it exceedingly hard to get any money together for school purposes." Even where money was available for the school, the local people often were parsimonious and uncooperative. F.W. Hobson, who taught in Beaver Cove near Alert Bay, reported that "this school district has no regular method of financing for school purposes, the amount collected occasionally being grudgingly paid by the residents. . . . The inhabitants in general are narrow minded."[59] The Survey noted that in some areas control over education was placed in the hands of local dictators (the three elected school trustees) who harbored "petty . . . jealousies toward each other," and as a result they pushed local control to an "illogical extreme."[60] Volatile local politics kept funds from being invested wisely. Interfamily disputes were rife, and the teacher had to be careful to remain neutral. In Pineview, thirteen kilometres from Prince George, R.R. Gordon-Cumming wrote confidentially to Victoria that:

The district is at present divided over a dispute on location and assessment for school, which makes it extremely difficult for the teacher to be friendly with both parties. I have had to build my own house to avoid antagonizing one party by boarding with the other. It requires much tact to keep on good terms with people all round owing to this dispute.[61]

Residents quarreled incessantly in Salmon River near Prince George and Sadie Johnston, who taught in West Demars south of Nakusp in 1928, recalled:

I experienced some small town jealousies there so that if I was friendly with one family, another would reject me. When I mentioned this to the Inspector he suggested I stay neutral and not patronize one family over another. This was not easy to do because the "hostile" family never did invite me to their home, explaining they couldn't as the husband has diabetes. There were only 3 families in the school. . . . I felt the small town jealousies hard to deal with, so decided to try for a new position.[62]

The uncooperative manner of the local people was often directly responsible for the teacher moving on. C.B. Christianson, in Cape Scott at the northern tip of Vancouver Island, observed that "a spirit of jealousy and general distrust seems to pervade this district. Present one is the only teacher who had held position more than 2 years." Mrs. Christine Kearne in Okanagan Landing similarly saw that "there is very little cooperation between parents and trustees and parents and teacher. Trustees do not work harmoniously together, consequently frequent change of teacher."[63] While for the most part the inspectors neglected the social aspects of the community, the Survey took care to mention the prevalence of alcoholism in some communities as a contributing factor to school inefficiency. It, however, saw this only in terms of money spent on alcohol vis-à-vis the school, instead of in respect to its harmful effects on pupils' upbringing, teacher's security, and community life generally.[64]

Also overlooked were the implications of the community's ethnic composition. The teacher was sometimes forced to deal with the idiosyncrasies of different languages and customs among both students and their parents. She was not only in a remote culture, but sometimes in an alien one as well. Where the inhabitants were from northern and western Europe, the teachers were usually favorable in their comments about them. Despite the long-standing antipathy of British Columbians to Japanese Canadians, teachers reporting in the TBR held their Japanese-Canadian students in high regard. Teachers in Doukhobor communities, however, such as Brilliant, Castlegar, North Kettle River and Pass Creek, were virtually unanimous in describing their charges and their parents as "difficult." Irregular and non-attendance was a perennial problem. Most Native children were by this time attending federally sponsored schools and thus were rarely found in public schools, although Metis and mixed blood children sometimes attended rural schools. Teacher opinion approximated the prejudices found in society generally.[65]

By the 1920s the in-school workday consisted of much more than simply teaching. Teachers were expected to take responsibility for the behavior of their students during lunch hours and school breaks such as recess. They were supposed to "improve" and beautify their school grounds, a daunting task in many communities where forest or sea lay close at hand. Modern health practices demanded that all teachers, rural and urban, inspect pupils for contagious diseases. Maintaining the compulsory school records consumed hours of busy work. Lighting fires, scrubbing the floor and blackboards (and sometimes painting the walls too) and general custodial duties were in many school districts the teacher's responsibility. Sometimes, with or without the school board's assistance, she would enlist the labor of one or more older students to carry out these onerous duties. Less often groups of parents helped out. But all too frequently the teacher's answer in the TBR as to whether or not the school employed a janitor was a blunt "no."

The figures from the TBR are very revealing on this account. Of 658 responses in the 1923 questionnaire to the query, "Does Board engage a janitor for school?", 352 teachers responded "yes" and 196 answered "no." The remaining 110 indicated a variety of alternatives including part-time janitors (only on weekends, once a month, or light fires only, to clean only), students, parents, or teachers as janitors, or both students and teachers as janitors. In other words, in 306 out of 658 schools (fully 46.5 percent) the teacher was either completely or partly responsible for janitorial duties herself or else had to supervise the work of someone else. The situation was marginally better in 1928. Then, of 722 responses to this question, the answer was "yes" in 435 cases, "no" in 160. The remaining 127 schools had a variety of makeshift arrangements over which the teacher retained supervisory capacity. In a total of 287 schools (or 39.6 percent), therefore, the teacher was either fully or partially responsible for janitorial duties. It was circumstances such as these that made the rural teacher feel much more akin in reality to a worker than a professional.[66]

Going to school at Carlin, 1913. "Students not only walked to school, but also rode horseback and in the winter used sleighs and dog sleds." (BCARS D-3248)

Finally, the temporary nature of some communities hindered school reform and contributed to teacher transiency. Many schools were located in areas where economic activity was seasonal, where extractive resource industries kept the community alive only until the minerals or timber were exhausted, or where railroad construction led to tie-making until the local stretch of line was completed. As a result of such activity, the teacher was never assured of the school's reopening the following year because the families, fearing unemployment, would migrate out of the area to make a living elsewhere. The Survey speculated that only one in three settlers in any given remote community was a permanent resident,[67] and in the AR the inspectors alluded to the periodic rural and assisted school closings (and openings) throughout the districts. Many of the schools suffered from chronic attendance fluctuation and in some areas, the teacher was teaching a "procession of pupils."[68] For the teachers, therefore, any long-range plans for the school in the way of physical improvements, even if the money were available, or the development of a structured pedagogical framework based on projected attendance figures were out of the question.

Parental decisions to withdraw their children from school were not always a measure of disinterest in or indifference to education as often interpreted by school inspectors. Economic factors, such as work or child-caring at home, were considered by parents as legitimate reasons for non-attendance at school. For example, the teacher at Telkwa in the Bulkley Valley reported in 1928: "Majority of farmers badly off – hence poor salaries – attendance is poor as farmers kept out boys to help on farms – unable to engage help."[69] When disputes arose between parents and teachers over the quality and type of education being provided, parents actually withdrew their children from school as a form of protest. Inspector A.E. Miller of the Kootenay District somewhat earlier in 1912 interpreted these incidents as examples of negative parental attitudes towards formal schooling. "Until the people living in such districts fully realize the importance of working with, and not against the teacher, the conditions of their schools must continue to be extremely unsatisfactory."[70] He went on to chastise such parents for contributing to the problem of poor attendance by their alleged "lack of interest" in public education. From another perspective, however, it might well be argued that these disputes by their very nature demonstrated not lack of interest but rather parental concern about who was teaching and what was being taught. To the disgruntled parents the disputes were hardly "petty," the common inspectoral designation.[71]

III

By the late 1920s the inspectors believed that rural-minded teachers were finally being created. The normal schools appeared to be training teachers successfully in the art of remote-school teaching. The evidence was there: better teachers' qualifications, better teaching, less transiency and more enthusiasm among the teachers. The inspectors were wrong, however, on several counts. First, the Survey's recommendations for normal school reform of rural school teacher training were either sluggishly applied or ignored. Of a total of twenty-three courses included in the Victoria Normal School curriculum in 1927, only one, nature study, dealt with a rural subject.[72] The much touted rural sociology was not even offered. For the teachers enrolled in Vancouver Normal School, practice teaching in a one-room school was restricted to one week if it existed at all. Even then, practice teaching schools were located in such communities as Burnaby, Richmond, North Vancouver, Delta and Surrey, which though sometimes "rural" in their surroundings, were hardly isolated enough for the teacher to experience the conditions of rural teaching. Practice teaching at the Victoria Normal School was similarly conducted within easy reach of Victoria. Even a brief session in a coastal school (for which student teachers' attendance figures are unavailable) would not have exposed the teacher to the pedagogical problems associated with rural community impoverishment, settler transiency and local politics. Moreover, throughout the latter half of the decade, both normal schools complained of problems which worked against the success of an efficient one-room school practice teaching program, in particular the lack of adequate facilities.[73] Each school set up a rural "demonstration" school within its main building, but the setting was inherently artificial. To illustrate, a teacher recalls that at the Victoria Normal School she "learned to correlate, that is, overlap timetables," a procedure that stood the beginning rural teacher in good stead.[74] But this was a far cry from practice in the isolation of a Quick, Rolla, Horsefly, Usk, Big Creek, Chu Chua, or Yahk.

The Summer School in Victoria was not as well attended as the inspectors believed. Despite their argument that better summer school attendance demonstrated the zeal of an increasingly qualified teachers' corps, in reality few remote school teachers attended, mainly because of its prohibitive tuition fees and inaccessible location for most of them. At most, 15 percent of all rural and assisted school teachers attended between 1925 and 1930 – as low as 9 percent in 1927 with a marked decrease in 1930.[75] Of the total 1 939 teachers who went to summer school during these five years (558 of whom were rural and assisted teachers), the total enrolment in all courses which pertained to rural living was only fifty-nine. In 1926, only six students sat in on rural science before the course was canceled the following year; in 1927, six teachers studied social science, which incorporated rural sociology (the course was dropped in 1928); and a high of twenty-two teachers attended nature study class in 1927, a course no longer offered by 1930.[76] Essentially, in the five years a total of only five rural courses were offered in summer school, while in any one year, at least fourteen other subjects were available in the curriculum.[77] Thus, not only were the vast majority of remote school teachers not attending summer school, but the few who did shunned the very courses which may have helped them better cope with rural contingencies. Most were probably looking for a first-class certificate and a job in the city.

As with normal school reform, other recommendations of the Survey were largely neglected. The salary structure for the rural schoolteacher remained the same – they were still underpaid vis-à-vis their urban counterparts – and the supervision of the teachers did not improve. The gulf between town and country schools was reflected in the hierarchy among teachers, with urban teachers accorded a higher place. The inspectors in rural districts were hampered constantly by inclement weather and poor transportation networks[78] and their brief visits to each school were occupied with administering standardized intelligence and achievement tests, one of the few recommendations of the Survey that was implemented. Margaret Lanyon remembered how little the inspectors cared about her welfare[79] and Miss M.J. Lynes in Crawford Creek responded to the inquiry for information from the Teachers' Bureau with a resentful "This is the first (official) request I have received."[80] She may well have been bitter because of the oft-reported aloof attitude many inspectors displayed towards the young school-teacher and the minimal contact she had with her inspector.[81]

An indication to the inspectors that the teachers were trying to upgrade their knowledge and expertise was the increased attendance at Teachers' Conventions. Held annually around Easter in a centrally located community, the Convention acted as a "medium for interchange of ideas; it is a sort of clearing house for teachers' problems and a source of information."[82] A safe inference can be made, however, that few remote teachers attended these conventions. They were held in some districts only and would have been inaccessible to many remote teachers who, because of their isolation, found that even collecting the weekly mail from a town a few miles away was a harrowing and laborious chore.[83]

Although the inspectors were wrong about normal school efficacy in creating rural-minded teachers and about signs of increased teacher conscientiousness, they were accurate in reporting an improvement in teachers' qualifications.[84] Progressively more rural and assisted school teachers had first-class certificates in 1930 than in 1925 (over a third as opposed to under a quarter).[85] Interestingly, however, fewer rural and assisted school teachers were attending university for an academic certificate, as the 5 percent who were working towards a bachelor's degree in 1925 dropped to 3.5 percent in 1930.[86]

The inspectors attributed this improvement in qualifications to normal school effectiveness when in fact formal instruction had little to do with the increase in more educated graduates. Inspector Leslie J. Bruce was one of the few officials to recognize a larger force at work – the labor market. "So many teachers are available," he wrote in 1927, "that school boards now have the opportunity to obtain teachers who are likely to do at least fair work." A.F. Matthews of the Kamloops inspectorate noted that the "supply of teachers in this province is now [1928] somewhat greater than is the demand for their services." J.D. MacLean, the Minister of Education in 1925, acknowledged the importance of market forces, especially their effect on teacher transiency.[87] In 1924 the AR noted an actual surplus of teachers.[88]

The following year the *Vancouver Province* observed that 500 teachers were out of work and the normal schools were turning out teachers too quickly.[89] Further evidence that the teachers' job market was constricting lay in normal school enrolment. Between 1924 and 1926, attendance in both normal schools dropped from 661 to 335 and fluctuated between 339 and 375 up to 1939.[90] This widening discrepancy between teacher supply and demand made teaching jobs more competitive; better qualifications were needed if the teacher hoped to secure employment. Once employed, she would be reluctant to relinquish her post considering the lack of alternative positions available.[91] The increase in teacher enthusiasm may have been somewhat superficial, therefore, because an indication of indifference on the part of the teacher could contribute to a negative inspector's report, subsequent dismissal, and possible unemployment. In essence, then, the normal schools were not responsible for producing more qualified graduates; rather the students were compelled to earn a higher certificate if they wanted a job.

IV

By 1930 rural school teaching conditions were probably no better than they had been at the start of the decade, perhaps even worse. Some speculation about the possible reasons why officials thought they were improving may be instructive. First, the administrators were getting the wrong impression of rural conditions. The TBR were distributed by a branch of the Department of Education, the Teachers' Bureau, primarily to assist local school boards in securing appropriate teachers and assisting unemployed teachers in obtaining positions. The education policy-makers may never have consulted these forms. The administrators' information about isolated communities came from the inspectors, the majority of whom spent only a few hours in each school annually. They would not have had the time, let alone the interest, to explore local problems.

Second, the inspectors' reports tended to be overly positive. Promotion out of the field, where in some cases thousands of miles of rugged terrain had to be traversed each year, must have appeared very attractive to the inspectors. A positive report of one's own district meant that good work was being done, a fine reference to have when a position opened up in the Department administration or closer to Vancouver or Victoria. Moreover, at this time of scrutiny and public criticism prompted by the Survey, the inspectors lauded the efforts of the normal schools to produce better graduates, a favorable impression which must have sat well with friends and colleagues in Victoria and Vancouver.

Third, policies affecting rural school reform that were proposed in the 1920s were not actually put into practice to any degree at that time. Chief among the new policy initiatives was school consolidation, which was also advocated in the Putman-Weir Report. The heralded closure of one-room schools and their replacement by multi-room consolidated schools required, however, the better part of the next half-century to accomplish. Significantly, there was no mention of school consolidation in the TBR. Likewise, the amalgamation of school districts as a move to provide a more efficient rural school administration and to overcome the sort of teacher complaints detailed above took another two or three decades before culminating in the seventy-five districts that now exist in B.C. The major step was taken in 1945 as a result of the Cameron Report of that year, which led to the amalgamation of most of the 650 school boards in the province. Both these measures encountered considerable resistance from local communities which accounts in part for the delay in their implementation.[92] As the lines of authority became more formal and increasingly standardized, the locus of power and decision-making shifted from the local school boards and parents to the central authority in Victoria. Supporters of the community-controlled school system struggled stubbornly against the forces of change and modernization represented by such progressive documents as the Putman-Weir Report.

Fourth, the administrators, and later historians, may have been blinded by progress in other areas of the educational system. During the late 1920s both school facilities and educational opportunity were expanding. New urban schools were being built, student population was increasing, and attendance levels were rising. High schools and superior schools in the larger rural areas were being established with a proportionate increase in school costs. The bureaucracy expanded as problems of growth were tackled and so unarticulated conditions of stagnation or decay were easily ignored. If one took account only of urban schools (both city and town), very real progress was in fact taking place.

Paradoxically, even while remote school teaching remained as difficult or became even more strenuous throughout the 1920s, the administrators seemed to grow less concerned. An overview of the entire decade reveals that they had little idea of the hardship and frustration experienced by hundreds of isolated teachers. More generally, by 1930 government officials were not nearly as worried about rural depopulation and the drift to the cities as they had been in 1910. By the late twenties the rural myth had almost dissipated in the province and the pre-eminent rural reform advocate, J.W. Gibson, had been eased out of his position as Director of Elementary Agricultural Instruction.[93] Despite the appointment of Lottie Bowron as Rural Teachers' Welfare Officer late in 1928, the rural teacher was even more without official solace and comfort at the end of the decade than earlier. The earlier argument from Gibson and others that the rural teacher at least had the advantage of better "moral conditions" by being in the countryside was by now no longer voiced. One can readily see from the circumstances described above how attempts at community leadership were most often futile.

In many ways the rural school problem in British Columbia was more intractable than on the Prairies. The latter certainly had its distances and isolation, but nothing to match this province's isolated mountain valleys.[94] Many of these almost inaccessible locations were difficult to service then and some are not much better today. The difficult terrain presented the authorities with a set of problems, much attested to in the journals of Lottie Bowron,[95] that were quite different from those found on the Prairies and in northern Ontario. Certainly, well into the 1930s within these small pockets of habitation throughout British Columbia, schools remained inefficient and teachers continued to struggle. In all of this, however, Miss Mary Pack, who taught in a one-room schoolhouse in 1923, seems to have remembered the ultimate purpose for schooling, whether rural or urban:

> It was a new experience for all of us – I don't think my pupils gained a high standard of scholarship ability or profound knowledge, but we did learn how to share and give, to take and to lead, to read and to seek.[96]

Notes

1. Interview with John Gibbard, retired schoolteacher, Vancouver, 24 February 1986. Gibbard was sometime professor in the Faculty of Education, University of British Columbia [UBC].

2. By "rural" we do not mean "agricultural," rather the land and people living outside the boundaries of incorporated urban centres, namely hamlets, villages, towns and cities. In 1921, by this definition, 277 000 of 524 000 residents of British Columbia lived in rural areas. Dominion Bureau of Statistics, *Seventh Census of Canada, 1931* (Ottawa: King's Printer, 1936), 364-69.

3. Aside from theses (see endnote 10) the secondary literature on the rural schools of British Columbia is scanty for the period between 1920 and 1930. General anecdotal studies on the nature of rural school life, while interesting, are not very substantial. See Jean Cochrane, *The One-Room School in Canada* (Toronto: Fitzhenry and Whiteside, 1981), and Joan Adams and Becky Thomas, *Floating Schools and Frozen Inkwells: The One-Room Schools of British Columbia* (Madeira Park: Harbour Publishing, 1985). See also for other regions, Robert S. Patterson, "Voices from the Past: The Personal and Professional Struggle of Rural School Teachers", in N.M. Sheehan, J.D. Wilson, and D.C. Jones, eds., *Schools in the West: Essays in Canadian Educational History* (Calgary: Detselig, 1986), ch. 6; Phillip McCann, ed., *Blackboards and Briefcases: Personal Stories by Newfoundland Teachers, Educators and Administrators* (St. John's: Jesperson Press, 1982).

4. See B. Anne Wood, "Hegelian Resolutions in the New Education Movement: The 1925 Putman-Weir Report," *Dalhousie Review*, 6, 2 (summer 1982): 254-77.

5. British Columbia, Department of Education, *Annual Report of the Public Schools* (hereafter AR] (1920), C34. At times, the inspectors referred to both rural and assisted schools simply as "rural" and for convenience we shall repeat this practice in this article. For more on Lord, see John Calam ed., *Alex Lord's British Columbia: Recollections of a Rural School Inspector, 1915-36* (Vancouver, UBC Press, 1991).

6. *AR*, 1918, 32-33.

7. *Revised Statutes of B.C.* (1924), ch. 226, sections, 25, 31, 110. In order to get the government grant, local parents were often ingenious in their definition of "school age." One memoir reports: "My youngest sister, age two, was enrolled and taken to school (Kaleden) every day." H.W. Corbitt, *The History of Kaleden* (Penticton: Kaleden Centennial Committee, 1958), 7. Boys in their late teens also enrolled in September: it allowed them the additional opportunity to size up the new female teacher. In actual fact many assisted schools operated in the 1920s with fewer than eight pupils average attendance. Often, the inspectors got around the stipulation by reporting, for example, that "more pupils are expected next month."

8. The number of assisted schools was 521. Figures for 1920-1925 are not obtainable because the lists in the *AR* did not distinguish between rural and assisted schools.

9. *Revised Statutes of B.C.* (1924), ch. 226, sections 113, 119-22.

10. Calculations based on information found in the Statistical Tables in the *Annual Reports*, 1918-1930. See Paul J. Stortz, "The Rural School Problem in British Columbia in the 1920s" (M.A. thesis, UBC, 1988), ch. 4. For Okanagan Valley rural schools, see Penelope Stephenson, "Portraits in the First Person: An Historical Ethnography of Rural Teachers and Teaching in British Columbia's Okanagan Valley in the 1920s" (M.A. thesis, UBC, 1993).

11. J.H. Putman and G.M. Weir, *Survey of the School System* (Victoria: King's Printer, 1925), 20. Hereafter the Putman-Weir Report will be referred to as the *Survey*.

12. Ivan J. Saunders, "A Survey of British Columbia School Architecture in 1930," *Research Bulletin* (Parks Canada), 225 (November 1984): 14.

13. *AR*, 1920, C 27.

14. *Survey,* 252, 128-31.

15. According to the 1925 *AR,* 79 percent of the rural and assisted school teachers listed (n=903) were female. Thus, for convenience, throughout this paper the teacher will be referred to in the feminine pronoun.

16. The *Teachers' Bureau Records* are officially known as *School District Information Forms for the Teachers' Bureau* [hereafter *TBR*], Department of Education, Victoria, B.C. They are located at Provincial Archives of B.C. (PABC), GR 461 and are organized alphabetically by school and year (1923 and 1928).

17. *AR,* 1922, C 11; 1923 F 11.

18. *TBR,* Harold J. Bradley, Burgoyne Bay, 1928; Abigail Nicholson, Kildonan, 1928.

19. *Survey,* 132.

20. See the *Survey,* 24-70. For a comprehensive study of Putman, see B. Anne Wood, *Idealism Transformed: The Making of a Progressive Educator* (Kingston and Montreal: McGill-Queen's University Press, 1985). Weir had considerable educational experience in Saskatchewan before coming to UBC. From being head of the History Department at Saskatoon Collegiate Institute he passed quickly (within a year) through being a school inspector to becoming a staff member at the new Saskatchewan Normal School in 1912. Saskatchewan, *Annual Report of the Public Schools,* 1911, 16; 1912, 5, 65; 1913, 35; 1918, 58-61.

21. Wood, "Hegelian Resolutions," 259.

22. John Calam, "Teaching the Teachers: Establishment and Early Years of the B.C. Provincial Normal Schools, *B.C. Studies* 61 (spring 1984): 30-63.

23. Thomas Fleming, "Our Boys in the Field: School Inspectors, Superintendents and the Changing Character of School Leadership in British Columbia," *Schools in the West,* ch. 15.

24. One historian, speaking of Ontario, has graphically characterized inspectors' reports as that "rich underworld of male administrative culture." John Abbott, "Accomplishing 'a Man's Task': Rural Women Teachers, Male Culture and the School Inspectorate in Turn-of-the-Century Ontario," *Ontario History* 78, 4 (December 1986): 313-30.

25. In the first five years of the decade, many inspectors commented on the teachers' lack of enthusiasm to attend summer school. See especially *AR,* 1921, F63; 1922, C 27; 1923, F29, F38; and 1924, T50.

26. *Survey,* 132. It seems certain that inadequate teacher supervision was a reason for the teacher's poor pedagogical practices. One annual inspectoral visit was often the norm in more isolated schools. See the *Survey,* 133, 252-56. For the minimal training which beginning teachers received in the New Education, see Neil Sutherland, "The Triumph of 'Formalism': Elementary Schooling in Vancouver from the 1920s to the 1960s," *B.C. Studies,* special issue on Vancouver 1886-1986, nos. 69/70 (spring/summer 1986): 175-210.

27. *AR,* 1923, F 29. For other inspectors' reports of rigid teaching practices in remote schools, see *AR,* 1920, C30; 1921, F28; and 1923, F28, F30.

28. *Survey,* 188.

29. *AR,* 1929, C26.

30. *AR,* 1922, C33.

31. *AR,* 1922, C40. For other reports on teacher transiency, see *AR,* 1922, C31, C25, C33, C37; 1923, F29; 1924, T53, T58; and 1925, M39.

32. For example, see *AR,* 1920, C27, C30, C37; 1921, F21, F24; and 1922, C31. See also the *Survey* for similar recommendations, 190-92.

33. *AR,* 1921, F36.

34. See the *AR* statistical tables.

35. *AR*, 1921, F39. For other reports that complained of teacher inability, see especially *AR*, 1922, C27; and 1923, F29, F39.

36. *Survey*, 18, 186-88. A teaching degree from a university was a three year program, while a first-class certificate required only one year of post-secondary study. A second-class certificate required one year of normal school and three years of high school, while a third-class certificate, abolished in 1922, demanded only one term (four months at normal school) and three years of high school.

37. David C. Jones, "Creating Rural-Minded Teachers: The British Columbian Experience, 1914-1924," D.C. Jones, N.M. Sheehan and R.M. Stamp, ed., *Shaping the Schools of the Canadian West* (Calgary: Detselig, 1979), 155-76.

38. *Survey*, 202, 194, 207-14; and of the inspectors' reports, see especially *AR*, 1921, F63; 1922 C28; and 1924, T42.

39. *Survey*, 194-95.

40. Norman Fergus Black, "Rural School Problems," *B.C. Teacher* (June 1924): 226-27.

41. *AR*, 1923, F31.

42. *Survey*, 184. See "British Columbia's Pioneer Teachers," chapter 10.

43. *Survey*, 177-79 and *AR* statistical tables.

44. J. Donald Wilson, "'I Am Here to Help If You Need Me': British Columbia's Rural Teachers' Welfare Officer, 1928-1934," *Journal of Canadian Studies* 25 (summer 1990): 94-118.

45. Mary O'Brien, "Sexism in Education," in Ratna Ghosh and Douglas Ray, eds., *Social Change and Education in Canada* (Toronto: Harcourt Brace Jovanovich, 1987), 263.

46. Calam, "Teaching the Teachers," 37.

47. *TBR*, F. Julian Willway, Stevenson Creek, 1928.

48. Interview with Mrs. Lexie Lawrie (neé McLeod), retired schoolteacher, Vancouver, B.C., Feb. 24, 1986.

49. Mildred E. McQuillan, Letters, 1927, PABC. McQuillan's diary is instructive because it contains her attitudes towards her work and community and gives an insight into the trials of a young remote schoolteacher. Her experiences encapsulate those undergone by countless other teachers in the 1920s.

50. Interview with Mrs. Edna May Embury (neé Hicks), 1986. Mrs. Embury was referring to the famous Chisholm murder near Prince Rupert which occurred in May 1926. The murderer was never apprehended nor the motive officially established.

51. *TBR*, Kathleen Murphy, Shutty Beach, 1928; Annie Haughton, Hunter Island, 1923; A.G.W. Dodds, Thetis Island, 1923; Odo A. Barry, Thetis Island, 1928; G. Bertrand, Soda Creek, 1923.

52. Kathleen S. Dewdney, "Christopher Tickel," *Okanagan Historical Society Report* 39 (1976): 84.

53. *TBR*, J. Harry Downard, Stuart River, 1928.

54. *Survey*, 178.

55. *Survey*, 128.

56. *AR*, 1921, F23; 1920, C26, C30; 1924, T55, T59; and 1925 M27.

57. See especially *TBR*, 1923; Miss Ferguson in Cache Creek; Miss Belle Mc Gauley in Champion Creek; Miss Frances H. Hampson in Cultus Lake; Miss Beatrice Tracey in Johnson's Landing; and Miss Ida M. Burnstill in Norwegian Creek. Also see McQuillan Letters, PABC, and Gerry Andrews, *Metis Outpost: Memoirs of the First Schoolmaster at the Metis Settlement of Kelly Lake, B.C., 1923-1925* (Victoria: Pencrest Publishers, 1985), 24.

58. *Survey*, 178.

59. *TBR*, 1923: North Dawson Creek, Beaver Cove.

60. *Survey*, 18. The Survey commented on the disproportionate amount of control the local trustees wielded as opposed to their financial contributions, as well as the tendency for the community administrators to use the money for interests other than education. See pp. 18-19, 124-27 and 172-79.

61. *TBR*, Pineview, 1923. For more on the experiences of Gordon-Cumming, see Jones, "Creating Rural-Minded Teachers," 170-71.

62. Letter from Mrs. Sadie J. Stromgren (neé Johnston), retired schoolteacher, New Westminster, B.C., Apr. 1986.

63. *TBR*, Cape Scott, 1923; Okanagan Landing 1923. For complaints about the obstinacy of the local people, see also *TBR*, 1923; Miss Harriet Sanborn in Bowie; Miss Inge Dohlmann in Burgoyne Bay; Miss Bess Roney in Kingcome Inlet; Mervin Simmons in Pouce Coupe; Miss Minerva Granger in St. Elmo; Miss Elvira Walters in Squam Bay; and Miss Helen A. Dewar in Winlaw.

64. *Survey*, 125-27.

65. For details on ethnicity as a factor in teachers' lives, see "The Visions of Ordinary Participants: Teachers' Views on Rural Schooling in British Columbia in the 1920s," J. Donald Wilson in Patricia E. Roy, ed., *A History of British Columbia: Selected Readings* (Toronto: Copp Clark Pitman, 1988), 239-55.

66. Michael Apple contends that teachers in the twentieth century are members of the petite bourgeoisie and the working class. Apple, "Work, Class and Teaching," in Stephen Walker and Len Barton, eds., *Gender, Class and Education* (New York, 1983), 53-67. For Ontario and Quebec see Marta Danylewycz and Alison Prentice, "Teachers' Work: Changing Patterns and Perceptions in the Emerging School Systems of Nineteenth and Early Twentieth Century Central Canada," *Labour/le travail* 17 (Spring 1986): 59-80.

67. *Survey*, 124.

68. *AR*, 1922, C23.

69. *TBR*, Alfred J. Clotworthy, Telkwa, 1928.

70. *AR*, 1912, 41.

71. For a similar analysis and a description of the importance of the "inspective function," that is, the administrative role of school inspectors, see Philip Corrigan and Bruce Curtis, "Education, Inspection and State Formation: A Preliminary Statement," *Historical Papers*, 1985 (C.H.A., Montreal), 156-71. For resistance to schooling and teachers, see Bruce Curtis, *Building the Educational State: Canada West, 1836-1871* (London, Ont.: Althouse Press, 1988), ch. 8.

72. See *AR*, 1927, M50 and 1929, R43. In 1928, 24 courses were offered in the Victoria Normal School; in 1929, 26 courses. See *AR*, 1928, V47 and 1929, R43. The curriculum for the Vancouver Normal School is unavailable for these years.

73. See especially *AR*, 1926, R51-52; 1927, M50-52; and 1929, R43. It is interesting to note that while principal of the Saskatoon Normal School, Weir had advocated the placement of practice teachers in conditions "that obtain in rural communities" rather than in urban schools. Saskatchewan *AR*, 1919, 101; 1920, 62.

74. Sylvia McKay (1929, Victoria Normal School), Normal School Project, University of Victoria, interviewer Judy Windle, tape recording 78-Y-27. Citation kindly provided by John Calam.

75. Indeed, a high of only 15 percent of all the teachers in the province attended during these years.

76. The average attendance of rural and assisted school teachers for each year between 1925-1930 was 112 as opposed to 388 average total enrolment per year. It is important to note that the one-room teacher enrolment in summer school and attendance in the various rural courses were perforce smaller than the figures given for rural and assisted school teachers.

77. All statistics were drawn from the *AR*.

78. See, for example, *AR* 1928, V28; and *AR*, 1927, M31, where the time consumed waiting for the boats "as the only means of conveyance in certain of [my] districts . . . [was] altogether out of proportion to the number of schools to be visited." For a fascinating study of transportation networks of the time, see Cole Harris, "Moving Amid the Mountains, 1870-1930," *B.C. Studies* 58 (summer 1983): 3-39.

79. Interview with Mrs. Margaret Manning (neé Lanyon), retired school teacher, Vancouver, 12 Apr. 1987.

80. *TBR*, Crawford Creek, 1928.

81. Interview, Mrs. M. Embury, retired schoolteacher, Vancouver, B.C., March 1986; interview, Mrs. Lexie Lawrie, retired schoolteacher, Vancouver, B.C., 24 Feb. 1986; interview, Mrs. Manning 1987; interview, Miss Mary Pack, retired schoolteacher, Vancouver, B.C., 25 Mar. 1986; and interview, Mrs. G.A. Steele (neé Smith), retired schoolteacher, Vancouver, B.C., 11 Apr. 1987.

82. *AR*, 1927, M37.

83. Unfortunately, attendance figures for the various annual conventions are not available. None of the retired school teachers interviewed recalled attending a convention while employed as a teacher in a remote school.

84. See especially *AR* 1926, R35; 1928, V21, 31; and 1929, R11.

85. Of all rural and assisted teachers in 1930, 34.5 percent had first class certificates versus 23 percent in 1925; 58.5 percent in 1930 had second class certificates versus 64 percent in 1925; 2.1 percent had third class certificates in 1930 versus 7 percent in 1925. The issuance of third class certificates had been stopped in 1922.

86. Changes in percentages for rural and assisted school teachers coincided roughly with the figures for other teacher classifications. All statistics were drawn from the *AR* tables.

87. *AR*, 1927, M34; 1928, V26; 1925, M11.

88. *AR*, 1924, T56.

89. Department of Education Newspaper Clippings, Provincial Archives, Victoria, B.C., 1925.

90. The statistics were drawn from the *AR*.

91. Just how important teaching qualifications were in helping to secure a teaching job was dependent mostly upon community requirements as perceived by the local school board. Interestingly, in 1926 Miss Margaret Lanyon landed her job in Black Canyon school in competition with a "shoe box full of 150 applicants" because she included a covering letter which described her father's recent industrial accident. Mrs. Manning was convinced that it was the sympathy expressed by the local school board for this event which assured her the teaching position (interview, Mrs. Manning, 1987).

92. David C. Jones, "The Strategy of Rural Enlightenment: Consolidation in Chilliwack, B.C., 1919-1920," Jones, Sheehan and Stamps, eds., *Shaping the Schools of the Canadian West*, ch. 9.

93. David C. Jones, "The Zeitgeist of Western Settlement: Education and the Myth of the Land," Wilson and Jones, eds., *Schooling and Society in Twentieth Century British Columbia* (Calgary: Detselig, 1980), ch. 3.

94. Cole Harris, "Industry and the Good Life Around Idaho Peak," *Canadian Historical Review* LXVI, no. 3 (September 1985): 315-43.

95. PABC, Additional Manuscripts 347, vol. 2, file 2/27 (incoming and outgoing correspondence); Additional Manuscripts 44 (travel diary). See J. Donald Wilson, "'I am ready to be of assistance when I can . . .'" Alison Prentice and Marjorie Theobald, eds., *Women Who Taught: Perspectives on the History of Women and Teaching* (Toronto: University of Toronto Press, 1991), 202-29. See chapter 14 of this book.

96. Letter from Mary Pack, retired schoolteacher, Vancouver, April 1986.

12

"Mrs Gibson Looked As If She Was Ready For The End Of Term": The Professional Trials And Tribulations Of Rural Teachers In British Columbia's Okanagan Valley in the 1920s

Penelope Stephenson

In 1975 John Calam lamented the fact that the teacher in history had, for the most part, been placed "at the periphery rather than at the centre of research attention" and called for historians to rectify this situation.[1] However, much of the early historical work on teachers was quantitative in approach, and thus even when teachers have been the focus of study the story has often been more in terms of what was done to them, or thought of them and about them, by others, rather than from the perspective of the teachers themselves. Female teachers especially have been treated as "nonpersons" and as "objects rather than subjects."

In the light of such concerns the importance of studying the subjective side of educational history in general, and the history of teachers in particular, has, and is, being increasingly advocated. As Richard Quantz, an American educational historian, contends:

> To understand teachers, we need to do more than treat schools as little black boxes with interchangeable parts which take inputs and create outputs and which are manipulated by those from outside them. . . . Attention to the larger forces of history provide a framework of understanding, but without a depiction of the finer detail of the participants' subjective realities, we fail to understand the dynamics of history. By following only microhistory we are in danger of reversing the common maxim and "failing to see the trees for the forest." In our eagerness to map out the great movements of "man," we sometimes forget that historical events often involved real women living in their own subjective, but equally real, worlds.[3]

However, as Gillian Creese and Veronica Strong-Boag have pointed out, identifying and documenting "women's actual experiences" is problematical because "much female experience has . . . gone unnoted in conventional sources" and been frequently "overlooked in men's accounts." Such difficulties have "led to a search for documents in which women narrate their own experiences" and thus "tell their own stories in their own words."[4] By exploring and analyzing first-person accounts of teachers' lives in letters, diaries, personal journals, memoirs and autobiographies, and also by way of oral testimony, historians have been able to examine the social context and meaning of teachers' lives. "Without such sources," Donald Warren suggests, "historians have trouble getting past the schoolhouse door."[5] Or, alternatively, as Richard J. Altenbaugh asserts: "Oral history enables educational historians to open the classroom door and investigate schooling from the perspective of one of its principal participants – the teacher."[6]

It is equally relevant to examine teachers in rural settings. Such a focus is in keeping with the increasing recognition that rural society needs to be examined in its own right and not just as the passive recipient of changes that were initiated in urban centres. Rural society was neither "passive" nor "homogeneous." Rather, historians have been able to document dynamic historical processes at work independent of any metropolitan forces. Indeed, rural life was the main feature of social formation for the majority of the Canadian population until the early decades of the twentieth century and as such must be accorded equal importance with urban society.[7] The study of the teachers who taught in rural areas in British Columbia is obviously central to such an agenda.

This essay offers a look at the dynamics of the rural classroom in the form of a case study of some of those who taught in the small rural schools of the Okanagan Valley in the Southern Interior of British Columbia in the 1920s.[8] The aim is to convey in intimate detail a portraiture of the multiple realities of rural teaching as expressed in the attitudes, perceptions and feelings held by individual teachers about their work experiences in the past. The framework of analysis centres exclusively on teacher experience within the confines of the schoolhouse itself. The pedagogical working conditions that rural teachers confronted on a daily basis in their classrooms and how they coped with their professional responsibilities, the nature of the relationships that developed between teachers and their pupils, and the response of students, and indirectly parents, to their rural schooling experience, are the focus of the discussion that follows.

A series of oral interviews conducted with surviving rural teachers and pupils from the 1920s, as well as various other personal history materials that the participants were willing to share with me, comprise the primary data for this essay. Personal narratives thus form the core of the text. Also used were the pertinent printed and manuscript records of the British Columbia Department of Education, authored by teachers,[9] school inspectors and other officials,[10] the Census of Canada, and local histories. In general terms the oral interviews complement the information in the official sources and provide insider perspectives of the events referred to in the written documents. More importantly, they generate primary source material about the undocumented areas of teacher experience or where the written documents are inadequate. Whilst attempting to remain true to the highly personal and unique nature of each individual teacher's experience I chose to thread together their accounts in order to convey the character of their collective experience. In this way the resulting narrative is the composite story of rural school teaching in the Okanagan Valley as told by the subjects.[11]

Rural teachers encountered and ultimately had to cope with a whole slew of pedagogical challenges which, for the most part, were beyond their control and which combined to produce considerable personal stress. A matter of major concern to all rural teachers was the problem of orchestrating the simultaneous instruction of a group of children of varying ages, abilities and attainments. The design and then implementation of a structured academic programme to serve all the various grades in the rural, and particularly one-room, school was an extremely difficult task, often made all the more time-consuming when the previous teacher had failed to leave any progress reports on the pupils. As Inspector A. R. Lord commented on the obviously trying situation facing Duncan P. Clark, a graduate of the Manitoba Normal School, who was appointed to teach at Mabel Lake School in September 1929: "Mr Clark is not familiar with either ungraded or primary school work [and] the outgoing teacher left literally nothing to assist him in organizing his school. Satisfactory results can scarcely be expected for a time."[12] Each teacher had to assess the level of attainment of individual pupils, and then group them together in appropriate grades in order to shepherd them through the prescribed curriculum. Some schools had high school classes which put added pressure on the teacher because the students' success or failure obviously reflected back on them. Thus Margaret Landon, who began her teaching career at Salmon Bench School in 1923, remarked of her experience at the school: "I was lucky enough to have a small group of pupils in grades 1 to 7 so there was no grade 8 to prepare for government examinations in June." In the case of children with special needs, whether learning disabled or gifted, rural teachers felt particularly frustrated because they had neither the training nor the resources, much less the time, to devote to them. Some pupils suffered from a lack of stimulation. In this context Alice Gibson regretted the fact that Sugar Lake "was such a small school" because "the smarter ones often had no-one to challenge them."

Timetabling and preparing individual lessons in every subject and for each grade, and then marking the assignments set, as well as keeping up to date with the compulsory school records such as monthly report cards for each pupil, was an administrative nightmare for rural teachers. Particularly for those with little experience, it demanded a seemingly inordinate amount of work. To Isobel Simard it seemed that "Every hour of the day practically I was preparing lessons." Marianne Nelson expressed similar sentiments when she stated: "I taught by one method, constant work, work, work, for me, that is."

Virtually all the former teachers interviewed considered the paucity of apparatus, in terms of instructional resources and supplies, to be their major stumbling block to effective teaching. Even an essential item of equipment such as the blackboard was often small and of inferior quality. In many schools they were, as in the case of Sugar Lake School, "painted wall-board" and therefore "not satisfactory."[13] The only other pieces of equipment that could generally be found in rural schools in the 1920s have been summed up by Lucy McCormick:

> Some schools had a roll of maps on spring rollers which, with wear and tear, shot up like cannon and had to be rewound with a fork. The most commonly seen map was one of Canada, a complimentary one from the Neilson Chocolate Company, advertising their chocolate bars. . . . A photo of the King, a Union Jack, a globe, and a school handbell.[14]

In the face of such limitations rural teachers, as Lucy's words imply, had to extemporise, modifying or varying their lessons according to the resources at their disposal, and also preparing their own materials. The dearth of textbooks was partially overcome by teachers spending substantial amounts of time laboriously copying out various exercises, assignments and notes onto the blackboard. Isobel Simard stated that at Kingfisher School she "always kept lots of work on the blackboard for them. I had to go down in the evening to prepare work on the blackboard for them." In fact she referred to the schoolhouse as "my home" because she "spent so many hours in that school." Alice Laviollette clearly remembered that as a pupil at Sugar Lake: "The teacher did everything on the board. . . . No textbooks. All our work was put up on the board." Some rural teachers made use of the "hectograph" or "jelly pad" duplicator. To Marianne Nelson the hectograph had been invaluable. She recalled spending long hours on many nights preparing and then pressing out worksheets and maps to keep her students busy the following day, and thus she suggested jokingly: "I had hectograph ink in my blood!"

"Really excellent accomodation for a school . . . well equipped, pleasant, comfortable, warm." Interior, Ellison School, 1927. (Courtesy of Bernard C. Gillie)

Rural teachers also learnt to utilize the natural resources on their school's doorstep to provide interesting lessons for their pupils. Anne Vardon recalled that as a pupil at Medora Creek School: "Our teachers took us on many nature rambles and there always seemed to be several large coffee jars with frogs' eggs hatching into tadpoles, at the back [of the classroom] on a table. . . . It seemed we were forever drawing any flower that was in season, or leaves or fruit."

Organizing instruction during the actual school day required that rural teachers develop considerable management skills to ensure that their pupils were productively occupied at all times and that their classrooms remained under control and running smoothly. For the most part teachers worked with each grade separately. Ila Embree described a commonly used strategy: "You bring the ones in the class to stand around your desk – grade 1 or 2 or 3 or whatever it is – and talk to them and teach them and then send them back to do it. Then you call up the next grade." This meant that at any one time the majority of pupils were working unsupervised. This situation posed a real dilemma for many rural teachers, as Margaret Landon explained: "To keep the classes going with suitable busy-work while I taught each class in turn was my biggest problem."

Finding themselves swamped with work a number of rural teachers reverted back to the old monitorial system of using older students to help those in the lower grades. Anne Richards remembered that at Okanagan Landing School one of her teachers "used to perhaps take somebody out of the grade 8 or 7 [who] was doing well and didn't need extra [help], and sent them down to look after the grade 1's and the grade 2's and help them with their work."[15] Many of those interviewed also recalled the situation as described by Margaret Landon who stated that at Salmon Bench School "the children helped each other and everyone was exposed to other classes so [they] could pick up on things they might have missed." Thus Mary Woollan, a pupil at North Enderby School from 1917-1924, recalled that "jumped grades were frequent as so much could be learned from listening to the senior classes and helping with the juniors."[16]

The extent to which an individual teacher was able to deal successfully with such exigent circumstances was dependent to a certain degree upon the level of enrolment at the particular school in which they taught. Schools with relatively small numbers on the roll were, after an initial period of trial and error, manageable. Alice Gibson, for example, likened her position as teacher at Sugar Lake, where the numbers never rose above eight in the four years that she taught at the school, to that of a "governess job." She explained that "with only six or seven pupils in three to four levels it wasn't difficult to keep a good working rapport." However, in some schools, those designated as "heavy" by teachers and inspectors alike usually because enrolment was at the level of thirty pupils or above, the organisational and instructional problems outlined above were of an order of magnitude greater than in schools with low enrolments.[17] As Marianne Nelson, who taught in a number of rural schools throughout the Okanagan Valley, reported:

> I was lucky to have had five years of experience in two ungraded schools with a school attendance of only twelve pupils or so. . . . When I taught in the larger ungraded schools I rarely went to bed before 12 p.m. to 1 a.m. as I had work answers and essays to correct, to find out how the pupils were doing. . . . [S]chools . . . with thirty pupils in eight grades, were, 'teacher killing' schools. I heard several cases where young beginner teachers quit at Christmas, or the next June after September, or had nervous breakdowns.

To control such a varied group of children in one room made maintaining discipline a concern for all teachers in rural schools. For some, keeping order in their classrooms was a substantial challenge. There was no place for the teacher who could not control her charges. Again such problems were magnified in schools with large enrolments. Overage boys, who often rivalled the teacher in size as well as age, could be particularly problematical. Anne Richards, who was a pupil at Okanagan Landing

School in the early 1920s, recalled that "some of those kids in grade 8 were practically grown up, sixteen, seventen years old. . . . They would be hard to handle too." Inspector Lord had designated Okanagan Landing an "unusually heavy ungraded school."[18] Laura Alcock was a pupil at Mission Creek School between 1918 and 1923. In 1922, just prior to the opening of a second classroom, enrolment at this one-room school had risen to forty-nine. Laura vividly remembered the "stress" that one of her teachers experienced in trying to control the "big boys" in her class: "There was no discipline at all. There would be amongst the smaller children because they were more afraid, but the bigger ones just dominated her with their saucy remarks. . . . I can remember her bursting into tears [because] they never did anything that they were told."

The designation "heavy" referred not only to those schools where class size made them difficult to organize but also, and in many instances simultaneously, to those where the pupil population included children from various ethnic backgrounds. Many teachers also had to accommodate children, often newly arrived in Canada, who spoke little or no English. After his visit to Norma Schroeder, a beginning teacher of less than twelve months' experience, at Benvoulin School in 1930, Inspector T. R. Hall reported: "This is the most difficult rural school which I have seen in the course of my work as an inspector. The attendance averages around fifty, all grades are represented, and a large proportion of the pupils are of foreign extraction."[19] It is important to note that the vast majority of rural teachers were not professionally equipped to deal with the difficulties of language and cultural change. In the 1920s, English as a Second Language (ESL) training for teachers, as well as the necessary curriculum materials, were undeveloped and certainly unavailable in rural schools.

The specific practices and strategies that rural teachers actually employed to effectively instruct non-English-speaking pupils were thus, of necessity, essentially pragmatic ones. When Ellison School opened in September 1927, Bernard Gillie, and his assistant Irene Cooper, had to accommodate a group of eighteen Austrian children, whose parents had recently moved into the district to work on the tobacco farms. Bernard explained in colorful detail the nature of the predicament he faced and how he attempted to cope with it: "[They] didn't speak a word of English . . . couldn't understand a thing I said and I had to provide an education for these people. I was completely stunned." With no information about the level of educational attainment of the children Bernard and Irene were at a loss as to how to grade them. In this situation, Bernard continued: "We lined them all up – this could hardly be described as reliable pedagogy – according to size and the nine or ten smallest ones went into Irene's room and the other ones came in my room."

What, and more importantly how, to instruct these children was the next problem. Lacking any appropriate language textbooks, and "in a state of panic" Bernard wrote to a former instructor at Normal School pleading for help. As a result he acquired a few copies of *English for New Canadians* to help him teach the Austrian pupils. Fortunately Bernard discovered that many of the young immigrants were proficient in arithmetic. He explained how he capitalised on this situation: "These poor little wretches. When I didn't know what else to do with them I put copious quantities of addition, subtraction, multiplication and division on the board and said 'O. K. Get busy and do this.'" Unable to speak to the children in English the only way that Bernard could communicate his instructions was by way of "waving my hands around and making signals and signs etc!"

Rural teachers also had to take account of the fact that many immigrant children found the process of adjustment to their new culture very bewildering. Mary Genier felt sorry for the "little German kids" at Medora Creek School who were obviously confused about their new schooling experience: "One little girl crawled under the desk for the first day . . . like a little wild animal, scared to death." Sometimes, of course, there was also prejudice. A number of former pupils, particularly those of German origin, related that they had experienced racial discrimination from both pupils and teachers. Anne Richards recalled that after the First World War "There was that terrible feeling against Germans. . . . You didn't let anyone know that you were German." In the same way Alice Laviollette stated that she and her siblings "had quite a hard time because we were classed as Germans and we didn't have many friends."

Rural teachers had to accept the probability that the level of attendance at their schools could be, and often was, both sporadic and unpredictable. Irregular attendance patterns were a common feature of rural education and for the most part were well beyond the control of the teacher. The attitude towards education varied considerably not only from one school district to another, but also between different families in an individual community, according to the home situation. Most of the former teachers interviewed reported that, in their experience, parental support for education in rural districts, in terms of whether they encouraged their children to attend school, was positive, and often enthusiastic. Ida Palmer recalled that her parents were very concerned that she and her siblings attend school in Okanagan Landing: "They wanted us to be educated so badly." Other children attended school, some teachers believed, only because they were compelled to do so. Thus the response of some rural parents to the education of their children was, so Alice Gibson asserted, "passive." The attitude held by Anne Richards' parents, who lived at Okanagan Landing, was typical of this perspective: "I don't think they thought too much about it or worried too much about it. They sent us to school and that was it. . . . I don't think they thought too much about . . . whether we were becoming educated or not." Such passivity can partially be explained in terms of the limited future prospects that the majority of young men and women in rural districts faced on leaving school. Most remained in the small communities in which they had been born and raised, to follow in their parents' footsteps, making a living farming or logging.

Ila Embree, who taught at Kedleston School, considered that: "Work and a job and bringing some money in was the main ambition of everybody in those days." Thus in isolated districts, schools were so closely adapted to the communities of which they were a product that the level of education children both required and received represented no more than the needs of rural society. It was a reflection of what rural parents expected. It is interesting, however, that even in those families where the parents had a minimal interest in education, their children often developed a strong desire to attend school. Alice Gibson suggested that at Sugar Lake: "There wasn't anything else to do for them. . . . There was nothing there." Significantly, the school was frequently the only social institution for children, and indeed often adults, in remote communities. One long-time resident of the Okanagan Valley has summed up the place of the "little one-roomed school" in rural districts by commenting that it was "really the center of our lives."[20]

"The means of entertainment were in our own hands. . . . We made our own fun."
Costume dress party at Sugar Lake School, 1926. (Courtesy of Alice Gibson)

Unfortunately, whether the attitude to education was "positive" or merely "passive" the isolation, harsh topography, transiency and chronic poverty so characteristic of many of the small rural settlements in the Okanagan Valley were factors which had a tremendous influence on the process of education in general, and could not help but impede school attendance. Moreover it is clear that in many instances pupil absence from school was often a direct result of these factors as opposed to being an indication of any disregard for the importance of education by their parents.

Even though in most cases rural schools were centrally located in a community, the scattered nature of settlement in the Okanagan Valley meant that the distance between home and school prevented some pupils from attending regularly. Aileen M. Halford reported such a problem at Hilton School: "Difference between average attendance [8. 4] and number of children of school age [14] is accounted for by great distance from school."[21] Most teachers and pupils travelled to school on foot, others came by horse and buggy or on horseback. Occasionally, however, severe weather conditions caused already poor roads to become impassable. This combined with inadequate or unavailable transportation to exacerbate the problem of distance. Alice

Gibson stated that for the pupils at remote Sugar Lake School "weather conditions would keep them home more than anything else." Many former pupils recalled the problems of trying to get to and from school, particularly in the winter. Millie Bonney still has very vivid memories of her journey to Springbend School: "It was pretty cold sometimes and you had to trudge through deep snow and [your] hands would be freezing when you got [there], almost crying with pain." On arrival at school during periods of severe climatic conditions rural teachers had to take precious time out of their already hectic schedules to ensure that their pupils were warm, dry and comfortable enough to concentrate on their lessons. On many occasions Marianne Nelson had to deal with "children, walking several miles to school, scantily clothed, who had to be warmed near the school stove, and for quite some time." Some schools closed completely, often for weeks at a time, due to inclement weather. Isobel Simard remembered this situation happening at Kingfisher School: "There was one winter that was so cold the school had to close in January for a week or two."

The level of school attendance was also dependent on the nature and extent of economic activity and hence available employment in an area. Transiency was a common feature of the settlement pattern in rural districts, particularly those based on struggling subsistence economies. This often posed a real problem for teachers who could unexpectedly be faced with the possibility of a sudden increase, or alternatively a decrease, sometimes substantial, in the number of pupils enrolled at their school.[22]

When the number of pupils in their schools dropped rural teachers not only had their work plans disrupted, but were also threatened with the likelihood of school closure, if enrolment fell below the required minimum to keep the school open. Bernard Gillie faced just this situation. In 1928, the enrolment at the two-room school at Ellison fell to thirty-seven, which was below the level to warrant a second classroom. Bernard was informed by Inspector Hall that unless he could find a way of bringing the enrolment up to the necessary level he was to lose his second teacher, and face the daunting prospect of converting the school into one-room and teaching all thirty-seven pupils himself, Bernard recalled his dilemma and how he eventually solved the problem, which he described as "enough to drive anyone to distraction:"

> I've never worked harder in my life than I did for that month. I worked fifteen to sixteen hours a day trying to prepare material. . . . I resorted to desperation. . . . I scoured the neighbourhood to find if anybody had a couple of youngsters that looked as if they might be of school age. Let's not worry about whether they really were or not. I found a couple and I persuaded their parents to send them to school. So that gave me my thirty-nine or thirty-eight or whatever I needed. . . . Nobody ever came and said 'Let me see the birth certificates of these two kids that you've got' . . . . For all [anybody] knew they could have been three years old.

Rural teachers also had to accept the fact that parents, struggling to provide the bare essentials of food, clothing and shelter, might withdraw their children from school in order for them to work. Often a child's contribution, either as an extra unit of labor on the family farm, or alternatively in terms of the additional few dollars they might earn working elsewhere in the community, was vital to a family's economic survival. For almost three months at the beginning of the school year in 1923, Miss M.E.A. McMynn, teacher at Westbank Townsite School, had a much reduced class to teach, because, as she explained: "Until nearly the end of November about half the pupils are absent to pick and pack fruit."[23] Amanda Singer recalled that her brother "missed so much school all the time. Dad would keep him home to cut firewood and things like that. Of course a book didn't mean much to him." Girls were sometimes required to care for siblings while parents were at work. Alice Laviollette reported: "[I] had to stay home lots of times to stay with the younger kids. . . . I was always the one who had to stay. . . . Lots of times I would have to take [the baby] to Mum where she was working because she was nursing then. Really I didn't go to school every day."

Farmwork and childcare aside, family impoverishment sometimes drove parents, often through shame or embarrassment, to keep their children at home when they could not afford to provide them with appropriate clothing or footwear, or with a lunch for noon hour. To quote Alice Laviollette once again: "The reason why I quit going to school was because we had nothing to eat in the house, absolutely nothing. We were just starving. . . . We had nothing to make lunch with. . . . We had no clothes and we were very, very poor." Thus rural teachers had to cope with children who were often hungry, undernourished and poorly clothed. Lloyda Wills, who taught Alice and some of her siblings at Hilton School recalled the desperate situation of the family. On one particular occasion, after they had been absent from school for three days, she decided to go to their home to ascertain the reason for their truancy, whereupon she found them "playing outside in their bare feet." Lloyda quickly realized why they had not been attending school: "They didn't have very much. They didn't have very much to eat either. They were quite poor. They didn't even have enough bread in the house for their lunches and that's why the mother didn't send them."

Finally pupil attendance in rural schools was affected by ill health. Outbreaks of contagious diseases spread rapidly from one pupil to another and could empty a schoolroom in a very short time. In his annual report on the Kelowna Inspectorate in 1924, which included sixty-one schools in rural districts, Inspector Hall noted:

> The work of the schools was greatly handicapped during the year by poor attendance, due to illness; in consequence of successive epidemics of whooping cough and measles many of the schools were closed for a time, while for several weeks the attendance was so broken that satisfactory work was out of the question.

There is no doubt that working under these strenuous conditions militated against any serious hopes that rural teachers might have harbored of developing, and then successfully implementing, a comprehensive, up-to-date and structured academic programme in their schools, such as was advocated in the Putman-Weir Report of 1925. Consequently the daily agenda for most pupils who attended rural schools consisted primarily of instruction in the basic skills of literacy and numeracy, and usually by way of word and phonic drill and rote memorization.

In addition to their strictly professional responsibilities, teachers in rural schools were also expected to find time in their already busy workdays to perform a number of other roles at the school. For many rural teachers one of their non-teaching "duties" was to act as school janitor. While 65 percent (59 of 91) of the teachers in the Okanagan Valley who completed and submitted a TBR to the Department of Education indicated that their respective School Board employed a janitor this did not however necessarily indicate either a full-time or an adult employee. In some districts individuals were appointed only part-time or to do a specific job. At Salmon Valley School, the teacher, Lydia Hayes, reported that a janitor was engaged "For firelighting 5 months only."[25] In a number of instances the School Board employed one or more children to carry out some, or all, of the janitorial work. Belle McGauley stated that "2 school pupils" were engaged at Ashton Creek School, and Alfred Hooper, teacher at South Kelowna School, noted: "One pupil paid to do sweeping only."[26] Children could not always be relied upon however, as R. N. Nesbitt clearly pointed out was the case for Ecclestone School: "Pupil, not well done."[27] Concomitantly this meant that even where a janitor was engaged rural teachers could also be liable for at least a portion of the work. They may also have had to supervise the work of others to ensure that it reached the required standard.

In at least 35 percent (32 of 91) of the rural schools in the Okanagan Valley teachers were entirely responsible for keeping their classrooms clean and warm. Vera Towgood recalled having been forewarned by an instructor at Victoria Normal "about the possibility that we might find a one-room school in 'a less than clean condition.' [He said] 'Don't hesitate to do what you can – sweep it out, scrub the floor & walls if necessary. Remember that all work is noble.'" Many of the former teachers who were interviewed confirmed that fullfiling such obligations had indeed been part of their rural teaching experience. Lucy McCormick stated that "as a rule" those who taught in rural districts also served as the "caretaker, firelighter, and general custodian of the school, especially if it was in an isolated area."[28] A number of others, such as Marianne Nelson, emphasized the multifarious nature of their work by describing themselves as a "general factotum" rather than exclusively an educator of children. Although rural teachers were not overly enthusiastic about their janitorial duties, in general they did not object strongly to the expectation that such work was their responsibility. Alice Gibson expressed a commonly held view of many of the participants: "All this was not a hardship as it was the status quo for most one-room teachers of that era. . . . [It was] one of the things you did."

Whereas chores such as sweeping the floor, cleaning the blackboards and general tidying up could be done after school, lighting a fire in the stove could only be done early in the morning. This made it imperative that those rural teachers arrive at the schoolhouse long before the start of the normal school day. Lucy McCormick lived in a teacherage in the grounds of Mabel Lake School and her daily routine began thus: "I'd light the fire in my own cabin and rush over and light the fire in the school." While teaching at Hupel School Marianne Nelson lived less than half a mile from the schoolhouse, whereas most of her pupils "walked several miles to attend school." So early each morning she "carried kindling, wrapped in newspaper from my boarding house to start the winter and cool-weather fires." Esma Shunter experienced real problems in trying to get the old Shuswap Falls School warm before her pupils arrived: "There was a big hole where the stove pipe went out and the snow would come down and the stove would be covered with snow and you'd have to sweep the snow off before you lit it."

Use of the school building in many rural areas for various community functions often increased the teacher's janitorial workload. Lucy McCormick recalled that "As the schools were frequently used for Saturday night dances and for church services on Sundays, on Monday mornings most of the desks would be in the wrong places and had to be reorganized."[29] Likewise Ila Embree reported that at Kedleston, "when there were any events in the neighbourhood they happened in the school yard or at the schoolhouse and you didn't know if it [would] have been cleaned up like you'd like to have it."[30]

Teachers in isolated districts also had to double as nurse, doctor or even dentist for their pupils when the situation arose. Complying with Provincial Department of Health regulations, rural teachers routinely checked their pupils for contagious diseases and administered general health care precautions. Wilma Hayes, former pupil at Ellison School, recalled how one of her teachers, Eldred K. Evans, acted on the advice of the local Public Health Officer to help reduce the incidence of goitre amongst the pupils at the school: "One such project that I recall was in the days before the use of iodized salt. Each noon hour every student lined up, under Eldred's supervision, for a glass of water containing several drops of tincture of iodine."[31] Some teachers even acted in the capacity of dentist. Marianne Nelson reported: "I used to pull teeth too. I got pretty good at pulling teeth."

Dealing with situations like those described above presented most rural teachers with few problems. However, when unpredictable crises struck such as a sudden illness or an accident at their schools they were often unprepared, and therefore unable to cope. Although the situations they faced were perhaps no worse than those confronted by their urban colleagues, the fact that expert medical care was so much harder to come by in rural areas made any problems potentially more serious. Lucy McCormick explained:

> She had to deal with any emergency. . . . Telephone service was non-existent, and medical services the same, with no Public Health nurse to turn to. The Medical Officer of Health . . . had such an area to cover that a school was lucky if they saw him every second year. If hospital care was needed it was a long way from Cherryville, Mabel Lake, or Trinity Valley by horse and buggy to Vernon.

A number of "unfortunate" incidents were related to me by former teachers where children needlessly suffered due to the lack of immediate and appropriate medical attention. At Mabel Lake School one young girl had her eye punctured by a stick and as a consequence lost her sight in that eye. At Medora Creek School another girl died as a result of a ruptured appendix. Teachers expressed the utter frustration and helplessness they felt in such circumstances. They not only lacked the necessary knowledge and expertise in medical procedures, but in most rural schools supplies to render even the most basic first aid did not exist, as Marianne Nelson's account of the contents of the medical facilities at Medora Creek School clearly illustrates:

> There was no equipment for first aid . . . nothing. With the exception of some clean white rags coming from the kind lady of my boarding place, I used a green salve for cuts, some tweezers to pull out slivers, and some needles and thread and safety pins, to save a pupil's dignity, should he or she rip clothes in play.

Marianne added resentfully: "Our Normal training should have included a course in first aid."

Finding time during the school day to take a few quiet moments alone was virtually impossible for the teacher in a rural school. Even during recess and noon-hour they were obliged to oversee their pupils' activities and to take responsibility for their behavior. Many rural teachers were also "ordered" to preside over the organization of a hot meal for their pupils at lunch-time. This usually consisted of a soup concocted from vegetables, either dried or in season, and would be cooked slowly on the school stove over the course of the morning. "So there goes the teacher," Lucy McCormick stated, "cook as well as nurse."[32] Some teachers, particularly those working in impoverished communities, like Marianne Nelson at Medora Creek School who felt deeply concerned about those of her pupils whom she regarded as obviously "deprived" and "underfed," initiated the provision of food for their pupils at lunch-time at their own expense. In such cases they did so, not because they were required to, but in response to a perceived need to ensure the children received at least minimal nutritional requirements. Marianne stated: "You should have seen those kids look forward to lunch." Anne Vardon, one of Marianne's pupils, recalled her kindness: "We were very poor at that time, and whenever she could she always helped out by bringing extra lunch that she thought we'd like, like extra cobs of corn or extra tomatoes or extra apples or something."

The in-school workday of the typical rural teacher was thus fully occupied. In trying to coordinate their time effectively and allocate it between their many responsibilites, they had, out of necessity, to become a jack-of-all-trades. A huge gulf existed between what was expected of them and what in reality they could achieve given the circumstances in which they were required to perform. Anne Richards, referring to one of her teachers at Okanagan Landing School, has encapsulated most rural teachers' inevitable situation, given the trials and frustrations they confronted on a daily basis: "I think she had more work than she could stand really. . . . But she was, well I guess, like all country school teachers, she did the best she could and that was all." Stan Wejr, a former pupil of Trinity Creek School, appreciated the huge undertaking it must have been to effectively manage a rural school in the 1920s when he wrote: "Believe me, that teacher earned her salary."[33]

The issue of whether the instruction teachers received during their months at Normal School actually equipped them to practice their profession in an isolated rural school was a moot point among the former teachers interviewed. When questioned specifically in this respect Esma Shunter's response, like that of many of the others, was emphatic: "No. I don't know how it could." Although they felt that their pedagogical training had been an important part of their lives in terms of their personal development, by the same token many of them also made vociferous complaints about what they regarded as the shortcomings of that training. Alice Gibson stated: "Normal School was a wonderful experience but there's no way it could prepare you for one-room teaching. The problems were different in every one." Lucy McCormick questioned how any Normal School program could feasibly instill in student teachers an awareness and understanding of the idiosyncrasies of living and working in remote districts: "The teacher training didn't do much to equip a young teacher to face a group of children and a community which could be very critical."

As noted earlier, the foremost stumbling block for new teachers was instructional: how to coordinate tuition in a multi-grade situation. The statements by former teachers indicate that in this regard they deemed their professional training to have been both impractical and irrelevant in the face of the actual circumstances they encountered in their rural classrooms. Facilities for practice teaching existed at both Vancouver and Victoria Normal Schools in the 1920s and most of those interviewed regarded such experience as the "most useful" and "valuable" aspect of their training program, because as Bernard Gillie suggested, it gave them "some idea of the importance of the continuity of lessons etc." Unfortunately, as Alice Gibson pointed out, "It was geared mainly to teaching one grade . . . situations in city schools." In 1927 Ruby Drasching did her "final two week practicum . . . at a rural school 'Happy Valley,' on the outskirts of Victoria," an assignment of far too short a duration and in a location that was hardly isolated enough to give Ruby any real sense of what teaching in the remote corners of British Columbia's hinterland really entailed. Her first teaching post was the one-room school at Grandview Bench where conditions were qualitatively very different from those she had experienced in suburban Victoria.[34]

The following account of Bernard Gillie's rude introduction to the very real world of one-room teaching highlights the immense training gap that existed as teachers tried to follow Department of Education policy and Courses of Study:

> One of the things that they taught us in Normal School was that you had to plan all your lessons. . . . [T]hat's theoretically a brilliant idea [so] I started out trying to do this. Here I am with six classes, some of them had only two or three youngsters in, including of course a group of eight beginners who had never been to school before. So if I tried to . . . write out a lesson plan for each one of those classes, for all day long, I needed a twelve day week. . . . This was hopelessly unrealistic. . . . I couldn't bridge . . . the gulf between theory and practice. . . . This was the experience of hundreds of teachers, dropped into one-room schools, totally inexperienced, not knowing how to go about really much [of] anything.

Bernard's experience as a novice teacher was replicated in countless other rural schools.[35] In this context, historian David C. Jones has suggested a rather cynical metaphor that is particularly pertinent here: "[N]ormal school training in the early twenties prepared trainees to teach on the moon better than in the typical one-room . . . school."[36]

The transition from training to employment was eased somewhat for those teachers whose own public school education had taken place in a rural setting. Bernard Gillie suggested that for him, as for many others in similar situations: "What we did in sheer desperation was think, 'Well, what did my teachers do?' I simply fell back on how they had done things." Ila Embree firmly believed that she was "much better prepared" to teach in a one-room school because she had "been through it" and thus "knew how to do it." She argued: "I learnt how to write, MacLean's Method,[37] and all that sort of thing at Normal and I specialized in Physical Education [but] if I hadn't gone to a country school . . . I would never have known how to teach at all."

Just as teachers in rural schools were inadequately prepared for the tasks they encountered in the classroom, they also suffered from a professional support system that was sadly lacking and did little to mitigate the daily frustrations of one-room teaching. Teacher anecdotes about the nature of their relationships with the inspectors who supervised their work manifested an ambivalent attitude towards these men. On the one hand teachers looked forward to visits from their inspector because they offered news of the "outside" and thus a welcome respite from the overwhelming feeling of isolation that was so common amongst those who taught in outlying rural districts. Often, as historian John Calam has pointed out, the inspector was the "sole educational professional in whom they could confide during an entire school year."[38] Generally, however, most teachers were not overly impressed with the quality of the service they received from their inspectors. In this context they cited a number of specific grievances related mainly to availability and utility.

For the vast majority of teachers contact with their inspector was minimal. Constrained by their heavy workloads – too many schools to inspect in too short a period of time – as well as the often unreliable nature of transportation and communication between scattered rural communities, inspectors were hard-pressed to meet the demands of their job. As Inspector A. F. Matthews noted in his 1922 report: "Six schools in isolated parts of the district were not inspected, as three of these were closed temporarily on the date of visit, and the difficulties of travel and lack of time proved obstacles in the case of the others."[39] Consequently visits from the inspector were rare and frustratingly brief, usually limited to a few hours twice, sometimes only once, a year. This was hardly sufficient time for him to gain an intimate knowledge and understanding of the precise circumstances each teacher faced, both in her school and in the local community. On one particular occasion Inspector Lord's visit to Esma Shunter and her pupils at Shuswap Falls School was cursory to say the least: "He never went inside the school. He came at recess and we were out in the yard playing and he came over and talked to me and then he left. . . . The only thing he talked about . . . was my older sisters: Where they were and what were they doing? and then he got in his little car and drove off."[40]

Many teachers also suggested that they received few practical or constructive suggestions from their inspectors on how to improve their performance in the classroom. Ila Embree's comments were fairly typical: "He just walked up and down and scared the dickens out of you and you wondered what he was thinking . . . ." Some also felt that their inspectors' reports were not very useful. Lucy McCormick recalled:

> When you got your report . . . it was just routine . . . it was terrible . . . it didn't mean a thing. . . . Also he usually left instructions with the teacher to approach the trustees regarding improvements. This was not an easy task, and by the time the Inspector's official report was received the term was over and his suggestions were conveniently forgotten.[41]

She added indignantly: "How was any young teacher going to go and tell the trustees that they should be doing this or that. That was *his* job!"

During the provincial inspector's visits his agenda was strictly administrative: to assess the pedagogical capabilities of the teacher, the academic progress of the pupils and the overall "standing" of the school. Other more personal issues were rarely addressed. Many inspectors seemed to express little concern, or even interest, in the life of the individual teacher outside of her professional responsibilities, surely a matter of crucial importance to a young teacher's survival in a remote school district. But as Lucy McCormick suggested, some inspectors gave her the distinct impression that "It was just a job. . . . Sometimes it depended on what kind of person he was, how well he got on with [teachers] who were sort of isolated in a community." Accordingly, in many instances a serious communication problem existed between inspector and the inspected in rural areas. But perhaps this was inevitable given the nature of the power relationship between the two parties. As historian John Abbott has summed up in relation to Ontario: "[M]ale inspectors, usually heads of families and well advanced in their careers, superintended a very young, inexperienced, minimally trained, and transient female teaching force."[42] Although the local school board had ultimate control over a teacher's tenure, a "poor" or "unsatisfactory" inspector's report could adversely effect a teacher's prospects of transferring to a better position in another school, could be instrumental in influencing a school board's decision to dispense with a teacher's services, or as Alice Gibson stated: "If you didn't do a good job, the Inspector might move you." Many teachers therefore found their bi-annual visits from the inspector more stressful than fruitful. Marianne Nelson reported: "I truly never felt at ease. . . . I was nervous." It was partly for this reason that Lucy McCormick suggested that some young girls were "really almost frightened" of their inspector.

The recollections of former teachers imply that there may have been more insidious aspects to the teacher-inspector relationship and that in some cases the latter used his position of trust to take advantage of those under his supervision. Lucy McCormick contended: "There was the odd inspector who wasn't a saint by any means." Marianne Nelson, speaking from personal experience, was more explicit. She felt extremely uncomfortable in the presence of one particular inspector: "I was quite busty and he was very fond of . . . looking down your clothes and so on, the old devil." She also suggested that some young women teachers, fearing the loss of their job, may have had good reason to permit such otherwise unacceptable behavior to occur: "It was such hard times that maybe a girl would do almost anything if she were destitute." In contrast, the participants referred to the visits of Lottie Bowron in very different terms (see chapter 14). To quote Lucy again: "She was very nice and . . . a very motherly sort of a person. She knew what to ask to find out for herself. I think probably teachers would open up to her more than they would to a man." Unfortunately Bowron's mandate did not include all female teachers but was restricted primarily to those in difficult situations. Consequently the typical rural teacher very often felt very much alone as regards professional help and support. As Alice Gibson so succinctly stated: "What do I remember about teaching in a rural school? That I was entirely on my own." Marianne Nelson reiterated Alice's sentiments almost exactly: "You were on your own. You were completely on your own."

Such professional isolation meant that rural teachers welcomed the annual Teachers' Conventions.[43] Lucy McCormick reported: "I always went. . . . That was part and parcel of our in-service training. . . . They were very useful because they were geared to small schools, mainly because there weren't that many big schools, and from the point of view of getting to know other people . . . with similar problems." Held in October in either Vernon, Kelowna or Penticton, the conventions not only provided rural teachers with professional enrichment and a chance to update their knowledge and expertise in the field, but also served an important social function as well. Indeed, for many lone rural teachers the annual meeting of their local teachers' association represented their only chance for contact with colleagues. Not all of the participants reported having attended teacher conventions during the 1920s however. The cost of travelling to the central location where the meeetings were held, as well as accommodation expenses for the duration of the convention, had to come out of the teachers' own pockets and were sometimes prohibitive. Moreover, to those working in very isolated communities serviced by inadequate transportation networks, the meetings were inaccessible. Many more, unfortunately, had simply been totally unaware of their ocurrence.

In many respects, the nature of rural school conditions and teacher experience in the Okanagan Valley in the 1920s were similar to those recorded in other studies relating to different regions of British Columbia,[44] as well as across Canada[45] and the United States[46] during the same time-frame. Irrespective of geographical location rural-teacher populations were typically comprised of young, single, and primarily female individuals. They were also generally inadequately trained and highly transient. Teaching in a remote country school in British Columbia in the 1920s, especially for the novice, could be an onerous assignment. It certainly was one which demanded the acceptance of considerable physical, mental, emotional and professional hardships. Rural teachers faced endless challenges in their classrooms. They toiled long hours in often primitive and poorly equipped buildings where they experienced seemingly insurmountable pedagogical difficulties and responsibilities. And in all of this many endured immense feelings of isolation and loneliness. Professional survival in a one-room school was thus a real challenge. Taken together such circumstances tested the will and stamina of the strongest of individuals and ensured that life for the lone teacher in a remote school district was at the very least trying. In this sense one can fully appreciate the significance of the comments of Lottie Bowron regarding the situation of the teacher at the one-room school at Reiswig, a tiny farming community thirty-seven kilometres east of Vernon, when she visited her in 1929. She simply stated: "Mrs Gibson looked as if she was ready for the end of term."[47]

An outsider might view the job of the rural teacher as a particularly onerous one that ostensibly offered little in the way of any recompense. Moreover, it is perhaps easy to understand why some individuals, finding themselves faced with such difficult and sometimes unpleasant circumstances, chose to move on to a situation they felt suited them better, often after only a brief time. Some found their circumstances intolerable and quickly and quietly left the profession altogether. But was the rural teaching experience a wholly negative one? This was not the general view of many of the former teachers interviewed. In fact in a number of cases the participant's own perspective was quite the opposite. None disputed the fact that they had endured often extremely strenuous working conditions in their rural classrooms, but, at the same time, they also made it quite plain that there had been some gratifying aspects to one-room teaching.

Motivated by a determination to succeed many participants regarded their experiences in rural schools, especially their inaugural year, as a challenge. Their sense of self-worth was enhanced by their ability to prove to themselves that they could survive under such adverse conditions. Moreover, many came to love their work and were deeply committed to their pupils. In relating their stories to me a number of former teachers stressed their degree of autonomy and immense sense of job satisfaction as least as much as the limitations of their work. For some, therefore, rural teaching clearly offered advantages that outweighed the negative aspects of the job.

Being far removed from any direct supervision meant that rural teachers were able to exercise a considerable degree of autonomy. While there were limits to what they could achieve given the paucity of instructional resources, equipment and supplies at their disposal, as well as community expectations and their own lack of preparedness and general inexperience, and although the content of the curriculum they were required to follow was determined by the Department of Education, ultimately rural teachers were a law unto themselves in their classrooms. Bernard Gillie recalled his situation at Ellison School, which he regarded as representative of other rural districts, as one where the "community was hardly aware of what you were doing." The general attitude was: "What happens in the school is the teacher's business." Esma Shunter reported the same scenario for Shuswap Falls: "Nobody interfered. . . . I never had anybody tell me what to do." Likewise Lucy McCormick stated that as the teacher at Mabel Lake she had been "absolutely autonomous. Nobody questioned [me] at all." With usually no principal to tell them what to do, or from whom they could seek advice, teachers in remote one-room schools had to make their own decisions and were thus in control of the daily pedagogical activities that took place in the school. They were free to set the pace of work to meet the needs of individual students, to alter their schedules if and when it suited them, or to experiment with different kinds of teaching methods to find the approach that worked best for them. In this sense some participants viewed their professional isolation as working to their benefit rather than to their detriment. Thus Janet Graham reported: "It made you responsible. You have the full responsibility of getting them through." As a young novice teacher Agnes Ball believed that teaching in a one-room school encouraged her to be "more independent. . . . It was a good start off for me. . . . A good grounding is what a person needs, to jump head first into something. I think that had done me a lot of good."

Participants also regarded the one-room school as a superior environment in which to teach in the sense of the highly personal nature of their work and their familiarity with the children they taught. Thus Lloyda Wills recalled: "I had such close contact with the pupils. . . . It was really a pleasure." The intimate atmosphere of the small rural community fostered the development of such special relationships because, as Vera Towgood suggested: "You know all the children and you know all their homes. You know what their backgrounds are. . . . My relationship with the pupils was close. Having so few, 11 or 12, I got to know them well." Lucy McCormick expressed a similar opinion: "This intimacy with families helped [the rural teacher] understand the emotional life of her pupils."[48] The bonds that developed between the rural teacher and her charges were often very strong and when participants recalled their pupils they spoke with affection and warmth. Many had obviously cared very deeply for their "kids" or "little ones." Significantly, many former teachers depicted their relationship with their pupils with family-like metaphors. Isobel Simard's attitude was typical: "The salary never bothered me at all. I never thought about that. All I thought about was the children and getting them through their grades and helping them. They were like my own children to me." Pupils also recalled the family atmosphere of the rural school and the way in which their teachers cared for them. Amanda Singer, a former pupil of Alice Gibson's at Sugar Lake, recalled Alice in a particularly poignant way:

> She was a really nice teacher, really nice. She was always kind [and] did everything she could to make us happy. . . . I always felt like she was my big sister. I could talk to her about anything. . . . That's what I really liked about her. You tell her that I just loved her and I'll never forget her.

Thus, at least for some individuals, rural teaching offered real rewards that helped to offset the hardships and for this reason they enjoyed their work.

The stories of former rural teachers clearly show that the quality of teacher experience in rural schools was by no means homogeneous. In fact the weight of evidence points to diversity rather than uniformity of experience. Thus, although rural teachers may have shared some common demographic characteristics, and undoubtedly had to cope with similar occupational and social problems and stresses, it was found that a crucial aspect of the rural teaching experience was the very personal nature of that experience.

The underlying relationship that existed between the individual teacher and the local world of education in rural districts was of fundamental importance in determining the nature of teacher experience. Localism ensured that each school and the community in which it was situated was different and ultimately played a predominant role in determining the nature of teacher experience. The unique economic, social, political and personal circumstances that existed in each community influenced not only the material conditions of the schoolhouse and its grounds, but also the social and learning environment within the school, that is, who was enrolled, when and why they attended or did not attend, and how they were educated. The recollections of former teachers also indicate that more personal factors were equally, if not more, significant. The extent to which teachers were disposed to adjust to the circumstances in which they found themselves depended primarily on their upbringing and social background, as well as their personality. In essence, how teachers actually perceived their experience was as unique as the community in which they taught. Thus to comprehend fully the historical experience of rural teachers it is essential to examine that experience in the context of the local communities in which rural teachers' lives were embedded and from the perspective of the individual teachers themselves.

Notes

1. John Calam, "A Letter from Quesnel: The Teacher in History, and Other Fables," *History of Education Quarterly* 15, 2 (Summer 1975): 136.
2. Richard A. Quantz, "The Complex Visions of Female Teachers and the Failure of Unionization in the 1930s: An Oral History," *History of Education Quarterly* 25, 4 (Winter 1985): 439.
3. *Ibid.*, 440-441.
4. See Gillian Creese and Veronica Strong-Boag, "Introduction: Taking Gender into Account in British Columbia," Creese and Strong-Boag, eds. *British Columbia Reconsidered: Essays on Women* (Vancouver: Press Gang Publishers, 1992), 5, 10-11.
5. Donald Warren, ed., *American Teachers: Histories of a Profession at Work* (New York: Macmillan Publishing Co., 1989): 4, 7.
6. Richard J. Altenbaugh, ed., *The Teacher's Voice: A Social History of Teaching in Twentieth Century America* (Washington D.C.: The Falmer Press, 1992), 4.
7. Chad Gaffield and Gerard Bouchard, "Literacy, Schooling, and Family Reproduction in Rural Ontario and Quebec," *Historical Studies in Education/Revue d'histoire de l'education* 1, 2 (Fall 1989): 201-202. For a review essay which discusses "some of the most sophisticated Canadian books in rural history of the last five years," see Catharine Anne Wilson, "'Outstanding in the Field': Recent Rural History in Canada," *Acadiensis* 20, 2 (Spring 1991): 177-190.
8. This essay is a revised version of chapter 7 of my M.A. thesis: "Portraits in the First Person: An Historical Ethnography of Rural Teachers in British Columbia's Okanagan Valley in the 1920s," (University of British Columbia, 1993). The thesis not only details the experience of rural teachers in the 1920s but also analyzes the role of those experiences in the context of the

life course as a whole. A map showing the locations of the schools mentioned in this essay is included in the thesis on page 124.

9. The Teacher Bureau of Records [hereafter TBR] are officially known as "School District Information Forms for the Teachers' Bureau, Department of Education, Victoria, B.C." They are located in the Public Archives of British Columbia in Victoria [hereafter PABC] in GR 461. They are filed alphabetically by name of school according to each year. Unfortunately only the records for the years 1923 and 1928 have survived the passage of time. Of the total number of 1 380 responses from these two years 91 were written by teachers who taught in the rural schools of the Okanagan Valley.

10. Multiple copies of the *Annual Report of the Public Schools* [hereafter *AR*] are located at the Main Library, UBC, and at the PABC. Inspector's reports for each district are not included in the *AR* after 1929. Copies of the inspectors' individual reports [hereafter IR] are available on reels of microfilm in the PABC (GR 122). They are filed chronologically under various categories: "Elementary Schools," "High Schools," "Superior Schools," etc. Within these categories the reports are arranged alphabetically by name of school. The inspectors for the Okanagan Valley between 1920 and 1930 were A.R. Lord, J.R. Hall, A.E. Miller, A.F. Mattheson and J.B. Delong. The reports of Lottie Bowron, the Rural Teachers' Welfare Officer, are included in the IR in the P.A.B.C. (GR 122). Her reports cover the period 1929 to 1933. Taken together the *ARs* and the IR provide the official view of teacher experience and professional development in the rural schools of British Columbia. Miss Bowron's reports offer a more intimate account of teaching conditions and teacher impressions of rural schools and community. The TBR provide a good complement to the reports of Bowron.

11. To assume that the complete picture of teacher experience in rural areas can be found in this essay would be a gross oversimplification. It is possible, and even likely, that many teachers would not be able to identify with the world of rural teaching presented here and that my sample of participants represents the exceptional rather than the average. Thus it is essential that the reader bears in mind that this essay relates specifically to the Okanagan Valley and most importantly to the experiences of those individuals about whom I have information.

12. IR, 3 October 1929. Significantly, Mr. Clark had resigned by November of that year.

13. IR, 18 September 1924.

14. See Lucy (Hill) McCormick, "Early Rural Schools of Vernon and White Valley," *Okanagan Historical Society: Report* (hereafter *OHSR*) 46 (1982):38.

15. See also Marguerite Hodgson, "Okanagan Landing School Days," *OHSR* 34 (1970): 116.

16. David Jones and Ruby E. Lidstone, In *the Shadow of the Cliff: A History of North Enderby* (Enderby: North Enderby Historical Society, 1976), 14.

17. Examples of schools described as "heavy" included Westbank Townsite (TBR, 1823), Deep Creek (IR, 9 October 1930), Falkland (IR, 14 November 1928), Lavington (IR, 11 June 1928 and 7 Nov. 1930), Mission Creek (IR, 1 December 1921 and 26 April 1922), Okanagan (IR, 2 Dec. 1921) and Rutland (IR, 6 March 1929).

18. *Ibid.*, 28 October 1921. See also IR, 26 September 1923.

19. IR, 21 November 1930. See also IR's for 12 March and 25 Sept. 1930. Similar problems existed at Rutland (IR, 27 Nov. and 20 Dec. 1927; 5 December 1929; and 2 April and 28 Nov. 1930); Mission Creek (Bowron Reports, 31 May 1929); Grindrod (IR 29 Nov. 1922; 8 Mar. and 7 Dec. 1923); 22 Jan and 10 Dec 1925; 17 Feb. and 21 Oct. 1927; 8 May 1930; and TBRs for 1923 and 1928); Coldstream (IR, 13 Dec 1928; 15 May and 25 Nov. 1929; and 8 April 1930), Hupel (IR, 13 May 1930), Mabel Lake (IR, 4 Nov 1930), Medora Creek (IR's 28 Oct 1926 and 16 June 1927), Okanagan Centre (IR, 6 Nov. 1930), Shuswap Falls (IR, 4 Nov. and 16 May 1930), Trinity Creek (IR, 14 May 1930 and TBR, 1928), Winfield (IR, 1929) and Woodville Road (IR, 17 May 1921).

20. Olive B. Clarke, "Peachland in the Pioneer Days," *OHSR* 39 (1975): 182.

21. TBR, 1923. See also TBR for Reiswig, 1928.

22. For example the schools at Okanagan Centre (IR, 23 September 1929); Mission Creek (*AR*, 1926-1928 and TBR, 1928); Bear Creek (TBR, 1923) and Ellison (TBR, 1928).

23. TBR.

24. *AR*, 1924, T53. See also IR's for East Kelowna and Peachland (Feb. 19 and 22 respectively). For examples of other schools where low attendance rates were caused by illness and disease, see IRs for Hupel (4 Dec. 1923), Kedleston (24 Sept., 1923), Mara (7 May 1930), Medora Creek (2 October 1929), Shuswap Falls (16 May 1930), and Westbank (10 Dec. 1921). In 1927 a serious outbreak of poliomyelitis had a marked effect on school attendanace. See *AR*, 1928, V28 and IRs for Okanagan Mission (7 December, 1927), Oyama High (14 March 1928), Peachland High (27 October 1927) Rutland (13 March, 1928). Salmon Bench (24 Oct. 1927), and Westbank Townsite (28 Oct. 1927)

25. TBR, 1928.

26. *Ibid.*, 1928 and 1923. Pupils were also employed at Ewings Landing (TBR, 1928), North Enderby (TBR, 1923). Okanagan (TBR, 1928), Silver Creek (TBR, 1923) and Westbank Townsite (TBR, 1923 and 1928).

27. TBR, 1928.

28. McCormick, "Early Rural Schools," 39.

29. *Ibid.*

30. References to the problems caused by schools being used for community functions are made in the minutes of the meetings of various school boards, see School District #23. Kelowna, South Okanagan Public School (3 May 1921), and Westbank Townsite Public School (7 Jan. 1929).

31. Iodine supplements were given to school pupils in the 1920s because prior to its use "25 percent of the Kelowna school children had large goitres." See David Green, "Dr. William John Knox 1878-1967: Beloved Doctor of the Okanagan," *OHSR* 33 (1969): 14. Lucy McCormick also noted that a "duty" of the rural teacher was to give "iodine tablets" to their pupils. See "Early Rural Schools," 39.

32. McCormick, "Early Rural Schools," 40.

33. Stan Wejr, "Memories of Trinity Creek Area in the 1920s," *OHSR* 50 (1986), 79.

34. The same was true of the Normal School in Vancouver where schools in places such as Surrey were used for practice teaching.

35. See for example inspectors' comments on May E. Burton (IR, Deep Creek, 8 Dec. 1925, 2 Dec. 1926, and 19 Oct. 1927), Ruby E. Drashing (IR Grandview Bench, Nov. 9, 1928 and May 29, 1929), Irene Pellow (IR, Falkland, Nov. 26, 1925 and April 15, 1926), Islay B. Noble (IR's, South Okanagan, Nov. 30, 1921 and March 1, 1922.) Miss E.L. Haywood (IR, Sicamous, Feb. 23, 1925), Vera M.Ford (IR, Hillcrest, Jan. 21, 1925), and Emily M. Melsted (IR, Silver Creek, April 6, 1925).

36. David C. Jones, *Empire of Dust: Settling and Abandonning the Prairie Dry Belt* (Edmonton: University of Alberta Press, 1987), 179.

37. Ila is referring here to The MacLean Method of Muscular Movement Writing introduced into the British Columbia school system in 1921. See *AR*, 1921, C10.

38. John Calam, ed., *Alex Lord's British Columbia: Recollections of a Rural School Inspector, 1915-36* (Vancouver: UBC Press, 1991), 18.

39. *AR*, 1922, C33.

40. Prior to becoming a School Inspector Lord was Principal of the Central Elementary School in Kelowna from 1910-1914. See Calam, *Alex Lord's British Columbia*, 4, 103-111. Lord had apparently taught Esma's older sisters in Kelowna.

41. McCormick, "Early Rural Schools," 40.

42. John Abbott, "Accomplishing 'a Man's Task': Rural Women Teachers, Male Culture, and the School Inspectorate in Turn-of-the-Century Ontario," *Ontario History* 78, 4 (December 1986): 313.

43. A number of teachers' associations existed in the Okanagan in the 1920s. In 1922 the Okanagan Valley Teachers' Association, the first of its kind in the area, was formed in response to "a need . . . felt amongst the teachers . . . for more unity." A local organization serving Armstrong, Enderby, Vernon, Lumby and Oyama was also established and called the North Okanagan Teachers' Association. See Lidstone, ed. *Schools of Enderby and District*, 64. In 1929 another association was formed to represent rural teachers working in schools further south in the Okanagan around the Kelowna area. See *AR*, 1929, R30.

44. The work of J.Donald Wilson and Paul J. Stortz is of primary importance here. See Wilson and Stortz, "'May the Lord Have Mercy on You': the Rural School Problem in British Columbia in the 1920s." *B.C. Studies* 79 (Autumn 1988): 24-58 (ch. 11 of this book); Stortz, "The Rural School Problem in British Columbia in the 1920s" (M.A. thesis, UBC, 1988); Wilson, "The Visions of Ordinary Participants: Teachers' Views of Rural Schooling in British Columbia in the 1920s," Patricia E. Roy, ed., *A History of British Columbia: Selected Readings*, (Toronto: Copp Clark Pitman, 1989), 239-255; Wilson, "'I am Here to Help You If You Need Me': British Columbia's Rural Teachers' Welfare Officer, 1928-1934," *Journal of Canadian Studies/Revue d'etudes canadiennes* 25, 2 (Summer 1990), 94-118 (ch. 14 of this book); and Stortz and Wilson, "Education on the Frontier: Schools, Teachers, and Community Influence in North-Central British Columbia," *Histoire sociale/Social History* 26, 52 (November 1993): 265-290. See also Joan Adams and Becky Thomas, *Floating Schools and Frozen Inkwells: The One-Room Schools of British Columbia* (Madeira Park, British Columbia: Harbour Publishing Company Ltd, 1985), for an interesting albeit less academically rigorous, account of rural schooling that is based on the reminiscences of former teachers and pupils.

45. For a scholarly study of the Prairies in the inter-war period see Robert S. Patterson, "Voices From the Past: The Personal and Professional Struggle of Rural School Teachers," Nancy M. Sheehan, J. Donald Wilson and David C. Jones, eds., *Schools in the West: Essays in Canadian Educational History* (Calgary: Detselig Enterprises Ltd., 1986), 96-111. See also the work of John C. Charyk whose approach to the subject is anecdotal rather than analytical but informative nevertheless. See *The Little White Schoolhouse,* Volumes 1-3 (Saskatoon: Western Producer Prairie Books, 1968-1977), *Syrup Pails and Gopher Tails: Memories of the One-Room School* (Saskatoon: Western Producer, 1983). For a popular piece that is based primarily on the personal recollections of former teachers who taught in rural Ontario, see Myrtle Fair, *I Remember the One-Room School* (Cheltenham, Ontario: The Boston Mills Press, 1979). Rural schooling and teaching in Quebec is described in Jacques Dorion, *Les ecoles de rang au Quebec* (Montreal: Editions de l'homme, 1979). For a general overview of Canada as a whole see Jean Cochrane, *The One Room School in Canada* (Toronto: Fitzhenry and Whiteside Ltd., 1981).

46. Particularly useful here are Mary Hurlbut Cordier, *Schoolwomen of the Plains and Prairies: Personal Narratives From Iowa, Kansas, and Nebraska, 1860-1920s* (Albuquerque: University of New Mexico Press, 1992); William A. Link, *A Hard Country and a Lonely Place: Schooling, Society, and Reform in Rural Virginia, 1870-1920* (Chapel Hill: The University of North Carolina Press, 1986); Andrew Guillford, *America's Country Schools* (Washington, D.C.: The Preservation Press, 1984) and Wayne Fuller, *The Old Country School: The Story of Education in the Midwest* (Chicago: University of Chicago Press, 1982).

47. Bowron Reports, 29 May 1929.

48. McCormick, "Early Rural Schools," 40.

13

The Diary of Mary Williams: A Cameo of Rural Schooling in British Columbia, 1922-1924

Thomas Fleming and Carolyn Smyly

On 5 September 1922, Mary Carolina Williams set out from her family home in Prince George to travel to her first teaching assignment in Mud River, about thirty kilometres east of town. She was just eighteen years old. In many respects she fit the profile of the "average" rural teacher described by school statistics of the period, 79 per cent of whom were female, and 91 per cent of whom were unmarried.[1] Like about two-thirds of her colleagues, she held a second-class teaching certificate, which in her case indicated she had finished junior matriculation at the High School in Prince George before attending Vancouver Normal School for one year. And, like many other young women teachers of the period, her time in the profession was short. After four years of teaching in British Columbia and Alberta, she left the profession to get married.

Mary was the fourth of ten children born in Vancouver to a "genteel" family. Her father, David Griffith Williams, had been a city newspaperman and a successful real estate agent. Her mother, Carolina McLellan, had taught school in the 1890s in Hall's Prairie and Kensington Prairie, both rural districts south of the Fraser River between New Westminster and the American border. Mary's older sister Margaret and her brothers Ben and Roscoe all followed their mother into the teaching profession. The Williams' family was also associated with provincial education in another way: Mary's grandfather had built Mt. Pleasant School in Vancouver. In 1915, the Williams family moved north, taking the steamship to Prince Rupert and, from there, the Grand Trunk to Prince George. Here Mary finished her schooling before returning to Vancouver for a year of teacher training.

Family photographs show Mary to be tall and athletic, with thick dark hair and shy brown eyes. She rode horseback and walked long distances. Nothing in her appearance suggests she would die at the age of thirty-five from tuberculosis. Yet, despite her tragically early death, Mary Williams is destined to be remembered and studied in a way that few other rural school teachers of her generation can be – because she kept a detailed diary of her two years at Mud River School.[2]

Context

Few other diaries of British Columbia teachers exist. One on deposit in the Provincial Archives is Mary's own mother's rough notebook which records a few months of her teaching experiences, likely at the Hall's Prairie School.[3] Another is Mildred McQuillan's brief chronicle of four months in 1927, in Orange Valley School, sixteen kilometres from Fort Fraser.[4] As a record of appalling living conditions, and a teacher's disgust with her assignment, the McQuillan diary is unmatched in content or style.

In contrast, the 102-page Williams' diary is more restrained in language, more descriptive of the community, more interested in people, and more analytical of interpersonal relationships. She seems to have begun it on the advice of the children's page editor of the *Edmonton Journal*, to whom Mary submitted short stories for publication. Her ambition to be a writer, like her father, as well as a schoolteacher, like her mother, no doubt explains the careful descriptions she made of the characters she encountered when she went to Mud River, as its third teacher. Her diary also likely served as an outlet for confidences she would have been unwilling to disclose to anyone else in the community. More than this, her diary offers a first-hand – and reasonably complete – account of a teacher's life in a country school over a two-year period. As such, it provides a more comprehensive chronicle of a rural teacher's experience in British Columbia than found in any other single source, and provides a counterpoint to the bureaucratic blandness of official reports which complained about, but did little to explain, the high rate of teacher turnover in rural schools.

The experiences of rural teachers in the province have been the subject of various studies.[5] Much of this historical writing has relied on composite kinds of evidence, shards of experience drawn from the lives of many individuals and assembled to create portraits of rural teachers' lives, or the institution that was the one-room school.[6] Several recent studies, in particular, have directly or indirectly, focused on the personal and professional trials of female teachers in the province's interior regions, and have suggested the similarity in their experiences.[7] These studies of rural teaching are essentially mosaic in construction: they have been pieced together from parts of government documents, notably inspectors' reports, superintendent's letters, annual reports of the public schools, teachers' bureau records, and the published works of commissions of inquiry.[8] Rich though they are in many respects, these sources yield, at best, fragmentary understandings of what teaching in rural British Columbia was actually like for any individual teacher in times past.

The importance of securing teachers' perspectives about rural life is underscored in Wilson's study of the 1920s.[9] Wilson challenges historians to direct greater attention toward "presenting the world of schooling from the angle of vision of teachers," as well as toward rural society, "a society little understood or studied in the face of the more exciting and more accessible urban environment."[10] He suggests that, by connecting rural and educational history, historians can provide better understandings of Canadian social development. While he cautions that observations made by rural teachers about their communities may not always be objective, he adds, "one has to begin somewhere . . . ."[11]

The following study of Mary Williams' diary is part of that beginning. The Williams' diary, recorded daily, with few exceptions, presents an opportunity too tempting to resist – an opportunity to explore the details of a rural teacher's existence over a period of time, more than average in length, if judged by teacher attrition rates of the period. It provides a sense of a teacher's life "in the round," that is to say a life set firmly in time and place – and in its entirety. Because it is a diary, it also offers more than a chronological structure of events, in essence a narrative about how someone felt about those events, a particular kind of prism through which to see the past. In Mary Williams' case, the diary entries range in character from the intimate to the ethnographic. Like that of many other eighteen-year olds, her writing is, at times, obsessively introspective, but, at others, possessed of an insight given only to those who are strangers in a new culture–which she clearly saw herself to be. Her perspective is thus, at once, both personal and removed. Mary Williams' diary is also appealing because it is the work of someone who wants to be a writer and who is interested in human and social relationships, especially those she has never witnessed before. There is a freshness about her words, an impression of things that goes far beyond the brief – and sometimes thin – responses made by teachers of her era to government questionnaires about schooling in rural society.

In other words, the Williams' diary, although not without its limitations, presents historians with a unique lens through which to view rural and educational life in 1920s British Columbia. In the narrowest sense, it furnishes the small details of living that might otherwise be forgotten or remain unobserved. In the broadest sense, it helps give historians a better feeling for the rhythm and texture of a rural community, a more complete view of how personal and professional autonomy was shaped by social structures, and a clearer vision of a teacher's role and the expectations society held for teachers at a particular time in the past.

Living Off the Land

The Mud River Valley to which Mary Williams came in 1922 owed its inauspicious name to the spring floods which turn the Chilako River into a turbulent muddy torrent.[12] The valley before settlement was thirteen kilometres of thickly-timbered bottom land interspersed by meadows growing natural hay. The hay meant that stock, both horses and cattle, could be sustained over the winter. Before the completion of the Grand Trunk Pacific Railway in 1914, all summer freight came into the Fort George district by road or river boat. During winter, when the rivers froze, the steamboats tied up at Fort George, and freight was re-routed by way of the Cariboo Road, pulled by long teams of draught horses. The horses needed hay and grain, a fact not lost on the valley's pioneer entrepreneurs who quickly realized that meadows full of wild hay, free for the cutting, could be hauled some thirty kilometres away into Prince George and sold for considerable profit to feed stores.

Similarly, the valley's timber meant railway ties, and building materials for houses and barns and corrals. Further up the mountains, the timber meant fur-bearing animals – mink, fisher, marten, fox and beaver. The valley was also rich in deer and moose, and fish were plentiful in the lakes and streams. For men who had skills in trapping, hunting, farming or ranching, and possessed of a sense of adventure, Mud River seemed like paradise. This view, as Mary Williams would learn, was not shared by the women in the valley.

A few families had come to the valley even before the completion of the Grand Trunk which, in itself, prompted further settlement. The Dominion Census of 1921 gave the total population of the Fort George district as 7 050, a region which included Prince George and the surrounding area as far west as Prince Rupert and as far south as Quesnel. The district's growth was no doubt due in part to the glowing prose of the Dominion Government's advertisements in Europe, which brought many newcomers to the prairies and to the British Columbia interior.

By the end of the Great War, three distinct groups had settled in the Mud River Valley – the "Russians" (or more properly, the Lithuanians), the Americans, and the British-Canadians who had some differences on either side of the hyphen but who shared a language, a system of government, and a monarch to distinguish them from the others. The ethnic mix was typical of many rural areas in British Columbia during the 1920s and thereafter, though the groups comprising the provincial population varied from area to area.[13] Teaching children in the classroom who scarcely spoke English was not yet covered by the provincial normal school curriculum but it was already part of the reality of life in rural schools. Nor was it likely that a young woman fresh from normal school was prepared for pupils who would bring to school each day the mutual suspicions and prejudices of three distinct backgrounds.[14]

Among those attending the Mud River School were the children of four Lithuanian families; two apparently-unrelated families of Millers, the Kaskas and the Malganuses. The Redferns and the MacDonalds were American families with children in the school. Children from the Tyner, Munro, Hughes, Breeze and Pallatt families represented the British-Canadian contingent. In addition to these families, there were a few families without children and a handful of itinerant male loggers, trappers and farm laborers, bringing the valley's population up to fifty to sixty people, depending on the season. The pioneers in Mud River, like adventurers elsewhere, had chosen their valley for its economic rather than its social opportunities. Until the log schoolhouse was constructed in 1920, the nearest school was in Prince George, some thirty kilometres away. When Mary Williams arrived two years later, the school was the settlement's sole institution, save for episodic meetings of the Farmers' Institute held at the school. All settlers were thus required to make a periodic trek to Prince George for supplies. In good weather, by car, it was a two hour journey.[15] In rainy or winter weather, with "a bad road" – and there was no other kind – travel could take over ten hours.[16] If the car broke down, or if mud and snow were deep, as was often the case, the trip might not be completed at all.

Prince George represented civilization. The 1918 British Columbia Directory indicates that in Prince George could be found a railway and road express to the outside world, telephones, a telegraph, a newspaper, three churches of different denominations, a bank, three lighting plants, two doctors, a small hospital, a lawyer, a dentist, a plumber, two blacksmiths, a jeweler, four hotels, two movie houses, five hay and grain stores, four men's furnishings stores, a millinery shop, a dry goods store, a grocery, a hardware store and an "auto" agent. Government agencies and officers in Prince George included the Provincial and Mounted Police, the Post Office, the Fire Warden, the Land Settlement Board, and the Road Superintendent. The Education Department was represented by the school doctor and the school inspector, G. H. Gower, who was based in Fort St. James, but who stayed in Prince George frequently as his rounds dictated.

The School at Mud River

By 1919, there were enough children of beginning school age in Mud River Valley – and several older children with little learning at all – that schooling became a necessity. The Education Office dictated certain procedures that called for a degree of community co-operation greater than previously required. Under law, the community was required to elect three school trustees from among district land owners, including women, one of whom was to act as board secretary. This individual was made responsible for communicating with the Education Office, keeping minutes of board meetings, and accounting for whatever monies the district received. The Education Office would supply teaching materials. And for an "assisted" school, as Mud River was, the provincial government would pay the teacher's salary. The board, however, would engage the teacher, set the salary, and provide the materials and local labor needed to erect the building.

In the summer of 1919, the school inspector, G. H. Gower, visited Mud River and ascertained that there were at least ten school-age children, the number required to warrant a school. Andy Miller, a Lithuanian and by one account, "the only man in the whole valley who could be called a successful farmer," offered the use of an outbuilding on his ranch for a temporary school, and "deeded" an acre of prime spruce trees, "ideal for building logs," as a permanent school site.[17] An election was held and Mr. Munro, Mr. Alexander and Mr. Pallatt were elected as trustees.

When Mrs. Katie Racklyeft, a widow and teacher with ten years experience, was hired in January 1919, she found herself teaching fourteen pupils in the two-room "temporary" building on Andy Miller's ranch, while the lumber for the new school lay on the ground waiting for the weather to improve. Gower's first report on the temporary school in March 1919 described it as "small, poorly lighted and ventilated" with no water closets except the privy belonging to the ranch. The desks were homemade and instructional materials were sparse – a globe, maps of British Columbia, Canada, the British Isles, North America and the world.

Building the new school proved more difficult than imagined. The daily exigencies of frontier life interfered with construction for the best part of a year, as one resident later recalled: "[E]veryone in the valley . . . wanted a school, was willing to help build one and donate his share of cash to buy lumber, windows and a door; but nobody had the organizing ability to get things started."[18]

Finally, in autumn 1919, the shell of the building was raised, a roof was laid, a floor installed, a door framed and hung, a large window cut in the north wall, and a stove placed in the middle of the floor with a tin chimney. When the desks and maps were moved across the river, the new building was seen to be ready.

Finding the old "school" a more convenient place to live than sharing a bedroom with the Millers' oldest daughter at the cost of $35 a month, board included, Mrs. Racklyeft moved into the school's back room and was promptly charged rent by Andy Miller, even although he had "given" the building to the school board. His generosity in donating the "temporary" building, and the deeded acre, were now estimated by some in the community to have had another motive – that of obtaining "room and board" money from the teacher. When Mrs. Racklyeft refused to pay rent for what she considered a school board teacherage, Miller would not release the trunk with her belongings until she did pay, and nearly came to blows over the issue with Fred Dyrhman, a local bachelor who had been "walking out" with the widowed teacher.

Katie Racklyeft lasted eighty-nine teaching days before leaving the community and, in September 1921, a new teacher, Jean McLarty was hired. She had attended normal school, but had withdrawn before finishing the program due to a family illness.[19] She was granted a temporary certificate upon application from the superintendent of schools in the Department of Education.[20] McLarty also "rented a shack," but not from Andy Miller. She too "walked out" with the same bachelor, Fred Dyrhman, whose romantic escapades caused a certain amount of amused gossip in the community. But, like many teachers of the interwar years, she would not remain for long in this assignment.[21] By the end of June 1922, Miss McLarty left to teach in Vancouver.[22]

Two weeks before Mary Williams' arrival, Inspector Gower summed up the state of rural schools under his supervision. "Conditions are far from satisfactory in many of the ungraded districts . . . the most important problem that faces the rural district is how to retain the services of competent teachers," he wrote.[23] The attractions of country life no doubt seemed small to many of the city-reared and city-educated young women who were obliged to earn a living teaching in rural schools.

An Institution Without Walls

The first entry in Mary's diary, 5 September 1922, records that she left Prince George the previous day in "a great rainstorm" and that, after a two-hour "unthrilling journey," by car she arrived in Mud River where, she too found herself "boarding at the Miller place and sharing a bedroom with one of her pupils, the Miller's eldest girl, Annie."[24] Like Katie Racklyeft, Mary Williams had contracted in advance for full room and board with the Miller's but, when she arrived, she was dismayed to find that the "room upstairs" was "not quite finished" and that she had to share accommodation. Within hours, she likewise found that Mud River's school was a far cry from the ideals of country teaching sometimes depicted at normal school:

> I went to the school which is not far . . . and the school was in a terrible state. Large shavings at least six inches in depth in some places covered the floor. The ceiling and one wall were finished but they had run out of lumber and had to stop. The blackboards were down also. Desks, lumber, and books everywhere. An old stove

still up and a new one on the floor. It was six o' clock then and I was to start school at nine next morning.[25]

To add to the difficulties, the school well had yet to be dug and water had to be carried from the river. The school board, she soon learned, was badly in debt and the school's official register – its most important document – was missing.[26] Moreover, the free text books promised by Victoria had still not arrived and, apparently, would not for some weeks, and the blackboards which the inspector had pointedly criticized for three years were still inadequate and would continue to be so for another year.

As her students trickled in during the weeks that followed, Mary began to adjust to the demands of life in a rural school . The first day of school, the youngest boys and girls came – the four Tyner girls, Annie Miller, and Albert Kaska, a youngster adopted by the Pallatts. As the harvest was completed in the weeks that followed, the older boys turned up, as did the bush rats which nested noisily in the new ceiling and had to be dispatched regularly in the middle of classes with an air rifle. By the end of the first term, Mary had thirteen pupils in five grades, as well as the oldest Tyner girl, Isabel, who was a high-school entrance student.

All fourteen pupils were instructed in writing, dictation, spelling and composition, arithmetic, nature, hygiene and drawing. Six studied geography, five learned English grammar and one, presumably Isabel Tyner, took English literature. All of them were also instructed in physical exercise and music. The diary makes no specific reference to the kind of physical exercise provided but music is mentioned. Even without a piano in the school, the children were taught singing and, reportedly, gave a creditable performance at Christmas concerts and the "social evenings" Mary held at school.

Given the complications of scheduling fourteen different subjects for fourteen pupils in one room, and with scant supplies, it is not surprising that something was overlooked in her first few months of teaching. When Inspector Gower made his first visit in October, he reported the children's oral reading had been neglected. Mary's reaction to Gower's inspection was typical of her – momentary depression followed by optimism: "I don't know what Mr. Gower's report will be but I am hoping for the best. But oh dear, I am feeling blue. I have neglected the reading and it was not up to the mark at all."[27]

Playing the role of the teacher gave her more trouble than the curriculum. She admitted to being rusty at grammar and hadn't "the slightest idea what to give the children for drawing" but, like her mother before her, she appeared more concerned about the tone of the classroom, and her ability to earn children's respect and obedience.[28] "I'm learning to smile in the schoolroom without damaging my dignity," her mother had written a quarter of a century before in her fragmented notes.[29] Her daughter's concern was similar as one diary entry reveals: "It is such a bally hard job to keep one's face straight in school. I can see their point of view so well since it was only a little over a year ago when I was [a student]."[30]

Her struggle to play the part of the teacher according to some internalized ideals clearly conflicted with her own youthful spirits and brought on bouts of anxiety from time to time during her first year:

Oh, I wish I could go home–or somewhere where I would not always have to be on the lookout not to do something a schoolteacher oughtn't to do. . . . I want to go home and be a *kid* for awhile. I am sick of being a grown-up young lady. If I tried to be a kid half the valley would be scandalized.[31]

But by the time of Inspector Gower's next visit in May 1923, she was beginning to have more confidence in herself: "Mr. Gower came today, and what the result will be I do not know. He told me I had more control on the class than before."[32] Like many of the inspectors, Gower was careful not to praise young teachers too fulsomely in written reports, but they were usually wise enough to get a good word back to a teacher in other ways: "Mrs. Pallatt told me that Mr. Gower told her husband that I had the makings of a dandy teacher. I got my report on Saturday. I got good for control and tone, the rest fairly good."[33]

From her diary entries, it is plain that Mary put greater stock in Gower's judgment of her abilities than in what the parents at Mud River had to say. Indeed, rather than live in fear of the inspector, as some teachers did, she generally looked forward to his visits, particularly when she had a problem and wanted the benefit of his advice and experience.[34] All in all, by the end of the first year, Mary's doubts about her capabilities seem to have resolved into a sense of professional confidence. Classroom problems regarding discipline, scheduling and poor equipment which upset her greatly in the early months were noted now as merely minor nuisances. Life proved more difficult, however, outside the school when Mary had to deal with the day-to-day life of the valley.

The Solitude of Rural Life

The teacher's life in small, isolated communities with one-room schools was, in certain respects, an alien existence. Mary Williams, for example, was the only resident in Mud River employed at a 9 to 5, Monday-to-Friday job. She was also the only permanent "public" official in the settlement, the keeper of the valley's sole public institution, and the only individual to be paid a regular salary from the public purse. Unlike teachers in cities or larger communities, she worked without colleagues for companionship, save for the inspector's bi-annual visits, and without the support of any other public agency, save for sporadic visits from the medical officer in Prince George. Nor could support for learning be found elsewhere in Mud River in the presence of a library, museum, or a community arts group. She was the best educated person in the valley, at least in terms of her academic credentials, and her social and professional existence was marked by the fact that there was no one of similar background – male or female – to socialize with, for instance a nurse, a librarian, or a pharmacist. In addition, she was also the only individual in the valley, apart from a handful of transient laborers, who had no family, friends, or relations in the community.

The social implications of Mary's situation did not take long to register in practical ways. In the first place, the valley's other residents were free to go to Prince George on weekdays and, in the tradition of family life throughout the country, usually remained at home on weekends. During the week defined by commerce, the men conducted business, did the banking, and purchased materials for the farm or ranch. Shopping and travelling were tasks easier for the women to complete on weekdays because the children were cared for in school and it simplified matters to leave them behind.

Mary Williams at Mud River, 1923.

This rhythm of rural life, however, played havoc with the social life of the only unattached female. Mary had no car and, if none of her neighbors went to town on a Friday night, Saturday, or Sunday, then neither did she. More specifically, it meant that she was unable to get home to visit her family in Prince George, maintain contact with the outside world by post, and enjoy opportunities for entertainment, or shopping. In effect, her mobility and, *de facto*, her personal autonomy, was prescribed and restricted by community routines.

Excerpts from the first months of Mary's diary suggest her dependence on others, and outline the solitude that characterized her life:

Sept. 11 – On Saturday nothing much happened. Nobody went to town so I haven't been able to send a single letter in yet.

Sept. 12 – My, I wish I could send those letters into town. Nobody seems to be going as it is a busy season, harvesting, etc.. Mother has not heard a word from me since

I left. It's harder to send a letter into town from here than it is from Vancouver more than 750 miles away by rail.

Sept. 18 – Went to town with the Miller's Friday afternoon. At Six-Mile Meadows the car broke down . . . I got home at seven.

Sept. 25 – Was not able to get into town this week.

Oct. 1 – Redferns were not going to town so I was not able to go.

Oct. 6 – I wish I could get home this weekend but it certainly looks as if I won't be able to.

Oct. 24 – I wrote Helen how tired I was of bachelors and how much I wished I had a girl friend close by.

Oct. 27 – Mr. Miller did not bring me any mail.

Nov. 1 – Mr. Miller returned last night but brought no mail for me. It gave me the blues.[35]

Finally, out of desperation, she closed the school on Friday, 7 November because it was the only day she could "catch" a ride to Prince George to see her family, whom she had not seen for nearly seven weeks. When she returned, it took her more than a week to make up the time she had missed at school, but confided to her diary that it was worth it: "I went to Dreamland Friday and the Rex [cinema] Saturday and to church three times on Sunday. . . . I got my [sewing] parcels from Eaton's and Ramsey's while in town so will have lots of work to do for awhile."[36]

As Mary's diary illustrates, the rural teacher's social world in 1920s British Columbia could be small, narrow, confined and isolated. As Mary put it: "You can hear the train nine miles north of here whistle as it comes to the station."[37] In Mary's case, her daily routine was comprised of a latticework of small chores and distractions. For example, the parcels she picked up in Prince George contained fabrics, which she used to make her own clothes and dresses for her younger sisters. When she was not sewing in the evenings, she read every book and periodical she could get – sometimes until her eyes hurt – and wrote dozens of letters. She paid $127, more than a month's salary, for a correspondence course in script writing so that her evenings would be spent profitably in learning how to write. Her aspirations to be a writer led her to submit a couple of short stories, and she was delighted when they were published on the children's page of the *Edmonton Journal* (to which she bought a six-month subscription). Apart from these activities, her time away from school was spent mostly in small pursuits – walking, visiting, berry picking, learning to ice skate with a chair, organizing school concerts, taking photographs, or playing cards in the evening. When she did get to Prince George during school breaks, or on the occasional weekend, she indulged herself by going to the cinema: "I cannot count the number of movies I went to see during the holidays," she wrote in one entry.[38]

After wrestling with her conscience for some time about the propriety of an unattached, young female writing to men, Mary joined what appears to have been a "lonely hearts" club, the Primrose Club, shortly after her arrival in Mud River. In December that year, she received one letter from an Alberta coal miner, and part-time boxer, but refused to answer it because "you never can tell where such a step will lead." After Christmas, she received letters from "that Mountie in the Yukon" and "a person in Vermont." "They are a safe distance away," she wrote, obviously relieved. Nevertheless, she did not continue the correspondence. By February, she was beginning to regret her rashness and confessed: "Somehow lately I feel as if I am cut off from the world in this little narrow valley. . . . Too much school does not agree with me!"[39]

Mary's homesickness and her longing for mail were not just because she was away from home. She had spent a year in Vancouver at Normal School, away from her family, and yet remembered it as the "happiest year of my life."[40] Nor was it the weather, of which she made infrequent mention. Her unhappiness seems to have been more related to the isolation and confinement she felt in Mud River, a feeling that life was passing her by while she marked time in a place which she sensed held no future for her, and upon which she could make little impression.

Unsettled States

Mary Williams' diary suggests that frontier life in early twentieth century British Columbia was far from pastoral. The so-called settlers who came to Mud River were, in many respects, far from settled themselves. There is a restlessness to many of the characters Mary describes, and a sense that their journeys — whatever they happened to be — were somehow as important as their destinations. Before coming to Mud River, these men and women had been on the road and, likely, would be again. Drawn by work and adventure to the unsettled states of the American West, or to the hinterlands of Alberta and British Columbia, they had stayed, but briefly and, then, moved on, undeterred by borders or changes in national identity. The emptiness and isolation of the places they chose seemingly reflected their own unsettled states of mind.

Within two weeks of her arrival, Mary sketched these brief social portraits of her neighbors:

> Mr. Yukano is also a Lithuanian. He lived near Estonia, was in the war for the greater half of it. Has been in Ireland, seen Cork, Dublin, and the Killarney Lakes. Mr. Lemen left Lithuania the winter before the war started. He was in the United States army but did not get overseas. Mrs. Miller came out here about 12 years ago and hopes to get back but has not had the chance yet. Alex lived with French people for about eight years, so he knows French well.

In following weeks, she added:

> Charlie Lemen, according to Mrs. Miller, is very hard to please. In Detroit, he examined a few girls for the position of Mrs. Lemen of Mud River! But one was too old, another too lazy, another too good, etc. . . . A divorcée from Detroit has written to him several times, it seems in an attempt to catch him but so far [he] has not condescended to respond.

> Mr. Pallatt and I had an interesting talk yesterday. He said he had to start working in a lumber camp when he was only 14. . . . Mr. Van Dyke of the Provincial Police

was at the Hughes' last night. Mr. Van Dyke is a Belgian. He left there in 1905 when he came to Canada. He went overseas with the Canadian forces. His accent is very pronounced but he is a well-educated man.[43]

Sometimes, the portraits were far from flattering and illustrated, in one case at least, that the entrepreneurial spirit of the frontier applied to more than business:

Mrs. A. Miller came out here to marry Andy Miller's partner, John Footless. With her was a girl who was going to marry Andy. She got frightened in the end and did not come. John Footless could not speak good English, and Andy could, so Andy went to meet the girls in Saskatoon. . . . Well, when Andy found his girl was gone, he told Miss Lemen, as she was then, that John had got another girl. What could the poor girl do? Alone, in a country the language of which she could not speak, and . . . deserted, as she thought, by her sweetheart. She had known John in Lithuania. Andy offered to marry her and she accepted. They were married in Kamloops. Mrs. Miller did not say what John did when they got home. . . . Not much, for Miss Lemen is still Mrs. Andy Miller.[44]

Throughout its pages, the diary observes a degree of geographic mobility not associated today with the rural past. For everyone who came, someone else left. In various entries, she reported:

The two Bagots are going to return to Australia soon. Mr. Alexander is . . . threshing in Alberta. Fred Dyhrman is down in California and Jack Seed is somewhere in the U. S. A. Joe has not been to school this week. He told me last week that Alex was leaving Miller's and that, as soon as the road work was over, he and Alex were going to Edmonton. The Slim Millers will be leaving here at the end of March. They are selling everything. [And], Mr. Derbyshire, who is thinking of locating in the valley . . . comes from Carmarthen, the same county in Wales as Papa did.[45]

If life in Mud River was distinguished by the mobility and restlessness of its inhabitants, it was also fraught with danger for those who worked the land, as the Williams' diary testifies. Accidents, threats of bears and cougars, temperatures reaching 46 °C below zero, impassable roads, a flooding river, and brush fires punctuated everyday life. On one occasion, a brush fire almost engulfed the school: "Frank . . . had been burning Saturday and the sparks jumped the road and landed on a pile of brush and logs near the woodpile of the school. A south wind was blowing and it drove the flames away from the school down the valley. It climbed the hill and burnt on the other side. Stanley stayed up all night to watch the school."[46] Overall, the diary presents a portrait of a rural society where the life and well being of individuals was far from assured.

The Daily Drama of Gossip

The women of Mud River had their own social network and visited informally with one another as the roads, the seasons and work allowed. Books, patterns and magazines – principally the *Ladies' Home Journal, Farm and Home,* and *Maclean's* were their currency of exchange. But these were not always enough. According to Williams, most were starved for entertainment and stimulation. Between visits to town, and before telephones and radios were introduced, they created their own form of daily drama fashioned from scraps of information and gossip about their neighbors. Gossip, in fact, constituted the valley's chief form of entertainment and its popularity was certainly not confined to women as the diary illustrates. By the end of the first school year, this young woman, now nineteen-years old, had been regaled in all quarters with tales of the valley's darker side – allegations of cuckolding, incest, infidelity, greed, bootlegging, drunkenness, treachery, temporary insanity and failure. Two weeks before school ended, she bemoaned the passing of her innocence: "I thought horrible things like this were only found in books. Yet here it is in the small place of Mud River. What a terrific amount of horrors and gossiping goes on in this world then, under the surface!"[47]

Much of the gossip had a racist edge and suggested that this small interior settlement, no larger than many medieval villages, had become a battleground for national differences that survived the Atlantic crossing. One English family regularly referred to the Lithuanians as "Bo-hunks" and "cattle."[48] In turn, the Lithuanians, some of whom were self-styled "socialistics," claimed that "the last war was made by the capitalists . . . that the king never has to work, [and] that he lives on 'strawberries, sugar, and cream,' so to speak."[49] Likewise, one American family did little to assist the cause of cultural integration by generally expressing "anti-British, anti-monarchist, and anti-Canadian views." Their refusal to sing in public "God Save the King," according to Mary, "jars many Canadians in the valley."[50]

For the men, easily more mobile than the women, the social universe was a little larger, according to Williams. They went to town regularly by horse, by car or even on foot to buy supplies and visit the saloon. The wives went too, but less often, tied down by children too young for school and by domestic responsibilities, though some could and did drive the family car or buggy. For the young unmarrieds, numbering less than a dozen, social life consisted mainly of cards and conversation in the evening around the oil lamp on someone's dining room table, a pattern broken by an occasional weekend visit to Prince George. "Arguments and stories formed most of the evening's talk," Mary wrote.[51] And elsewhere: "Charlie Lemen proposed having a dance in the schoolhouse soon. . . . I have told him that I'll do no dancing but they think I'll change my mind."[52]

The cinemas and saloons of Prince George were the only sources of solace for bachelors when young ladies, like Mary, sought to preserve their dignity and reputations. But even there, little was secret. As Williams observed: "Stanley went to town with Mr. Miller Monday and has not returned yet. It is understood here that he is on a spree and is gloriously drunk!"[53]

Such was Mud River Valley in the years following the Great War, a community that was not quite a community, held together more by topographical features and isolation than social ties, a place where people were dependent on each other for labor at times, drawn closer on rare occasions by death or disaster, but generally held apart by jealousy, cultural prejudice, clannishness, and fear – fear of appearing weak, fear of gossip, and fear of losing the spirit of independence prized by so many. This was the social world that Mary Williams had entered.

A Frontier Finishing School

When Mary Williams came to Mud River, more than the geography of the valley was unfamiliar. The settlement was not simply a new place to her but, evidently, a new cultural world. For the first time in her life, she was forced by circumstance to live and deal with people and nationalities she had never encountered, at least in the sense of sharing a social space. What she found challenged her own beliefs and whatever British-Canadian certainties she had learned growing up. Living with a family not her own – and a Lithuanian one at that – meant a difficult adjustment for Mary. In the first place, the Millers spoke broken English and Mary's experience of "foreigners" had been limited: "School-teaching has a very broadening effect on one's mind. Before I came here I had a half conceived notion that the foreigners who spoke broken English did not know much but I'm mistaken."[54]

From Frank Yukano she learned something of Russian life under the Czar, "first-hand," as she put it, and, from Mr. Pallatt, the Fenian raids. Andy Miller instructed her in the rudiments of Bolshevism and advanced arguments for atheism, saying that "his religion is . . . to believe only what he sees."[55]

Such discussion and debate, at times shocking and disillusioning, seemed welcomed by Mary, who found to her dismay, that the frontier was its own kind of finishing school about intellectual and other worlds far beyond provincial borders. Above all, these discussions acted as a crucible which served to forge her own views, especially about the importance of the teacher's social role. Reflecting on one argument with a Lithuanian family, she wrote:

> Their viewpoint is too narrow. . . . They think that the capitalist is a person who looks on the labouring class as an animal to be starved and driven. They cannot see that there is good and bad in both. They are not products of the Canadian schools, and it is there that the duty of the teacher comes in. They must give the newcomer's children the Canadian viewpoint, a broad viewpoint, show them that everyone does not think alike and it takes many kinds of people to make a world.[56]

Mary's intellectual resilience, for the most part, was greater than her social confidence. For one thing, she was unsure about how to balance her role as a schoolteacher with that of being a "member" in a new family. Her first instinct was always to withdraw – to hide in her room when the parlor filled up with Lithuanian bachelors, as it did every night, or to retreat to the safety the pages of a book offered, where she could be, at once, present but detached from the worldly ways of "foreigners." Her lack of confidence was borne out in confessions to her diary: "Yesterday afternoon when I came home Frank Yukano . . . was at Miller's but I kept strictly to my room. . . . Ditto last night."[57]

At times, Mary was tempted to stay at the school house and not go home to the Millers, but it was impossible to stay apart, so with as much grace as she could muster, she forced herself to "entertain" in the only way she felt comfortable–by extending the schoolroom into the Miller household. She began to join what she called the "regular debating club" and, sometimes, talked until "about half past ten about almost every country in the world."[58]

When the discussion became too intense, Mary began to play cards with the bachelors but, unexpectedly, found herself in conflict with her own conscience. The Saturday night card games – and the card tricks she learned from Stanley, Frank, and Charley Lemen – were innocuous enough, but they crept over into Sunday, causing Mary to battle with her upbringing about the immorality of playing cards on the Sabbath. Furthermore, if she was not to make a practice of it, how would she explain her reasons for refusing to play? "Last night, when I was asked to play I could not think of no real good reason why it was wrong to play cards on Sunday. But I must not put any more down. Somehow saying that seems irreligious."[59]

But this was not the only cause of her social unease. In the Miller's parlor, Mary came up against male chauvinism in its virulent northeastern European form. All the Lithuanian bachelors seemed to be interested in was finding "housekeepers," who had to be pretty, good cooks, hard workers, and fertile. In their view, women should not want to spend money on clothes or frivolities but be content with what their husbands offered. She described a woman who admitted her husband "doesn't care" for her anymore: "'Says I'm an old woman.' She is only 33. Her brother is older than her by a year and a half and she said he wanted a young wife! The men are very particular about themselves. . . ."[60]

Whatever quiet hopes of romance Mary Williams might have entertained, and there are frequent references to show that she kept close watch on every bachelor newcomer to the valley, she was heartily disillusioned by the pragmatic search for "a missus" evidenced by the young men she met at the Miller's. Nevertheless, when the "wondrous Fred Dyrhman" was rumored to be returning from a trip to the United States–he who had "walked out" with the previous two school teachers–she found herself interested: "I wish he would for what I hear he has lots of life in him and Mud River certainly needs to be enlivened. It is absolutely dead, and it makes me feel like dying."[61] Dyrhman, however, was not one of the Lithuanian bachelors who turned up nightly at the Miller household – no doubt because of a past disagreement over the widow Racklyeft's trunk.

Changing Places

Mary Williams was faced with the obstacle common to rural teachers of her generation–that of finding and keeping suitable board and lodging.[62] Shortly after the end of her first month in Mud River, she became embroiled in a dispute with Andy Miller, her landlord. It began innocently enough during a lunch-time argument about politics. The Millers' were, to use their own term, "socialistics," which apparently meant a wholehearted disbelief in any government interference, together with an equally firm suspicion that capitalists, bankers, and real estate men were chiefly responsible for society's evils. "At noon," Mary reports, "Mr. Miller and I got into such a big argument that I was almost late for school. It was on Socialism. . . . I always like an argument but when they make some ridiculous statements, rather truths that are only half-truths, and believe them thoroughly . . . I almost lose my patience."[63]

Unfortunately, the argument did not end there. In the weeks following, Andy Miller continued his derision of the capitalist class, especially real estate men. The fact that Mary's father was in real estate prompted her to issue hot replies and fierce arguments in support of her upbringing. On 1 December, things came to a head, as Mary explained:

> Monday night the bailing crew were at Millers' and I had to eat supper with them. By mistake, I did not sit in my usual place but beside Mr. Miller. When asking me if I wanted some salt, I think it was, he added 'dear.' I was mad. Have been ever since and have not spoken to him since.[64]

She had weathered blasphemy, attacks on her father's profession, and challenges to her beliefs, but this affront to her young dignity was intolerable. She had been called "dear" in front of the harvest crew, a small piece of paternalism that proved to be the last straw. On January 10, following the Christmas break, she reported: "Well I have gone and done it so to speak. I went to [the] Hughes' to board yesterday. Mrs. Miller did not say much but I am very much afraid that there is a break between us [that] time alone will heal."[65]

Moving in with the Hughes' family did not solve all her social problems, but it was a secure haven compared to the turbulence of the Miller's: "The things at Hughes' are more convenient and nicer, and I have more room for myself, although the house is colder than the Miller's."[66] Despite the cold, she was sufficiently comfortable to remain boarding with them until she left the valley in June 1924.

A Youngster Teaching Youngsters

After the first couple of months of school, Mary developed considerable confidence about her work in the classroom, despite the fact that she was a youngster teaching other youngsters. The diary suggests by its virtual silence that on few occasions did she have cause to reflect on the pedagogy she employed. On one such occasion, likely common to all members of the profession, past and present, she wrote: "Two weeks of school gone. What is there to show for it?" In another: "Today I taught singing at school. I do not know if it will be successful or not."[67]

Otherwise, most of the comments she made about her work concerned the children she taught, their comings and goings, their health, and their behavior. To illustrate:

> Two more pupils came today – A Constantine Malganus and Billy Hughes. The former is just as hard to handle as his name.
>
> Kept four children in today. Had nine pupils, the most I have had yet.
>
> The north wind has been blowing for the last five days. It was 46 below zero this morning. I had only five pupils.
>
> All my pupils were at school today. I have had quite a good attendance lately.[68]

Some children's names appear as threads throughout her narrative – youngsters in whom she developed a special interest, or who were causing her problems of one kind or another. "Winnifred Tyner," she wrote, "is a curious child. So grown up in some ways and yet a great child in others. I have not just decided upon her character yet."[69] Of another, she wondered: "I wish I knew for certain if there was any chance for Isabel. In arithmetic she is so slow and makes such silly mistakes. I wish Mr. Gower was coming soon so I could ask his advice."[70] And of the boy, Constantine Malganus, who proved, as she suspected, to be as difficult as his name: "A minute or so ago I did it. That which I was afraid would come: [I] strapped Constantine. . . . I believe I was as shaky as he but it had to be done."[71]

Apart from such notations, the diary reveals relatively little about the nature of Mary's instructional techniques, how she planned her lessons, or how she organized the class to keep more than a dozen children, some studying different subjects at different levels, busy. But she does provide details about the small rituals of rural school life, including collecting money for school concerts, "celebrating the King's birthday," making Valentine's Day cards, and organizing beginning and end-of-term picnics.

What is clear from the diary, however, is that, at times, Mary was more than a little unsure about the nature of the career she had chosen. In mid-June 1923, on the eve of the school term's end, she reflected on the course her life was taking:

> My life's work is teaching? Somehow I never thought of spending my life at it. It was only to be a stepping stone. I intended to write after I had experience. I think experience takes all your dreams from you. Therefore I must write before all my dreams are gone. They are going fast, very fast.[72]

Finding and Losing Her Footing

"Here I am back on the old job again," Mary wrote on 11 September 1923, on the first day of her second school year at Mud River.[73] But things were different: if the job was the same, then Mary's attitude or perspective had somehow changed, at least judging by the tone of the diary's entries during her second year. Irritations such as poor mail delivery and the infrequency of her trips to Prince George, which plagued her the first year, were summarily dealt with, suggesting that she had adapted to community routines or, at least, learned how to work within the system to secure rides to town or whatever else she needed.

For much of the first term, her diary entries were animated by a sense of the positive. The school's inaugural picnic "came off splendidly." Her four new pupils were "handsome." A party at the Hughes' featured nothing less than music by Handel, Beethoven, and Bach, and was enjoyed by all. The "free textbooks" arrived from Victoria but she continued to teach phonics the old way because she was confident that it worked. At long last, she met the bachelor Percy Peacock, who looked "English." She wondered if she should have her fortune told and tried to skate. Even the composition of the school board had changed for the better. The three trustees were now Andy Miller, as the newly-elected trustee, as well as Mr. Pallatt, and Mrs.

Hughes, who served as board secretary. With Miller's characteristic drive and energy, which she was quick to credit, work on the school was advancing more quickly. A stable was being built at the back of the school for children's horses. And, a new school floor was to be installed over Christmas.

Aside from the gossip, which seemed incessant, the only dark spot in a bright and, otherwise, uneventful term was a community quarrel over the school pump, long unreliable. In early November, Mrs. Pallatt threatened to withdraw her son Albert's services as janitor if he had to carry water from the river to mop the floor. Instead of asking for the pump to be repaired or replaced, Mary made the mistake of asking the Tyner girls, Winnifred and Isabel, if they would like to earn money cleaning the school if Albert resigned, which he did. Despite the fact that she had prompted Albert to quit, Mrs. Pallatt was furious about her son "losing" the janitor's job. Mrs. Hughes, now Mary's landlady and secretary of the school board, in turn, "got awfully hot" because Mrs. Pallatt withdrew Albert's services. In Mary's words, "that is what started the commotion."[74]

To this point in the diary, nothing suggests that Mary was actually contemplating leaving Mud River, although she had expressed her unhappiness about the community's isolation several times during her first year. "Somehow lately," she wrote in the midst of a winter storm in February 1923, "I feel that I am cut off from the world in this little narrow valley."[75] And, a few days later: "I have lost the footing somehow that I had at the start and wish the monotony, the endless days of doing the same thing over and over again would go."[76]

Nine months later, Mary's mood of unease had obviously deepened, brought on this time by the bitterness she saw around her. On 3 December 1923, she reported: "The valley is all divided up. Quarrels! My goodness! Hughes and MacDonalds, Tyners and Breezes, MacDonalds and Alexanders, Pallatts and Malganuses, and strained relations between Mrs. Pallatt and me. It is about time a new year came to wipe these out. I doubt if it will."[77] On December 11, in her last entry for the 1923 school year, she recorded: "Mr. Gower advised me to take a third grade class in a graded school near Vancouver next year. . . . He advised me never to take my home school. What will mother say to that, she has always wanted me to teach in Prince George?"[78]

Whether this suggestion to leave the valley was entirely Gower's, or whether the inspector and Mary had earlier discussions about the possibility of her teaching elsewhere is unclear. However, if it had been discussed earlier, it is likely that Mary would have noted it in an entry. In any event, regardless of whether her mind was made up at this time, circumstances after Christmas ensured that she would leave.

A Convenient Battleground

The new year proved to be anything but new in Mud River as old unresolved conflicts focused themselves around the schoolhouse. Since the previous September, community tensions had run high. The Millers' horses had been found grazing in the

Hughes' oat field. Then, someone else deliberately turned a horse loose on the Hughes' land. Meetings of the Farmers' Institute grew more unpleasant. One cattleman reported another's livestock to the police, resulting in a fine. Then someone else informed on the informer. Accusations and complaints were traded back and forth about various issues, including the Institute's management.

The community's general unhappiness and mood of distrust eventually spilled over to the school. While Mary had been visiting her family during the Christmas holidays, a public meeting about the school and the teacher had been called, but not by the school board. During the meeting, convened by a few dissatisfied families, Mary was criticized, among other things, for not advancing Slim Miller's son, Tommy, along with his sister Allie because he was "not as bright" as his sister. Mrs. Tyner, whose daughter Sarah suffered from poor vision, blamed Mary for the poor quality of the school's blackboards, still deficient after four years, and informed the audience that she had already complained to the inspector about Mary during the summer, especially her leniency toward students. Minutes of this extra-legal meeting were sent to Mr. Gower, describing Mary as "careless," and indicating that some residents wanted a new teacher. Upon receiving them, the inspector told Mary of the meeting and reassured her that it "did not seem important to him."[79]

Deciding to Leave

By mid-February, Mary's growing disengagement with the community was apparent in her diary entries: "This is some life," she wrote. "Believe you me. The person who considers it an honour to be a schoolteacher is a couple of centuries behind time."[80] She also noted that Mrs. Tyner, who complained so vigorously about the school's blackboards, refused to help in bringing new ones out from Prince George – and threatened to keep her daughter out of school if someone else did not deliver them. This lack of co-operation was, of course, nothing new.[81] Referring to another source of her problems, Mary added that "Mrs. Pallatt said she was satisfied with Albert, but behind my back she talks about the janitor business."[82] By May 12, Mary's decision was made. "I'm glad I'm not coming back here," she wrote, "I'm beginning to realize that teaching is hard on the nerves."[83] On June 27, the diary records her final words on Mud River:

> I started this diary almost two years ago, the first day I taught here, and this is my last. . . . I've got my first taste of what life is here. Several different tastes in fact – but I hope that if I get worse tastes in the future I'll meet them with head up.[84]

Mary Williams went to Park Court, Alberta, in August 1924, where she taught school for a year and met her future husband. She returned to Prince George to teach the following year before returning to Park Court in 1926 where she married and taught for a brief period. She died in 1938, at thirty-five years of age, of tuberculosis.

Mud River continued to wear out its teachers. Miss Bessie Miller – no relation to either of the Miller families in the valley–taught the 1924-1925 school year. Miss V. Sleightholm taught the class of 1925-1926, and managed to return for a second year as well. On the school district information form of 1927, she confirmed much of what Mary had learned: "It would not be a wise policy to send an inexperienced teacher here, for the community does not have much cooperative spirit, or harmony, so that it makes a teacher tread most carefully to keep on friendly terms with all."[85] The next three teachers – one of whom was male – lasted just one year each. The effects of the Depression hit the interior region hard in 1931 and the next teacher, possibly because of the uncertainty of securing other employment, stayed three years before leaving. Even allowing for this record tenure, the Mud River school had been staffed by ten different teachers in the sixteen years since it was built.

So, too, was Mary's view of the community confirmed when the Rural Teachers' Welfare Officer, Lottie Bowron, reported on Mud River in the late 1920s and early 1930s. Miss Bowron, charged specifically by the Department of Education with investigating the general welfare of female teachers in isolated parts of the province, wrote that the district's social conditions were "not very good," that it was not "an easy district" to work in, that is to say, a "lonely one," and that she could not call the living accommodations "very satisfactory."[86] She concluded: "I was glad to find an older woman at Mud River this year and not a young girl. I have in the past recommended that a man be sent here."[87]

Significance of the Diary

What does this diary, subjective though it is as a source, offer to social and educational historians? Does it prompt the reader of provincial history to reconsider in any way the historical record? And, if so, in what respects?

First, to the question of the diary's overall value, the entries made by this young woman over a period of two years reveal relatively little about life in rural classrooms in the decade after the Great War. It is evident that Mary Williams, like many teachers, as Lortie points out, defined her work largely in terms of her relationship with the children she taught.[88] Few references pertain to what she taught, how she taught it, or what she had learned at normal school to guide her practices in school. Her interests were obviously elsewhere.

However, the narrative Mary provides has considerable value in other respects. It is highly descriptive as a source in setting the experiences of one teacher within the confines of a small rural community in the 1920s. Its pages offer interesting glimpses into the social and human forces that shape the contours of a teacher's relationship with a community, how the routines of a rural society served to check a teacher's personal autonomy, and how the school as an institution, and the teacher, together acted as a lightening rod around which other civic issues gathered in search of expression or resolution. The great advantage of the diary as a record in this regard is that it not only indicates the nature of the connections between the teacher and the community, but it also documents how the teacher personally felt about events acting upon her.

The diary shows, that, in Mary's case, the community's expectations of her were never clearly stated, or at least never stated so obviously that she felt obliged to record them. Whatever sense she had of what it was to be a teacher she seems to have brought with her to the valley. Her understanding of the teacher's role, as she wrestled to define it, seems to have been more directly influenced by family tradition than by anything learned at normal school. References to her teacher training are conspicuous by their absence. The diary also shows that the decisions she made were generally the result of a cumulative process. There are few defining moments in her life; things assume a form over time, which the diary records, sometimes in meticulous detail.

No doubt, the diary's greatest value lies in its portrait of Mud River. Page after page, it illustrates in small ways the character of this settlement, its folkways and rituals, as well as its cultural codes. As such, it is an extremely important document in rural history, even as an inside-out view, comprised of small photographs taken from within school walls by someone who is a stranger. The images Mary presented may, of course, not always be accurate. However, judging by the diary's ruminative character, her obvious willingness to hammer away at things to secure more complete understandings over time, as well as her manifest good naturedness, it is likely that the portrait she presented is a reasonably fair version of events to the extent she understood them. In the singularity of its scope and depth as a commentary on a teacher's experience in a rural community, the diary is valuable in its own right.

Mary's biographical sketches of the valley's residents are also useful in that they furnish a much-needed human dimension to the public around the schools, a public too often invisible in much of educational history. Through her words, readers learn of the extraordinary cultural differences that confronted this young teacher and the educational and social challenges they presented.

Similarly, the diary is unquestionably valuable as autobiography. In many respects, the writer is her own best subject. Her notations over a two-year period show her to be a kind and sensitive young woman, more than a little unsure of herself but, nonetheless, courageous. Mary Williams appears to be someone much like Voltaire's Candide, a young individual who has entered an unfamiliar world expecting the best of others, and somewhat reluctant to believe the worst in people when she finds it. Also, in the manner of Candide, the diary represents a chronicle of a personal odyssey from innocence to experience.

And what of the historical record? Does the diary add in other ways to understandings of rural schoolteachers in the years after the Great War? Certainly, it can be argued that the diary fleshes out parts of the historical record that require additional texture. To illustrate, neither the inspector's reports on Mary, nor Mary's own description of Mud River in the school district information form, suggest why this teacher refused to return for a third year in September 1924. Inspector Gower wrote that "the tone and general standing of this school have improved under Miss Williams." Mary herself wrote that the condition of the school was "quite fair," that the winter weather was "quite fair" for those used to it, that mail came "once a week," and that the boarding place (at the Hughes') was "congenial." In other words, the government records that provide the foundation for much of what we know about rural teachers' lives is silent in Mary's case – and, indeed, in many others – in defining a motive for leaving.

Because of its reflective character, however, the diary provides an understanding that goes beyond the "low salary and poor living conditions" commonly given as reasons by Inspector Gower and other inspectors to explain high rates of teacher attrition in rural areas during the 1920s and 1930s. It confirms, albeit as a single source, that Lottie Bowron's estimation of the problems besetting female teachers in rural areas was considerably closer to the mark than that offered by school inspectors generally.[89] If Mary William's story is illustrative of others – namely that teacher turnover was a function of poor social relationships between communities and their teachers – it also serves as a reminder about just how powerless the Department of Education and its officers actually were in attempting to remediate problems of high attrition.

The diary is interesting in two other ways. Although this discussion has not compared the lives of rural and urban teachers during this period, it is reasonable to suggest that one important difference between these two groups may involve the implicit kinds of social contracts formed between teachers and their communities. Urban teachers of this generation, especially in large centres, were likely freer of the explicit and subtle day-to-day constraints that influenced the lives of their rural counterparts, such as Mary Williams. The implicit social contract they had with their communities was of a different order. This difference between urban and rural norms and expectations may even hold true between country towns, such as Prince George and their rural satellites, like Mud River.

Likewise, in its portrait of a geographically mobile rural society, the Williams' diary may prompt us to reconsider the meaning that various sources, principally inspectors' and other government reports, have given to retention and attrition rates in rural schools. Rates of attrition in rural districts have been judged high perhaps because they have generally been compared to attrition rates in urban districts. In describing the mobility of Mud River's residents, the William's diary suggests that rural teachers were not the only individuals to change addresses frequently, and that it may be more insightful to re-calibrate the historical meaning given to teacher attrition rates in rural British Columbia against a standard other than that of urban districts, for instance against the mobility of farm laborers or other occupational groups who, like teachers, enjoyed a certain freedom in offering their labor to various employers. Measured against such groups, teachers may not have been as unstable a workforce as we generally have held them to be.

Notes

I am indebted to Robin Bright of the University of Lethbridge for her assistance in the early stages of this project and to Jean Barman at UBC and Tara Toutant at the University of Victoria for their editorial suggestions. Appreciation is also owed to Joyce Greenwood, Mary Williams' daughter, for the information and photographs she kindly supplied. This study was made possible by a grant from the SSHRC.

1. These statistics are derived from counting the number of rural, female school teachers, married and unmarried, in the British Columbia Department of Education, *Annual Report of the Public Schools* [hereafter ARPS] (Victoria: King's Printer, 1922).

2. Mary Carolina Greenwood, *Personal Diary of Mary Carolina Williams* (hereafter *Williams' Diary*), Provincial Archives of British Columbia (hereafter PABC), Victoria, British Columbia, Add. MSS 261. For other diaries and first hand reports on rural schools in British Columbia, see for example: Carolina McLellan Williams, *Notebook*, PABC, Add. MSS 558; Mary Lenore Nichols, Correspondence, PABC, Add. MSS 2459; Lillian V. Williams, Letter to Lillian Anderson from Lorraine Johns, 1922, PABC, Add. MSS 2796; and, Annie Monk, Brief Notes, PABC, Add. MSS 2821.

3. Carolina McLellan Williams, *Notebook*, PABC, Add. MSS 558.

4. Mildred E. McQuillan, *Personal Diary*, PABC, Add. MSS 1252. To illustrate with an entry form October 23, 1927: "I get out some dough to pay my board and holy dying catfish, church on fire, suffering tom-cats, holy smokes, ye gods, my stars, dirty dying Dora, outrageous, I have to pony up 35 bones for this dive."

5. See for example: Joan Adams and Becky Thomas, *Floating Schools and Frozen Inkwells: The One-Room Schools of British Columbia* (Madeira Park: Harbour Publishing, 1985); Jean Cochrane, *The One-Room School in Canada* (Toronto: Fitzhenry and Whiteside, 1981); John Calam, ed., *Alex Lord's British Columbia: Recollections of a Rural School Inspector, 1915-1936* (Vancouver: UBC Press, 1991); John Calam and Thomas Fleming, *British Columbia Schools and Society, British Columbia Royal Commission on Education*, Volume 1 (Victoria: Queen's Printer, May 1988); J. Donald Wilson, "The Visions of Ordinary Participants: Teachers' Views of Rural Schooling in British Columbia in the 1920s," Patricia Roy, ed., *A History of British Columbia: Selected Readings* (Copp Clark Pitman: Mississauga, Ontario, 1989), 239-255; J. Donald Wilson and Paul J. Stortz, "May the Lord Have Mercy on You: The Rural School Problem in British Columbia in the 1920s," *B.C. Studies* 79 **(Autumn 1988): 24-57 (see ch. 11 of this book)**; Thomas Fleming, Carolyn Smyly, and Julie White, "Lottie Bowron Within Organizational Realities and Bases of Power: British Columbia, 1928-1934," *Journal of Educational Administration and Foundations*, 5, 2, (1990): 7-31; and J. Donald Wilson, "'I am Here to Help if You Need Me': British Columbia's Rural Teachers' Welfare Officer, 1928-1934," *Journal of Canadian Studies* 25, 2 (Summer, 1990): 94-118.

6. This seems especially true in the case of Wilson, "The Vision of Ordinary Participants," and Fleming, Smyly, and White, "Lottie Bowron Within Organizational Realities."

7. See, for example, Wilson and Stortz, "May the Lord Have Mercy on You;" Wilson, "The Vision of Ordinary Participants"; Fleming, Smyly, and White, "Lottie Bowron Within Organizational Realities;" Wilson, "'I am Here to Help.'"

8. See, for example, British Columbia Department of Education, *Inspectors' Reports*, PABC, GR 122, GR 456, GR 1492, GR 2566; British Columbia, *Superintendent of Education*, PABC, GR 450 and GR 1445; British Columbia, Department of Education, *Teachers' Bureau*, PABC, GR 461; British Columbia, Department of Education, *ARPS*, 1872-present; and J.H. Putman and G.M. Weir, *Survey of the School System* (Victoria, British Columbia: King's Printer, 1925).

9. J. Donald Wilson, "The Visions of Ordinary Participants," 239-255.

10. *Ibid*, 251-52.

11. *Ibid*.

12. The Chilako is a tributary of the Nechako which joins the Fraser River to Prince George.

13. In Ladner, for example, many Japanese families settled. Creston, in contrast, became home to many Doukhabors.

14. Earl Baity, *I Remember Chilako* (Prince George, B.C.: Prince George Press, 1978).

15. *Williams' Diary*, 5.

16. *Ibid.*, 51.

17. Baity, *I Remember Chilako*, 53-54.

18. *Ibid.*, 55.

19. *Williams' Diary*, 11.

20. The Education Office was re-named the Department of Education in 1920.

21. In 1920, Inspector Gower estimated that only 10 per cent of the teachers within his inspectorate (then #13) returned to their schools after their summer vacations, and that 25 per cent of classrooms experienced a change of teacher during the school year. See ARPS, 1920, C37.

22. *Ibid.*, 22. Williams reports that Miss McLarty spent but one year in Vancouver before returning to another rural school.

23. ARPS, 1922, C40.

24. *Williams' Diary*, 2.

25. *Ibid.*

26. *Ibid.*

27. *Ibid.*, 14.

28. *Ibid.*, 2 and 9.

29. Caroline McLellan, *Notebook*, Wednesday, March 30.

30. *Williams' Diary*, 13, 2 and 3.

31. *Ibid.*, 32.

32. *Ibid.*, 47.

33. *Ibid.*, 50

34. For descriptions of inspectors' relationships with teachers, see John Calam, ed., *Alex Lord's British Columbia*; and Thomas Fleming, "Our Boys in the Field: School Inspectors, Superintendents, and the Changing Character of School Leadership in British Columbia," in Nancy M. Sheehan, J. Donald Wilson, and David C. Jones, eds., *Schools in the West: Essays in Canadian Educational History* (Calgary: Detselig Enterprises Ltd., 1986), 285-303.

35. *Williams' Diary*, 3, 4, 5, 6, 7, 8, 10 and 17.

36. *Ibid.*, 18.

37. *Ibid.*, 5.

38. *Ibid.*, 26.

39. *Ibid.*, 40.

40. *Ibid.*, 68.

41. *Ibid.*, 5-6.

42. *Ibid.*, 8.

43. *Ibid.*, 29.

44. *Ibid.*, 21.

45. *Ibid.*, 42, 58, 62, 71, 72, and 73. Even within Mary's own family and circle of friends, someone always seemed to be coming or going: "Cousin Lilian, she is at Bellingham going to Normal [School]." "Margaret is still in the States." "Papa has gone to Vancouver and he may go across to Victoria and see Roscoe." "George is down in California." And, "Masie Golder phoned up . . . while I was in town [Prince George]. She had just arrived from Seattle." Even Mary, herself, admitted to a certain restlessness: "If only I could have enough money to travel

everywhere or anywhere during the summer, I know I could come back to Mud River . . . ready for another year's work."

46. *Ibid.*, 48.
47. *Ibid.*
48. *Ibid.*, 59.
49. *Ibid.*, 10.
50. *Ibid.*, 27.
51. *Ibid.*, 16.
52. *Ibid.*, 17.
53. *Ibid.*, 17.
54. *Ibid.*, 4.
55. *Ibid.*
56. *Ibid.*, 12.
57. *Ibid.*, 2.
58. *Ibid.*, 4.
59. *Ibid.*, 5.
60. *Ibid.*, 7.
61. *Ibid.*, 20.
62. For example, see: Fleming, Smyly, and White, "Lottie Bowron," 7-32.
63. *Williams' Diary*, 11.
64. *Ibid.*, 22.
65. *Ibid.*, 26.
66. *Ibid.*
67. *Ibid.*, 33.
68. *Ibid.*, 2-15.
69. *Ibid.*
70. *Ibid.*, 43.
71. *Ibid.*, 29.
72. *Ibid.*, 52.
73. *Ibid.*, 55.
74. *Ibid.*, 64.
75. *Ibid.*, 32.
76. *Ibid.*, 33.
77. *Ibid.*, 68.
78. *Ibid.*, 69.
79. *Ibid.*, 70.
80. *Ibid.*, 71.
81. *Ibid.*, 22. More than a year before, Mary had commented: "The bookcase is in town, if someone will only bring it out."
82. *Ibid.*
83. *Ibid.,* 77.
84. *Ibid.*, 81.
85. British Columbia Department of Education, *Teachers' Bureau, School District Information Form*, Mud River, February 21, 1927, PABC, B6666.

86. British Columbia Department of Education, *School Inspectors' Reports, Reports of Rural Teachers' Welfare Office (Women)*, 1930.

87. *Ibid.*

88. Dan C. Lortie, *Schoolteacher: A Sociological Study* (Chicago: University of Chicago Press, 1976).

89. This point is made in Wilson and Stortz, "May the Lord Have Mercy" and in Fleming, Smyly, and White, "Lottie Bowron Within Organizational Realities."

14

"I am ready to be of assistance when I can": Lottie Bowron and Rural Women Teachers in British Columbia

J. Donald Wilson

On the morning of 14 November 1928 officials of the Cowichan Lake Logging Company came upon a grisly scene in the teacher's residence at Nixon Creek, an isolated logging camp on the southwest shore of Cowichan Lake on Vancouver Island. Upon entering the three-roomed dwelling they were horrified to find the body of the teacher, twenty-year-old Mabel Jones, stretched out on her back on the floor in the sitting room with a .22 rifle beside her. The post-mortem report coldly described "a bullet wound of entrance on the front of the chest just to the left of the mid-line with about it a powder burn."[1] A note was found. In a letter to the managing director of the logging company, which had that fall "built and equipped an excellent school building" at Nixon Creek, Miss Jones wrote: "There are a few people who would like to see me out of the way, so I am trying to please them. . . . I know this is a coward's way of doing things, but what they said about me almost broke my heart. They are not true. Forgive me, please. Say it was an accident." The complaints registered against Mabel Jones by some parents (out of twenty-two children, the parents of only three were responsible for these criticisms) were enumerated as follows: the flag was continually flying; the children were allowed to march into school in a careless manner; schoolroom discipline was lacking; and the teacher was allowing the children to "waste their scribblers."[2]

Later in the month a coroner's inquest was held before which a number of witnesses appeared, both company officials and local residents. The verdict was straightforward: "Mabel Estelle Jones came to her death whilst temporarily insane." The jury added, however: "we are further of the opinion that the mental state was the result of unjustifiable, unfeeling and underhanded criticisms of her work on the part of two members of the school board." It recommended finding ways in future to free teachers in such small, isolated school districts "from the gossip of irresponsible and petty citizens."[3]

Public outrage about the Mabel Jones case was immediate. Typical of newspaper reaction was the Vancouver *Province*'s editorial which lamented the tragic death of "poor little Mabel Jones" who "took her own life because it had become intolerable to her in that lonely settlement in the deep woods of Vancouver Island." But there was a positive side to this tragic affair, the newspaper continued, because "her pitiful story has done more to arouse public interest in the problem of our rural schools than anything else that has been done or said in this province for years."[4] Women's groups such as the influential Local Council of Women in Victoria were upset and Joshua Hinchliffe, the new Conservative minister of education, dismissed the Nixon Creek board, replacing it with an official trustee.

Ironically, only three weeks before Mabel Jones' death the school inspector for the area, A.C. Stewart, had complimented her on her "good" work. Her school management and control were described as "satisfactory," the character of teaching, her grading of pupils, and her attitude to work as "good." In his previous report of January 1928 he described Jones as "very interested in the welfare and progress of the pupils" and complimented her on their behavior. In his 1927 report on his inspectorate as a whole, Stewart had pointed to the need for local communities to be charitable in their criticism of inexperienced teachers in remote situations. By the same token teachers had to learn to live with local criticism. "We all have the same burden of human defects and need all the helpfulness, sympathy, and encouragement possible from the community in which we serve in order that we may rise in some measure and in some degree to the height of the service required and demanded of us. Whatever the baffling conditions, whatever the adverse and apparently unjust criticism, if we honestly and sincerely try and strive we shall at least enjoy the luxury of self-respect."[5]

Hinchliffe launched an immediate investigation into conditions as they affected the lives of teachers in rural and assisted schools.[6] The investigators recommended a revision of rural school classifications, higher salaries for assisted school teachers, and a system whereby the provincial police would periodically visit teachers in isolated schools. While none of these recommendations was acted upon, Hinchliffe did take one positive step: he appointed a Rural Teachers' Welfare Officer whose duty was to "visit the rural districts of the Province where the living and social conditions under which young female teachers are working are not found to be satisfactory." To the one-room school teacher the welfare officer was to act as a "friend and good counsellor who will ever be ready to respond to any call that may come for advice or assistance."[7] The person chosen to carry out this important duty was Lottie Bowron, like Hinchliffe a staunch Anglican. Effective 1 April 1929, her title was fixed as Rural Teachers' Welfare Officer (Women) in the Department of Education. She began work, however, immediately after the Jones tragedy in November 1928, issuing her first report on 11 January 1929.[8]

Instead of choosing to make the structural changes he might have – revised school classifications, higher salaries, and police visits to teachers – Hinchliffe chose to shore up individual teachers by naming someone who could offer pastoral care to the troubled female teachers in the province's isolated areas. The appointee was a noted club woman rather than an experienced teacher, whose culture was one of sociability, service and subordination. The decision to appoint Bowron was made, therefore, without intention to attack the rural school problem at its roots.

I

Lottie Mabel Bowron was born in Barkerville on 20 November 1879, the daughter of John Bowron, one of the original Overlanders in 1862 who had settled in the Cariboo the following year. She received her early education in Barkerville and later attended All Hallows School in Yale in 1891-2 and the Annie Wright School, a private girls' school in Tacoma, Washington.[9] In 1904 she was appointed clerk and stenographer in Conservative premier Richard McBride's office, beginning an association that lasted until his death in 1916. In 1909 she became his personal secretary, a post she held until December 1915 when McBride resigned as premier and assumed the post of British Columbia's agent-general in London. Bowron then became secretary to the provincial minister of mines, but departed for England on leave of absence when the Liberals came into office late in 1916. In London she worked in the Admiralty from March 1917 till November 1918. On her return to Victoria the Liberal government under John Oliver showed her little consideration, offering her only, "under pressure" as she phrased it, a temporary position as stenographer at half her salary with McBride. Work in the premier's office was specifically denied her.[10] Upset and disappointed, Bowron left the civil service and served as a public stenographer at the Empress Hotel and assisted for a brief period in the lieutenant-governor's office until her appointment as Rural Teachers' Welfare Officer under the new Conservative government of S.F. Tolmie in 1928.

Lottie Bowron as a young woman: "I am here to help if you need me."
(BCARS G-9949)

288 Becoming and Being a Teacher

After returning to Victoria in 1919 Bowron, now in her forties, became an active club woman. She was the founding president of the Kumtuks Club (Chinook word meaning "to know, understand"), the forerunner of the Victoria Business and Professional Women's Club.[11] Later she was active in the Local Council of Women, the women's auxiliary of the Canadian National Institute for the Blind, assistant secretary of the White Cane Club, and a member of the B.C. Historical Society.

Given the large number of congratulatory notes she received upon her appointment as Rural Teachers' Welfare Officer, Bowron was well respected, certainly amongst elitist groups and organizations. Among her well-wishers were the Vancouver Club, the Native Daughters of British Columbia Post #1, the Imperial Order Daughters of the Empire and the Children of the Empire, the Victoria Local Council of Women, and many personal friends. One acquaintance, Maude Palmer, wrote: "good for the Conservative Government they couldn't have chosen a more suitable woman to fill the bill." Then she added, "I certainly think that you will make the lives of those often lonely girls much brighter – and you will love doing it." The president of the National Council of Women joined in: "I think you are the first to hold such a position and I am delighted for I am sure that you will set a splendid precedent."[12] Such comments underline the perceived service component of her task. Neither Hinchliffe nor Bowron herself imagined that her job would produce significant structural changes affecting the lot of rural teachers. Certainly fundamental improvements in rural education were not to be effected during his term of office.

II

The conditions that contributed to Mabel Jones' suicide were by no means unique to Nixon Creek. Hundreds of young female teachers in rural British Columbia in the 1920s faced similarly difficult circumstances. The following year, for example, at Lily Lake, a "difficult place" south of Fort Fraser, the inspector reported that the teacher was a victim of "petty persecution" from one of the families living in the district. Although the inspector was not specific about the nature of the problem, he expressed concern about the physical safety of the teacher and recommended the appointment of an official trustee. If "serious consequences" should develop, he warned, he did not want to be held responsible for not acting on the situation. He and Lottie Bowron actually alluded to the similarities between this case and the harassment Mabel Jones suffered before taking her life.[13] Fortunately, nothing so serious transpired.[14]

Loneliness, isolation, difficult and unfriendly trustees, parents, and landlords confronted many teachers. Yet compared to domestic service, working in a cannery or factory, or even early marriage, teaching offered numerous attractions. It was certainly a genteel occupation offering sometimes the opportunity to meet respectable eligible members of the opposite sex. It paid not handsomely but reasonably well compared to other occupations open to women, and required little special skill or equipment. At a minimum, a high school graduation diploma and one term (four months) at normal school were sufficient, although by 1922 one year at normal school in Vancouver or Victoria was expected of all prospective teachers. The average weekly wage in Canada in 1931 was $22.56 for men and $12.01 for women.[15] At about the same time the average salary for a teacher at a rural assisted school was $1 080 per annum or $20.76 per week. So in terms of disposable income, rural female teachers, especially if single, were not badly off compared to women in other female occupations such as domestic servant, stenographer and typist.[16]

Despite the material difficulties presented by rural British Columbia, many female teachers thrived on the independence and modest social status afforded them. The economic opportunity to live away from home made teaching a desirable transition stage between schooling and marriage, the ultimate "vocational" goal for most women of the time.[17] For a minority of women, however, teaching was "less a preparation than a substitute for woman's divine calling in the home."[18] For these women teaching became a vocation, in fact often a lifetime career. For some, rural school teaching satisfied a sense of adventure. As one such teacher reminisced: "It sounds like teachers had a hard life in those days but we thought of ourselves as adventurers – like Olympic Torch-bearers in our gumboots and mittens."[19] Finally, as work, teaching provided the challenge, satisfaction, and sense of accomplishment that came from reaching the minds and hearts of young children.

A word about the context of rural schools in British Columbia in the 1920s. Whether there was a school or not and whether the school was in good or bad condition, depended on local enthusiasm and support. The building itself was a product of local initiative. Only after it was built and ten students enrolled did the government reimburse the building costs and supply a grant to pay the teacher. Consequently, even in the 1920s many schools were built of logs; almost all the rest were frame structures, as was true throughout western Canada. Unlike southern Ontario, where brick was commonly used by this time for rural schools, wood was the normal material of construction. The diversity in appearance of British Columbia's one-room schools belied Department of Education efforts seeking uniformity of design. The suggested 1911 Public Works designs for provincial one-room schools were a joke.[20] In reality, rural schools expressed community conditions, initiative and reliance on local materials. They were manifestations of local, and particularly family, control. By contrast multi-roomed city schools dotting the landscape of Vancouver and Victoria represented state power, the architectural designs bespeaking a uniformity that extended beyond the structure itself. The rural school blended into the topography whether it be prairie, mountain valley, or west coast rainforest. In a culture where the family was central to everyday life and the family economy still persisted, it should not surprise us that the school was family-dominated. By the same token, as most regions were impoverished, the schools were poor and makeshift, materials were at a premium, and upkeep varied from loving attention to none at all.[21]

The way rural British Columbians organized their schools reflected their surroundings and what they valued in their lives and for their children. Localism ensured that rural schools would become distinctive and reflect the attitudes of the communities creating them.[22] The desire of settlements, even very small ones, to have their own schools led to a proliferation of schools. The process continued in the 1920s in the face of recommendations to the contrary emanating from the department and the likes of the Putman-Weir Report of 1925 on how to solve the perceived "rural school problem" created by small, ill-equipped, one-room schools with inefficient teachers and lack of financial resources. One solution proposed was amalgamation or consolidation of these tiny schools into multi-roomed, urban-like structures, to shift the control from the individual community where it had resided for half a century to the Department of Education in Victoria and its officials, in particular to the inspectorate, the system's representatives in the field.[23] Although by legislation responsibility accrued to local trustees, they were, in the final analysis, "creatures of provincial authority" and even "subject to the constant scrutiny and, if warranted, intervention" of provincial officers.[24] Bureaucratic centralization raised the spectre of control by "outsiders" and resistance to it persisted right up to the Second World War. In other words, rural parents supported basic schooling but resisted outside intervention.

For rural parents "school" meant much more than the designation of a building; it signified a whole series of interactions inside and outside the building between teacher and students. Despite the pretensions of the central authorities, the very existence of a rural school depended primarily upon two factors; the teacher's ability to adapt it to community desires, and parents' willingness to support the school by enrolling their children and seeing that they attended.[25] The existence of the school was what mattered, not the precise nature of its construction. Throughout the 1920s inspectors' reports continually recommended to local school boards school improvements that went unheeded. By 1920, while attendance rates in urban schools were much improved over prewar years, in rural British Columbia students, especially older ones, attended only when school did not compete with other, more pressing demands or when the weather was not inclement. Attendance was also affected by distance.[26]

By virtue of its focus on the Rural Teachers' Welfare Officer, this essay concentrates on the condition of rural rather than urban teachers and particularly teachers in remote and one-room schools; on female rather than male teachers (only one out of five rural teachers was male); and on female teachers in trouble rather than those who were coping well. Bowron's responsibility was confined solely to female rural teachers experiencing difficulties. One should not assume that male rural teachers did not experience problems in their rural schools and communities; they did.[27] Nor should one imagine that all female rural teachers had difficulty coping; they didn't. Although in the course of her visits Bowron did talk to teachers who were coping well she said little in her reports about them because the point of her job was to resolve as best she could problems women teachers faced in remote schools.

III

Now to return to Lottie Bowron's story. Tall, striking in appearance, and forty-nine years of age, Bowron set to work promptly in the new year of 1929 to visit schools.

Her normal mode of operating was to choose an area of the province, such as the Peace River or the Bulkley/Nechako valleys, and plan a visit to most of the one-room schools with female teachers in the area. She might stay at a school only a few minutes or at most a couple of hours since her main task was to chat with the teacher, not observe her class in progress. Bowron, after all, had never been a teacher. Sometimes, if her schedule allowed no more, she met her charges at a freight way station during a brief train stop or on a wharf. But at "difficult" schools or in cases where her assistance had been requested (most often by the teacher herself), Bowron might stay up to two days sorting out a problem.[28] She usually met around 250 teachers a year.

Typical of Bowron's trips into the Interior was her visit to the Peace River Block in February-March 1931. As recorded in her diary, she left Victoria for Vancouver on 18 February and boarded the train for Edmonton via Kamloops and Jasper. While in Edmonton she went to the "House" to hear the budget speech. The next day, 21 February, she took the Alberta Northern Railway to Pouce Coupe where she noted "a great change" since her previous visit. Two days later she was "still waiting for car to take me to Fort St. John. Same old story of 18 months ago." Finally she left late in the day, but unfortunately the car broke down on the way, and so she did not visit her first school in Fort St. John until the afternoon of 24 February. Using this town as a base, she visited over the next week nearby schools, on the average two a day, including Fish Creek, Clayton, North Pine, Rose Prairie, Charlie Lake, Crystal Springs, Montney, and Taylor Flats. On 27 February she returned to Fort St. John in order to attend in the evening a "tremendous meeting of about 300, keen looking men – and women" including the mayor. The purpose of the gathering was to discuss the lack of "fairness re roads this side of [Peace] River." Resolutions were passed. She ended the entry cryptically with: "[met] a youngish type of man – afterward stayed to dance for a time." On 4 March she returned to Pouce Coupe, Rolla, Roe Creek, Shearerdale, Landry, Sunset Prairie, Progress, Devereaux, Dawson South and Saskatoon Creek. On Friday evening she attended "Masons' banquet" at Rolla. "Danced afterward. Got home about 1:30. Enjoyed it." The last week of her stay in the Peace, again using Pouce Coupe as a base, she visited teachers at Swan Lake, Hays, "missed Tupper Creek," Riverside, East Pouce Coupe schools, Rolla, Sweetwater, and Arras. By the end of three weeks, Bowron calculated she had travelled nearly 900 miles in the "Block."[29]

Three weeks later Bowron set off again on a lengthy trip, this time to the Nechako and Bulkley valleys along the Grand Trunk Pacific west of Prince George and the Cariboo Country. On 9 and 10 April she attended a teachers' convention in Prince George where she gave a talk on "Love of Country" in the afternoon, spoke at the banquet in the evening, and left for the hotel at 2:30 the next morning after staying for the dance. "Such a nice lot of men and girl teachers," she confided in her diary. While in Prince George she visited both socially and professionally with the district inspector Mr. Gamble. On 14 April she began working her way along the GTP rail line visiting schools located along the line and making excursions to others north and south of it. The first week she got as far west as Decker Lake, just west of Burns

Lake. The second week she worked out of Vanderhoof, visiting as many as five nearby schools in a day. Toward the end of the week she headed north by car to Fort St. James. The trip took three and a half hours, but it was worth it: "This is a most glorious site. The Hudson Bay Company and Indians facing the lake — most romantic." The third week, having returned to Prince George, she drove south to Quesnel. Her chauffeur for much of this section was a police constable. Stops included Dragon Creek, Castle Rock, Bouchie Lake, Sister's Creek, Australian, and Alexandria. From Alexandria she took the Pacific Great Eastern to Williams Lake which became a base for the next two days' work. On 1 May she headed south by car over the "old Cariboo Road" to Cache Creek, Savona, and Kamloops. From there she caught the train back to Vancouver.[30]

Bowron also made special trips to problem schools when asked to. Such was the case with the teacher at Nicomen Island in the Fraser River near Dewdney. "Miss Martin had written to me," Bowron reported, "asking me to visit her as conditions were rather discordant." She met her at the school together with the trustees and the two complaining parents who were upset about what they termed a lack of discipline. A solution was reached: the trustees concluded "the parents were not to visit the school and complain to the teacher but were to send in writing to them [trustees] any remarks they had to make." Another special visit, this time to Gabriola South, was also typical. The teacher Jennie Szlater, had written Lottie Bowron asking for help. Two days later Bowron left for Gabriola. One or two parents had questioned the teacher's discipline, and wished to have a small boy expelled. In her meeting with the secretary of the board and one of the disgruntled parents she learned that the ratepayers wanted a new teacher. For her part Miss Szlater did not want to give up her job because she was helping her mother out financially. Declaring it was "not an easy school for a young girl" (Szlater was in her second year of teaching), Bowron then talked over the situation with Inspector Stewart, got him to agree to visit the school, and hoped that he "can assist in a solution." Meanwhile, the residents agreed to a ratepayers' meeting to discuss the problem.[31]

For each teacher she talked to, Bowron filled out a form recording information on the teachers' name and school, as well as on living conditions and other pertinent information, all of which varied greatly. Often little more than a comment was made as to whether the living accommodations or social life were satisfactory. Phrases such as, "This is a heavy school," "This is not an easy place," "This is a hard place for a young teacher," appear repeatedly in Bowron's reports. Some reports, however, were more detailed, no doubt bespeaking a particularly difficult school or community. Typical was her report for Bainbridge, north of Port Alberni, in January 1929:

> The living accommodation is not good. Mrs. Sterling was living in one of the Company's houses. The mill having closed down the place is desolate . . . . This is a lonely place for a teacher . . . 7 children – 4 of one family – 3 of another – and all have to walk over 2 miles. All young . . . I consider this rather a hard situation for a teacher.[32]

Many of her reports spoke of "quarrels with locals" (Beaver River), "locals obstinate" (Chilco), "troubles with parents" (Heriot Bay), "factions" among parents (Lily Lake), and "parents not liking the teacher" (Three Valley).[33] In all cases Bowron tried her best to smooth things over by actually confronting the troublesome parents or by offering advice to the often distraught teacher as to how she might best resolve the problem she faced. In some cases the situation was considered so difficult that Bowron simply designated the school "a man's school" in hopes that female teachers, especially young inexperienced ones, not be hired there in future. In July 1929 she wrote the superintendent of education enclosing a list of rural schools "best served by a) male teachers and b) male teachers or married women." In her 1932 report she added to these categories a list of schools headed "c) *not* for inexperienced women teachers." Railway towns like Field and Begbie, mining towns like Duthie Mines, Lorne Mine, and Coal Creek, and logging camps like Roy and Jackson Bay were definitely "best served" by men.[34]

Another phrase commonly found in Lottie Bowron's reports was the term "a lonely school." As a gregarious woman herself, she was clearly concerned that her female charges should have access to some sort of social life. Unfortunately, many of these communities offered little or no social life at all, a point Bowron frequently noted. The rural teaching force was overwhelmingly single and female. In 1925, for example, out of 903 rural and assisted school teachers, 79 per cent were female, 91 per cent of the females unmarried, and their average age was 23.6 years. By 1930 the proportion of women teachers rose to 83.5 per cent and those who were single climbed to 92.5 per cent.[35] Yet the notion that the rural areas were too rugged and wild for the delicate sensibilities of the young female permeated teacher correspondence with the educational authorities in Victoria well before Bowron's appointment.

In the 1920s many rural school locations became designated by inspectors and others, including teachers themselves, as "a man's school." In her answer to a questionnaire from the Teachers' Bureau,[36] Mrs. K.E. Easton of the Fort St. John School warned in 1923 that this was a "pioneer settlement," and she would "not advice [sic] a lady especially a young one to come here . . . Zero ladies here." Janet A. Mill, who taught near Pender Harbour, cautioned: "At Donley's Landing no place for young Lady Teacher living alone – no society, etc. . . . The situation here I would say is not very good – There is no water at school – no toilet accommodation [sic] for teacher. It is only suitable for a male who likes catering for himself. Rowing and fishing can be had as a pastime." George S. Quigley who taught in Glencoe eleven kilometres from Soda Creek wrote that the school was "suitable for married couple or male. Must be prepared to supply own bed and table linen, crockery and cutlery. Water difficult to obtain during winter. Snow and ice good substitutes." In the far north at Telegraph Creek on the Stikine River with an average winter white population of twelve, Clare Tervo found life "rather lonely socially." Despite the "beautiful scenery" and "healthful climate" this "typical frontier town" to her mind deserved "a man's school." Similarly, the teacher at Pender Harbour, then a female, had "no woman neighbors, practically no social life at present." As late as 1932 Lottie Bowron found Pender Harbour still "a difficult community to live in." Yet some communities were far more isolated than Pender Harbour. Dog Creek, for example, ninety-five kilometres south of Williams Lake in Cariboo ranching country, was so inaccessible that Pansy Price was not able to get out at Christmas or Easter for holidays. "The trip is too cold and too long at these times . . . 10 months is the full term here." So Lottie Bowron's observations in the late twenties and early thirties about the prevalence of "lonely schools" and the lack of social life was not news to Department of Education officials in Victoria. Some locations were so difficult, however, that "even a man might find it hard," – Bowron's description of Hulatt, a few miles east of Vanderhoof, a "hard bootlegging district."[37] In large part Lottie Bowron was trying to combat the effects of isolation on her female charges.

Occasionally a community could actually prove dangerous for young female teachers. A case foreshadowing that of Mabel Jones in the horror surrounding it was the murder of Loretta Chisholm, a twenty-one-year-old teacher at Port Essington near Prince Rupert. One Sunday morning in May 1926 she left her boarding house for her customary walk before church. She never returned. Her body was found the following day in the bush near a walking path, her chest and the back of her head crushed, jaw and nose broken, and moss forced down her throat probably to stifle her screams. The autopsy revealed that she suffocated to death. A local Indian was indicted, then later acquitted on appeal for lack of evidence. The jury declared that, "the deceased came to her death as a result of foul play on the part of some person or persons unknown." The Prince Rupert *Daily News* commented on the hazards of the locality. "All kinds of characters' gathered in the village during the fishing season but despite warnings about this sort of people, Miss Chisholm persisted in taking her solitary Sunday walks.[38]

Some situations female teachers experienced were more bothersome than dangerous. On Mayne Island Irene Hawes, only eighteen and fresh out of normal school, found the advances of a seventeen-year-old male grade 7 student more than disconcerting. A report recounts how the student "took one look at the attractive young schoolmarm and decided to lay siege to her, since she was the finest looking maiden he had ever seen. At recess he proceeded to make his intentions known, and the little lady had to beat a strategic retreat." Mildred McQuillan, who taught at Orange Valley west of Vanderhoof in 1927, reported that the closest she came to a romantic evening was at a monthly dance where she danced with the only man in the hall who attracted her, but was reluctant to become intimate with him for fear of the rumors that she would start in the community. At Hays in the Peace River District a problem arose in 1932 over the teacher entertaining a man in her house. "The Secretary, I believe, was on the point of asking for a visit from me so I was very glad I arrived when I did," wrote Bowron. She ended her report with the following advice: "Miss Teeple's case is one which assists me in coming to the conclusion I came to last year, that no girl – young girl – just out from Normal, should go to the Peace River country, unless she has relatives there, nor is it wisdom for a teacher to stay in the community for her summer holidays." At Alexander Manson School in the remote Ootsa Lake ranching settlement, a teacher's dismissal was pending on account of the company she kept. Bowron reported:

> Miss Beechy is . . . engaged to a man whom the community does not care about, and this man spends far too much time in Miss Beechy's house, having his meals there, etc., and this, with some school problems, has caused the trouble. I called on . . . one of the trustees who informed me that the Board was going to dismiss her . . . and I believe [it is] willing to give her an opportunity to resign.

Miss Beechy did not return to the school the following year.[39]

Although documentary evidence of amorous adventures is slim, the fact that the teacher was usually young and unmarried presented problems. She had to be careful in her selection of friends. Indiscreet fraternization in an isolated area, as we have seen, could lead to alienation from the community and, in the extreme, physical harm. The teacher, therefore, had to choose her acquaintances carefully if she were to survive unscathed.[40] An empty social and love life may have embittered her. Often in the remote communities, eligible males were so few that the teacher became eager to leave the area for one with a larger marriage market. Lexie McLeod left Lower Nicola to "grab a husband" in Vancouver, while Mildred McQuillan married shortly after leaving Orange Valley in December 1927. Margaret Lanyon, who taught in Black Canyon near Ashcroft from 1926 to 1928, felt "stuck" in the community and eventually left for a less isolated school at Dewdney even though she took a pay cut. Lottie Bowron seemed particularly sensitive to this problem. When she visited Lewis Island near Prince Rupert in June 1929 she found that "there was not one man on the island" as they had gone away fishing. At Elk Prairie fourteen kilometres from Natal she noted that there were simply no young people for a teacher to associate with.[41]

Unfortunately, as Bowron discovered, many teachers did not find their initial boarding place to their liking. For those who moved, problems stemming from the original family quite often ensued. According to one teacher in Grant Mine near Wellington on Vancouver Island, "matters are not very harmonious in the district, one of the main causes being because she [the teacher] changed her boarding place." In Flagstone in the West Kootenays the teacher (Miss Elwood) "lost heart and says she will not teach again" following "a rather trying time no doubt the fact of Miss Elwood leaving their home [playing] a big part." In still another community, Lakeshaw on Shawnigan Lake, the teacher felt that the family she had previously lived with had "endeavoured to make things unpleasant for her [and that the father] was trying to get rid of her."[42]

Whether the teacher batched, boarded or lived in a hotel, Bowron had another concern. This was the distance the teacher had to travel in order to reach the school. Some teachers had to walk as far as five and a half kilometres to school, a particularly hard grind in the winter. Even a shorter trek could prove difficult over some terrain. One teacher struggled a kilometre through the woods twice each day over a very steep rough trail with a log as a makeshift bridge across a stream. Yet another teacher, an older woman with twenty-seven years teaching experience, had to "climb down a steep bank to the Kootenay River, cross in a small boat and climb up the other side."[43]

Some teachers, of course, were more fortunate in that they lived within easy reach to the school and a few even had teacherages on the school property.

Another challenge facing many teachers was instructing children of various ethnic backgrounds.[44] Lottie Bowron was especially conscious of teaching problems faced in ethnically diverse classrooms. A typical comment was her dismay over the situation she found in Mission Creek, in the Okanagan, in 1929: "this room has 7 nationalities in 42 pupils and is too heavy for any but an experienced teacher and even this is too heavy for one." In Cultus Lake she found the district not just a lonely place but a difficult one too: "the children [were], all but three, Czecho-Slovakians." At Vesuvius on Salt Spring Island she recorded the presence of "Whites, Japanese, Negroes and one or two halfbreeds." Students' lack of fluency in English could make a teacher's task that much more difficult. In Ucluelet on the west coast of Vancouver Island she noted "of 37 pupils 26 . . . are Japanese, [and] this, of course, makes the work of the teachers very strenuous." In Ucluelet East eighteen of nineteen pupils were Japanese, and a high percentage was to be found in Tofino as well. Some ethnic groups, such as Finns and Ukrainians, were distinguished by their radical political leanings. At Greenslide, just south of Revelstoke, Bowron appended a note to her official report: "I was told that after school the children went to a community hall to be taught their own language – Ukrainian, music, etc. Other people say this is propaganda and communistic teachings."[45]

Topping the list of "difficult" ethnic groups were the Doukhobors of the West Kootenays. Not only was attendance irregular – sometimes girls did not attend at all – but the teacher's safety was occasionally at risk. Schools were ideal targets for arsonists protesting, among other things, government interference with Doukhobor private lives, in particular its insistence that Doukhobor children attend public schools. Police patrols increased with the number of incidents so that by 1931 the schools in Brilliant, Carson Fruitove, Glade, and Winlaw were all patrolled at night by either the police or a guard. Not one to exaggerate, Bowron stated that one teacher in Brilliant "had become a little nervous" after threats to the school had been made and after "someone had tried to break into her residence." Similarly, in regards to teachers in Fruitove she counselled, "there is no doubt that the experience of a bomb having been placed under the building rather unnerved them, nor is it at all to be wondered at." Bowron even recounted her own run-in with a Doukhobor parent at Brilliant. "While visiting the teacher in her rooms before school opened," she reported, "a nude fanatic woman came to see me, her excuse being that some children were fighting and she wanted me to tell them not to fight." Bowron refused to see her.[46]

It is not surprising that facing such events teachers would become distraught. More surprising is how well the teachers stood up to this kind of stress and harassment. Bowron noted that most teachers reacted very well and, as best they could, seemed to take these matters in their stride. Writing about one stalwart soul she remarked, "this teacher had rather a trying time recently when an attempt was made to burn her school. . . . These things are very unsettling and while the teachers say little about it, one feels that at times they have their unhappy moments, but are very plucky."[47]

Children at Pemberton Meadows, the first school. "August Newman [was] away from school this A.M. I asked Cecil his brother where he was and this was his reply – eh, August had to stay home cause he had a hole in his pants." Diary of Mildred McQuillan, Orange Valley School, 1927. (BCARS C-1015)

Lottie Bowron could do little to stop what she termed "fanatics" in these communities, but she did recommend that teachers in Doukhobor communities have "special considerations." Although she did not give further details as to what these considerations might be, she did provide suggestions to individual teachers which she hoped would put them more at ease. In Fruitove she recommended that "if big lamps were placed at either end of the school and lighted during the night a sense of protection might be afforded [the teacher]." In Glade, whose school was across the river "where only Doukhobors live" and the only ferry was run by Doukhobors, Bowron recommended that "a telephone be placed in the school."[48] Finally, her very support of the teachers and her praise of their courage must have reassured them, if only in a small way.

Bowron's support for her teachers, or her "girls" as she called them, became legendary. As she reassured a troubled teacher, "I am here to help if you need me."[49] When problems did occur she could be counted on to investigate the matter promptly. When the wife of the secretary of the school board in Devereaux, north of the head of Knight Inlet, was giving the teacher "an unhappy time," Bowron approached the secretary and "asked him to do his best to see that the persecution cease." Concerning another parent at Lee in the Cariboo, Bowron visited the teacher, two of the trustees, and "nearly all the people in the community." Having found that these people supported the teacher and "that when discord arose in this district it emanated from the Brown Family," Bowron spoke to the offending man and his children. Although she found it "rather difficult to get to the bottom of anything he was supposed to have said," he did admit that he had no actual complaints against the teacher. Furthermore, Bowron left him with the warning that the "persecution of the teacher must cease or a way would be found to have it cease." Despite her no-nonsense manner, problems in other communities were more difficult, if not impossible, to resolve. In Coleman Creek near Port Alberni, for example, the secretary informed Bowron that "while he had nothing against the present teacher, he was not in agreement with married women teaching." Still less hopeful was the situation in another community (said to be a quarrelsome one) about which she wrote, "the people here are always threatening to get rid of the teacher – any teacher."[50] Much teacher/parent, teacher/trustee trouble seems to have derived from the fact that parents expected to exert control over the teacher and she often resisted these efforts. Teachers not from the community – the majority – were "outsiders," and common sense tells us that a reasonable length of stay in the community was a prerequisite for such teachers to win the trust and respect of the community. And yet teacher transiency was very high in rural British Columbia.[51]

Bowron took her work seriously and was pleased to note in her second annual report that "it is seldom indeed that I leave a teacher without an expression of appreciation for the visit and again and again I am told that the knowledge of such an appointment gives them a sense of security."[52] Certainly, she went beyond her official duties in extending aid to many teachers. In addition to her visits, she frequently wrote teachers giving advice, moral support, and occasionally a message from home. She even visited teachers' families, offering them reassurances about their daughter's situation. The teachers reciprocated with news of their district in addition to any concerns they might have and spoke warmly and openly to her. In response to one letter in which a teacher was having a hard time fitting in, Bowron replied:

> Just remember this, someday you will be the 'other teacher.' I find in the course of my visits that so often it is the previous teacher, so I am told, who was either splendid, or poor, or good at this or that, or pretty or plain or something. So don't let that worry you in any way. You, I am sure, are doing good work where you are and trying to find your place as you think a teacher should. Can you do more?[53]

In addition to letters of this kind, Bowron performed many other small acts of kindness. Knowing how scarce resources were, for example, she sent a pretty poster to several schools. In her files of letters one can find thank-you notes from children to whom she sent valentines in Sinclair Mills east of Prince George.

Periodically Bowron addressed students at both Victoria and Vancouver normal schools. Forever concerned with teachers' well-being, she remarked in 1930 that the visit to the normal schools not only served to introduce the welfare officer to the students but also afforded "a splendid opportunity of placing before [them] some of the problems likely to arise in the social and living conditions which they may encounter, and, as well an excellent chance to give some practical advice which may prove of service later on."[54] Such advice about remote school situations was sorely needed. Many normal school students, aside from those from rural areas, had little idea about what rural teaching in the province was really like. For the student teachers enrolled in Vancouver Normal School, practice teaching in a one-room school was restricted to one week if at all. Even then, practice teaching schools were located in such communities as Burnaby, Richmond, Coquitlam, North Vancouver, Delta, and Surrey which, though sometimes "rural" in their surroundings, were hardly isolated enough for the teacher to experience the conditions of rural teaching.[55] Practice teaching at the Victoria Normal School was similarly conducted within easy reach of Victoria in school districts unused to rural community impoverishment, settler transiency, and disruptive local politics. To try to acquaint its students with rural school problems, each normal school set up a rural "demonstration" school within its main building, but the setting was inherently artificial. A teacher recalls that at the Victoria Normal School she "learned to correlate, that is, overlap timetables," a procedure that stood the beginning rural teacher in good stead.[56] But this was a far cry from practice in the isolation of a Quick, Rolla, Horsefly, Usk, Big Creek, Ootsa Lake, Chu Chua, or Yahk.

IV

In late February 1934, Lottie Bowron was unceremoniously dismissed by the new Liberal minister of education, George M. Weir. Arriving back in Victoria on 9 March from an extensive trip to the Peace river country, Bowron recorded in her diary how "the first letter I opened was saying the Rural Teachers' Welfare Officer was to be done away with – a nice greeting after five years of hard work – where is justice I wonder?" The next day she had "a straight talk" with superintendent of education S.J. Willis who claimed the dismissal was a cabinet decision and offered "no complaint of any sort against my work." The next week she called on Premier Duff Pattullo "who flew in[to] a petulant state, begged me to go – would see me after session [of the Legislature]. Said it [her post] was a political job [,] always thought so and would have attacked earlier if it not for me." Bowron scribbled in the margin "a very strange interview." The next day she tried to see Weir, but he "can't or won't see me until Tuesday," she confided to her diary. "It seems like a fight for justice," she wrote, and added in typical fashion "must not forget the teachers. . . . I'm going down if I have to, with flags flying." Finally on 20 March, Bowron had an interview with Wier. "I found him quite 'listenable.' I felt as though he were learning something about the post – something he didn't know."[57] Significantly, there is no record that Bowron's case was raised in the House, nor did any of the male inspectorate come to her defence, publicly at any rate. Perhaps they too saw hers as a political appointment or preferred to keep the bureaucracy uniformly male. In any case, as employees of the state the inspectors would not be likely to criticize publicly a decision of the minister of education.

"Lottie Bowron on tour, 75 mile post, Cariboo Road"
(Royal B.C. Museum)

Bowron's letter of dismissal had specified that her duties were to end on 1 April 1934, at which time she would be granted leave-of-absence without pay until 20 November, "when you will be retired from the service of the Department on pension." Despite her pressing pleas in person and by letter to Weir to be allowed to "carry on in my position to the end of June," he remained adamant about his earlier decision to abolish the post, although he did eventually agree to pay her salary until the end of the school year.[58] By the end of March Bowron was thoroughly discouraged. "I feel as though I am almost a culprit," she confessed. "Someday the worth of this past five years will come out." Her depression deepened; by the end of April she lamented in her diary, "what's there to write about – only self."[59] From the first of June till the beginning of August she wrote nothing in her diary, where she had formerly filled each day's space with news of the day's activities, both personal and professional.

Bowron's dismissal, more accurately a forced retirement, raises a number of questions. Clearly there was a continued need for the service she was performing and there is every evidence that she was carrying out her duties in an exemplary fashion. Perhaps the new Liberal government of Duff Pattullo reasoned that it could not afford the post during the Depression. That she was not replaced lends credence to this hypothesis. On the other hand, nowhere in the correspondence between Bowron and the government officials or in her diary entries is economic restraint suggested as the reason. She may have been fired because hers was a patronage appointment of the previous Conservative administration or because of her earlier close association with Premier McBride. She and others suspected political reasons were responsible for her dismissal.[60] In offering to take up her case with Dr. Weir, the Anglican bishop of the Cariboo, Walter Adams, observed: "You might not be continued, for whatever your associations were or were not, your appointment 5 years ago would be suspect." Still he personally found it "extremely difficult to believe that the new party [could] be guilty of such stupidity to economize on a piece of supervision that hard facts had proven to be necessary." Bowron seems to have been forewarned about her possible dismissal, as hard on the heels of the Liberal election triumph she recounted in her journal how on meeting family friend Bishop Adams in Nelson in January 1934 he had "said to let him know if I had heard anything about my work ceasing."[61]

Retired at age fifty-four, Bowron lived on for another thirty years, returning each summer to Barkerville where she became a vocal supporter of the government restoration of the historic gold rush community. While remaining an active club woman and church-goer, she lived out her days as a resident of the Strathcona Hotel in downtown Victoria, having friends to tea and attending luncheons and dinners with her many friends and relatives in the provincial capital.[62]

What are we to make of Lottie Bowron's brief term of office? Her efforts had little long-term effect on the state of rural schooling in the province. This should not surprise us since her duties as both she and Hinchliffe understood them were meant to be pastoral not reformist in nature. Her annual reports to the Department were short and perfunctory, carrying few general recommendations for change. It was rather at the level of the individual school and teacher that Bowron made the greatest impact. Her chief concern was to aid her "girls," to make their lives a little easier and more bearable in their often remote locations. To that end she was willing to confront difficult board members and obstreperous parents on behalf of her charges. She continually urged authorities in Victoria to designate certain schools men's schools to be avoided by female teachers. But hiring teachers remained a local responsibility and female teachers still presented themselves as candidates for jobs in rural schools.

Throughout her tenure Bowron seemed to have very cordial relations with the school inspectors – all male – who functioned in the same regions. I found no evidence of animosity toward her nor any sense that she was seen to be infringing upon their territory. On the contrary, the inspectors often drove her around on school visits and frequently cooperated with her in trying to solve teacher problems. Their respective tasks were quite distinct. The inspectors' job was to pass judgement and offer recommendations on teacher pedagogy, teaching materials, the state of school building and grounds, and any desirable structural changes to the rural school system. Bowron was to minister to the needs of the female rural school teacher, to offer comfort and solace, and to ameliorate, if possible, the living and working conditions her charges experienced. She was a counsellor rather than an inspector, and if her correspondence to and from teachers is any indication, she was extremely successful in tending to her "girls'" social and psychological needs. Teachers' letters still on file sing her praises, and in many ways she seems to have acted as a surrogate mother, especially to the younger female teachers. There is clear evidence of the merits of same-sex support systems, for these teachers often turned to Bowron for help rather than to the all-male inspectorate.[63] On the other hand, there is little evidence of the existence of female networks between the teacher and the women in the community. My sources, of course, may have served to prejudice this conclusion, but the female teacher may have represented escape from the community and a life most women in it could not have. She was a challenge to their own choices and an alternative model to their daughters. Most people deemed it easier for a male teacher to find company among married and unmarried men alike – to "go native" – but for female teachers, friendship with married women may have been problematic.

Bowron's experience as a well-known club woman in Victoria before her appointment undoubtedly stood her in good stead as she went about her visitation duties. Previous experience as a teacher was not so important to her work as the resilience, fortitude, and concern for others she had learned as a club woman. Personal autonomy was a characteristic Bowron displayed throughout her life, and she encouraged her teachers to cultivate the same attitude to theirs. By the same token her approach to problem-solving was highly individualistic. She advocated no collective approaches to resolving teachers' work problems. To do so would not have been in keeping with the club woman's credo not to challenge existing socio-economic structures or women's cultural subordination in that area.[64] Lottie Bowron had struggled on an individual level, ministering as best she could, and often with great success, to her many charges. Her motto might well have been, as she told one of them, "I am ready to be of assistance when I can."[65]

Notes

1. Provincial Archives of British Columbia (hereafter PABC), Attorney General's records, Inquest no. 351, 6, report of coroner's inquest; p. 4, autopsy report by Dr. G.W. Bissett, 16 Nov. 1928.
2. PABC, Department of Education Newspaper Clippings, Vancouver *Province*, 21 Nov. 1928; see also coroner's inquest and the testimony of Chris Gibson, president of the Cowichan Lake Logging Company, p. 12.
3. Inquest 16 Nov. 1928, 1, 36. Temporary insanity was a common cover-up for suicide.
4. Dept. of Educational Newspaper Clippings, editorial "Our Rural Schools," Vancouver *Province*, Nov. 1928; see also *ibid.*, "Protect Young Girl Teachers."

5. PABC, Dept. of Education, School Inspectors' Reports, Nixon Creek, 24 Oct., 18 Jan. 1928; Dept. of Education, *Annual Report of the Public Schools*, 1927, M31.

6. Rural status implied a school that was neither urban nor consolidated, and as a result was without the benefit of centralized municipal administration or finance. Still, the rural school on the average was more properous than the assisted school which ws so impoverished that the teacher's salary and a grant for the school equipment and supplies were underwritten entirely by the provincial government. Provision of the schoolroom or building was the responsibility of the parents and other interested persons.

7. *Annual Report*, 1929, R10.

8. Dept. of Education, School Inspectors' Reports, Reports of Rural Teachers' Welfare Officer (hereafter Bowron Reports), 1928-9. Each school report has been filed alphabetically by school year. Bowron's post was referred to by different names, but the designation "Rural Teachers' Welfare Officer (Women)" was commonly found in correspondence from the superintendent of education, on her business card, and in the way in which she signed her letters. Other titles used in the department's annual reports were Rural Female Teachers' Welfare Officer and Welfare Officer of Rural Female Teachers.

9. The Bowron Lakes in the Cariboo are named after her family. For her attendance at All Hallows School, see student list compiled in Nov. 1939 by Heber Greene, Anglican Archives, Vancouver. For a description of the school, see Jean Barman's "Separate and Unequal: Indian and White Girls at All Hallows School, 1884-1920" [ch. 17 in this book]. Annie Wright School was a popular destination for B.C. girls from well-to-do families. One of its most distinguished graduates was Mary McCarthy, author of *How I Grew* (San Diego 1987) and *Memories of a Catholic Girlhood* (New York 1957).

10. She was gazetted on 18 March 1904. Bowron to J. Hinchliffe, 30 Jan. 1930, PABC, Add. mss. 347 (McBride/Bowron Papers), vol. 2, file 2/28. McBride died in London on 6 Aug. 1917. Re: denial of work, see W.H. MacInnes (Civil Service Commissioner) to Bowron, 7 Feb. 1919.

11. *Victoria Times*, 17 Jan. 1921

12. McBride/ Bowron Papers, vol. 2 (2/27). Palmer to Bowron, 17 Dec. 1928; Mrs. J.A. Wilson to Bowron, 2 Aug. 1929.

13. PABC, Bowron Reports, Lily Lake, 18 Sept. 1931; Dept of Education correspondence, A.H. Gower, Prince George, to S.J. Willis, 22 April 1929.

14. McBride/Bowron Papers, vol. 2 (2/27). Ethel Wilson, Fort Fraser, to Bowron, 15 May 1929. Wilson compliments Bowron for "heartening up" the teacher in question.

15. *Census of Canada*, 1931, vol. 1, 296. In 1929 the average weekly industrial wage stood at $29.20. Margaret A. Ormsby, *British Columbia: A History* (Toronto: Macmillan, 1964), 441.

16. Teaching as respectable employment for women had been accepted from at least the mid-nineteenth century. See Bruce Curtis, *Building the Educational State: Canada West 1836-1871* (Lewes: Falmer Press, 1988), 255.

17. Marriage and children was for the time every "true" woman's ambition. See Veronica Strong-Boag, *The New Day Recalled: Lives of Girls and Women in English Canada, 1919-1939* (Toronto: Copp Clark Pitman, 1988); also Alison Prentice et al., *Canadian Women: A History* (Toronto: Harcourt Brace Jovanovich, 1988), Part 3.

18. Marta Danylewycz, Beth Light, and Alison Prentice, "The Evolution of the Sexual Division of Labour in Teaching: A Nineteenth-Century Ontario and Quebec Case Study," *Histoire sociale/Social History*, xvi, no 31 (May 1983), 82. For a fascinating account of teacher behavior in the United States, see Barbara Finkelstein, *Governing the Young: Teacher Behavior in Popular Primary Schools in 19th Century United States* (New York: Falmer Press, 1989).

19. Letter from Edna May Embury to Paul Stortz, West Vancouver, 11 March 1988.

20. Ivan J. Saunders, "A Survey of British Columbia School Architecture to 1930," *Parks Canada Research Bulletin*, no. 225 (Nov. 1984).

21. For an extended discussion of the rural school problem in British Columbia in the 1920s, see J. Donald Wilson and Paul J. Stortz, "May the Lord Have Mercy on You: The Rural School Problem in British Columbia in the 1920s," *B.C. Studies*, no. 79 (autumn, 1988), 24-58 [chapter 11 in this book]; for a case study of the Bulkley and Nechako Valleys, see P.J. Stortz, "The Rural School Problem in British Columbia in the 1920s" (MA thesis, UBC, 1988), ch. 3-4; and for the Okanagan Valley, see Penelope S. Stephenson, "Rural Schooling in the Okanagan in the 1920s" (MA thesis, UBC, 1993).

22. For confirmation about the importance of localism in the lives of British Columbians, see Cole Harris, "Reflections on the Surface of the Pond," *B.C. Studies* 49 (spring, 1981): 86-93. Similarly a political scientist concludes that "geographically based parochialism" made local rather than provincial concerns pre-eminent until after the Second World War. R. Jeremy Wilson, "The Impact of Communications Developments in British Columbia Electoral Patterns, 1903-1975," *Canadian Journal of Political Science*, 13 (Sept. 1980): 512, 534.

23. Thomas Fleming, "'Our Boys in the Field': School Inspectors, Superintendents, and the Changing Character of School Leadership in British Columbia," in N.M. Sheehan, J.D. Wilson, and D.C. Jones, eds., *Schools in the West: Essays in Canadian Educational History* (Calgary: Detselig, 1986), 285-303.

24. L.W. Downey and A.E. Wright, "The Statutory Bases of the B.C. Educational System: A Report of an Analysis" (Vancouver: University of British Columbia, 1977), 9.

25. For a discussion of similar factors at work in eastern Ontario in the late nineteenth century, see Chad Gaffield, *Language, Schooling and Cultural Conflict: The Origins of the French-Language Controversy in Ontario* (Kingston and Montreal: McGill-Queen's University Press, 1987).

26. For a detailed discussion of attendance problems in the Bulkley and Nechako Valleys, see Stortz, "The Rural School Problem," chap. 4.

27. See David C. Jones, "Creating Rural-Minded Teachers: The British Columbia Experience," in D.C. Jones, N.M. Sheehan, and R.M. Stamp, eds., *Shaping the Schools of the Canadian West* (Calgary: Detselig, 1979), ch. 10.

28. For example, Bowron Reports, Houston, 11 Feb. 1930.

29. PABC, Add. mss. 44, Lottie Bowron's *Daily Journal, 1931*, 18 Feb. – 13 Mar. For a first hand account of life in the Peace River Block at this time, see W.L. Morton, ed., *God's Galloping Girl: The Peace River Diaries of Monica Storrs*, 1929-1931 (Vancouver: UBC Press, 1979). The block was restored to British Columbia by the federal government in an agreement signed on 20 February 1930. For a description of this, see Dorothea Calverly, "Peace River Block," in Lillian York, ed., *Lure of the South Peace: Tales of the Early Pioneers to 1945* (Fort St. John, Dawson Creek: Alaska Highway Daily News and Peace River Block News, 1981), 7-8.

30. Bowron, *Daily Journal, 1931*, 7 April – 2 May.

31. Bowron Reports, Nicomen Island, 3 May 1929; Bowron, *Daily Journal, 1931*, 29 March; Bowron Reports, Gabriola South, 31 March 1931.

32. Bowron Reports, Bainbridge, 1928-29, Jan. 1929.

33. *Ibid.*, Jan.-April 1929.

34. The implication here is that men were better able to cope with the problems presented in communities like these. I am not suggesting that Bowron was right in her contention, but only that this was certainly her perception. In a study of Ontario teachers in the late nineteenth century, Harry Smaller found that it was not necessarily true that "men were better." H.J.Smaller, "Teachers' Protective Associations, Professionalism and the 'State' in Nineteenth Century Ontario," (Ph.D. thesis, University of Toronto, 1988).

35. J.H. Putman and G.M. Weir, *Survey of the School System* (Victoria: King's Printer, 1925), 177-9, and *Annual Reports*, statistical tables.

36. The Teachers' Bureau Records are officially known as *School District Information Forms for the Teachers' Bureau*, Dept. of Education. They exist for only two years, 1923 and 1928, and are located at the PABC, GR 461, organized alphabetically by school and year. Hereafter known as *TBR*.

37. *TBR*, Glencoe, 1923; Telegraph Creek, 1928; Pender Harbour, 1923 and 1928; Bowron Reports, Pender Harbour, 20 May 1932; *TBR*, Dog Creek, 1928; Bowron Reports, Hulatt, 1928-9. About this time a thoughtful inspector advised a male teetotalling teacher at Hulatt to take more account of the community he was in: "You had better learn to drink a little or you just can't communicate with these people. This is a very heavy drinking country. I'm not suggesting you drink like they do, but if you're a complete teetotaller, I don't think you'll get along with them at all." Quoted in Joan Adams and Becky Thomas, *Floating Schools and Frozen Inkwells* (Madeira Park: Harbour Publishing, 1985), 79.

38. The case was never solved. For a full description of the murder and legal proceedings, see Prince Rupert *Daily News*, 27 May – 16 June, 1926 and 22-5 Nov., 1926, and for the appeal, New Westminster *Columbian*, 7 April, 1927. The official inquest report is unavailable. Interestingly, when Lottie Bowron visited Port Essington in September 1931, she mentioned in her diary how a local trustee insisted upon relating the "tragedy of poor Miss Chisholm." PABC, Add. mss. 44, Lottie Bowron's *Daily Journal*, 1931, Sept. 30.

39. Jesse Brown, ed., *Mayne Island Fall Fair* (Mayne Island: Agricultural Society and Fall Fair, 1971), 35-6. PABC, Mildred E. McQuillan Diary, 1927. McQuillan's well-written diary reveals her attitudes towards her work and the community she served. She specifies the trials she faced as a young teacher in a remote school – experiences no doubt common to countless other rural school teachers in the 1920s. Bowron Reports, Hays, Oct. 1931, Alexander Manson, Sept. 1931.

40. The importance of keeping up appearances as well as facing up to sexual harassment and lack of respect from suspicious parents, rate-payers, and niggardly trustees is underlined in Robert Patterson's account of Prairie rural teachers at the same time. See his "Voices from the Past: The Personal and Professional Struggle of Rural School Teachers," in Sheehan et al., *Schools in the West*, ch. 6.

41. Lawrie (McLeod) interview, 1986; "McQuillan: Backwoods Teacher," Victoria *Times-Colonist*, 31 Aug. 1981, p. 35. Interview with Mrs. Margaret Manning (née Lanyon), retired school teacher, Vancouver, 12 April 1987. Bowron Reports, Lewis Island, 22 June 1929; Elk Prairie, 16 June 1932.

42. Bowron Reports, Grant Mine, 12 June 1931; Flagstone, 14 June 1932; Lakeshaw, 28 Oct. 1931.

43. *Ibid.*, Surge Narrows, 1 Nov. 1929; Champion Creek, 14 Jan. 1932.

44. For a discussion of rural teachers' perceptions of children of ethnic minorities, see J. Donald Wilson, "The Visions of Ordinary Participants: Teachers' Views of Rural Schooling in British Columbia in the 1920s," in Patricia E. Roy, ed., *A History of British Columbia: Selected Readings* (Toronto: Copp Clark Pitman, 1989), 239-55.

45. Bowron Reports, Mission Creek, 31 May 1929; Cultus Lake, 14 May 1931; Vesuvius, 9 Dec. 1931; Ucluelet, 15 March 1930; Ucluelet East, 15 March 1930; Tofino, 16 March 1930; Greenslide, 29 Jan. 1931.

46. Mary Ashworth, "The Doukhobors," *The Forces Which Shaped Them* (Vancouver: New Star Books, 1979), ch. 4; Bowron Reports, Brilliant, 20 Jan. 1931; Fruitove, 22 Jan. 1931; Brilliant, 9 June 1930.

47. Bowron Reports, Brilliant, 13 Jan. 1931.

48. *Ibid.*, Glade, 21 Jan. 1931; Fruitove, 22 Jan. 1931.

49. McBride/Bowron Papers, vol. 2 (2/27). Bowron to Miss L. McCall, Bednesti, 6 Feb. 1932.

50. Bowron Reports, Devereaux, 16 March 1932; Lee, 1 Nov. 1930; Coleman Creek, 21 March 1932; Begbie, 13 April 1929. Normally, in those days, female teachers left teaching when they married. This practice was more strictly enforced in urban than rural areas. Exceptions occurred where trustees were desperate to secure a teacher, a teacher married a local man, or a married woman was forced into paid employment for a variety of reasons.

51. For details, see Wilson and Stortz, "'May the Lord Have Mercy on You.'"

52. "Report of Rural Teachers' Welfare Officer (Women), 1929-30," in *Reports on Public Instruction* (Victoria: King's Printer, 1930).

53. McBride/Bowron Papers, vol. 2 (2/27). Bowron to L. McCall, Bednesti, 6 Feb. 1932.

54. "Report of Rural Teachers' Welfare Officer (Women), 1929-30."

55. For example, Bowron reported encountering normal students on practicum at Glen (Coquitlam), Boundary Bay (Delta) and Surrey Centre. Bowron Reports, 23, 24, and 20 Jan. 1930.

56. Sylvia McKay [1929, Victoria Normal School], Normal School Project, University of Victoria, interviewer, Judy Windle, tape recording 78-Y-27.

57. Bowron, *Daily Journal*, 9, 10, 15, 16, 17, 20 March, 1934.

58. McBride/Bowron Papers, vol. 2 (2/27). S.J. Willis to Bowron, 28 Feb.; Bowron to Weir, 31 March; Weir to Bowron, 9 April 1934.

59. Bowron, *Daily Journal*, 1934, 26 March, 30 April.

60. *Ibid.*, 1 April 1934. Patronage was certainly a central feature of government at this time in British Columbia. See Robert A. Campbell, "Liquor and Liberals: Patronage and Government Control in British Columbia, 1920-1928," *B.C. Studies* 77 (spring, 1988): 30-53.

61. McBride/Bowron Papers, vol. 2 (2/27). Walter Cariboo to Bowron, 17 March 1934; Bowron, *Daily Journal,* 18 Jan., 1934.

62. PABC, vertical file. Victoria *Times*, 9 Aug. 1960, p. 19; *Colonist*, 2 Feb. 1962, p. 5; *Colonist*, 5 Feb. 1964, p. 5; *Times*, 24 Feb. 1964, p. 13. Bowron's entire estate at death amounted to $2 575. Probate documents, 1 April 1964. Provincial court registry, Victoria.

63. For the same time period, Veronica Strong-Boag speaks to the importance for many single women of same-sex relationships: see *The New Day Recalled*, 104-6, 218.

64. Gillian Weiss, "'As Women and as Citizens': Clubwomen in Vancouver, 1910-1928," (Ph.D. thesis, University of British Columbia, 1983).

65. McBride/Bowron Papers, vol. 2 (2/27). Bowron to F.L. Richards, Bridge Lake, 14 April 1932.

15

From Normal School to the University to the College of Teachers: Teacher Education in British Columbia in the Twentieth Century

Nancy M. Sheehan and J. Donald Wilson

This article examines the history of teacher education in British Columbia over this century. It argues that from subject-based examinations to the development of Normal Schools to the transfer of all teacher education to the universities, British Columbia's system for the education and certification of teachers was much like that found in most Anglo-Saxon countries. The enactment of the Teaching Profession Act in 1987, establishing the B.C. College of Teachers as a professional body with jurisdiction over certification and discipline, challenged this unified approach. We review the College's efforts to establish itself and exercise its legislative mandate, conclude that despite problems the College has raised the awareness and importance of teacher education in BC and may help forestall the move to school-based and/or alternative certification practices found in Britain and in the United States.

Introduction

In 1983 a publication appeared entitled Historical Inquiry in Education sponsored by the American Educational Research Association.[1] Of the fifteen chapters devoted to various topics in educational history, not one was concerned with the history of teachers or teacher education. Significantly, just six years later the same association sponsored another fifteen-chapter publication devoted this time exclusively to the history of teachers and teaching in the United States.[2] The last several years have seen a similar development in Canada of interest in the subject of the history of teachers and teacher education.[3] This paper is an attempt to extend this historical interest to British Columbia, and to focus particular attention on the creation of an institution unique to Canada and the United States, namely the B.C. College of Teachers. Since 1988 this latter body has had the authority to exercise control over the certification, discipline and professional development of teachers in this Province in a fashion similar to that of other professional bodies operating in the interests of doctors, lawyers, and engineers. The presence of the College of Teachers has had immediate effects on teachers themselves, their professional association (the British Columbia Teachers' Federation), and the provincial universities which, for close to forty years, had operated teacher education programs with little involvement from the profession.

Early Developments – the Normal Schools

It may be wise to begin with some historical background. Significantly, one of the first acts to pass the new British Columbia legislature after the Province entered Confederation in 1871 was the Public Schools Act of the following year. Wherever a handful of settler children could be gathered together, a free non-denominational public school was to be opened and operated. Despite this generous state provision for universal schooling, no institution was created for training teachers until some thirty years later when the Province's first normal school opened its doors in 1901. Thus during that intervening time to become a teacher it was only necessary to pass a knowledge-based examination set by the Superintendent of Education of the Board of Education in Victoria, and with subject matter roughly equivalent to that taught in the high school. The passing mark for a certificate good for one year was 30 percent. Higher grades earned a longer-term certificate. Even those trained in other provinces had to take this examination. The "opportunity cost" to be a teacher was thus not great because there were no classes to attend and one could continue with one's regular occupation while studying for the examination. There was no screening or weeding out process as found in Ontario or the Maritime provinces, each with its own normal school.[4] There was no formal indoctrination of the teacher-to-be, something which Egerton Ryerson had put great stock in in mid-nineteenth century Ontario. To become a teacher in this era was largely a matter of self-selection.

Before 1901 very few teachers from elsewhere came to British Columbia specifically to teach.[5] More frequently, they were men and women simply looking for better opportunities, as the first Superintendent John Jessop himself had done when he arrived from Ontario in 1860 to seek his fortune.[6] From 1872 to 1901 and especially after 1886 with the arrival in Vancouver of the transcontinental railway, the number of elementary schools rose dramatically and thus the corresponding need for teachers.[7] Since the supply never quite met the demand, it was not difficult to secure a position, even for a year or two. Using a number of diaries, letters and reminiscences and the letterbooks of the Superintendent of Education, Jean Barman has identified five categories of individuals who became teachers before 1901: girls just out of school, often filling the transition period between school and anticipated marriage; young people determined to get ahead and seeing teaching "as a stepping stone toward what they really wanted out of life," such as law, medicine or the church; females forced to fend for themselves as a result of unforeseen circumstances, for example, death of parents, widowhood; men in need of ready cash, who moved in and out of teaching as need dictated, or who combined teaching and farming; and experienced teachers, those who had made some lifelong commitment to teaching.[8] For almost all men and for a considerable proportion of the women, Barman concludes, the motivation to be a teacher was economic, "the necessity to earn a living or to contribute to the family economy in geographical and socioeconomic circumstances where the range of possible occupations was limited."[9] That teaching was seen as a legitimate goal for a certain class of young women to aspire to is underlined by the fact that females could become teachers at age sixteen while males had to wait to age eighteen. For most girls, however, marriage remained their true and ultimate vocational aim.

With the inauguration of the normal school in Vancouver in 1901, professional educational credentials became accepted in lieu of provincial examinations held annually in Victoria. Local boards still did the hiring of teachers, but the Province, through its licensing standards, defined those people qualified to teach in the Province. Providing teachers for the ever-expanding population of school-aged children made it difficult to improve the education qualifications of teachers. For example, it was not until 1922 that the lowest qualification, a third class certificate (three years of high school and four months of normal school) was abolished. An oversupply of teachers in the depression years of the 1930s, however, allowed the Department of Education to raise the minimum requirement for admission to one of the two provincial normal schools to senior matriculation (four years of high school). All this changed in the war years as normal school enrollments dramatically declined and by 1942-43 a teacher shortage resulted in lower standards of admission (back to three years of high school).[10] During this time high school teaching certificates were differentiated from elementary ones and salaries were affected accordingly.

The introduction of contracts for teachers had the desirable effect of providing a measure of security of employment. On the other hand, dozens of responsibilities, such as janitorial duties, and proscriptions against certain behaviour were made part of the contract. Typically female teachers were restricted in their social contacts with men, they were prohibited from marrying, and were obliged to terminate their employment once they married. Exceptions to this last provision occurred but were not at all common, and were most often found in rural areas where a widow might be hired or a female teacher married to a local resident might be employed in preference to an unknown stranger. Both the community and the individual female teacher believed, with some exceptions, that married women and mothers belonged in the home not in the classroom. Single women teachers might well play an important role in building the nation and the province through their teaching efforts, but once married they were expected first to build their own families. Their prime and true vocation was in the home not the school. The right of married women to continue teaching in British Columbia schools was not confirmed until 1950.[11]

In early twentieth century British Columbia, about the time that the British Columbia Teachers' Federation came into being in 1917, it was difficult to tell whether teaching was a profession or not. The pay was certainly poor and teachers' work was highly supervised. In that sense teaching was hardly "professional." One might even argue that teaching resembled more a working class job with low status, little autonomy, strict supervision and few educational requirements. Manual tasks such as lighting the fire and cleaning the school were often expected of teachers. Paperwork grew and much of this was purely mechanical and clerical and not the sort of work done by other professionals. Teaching, at least at elementary school, was not exactly "mental" work either. Much of it was routinized around standardized textbooks and classroom procedures, and supervision from male principals, inspectors and school trustees continued to increase as the educational bureaucracy became firmly established.[12]

The undeveloped nature of the teaching profession in the interwar period is perhaps best summed up by reference to the critical appraisal of B.C. teachers in the Putman-Weir Survey of British Columbia education done at government behest in 1925:

> Too many unmarried teachers; the immaturity of the teachers, especially in rural schools; lack of vision and professional pride; deficient academic and professional qualifications; unwillingness to take additional professional training beyond the legal minimum; lack of experience; inability adequately to profit from experience; tendency to change schools too frequently . . . . [13]

Ironically, the path which British Columbia teachers took to try to improve their professional status was to form a teachers' union in 1917. Thus the most prevalent instrument of class consciousness at the time, the trade union, became the means by which teachers sought to achieve a sense of definition for their work and to better their working conditions. The debate over whether the BCTF should play by the rules of the trade union or the professional association was to extend over close to three decades before the Federation formally affiliated with the Trades and Labour Congress in 1943. But support for labour affiliation within the Federation was always precarious, divided as it was between those who favoured unionism as such and those who preferred to develop a professional association. The Federation thus broke with the TLC in 1956. In the mid-1970s renewed efforts were made to re-affiliate with the trade union movement but they proved unsuccessful.[14] As late as March 1992, the BCTF in its Annual General Meeting voted against a resolution calling for affiliation with the Canadian Labour Congress.

Mid-Century - Transfer to Universities

By the end of World War II, the normal pattern of teacher education across Canada was as follows. Secondary school teachers were expected to have a bachelor's degree followed by a one-year post-baccalaureate course leading to certification. Elementary school teachers, for the most part, took a one-year course following high school graduation in what was called a normal school. Following American practice, in some provinces the name "teachers' college" came to replace the latter. Also following the lead of the United States, in one province after another responsibility for the training of elementary school teachers was assumed by the universities – in Alberta in 1945, in Newfoundland in 1946, in British Columbia in 1956, in Saskatchewan in 1964, and in Manitoba in 1965. By 1970 the transfer to universities either had been accomplished or was about to be in all other provinces with Quebec and Ontario being the last to make the change. Most elementary teachers were by then receiving at least two years of university education and the goal of a B.A. or B.Ed. for all teachers was within sight. Thus, we see that British Columbia was among the first Canadian provinces to transfer all teacher education to the university. In 1961-62, British

Columbia led the provinces in the proportion of its teachers holding university degrees – at 37 percent. Also, in 1962 three years' study toward the B.Ed. degree became the requirement for a permanent certificate for elementary school teaching.[15]

By the same token, it is worth noting that the supply of and demand for teachers had a continuing effect on certification requirements. In the two decades after the war the demand for teachers across Canada severely outstripped the supply as the effect of the "baby boom" ran its course through the schools. Whereas the teaching profession advocated lengthening the period of teacher preparation, the provincial departments of education, concerned about putting teachers in classrooms, delayed the introduction of longer training periods and more stringent certification requirements. To this end, some provinces, such as Ontario, introduced emergency short courses requiring only two summers of teacher education with an intervening year of "supervised" teaching at full salary. By these arrangements the various provincial departments of education managed to direct and exert control over both the training and licensing of teachers in the various public school systems. This situation contrasted sharply with other professions in Canada, such as law, medicine and dentistry, where both education and self-regulation were supervised by their respective professional bodies. If the notion of a profession involves the use of a professional organization, belief in public service, sense of calling, belief in self-regulation, and a large degree of autonomy in its day-to-day operation, then teaching in Canada had some way to go at least with respect to the last two points.[16]

Three decades ago, in a wide-sweeping critique of public education for being overburdened by politics and the state, the political scientist, Frank MacKinnon, in a book entitled *The Politics of Education*, advocated delegating more responsibility and freedom to Canadian public schools and teachers. His criticism may be summarized as follows:

> To the schools the state gives no power of their own; and the teaching profession is a kind of low-drawer civil service, trained, licensed, hired, inspected and directed by the state. No other activity, institution, or profession is in this extraordinary position; education in North America is now the most completely socialized activity in modern society.[17]

In place of this situation which he roundly deplored, MacKinnon advocated granting a large amount of local control to the public schools, even down to the individual school, and recommended that teachers should become a true profession by virtue of being allowed to regulate themselves as to certification, discipline and professional development in much the same way as Canadian doctors, engineers and lawyers were able to do. "Most institutions and professions which serve the public," he continued, "are able to do so largely on their own terms and with some protection from political interference."[18] Why not teachers? MacKinnon centred his critique on the fact that at that time teaching was the only profession where the State controlled both training and licensing. He contrasted this with the other professions where "the requirements are set and administered jointly by a university and the professional organization concerned, and the licence is given by the profession after certification by the university. For teaching, however, the teacher's licence was "a State permit, not a professional diploma."[19] It was not until the late 1980s that MacKinnon's recommendations were to be seriously addressed, and this occurred in the Province of British Columbia.

By the 1980s, despite the lack of autonomy accorded other professions, teachers – both men and women – had made great strides. The development of the British Columbia Teachers' Federation enabled teachers to focus on both economic and working condition issues and on professional development. Decent salaries, pensions, benefits and contracts became commonplace; negotiating on working conditions, class size, preparation time and extracurricular activity gave teachers some control over their day-to-day lives. At the same time professional issues received attention and membership on ministry curriculum committees, educational commissions and task forces were demanded and accepted. The establishment of professional specialist associations enabled teachers to work together to improve their own professional development.[20]

The transfer of all teacher education to the universities also helped professional development. In many ways this transfer was akin to a shot-gun marriage and it has taken many decades for both parties in this marriage – teachers and universities – to come to appreciate one another. There is no question that despite many difficulties the move to universities has been beneficial to teacher education and to the professional development of the teaching force in the Province. First of all, virtually all teachers now have degrees and can be said to have a broad liberal education as well as a grounding in the professional aspects of teaching, learning and education generally. Second, because research is integral to the university and separates it from colleges, institutes and normal schools, research on teaching and teacher education, as well as on other areas such as the curriculum, has developed to the extent that it is having an influence on teacher education programs, policy decisions at the Ministry level, and the development of curricula and resource materials. Third, the emphasis on graduate studies has helped develop a cadre of career professionals – administrators, counsellors, curriculum developers, specialists of all kinds. The theoretical knowledge base, professional understanding, and skill development that these teachers and specialists bring to their school and classroom practice ensure that teaching in British Columbia has attained a professional status recognized by parents and the public generally.[21]

Despite this progress, criticism of faculties of education in Canada has remained fairly strong. It is difficult to support or critique such criticism since there has been no comprehensive study done of university faculties of education in Canada over the last three or four decades. For the United States, William R. Johnson has concluded that during this time period, "first, university schools of education have tended to distance themselves from the training and concerns of classroom teachers; second, the research agenda has not often produced knowledge useful to the practitioner nor has it often gained respect among members of the traditional academic disciplines; third, university schools of education have produced no permanent, durable models of teacher training."[22] Clifford and Guthrie, in *Ed School*, an insightful and critical look at schools of education in the U.S., agree with the conclusion of a committee in California which stated: "Education schools have been unable either to establish the degree of academic prestige enjoyed by schools such as law and medicine, or to obtain a perception of indispensability on the part of the education profession."[23] The Carnegie Report, *A Nation Prepared: Teachers for the 21st Century* (1986), the report of the Holmes Group (1986), and John Goodlad's trilogy (1990), all conclude that schools/colleges/faculties of education need reform.[24]

In Canada the Fullan/Connolly Report on Teacher Education in Ontario, produced in 1987, was quite damning. "The qualifications of most faculty members presently teaching is a serious concern. In the perception of their critics, many of them lack the training or desire to engage in research, some of them do not keep up-to-date with the research that is being done, and others do not fully appreciate the value of educational research."[25] On the other hand a good number of education professors have learned to play the academic game. The 1988 Birch/Robitaille Canada-wide study documents the refereed journals, grant proposals and research teams that have been established.[26] As education professors felt obliged to establish academic credentials and to forge academic careers, that is succumb to "publish or perish," their research became more and more sophisticated methodologically and theoretically and thereby, less and less acceptable to practitioners. A chasm opened between theory and practice. Professors of education, members of research institutions but with a professional commitment to schools and teachers, have found themselves pulled in opposite directions. Unlike other professional faculties – medicine, law, business, engineering – faculties of education have not been as successful in gaining the respect of either the university or the professional community.[27] One reason for this may be the history of the move from the normal school to the university; another may be the lack of professional autonomy including control by teachers over certification and discipline.

Recent Developments – The British Columbia College of Teachers

In 1987, without warning, the British Columbia Government led by a right-of-centre party (Social Credit) gave teachers professional autonomy, i.e. control over who may become and continue to be teachers. Bill 19, The Industrial Relations Act (1987), gave teachers the right to strike, bargain collectively for wages and working conditions, put principals and vice-principals on contract as managers and therefore not eligible for membership in the BCTF, and legislated either independent local teacher associations or unions within the BCTF.[28] Bill 20, The Teaching Profession Act (1987), created the British Columbia College of Teachers (BCCT).[29] The legislation was developed without consultation with teachers, the universities or other members of the education community. Although it is unclear why the Government acted as it did, there is some speculation. For several decades and increasingly in the 1980s, the BCTF had an agenda which many have argued has been at odds with the agenda of the Government. Each approached education from a very different ideology resulting in growing antagonism between the two.[30] It has been suggested with much plausibility that Bill 20, in creating a second body of teachers, and Bill 19 which allowed independent local teacher associations, was intended as a way of undermining the control and authority of the BCTF. A second conjecture suggests that the Socred Government had already adopted a policy of privatizing many government services. By creating an independent College with control over certification and discipline the Government decreased its costs. The price of professional control was the institution of fees. Accordingly teachers now pay for a certification service formerly supplied by government.

The enabling legislation established the College as a professional body of teachers with a College Council of twenty individuals as the governing body. Membership on the Council was composed of fifteen teachers elected by teachers in each of the fifteen zones in the Province, two members appointed by cabinet, two appointed by the Minister of Education, and the last a representative of the Deans of the Faculties of Education in the Province appointed by the Minister but selected by the Deans.[31] The Teaching Profession Act was proclaimed in August 1987, elections were held in the fall, and the College and the Council began operations in January 1988. Control over certification, discipline and professional development was henceforth to be in the hands of the teaching profession. To teach in the public schools of British Columbia membership in the College was made mandatory.

All fifteen teacher members first elected in the fall of 1987 had been supported by the British Columbia Teachers' Federation. Many had at one time or another held executive positions in either a local branch or the provincial association. The Chairperson of the Council elected at the first meeting was Bill Broadley, a former President of the BCTF. The BCTF announced it had control over the Council of the College and believed that it had circumvented the legislation which had created a second body of teachers.[32]

The Council members had a difficult first term as they struggled to clarify the meaning of the Act and determine their responsibilities. The College of Teachers was the first attempt, certainly in North America but possibly world-wide, to put control of teacher certification, discipline and professional development in the hands of the profession. Therefore, it had no precedent upon which to base its decisions.[33] It had authority over certification of teachers in B.C. and yet it had no officers, no registrar, no system in place to handle certification. The College had authority to approve the programs for teacher certification at the three universities and yet it had no way of establishing whether these programs should be accredited. It had by legislative authority control over teacher discipline and yet it had no disciplinary by-laws and did not have a system in place to handle either new discipline cases or those turned over to it by the Ministry. It had control over professional development and yet it was cognizant of the fact that the BCTF and the Provincial Specialists' Association of the BCTF had been involved in professional development for some time. In its first six months of operation the College of Teachers gave interim approval to the teacher education programs at the three provincial universities, hired a registrar, rented space, designed membership and service fees, developed a budget and proceeded to establish committees which would produce by-laws.

The creation of the College of Teachers has produced a number of issues affecting teacher education in the Province. Although the College has had to deal with many questions connected with membership and discipline and with reactions from the Government, other education groups and the public, in this paper we shall concentrate only on those which affect teacher education. It is noteworthy that on a Council of twenty individuals who have authority over the approval of teacher education programs for certification purposes, only one member is a teacher educator.

The legislation gave the College control over professional development. However, as noted, the BCTF had exercised a professional development mandate since its founding and numerous provincial specialist associations operated under the banner of the Federation. The College made the decision not to exercise its mandate in this area and appealed to the Government to change the legislation, mandating a Standing Professional Development Committee as one of three standing committees. The Government agreed and, in 1993, substituted a Teacher Education Programs Committee. Professional development for teachers in B.C. is thus separated from pre-service. This has caused some discomfort among those who see teacher education as a continuum of pre-service, induction and in-service professional development.

The certification process and the approval of programs for initial teacher certification at the three universities (U.B.C., Simon Fraser, and the University of Victoria) have provided interesting challenges for the College. In the initial months of its operation the College adopted the certification practices of the Ministry and gave interim approval to the three universities' teacher education programs. Over time it has developed certification policy, by-laws and appeals procedures. One of the areas of some contention and the source of many appeals has been the qualification of teachers from out of province, especially teachers who don't meet the academic requirements but who have many years of successful classroom teaching.[34] Another issue has been the more stringent requirements of the three faculties in the Province compared to requirements in other universities in Canada and whether it is inequitous to B.C. graduates to certify out-of-province candidates whose qualifications are less. In some instances the practices of the College in reviewing nominations for certification from B.C. universities have been more specific and the interpretation of certification criteria more literal than Ministry practice had been. This poses problems for admission decisions of the Faculties as they attempt to judge whether an applicant's previous academic work meets the College's specific criteria. The Universities believe that they should be able to exercise their academic and professional judgment as teacher-educators on such matters as the waiver of a particular course, or the substitution of one course for another, without constant referral to the College Registrar's staff for approval and decision. Traditional university autonomy has thereby been challenged.

Another issue that has affected the Universities has to do with the establishment in the Province of University Colleges which, in association with a university, offer degree programs.[35] The students attend the colleges where they register, pay their fees, and receive student numbers. The courses they take are university courses. At issue is that only the programs at the universities have been approved for certification by the College and a university transcript is required as evidence. The students at the university colleges are registered as college students and receive a college transcript. The question of how to grant B.C. certification to these students and not violate the policy that only the universities have received approval for programs has been a difficult one to resolve. A third issue causing some contention among Council members and the BCTF is the request by the Universities to have some students do the major portion of their practicum in independent schools. Schools in question are government funded, use the B.C. curriculum, and have teachers who are members of the College. This issue has been before the Council for two years without appreciable movement toward a solution. The ability of the faculties to exercise judgment on suitable placements for practica is being challenged by the College as is the right of students who wish a career in independent schools to get some practice and exposure in them.

The major effort of the College affecting the faculties of education in B.C. has been a review of the universities' pre-certification programs. In 1989 the College requested that each of the three faculties of education produce a self-study; asked for briefs from all education partners in B.C.; surveyed practising teachers, cooperating teachers who worked with the practicum teachers, faculty advisors and students; held two forums on teacher education; and conducted on-site visits by a three member team — one teacher-educator, one teacher chosen by the BCTF and the Chair of the College of Teachers, Bill Broadley, also a teacher. This work was facilitated by a consultant, Jim Bowman, a former teacher and BCTF staff officer, who coordinated and summarized the briefs and other documentation and wrote a report, *Teacher Education in British Columbia*, which was circulated for discussion and considered at a third forum (1991).[36] From this forum and other feedback the College established criteria for approval of new teacher education programs and approved on an on-going basis those currently in existence. It also established an on-going process for working collaboratively with the Faculties for the improvement of teacher education.

The review process and the report presented to the College engendered much discussion. The meaning and purpose of the review were viewed differently by College members and by members of the university community who deal with various kinds of accreditation bodies. Issues such as the nature of university autonomy versus the authority of the College, the desire to make specific recommendations against the need for flexibility, idealistic suggestions which in practical terms could not be implemented, and the relative emphasis given to pre-certification programs by the faculties, have all been part of the debate.

Heated discussions have taken place on the role of faculties of education in the university community, and the place and prestige of teacher education in faculties which serve purposes other than the provision of teacher education programs, such as graduate and diploma programs and fundamental and applied research. These are important issues to faculties of education which are part of the university community and must play by its rules not only those of the College of Teachers. They are also important issues for the teaching profession in its search for status, improved practice and the knowledge to handle its increasing social, as well as educative, role in society. Moreover, many practising teachers have a vested interest in that they are engaged in some form of graduate study. Finally, suggestions which would seem to separate pre-service from the full continuum of teacher education have caused much comment, with overwhelming support among practitioners as well as faculty members for the continuum of pre-service and in-service including a central but not a separate role for pre-certification teacher education programs.

The College is struggling to establish its approaches and its methodologies. The review of programs provided one example of the tasks. There is no question that, without precedents in place, it will take some time for the College to develop an effective accreditation process. A willingness by all parties involved to recognize this and work together should help to facilitate the process and enable the College to gain its own sense of maturity.

Conclusion

This brief look at teacher education in British Columbia suggests several conclusions. First, if one looks back over the century from the pre-normal school days when almost anyone could teach provided they passed a written examination, to today's very explicit by-laws and policies of the BCCT, the change is profound. However, almost all jurisdictions in Canada moved from a written subject-based examination, to normal schools, to university or control of teacher education. Most jurisdictions also moved from very short programs of four months to one or two years following junior matriculation, to the requirement of a degree, either a B.Ed. degree or a first bachelor's degree followed by a certification program. Most jurisdictions have also changed from a concentration on school subject-based knowledge to a combination of liberal arts, professional courses and an extended practicum. The difference in British Columbia is not in the content or length of programs; it is in the locus of legal authority for these matters and the ways that legal authority is exercised.

For the greater part of this century in B.C. and in most other jurisdictions the legal authority for teacher education and certification has been with the government of the particular province or state. When teacher education was transferred to the university that legal authority did not change. However, in practice governments accepted the recommendations of the universities without question. Faculties of education, in making curriculum and/or program changes, were bound by the regulations of the Senate of the university. The government, at least in British Columbia, did not review such changes and did not establish a mechanism to approve program requirements. De facto, the universities controlled who received certification within the province. Clearly that has changed with the establishment of College By-laws and Policies and the exercise by the College of its authority. It will be unfortunate if the bureaucratic and minute attention to detail practised by the College prevents or delays university attempts to change teacher education programs. Change is always difficult and faculties of education now have two hurdles to overcome in making change – the traditional university mechanism of faculty and senate approval, and now as well the mechanisms for approval established by the College.

A second point involves the review of teacher education and the Report prepared by Jim Bowman. The results of this are equivocal. Certainly, members of the Council learned quickly how complex a matter it is to design and prepare programs to educate teachers for the classrooms of the nineties. They were unprepared for the variety of courses that individuals and groups argued should be included in pre-service teacher education programs. The critical role that classroom teachers have in the success of the practicum and the cavalier attitude that many principals and teachers displayed toward this task became evident. The lack of relevant knowledge, attitudes toward faculties of education based on out-dated information and the prevalence of biases and assumptions all played a part in this review.

For the faculties, the requirement to articulate their programs, the need to justify the balance between theory and practice, and the results of surveys of both practising teachers and pre-service students on various aspects of the programs resulted in numerous committees being struck in the faculties to look at and analyze the program components and their delivery. Nonetheless, despite thirty-two recommendations in the Bowman Report, the courses and programs of the three faculties of education have not changed as a result of this review.

Third, the enactment of The Teaching Profession Act (Bill 20) creating the B.C. College of Teachers has served to focus more attention on teacher education than has heretofore been the case in British Columbia. The review, with its numerous surveys, questionnaires, site visits and forums, has raised the level of interest in the faculty programs, the supporting role of the school and classroom teachers, and some awareness of the complex nature of the task. Teachers, administrators, Ministry personnel, trustees and faculty members have debated with good humour and a genuine interest in each other's point of view. The BCTF has elevated the attention given to teacher education and produced a revised position paper for approval by its membership. At the same time, however, the College and the BCTF are in conflict over control. At its Annual General Meeting in March 1992, the BCTF adopted a motion calling for the repeal of the Teaching Profession Act and the closure of the College created by Bill 20. In place of the College, a Teachers' Professional Certification Council was proposed composed of fifteen members appointed by the BCTF and five members appointed by the provincial government. In addition, the new council would be financed by the Ministry of Education instead of the teachers themselves.[37] To date the Government has not dealt with this request. Although there is disagreement around the issues of control and financing, the level of interest in the education community is healthy, and one which, if nourished appropriately, should provide a basis for continuing dialogue and the improvement of professional practice in the education system.

Finally, although it may have been unintentional, the Government, in creating the College, may have helped prevent a trend, prevalent in some states of the U.S. and in Britain, from gaining a foothold in B.C. In the U.S. alternative certification practices put individuals in schools without professional courses or practicum, relying instead on academic preparation in the subject field.[38] In Britain the move of teacher education out of the institutions of higher education and into schools would seem to put emphasis on practice as opposed to theory.[39] The acceptance of the College as a strong player in education in B.C., the heightened awareness of teacher education in the ultimate success of schools and the willingness of all parties to work together may be the antidote necessary to resist such developments. In the final analysis it is important that the B.C. College of Teachers thrives and succeeds in giving the teaching profession control over certification and discipline. To fail may indicate that teachers cannot manage their own affairs and that would be devastating to teachers, teacher educators and the profession generally.

Notes

1. John Hardin Best, ed., *Historical Inquiry in Education: A Research Agenda* (Washington: AERA, 1983).

2. Donald Warren, ed., *American Teachers: Histories of a Profession at Work* (New York: Macmillan, 1989).

3. See for example, Robert S. Patterson, "Voices From the Past: The Personal and Professional Struggles of Rural School Teachers," in *Schools in the West: Essays in Canadian Educational History*, eds. Nancy M. Sheenan, J. Donald Wilson and David C. Jones (Calgary: Detselig, 1986), 91-111; John Abbott, "Accomplishing a Man's Task: Rural Women Teachers, Male Culture, and the School Inspectorate in Turn-of-the Century Ontario," *Ontario History* 78, 4 (Dec. 1986): 313-30; J. Donald Wilson and Paul J. Stortz, "'May the Lord Have Mercy on You': the Rural School Problem in British Columbia in the 1920s," *B.C. Studies* 79 (Autumn 1988), 24-58 [ch. this book]; J. Donald Wilson, "The Visions of Ordinary Participants: Teachers' Views of Rural Schooling in British Columbia in the 1920s'" in Patricia E. Roy, ed., *A History of British Columbia: Selected Readings* (Toronto: Copp Clark Pitman, 1989), 239-255; J. Donald Wilson, "'I am ready to be of assistance when I can': Lottie Bowron and Rural Female Teachers in British Columbia," Alison Prentice and Marjorie Theobald, eds., *Women Who Taught: Perspectives on the History of Women and Teaching* (Toronto: University of Toronto Press, 1991), 202-29 [see ch. of this book]. John Calam, "Teaching the Teachers: Establishment and Early Years of the B.C. Provincial Normal Schools," in *Schools in the West*, 75-97.

4. Alison Prentice, "'Friendly atoms in Chemistry': Women and Men at Normal School in mid-Nineteenth Century Toronto." David Kean and Colin Read, eds., *Old Ontario: Essays in Honour of J.M.S. Careless* (Toronto: Dundurn, 1990), 285-317.

5. Jean Barman, "Birds of Passage or Early Professionals? Teachers in Late Nineteenth-Century British Columbia." *Historical Studies in Education*, 2, 1 (Spring 1990): 19.

6. F. Henry Johnson, *John Jessop: Gold Seeker and Educator* (Vancouver: Mitchell Press, 1971).

7. Between 1891 and 1901 enrolment in provincial public schools rose from 9 260 to 23 615. Timothy A. Dunn, "The rise of mass public schooling in British Columbia, 1900-1929." J.

Donald Wilson and D.C. Jones, eds., *Schooling and Society in Twentieth Century British Columbia* (Calgary, Detselig, 1980), 26.

8. Approximately 1 500 individuals worked as teachers in British COlumbia between 1872 and 1901. Jean Barman, "Pioneer teachers of British Columbia." *British Columbia Historical News*, 25, 1, (Winter 1991-92): 15-18 [see ch. 10 in this book].

9. Barman, "Pioneer teachers of British Columbia."

10. F. Henry Johnson, *A History of Public Education in British Columbia* (Vancouver: UBC Publications Centre,1964), 213-14.

11. William A. Bruneau, "'Still Pleased to Teach': a Study of the British Columbia Teachers' Federation, 1917-1978" (unpublished manuscript, 1979), 31.

12. Marta Danylewycz and Alison Prentice, "Teacher's Work: Changing Patterns and Perceptions in the Emerging School Systems of Nineteenth and Early Twentieth Century Central Canada." *Labour/le travail*, 17 (Spring 1986): 59-80; Wilson and Stortz, "'May the Lord Have Mercy on You.'"

13. J.H. Putman and G.M. Weir, *Survey of the School System* (Victoria: King's Printer, 1925), 174.

14. Bruneau, "'Still Pleased to Teach,'" 36-7.

15. F. Henry Johnson, *A History of Public Education*, 222.

16. R. Hall, "Professionalization and Bureaucratization." R. Hall, ed., *The Formal Organization* (New York, Basic Books, 1972).

17. Frank MacKinnon, *The Politics of Education: A Study of the Political Administration of the Public Schools* (Toronto: University of Toronto Press, 1960), 4.

18. *Ibid.*, 6.

19. *Ibid*, 89.

20. See, for example, *Members' Guide to the BCTF, 1978/79* (Vancouver: British Columbia Teachers' Federation [BCTF], 1978). A *Member's Guide* is published each year and includes a history of the BCTF and of B.C. education to date.

21. See, for example, W. Robert Houston, ed. *Handbook of Research on Teacher Education* (A Project of the Association of Teacher Educators, New York: Macmillan, 1990); M. Fullan and F. M. Connolly, *Teacher Education in Ontario: Current Practice and Options for the Future* (Toronto: Ministry of Colleges and Universities, Ontario, 1987); Geraldine Joncich Clifford and James W. Guthrie, *Ed. School: A Brief Professional Education* (Chicago: The University of Chicago Press, 1988); John J. Stapleton, "Preparing Teachers for More Complex Classrooms: An Overview of the Pressures for Extension and/or Reform in Teacher Education Programs" in *Extended Programs of Teacher Education* (Ottawa: Canadian Teachers' Federation, 1988), 3-23.

22. William R. Johnson, "Teachers and teacher training in the twentieth century." Donald Warren, ed., *American Teachers: Histories of a Profession at Work* (New York: Macmillan, 1989), 243.

23. Clifford and Guthrie, *Ed. School*, 324-25.

24. Carnegie Task Force on Teaching as a Profession, *A Nation Prepared: Teachers for the Twenty-first Century* (New York: Carnegie Forum on Education and the Economy, May 1986); Holmes Group, *Tomorrow's Teachers: A Report of the Holmes Group* (East Lansing, Michigan: Holmes Group, 1986); John I. Goodlad, *Teachers for our Nation's Schools* (San Francisco: Jossey-Bass, 1990). Further references: John I. Goodlad, Roger Soder, and Kenneth A. Sirotnik, eds., *The Moral Dimensions of Teaching* (San Francisco: Jossey-Bass, 1990); Goodlad, Soder, and Sirotnik, eds., *Places Where Teachers are Taught* (San Francisco, Jossey-Bass, 1990)

25. M. Fullan and F.M. Connolly, *Teacher Education in Ontario: Current Practice and Options for the Future* (Toronto: Ministry of Colleges and Universities, Ontario, 1987), 20.

26. Daniel R. Birch and David R. Robitaille, "Canadian Educational Research: an Assessment and Strategies For Achieving Excellence." H.A. Stevenson and J.D. Wilson, eds., *Quality in Canadian Public Education* (Philadelphia: The Falmer Press,1988), 67-84.

27. Clifford and Guthrie, *Ed. School*; David D. Dill, "Transforming schools of education into schools of teaching." David D. Dill and Associates, *What Teachers Need to Know: the Knowledge, Skills and Values Essential to Good Teaching* (San Francisco: Jossey-Bass Publishers, 1990), 224-239.

28. *Industrial Relations Act*, 1987. Statutes of British Columbia.

29. *The Teaching Profession Act*, 1987. Statutes of British Columbia.

30. Charles Ungerleider, "Power, Politics and Professionalism; the Impact of Change in British Columbia on the Status of Teachers and Their Professional Conduct," presented to the Teacher Development: Key to Educational Change Conference, Vancouver, B.C., 1991.

31. To date the two members appointed by the Cabinet have been political appointments; of the two appointed by the Ministry of Education one has been a Ministry official and the other an individual from the independent schools sector; the Deans' appointee has been Dr. Nancy Sheehan, Dean of Education at the University of British Columbia.

32. *BCTF Newsletter*, vol. 27, no. 4 (Nov. 1987) and vol. 278, no. 5 (Dec. 1987) *Teacher: Newsmagazine of the B.C. Teachers' Federation* (March 1988): 8-9.

33. The only other jurisdiction to give substantial control over who should be admitted to the Register of Teachers and, therefore, entitled to teach, is Scotland, where the General Teaching Council for Scotland was established in 1965. This Council has a much broader membership and, although teachers are in the majority, there is substantial representation from the teacher education institutions. The Council and the institutions are also subject to decisions by the Scottish Education Department in such areas as policy, course approval and degree stipulations. See Gordon Kirk, "Persistence and change in teacher education." S. Brown and R. Wake, eds., *Education in Transition: What Role for Research?* (Edinburgh: The Scottish Council for Research in Education, 1988).

34. Certification requirements specific to individual provinces have been a source of dissatisfaction in Canada for all of this century. There are a few reciprocal agreements on certification between Canadian provinces at present but none involving British Columbia.

35. The Government's Access Program was developed in 1988 with a goal of creating 15 000 new places for university students. One aspect of this program was the creation of university colleges at three of the Province's colleges. In association with a university these colleges are granting certain degrees and, over time, hope to become autonomous degree-granting institutions. See Province of British Columbia News Releases, Ministry of Advanced Education and Job Training, and MInistry Responsible for Science and Technology. "Hagen Provides Details on University Degree Programs in Kelowna"; "Hagen Provides Details on University Degree Programs in Kamloops"; "Hagen Provides Details on University Degree Programs in Nanaimo," March 21, 1989.

36 Jim Bowman, *A Report to the College of Teachers on Teacher Education in British Columbia* (Vancouver, B.C. College of Teachers, 1991).

37. News release from the BCTF dated March 19, 1992.

38. Sheryl E. Stein, *Teacher Education Policy in the States: a 50-State Survey of Legislative and Administrative Actions* (Washington: American Association of Colleges for Teacher Education, 1990). Hendrik D. Gideonse, *Teacher Education Policy: Narratives, Stories and Cases* (Albany: State University of New York Press, 1992).

39. Don Gutteridge and Geoffrey Milburn, 1992. Forward: "To the Canadian reader." J. Wilson, *Reflection and Practice: Teacher Education and the Teaching Profession* (London: The Althouse Press, 1992).

Organizing and Reorganizing Schools
Part 3

16

Reflections on the Role of the School
in the Transition to Work in British Columbia Resource Towns

Jean Barman[1]

For some time I have been researching a company town that existed relatively unchanged for half a century, from 1910 to 1960, along the British Columbia coast. My particular interest in examining the history of Powell River has been with generational continuity. I wanted to know why sons did, or did not, follow their fathers into the pulp-and-paper mill that provided the almost sole basis of employment in the community. Increasingly, I realized that I was simply assuming the role played by the school in the transition to the workplace, rather than stepping back to consider exactly what it might have been. The more I have reflected, the less certain I have become. What happened in the schools of Powell River and other resource communities may have done little or nothing to expand options in the workplace, and is this not, after all, what public education is meant to be all about?

The significance of such speculation goes beyond Powell River or even British Columbia. Single-industry or resource towns, many of them owned by private companies, have been a prominent feature of human settlement across Canada.[2] While their existence over the long term depends ultimately on national and international markets for the commodity being produced, quality of life within towns helps to determine not only economic stability in good times but the extent to which residents are willing to endure downturns in the interest of community survival. For families, one of these elements must be the character of the local schools, schools which ironically may have been limited rather than expanded options for their children.

To make the case, I want to relate two quite different vignettes of British Columbia resource communities. The first comes from the coal mining towns of Nanaimo and Wellington in the late nineteenth century, the second from Powell River in the 1920s. Before doing this, I briefly want to review the history of public schooling as it developed in British Columbia.

The Development of Public Schooling in British Columbia.

A review of the development of public schooling in British Columbia suggests that the system failed resource towns because, quite simply, it did not take communities like Nanaimo, Wellington and Powell River into account. Put another way, the "public" to which "public" education in British Columbia was addressed did not extend as far as the "public" living in resource towns.

Public schooling in British Columbia had its origins in the mid-nineteenth century. By the time British Columbia joined Canada in 1871, consensus existed that the public education system should be modeled on Ontario, except that it should be non-denominational without special concessions for religious groups.[3] Control at the local level was vested in elected boards given various responsibilities including raising the proportion of school funding levied on property. British Columbia's provincial capital lay on Vancouver Island, and it was from Victoria that British Columbia's first intrepid Superintendent of Education John Jessop undertook his annual tours of inspection of each public school in operation across the far flung province.

So far so good, but the system soon turned inward. Subsequent superintendents skipped the most distant schools, so much so that Barkerville with its origins in the Cariboo gold rush was not inspected once between the late 1870s and the turn of the century.[4] In line with the dominant rhetoric of the day, Jessop's successors were most concerned with efficiency and progress. The department's 1878 annual report asserted without equivocation that the principal measure of a school should be "whether it is efficient or not." Schoolmen equated efficiency with uniform curriculum, compulsory attendance, graded schools and the most modern buildings. These goals were most realizable in populous areas. Imposing new urban schools with their massive brick facades and glistening porcelain indoor plumbing so gladdened school men's hearts that they were described in annual reports in almost rhapsodic tones.[5]

Larger social and economic factors encouraged the move toward urban models. Not only Victoria but the province's other two largest cities of Nanaimo and New Westminster were located in the province's far southwestern tip. With the completion of the transcontinental railroad in 1886, its terminus of Vancouver came to dominance as British Columbia's principal metropolis and service centre. It too was located in the extreme southwest. By 1891 the area extending from Vancouver Island through Vancouver and the lower Fraser Valley contained almost 80 per cent of British Columbia's population, a percentage that has leveled off at about 70 per cent through the twentieth century.[6]

Thus, schoolmen's urban assumptions only reflected the perspective of the majority of the province's population. What this majority wanted, so it was perceived, was more schooling which would then lead to greater employment opportunities. The first high school appeared in Victoria in 1876 and in the province's other three urban centres in the next decade and a half. Their initial programs of study were classical, intended as preparation for the professions or teaching. The Department of Education's goal was evident in the complaint of the principal of one of the feeder schools that he "was made to feel that my work was to pass pupils in to the High School and that my success in doing so would form the basis of the popular judgment as to my fitness for the position I held."[7] Reflecting schoolmen's urban blinkers, only after the turn of the century did the first high school appear outside of the province's densely populated southwestern tip.[8]

In the early twentieth century some realization grew that the rest of British Columbia had been ignored. Schoolmen's attention turned, at least perfunctorily, to what was perceived as the rural "problem." While the actual schooling that went on in the rural classroom did not move away from the dominant urban model, some shifts occurred. Superior schools were established, permitting children to continue through grade 9 and 10, but high school education was considered more the exception than the rule. In the 1920s two surveys were carried out to ascertain teaching conditions in non-urban schools. By then, or soon after, most prospective teachers were being given little lectures on what to expect when teaching in rural communities. The emphasis was on teachers coping with existing conditions as opposed to their using the school to effect change. Overall, what the Department of Education sought was to shift the blame for failure from itself to the locality, to rural trustees supposedly unconcerned to do anything, to uncaring parents and to irresponsible teachers. As J. Donald Wilson and Paul Stortz have elucidated, the initiatives were essentially gestures rather than a true change in direction away from urban priorities.[9]

This division of the public system into urban and rural obscured a third dimension. The special circumstances of children, more particularly boys, in resource communities were ignored. This cannot have been through lack of information. In the two 1920s surveys, for instance, teachers repeatedly referred to the uniqueness of company towns in particular. "Company town, School Board three company appointments." "Influence of company town very present." "This is one of the 'Company Towns.'"[10] Yet such key policy documents as the Putman-Weir Report of 1925, which set the agenda for public education in British Columbia until after the Second World War, did not even mention resource towns. Company towns received passing attention and then only in the section on finance, where Powell River's "taxable real property" was deemed to be able to supply a greater proportion of school funding that currently the case.[11] Over 550 pages in length, the report focused almost exclusively on urban, mostly Vancouver, schools and to a much lesser extent on the perceived limitations of their small rural counterparts.

It may have been that from the perspective of schoolmen, resource communities did not warrant attention away from urban priorities. From the late nineteenth century "the chief aim" of the schools was "to prepare the children of the Province, on entering upon the active duties of life, to become good and useful members of society." The Putman-Weir report put the "general aim of education" as "to enable the child to take his place as an efficient participant in the duties and activities of life."[13] Schoolmen, rather than viewing their role as giving children the opportunity to choose how they should best become "good and useful members of society," may have confused means and ends. Students' ease in entering the work force in company and other resource communities may have been interpreted as a measure of success. In other words, the Department of Education was so determined to measure success in terms of outcomes that it lost touch with the means to that end. The consequence was that, rather than expanding occupational opportunities for children, schools in resource towns narrowed them.

Nanaimo and Wellington in the Late Nineteenth Century.

The first of the snapshots or vignettes to make the argument comes from the coal-mining communities of Nanaimo and Wellington in the late nineteenth century. Nanaimo had its beginnings in the early 1850s when two dozen families were brought over from England to work nearby coal deposits. One of the first public schools to be established in the British colony of Vancouver Island was located in Nanaimo. As other mining communities grew up nearby, notably Wellington about eight kilometres distant, so schools also appeared there.

From the earliest days the schools at Nanaimo and Wellington refused to conform to schoolmen's expectations, and they finally simply washed their hands of them rather than attempting to redefine their priorities to meet the special circumstances of resource towns. Superintendent Jessop noted despairingly in his very first report of July 1872 that on the day he visited the Nanaimo school just eleven boys and sixteen girls were present whereas the community likely contained about 175 children of school age. Numbers gradually rose but twice as fast for girls, and Jessop noted somewhat wryly that "there are probably as many boys as girls in the town."[14] In 1876 Jessop estimated that a fifth of the school-age population was still not enrolled.

Those in school did not give cause for enthusiasm. "When the school was visited, the senior classes in both departments was little advanced in their studies. The boys were noisy and disorderly."[15] As would later happen with rural schools, Jessop put the blame squarely on parents. "A disposition on the part of many parents to send their children into 'the pit' at an early age is exercising a prejudicial influence on the rising generation by depriving them of the advantages of free school education."[16]

In 1876 the first written examination was held for admission into the new public high school just established in Victoria. Whereas fifty-four out of seventy Victoria students who took the exam passed, not one of the 26 sitting for it in Nanaimo did so. The average score was 277 in Victoria, 139 in the mainland city of New Westminster and just fifty-three in Nanaimo.[17] A year later no one from Nanaimo even bothered to take the high-school entrance examination. Jessop lamented,

> It is a difficult matter to raise and maintain a high standard of attainment in the senior division [of the elementary school] in consequence of pupils being withdrawn from school at a much earlier age than they ought to be. Parents should not under any consideration send their children into the mines, or give them employment above ground, till the before mentioned examination has been creditably passed.[18]

Over time, some Nanaimo boys did sit for the exam, but very rarely did the few who passed then go on to high school.[19]

In 1886 a high school opened in Nanaimo itself. Just twelve pupils enrolled. The problem lay, authorities acknowledged, in many being "engaged in pursuits by which they were enabled to support themselves or assist their parents."[20] In the late 1880s growing racism led to Chinese being prohibited from working underground. The school inspector lamented: "Owing to the exclusion of Chinese from the mines, a great many of our boys left school to fill their places, and consequently deprived us of some of our best material."[21] The high school by this time contained 9 boys and 16 girls, whereas Nanaimo's elementary schools enrolled 430 children. Conditions changed little during the next decade, a typical condemnation from the visiting school inspector reading:

> The great inducements held out to boys of thirteen to fifteen years of age to work in the coal mines naturally draws large number from the school every year, and place the senior divisions at a great disadvantage. You will notice, by the list of pupils, that quite a number of the boys of the age above mentioned have gone to work, thus carrying off the material that should go to the High School.[22]

Until the mid-1890s numbers in high school remained skewed by sex, fourteen boys vs. twenty-five girls in 1892-93, nineteen vs. twenty-nine the next year.[23] Thereafter they levelled out.

If Nanaimo was bad, Wellington, just a few miles distant, was worse. Average daily attendance in the mid-1870s was just 25 per cent of enrolled children.[24] Labor unrest was greater in its mines than in those at Nanaimo, and insecurity of employment seemed to have equally negative consequences to Nanaimo's assurance of steady work. By 1877 Jessop had virtually despaired of parents:

> Family difficulties, arising out of the unfortunate colliery strike and disputes, have seriously retarded school progress in the district during the year. The result has been a very large amount of irregularity, a low average, and little or no advancement among the pupils.[25]

An atmosphere of hostility sometimes became open animosity against the school as an institution, as in 1885:

> For a long time the destruction of the school property has been a favorite amusement with the hoodlums of Wellington. The school has been repeatedly disturbed by them while in session; a large proportion of the windows have been broken; a number of panes have been entirely cut out; the locks were broken or wrenched off the doors; the outhouses were destroyed; the stoves were broken into pieces and the stovepipe stolen &c &c. In consequence of these proceedings, the school-house became in cold weather unfit for habitation. Every year the school-house, and its appurtenances, are renovated and restored; but immediately after these repairs the work of wanton destruction begins anew, and by the end of the fiscal year (indeed, long before that time) there is again little left but the bare walls.[26]

Unlike Nanaimo, Wellington boys could not be persuaded to sit the high-school entrance exam, much less contemplate attendance.[27] The school inspector commented that it was "not difficult to assign reasons for their comparative indolence." Again, the blame was fixed squarely on parents.

> At an early age boys are able to earn in the mines (at employment requiring neither strength nor skill) almost as much wages as are given to adults in the Atlantic states. There is thus an inducement for parents to send their boys to work as soon as they are legally entitled to do so. On the other hand, if a boy distinguished himself by his proficiency at school there is no immediate prospect that he will be able to turn his

acquirements to account. Suppose, as generally happens here, his parents are unable to support further expense in fitting him for a profession, then he must be a clerk or a teacher. In this Province clerkships, if at all valuable, are few and not so easily obtained. As to teaching, about as much money can be got by ordinary unskilled labor as is given in most of the schools to the majority of teachers. Under such circumstances is it to be expected that boys should be inclined to make painful and laborious efforts in the acquisition of knowledge?[28]

As the public school system as a whole turned its attention to efficiency and more specifically to the necessity for children not only to be enrolled but to attend school regularly, schoolmen found ever greater reason to despair of Nanaimo and Wellington parents. Expectations were set out in no uncertain terms:

The allowing of children to be frequently absent from school on the merest semblance of an excuse, or on any avoidable pretext, tends to create in them a desire for freedom from the labors and restraints of the school-room, and too often causes the habit of irregular attendance to become chronic.[29]

Even tardiness could become a precursor of adverse lifelong habits:

Want of promptitude in arriving at the school is a loss to the pupil of possibly one or more recitations of lessons, disturbs those who are punctual, is an annoyance to the teacher, and, what is worst of all, tends to cultivate the wretched habit of procrastination.[30]

Cases of "truancy" were always especially high in Nanaimo and Wellington. In 1880-81, for instance, 23 cases occurred among 310 enrolled boys in the provincial capital of Victoria, whereas Nanaimo recorded 70 cases among just 148 enrolled boys.[31]

The blame for conditions in Nanaimo and Wellington lay unequivocally, in the opinion of Jessop and his successors, at the local level. Not just teachers, but trustees were to blame.[32] Whereas trustees came in for repeated criticism for their supposed disinterest in school matters, the minutes of the Nanaimo and Wellington school boards paint quite a different picture – that of harassed boards trying to cope as best they could in the face of relative disinterest by provincial authorities. The Wellington board perennially operated on the financial margin. It repeatedly requested urgent help to keep the school open. "Our present school years grant is now presently exhausted and we stand at present indebted to R.D. & Sons for 6 ½ tons of coal. The trustees do not feel justified in going any further in debt." We require immediate help from the Department "to unable us to continue school uninterrupted through out the term . . . as the children cannot attend without endangering health."[33] Two years later Wellington trustees again sought rescue.[34] A year later they were in such dire straits that they could not afford to have the outhouses cleaned out. "There is an attendance of 300 children. The condition of closets can better be imagined than described."[35] The Superintendent of Education's response seems to have been "to reduce staff to three teachers." According to the school board minutes, "trustees were of the opinion that present indications do not justify the reduction of staff to three teachers," but they could do nothing except to acquiesce.[36] Even while fighting off disaster, the Wellington trustees firmly believed that their children should receive the best possible education. The board repeatedly expressed its concern over crowded elementary schools.[37] They came out against the use of corporal punishment for pupils "failing to have lessons" and wrote to the provincial ministry to see whether they could act in the matter.[38] The minutes do not record a response.

In nearby Nanaimo, the school board not only responded as best it could to local conditions, but repeatedly took initiatives to improve the level of schooling for all children. It contacted the Superintendent to see if kindergarten could be offered.[39] The answer was no.[40] The board requested that an unsuitable school text be replaced. The answer was no.[41] School attendance of 50, 60 and upwards to 100 pupils in a single classroom prompted the board in November 1891 "to write to the Supt of Education drawing his attention to the overcrowded state of our schools, and the urgent necessity of having two assistant teachers appointed without delay."[42] The next spring one school was so full only standing room remained.[43] Shortly thereafter it was brought to the board's attention "that children have for some time since been refused admittance to the school and had to be kept at home for the want of school accommodation."[44] The board petitioned the Superintendent of Education and the city council for construction of additional facilities. The council refused to do anything, and the Superintendent sent only his regrets.[45] Eventually board pressure forced the council to change its mind.[46] Within half a dozen years overcrowding was again the issue. In one elementary classroom, "while there was only seats for 80 the actual average attendance for the past month had been 91."[47] The only solution, the board decided in 1899, lay in having "one half of these divisions attend school in the morning and one half in the afternoon."[48] Near the end of the year sixty elementary children were moved into the high school building, which was still underused.[49]

The impression left from juxtaposing the Department of Education's perspective with that of local boards is of a relatively intransigent provincial system so concerned with an urban model that it was unable to contemplate, much less respond to, any alternative set of circumstances. To the extent conditions eventually altered in Nanaimo and Wellington, it likely came through anti-child labor legislation which, it might be argued, was linked more to adult demands for employment that to pressure from the education system. The earliest regulations restricted boys under fourteen from working underground except with special ministerial permission. After the turn of the century boys under fourteen were completely banned from the pits. Even then they could still do clerical work above ground.

Powell River in the 1920s.

The second, very different snapshot bearing on schooling in resource communities comes from the company town of Powell River. Powell River was an educational paradox. Externally its schools were eminently satisfactory, but this had little if anything to do with the province's role in schooling. An elementary teacher from the interwar years recalled in admiring tones that Powell River was the only school she ever taught in that had "two pianos." Such praise was exactly what the Powell River Company that owned the town sought. Good schools were a very visible component of a deliberate policy intended to keep workers and their families acquiescent and quiescent. In the early 1920s trouble had erupted in the pulp-and-paper mill that dominated the town and the company was determined that it would not happen again. Workers had unionized at the time of the First World War. Between late 1921 and the spring of 1923 poor economic conditions were made the pretext to fire union leaders for supposed "disloyalty to the Company" and threaten to discharge the entire membership unless locals voluntarily disbanded.[50]

Once the unions were crushed the company set about putting in place the social infrastructure necessary to create what a Canadian company town planner of the 1920s termed "greater loyalty from . . . more contented and efficient workers."[51] Company houses in Powell River contained the most modern conveniences at minimum rent. Even light bulbs were free. Workers shopped at the company store, ate eggs laid by company chickens and produce grown at the company ranch, swam at the company beach, read books from the company library, attended dances in the company hall, golfed on the company greens, played badminton in the company gymnasium, and gave birth and died in the company hospital. Powell River's children were central to the strategy. Workers had to be convinced that not only their future but that of the next generation was assured. Organizations like the Boy Scouts and Girl Guides were subsidized. The company's glossy monthly magazine, the *Digester*, which was distributed free to every household in Powell River, regularly included attractive photos of children of all ages from healthy babies to academically outstanding students and sports stars.

Powell River's schools were from the beginning under company control. The first school was opened as part of the company's initial construction of the mill in order to encourage families to move to the remote coastal site. By provincial law only property owners could sit on local school boards. Since the company was virtually the sole property owner, its appointed representatives were in effect the board.[52] The company's control over the system was assured by its payment of virtually the entire local assessment levied by the Department of Education.[53] Schoolmen basically removed themselves from any role in Powell River's schools, apart from inspection of what were by any measure eminently satisfactory facilities.

Indeed, Powell River's schools simply became better and better. As early as 1916 three pupils qualified for high school entrance. Three years later a superior school was established, making it possible to take the first two years of high school in Powell River.[54] By 1921 the superior school had proven so popular that it became a regular high school.[55] In June 1924 the entire completing class successfully wrote university matriculation exams, a distinction attained by just three other schools across the province.[56] The same autumn the *Digester* reported proudly the visiting high school inspector's pleasure "with the general tone of the school and the quality of the work."[57] The next year growing numbers of pupils led to the construction of a second elementary school, again located on company land and built with a generous injection of company funds.[58]

The company's goal was to retain as many of the second generation of males as possible in the town. Believing that the best workers were the best-educated workers, the company's mouthpiece, the *Digester*, was straightforward in its admonitions to parents: "It is up to parents to keep the children at school as long as possible. It is an indisputable statement that the more instruction a child gets at school the better fitted the child will be for the battle for existence when maturity is reached."[59] To ensure that the "battle" would be fought in Powell River, curriculum were adapted to company purposes. In 1928 a two-month course in papermaking was introduced into the high school curriculum as part of General Science. The Powell River mill made newsprint and the course's goal was for pupils to be able to place "the manufacture of newsprint in its proper perspective as only one branch of a very great and varied industry."[60] Two years later the course was expanded into a three-year technical program especially designed by company management in cooperation with the Department of Education's organizer of technical education to appeal to secondary students wanting to make a career in the mill.[61] Two dozen boys enrolled the first year.

Activities in the classroom were complemented by outside opportunities encouraging boys to identify with the town and its mill. Outstanding players on football and baseball teams, as well as in field sports, received letters, sweaters and shields from the school board, in effect from the company. Summer and weekend jobs in the mill were available to male teenagers in preparation for a permanent job once they completed their education. Preference was always given in hiring to local as opposed to outside applicants Even where boys persisted in taking not the special technical course but the general academic course and then going on to university, they could count on summer jobs back home. At least some of them returned permanently in managerial positions.

In Powell River schools were an integral component of a resource company's larger agenda. While, as school board minutes testify, trustees regularly communicated their initiatives to provincial authorities, the local trustees were essentially the actors. The Department of Education's agenda, urban focused with a condescending nod to rural schools, probably made it grateful that Powell River demanded so little in terms of direct action on its part. Schools in Powell River did play a role in the transition from school to work, but only in terms of the agenda set by the company that owned the town. Alternatives were not encouraged, and the Department of Education did nothing to ensure that pupils were acquainted with occupational options. Rather, schoolmen through their passivity assisted the company in its ongoing goal of maintaining control over the lives of workers and their male offspring.

Reflections

What then might we learn from these two vignettes? On the surface they appear quite different, not only in time period but in the quality of the schooling being provided local children. Their very diversity makes a fundamental point, and that is the social and psychological distance that has sometimes existed between public systems of education and the real world of resource towns. The measures that schoolmen used to gauge schools' "efficiency" and "progress" were essentially those which could be quantified and standardized, from layout of buildings to records of attendance. They sought uniformity, a uniformity grounded in the urban models that appeared to them the most up-to-date and efficient, as well as the most visible from their base in the province's densely populated southwestern tip. Had they looked closer as opposed to wearing urban blinkers, realization might have come that the role of the school in some resource towns, as with Powell River, was not to open up opportunities in the workplace but only to fit the child to a particular workplace. This was certainly a situation in which many families concurred, but not necessarily one which the Department of Education ought to have indulged. Maybe nothing would have changed had schoolmen included resource communities within their frames of reference. Maybe the appeal of the local workplace would have continued to take precedence. Because the public school system did not try and, as in Nanaimo and Wellington, did not even respond when localities sought assistance, we will never know.

An equally important question becomes what these snapshots tell us for today. Generalizing from the experiences of Nanaimo and Wellington and Powell River, it may be that to, the extent education can expand horizons, it will not occur through the school. The appeal of immediate employment may simply be too overwhelming. This perspective comes through in a recent survey of British Columbia sawmills commissioned for the Council of Forest Industries and the International Woodworkers of America to measure employees' literacy levels.[62] Over 200 employees, 60 percent of them born in Canada, were interviewed to investigate the extent of agreement between written workplace materials and employees' reading comprehension levels. The most interesting findings relate to the small proportion of workers having taken work-related training courses. Of the 70 percent who had taken no courses, half said they felt "no need." Asked for the circumstances in which they would likely take a course, the two most frequent responses were "course needed to get better job" and "course needed to keep job." Practical, immediate utility holds the key.

It may be that, both in past and present, the central educational issue for workers in resource communities is not the transition from school to work but rather access to schooling at points of crisis. These will likely become more frequent, both as the Canadian economy redefines itself and as technology grows in importance. The number of jobs held by individuals with only a high school diploma or less is steadily shrinking as opposed to the growing number available to individuals with some post-secondary education. In the case of resource towns better access to post-secondary technical training and two-year colleges is clearly part of the answer, but so also is great sensitivity by public systems of education to the diversity of children's lived environments. As these vignettes from the late nineteenth century and early twentieth century testify, the particular circumstances of resource communities are not new. Perhaps we can learn at least a little from the experience of past generations.

Notes

1. The research for this essay was made possible by SSHRC grants to the Canadian Childhood History Project and, to study generational continuity in Powell River. I am grateful to the Social Sciences and Humanities Council and to members of the School-to-Work Network centred at York University for their comments on an earlier version of this essay. I owe a special debt to Helen Brown and Chris Anstead for their incisive critiques.

2 The Canadian literature is summarized in Robert Robson, *Canadian Single Industry Communities: A Literature Review and Annotated Bibliography* (Sackville: Rural and Small Town Research and Studies Program, Department of Geography, Mount Allison University, 1986), and Rolf Knight, *Work Camps and Company Towns in Canada and the US.: an annotated bibliography* (Vancouver: New Star, 1975). Estimates of numbers of communities historically can be inferred from *Single-Enterprise Communities in Canada: A Report to Central Mortgage and Housing Corporation* (Kingston: Institute of Local Government, Queen's University, 1953).

3. See chapter 1.

4. Department of Education, *Annual Report* [AR], 1876: 91, and 1901: 263.

5. See, for instance, Department of Education, *AR*, 1894: 192 and 194-5 and 1895: 254.

6. For details, see Jean Barman, The West beyond the West: A History of British Columbia (Toronto: University of Toronto Press 1991), Table 14, 371.

7. Department of Education, *AR*, 1885: 316. Emphasis in original.

8. A high school opened in Nelson in January 1901, followed by a second in Rossland in September 1901 and a third in Vernon in January 1902. Department of Education, *AR*, 1901: 235.

9. See chapter 11 and Paul J. Donald, Stortz and Wilson, "Education in Rural British Columbia: A Case Study of B.C.'s North-Central Interior in the 1920s," *Histoire sociale/Social History* 26 (1993): 265-90.

10. Department of Education, Teachers Bureau, School District Information Forms, 1928, Granby Bay, Westview and Woodfibre, held in British Columbia Archives and Record Service.

11. J.H. Putman and G.M. Weir, *Survey of the School System* (Victoria: Province of British Columbia, 1925), 293, 297 and 299, also 20.

12. Department of Education, *AR* 1893: 626.

13. Putman and Weir, *Survey of the School System*, 44.

14. Department of Education , *AR*, 1874: 17.

15 *Ibid.,* 1876: 94.

16. *Ibid.,* 1876: 94.

17. *Ibid.,* 1876: 128.

18. *Ibid.,* 1877: 19.

19. *Ibid.,* 1885: 313.

20. *Ibid.,* 1886: 144-45.

21. *Ibid.,* 1888: 199.

22. *Ibid.,* 1893: 542.

23. *Ibid.*, 1894: 199.

24. *Ibid.*, 1885: 324.

25. *Ibid.*, 1877: 19.

26. *Ibid.*, 1885: 324. The same thing happened in Nanaimo, although to a lesser extent. In 1893 the Nanaimo girls' school was broken into, doors damaged, some articles removed, and blackboard covered with obscene writing. Nanaimo School Board, Minutes [hereafter NSBM], meeting of 6 November 1893. Three years later windows were repeatedly broken. Nanaimo School Board, Minutes, meetings of 7 March and 12 December 1896. In 1898 outhouses were damaged. NSBM, meeting of 22 October 1898, held in Nanaimo School Board offices.

27. Department of Education, *AR,* 1891: 183.

28. *Ibid.*, 1887: 222.

29. *Ibid.*, 1891: 261.

30. *Ibid.*

31. *Ibid.*, 1881: 270-71.

32. *Ibid.*, 1874: 17.

33. Wellington School Board, copy letter of 5 March 1896, held in Nanaimo School Board offices.

34. Wellington School Board, copy letter of 19 March 1898, to S.D. Pope, Superintendent of Education.

35. Wellington School Board, copy letter of 8 June 1899, to Joseph Martin.

36. Wellington School Board, Minutes, [hereafter WSBM] meeting of 8 December 1900, held in Nanaimo School Board offices.

37. WSBM, 9 December 1896.

38. WSBM, 27 October 1896.

39. NSBM, 5 October 1895.

40. NSBM, 19 October 1895.

41. NSBM, 3 and 10 April 1897

42. NSBM, 13 October 1891 and 8 February 1892.

43. NSBM, 8 April 1892.

44. NSBM, 13 May 1892.

45. NSBM, 12 March, 8 April and 8 July 1892.

46. NSBM, 8 and 12 August 1892.

47. NSBM, 2 October 1897, also 1 and 6 October 1898.

48. NSBM, 2 September 1899, also 2 December 1899.

49. NSBM, 28 December 1899.

50. A. Lewthwaite, secretary of Local 76, Powell River, to John Burke, president of International Brotherhood of Pulp, Sulphite and Papermill Workers, 5 January 1922, in correspondence between the local and international union, 1918-22, copies held in the offices of Local 76, Powell River.

51. J.A. Walker, "Planning of Company Towns in Canada," *Canadian Engineer* 53, 3 (1927), 147.

52. Initially one or two of the few independent property owners sat on the board, but by the 1920s it was entirely a company enterprise. For the history of schools, see Alice Cluff, *Powell River and District Schools 1899-1983* (Powell River: Powell River Phoenix Printers, 1983).

53. Powell River School Board, Statement of Operating Expenses 1920-21, held by Powell River School District.

54. Powell River School Board, Minutes [hereafter PRSBM], annual meeting of 12 July 1919.

55. PRSBM, 7 September 1921.

56. *Digester* 5, 1 (January 1925), 8-9, held in Powell River Archives.

57. *Ibid.*

58. PRSBM,13 July and 7 December 1925.

59. *Digester* 5, 9 (September 1926), 9.

60. *Digester* 7, 9 (September 1928), 19.

61. *Digester* 10, 1 (January 1931), 2, and 10, 11 (November 1931), 20.

62. COFI and IWA-Canada, *A Preliminary Study of Job-Related Communications Skills in British Columbia Sawmills* (Vancouver: JCP Research, 1991).

17

Separate And Unequal: Indian And White Girls At All Hallows School, 1884-1920[1]

Jean Barman

During the first decade of this century, Indian, or Aboriginal, education in Canada underwent re-evaluation. Previously, federal policy had been directed toward the immediate assimilation of educated young Indians into the dominant socio-economic order. But, so the Department of Indian Affairs argued, most pupils were returning home to their reserves rather than settling down in White society. In 1910, the department's goal became "to fit the Indian for civilized life in his own environment" rather than "to transform an Indian into a white man."[2] The move away from assimilation altered the course of Aboriginal history in Canada and so merits explanation. The federal government argued that educated young Indians were themselves responsible for the shift because of their unwillingness or inability to make the transition. A close examination of the policy shift within the context of a specific school admitting both Indian and White pupils suggests that the failure of government policy became inevitable because of federal parsimony and White prejudice. The case in point is All Hallows School in British Columbia, in existence of a third of a century between 1884 and 1920.

Origins

All Hallows School developed as a result of similar interests between Christian missionaries and the federal government in the late nineteenth century. Almost as soon as the first White settlers arrived in British Columbia, the major denominations began demarcating spheres of influence for the purpose of Aboriginal conversion.[3] The Anglican claim to the southwestern interior was consolidated with the arrival from England of the first bishop of the diocese of New Westminstser in 1880.[4] Bishop Sillitoe quickly became convinced that the establishment of schools not only was essential to carry out God's work among the 3 000 Indians in the Yale district but was also deeply desired by the Indians. His travels about the mission showed him "examples enough of self-improvement under the present very limited opportunities to warrant the highest expectations" if schools were begun.

> When we shall have been allowed to accomplish this, we shall have wrought a social revolution in the land, for we shall have elevated the people from the servile condition of hewers of wood and drawers of water and given them an equal chance in the race of life.[5]

To this end, the bishop enticed out from England both missionary clerics to establish a boys' school and Anglican nuns to work with Indian girls.

Unfortunately, by the time three sisters of the order of All Hallows arrived in British Columbia in October 1884, the diocese's finances were in disarray, the bishop's enthusiasm having far outstripped resources, which were limited to a small endowment and voluntary contributions from Britain.[6] The sisters had come on the understanding that financial support for a boarding school would be forthcoming but instead found themselves isolated at Yale, "forced to take in washing to make ends meet."[7] The community, nestled in the steep mountains of the Fraser canyon, had originated a quarter of a century before, during the gold rush, and had received its second life as a construction centre for the transcontinental railroad. Now it was "gradually decaying."

Despite their onerous condition, the sisters immediately began a day school, but irregularity of attendance soon confirmed the absolute necessity of a boarding school.[8] The bishop proposed an expedient. Among projects initiated in his original spate of energy had been two church schools for White girls, intended to counter the non-denominationalism of the province's public system. Neither was self-support-ing. If the sisters would also commit themselves to take on this work, then funds granted by an English mission society for their capital costs could be used at Yale.[9] The sisters acquiesced, and White fee-paying boarders began to be accepted along-side Indian girls. Additional funds still had to be raised, however. Bishop Sillitoe turned to the Department of Indian Affairs, which he had first approached without success at the time of the sisters' arrival.[10] In June 1888, an agreement was concluded to subsidize up to twenty-five pupils and construction of a dormitory.[11] Thus All Hallows was established, with enrolment eventually reaching thirty-five Indian and forty-five White pupils, the latter almost all the daughters of Anglican families in the New Westminster diocese.[12]

Reasons for Attendance

Pupils were attracted to All Hallows for a variety of reasons. Many early White pupils were the daughters of Anglican clergymen, who were sent primarily because All Hallows' religiously based instruction replicated what their parents, almost all of English origin, had themselves experienced. Other girls came for lack of alternatives. Almost half of the White pupils at All Hallows in the years for which enrolment data has survived – 1899-1901, 1906, 1908-09 and 1911 – came from areas of British Columbia without a public high school, what one pupil has remembered as "small places."[13] Fathers were often establishment figures such as the CPR or government agent, owner of the general store cum post office, or possibly the cleric or doctor. Some White girls came from very remote areas without even a primary school, their father a farmer, rancher or mining engineer. Typical was the writer Charles Mair, who shortly after settling in the Okanagan Valley, reported: "There is no school here as yet which is a draw-back, but there is a fine school at Yale, kept by lay-sisters of our church, and we shall send Mabel, and perhaps Bessie, there in spring."[14] In some cases, a paucity of alternatives was more a matter of perception. A young girl growing up on a ranch in the Kootenays has remembered her first school being two miles down the valley and her English mother deciding, a year later, that she "should not be taught by anybody whose grammar was all wrong." The alternative was All Hallows, where "the disinctiveness of their enunciation" suitably distinguished pupils from average "Canadians."[15] In time All Hallows became fashionable and also attracted numerous daughters of prominent Vancouver families.

Since young Indians were not yet legally compelled to attend school, they had to decide themselves if they wanted a formal education. By the time of All Hallows' foundation, Indians of the Yale district had experienced a quarter century of White contact, and lifestyles were changing. Thus, according to a contemporary, while few "parents can read or write (the mothers certainly cannot)," many families accepted the utility of offsprings learning English, becoming literate and acquiring some familiarity with White culture.[16] As one All Hallows' pupil explained, she was sent "to learn White people's ways."[17] From the late 1890s, All Hallows had little difficulty attracting sufficient pupils and was compelled more than once to refuse applications for lack of room. To quote the order's magazine in 1897:

> The present difficulty is not to secure children for the school, as in former years, when we had to go to the Indian Reservation to coax the parents into sending their children to school and the children into coming but to find room for those who are desirous of admission.[18]

The local Indian agent reported in 1900 that Indians of the Yale band "take a good deal of interest in the education of their children and are anxious in this respect to see them on a par with their white neighbours." The same year a local chief expressed his pleasure to the sisters that Indian pupils were now "growing up together" with "the children of the white people." A decade later, another elderly chief in the area "complained" to the local Indian agent that their "children were not taught enough": "'We wish our children taught the same as the whites. They go to school, maybe, five, six, seven years. They learn read [sic] a little. That's all. Not much use.'"[19]

In some cases the local Anglican cleric urged attendance. The Yale district contained about 1 200 baptized Indians. More than one family must have agreed because the request that their children attend the school came from a representative of the church. An Indian pupil recalled how the local cleric would regularly "pick up girls that wanted to go to school." As remembered by another, who in 1894 at the age of eight joined her older sister and cousins at All Hallows, "Archdeacon Small, you see, was in charge of that part of the parish, and it was him that got these girls in and finally talked mother into letting me come."[20]

Family dislocation also brought Indian pupils to All Hallows. For example, during Holy Week 1901 a "very pale thin child, with a care worn face," appeared on the school's doorstep, volunteering only that her name was "Tuchsia." Some time later a telegram arrived from her mother, a former Indian pupil not remembered for her academic abilitiy: "I sent my little girl to you pecause [sic] I am dying. Dake care of her, make her to pe goot." Among the Indian girls Tuchsia joined at school was "a loving soft dumpling" named Grace who had arrived a year earlier at age two after her mother, also an ex-pupil, died. Grace was still too young to understand when a few months later her father was killed in a mine explosion.[21] No data exist to determine the proportion of Indian girls who came to All Hallows as a result of family dislocation. The sole surviving school register, for the years 1910-18, contains only partial information, but it indicates that many girls had only one living parent or that parents were separated.[22]

Another reason bringing Indian pupils to All Hallows was lack of educational alternatives. According to the Department of Indian Affairs, only "in a few instances" across Canada could "Indian children attend the white children's schools." For a time exceptions existed in British Columbia, but in 1911 came the observation that "a very marked prejudice exists, I might say, generally among the whites against association with Indian children." The next year pupils in several schools were told to discontinue attendance. The All Hallows' register for 1910-18 notes only two occasions where a pupil also attended a public school.[23]

Physical Separation of Pupils

The peculiar circumstances of All Hallows' creation offered a unique opportunity for young Indians and Whites to learn to live together in a physical environment relatively isolated from the larger society. But such was not to be the case. Originally, a certain amount of contact existed. So long as only a handful of White boarders enrolled at what was in essence an Indian school, they could not remain apart, nor did they. Indeed, in March 1888 Bishop Sillitoe commented approvingly that "no prejudice seems to exist among white parents against sending their children to the same school." Christmas 1889 was celebrated, to quote a participant, by "twenty of us Indians and half-breeds, and only two young ladies," one of whom was "going to be Father Christmas, and she is followed by four Christmas spirits."[24]

Then came physical separation. Late in 1890 an anonymous letter appeared in the New Westminster newspaper "raising the question of mixed classes" at All Hallows. While denouncing the letter as "abusive and slanderous," Bishop Sillitoe in effect acquiesced as evidenced by his statement that "there are certainly two classes of children in the Yale School." He went on to assure present and prospective parents that the school's seven White boarders were, or would be, treated in a manner consistent with their station in life and thus were lodged separately: "Even in the play ground they only very occasionally mix with the other children." The visiting examiner that spring commented that "the school is, it may perhaps be well to note, having regard to racial and other prejudices, entirely distinct from the Indian Mission work of the All Hallows Sisterhood."[25]

Such arrangements continued. On Christmas 1895, as two of seven White girls remaining at school alongside twenty-five Indian pupils reported somewhat wistfully, no common events occurred as had been the case previously:

At midnight [on Christmas eve] there was a celebration of the Holy Communion in the school chapel, to which the Indian children and about sixty Indians went. We were not allowed to go to this, but from our dormitory we tried to listen to the singing.

Two days later, a party was held around "the Indian Christmas-tree."

We were not allowed to go to it, only to peep in through the open door for a little while, and I will tell you what I saw. . . . The Indian children of the school stood on the platform at one end of the room singing carols. They all wore dark frocks and red pinafores and looked very nice.

A report to the order's mother superior in England summed up the new arrangements: "In accordance with the wishes of the English parents, the white children and the Indians do not mix." Eventually the only activity shared by all the girls were the daily religious services. Even then they attended as two separate groups. As a thirteen-year-old White girl explained, "the seats are on either side, and the Indian school in red caps and pinafores sit on one side, and the Canadian school in white veils on the other."[26]

Pupil recollections confirm the entirety of separation. As put by an Indian girl at school from 1894 to about 1900, "We didn't mix at all." However, to defend the sisters, whom she deeply admired, she put the case in favor of separation: "I think the sisters were very wise in keeping us separate because we didn't begin to have the nice things the other children had because our people couldn't afford it." The only

Early All Hallows pupils, 1886. (BCARS)

time she recalled talking with a White girl was once when they were both happened to be folding linen. According to a White pupil at All Hallows from 1909 to 1914, "Whites and Indians were never together, that I can tell you." "We didn't think about mixing in those days." Another has summed up, "There was no contact at all." And another, "We weren't allowed to speak to them." A fourth White girl has made the same point: "We weren't allowed to look at the Indian girls, were not even supposed to look at them in chapel which was the only time we ever saw them."[27]

Physical Separation but Educational Parity

While the physical separation put in place at All Hallows between Indian and "Canadian" girls was significant enough on its own terms, its consequences would have been immeasurably compounded if accompanied by inequality. In All Hallows' first years inequality remained relative, with parity existing to the fullest extent possible given the assumptions of the age. The churches believed, and the Department of Indian Affairs concurred, that Christianity and civilization were coterminous and, more specifically, that civilization was a White prerogative. To Christianize an Indian was to civilize him, and to civilize him was to socialize him into the dominant culture.

Thus Indian girls arriving at All Hallows at age five or seven or nine from an affectionate environment without restraints or punishments, familiar only with the world of their family and band, and very probably knowing no English, were immediately thrust into a closely regulated alien environment. Family clothing had to be exchanged for garments provided by the school, consisting in winter of chemise and drawers of unbleached cotton, heavy red or grey flannel petticoat, long woollen stockings, high leather boots, dark blue serge longsleeved dress, red pinafore, and red cloak for outside. New pupils had their own sleeping area, in order "to acquire habits of cleanliness and order" before moving to a dormitory housing eight to twenty-five girls. Thereafter came a relentless routine whose infringement brought such traditional European punishments as being "sent to bed early, put in the corner," or deprived of "Sunday pudding." Once in school, Indian pupils had little choice as to whether or not they wished to be "civilized."[28]

A second critical assumption of the nineteenth century held that status at birth was decisive in determining status in adulthood. A principal function of education lay in preparing each individual for his place in the socio-economic order as foretold by his conditions of birth. Thus, in an English orphanage also under the auspices of the sisters of All Hallows, poor White girls were "trained for domestic service, were confirmed, and were employed in performing the household chores of the main school whose pupils were also orphans but of the Upper Class." Similarly, the Protestant Orphans' Home in Victoria, British Columbia, taught its female residents "to wash clothes, scrub floors, wash dishes and attend young children and all domestic work as a most important part of their education."[29]

White pupils at All Hallows at Yale, born into the middle or upper class, had by force of circumstance to be suitably prepared to assume that lifestyle. On the basis of their birth, All Hallows' Indian pupils had not even attained the bottom rung of the White socio-economic order. Their education must therefore have as its first goal that achievement, which meant training not unlike that meted out to White orphans of the day. The Department of Indian Affairs assumed that "semi-industrial" schools like All Hallows would give "domestic training in cooking, housework, laundry, waiting, gardening and needlework."[30] In part for reasons of economy, All Hallows' Indian pupils had always been expected to "assist in the domestic arrangements of the house." As the school grew through the admission of White boarders, the Indian girls, as part of their training, became responsible for all household duties, including food preparation.[31] As summed up by a White pupil, "They were the servants; they did the work."[32]

Consequently Indian girls rose earlier than did their White counterparts in order to do an hour of "House work" before the joint chapel service at 7:30. Whereas White pupils spent the hours from 9 a.m. to 3 p.m. wholly in the classroom, Indian girls interspersed classes with another hour of housework. When White girls went "up to dress for dinner," their Indian counterparts set the table and lit the lamps. At the end of the year on Prize Day, both groups received awards for academic performance and conduct, but Indian girls were also commended in such areas as "bread-making" and "laundry-work." The only work activities performed by All Hallows' White pupils appear to have been making their beds each morning after chapel and darning their stockings on Friday evening.[33]

Originally, inequality in work was offset by parity in the classroom. The concept of assimilation foresaw some opportunity for individual advancement beyond the bottom rung of White society. The potential in education was perceived as enormous, not only by Bishop Sillitoe but by federal authorities. "The Indian problem exists owing to the fact that the Indian is untrained to take his place in the world. Once teach him to do this, and the solution is had." Individual ability would make the difference and some would do better than others. In 1892 the Department of Indian Affairs commented on "the prospects of being considered fit for promotion to schools of a higher type, seeming to act as a stimulus to the pupils to excel." Already "the Indian race of Ontario has its representatives in all the learned professions, as well as in every other honourable occupation," and "no doubt the same satisfactory results will in time follow" elsewhere in Canada.[34]

No question exists but that the sisters of All Hallows considered their Indian charges to be academically capable human beings. The external examiner of spring 1887 spoke of,

> the careful and successful teaching; of the readiness and accuracy with which my questions were almost invariably answered; of their quickness of apprehension and the clear understanding of the subjects treated of in the examination. . . . The children seemed to brighten up and look pleased when I laid aside the books and appealed to their intelligence rather than to their memories.

A year later the bishop himself held "a very rigid examination" to discover "the answers in all respects being equal, and sometimes superior, to anything that could be expected from white children of the same age."[35] From 1893 federal authorities required that the academic level of Indian pupils be assessed annually. In British Columbia residential schools in general over half of the pupils were in the two lowest grades, just 14 percent in grades 5-6. At All Hallows 45 percent were in grades 1-2 and fully 28 percent in 5-6.[36] As summed up by an Englishman visiting All Hallows in 1897, "Education goes on in much the same methodical routine as in England, only at Yale it is rather two schools under one roof."[37]

Individual pupils made great strides. For example, "'Mary' came to us three years ago, not knowing her letters nor a word of English; she is now in the *Third Canadian Reader*, and in the compound rules, weights and measures in arithmetic; she can also say the Church catechism perfectly." During her holidays Mary wrote a long letter to the sisters which suggests her progress:

> It was raining very hard when I got off the train. I got so wet, and my poor little dolly was wet too, because she had no hat on. . . . Oh, Sister dear, if you can't find my Communion little catechism book, I got it here. It was inside of my Bible, that's why I didn't see it. If you wanted I'll send it to you. Now that is all I can say, so with best love, dear Sister, I remain your loving naught [sic] child.

Equally representative of pupil work is an essay "About Music" by twelve-year-old Emma:

> God made everything, and He gave power to the birds to have music, and to the brook, and to the wind too. If you stand near the telegraph wires when the wind is blowing you will hear lovely music. Some birds have hardly any music. The pretty birds cannot have a nice music, because they have something pretty already; and the birds that are plain have a lovely music in their throats, because they have only dull feathers to cover them – they are not pretty outside. . . .
>
> There is music in everything. Someone told me there was music too when everything was quite still, you could not *hear* that kind of music, but you could feel it in your heart.[38]

Talent was also encouraged in other areas. The bishop's mother-in-law reported with some astonishment in 1895 "that of the teachers standing before their classes, *two* were Indian girls, being in fact the more advanced pupils" who have become "efficient teachers, and are occupied in tuition five hours for five days each week." She received a note inviting her to an evening party organized by the Indian girls "quite by themselves . . .the writing inside (one now lies open before me) such as no English maiden need be ashamed to own." To her pleasure, "Among the attractions were a piano-forte duo, a piano solo (a well-known Mazurka, I have forgotten by whom). The execution of this last was a marvel to me; no mistakes were made, and the quick running passages given with light, easy fingering." A year later Rosie passed the Royal Academy of Music examinations alongside eight White pupils.[39]

Achievement did not necessarily come at the cost of complete alienation from traditional Indian culture. While pupils went home only during the summer holidays, contact did not disappear. Because the sisters also ministered to local Indians, including many pupils' families, they were regularly invited to Christmas festivities and the spring Prize Day. Moreover, "whenever there is a service for the Indian adult congregation in the school chapel, and this happens about twelve times a year, the children are allowed to attend, and are taught to take their part in the portion of the service sung in the Indian language."[40] When girls did go home for the summer, many like Mary wrote freely to the sisters about their adventures, suggesting a lack of strictures on behavior.[41]

On the other hand, there is no question but that pupils had to reconcile the two cultures in their minds. Indicative of the dilemma is a long letter written to the sisters in 1900 by Mali, a pupil at the school from 1885 to 1897. She had just attended a potlatch, even though they had been forbidden by law since 1884. The letter is significant because Mali could accept both traditional Indian culture and Christianity, because she felt free to share her views with the sisters, and because they then considered it suitable to publish the letter in the school magazine. Mali began by detailing how,

> after an absence of many years, I went back to live among my people for few months, and I saw again some of their customs which must appear to white people as very strange, and sometimes very wrong – but I think it is because they do not understand.

She went on to explain how the potlatch is "our way of praying for the burial of our dead. . . . I think you would call it etiquette, and the Indians are very particular about it." A lengthy analysis of the ceremony followed, and Mali summed up:

> Potlatch is an old custom, and I do not think the Indians will ever give it up. . . . I think if some of our friends, I mean our *real* white friends like the Sisters and Miss Moody [a longtime teacher] would come, they would see for themselves; you cannot understand unless you see, and the Indians would be so glad, and there would be a chance to teach them more to be good Indians and Christians too, and not what they often feel, that to be Christians they must leave off being Indians and try to be like white people, giving up even what is harmless in their old customs.

Although no evidence exists that any of the sisters or Miss Moody ever took up Mali's invitation, it is clear from her letter that they were not unreceptive to discussion of differences between the two cultures.[42]

Thus, while Indian pupils at All Hallows rapidly became physically separate and unequal in work duties, they were recognized through the turn of the century as possessing comparable intellectual capacity. Individual advance depended on individual ability and initiative, and many achieved much. As a knowledgeable observer of the national scene reported to the Department of Indian Affairs in 1904: "It is beyond doubt that Indian children have the capacity to learn and that the reason of nonsuccess in education is not to be found in want of intelligence."[43]

Educational Inequality

Despite demonstrated intellectual capacity, the paths of Indian children diverged from those of young Whites both at All Hallows and across Canada after the turn of the century. At the time of All Hallows' foundation public education had been relatively simplistic, few children remaining in school more than half a dozen years. Gradually public schools became more attractive. To remain competitive, All Hallows had to raise its academic appeal for White families, which it did by appointing a Queen's University graduate as "headmistress" in 1899. The results were soon apparent. In 1907 an All Hallows' pupil came first in British Columbia and sixth in all of Canada in the entrance examination to McGill University. The next year another pupil received the first gold medal awarded in Canada by the Royal Academy of Music.

The explanation for the growing inequality of Indian pupils must be sought primarily at the federal level. Disenchantment with the goal of assimilation can be dated from the assumption of ministerial responsibility for Indian affairs by Clifford Sifton in 1896. As his biographer has concluded, Sifton demonstrated during his ten-year tenure "an unvaryingly parsimonious attitude toward the Indian."[44] Up to that date it was generally accepted that, while residential education was expensive, it must be regarded, "when viewed with relationship to the future interests of the country, as an excellent investment." Just a year into Sifton's tenure came the assertion in the department's annual report that "only the certainty of some practical results can justify the large expense entailed upon the country by the maintenance of these schools." The report went on: "to educate children above the possibilities of their station, and to create a distaste for what is certain to be their environment in life would be not only a waste of time but doing them an injury instead of conferring a benefit upon them."[45]

The die was cast. In retrospect it seems clear that the move away from assimilation would have less to do with the lifestyles of ex-pupils than with the inability of Sifton and, more generally, White Canadian society to accept Indians even at the bottom rung of the dominant socio-economic order, much less as equal human beings. Indeed, Sifton's eventual successor stated as early as 1897, "We are educating these Indians to compete industrially with our own people, which seems to me a very undesirable use of public money."[46]

Supposed Indian "inability to mingle freely with white communities" became the pretext for a change in policy which was probably already inevitable.[47] Sifton himself led the way: "I have no hesitation in saying – we may as well be frank – that the Indian cannot go out from school, making his own way and compete with the white man. . . . He has not the physical, mental or moral get-up to enable him to compete. He cannot do it."[48] The focus soon became "the danger . . . of inculcating habits, tastes and ideas calculated to produce unfitness for and discontent with a subsequent environment from which the prospect of escape is most remote." And: "Great caution has to be observed to avoid the danger of unfitting the pupil for the surroundings to which their destiny confines them."[49]

A decade and more of federal discontent with assimilation culminated in 1910 in a revised, more frugal policy intended "to fit the Indian for civilized life in his own environment. . . . To this end the curriculum in residential schools has been simplified, and the practical instruction given is such as may be immediately of use to the pupil when he returns to the reserve after leaving school. . . . Local Indian agents should carefully select the most favourable location for ex-pupils" with "most careful

All Hallows White pupils, 1903-04. (BCARS)

thought given to the future of female pupils" in order that they be "protected as far as possible from temptations to which they are often exposed." Since such temptations were perceived as emanating primarily from contact with White men of "the lowest type," this meant in effect young Indian women's exclusion from any independent role in White society. "If we can keep them on their reserves, in their homes, they will not be in the way of temptation." The problem with boarding schools'curriculums as they had previously existed was quite simply that "the girls are made too smart for the Indian villages."[50]

While raising the per-pupil subsidy, the new policy effectively restricted enrolment in existing residential schools through health regulations requiring more space per child and physical improvements whose cost had to be borne principally by the religious group operating a school. In the provision of new facilities, emphasis was on fairly simple day schools offering a little education to more children at far less cost to the federal government; the goal was less alienation from the culture to which pupils must now return. Any threat of the young Indian successfully entering White society was thus effectively removed.

The changing federal attitude soon rebounded on All Hallows. The school's mother superior had early opposed any change in federal policy, writing to authorities as early as 1901:

Many people urge a shorter period of education and training as being more profitable both to the church and to the state by enabling greater numbers to pass through the school; but seventeen years experience has proved the great unwisdom of this advice.[51]

Yet the school gradually accepted the federal shift away from academic achievement, perhaps in part because a new mother superior arrived from England in 1907 less familiar with the school's traditional objectives. A White pupil has even suggested that she was "second-rate," lacking her predecessor's "knowledge of *human* nature, not so good to judge character."[52]

Up to that time, both the school magazine and the annual report submitted to the Department of Indian Affairs stressed Indian pupils' intellectual growth and academic progress. Thereafter neither did. The school magazine turned its attention to the activities of White pupils, whose social events alone merited four pages in 1908 compared with under a page for those of Indian girls. White pupils studied in increasing numbers for McGill matriculation examinations and external music and drawing examinations, and in 1908 one pupil received the first gold medal awarded in Canada by the Royal Academy of Music.[53] The greater academic accomplishments of White pupils also reflected more general shifts occurring in British Columbia. Expectations concerning mean length of schooling were rising, as evidenced by an increase in the number of public secondary schools across the province from four in 1900 to thirty-one a decade later and forty-nine by the First World War.[54] Thus, even as federal authorities were moving to curtail educational opportunities for young Indians, White Canadians were raising academic standards for their own offspring.

The annual reports submitted by All Hallows to the Department of Indian Affairs similarly turned their attention away from Indian girls' academic accomplishments. In 1904 the report had stressed how Indians "compare very favourably with white children of the same age; in fact, in several examinations where they have had the same papers, the Indian girls have gained the higher marks of the two."[55] Through the first decade of the century virtually all Indian pupils at All Hallows completed the allowable six grades as evidenced by a total during these years of 31 percent enrolled in grades 1-2, 35 percent in grades 3-4, and 34 percent in grades 5-6.[56] From 1907, however, the emphasis in reports to federal authorities shifted to girls' acquisition of practical skills suitable for life on the reserve. The 1908 report highlighted, for instance, the introduction of traditional cedar basket-making as "some practical handicraft which will stand them in good stead when returning to their homes."[57] No further mention was made either of classroom achievement or of pupils' preparation for external music or drawing examinations.

All Hallows accepted changing federal priorities and, publicly at least, the notion of almost inherent inequality between Indians and Whites, inside as well as outside of the classroom. In the years between 1910 and the closure of the "Indian school" in 1918, the proportion of Indian pupils reaching the two upper grades fell sharply to just 18 percent, compared with fully 49 percent enrolled in grades 1-2.[58] No longer was academic achievement a priority.

During these same years the factors leading to the eventual collapse of All Hallows White school were also becoming apparent. The demand for exclusive private schooling responsible for All Hallows' success also encouraged more accessible alternatives, such as Vancouver's Crofton House School "with all city advantages culturally."[59] Yale had never offered much beyond the school itself, one visitor noting the "abandoned stores & dwellings" along "the old main street."[60] Public high schools were also being opened at more and more locations around the province. Then came the severe economic recession beginning in 1913, followed by the onset of war a year later. The fees of White pupils had always subsidized the Indian school and, as numbers of fee-paying White girls fell, so the Indian school's finances became increasingly tenuous.

In 1910 the federal funding policy for Indian schools had been officially changed. More stringent health regulations meant that, in order to receive full funding and so become financially viable, All Hallows had to riase at least $10 000 on its own to construct a new dormitory. Just half of that sum had been acquired by 1917. At that time, an English mission society which had recently established a boys' school at nearby Lytton offered to take over All Hallows' pupils. The sisters, emotionally exhausted from a third of a century of financial hardship in conditions of extreme physical isolation, gratefully accepted the proposal. Their Indian school was closed, followed by its White counterpart two years later in 1920. The sisters returned home to England.[61]

The Life Styles of Former Pupils

In comparison to White pupils at All Hallows, who easily melded into the upper ranks of the dominant society in British Columbia, principally as wives and mothers, the Indian pupils had more complex decisions to make about life styles. Based on the number of Indian pupils annually admitted into grade 1, about 250 girls passed through All Hallows, remaining on average about three years. At a cost certainly of considerable alienation from traditional Indian culture, pupils were indoctrinated into Christianity, made conversant in the English language, given at least basic literacy, and familiarized with European methods of housekeeping and cleanliness. As well, in the words of one young pupil, "we were taught very nicely too [sic] behave ourselves, learn our manners and taught how to behave ourselves when we leave here and go out into the world."[62]

To prepare girls to "go out into the world" was a prime function of the school. From its earliest years, the sisters were committed to pupils becoming, if they so chose, "a very useful, permanent element of the working community of the Province."[63] Their practical training in household duties was intended to permit them to obtain the bottom rung of the White socio-economic order, while their academic achievement gave some girls the possibility of rising further. For young White women of similarly modest background, few employment opportunities existed in the late nineteenth century. The work viewed as most viable for Indian girls was domestic service, which also allowed acquisition of additional familiarity with the dominant culture in semi-sheltered conditions.

As early as 1886, a pupil was sent out "into service" in Victoria. The report two years later was that not only was she performing her job but she had also been persuaded to teach Sunday school at the Anglican cathedral. Soon additional girls were placed into service, "giving satisfaction." In the autumn of 1899, an older pupil recorded being taken by Miss Moody to the provincial exhibition and having the

Two former All Hallows Indian pupils in domestic service, 1902. (Department of Indian Affairs, Annual Report, 1903)

opportunity to visit with Mali and Rosie, both nursemaids in Vancouver. Her one disappointment was not having time to accompany Mali to see the monkeys in Stanley Park, the incident suggesting that Mali, who had left the school two years previous, had already achieved some familiarity with the city. It is clear from the varying bits of evidence which survive that numerous pupils went into domestic service, some of them becoming nursemaids or governesses, and at least one a nurse.[64]

On the other hand, the sisters were always quite content that their pupils should marry and thus "carry the leaven of Christian training into their Indian homes." As early as 1900 the local Indian agent was commenting that girls "who have been educated and who have taken up housekeeping show a marked improvement in their homes as compared with those of their less fortunate neighbours who have never received any education." Other girls married after several years in domestic service or some other occupation, not necessarily to fellow Indians. "Some have married respectable Englishmen and are comfortable settlers." Soon former pupils were sending "their little daughters to be brought up and educated in the old school which sheltered the childhood and girlhood of these young mothers."[65]

Other pupils directly returned home, sometimes to care for motherless siblings or invalid parents. Experience as a pupil-teacher was often put to good use, the mother superior noting in 1901 that "from more than one quarter pleasing testimony has been afforded as to the success of former pupils in carrying on this work after they have returned to their own people." Exemplary was Christina, an early pupil whose mother had died while she was at school. The cleric at Lillooet reported in 1900 that she was "going heart and soul into the teaching of the younger family."

> I spent Tuesday there and examined her pupils during the evening. . . . She has a regular system of marks, and gives conduct marks also, for the time out of school hours. You may well feel encouraged at finding your seed sown in the past, thus being fruit.[66]

For lack of information, it is impossible to be more than suggestive concerning the life styles chosen by All Hallows' pupils during these early years, when federal policy favored assimilation. Their choices were not easy, nor necessarily did they reach their goal. As All Hallows' longtime teacher Althea Moody wrote in 1900:

> It is very probable that the results, of the first efforts in this direction, may not meet with marked success, but "Rome was not built in a day," and no work that is worth doing in this world succeeds all at once. . . . Still it is obvious that a thing has no chance of success until it is at least *begun!*[67]

What is clear is that pupils from All Hallows, as well as from other schools, did for a time retain the option to choose their destiny. The reports of Indian agents in British Columbia reveal that many educated young women entered domestic service, while others became teachers in mission day schools about the province. In 1903 came the assessment that "among the younger Indians English is freely spoken, and their ambition to a greater extent inspires them with a desire to attain that condition which will put them on a level with the white man." The report a year later from the agent in the Lytton area was similar: "They dress well and live more like their white neighbours than was formerly the case. These improvements are more noticeable among those who have attended school." British Columbia's Indian agents agreed with Miss Moody in seeing pupils as a transitional generation:

> The ex-pupils find their education so convenient in their ever-increasing intercourse with the whites that there is no doubt that they will be anxious to see their children in turn acquire an education, and from these children better results may be expected.
>
> It is considered by many that the ultimate destiny of the Indian will be to lose his identity as an Indian, so that he will take his place fairly and evenly beside his white brother. It is only by systematically building from one generation to another that this will be accomplished. The ex-pupils merely form the second link in a chain between barbarism and civilization. Some of them are married and have children attending the schools, but they will only be the third link.[68]

However, that third link was not to be.

All Hallows' acquiescence to the federal shift away from assimilation paralleled its de-emphasis on academic achievement. In 1907 concern was expressed for the first time over "the dangers and temptations to which the Indian girl is specially exposed in our great cities." Increasingly, pupils' aspirations were directed homeward rather than outward toward the larger society. Not only was basket-making introduced; pupils were now taught when doing laundry not how to use appliances available if going into domestic service but rather "to make use of such simple, homely contrivances as they would be likely to have to use in after-life, as, for instance, boiling their clothes in coal-oil tins to which wooden handles have been attached." In 1912 came almost a verbal sigh of relief that "very few, as a rule," were choosing to go into domestic service. A year later, the admission was voiced that only those "who had no homes, have lately been placed out in service," for we "prefer, when possible, to send them home."[69] Pupils from All Hallows, like young Indians across Canada, had lost their freedom of action.

With the closing of All Hallows came another blow affecting many lives. For some girls, the school had been the only home they ever knew, for most of them it remained a centre of permanence to which they would periodically return and be refreshed. As a visiting English cleric observed, All Hallows "has produced amongst the pupils a deep spirit of loyalty, equally towards their teachers and their Alma Mater."[70] Numerous girls visited each Christmas and Prize Day, and many were regular correspondents. While the latter exchange continued, in some cases for decades after the school's closure, the living link disappeared. Not only was direct physical contact made impossible, but educational aspirations for many daughters were quashed.

Conclusion

During the third of a century that All Hallows was in existence, 1884-1920, separation and inequality became the norm for young Indians not only at that school but across Canada. The Anglican church under whose auspices All Hallows was founded had believed in Indians' equal potential given educational opportunities. The school's concern that pupils utilize their intellectual capacity as well as obtain work skills coincided with the policy of assimilation advocated by the Department of Indian Affairs during the late nineteenth century.

Despite a difficult transition to school life, many Indian pupils achieved much within a short time period, and some at least were able to reconcile differences between Indian and White cultures within their own minds. A number ventured out into the dominant society and, while only scattered evidence survives, it seems fairly clear that a few at least chose to remain there either through occupation or marriage. Certainly, All Hallows influenced lifestyles, as is evident by the many who maintained contact and those who sent daughters back to the school. Most importantly, through the turn of the century the schooling provided at All Hallows maximized the opportunity for educated young Indians to choose their destiny rather than having it imposed upon them.

Federal parsimony together with White refusal to accept educated young Indians into the dominant socio-economic order reordered All Hallows' priorities. The school's orginal difficulty in securing federal funding makes clear that the Department of Indian Affairs was never overly generous with its support. If assistance had come earlier, no "Canadian School" would have existed. Even with federal support, All Hallows was still expected to obtain additional funding to cover part of its expenses. In short, no federal expectaton had ever existed that the conditions of Indian education ought as a matter of course to be made maximumly conducive to achieving its goal of assimilation. For that reason alone, assimilation was never given a fair chance of success.

Much more importantly, the possible success of assimilation very rapidly became of itself an undesirable outcome. White Canadians did not want young Indians entering their socio-economic order, even at the bottom rung. That such a threat was perceived is perhaps the best evidence that the assimilation policy was having an effect. To what extent Indians would have been successful in White society, if the federal policy in favor of assimilation had been allowed to continue, is of course impossible to know. Contemporaries in British Columbia familiar with conditions among that province's Indians believed not only that change was occurring, but also that its effect would cumulate with each successive generation. The principal opposition to assimilation did not come from Aboriginal peoples but rather from the dominant society. First came the demand for physical separation in the classroom, then more general unwillingness to allow educated young Indians into the work force.

What is certain is that the federal reversal of policy in 1910 removed even young Indians' option to enter the larger society with all its discrimination and prejudice. Their potential to mitigate some of that prejudice through the example of their own lives was also taken away. Young Indians were forced back onto the reserve, and the dominant society was for a generation and more left comforted in believing that Indians were after all, inferior. As one White pupil at All Hallows observed, only at a school reunion in the late 1950s did she finally meet any of the school's Indian girls and discover that "the rules of the old days were rather silly."

Notes

1. The Sisters of All Hallows at Ditchingham, Norfolk, and especially Sister Violet, have generously provided both hospitality and access to the order's archives. I am also grateful to Garth Walker, for assistance in locating materials.

2. Department of Indian Affairs [DIA], *Annual Report* [*AR*], 1900, 132-33, and 1910, 273: and Duncan R. Scott, "Indian Affairs. 1867-1912," in *Canada and Its Provinces*, ed. Adam Shortt (Toronto: Edinburgh University Press, 1914), 616.

3. DIA, *AR*, 1872, 12.

4. The history of the diocese is recounted in Lyndon Grove, *Pacific Pilgrims* (Vancouver: Fflorbez Publications, 1979).

5. Herbert H. Gowen. *Church Work in British Columbia* (London: Longmans, Green and Co., 1899), 113-17.

6. *Ibid.*, 85-89, 122-24, 137-45; also *New Westminster Quarterly Paper* [*NWQP*] 6 (November 1885): 7-13.

7. *NWQP* 2 (October 1884): 9,19: and *Sister Violet, All Hallows, Ditchingham: The Story of an East Anglican Community* (Oxford: Becket Publications, 1983), 37.

8. *Churchman's Gazette* [*CG*] (March 1884): 331 and 335; Gown, *Church Work*, 132-34; and *NWQP* 2 (Oct. 1884): 9, 18 and *NWQP* 4 (April 1885): 23-27.

9. See *CG*, February 1891, 794-801; August 1888, 540; February 1889, Supplement, 580; February 1890, 5; *NWQP* 7 (June 1886): 11-13; *NWQP* 9 (Nov. 1888): 33; and *NWPQ* 67 (Mar. 1896): last page; and *All Hallows in the West* [school magazine, henceforth *AHW*] 2, 3 (Christmas 1900): 63-64.

10. DIA, *AR*, 1885: 123; *NWQP* 10 (November 1888): 25; and *East and West* [the order's magazine, published in England], All Saints 1888, 34-35.

11. *NWQP* 11(March 1889): 27-28; *CG*, August 1888, 539; Diocese of New Westminster, *Monthly Record* 4 (December 1889): 5; and DIA, *AR*, 1896, xxxvii.

12. *NWQP* 11 (March 1889): 28; 65 (May 1895): 7; *CG* August 1888: 540; and *CG* supplement February 1889: 580; Februrary 1890, 5; *CG* July 1890, 725; August 1890, 730; and, February 1891, 794 and 801; Diocese of New Westminster, *Monthly Record* 12 (August 1890), 6; Over the Rockies, April 1897, 15, and July 1900, 24; and Work for the Far West [hereafter WFFW], 1909, 18.

13. Interview with Mrs. Lorraine Pindemoss, Vancouver, 12 February 1980. Lists of White pupils included in AHW 1, no. 2 (Michelmas 1899): 20-21; 1, no. 3 (Christmas 1899): 41-42; 2, no. 1 (Ascension 1900): 9; 2, no. 2 (Michaelmas 1900): 31; 2, no. 3 (Christmas 1900): 56; 3, no. 1 (Ascension 1901): 12-13; 3, no. 3 (Christmas 1901): 76; 6, no. 8 (Ascension 1906): 519-20; 8, no. 11 (Whitsun 1908: 74-75; 8, no. 12 (All Saints 1908): 100-01; no no. (Christmas 1909): 16; no. 13 (Easter 1909): 15-16; and no. 15 Canadian number (Midsummer 1911): 17-18.

14. Letter of Charles Mair to George Denison, Kelowna, 5 Dec. 1892. I am grateful to Dr. Duane Thomson of Okanagan College for access to this correspondence, in his possession.

15. Interview with Mrs. Doris Lazenby, North Vancouver, 4 Feb. 1980, and WFFW, no month, 1908, 18.

16. *NWQP* 65 (May 1895): 8.

17. Interview by Imbert Orchard with Mrs. Clara Clare, Yale, 1964, accession no. 400, Aural History Division, British Columbia Archives and Records Service [BCARS].

18. *East and West*, All Saints 1897, 516, and All Saints 1898, 564-65; and *WFFW*, 1901, 15.

19. DIA, *AR*, 1900, 254; 1903, 271; 1904, 236; and 1911, 381.

20. Interview with Mrs. Lavinia Brown, Lytton, 4 October 1983; and Clare interview. For the role of local clerics, see also *AHW* 1, 2 (Michelmas 1899): 23.

21. *AHW* 2, 1 (Ascension 1900): 18-20; 3, no. 1 (Ascension 1901): 4, 19-20; Indian number, no. 1 (Easter 1911): 8; 8, no. 11 (Whitsun 1908): 78; and 1, no. 3 (Christmas 1899): 36; *East and West* (Winter 1893): 240-41; and *NWQP*, no. 4 (April 1885): 25-27. Until All Hallows' last years. Indian pupils had only a Christian first name, given at baptism. See *East and West* (Winter 1893): 237-40.

22. "Record of Indian Girls [at All Hallows and St. George's Schools], 1910 to 1922," in possession of Rev. A.W. Harding, Lytton Hospital, Lytton. James Redford has determined that at two other British Columbia residential schools, Methodist Coqualeetza and Catholic Kuyper Island, both coeducational, fully 45 and 50 per cent of pupils during these years had lost one or both parents. See his "Attendance at Indian Residential Schools in British Columbia, 1890-1920," *BC Studies* 44 (Winter 1979/80): 48.

23. DIA, *AR*, 1895, xxiii; 1900, 256, 290; 1903, 317; 1907, 259; 1908, 270; 1910, 334,340; 1911, 378; 1912, 295; 1913, 407; and "Record of Indian Girls," entries 157 and 166.

24. *CG*, April 1888: 502; August 1890: 729; Diocese of New Westminster, *Monthly Record* 11 (July 1890): 6; and "Yale's Mission School," *Vancouver Daily World*, 5 July 1890.

25. *CG*, Feb. 1891: 794-95, and August 1891: 842.

26. *NWQP* 67 (March 1896): 19; *East and West*, Winter 1895: 375; *WFFW*, 1897: 14; and *AHW* 2, no. 3 (Christmas 1900): 63; 3, no. 3 (Christmas 1901): 72.

27. Interviews with Mrs. Lily Rogers, Vancouver, 7 March 1980; Mrs. Mary Hickman, Chilliwack, 17 December 1983; and Lazenby, Pindermoss, and Clare interview.

28. Brown interview: AHW 6, no. 8 (Ascension 1906): 544-46, and Indian number, no. 1 (Easter 1911): 25; and DIA, *AR*, 1896, 593-94; 1911, 390; and 1913, 404, 409.

29. *East and West*, 1886-1919; Sister Violet, *All Hallows*, 25.

30. Victoria Orphans Home. *AR*, 1886, quoted in Patricia T. Rooke and R.L. Schnell, *Discarding the Asylum: From Child Rescue to the Welfare State in English-Canada* (New York: University Press of America, 1983), 165.

31. DIA, *AR*, 1896, 394.

32. *CG*, Aug. 1890: 729; Diocese of New Westminster, *Monthly Record* 14 (October 1890): 3; *NWQP* 65 (May 1895): 7; *WFFW*, 1897: 15; AHW 2, no. 3 (Christmas 1900): 64; and DIA, *AR*, 1909, 409; 1910, 516; and 1913, 532.

33. Hickman interview.

34. *AHW* 3, no. 3 (Christmas 1901): 71-73; 6, no. 8 (Ascension 1906): 518 and 539; 8, no. 12 (All Saints 1908): 91; and Indian number, no. 1 (Easter 1911): 18-19.

35. DIA, *AR*, 1895, xxii; 1891, xii; and 1892, xiii-xiv. Also 1896, xxxvii.

36. *CG*, (August 1887: 433; and April 1888: 502.

37. DIA, *AR*, 1894-97. Only schools in existence long enough for pupils to have reached the upper grades were included in the calculations.

38. *WFFW*, 1897: 14.

39. Diocese of New Westminster, *Monthly Record* 13 (September 1890): last page; and *WFFW*, 1901: 14. Letters were not edited for publication, and many girls did have trouble with English grammar; see *AHW* 1, no. 2 (Michelmas 1899): 27-28. Pride in Indian pupils' academic accomplishments is also evident in "All Hallows School." *Vancouver Daily World*, 3 August 1899.

40. *NWQP* 65 (May 1895): 7-8; *WFFW*, 1896: 13; *East and West*, 1894: 308; and *AHW* 1, no. 2 (Michelmas 1899): 25, and 2, no. 3 (Christmas 1900): 64.

41. DIA, *AR*, 1906, 442-44. See also *AHW* 1, no. 2 (Michelmas 1899): 30; 2, no. 1 (Ascension 1900): 17-20; 3, no. 1 (Ascension 1901): 20-21; Indian number, no. 1 (Easter 1911): 22: *East and West,* Winter 1894: 307 and 310; and *Sh'Atjinkujin: Parts of the Communion Service of the Church of England, Privately Printed for the Use of the Lower Fraser Indians in the All Hallows' Mission Chapel,* Yale, B.C. (London: Darling & Son, 1894), copies of which are in BCARS.

42. See, for example, *AHW* 1, no. 2 (Michelmas 1899): 21-22; 1, no. 3 (Christmas 1899): 41; 2, no. 2 (Michelmas 1900): 33-34; and Indian number, no. 1 (Easter 1911): 17 and 25.

43. *AHW* 2, no. 3 (Christmas 1900): 66-67; and DIA, *AR*, 1884, 104. For other, less introspective letters, see *AHW* 1, no. 2 (Michelmas 1899): 23-24, and 2, no. 2 (Michelmas 1900): 35-36.

44. Inspector of Indian Agencies to Deputy Superintendent General, 4 June 1904, in DIA, School Files, vol. 6001.

45. D.J. Hall, "Clifford Sifton and Canadian Indian Administration, 1896-1905," *Prairie Forum* 2 (1977): 128. See also his *Clifford Sifton,* vol. 1: *The Young Napoleon, 1861-1900* (Vancouver: University of British Columbia Press, 1981), 127-28 and 268-71. Sifton was also minister of the interior; its budget nearly quintupled during his tenure, while that of Indian affairs rose less than 30 per cent. The national budget doubled. On the policy shift, see E. Brian Titley, "Duncan Campbell Scott and Indian Education Policy," in *An Imperfect Past: Education and Society in Canadian History,* ed. J.D. Wilson (Vancouver: CSCI, U.BC, 1984), 141-53.

46. DIA, *AR*, 1894, xxi; 1897, xxvii; and 1898, xxvii. For evidence that the shift came directly from Sifton, see Hall, "Clifford Sifton," 13, 3n 32.

47. Canada, House of Commons, *Debates,* 1897, col. 4076, 14 June 1897, quoted in Hall, "Clifford Sifton," 134. Widespread fear of economic compettition is suggested by the assurance contained in a 1901 brief to the Department of Indian Affairs offering to assist young Indians' assimilation into White society: "Nothing that we propose doing for the Indian is going to injure the propects of the white labourer." See Katherine Hughes on behalf of Association for Befriending Indian School Graduates to DIA, 15 September 1901, in DIA, School Files, vol. 6001.

48. See DIA, *AR*, 1911, 388; 1900, xxxiii; 1901, xxvii-xxix; and 1904, xxvii and xxix. No evidence exists in the school correspondence files of the DIA that Indians themselves were ever consulted about the proposed change in direction.

49. *Debates,* 1904, cols. 6946-56, 18 July 1904, quoted in Hall, "Clifford Sifton," 134.

50. DIA, *AR*, 1903, xxvii; and 1905, xxxiii.

51. Scott, "Indian Affairs," 616; and DIA, *AR*, 1909, xxxiv; 1910, 273-75; and 1911, 337.

52. DIA, *AR*, 1901, 415.

53. "Notes of reaction-elaborated" in the Rev. Heber Greene papers. British Columbia Provincial Synod Archives, Anglican Church of Canada, Vancouver School of Theology, UBC.

54. *AHW* 8, no. 12 (All Saints 1908), 96.

55. British Columbia, Department of Education, Annual Report, 1915, 20; and F.Henry Johnson, *A History of Public Education in British Columbia* (Vancouver: University of British Columbia Press, 1964), 61. Totals include both high schools and superior schools offering instruction through grade 10.

56. DIA, *AR*, 1904, 402. See aslo 1905.

57. DIA, *AR*, 1908, 416

58. A similar decline to 18 per cent occured at residential schools across the province. Even then the proportion was somewhat higher than at residential schools throughout Canada. In the years 1910-18, 53 percent across Canada were enrolled in grades 1-2, just 14 per cent in grades 5-6.

59. "Notes of reaction-elaborated" in Greene papers.

60. Typescript of Bishop George Hills' diary, 8 July 1892 entry, in British Columbia Provincial Synod Archives.55. By comparison across British Columbia just over a fifth of all young Indians enrolled in a residential school reached the two upper grades.

61. *East and West,* All Saints 1911: 2033; Winter 1912: 30; Winter 1913: 76; Winter 1914: 19; and All Saints 1917: 26-27.

62. *AHR* 1, no. 2 (Michelmas 1899): 27.

63. *East and West,* All Saints 1890: 33; Diocese of New Westminster, *Monthly Record* 14 (October 1890): 3; and DIA, *AR,* 1898, 390, and 1900, 421.

64. *East and West,* All Saints 1888: 36; Easter 1889: 31; All Saints 1889: 31; All Saints 1896: 466; All Saints 1897: 515-16; *CG* August 1888: 539; August 1891: 843; *NWQP* 9 (March 1888): 15; and *AHW* 1, 3 (Christmas 1899): 47-48.

65. *NWQP* 65 (March 1895): 8; *East of West,* Winter 1895: 380, and Winter 1903: 800; and DIA, *AR,* 1896, xxxviii; 1903, 423; 1900, 255; 1908, 448; 1905, 367; and 1910, 517.

66. DIA, *AR,* 1901, 413; *East of West,* Winter 1899: 600; and *AHW* 1, 1 (Ascension 1900): 13.

67. *AHW* 2, 2 (Michelmas 1900): 41-42.

68. DIA, *AR,* 1908, 270; 1903, 317; 1904, 236; 1911, 374; and 1913, 400. Rolf Knight argues that "the pinnacle of Indian labour and entrepreneurship within the broader economy [of British Columbia] was reached during the period 1890 to WW1." See his *Indians at Work: An Informal History of Native Indian Labour in British Columbia, 1858-1930* (Vancouver: New Star Books, 1978), 185.

69. DIA, *AR,* 1907, 407; 1910, 516; 1912, 501; and 1913, 532. A contemporary has suggested that the change came much earlier, writing in 1901 that schools "seem to have withdrawn their encouragement for the outward movement" of female pupils into domestic service. See Hughes brief.

70. DIA, *AR,* 1903, 424; 1906, 443; 1912, 583; 1913, 532; *AHW,* Indian number, no. 1 (Easter 1911): 28-29; and Clare interview.

18

Growing Up British in British Columbia: The Vernon Preparatory School 1914-1946

Jean Barman[1]

In 1967 the final report of the Royal Commission on Bilingualism and Biculturalism objected "in the strongest terms" to the "common practice in Canada to restrict the term 'ethnic' to groups which are neither British nor French."[2] Yet Canada's largest ethnic group, the British, has continued to be ignored by social scientists interested in understanding the Canadian mosaic. To dismiss or discount the existence of ethnicity among British immigrants is both illogical, in its summary denial to one group of attributes granted all others, and careless of the realities of the past.

Using evidence from the history of private education in British Columbia, this essay argues that ethnicity clearly existed among British immigrants. The term ethnic, as used here, is derived from Leo Driedger's definition that "territorial, institutional, and cultural factors . . . tend to reinforce each other, so that when individuals of a given ethnic group identify with their ingroup along these dimensions, they tend to remain more distinctive."[3] This is precisely what occured among British immigrant groups to British Columbia who settled near each other and through private schooling, as well as clubs and close personal relationships, maintained a separate cultural identity within the area and the province well into the second generation.

Since the mid-nineteenth century, the private boarding school has been a fundamental mechanism transferring across generations British "official" culture: education first at a preparatory school and from about age thirteen at a public, i.e., private, school has enabled the offspring of the middle and upper class, whether at home or abroad, in Perth or Buenos Aires, to grow up "British."[4] Boarding schools on the British model were established early in Canada, especially in Ontario.[5] Private boarding schools in British Columbia were not, however, extensions of their eastern Canadian counterparts, which would have been the case had they been an Anglo-Canadian phenomenon moving into more recently settled areas. Rather, boarding schools in British Columbia were direct replications of English institutions, founded, as one prospectus emphasized, to facilitate growing up British in British Columbia:

> For some time a demand has existed in British Columbia for a school run on the lines of the great English and Scotch Public Schools. Parents who want to send their boys to England to get what is usually called English Public School Education are now [1923] faced with serious obstacles – both fees and travelling costs have increased tremendously. . . . These obstacles will be overcome by a school founded in B.C. for boys thirteen-eighteen and on English Public School lines.[6]

As with other immigrant groups in Canada, British settlers in British Columbia turned to education to maintain the culture they knew, in this case the British "official" culture of the middle and upper class.

Little is known about the precise nature of private education in British Columbia. Schools have until very recently been exempt from public regulation and the internal records of the separate institutions have not generally been accessible to outsiders. Fortunately, the remaining papers of the Vernon Preparatory School, which began in the Okanagan Valley in 1914 and closed finally in 1972, are available.[7] They leave no doubt but that the maintenance of British ethnicity, of a British cultural identity, was the most powerful constant determining the formation, location, objectives and acquisition of clientele.

Formation

Like most private schools in early British Columbia, the Vernon Preparatory School was an independent venture by a single British immigrant.[8] The Rev. Austin C. Mackie came to Canada late in 1913 specifically to start a school after learning from his nephew, who had visited British Columbia the previous year, that "high class" education was in short supply. Gordon Mackie had written home to England telling of the rapid agricultural development taking place in the interior of the province. British settlers were arriving in great numbers into the Okanagan Valley, and "a large percentage of them are English all of the better class," many even "English ladies & gentlemen."[9] He had spoken to several recent immigrants to the Vernon area about the problem of schooling – to "Mr. Bird, an old Rugby boy who at present sends his boys to govt. schools but wants something better & can't afford Victoria," and to Mr. Richardson, "an old Harrow boy with a large family the eldest of whom just left Harrow before they came out 2 years ago" and who had sent his younger sons to University College School in Victoria. Gordon Mackie summed up:

> There is a large class of parents in the Valley who cannot afford to send their boys all the way to Victoria or else don't like to have them so far from home & I feel certain that if a small high class school were started in some central place – Vernon or Kelowna – there would not be the slightest difficulty in getting all the boys one wanted. . . . Everyone I have spoken to recognizes the fact that the education of their sons is going to be one of the difficulties of the future.[10]

This was all the challenge Rev. Mackie needed. For a decade after graduation from Cambridge University he had held a succession of rather monotonous positions as tutor and cleric while trying unsuccessfully to secure an administrative position in education. The problem lay as much with English society as with Rev. Mackie. Without connections or private means – which, as a younger son in a large Anglican clerical family, he simply did not possess – ambition and intelligence did not assure success. Now there suddenly appeared a chance to be his own man in a newer, less rigid society and Rev. Mackie was determined to make a success of the unexpected. Within a month of his arrival in Canada he had issued a prospectus announcing the opening of a school. His vision of the future was clear in its first lines:

The school will be conducted, with necessary modifications, on the lines of an English Preparatory School; its aims will be to give boys an all-round education fitting them for an English public school or for Canadian life, and to train them to be God-fearing, well-disciplined, clean-minded and honourable.[11]

The prospectus included as referees two English bishops and two Earls, names especially chosen, as Rev. Mackie later admitted, to attract "all the decayed nobility and disillusioned gentry in the neighbourhood." At the same time he was already aware that Anglo-Canada was not Britain and added the names of the local member of the provincial assembly and the Anglican rector "as a sop to Cerberus vis., democratic parents."[12]

The Vernon Preparatory School, intended for boys seven to fourteen, opened in January 1914 with five pupils but within a half decade almost reached its full complement of forty to fifty boys. Rev. Mackie soon convinced his brother and sister-in-law, Hugh and Gracie Mackie, to join in the school. Hugh Mackie had trained in England as a solicitor and, in his mother's words, was even more than his older brother "fired with a desire to try his fortune in the new country."[13] The three Mackies ran the Vernon Preparatory School jointly from 1916 through 1946, during which time they never deviated from the goals of the original prospectus. In 1945, on the eve of retirement, Rev. Mackie summed up their philosophy:

V.P.S. has always been run on the lines of an English Preparatory School with results apparently acceptable both to parents and boys. We believe the English Private School System to be the finest in the world. We are unblushing and unrepentent champions of the "Old School Tie" and all for which it stands. We strongly hold that the future welfare of Canada depends on a steady inflow of settlers of British stock and British traditions to enrich her national life.[14]

Location

The location chosen for the Vernon Preparatory School, a secluded valley in the area known as the Coldstream, about six kilometres southeast of Vernon, symbolized the Mackies' desire to maintain distance between the school and all outside influences, including those of Anglo-Canada. Rev. Mackie described the setting:

There was a 10-acre orchard of good commercial varieties of apple, pear and prune; the Coldstream Creek formed its southern boundary and along its banks were a dense growth of pine, fir birch and cotton trees of good size. It lay off the main road and was hemmed in by orchards, but there were only two residences within sound or sight and easy access was had to the almost unlimitable range-land and forest to the south. Indeed the situation for a school was ideal.[15]

Isolation was essential to the school's success, for:

A School is a little world of its own – self-contained – with the same strange mixture of character & talents we find elsewhere – but with this difference. The citizens are in a plastic form like moist clay which can be moulded according to the will of the potter into vessels of beauty or usefulness or both.[16]

Delivering a sermon to his students in 1922, Rev. Mackie built on the relationship of the school to its physical environment:

> A schoolmaster is like an orcharist; his trees are his boys and tho [sic] some may wither & others be backward & stunted in growth; others just miss the full measure of health or vigorous growth, some will have deep roots & show beauty of form and symmetry, abundance of foliage and in due time a bounteous harvest.[17]

Former pupils are still aware of how fully the school existed within a context of its own creation. A boy from the early 1920s remembers it as "a world unto itself with all its rules, regulations and shibboleths" and one from a half decade later simply as "a little England."[18] The sense of separation was heightened by the school's economic independence, for most of the food eaten by the boys – from meat, game and fish to fruit and vegetables – was quite visibly being grown or acquired around them. Moreover while students were allowed to roam freely through the hills and valleys surrounding the school on every side, they were not allowed to enter any built-up area, much less Vernon itself; one former student still remembers with nostalgia the little Chinese-run store visible on long walks but nonetheless forbidden, another the tantalizing prospect of being allowed to walk through his father's orchard located near the school but to do no more than wave to his parents in passing.[19]

All the same, the larger environment of the Vernon Preparatory School was just as British as was the school itself. The Coldstream, visited by Gordon Mackie in 1912, was a planned community consciously designed to attract British immigrants of a particular social background. The area took its name from the large ranch purchased by Lord Aberdeen in 1891, shortly before he became Canadian Governor General.[20] The Aberdeens experimented with fruitgrowing on the ranchland and by 1894 were, according to Lady Aberdeen, selling off "fruit-lots" to English settlers "of very good class."[21] The Aberdeens wanted to develop "a really high-class little community" and, for instance, refused to sell land on long-term financing since they feared "many of the Vernon people would take up lots under these terms."[22] According to a contemporary observer of the 1890s, as "English people from the so-called upper classes" arrived to grow fruit, "a distinct exclusive 'social set'" developed, likened by him to "the social life of some Indian station as described by Kipling in 'Plain Tales from the Hills.'"[23]

In the years before the First World War English and Scottish settlers with sufficient means to maintain themselves until trees came into production continued to be enticed into the Coldstream "to shoot bear and catch salmon, and incidentally to grow a few apples."[24] Coldstream was incorporated as a separate municipality in 1906, and four years later its residents established a private club on nearby Kalamalka Lake which would be the focus of British society for the next several decades.[25] As late as 1937 a full-page advertisement for the Coldstream was headed "The delights of Rural England – at one-tenth the cost" and described the area as one "where Anglo-Saxon settlement is thoroughly predominant and has been for 40 years."[26]

The immediate neigbors of the Vernon Preparatory School exemplified the Coldstream settlers. Across the creek lived Major W.R. Grieve, educated at Rugby and Cambridge, who had immigrated to the Coldstream in 1906 after first trying his hand at sheep in New Zealand.[27] Just a little further away was Captain Thomas Brayshaw. After attending Giggleswick, a private school in Yorkshire headed by his father, he had worked his way out to the Coldstream via positions as a draughtsman in a Newcastle shipyard and as an insurance salesman in Vancouver. Capt. Brayshaw, who was well-known for his angling ability and his wooden lifesize carvings of salmon, supplemented his orchard income during the 1930s by teaching mathematics at the Mackies' school.[28] Also close friends and neighbors were the Kidstons, whose elegant house on Kalamalka Lake boys from school were allowed to visit as a special Saturday treat. John Kidston, educated at Loretto, a leading Scottish public school, had married the daughter of a wealthy Glasgow shipbuilder and gone out to Calcutta with a life insurance company. In London on leave in 1903, he fell for the assurances of the Agent-General for British Columbia that the future lay with fruit and brought his family out to the Coldstream, "complete with cook, nurse and gardener."[29] The sons of the Grieves, Brayshaws and Kidstons attended the Vernon Preparatory School almost as a matter of course.

Beyond the Coldstream lay the town of Vernon with which the school and the British settlers in its vicinity maintained a limited and ambivalent relationship. From 1892, when the town of 600 became a railroad terminus and was incorporated, Vernon grew rapidly as the administrative centre of land development in the northern Okanagan Valley.[30] The attitude of the Aberdeens toward Vernon residents attests to a certain tension having existed between the growing British immigrant community and the merchants and professionals of the towns, considered "mere 'colonials'" or at best, "Canadians."[31] While the life of the town, which "up to this time had been very free and easy and unspoiled by any sense of 'class,'" became noticeably more rigid, townspeople were never accepted into the society of the Coldstream, which remained a closed ethnic community.[32] The Kalamalka Country Club was, for instance, largely off limits to Vernon residents through the 1930s.[33]

At the same time, the Vernon Preparatory School and the town of Vernon maintained a mutually beneficial business relationship. The Mackie family made a point of purchasing all their needs in Vernon, and several merchants regularly advertised in its magazine as purveyors to the school "By Special Appointment."[34] Moreover, the school held a certain attraction to leading townspeople: the sons of the first two bank managers, one from a London shipowning family and the other a Quebec native of Scottish ancestry, were both students, as were the sons of the doctor, the dentist, the postmaster, the magistrate and the public notary.[35]

The rapid growth of Vernon in the decades before the First World War reflected the boom in fruit-growing which swept the valleys of the Okanagan and the Kootenays. The development companies that divided up ranchland and promised water for irrigation normally directed their advertising toward prospective purchasers in a specific place, such as the Canadian prairies or southern England.[36] As a result, settlements, described by an early visitor as "little excluded communities, shut off until yesterday from the outer world," frequently had strong ethnic and even class homogeneity.[37] The groups of British settlers – "those who have, by force of circumstance, been drawn together on the isolated fringes of an Empire in the making," to use the words of one such pioneer whose son attended the Vernon Preparatory School – were determined to retain their culture.[38] In Lavington, an area on the other side of Vernon from the Coldstream, a group of families decided early on that the "government school" would not do and, after hiring a young Irish woman to teach the basics, packed off their sons to the Mackies. Why? As one of these boys explained, "They didn't want their children losing their accents and mixing with ordinary family types in the district."[39]

Principles and Practices

As the orginal prospectus made clear, Rev. Mackie had decided even before the Vernon Preparatory School opened that it would be run "on the lines of an English Preparatory School." The school's location, both its isolated rural setting and its proximity to a British ethnic community, was deliberately chosen. More importantly, the Vernon Preparatory School could successfully replicate its British counterparts precisely because this was the education families wanted for their sons in order to maintain their ethnicity, their cultural identity, into the next generation. Most fathers were products of the same British boarding school tradition as were the Mackies. Both brothers ahad attended St. John's, Leatherhead, a "very moderate" public school near London intended to give sons of Anglican clergymen an education equivalent to that of the "great schools."[40] The Vernon Preparatory School was consciously patterned after St. John's and consequently after the "great schools" whose principles of education had originated in the first half of the nineteenth century.[41] Building on their original definition by Thomas Arnold of Rugby and their elaboration by such headmasters as Edward Thring of Uppingham, these principles were so monolithic by the last decade of the century, when the Mackies were school boys, that they formed the basis of British "official" culture. Almost all middle and upper class boys, even some of the girls, passed through a similar boarding school experience and emerged with virtually identical beliefs, values and ideas about the nature of society.

At the centre lay belief in Christianity as compounded by Social Darwinism. In the words of Rev. Mackie, as preached to his students from the school chapel, "life itself is a battle," but among the "laws of God" are "victory through struggle" and the "survival of the fittest."[42] From hence derived the awesome responsibility of educators to ensure that the young became not only believing Christians but the fittest possible Christians. It was for the schools to be the "exponents of true X^n [sic] manliness," the developers of "character along the right lines."[43] On the one hand, each boy must "grow up to be a Christian gentleman" imbued with "the ideals of courtesy, self-effacement, chivalry toward women, honour in business and a sense of noblesse oblige."[44] As expressed by the fictional Squire Brown in ruminating about the schooldays of his son Tom, "If he'll turn out a brave helpful truth-telling Englishman, that's all I want."[45] On the other hand, each boy must be properly prepared for the "fierce and endless struggle" of this life, able to:

play the Game of Life in the true sporting spirit, struggling to our feet as often as we are knocked down, giving forth every ounce of all that is best in us until the final whistle blows and we leave the ranks of the Church Militant here on earht & join the Church Expectant in the Great Beyond.[47]

The importance of producing "Christian gentlemen" fit to "play the Game of Life" explained much about the nature of the school experience. A residential environment was essential, such as that at the Vernon Preparatory School, which the Rev. Mackie likened to "a little world of its own" in which the potter moulded and the orcharist pruned. The loneliness which resulted from separation from family at age eight or ten had long been part of the British education tradition. It was no stranger to the Mackies, as evidenced by a letter written in the 1890s by a very young Austin, sent off to school for the first time, to his brother Hugh, still at home:

Only 5 weeks and 3 days more and I shall be once more at home, won't it be fine. . . . We shall be able to go to the minnow farm shall we not for the holidays. Oh! I wish they would hurry up & come don't you, only 38 days more never mind.[48]

Vernon Preparatory School choir, 1940, with the Rev. A.C. Mackie and Grace Mackie in the centre.

Separation was thought to enhance family relationships, for it taught the boys "to learn to love your parents & your homelife as you have never loved them before & as you never could learn to love them till you left them."[49] The central purpose of living in a boarding environment away from the family ten months of the year was, however, more longterm.

You have also come here to mix with other boys of your age & station in life, to make innocent and happy friendships, to have the corners rubbed off by contact with others, to learn to give & take & to subordinate you own wishes to the wishes of others, to be helpful by helping others, to learn to be independent & to do things for yourselves instead of expecting others to do them for you, to be patient towards the weak, the champion of the oppressed, to be courteous toward ladies, to be respectful towards your seniors – in a word to be a gentleman.[50]

Deeply interwoven with learning to "play the Game of Life" was the strong emphasis on games and organized activity which characterized every British boarding school. All boys at the Vernon Prepartory School played cricket in the spring and summer, soccer in the autumn, and went on "grinds," closely marked out runs, when the weather was inclement. Rev. Mackie explained the significance of games in a sermon he gave his students:

> The importance of regular, organized, supervised games cannot be exaggerated; it is on the playing field that a boy learns to play the game of life by giving & taking hard knocks, & nasty falls without whimpering or losing his temper, by putting the honour of his side before his own by scorning to win except by fair means, by distaining to employ mean or underhand tricks such as tripping or fouling, by taking defeat cheerfully like a good sportsman & by being modest in victory; all this is what is meant by team work and it is one of the most valuable lessons a boy can learn. Therefore, I say play your games to the very limit of your powers, not of neccessity & under compulsion but because they will give you a sound healthy body without which you are little likely to have either a sound mind or a healthy soul.[51]

It is not by chance that tucked among the well-thumbed sermon notebooks of Rev. Mackie still lies a yellowed copy of the Edwardian poet Henry Newbolt's "Vita Lampada," whose every stanza ends, "Play up! Play up! and play the game!"[52]

The rhythm of life at the Vernon Prepartory School was carefully structured along the touchpoints which had worked for generations of British school boys – early rising, cold showers, daily chapel, rote learning, immersion in the classics, corporal punishment, mandatory games, and spartan life style. The traditional holidays of the British boarding schools, such as Shrove Tuesday and Guy Fawkes' Day, were carefully observed. Performance and punishment were closely linked, lying and working below individual capacity being the worst offenses:

> We have made it a rule here that very little if any punishment is meted out to a boy who, having done wrong, owns up to it; when a boy does wrong & lies about it he is punished not for doing wrong but for telling a lie.[53]

> I urge all of you to make up your minds to work your very hardest, for the lazy boy makes his school-days miserable for himself and his teachers.[54]

Prefects chosen by the Mackies from among the eldest boys not only helped to maintain order but deliberately recreated at school the concept of responsible leadership within a hierarchical and deferential society. These leaders had specific instructions:

> Your duty is to study the character of the boys & learn to handle them wisely – never driving when you can lead – nor using your authority in a highhanded way, but proving yourselves examples.[55]

> Make your office easy by keeping yourselves somewhat aloof from your charges – let them learn to respect you & you will have no difficulty in leading them.[56]

While the Mackies believed totally in the British system of education, they were not unaware that most of their students would "play the Game of Life" in Anglo-Canada. The advantages the Mackies perceived in the new country were not minimized: for instance, unlike in Britain, "no one is thought the worse of because he has chosen to work with his hands."[57] Rev. Mackie's Sunday sermons touched several times on "the adventures of the men who opened up the unknown places on this continent – of Simon Fraser, of Alexander MacKenzie & even of our own valley – heroes like Ellis, Fortune & others," and on the opportunities still awaiting the younger generation to be "explorers in the uncharted unknown regions of this country."[58] In identifying "the many fine features of Canada" in 1945, Rev. Mackie pointed to,

> the beauty of its hills & valleys, its wide open spaces awaiting settlers to cultivate it, the hospitality of its people & above all, the atmosphere of sturdy independence & freedom, a freedom which cannot be matched even in the Old Land, the fountain & champion of freedom & independence.[59]

Hugh Mackie, who of the two, kept the boys much more in touch with current events in Canada and elsewhere, summed up what mattered to him quite simply as "the sunshine and outdoor life of the Okanagan Valley."[60]

Vernon Preparatory School cricket team, 1942. (BCARS)

By bringing references to Anglo-Canada – particularly its physical dimension as reflected in the beauty of the Okanagan Valley – into the life of the school, the Mackies seriously strengthened the purposes for which the school was established. Assuming, as has been concluded about the English boarding school, that the Vernon Preparatory School also provided "a certain class confidence, a confidence that their pupils should and could lead, and the useful disciplines and stability that go with self-control and conformity," then the added sense of place which such references gave must have made it even more possible for students to succeed in Anglo-Canada.[61]

There was never any question but that the boys should push themselves as far as possible, certainly toward the "wider sphere which a University offers."[62] Only thus would they, as Rev. Mackie reminded them frequently, "take your proper place as a cultured men, moving as equals among others of your own status in life."[63] Put more directly, "ambition is one of the gifts of God and it should be the aim of every boy to take a high & honoured position in his community."[64] How better to maintain British traditions in Anglo-Canada than to have it guided by individuals who had grown up British?

Clientele

Through the 1920s a clear symbiotic relationship existed between the Vernon Preparatory School and British immigrant families of the interior of British Columbia. Boys from the Coldstream, Lavington and Vernon, together with their counterparts from elsewhere in the Okanagan and from the Kootenays, dominated the school. Of the 200 boys who entered up to 1929, 55 (28 percent) were from the vicinity of the school, 82 (41 percent) from other parts of the Okanagan and the Kootenays, 43 (22 percent) from greater Vancouver, and the remaining 20 (10 percent) primarily from outlying areas of British Columbia and Alberta.[65]

Of these 200 boys, it has been possible to trace fathers' birthplace for slightly over half (n = 111), and it is hardly surprising that over 80 percent of the fathers were born in Britain. Examination of the families where the father was born elsewhere is of some interest, for it suggests the complexity of ethnicity as an explanatory factor in matters of education. Half of the fathers were born in Canada, most of British stock. Not untypical were the sons of the Vernon banker from Quebec; the grandson of one of the Cornwall brothers who in the 1870s imported foxhounds from England to hunt coyotes on their ranch at Ashcroft; or the eldest son of Clarence Wallace, a future lieutenant-govenor of British Columbia whose father had emigrated from Devon to become a pioneer Vancouver shipbuilder. Although such families still identified with their British origins, they were clearly not a part of an ethnic community like the Coldstream. Another minority of boys had American fathers and in at least two cases were sent for very practical reasons: in one the mother a single parent working full-time, in the other the father a mining engineer in remote parts of the province.

In the 1930s the clientele of the Vernon Preparatory School changed dramatically. Of the 250 boys who entered, 1929-1946, the largest number, 111 (44 percent) were from greater Vancouver and another 12 (5 percent) from Vancouver Island. Only 13 (5 percent) were from the vicinity of the school, 59 (24 percent) from the Okanagan and the Kootenays, and 29 (12 percent) from remoter areas. Twenty-seven (11 percent) came as students sent from Britain at the outbreak of World War II. The dominance of the school by boys from the coast reached almost 60 percent during the 1930s. Between 1932 and 1942 such boys always formed the majority of the forty some students at the school at any one time. Their presence was even instituuionalized through the provision of a special train car complete with its own attendant to take them to and from Vancouver each term.

There are several reasons why the clientele of the school shifted. The intensive, clustered immigration of the "better classes" from Great Britain into the interior of British Columbia largely ceased with the First World War, which also disrupted many families already there. Most of the male immigrants had arrived at a decisive stage in their life cycle, either as young men out of boarding school looking for a first career or as middle-aged military men searching for a second one. By the end of the 1920s the sons of this generation of settlers had largely reached school age. Moreover, economic conditions in agriculture – persistently low fruit prices and then the Great Depression – made many families consider carefully the necessity of private education. Only the most resolute against accomodation with Anglo-Canada could afford to resist the temptation of free public schooling.

The new clientele of the Vernon Preparatory School was dominated by the sons of leading Vancouver families in lumbering, business and the professions. Their reasons for choosing the school were varied. Health was an important factor in many cases: a leading Vancouver pediatrician of the 1930s whose practice included the prestigious Shaughnessy area regularly recommended the school, located in a dry climate, to parents of asthmatic or bronchial boys.[66] Particular aspects of the school, especially its isolation, spartan life style, emphasis on games, and traditional education, had appeal to many families interested in living comfortably themselves but in insulating their impressionable offspring from the excesses of city life. The impact of things American, movies and comic books as well as attitudes and values, was a matter of concern to many British Columbian families in the 1930s. Where fathers were British-born, ethnicity may have played a direct role; on the other hand, many fathers Canadian by birth were, to quote a scholar writing in the 1930s, "pseudo-English" or "English by social ambition."[67] To an extent, the school simply became fashionable so that when some leading families were seen to be sending their sons other parent decided that nothing could be better for their own offspring.

There is no evidence that the shift in clientele altered the school's objectives or practices. The Mackies were in a strong, independent socio-economic position. By the early 1920s they owned outright the fruit ranch on which the school stood. Enrolments were virtually always filled or oversubscribed, except during the height of the Depression when they did not decline long enough to cause serious financial problems. The Mackie family provided the backbone of the teaching and custodial staff with the occasional outsider coming from the local Coldstream community, as did Capt. Brayshaw, or being a former student at the school. The Mackies remained completely insulated from contact with Anglo-Canadian society except on their own terms or through necessary contact with parents of students.

From the very first years, the Mackies had taken the high road in their relationship with parents, stressing that not only was the school in *loco parentis* but that it was the duty of parents to cooperate with the objectives of the school rather than the reverse:

> If parents and teachers pull the same way the effect is irresistible, if the boy is torn between the conflicting claims & standard of home & school, he will probably adopt those of the home . . . ; in any case the resulting conflict will be disturbing to his mind & bad for his character. . . . So I urge parents in the highest interest of their boys to cooperate with us in all such matters that together we may produce the desired effect upon the boy's character.[68]

Rev. Mackie was not adverse, however, to his boys reflecting favorably on the school during their holidays, especially with their mothers:

> Many a mother's holiday is spoilt because all the work is thrown on her shoulders & when the holidays are over she herself is worn out in the service of her children.[69]

> Remember that the extra labour & expense of your holidays falls upon your parents – especially your mother; she needs a holiday far more than you.[70]

The attitude toward parents is epitomized in a story which has become legend among former students. In the mid-1930s a most influential Vancouver father arrived to take his son out on the single half-holiday allowed each term. On leaving he remarked that, since he had made a special trip from the coast, he might keep his son out overnight. Rev. Mackie reminded him that 6 p.m. was the time for return. "But there couldn't possibly be any objection if an automobile just happened to break down and couldn't be repaired until the next morning?" "No," replied Rev. Mackie, but when he did return, his son's trunk would be packed and waiting at the side of the road. The son was back at 6 p.m.

If anything, the new clientele reaffirmed the objectives and practices of the Vernon Preparatory School. One close observer of the school in the 1930s has suggested that, rather than the school being altered by its more Anglo-Canadian students, what occurred was "in fact, the reverse; it became more British." A socially prominent Vancouver mother is said to have told Mrs. Mackie that it was precisely because the school offered such an alternative that her son was there: "The appeal of the school was the spartan existence, the traditional values, so different from home values."[71] The experience at the school of English students evacuated to Canada at the beginning of World War II confirms how closely the school replicated its British equivalents. Not only were they generally happy at the school but many returned home to go almost directly into such leading public schools as Blundell's, Eton and Rugby. One boy from this period who went on to school in England summed up, "VPS was very English indeed, inculcating entirely English values."[72]

Conclusion

The case of the Vernon Preparatory School, 1914-1946, argues strongly for the existence of British ethnicity in British Columbia. The school as an institution and the Mackie family as its personification acted consistently to maintain among students the British "official" culture embodied in the boarding school monolith.

Deliberate isolation from the larger environment of Anglo-Canada contributed to the school's ability to maintain its identity and to ignore changes occurring elsewhere.

Both the formation of the school and the implementation of its principles were greatly facilitated by a symbiotic relationship with the British immigrant communities formed in the Okanagan and the Kootenays in the two decades before the First World War. These settlers, primarily from the middle and upper classes, were concerned to retain their cultural identity into the next generation. The school assisted them in this maintenance of ethnicity through providing for their sons precisely that education which they themselves had experienced in Britain and which was an essential element of the culture to which they clung. In 1938, just months before sending his own son to the Vernon Preparatory School, UBC academic Henry F. Angus called attention to these offspring of English "public school" settlers in British Columbia:

> Its descendents are young men and young women who have received their education in the Province, but who have been brought up in close contact with English ideas, English periodicals, letters from relatives, visits to England and visits from relatives. This group is apt to feel – and not altogether without reason – a certain superiority in education, ideals, and civilization to the community to which it has migrated. Its "values" are definately English values.[73]

Clearly, a British ethnic community not only existed in British Columbia but could, and did, pass on its cultural identity to the second generation.

In the 1930s the Vernon Preparatory School attracted a new clientele, primarily from greater Vancouver. Sons were sent not so much to maintain ethnicity but, at least indirectly, because the school provided what was in effect an ethnic education. To some, it perhaps represented a class education. For whatever reasons they came, these boys received from the Mackies precisely the same set of values and the same belief system as had earlier students. They too grew up British in British Columbia.

Notes

1. I am indebted to Patrick Mackie, Dr. George O. Mackie, Dr. William Bruneau, and Dr. Margaret Ormsby for their encouragement and practical assistance. In addition, many former students of Vernon Preparatory School, to whom I have promised anonymity, have provided invaluable recollections of their experience at the school.

2. Royal Commission on Bilingualism and Biculturalism, *Final Report* 1 (Ottawa: Queen's Printer, 1967): xxiv.

3. "British" refers to the English, the Scots and the Welsh. The series, "A History of Canada's Peoples," does include a volume entitled *The Scottish Tradition in Canada*, W. Stanford Reid, ed., (Toronto: McClelland and Stewart in association with the Multiculturalism Programme, Department of the Secretary of State of Canada and the Publishing Centre, Supply and Services Canada, 1976), but it never directly considers the matter of cultural identity or ethnicity.

4. Leo Driedger, "Ethnic Identity in the Canadian Mosaic," in Driedger, ed., *The Canadian Ethnic Mosaic: A Quest for Identity* (Toronto: McClelland and Stewart, 1978), 17.

5. The leading school on the British model in Perth is Hale School, in Buenos Aires St. George's.

6. Prospectus for Brentwood College School, Mill Bay, B.C., opened 1923, quoted in Carol Gossage, *A Question of Privilege: Canada's Independent Schools* (Toronto: Peter Martin, 1977), 254.

7. The records of the Vernon Preparatory School have been given by Patrick Mackie to the British Columbia Archives and Records Service [hereafter BCARS]. These records consist of Mackie family papers going back to the nineteenth century; the school magazine, *The Chronicles of the Vernon Preparatory School*, issued thrice yearly, 1918-1950; the *V.P.S. Old Boy's News Letter*, issued yearly, 1951-1961; the sermons given by Rev. A.C. Mackie at the school; Rev. Mackie's personal scrapbooks of clippings about the family, the school, and former students; and photographs. There are, unfortunately, no administrative records.

8. See Jean Barman, Growing Up British in British Columbia: Boys in Private School (Vancouver: University of British Columbia Press [hereafter UBC Press]

9. Letter of Gordon Mackie to his father, George Mackie, Coleville, Saskatchewan, 21 July 1912.

10. *Ibid.*

11. Printed prospectus entitled "Vernon Preparatory School."

12. "V.P.S. History: Childhood," *Chronicle of the Vernon Preparatory School* 12, 1 (Easter 1929): 6-7.

13. Manuscript diary of Anis Mackie, 1: 300.

14. "School Notes," *Chronicle* 29, 3 (Christmas 1945): 3.

15. "V.P.S. History: Infancy," *Chronicle* 14, 1 (Easter 1931): 11.

16. Separate notes in hand of Rev. A.C. Mackie, dated by handwriting as from early 1920s.

17. "Farewell Sermon," given June 1922, in manuscript notebook of sermons entitled "Ascension Tide/22-Rogation Tide/23" (hereafter vol. 3).

18. I interviewed a variety of former students with an assurance of anonymity. Each interview is here identified by the date on which it was held. 4 March 1979, a.m., and 18 April p.m., no.1.

19. Interview, 18 April 1979, p.m., no. 2, and 19 April a.m.

20. Mary Kitcher, "Coldstream Ranch Goes Back One Hundred Years," Okanagan Historical Society, *Report* 27 (1963): 119-20.

21. *The Canadian Journal of Lady Aberdeen, 1893-1898*, John T. Saywell, ed. (Toronto: The Champlain Society, 1960), 141, entry for 30 Oct. 1894.

22. *Ibid.*

23. C.W. Holliday, *The Valley of Youth* (Caldwell, Idaho: Caxton Printers, 1948), 189-90.

24. Normal Noel, *Blanket-stiff or a Wanderer in Canada 1911* (London: St. Catherine Press, 1912), 2, quoted in David R.B. Dendy, "One Huge Orchard: Okanagan Land and Development Companies Before the Great War" (Honors B.A. thesis, University of Victoria, 1976), 45. See also Dendy, 11-14, 51.

25. Jean Webber, "Coldstream Municipality," Okanagan Historical Society, *Report* 15 (1951): 79; and J.R. Kidston, "Country Club is a Splendid Asset to District of Vernon," *Vernon News*, special edition, 1937, unpaginated.

26. *Vernon News*, 1937, special edition.

27. Biographical information on separate students obtained from *Chronicle: Old Boys' News Letter*; scrapbooks of Rev. Mackie containing primarily undated clippings from *Province* newspaper, Vancouver, and *Vernon News*: vertical file of BCARS; alumni records of UBC; interviews with former students and with Dr. Margaret Ormsby, Vernon, and Prof. Keith Ralston, UBC.

28. Stanley E. Read, *Tommy Brayshaw: The Ardent Angler-Artist* (Vancouver: UBC Press, 1977), is concerned about Brayshaw's career as a teacher only in passing but does present an excellent portrait of the man in his environment.

29. J.R. Kidston, "Anna Euphemia Kidston," Okanagan Historical Society, *Report* 24 (1960): 108.

30. Special 1937 edition of the *Vernon News*: E.A. Orchard, *Orchard's Guide and Directory to the Okanagan: A Ready Reference for Business Men, Tourists, Sportsmen, Capitalists and Prospective Settlers* (Vernon: Vernon News, 1909), 25-49; *Vernon, British Columbia, Canada: The Commercial City of the Famous Okanagan Valley* (Vernon: Board of Trade, n.d.); and various articles in Okanagan Historical Society, *Report*..

31. Holliday, 189.

32. *Ibid.*

33. Interview, 4 Mar. 1979, p.m.

34. *Chronicle*, passim.

35. Eric Henderson, "Pioneer Banker," Okanagan Historical Society, *Report* 31 (1967): 79, 83.

36. Dendy, 21, 30, 36, 42-44. Also see Margaret Ormsby, "The History of the Okanagan Valley" (B.A. thesis, UBC, 1929), and her "A Study of the Okanagan Valley of British Columbia" (M.A. thesis, UBC, 1931).

37. Duane Thomson, "Charles Mair's Letters from the Okanagan," Okanagan Historical Society, *Report* 42 (1978), 66.

38. Phyllis Warren, [*West we go*] (n.p.: n.p., 1959?), 11.

39. Interview, 5 Mar. 1979, a.m.

40. "St. John's Foundation School, Letherhead," *Illustrated Church News*, 7 July 1899. The development of the school is described in E.M.P. Williams, *The Quest Goes On, Being a Short History of the First Hundred Years of St. John's School, Leatherhead, 1851-1951* (Leatherhead, Surrey: St. John's, 1951).

41. Interview, 6 Mar. 1979, p.m.

42. "Radio Address I: A good Warfare," 1 Mar. 1948, and 11 Feb. 1951, in vol. entitled "1938 to" (vol. 10); "Flower Service," 16 June 1929, and unknown date in "Flower Service: June 16th 1929 to Quinguagesima 1932" (vol. 8); and "Disarmament conference," 13 Nov. 1921, in "Advent-Ascension, 1921-22" (vol. 2).

43. "1st S. after Easter," 1922, 15 Apr. 1928, 19 Apr. 1929, and 19 Apr. 1942, vol. 2; and "Heaven," late fall 1922 and 19 Oct. 1925, vol. 3.

44. "Summer Farewell," June 1929, vol. 8.

45. Thomas Hughes, *Tom Brown's School Days* (New York: American News. Co., n.d.), 91; original ed., London, 1857.

46. "Flower Sunday," 1923 and 1926, in vol. entitled "Ascension/ 23-Epiphany/24" (vol. 4); and "All Saint's Day," autumn 1922, 1 Nov. 1931, 2 Nov. 1941, and 31 Oct. 1948, vol. 3.

47. Austin Mackie to Hugh Mackie, St. John's, Leatherhead, no month 6, 1892.

48. "Opening of School Year," fall 1929 and 9 Sept. 1933, vol. 8.

49. *Ibid.*

50. *Ibid.*

51. Also in Henry Newbolt, *Collected Poems, 1897-1907* (London: Thomas Nelson, n.d.), 131.

52. "Truthfulness," autumn 1933, in vol. entitled "Lent I 1932 to" (vol. 9).

53. "Opening of Term," Sept. 1926, in vol. entitled "November 1924-June 9th 1929" (vol. 6).

54. "Beginning of Term," 28 Apr. 1918, and 1925 in vol. entitled "School Addresses" (vol. 1); repeated almost verbatim in "Opening of Term," autumn 1924 and autumn 1925, vol. 4.

55. "Opening of the School Year," autumn 1929 and 17 Sept. 1933, vol. 8.

56. "Careers," late 1923, vol. 4.

57. "Epiphany," early 1934, vol. 9; also "The Great Adventure: Epiphany," 1926, vol. 6.

58. "End of School Term," 17 June 1945, vol. 10.

59. Hugh de Fylton Mackie, "Reminiscences of School Teacher," Okanagan Historical Society, *Report* 38 (1974), 35.

60. Jonathan Gathorne-Hardy, *The Public School Phenomenon* (London: Hodder and Stoughton, 1977), 228.

61. "The Next World," spring 1930, vol. 8.

62. "Thankfulness," 24 Feb. 1918, and 10 May 1925, vol. 1.

63. "Careers," late 1923, vol. 4.

64. These calculations are derived from biographical data accumulated about individual students. Home town is usually given in the *Chronicle* at time of admission to the school.

65. Interviews, 26 Feb. 1979, p.m.; 17 Apr. 1979, p.m.; and 22 Apr. 1979, p.m. Also *V.P.S. Newsletter* 8 (1958): 5.

66. H.F. Angus, ed., *Canada and Her Great Neighbor: Sociological Surveys of Opinions and Attitudes in Canada Concerning the United States* (Toronto: The Ryerson Press and New Haven: Yale University Press for the Carnegie Endowment for International Peace, 1938), 58.

67. "Cast Your Nets Upon the Right Side, Ascension 1933, vol. 3; and "Reunion & Ascension," 21 May 1939, and 21 May 1944, vol. 10.

68. "Summer Farewell," June 1928, in vol. entitled "May 1st 1927-June 9th 1929" (vol.7).

69. "Summer Farewell," June 1929, vol. 8.; same idea expressed in "Summer Farewell," June 1931 and 19 June 1949, vol. 8., and in "Summer Farewell," June 1933 and 1937, v.9.

70. Interview, 6 Mar. 1979, p.m.

71. Interview, 18 Apr. 1979, p.m., no. 2

72. Letter from former student, 15 June, 1979.

73. Angus, 57-58.

19

"Due to their keenness": [1]
The Education of Japanese Canadian Children in the British Columbia Interior Housing Settlements During World War Two

Patricia E. Roy

In 1942 the federal government ordered the evacuation of all persons of Japanese racial origin from the coast of British Columbia; the province rejected any responsibility for educating the children. Despite the concern of the Japanese for education, only one was a qualified teacher with experience in the British Columbia public schools. Nevertheless, with minimal assistance from the federal government, which was anxious to have them move east of the Rocky Mountains, "their keenness regarding education" allowed teachers and students in the interior housing settlements to get "the utmost" out of the elementary schools set up for them during the war years.

I

Before the war, Japanese Canadian children had such well deserved reputations as intelligent and hard-working students in British Columbia's public schools that when a recent immigrant took first place in the province-wide high school entrance examinations some observers fretted that the "yellow peril" was not "yellow battleships nor yellow settlers, but yellow intelligence."[2] Municipal school trustees complained about the cost of educating Japanese children while admitting their ready adoption of Canadian customs. At the same time, over the protests of the children, some controversy within the Japanese community,[3] and suspicions of whites that they taught "a flood of jingoistic nationalism,"[4] Japanese language schools operated after public school or on Saturdays wherever there was a significant Japanese population.

Given their interest in education, it is not surprising that a significant proportion of the Japanese went to high school and to university even though their entry to the professions was limited. A few *Nisei* graduated from the Provincial Normal School, but only one, Hideko Hyodo, was employed by a public school board. She had a first class certificate and from September 1926 until the spring of 1942 taught an all Japanese Grade 1 class at Lord Byng School in Steveston.[5]

For several weeks in the spring of 1942 Miss Hyodo taught at Steveston and then "rush[ed] out to Vancouver's Hastings Park" where she voluntarily organized 12 people teaching 261 students in Grades 1 to 3.[6] After the Canadian government decided in February 1942 that, because of the war, people of Japanese ancestry must be removed from the coast, Japanese from outside greater Vancouver had been gathered at the Park to await their removal to interior points.[7]

After the evacuees began arriving at Hastings Park, the British Columbia Security Commission (BCSC),[8] the federal agency established to look after the evacuation, "borrowed" W.S. McRae from the Vancouver School Board to supervise recreation and education. His specific instructions, he recounted, were "to go as far as I liked provided that it didn't cost the Commission any money."[9] In such circumstances, the classes at Hastings Park depended on volunteer teachers chiefly missionaries and evacuees with high school or university education. To train the Japanese assistants, McRae and his associates set up "teacher-leadership" classes, invited prominent local educators to give lectures, and arranged visits to the Model School of the Vancouver Normal School.

A class in a downtown eastside Vancouver school in the 1930s. Trustees "complained about the cost of educating Japanese children while admitting their ready adoption of Canadian customs." (Vancouver Public Library [VPL], S-50495)

The civil servants in the BCSC persuaded their political masters that educating children in the interior housing settlements was "a matter of fairness to the future of the children" and "in the national interest" since it would help with "their assimilation into normal Canadian community life after the war."[10] In practical terms, the Commission staff expected the schools to improve morale, reduce the likelihood of juvenile delinquency, give families a certain amount of security so that fathers of school age children would feel easier about leaving for outside employment,[11] and assuage the Spanish Consul who, acting as the Protecting Power for Japan, had made embarrassing inquiries about education.[12]

Japanese Canadian children being escorted home after they had been removed from their school in Vancouver, 1942. "The RCMP came in and took out all the Japanese kids." (VPL 1345)

The BCSC, however, wanted minimal involvement in education. It refused any responsibility for schooling beyond Grade 8 and wherever possible it sought to have others educate approximately 4 000 children of elementary age.[13] It persuaded Alberta and Manitoba to accept evacuee children into public schools in return for assistance with the cost; similarly, it accepted the offers of the Roman Catholic and United Churches to provide schooling at the Greenwood, B.C. settlement in return for some financial assistance and minimal supervision. Later, it accepted offers from those churches and the Anglicans to operate kindergarten and high school classes.

In British Columbia, where most evacuees resided, the BCSC believed the province should be responsible since as "Canadian citizens . . . they [the Japanese] are entitled to their education, by Government grant or otherwise."[14] At the very least, the Commission hoped the province would pay for teachers and textbooks. The provincial cabinet, however, decided that, in this case, education was a federal responsibility.[15] Despite a direct appeal from federal Labour Minister Humphrey Mitchell to Premier John Hart for the "advice and assistance of the experienced educational administrators in your Department of Education" to help give "these young Canadian subjects a proper British education," the province would do no more than sell copies of elementary correspondence school lessons, textbooks, and school supplies at cost. Reluctantly, it loaned answers to correspondence lesson exercises and examinations so the Commission might mimeograph and distribute them to its teachers.[16]

By the time the 1942 school year began in September, evacuation to the interior housing settlements was almost complete. Several West Kootenay communities, namely Sandon, New Denver, Kaslo, and Greenwood, were developed around declining mining towns where the new residents were largely housed in rehabilitated buildings. In the three settlements at Slocan (Bay Farm, Popoff and Lemon Creek) and at the brand new community of Tashme, twenty-two kilometres east of Hope, the Commission had to construct many new buildings. Housing was the priority.

The lack of schooling concerned parents. By early October the Commission noted "a great deal of unrest . . . due to the lack of information regarding the educational programme to be followed. . . ." Before opening the schools, the Commission informed parents that it would "solely" dictate "the educational program," that the Japanese school supervisors were responsible to it, and that all teaching would be in English.[17]

Such warnings were necessary because some evacuees, believed to be sympathetic to Japan, had tried "to assume certain responsibilities in connection with the schools." Subsequently, in several instances, parents demanded a say in the appointment of teachers and, at Tashme, protested the dismissal of a popular principal. Yet, even at Tashme where the community was divided on many issues, parents set aside their "petty complaints and dissatisfactions, when the subject revolves around education."[18] The BCSC encouraged the formation of Parent-Teachers Associations which it hoped would organize sports days and similar activities and raise money to purchase library books, sports equipment and other extras. A few schools were disappointed by apparent indifference when few parents attended Open Houses. At most, however, parents attended PTA meetings regularly, asked "intelligent questions," and co-operated in improving discipline in and around the schools.

Because the availability of physical facilities varied from community to community, the schools did not open simultaneously. In Kaslo, one of the first "ghost towns" to be settled,[19] school started in temporary quarters in September.[20] At Tashme and Slocan, construction delays meant classes did not begin until early 1943 and then, some classes operated on shifts because of overcrowding. The number of classes varied from four at Rosebery (near New Denver) to twenty-seven at Tashme.

The BCSC had feared jealousy if it provided better conditions or services than were available to nearby white children. It had no worries on this account insofar as its classrooms were concerned. None was ideal. Lighting was often poor; blackboards, inadequate in quality and number; and poor partitions made classrooms noisy. The worst situation was at Tashme where the heating in the main school building, the upper storey of a renovated barn, was so poor that the medical health officer ordered that children be sent home if the temperature fell below 13°C (56 F). Although the BCSC gradually improved the physical facilities, one of its officials complained that so doing made "it just that much tougher . . . in getting these families moved elsewhere."[22]

II

Unlike its American counterpart, the War Relocation Authority, which had the advice and assistance of professional educators who saw the relocation camps as an opportunity for experiments in creating a curriculum that would provide "an effective instrument of community planning and building" leading to "democracy in action,"[23] the BCSC simply adopted the existing British Columbia curriculum. That had practical advantages. Most students and their neophyte teachers were familiar with it, textbooks were available, and provincial elementary correspondence lessons provided guides beyond the prescribed texts and workbooks.

The curriculum also conformed to the belief of some officials of the BCSC that one of their objectives was to promote a Canadian identity among its students. At the first Summer School for teachers, Howard Pammett of the federal Department of Labour which was responsible for the BCSC, told student-teachers to remember "that you are teaching young children to be Canadians, future citizens of this vast rich country. . . ."[24] Summer School instructors helped "lead pupils to think and talk and act as Canadians." Thus, for example, the Health and Physical Education instructor arranged his course to improve the "everyday patterns of living" of the student-teachers so they "would more closely conform to that of the ideal for Canadian youth, so that they, possessing some ideals, might guide their Japanese pupils in the same pattern."[25]

Because of a severe teacher shortage in British Columbia,[26] the BCSC could not consider the practice of its American counterpart of recruiting a large number of caucasian teachers.[27] The Commission planned only to hire Miss Hyodo, an assistant, and fourteen supervisors who would be qualified teachers or high school or university students who had had some teacher training at Hastings Park. These paid supervisors would look after books and supplies and organize "a voluntary staff of Japanese High School and University students" to help coach or teach the younger children.[28] The prospective coaches or teachers, however, insisted on being paid. But there were savings. The teachers' salaries were included in their families' incomes; what the Commission paid out in salaries, it largely saved in maintenance or welfare allowances.[29] The proposed salaries were so low that few university students or graduates accepted teaching positions. By the time the schools were operating, Miss Hyodo was being paid $75; Miss Hidaka, $65;[30] the principals of the eight schools, $55 and the assistant teachers, $40 or $45.[31] Early in 1944 because of its dependence on Hyodo and Hidaka, the Commission recommended raising their salaries to $100 and $75 respectively and that of the principals of the three largest schools to $60. The teachers generally accepted their salaries as given. Early in 1944, however, when some of the $40 teachers at Tashme were denied a $5 raise, seven of them, inspired by their parents and the Japanese Committee in Tashme, possibly as part of a larger factional dispute within the settlement, submitted their resignations. The resignations were not accepted and, in due course, a new salary scale was worked out based on experience and attendance at Summer Schools rather than on "actual teaching merit."[32] Nevertheless, the salaries remained significantly lower than the $1 300 per annum average salary in provincial rural schools.

The Commission believed it could not "throw the whole burden of administering the education of 2,800 chidren" upon Misses Hyodo and Hidaka and thought a serious weakness of its schools was the lack of "any experienced white educational administrators."[33] It also feared criticism that by "employing all Japanese teachers and a Japanese Educational Director, we are giving these children a Japanese rather than a Canadian education."[34] But without the co-operation of the provincial government, the Commission could find no suitable person to take the job on a permanent basis nor could it find white supervisors. Thus, Miss Hyodo, who was based in New Denver, or her assistant, Miss Hidaka, visited all the schools on a quarterly basis. Because of problems at Tashme, Miss Hidaka, who was based there, could seldom travel.

To assist them, the BCSC hired retired public school teachers as part-time advisors. The first, Miss Ella Robertson of Vancouver, visited the Commission schools for a month in the spring of 1943 observing teachers, giving demonstration lessons, and discussing school organization.[35] Subsequently, the Commission hired Arthur Anstey, the retired principal of the Provincial Normal School at Vancouver, as Educational Director. He visited the schools twice a year reporting on physical facilities, giving demonstration lessons, discussing problems with teachers, and administering the standardized tests used to assist in grading the children. Miss Hyodo and her principals reported regularly to Mrs. Cleo V. Booth of the Commission's Vancouver Office. Mrs. Booth offered advice but admitted she had no educational background; before the war she was a stenographer in the Japanese consulate in Vancouver.

Although the records of the B.C. Security Commission are rich in many details, they are disappointingly thin on the actual process by which it selected teachers and on personnel details. Loyalty to Canada, however, was a factor. All were "thoroughly investigated" through RCMP records and a few who had received or sent "epistles considered as somewhat subversive" were reprimanded.[36]

There is some evidence of the Commission occasionally requesting the dismissal of certain teachers for reasons it could not reveal to Miss Hyodo but normally she was responsible for dismissing or reassigning teachers whose classroom work, usually discipline, was unsatisfactory. At least once she dismissed a teacher whose teaching was satisfactory but whose personal conduct was not.[37]

Because the relocation program took priority over education and its mistaken claim of plentiful opportunities for good jobs for young men in eastern Canada, the Commission was reluctant to authorize the use of male teachers except where they were required as physical training instructors or to maintain discipline in the higher grades.[38] Thus, most teachers were female. Few had more than high school graduation; some had less. Most were in their late teens; one grade 2 teacher was only fifteen. None had any experience as a classroom teacher. As David Suzuki recalled, "Our teachers were girls barely out of high school, ill-prepared to handle the job."[39]

Class sizes varied from about 15 in the primary grades to an average of twenty-five in the other grades. Two children shared a set of texts in Grades 1 and 2. Due to what Mrs. Booth described as "the natural docility of the Japanese children, and the encouraging attitude of parents towards Education," the system worked well in the lower grades. In the higher grades, at least at the beginning, it was another matter. The initial plan was to supply one set of correspondence lessons for every four students and to have the children study directly from them with the assistance of the teachers. While the Commission believed that "children who study from correspondence courses have a much better grounding in the fundamentals of education than the average school student," teachers soon discovered the lessons were "rather inadequate when applied to group instruction."[40]

The papers were boring. Shizuye Takashima in her autobiography, *A Child in Prison Camp*, recalled "those stupid correspondence courses. We have to answer hundreds of questions. . . . I don't understand any of them."[41] Only a set of the Grade 6 papers has survived but a perusal of them confirms Takashima's assessment. In Social Studies, for example, each correspondence lesson generally included a practice exercise of about fifteen questions requiring a response of True or False, one word, or possibly one sentence. The Mastery Work consisted of five to ten questions requiring about a sentence to answer.[42] Similarly, the Literature lessons directed students to specific pages in the *Highroads to Reading*. Occasionally, the lesson explained some term or phrase in a poem or story. It always included questions such as "Name three things the author of 'Hymn for Canada' hoped God will make possible in Canada" or asked students to answer questions following the selections in the text.[43]

A more practical problem was that the lessons were not easily shared; subjects such as arithmetic and language required the simultaneous use of the teaching and practice booklets and the text book. In addition, the Health, Nature, and Geography lessons were often incomplete and, in the early stages at least, there were many production errors in which pages or lessons were missing and others were duplicated. Some teachers decided it was "more convenient to do most of the teaching" themselves and use the correspondence courses only as guides to be supplemented by reference books. Despite burning midnight oil, teachers were often "very little ahead of the pupils."[44]

Most teachers recognized their serious responsibilities. As Takashi Tsuji, an ordained Buddhist priest[45] and president of the student council at the first Summer School for teachers, admonished his classmates:

> We, who were store clerks, stenographers, domestics and high school students made up our minds to become teachers and to participate in the important programme . . . must fully realize, that although the system itself may be temporary, whatever mental and spiritual wealth we give to the children to-day, will bear upon them a life-long influences. . . .[T]eaching . . . is a sacred work – work we must undertake with our hearts and souls.[46]

Even before all the schools opened, BCSC officials recognized the need for teacher training. Thus, they gladly accepted the offer of Principal A.R. Lord of the Vancouver

Normal School and some of his staff to operate a summer school. F.C. Boyes, the Social Studies Instructor at the Normal School, acted as Principal of the New Denver Summer School. His assistants came from the Normal School, the Model School and a Vancouver city school.

After teaching at the month-long Summer School, Boyes reported "No student body ever worked harder." The principals attended daily meetings with Lord or Boyes to discuss administration, curriculum, testing and discipline. The classroom teachers had a full schedule including a daily one hour Physical Education class because many "were inclined to be too serious and unable to relax." They also spent three hours on "Methods" courses related to the grades they were teaching. The afternoons were spent on study and extra curricular activities including arts, crafts, music and dancing. Although an old-time resident of New Denver described them as "a very lighthearted merry crowd," they were serious.[47] They had little interest in purely recreational activities such as baseball and tennis and requested "extra work in English." Organized groups practiced Oral and Written English through such activities as public speaking, a school paper, and a drama club which publicly performed a play written about the local area by the History group. A Student Council provided experience in organizing meetings and activities including concerts and a dance.[48]

Summer School training combined with the teachers' increasing experience benefitted their students. By the fall of 1943, many teachers abandoned the correspondence lessons and taught directly from the provincial Programme of Studies and organized more extra-curricular activities.[49] All centres held Christmas Concerts complete with the usual fare of songs, dances, and playlets. Some schools also produced newspapers, held assemblies and seasonal concerts, developed school songs[50] and, at Lemon Creek, teachers sought to "create better understanding between their students and their Canadian friends out in the East," by initiating a pen pal programme with students in Ingersoll, Ontario.[51] Such activities provided enjoyable practice in English expression and relieved some of the isolation of the interior housing settlements.

Isolation was a fact of life. At the first Summer School Boyes had noted that his students lacked the broad background necessary "to teach Social Studies in an interesting manner." He blamed the ban on radio receivers and the meagre supply of reference material.[52] Similarly, early in 1945 the principal of Bay Farm School was shocked when a questionnaire given to children in Grade 5 and up revealed that 74 of the 228 students did not know the name of the prime minister. He concluded that his students were "shut inside a huge stone wall, utterly oblivious of the gigantic change outside." Indeed, some teachers arranged ball games with nearby Commission schools so children would at least gain a little knowledge of neighboring communities. In several schools National Film Board films offered a view of the outside world.[53]

The success of the first Summer School led to the holding of a second in the summer of 1944 under the direction of Lord and many members of the original staff. Of the students, 101 were returnees, 25 had little or no teaching experience, and 11 were principals or supervisors. The returnees were placed in advanced classes; a preliminary class was held for the beginners and a special programme in Administration was devised for the principals. Because of demonstrated problems with the children's use of English, the School gave special attention to English usage including the writing and production of a four act play on the history of the Japanese in Canada and special courses in public speaking, drama, and vocal music. The results of the intensive English programme were striking. The median score in the Dominion Language Test had been 79.5 at the beginning of the session, it was 92 at the end.[54]

Children attending one of the make-shift schools in the Hastings Park Clearing Station, Vancouver, 15 July 1942. (National Archives of Canada, C-24454)

Weakness in English was not a new problem; the Japanese themselves were well aware of it.[55] The Commission also recognized that "the children as a whole are far below average in the subjects belonging to the language group." In largely Japanese communities, language skills could deteriorate further. This was particularly true at Tashme, an all-Japanese community, where pre-school children spoke Japanese almost exclusively but it was also noticeable at Kaslo where, despite considerable integration of the Japanese and caucasian communities outside the elementary schools, Japanese children chattered in the streets in "a foreign and enemy tongue." Teachers realized the academic implications, namely the poor results in the Stanford Achievement Tests administered in June 1944 and reports from the High School about poor English hindering students academically and socially, but had limited success in checking the use of Japanese and encouraging the use of English.[56]

Despite the stereotype of the docile Japanese child, maintaining discipline was a problem for inexperienced teachers especially in Grades 5 and 6 where there were always a few mischief makers. Solutions varied. A child who broke a window with a snowball was sent to apologize to the superintendent of the settlement; boys who misbehaved at a concert were reprimanded and one who refused to apologize was effectively required to withdraw from school; ill-mannered students were instructed in manners; a boy who swore at a primary teacher was strapped but apparently learned his lesson; when swearing became a general problem at one school, students were fined 1 cent; a smoking problem was dealt with by the PTA which asked parents and stores to cooperate in stopping it; and "a sudden epidemic of slingshots" was resolved when the Student Council decided that after one general warning, it would confiscate slingshots. At Riverview School, the fine for eating in school was 25 cents. Since children had little pocket money, they had to ask their parents for it. This request required an explanation and usually resulted in a parental lecture. The school secretly returned the fine money to the parents.[57]

Gradually, many schools acquired student councils and systems of prefects who made and enforced school rules. At New Denver, where the students asked for a prefect system, the prefects saw "that students line up, obey school rules set by the council and staff, [and maintain] order on the school grounds." To punish offenders, student council set up a detention room. The Student Council, which selected the prefects, considered its choices carefully and sometimes appointed "problem boys who might benefit by being given the honour, and couple them with dependable boys." Bay Farm School eliminated discipline problems with a House System and Monitor's Court based on a program devised at Vancouver's Templeton Junior High School. The Student Council imposed such punishments as washing windows, scrubbing desks, and snow clearing. At Lemon Creek, after the principal discovered some children taking advantage of the absence of teachers at lunch time, the Student Council decided that "no matter how cold the weather," the children could not re-enter the building until 12:40 when the prefects would be on duty. At Popoff, however, the prefect and Students Court system did not work initially because "the pupils were too loyal to each other, and would not sentence their friends."[58]

Principals recognized the need to provide children with extra activities since few constructive diversions were available. In several settlements, the establishment of Boy Scout and Girl Guide troops was encouraged to teach "fair play, courtesy, obedience [and] responsibility." In some cases, Scouts provided Physical Education for older boys.[59] Guiding and Scouts were also expected to help promote a Canadian identity.

Because the Commission hoped to disperse the Japanese across Canada, it was anxious to insure that its students could transfer easily to regular public schools. This meant that pupils had to be properly graded. Beginning in the fall of 1943 the Commission administered Stanford Achievement Tests in all schools before regrading and promoting a large number of children.[60] Overall, these tests revealed the students had "remarkably high" marks in drill subjects such as arithmetic and spelling and were "far above the accepted standard" of American schools in all subjects except paragraph interpretation and word meaning.[61]

The Commission expected most Japanese would remain in Canada. In practical terms this was reflected in its educational policies. Although it considered offering Manual Training and Home Economics to Grade 8 graduates in order to provide them with marketable skills in eastern Canada, it ultimately confined manual training and home economics to Grades 7 and 8 where they were part of the provincial course of studies. In some cases the course was adapted to prepare students "to take up remunerative work at the end of their elementary school education." At Tashme, for example, laundry work and bed-making were added to the Home Economics curriculum "so that a graduate of these classes will be fully trained in domestic work." Similarly, the Commission encouraged boys to attend cooking classes as a Club activity since cooking was "well suited to the Canadian Japanese from an employment angle." The Commission also refused to "freeze" teachers in their employment since "the satisfactory relocation of persons outside the centres is of more importance than a slight loss which the Education Department may suffer by the departure of a few teachers. . . ." By early 1944 some teachers were leaving because of marriage or because they had accepted the Commission's advice to move east. When parents expressed concern about the loss of experienced teachers, *The New Canadian*, the *Nisei* newspaper, suggested that for the well being of their children, parents should also consider relocation.[62]

The Commission had recognized "the fundamental error in the present system is the lack of association of these Japanese Canadian children with Canadian children of British and other racial origins. The Japanese home influence becomes increasingly strong without the counteracting influence of purely Canadian teachers and associates." At the first Summer School Pammett advised that children should be encouraged to use English since "children who talk Japanese among themselves also think in Japanese and therefore cannot get the most out of a Canadian education given to them in English. That defect will handicap their lives wherever they live in Canada."[63]

The teachers followed instructions to discourage the use of Japanese. By the summer of 1944, the BCSC reported that none of its officials had ever heard a word of Japanese in the schools. One principal, who found some children persistently using Japanese, organized a house system and issued demerits for any child using Japanese. Thus, in the winter of 1945, the Commission was surprised by an unsubstantiated report that possibly half its teachers were "nationalistic." The Commission could do little except "keep them under constant check and warn them not to deviate from the regular teaching curriculum." The cause, Pammett speculated, was that family influences were stronger than the Canadianizing influences of the Summer Schools. The Commission also believed that clandestine Japanese language schools were operating at Tashme and at Lemon Creek. But, apart from reminding parents that the use of Japanese at home and play would handicap their children in school and in "every phase of Canadian life when they grow up" and antagonize other Canadians, it did nothing.[64]

In August 1944 Prime Minister King announced that residents of the settlements must choose between relocating east of the Rockies or accepting "repatriation" to Japan. Children were well disposed to relocation but parents waited for "definite action" by the government.[65] By the end of 1944, the school population had only dropped to 2 209 from its October 1943 peak of 2 449. Finally, in March 1945, the government announced definite action; residents of the interior housing settlements must move east of the Rockies or sign for "repatriation to Japan." Although some children seemed upset by the move, others appeared unaffected. Their teachers, however, experienced uncertainty. A few teachers moved east on their own and the number of teachers declined to 104 by December 1944. Since most teachers now had some experience, it was possible to increase class sizes. Teachers then heard conflicting rumors that they would be cut off the payroll as soon as they said they intended to go east; others claimed teachers could not leave until they found substitutes. In fact, some teachers who announced they were going East, received notices quickly; some who had not stated their intentions also received notices; others were left in place. From the point of view of school administrators, the movement was confusing; some teachers left sooner than expected and finding replacements was not always easy. Indeed, as the 1944-45 school year ended, some schools had few teachers but enrolment had only declined to 2 115.[66]

Among those who were departing was Miss Hyodo. To assist her successor, Miss Hidaka, and to act as principal at Tashme, the Commission appointed Kayou Ochiai who had had three years' of Normal School Training in Japan, attended all three summer schools at New Denver, and served as principal at Rosebery for two years. The Commission expected about half the staff for the 1945-46 school year would be beginners so it held another Summer School. Although three-quarters of the Summer School students had signed for repatriation, they were co-operative and interested.[67]

Because many young adults signed for repatriation, there were few problems in staffing the schools at Tashme and in the Slocan where the repatriates were concentrated.[68] If the surviving records are indicative, the Commission had little interest in these schools and even permitted Japanese language teaching during the last hour of the school day if parents so requested. The atmosphere in these schools reflected the widespread uncertainty particularly among those who now realized that the Canadian government really meant it when it had offered them the opportunity to go to Japan.[69] By the fall of 1945, senior students at Bay Farm in Slocan were restless, they understood their life there was temporary, they adopted a "what's the use attitude" and lost their incentives to study. Moreover, the thought of having to go to Japan weighed heavily on them.[70] In the end, not all had to go to Japan, a land most of them had never seen.[71]

In the relocation settlements, the Commission expected it would need only about thirty-three teachers for the 1945-46 school year. While it was anxious to promote relocation in the east as quickly as possible, it decided not to press any teachers to move during the year as long as their services were required and there were no substitutes. By the spring of 1946 as the movement to the East got underway on a large scale, school populations fell. In some cases, the Commission transferred students to local boards and paid tuition fees on their behalf. In New Denver, where families who wished to remain in Canada but could not be easily relocated had been assembled, the Commission operated a small school until the end of the 1946-47 school year when the remaining students and two teachers transferred to the local public school.[72] Indeed, for some teachers, their experience opened new careers. Between 1945 and 1948 nine different Japanese names appeared on the payrolls of British Columbia's public schools. Others found teaching positions in Ontario.[73]

III

After visiting the schools in the fall of 1943, Anstey emphasized the "great credit" due to those who initiated the venture, to the supervisors, to the teachers and "to the patient group of some 2,500 *children* who (with the backing of the home) are doing their best to benefit from the opportunity that is being offered them."[74] The ideal test of whether or not they "got the utmost" out of the "opportunity" would be a detailed analysis of the subsequent careers of students and teachers. Such an examination is theoretically possible but the problem of tracing and questioning approximately 2 500 individuals who were subsequently scattered across Canada or "repatriated" to Japan would be exceedingly difficult.

Thus, we must rely on very limited, mixed, and mainly anecdotal evidence. David Suzuki, the geneticist, has remarked, "Somehow, those years at Bay Farm School didn't turn me off" but he attributes his interest in study to his father's great interest in learning. One student of Tashme High School recalled how her little brother who did Grades 3 through 5 there had no problems in Grade 6 when the family moved to Alberta. Yet, at Tashme a United Church High School teacher reported that "each year the class of pupils entering grade 9 showed a poorer grounding in basic subjects such as English and Mathematics than the previous class, showing the effect of partially trained teachers and of the gradual increase in the use of the Japanese language in the community." Joy Kogawa's semi-fictional heroine, Naomi Nakane, who attended school at Slocan, found in Alberta that "arithmetic is easier and spelling is harder."[75] This suggests she was reasonably well taught but it contradicts some of the only "scientific" evidence, the Stanford tests.

In June 1945, 74 per cent of the 61 classes in Grades 4 through 8 tested, reached or exceeded the American norm for their grade as compared to 54 per cent in 1944 and only 31 per cent in December 1943. The students continued to be strong in arithmetic and spelling but weak in English language. Indeed, on the basis of American norms, only 66 per cent of the children qualified for promotion though that was a dramatic increase from the 50 per cent a year earlier. However, some students were promoted because they were overage or their term work justified it and the pass rate was 75-80 per cent. What struck Anstey was that few Grade 4 classes reached American standards. He did not know whether that was the result of poor teaching, the relative lack of previous exposure to an English-speaking environment, or the unreliability of such tests for younger children. Nevertheless, Anstey concluded, "it is a pleasure, perhaps somewhat of a surprise, to testify to the genuine quality of the work that is being done, to the unstinting efforts of principals and class teachers, to the hearty co-operation of student-councils and senior pupils, and to the help given by the two supervisors and – in most localities – by the parents. Without this desirable spirit of 'working together' results would have been meagre indeed."[76]

Perhaps the last word should be left to the valedictory of the principal of Bay Farm School in June 1945:

> We, who have chosen to leave the staff in order to start life anew in other parts of Canada cannot help but look back upon our three years with the children and know that we will certainly miss them. They might have been discouraging at times, and we might have had spells of disappointment but at this time of leaving, we know that we did try to do our very best for the young pupils, and they in turn tried so hard to please. It has been a time well spent and we shall all leave with a satisfied and happy feeling. . . .[77]

We did try to do our very best" was the theme of most teachers. "Due to their keenness regarding education," they, and their students, got "the utmost out of the whole plan."

Notes

1. J.A. Tyrwhitt to F.B. Pearce, 24 September 1942, National Archives of Canada [hereafter NAC], British Columbia Security Commission [hereafter BCSC] *Records* 12: 500.
2. *Vancouver Sun*, 24 July 1925. I wish to think Michiko Midge Ayukawa, Jean Barman, Dan Hawthorne and Wyn Millar for their helpful comments on the manuscript.
3. Rigenda Sumida, "The Japanese in British Columbia" (M.A. thesis, University of British Columbia [UBC], 1935), 521ff.
4. Arthur Laing to G.M. Weir, 20 August 1940, British Columbia Archives and Records Service [hereafter BCARS], Premiers' Papers, GR1222, vol. 27:1.
5. British Columbia, Public Schools, *Annual Report,* 1926-27 (Victoria: King's Printer, 1927), M57.
6. The anonymous interviewee in Barry Broadfoot, *Years of Sorrow, Years of Shame* (Toronto: Doubleday, 1977), 241, is clearly Miss Hyodo.
7. For a detailed account of the experience of Japanese Canadians during World War II, see Patricia E. Roy, J.L. Granatstein, Masako Iino and Hiroko Takamura, *Mutual Hostages: Canadians and Japanese During the Second World War* (Toronto: University of Toronto Press, 1990). For another interpretation see Ann Gomer Sunahara, *The Politics of Racism: The Uprooting of Japanese Canadians During the Second World War* (Toronto: Lorimer, 1981).
8. The British Columbia Security Commission was formed in March 1942 and officially dissolved in February 1943 when its duties were transferred directly to the Department of Labour. However, the name continued in popular use and in this context is used in this paper.
9. W.S. McRae, *Report on Educational Services for Children of Japanese Parents,* July 1942, BCSC, vol. 11: 500.
10. MacNamara to Minister of Labour, 9 February 1943, NAC, Ian Mackenzie Papers, vol. 25; Pammett to MacNamara, 4 February 1943, BCSC, vol. 13: 503. The Commission advised

supervisors of the settlements that until it set up schools, the evacuees would have to organize their own classes. Some tried but their resources were limited.

11. Report of BCSC Welfare Committee, 28 October 1942, and Minutes, Maintenance Advisory Committee, 24 November 1942, BCSC, vol. 7: 163.

12. The Swiss, who also acted for Japan, also inquired about educational opportunities for evacuee children. A. Rive to High Commissioner, London, 3 December 1943, NAC, Department of External Affairs Records, vol. 3005, file 3464-M-40. Representatives of the International Red Cross, who visited the settlements from time to time, mentioned education but made no particular comments.

13. By October 1942, 2 423 students resided in the interior settlements and 571 in the self-supporting groups. The difference between the initial estimate and the actual number is partly explained by the departure of some families to Alberta and Manitoba and the movement of self-evacuees to scattered points in the interior of British Columbia, notably the Okanagan Valley.

14. W.A. Eastwood to MacNamara, 8 August 1942, BCSC, vol. 13: 503.

15. So determined was the province to be free of the responsibility of educating evacuees that only a veiled threat to disallow any such amendment to the Public Schools Act kept it from forbidding local school boards to accept Japanese students.

16. J.S. Willis to Tyrwhitt, 6 October 1942, BCARS, British Columbia High School Correspondence Branch Records, vol. 1: 1; Mitchell to John Hart, 12 April 1943, Premiers' Papers, vol. 163: 4; Anna B. Miller to Tyrwhitt, 19 October 1942, BCSC, vol. 12: 500; J.E. Read to King, 10 February 1943, NAC, W.L.M. King Papers, #C249486-7; King to Hart, 12 February 1943, Mackenzie Papers, vol. 25. Since few school boards admitted Japanese students, the Commission had to provide some supervision and limited financial assistance towards education in the self-supporting settlements in the Lillooet area where evacuees paid local school taxes but had to arrange private schooling for their own children. In a few cases, local school officials were co-operative. At Grand Forks, in return for tuition fees paid by the Commission and parents, the School Board accepted about forty Japanese children into the public school. Teachers in the New Denver and Kaslo schools invited the Japanese teachers to observe their classes but in Slocan the hostility of the local principal prevented this.

17. Tyrwhitt to MacNamara, 5 October 1942, BCSC, vol.12: 503. Tyrwhitt to Eastwood, 8 November 1942, BCSC, vol. 12: 502.

18. Booth to Eastwood, 17 March 1943, BCSC, vol. 13: 503; Booth to George Hoji, President, PTA, Bay Farm School, 11 August 1943, BCSC, vol. 11: 300. (Because of Access to Information restrictions, not all the information about the Tashme case is available); Stephen A. Kamino to Booth, 13 October 1943, BCSC, vol. 21: 716.

19. See my article, "A Tale of Two Cities: The Reception of Japanese Evacuees in Kelowna and Kaslo, B.C.," *BC Studies* 87 (Autumn 1990): 23-47.

20. It was housed in temporary quarters and had 9 teachers and 212 students in Grades 1 to 8. It used desks borrowed from the local school board. Later, a renovated hardware store accommodated all nine classes and had adequate partitions and lighting.

21. Collins to MacNamara, 7 September 1943, BCSC, vol. 13: 503; C.G. McNeill M.D. to T.C. Orford, 21 October 1943, BCSC, vol. 21: 716.

22. E.L. Boultbee to George Collins, 10 August 1943, BCSC, vol. 1/20.

23. Quoted in Thomas James, *Exile Within: The Schooling of Japanese Americans 1942-1945* (Cambridge: Harvard University Press, 1987), 39-40.

24. *Summer School Echoes*, 3 August 1943.

25. "New Denver Summer School, 1944," BCSC, vol. 13: 514.

26. Perry to Tyrwhitt, 28 August 1942, BCSC, vol. 13: 503.

27. James, *Exile Within*, 43.

28. Tyrwhitt to all Supervisors in Interior Housing Settlements, 6 October 1942, BCSC, vol. 12: 500.

29. Taylor to MacNamara, 27 October 1942, BCSC, vol. 13: 503. The Commission proposed to pay Miss Hyodo $65 per month; her assistant, Miss Teruko Hidaka, $50; $40-$45 per month to senior tutors who had some teacher training or university experience and $30 to junior tutors. The BCSC paid $25 per capita to Manitoba for Japanese students and $65 to Alberta.

30. Miss Hidaka had graduated from Maple Ridge High School and the Provincial Normal School. The Maple Ridge School Board hired her as a substitute teacher but after some parents withdrew their children from her class, the school board decided not to hire any teacher who was ineligible to vote. Since Japanese could not vote in British Columbia that ended Miss Hidaka's career as a public school teacher. (Sumida, "The Japanese," 579ff.) She later taught in a kindergarten operated by the United Church.

31. Booth to Eastwood, 17 March 1943, BCSC, vol. 13: 503.

32. Booth, "Education, British Columbia, January to June 1945," BCSC, vol. 13: 514.

33. Pammett to MacNamara, 4 February 1943, BCSC, vol. 13: 503. At first, the Commission had proposed that a white supervisor and ten white principals would supervise the work of about 135 Japanese teachers or "coaches." (Tyrwhitt to Perry, 29 July 1942, BCSC, vol. 13: 500).

34. MacNamara to Collins, 27 July 1943, BCSC, vol. 13: 503.

35. Booth, "Education in British Columbia," 15 April 1943, BCSC, vol. 13: 513.

36. Booth, "Education in British Columbia," 15 April 1943. The mail to and from the housing centres was censored.

37. Booth to Hyodo, 5 and 19 February 1943; Hyodo to Booth, 17 March 1943; Hyodo to Booth, 5 June 1943; Booth to Hyodo, 28 June 1943; BCSC, vol. 12: 501.

38. Booth to Hyodo, 16 November 1943, BCSC, vol. 12: 501.

39. Tyrwhitt to Hyodo, 22 December 1942, BCSC, vol. 12: 500; Booth to Okuda, 17 February 1943 and Lists of Applicants and Teachers Appointed, Tashme, c. early 1943, BCSC, vol. 21: 716; Booth to MacNamara, 3 February 1943, BCSC, vol. 13: 503; David Suzuki, *Metamorphosis: Stages in a Life* (Toronto: Stoddart, 1987), 67.

40. Booth to Eastwood, 17 March 1943, BCSC, vol. 13: 503; Booth to H. Okuda, 27 January 1943, BCSC and Hidaka to Booth, 23 February 1943, BCSC, vol. 21: 716.

41. Shizuye Takashima, *A Child in Prison Camp*, (Montreal, 1971), n.p.

42. "Honor Work" allowed students to prepare booklets including relevant pictures or stories and drawings of their own creation. Among the possible answers were freedom from oppression, justice, and courage. Copies of the lessons may be found in BCARS, Department of Education, Elementary Correspondence Branch, vol. 7.

43. Hidaka to Booth, 23 February 1943, BCSC, vol. 21/716; Booth to Miller, 18 January 1942, BCARS, Elementary Correspondence Branch, vol. 14.

44. I am indebted to Michiko Midge Ayukawa for this information.

45. *Summer School Echoes*, 4 August 1943.

46. J.C. Harris, "Our New Canadian's Problems," September 1944, BCARS, J.C. Harris Papers, vol. 3: 12.

47. F.C. Boyes, "British Columbia Security Commission, New Denver Summer School, July-August 1943," BCSC, vol. 13: 513.

48. Booth to Miller, 14 October 1943, Department of Education, Elementary Correspondence Branch, vol. 14.

49. In her partly autobiographical novel, *Obasan*, Joy Kogawa records some words of her school song: "Slocan get on your toes/We are as everyone knows/The school with spirit high!/We

all do our best/And never never will rest/Till we with triumph cry...." (Toronto: Lester, Orpen & Dennys, 1981), 157.

50. Lemon Creek School Report, January 1945, BCSC, vol. 13: 513.

51. "New Denver Summer School, 1944," BCSC, vol. 13: 514.

52. Takashi Tsuji, Bay Farm School Report, 2 February and 1 March 1945.

53. "New Denver Summer School, 1944," BCSC, vol. 13: 514. The median score in the Dominion Language Tests for students entering the Vancouver Normal School was 82.

54. Sumida, "The Japanese in B.C.," 513.

55. Booth, "Monthly Educational Report, April 1943"; Booth to MacNamara, 3 February 1943, BCS, vol. 13: 503; *Kootenaian*, 10 February 1944; *The New Canadian*, 19 February 1944; *The New Canadian*, 4 March 1944; *Kaslo School Reports*, 2 May 1944, 30 September and October 1944, BCSC, vol. 13: 513.

56. *Lemon Creek School Report*, February, March and April 1944; *Sandon School Report*, March 1944; *Riverview School Report*, March 1944 and November 1945; *New Denver Orchard School Report*, October 1944, vol. 13: 513.

57. *New Denver Orchard School Report*, February and October 1944; *Bay Farm School Report*, December 1945; *Lemon Creek School Report*, February 1944; *Popoff School Report*, November 1945, all in BCSC, vol. 13: 513.

58. *Popoff School Report*, November 1944 and Booth, "September-December 1944," BCSC, vol. 13: 514.

59. Anstey defended these tests as measurements of achievement, intelligence, and "the ability to use facts, to relate them one to another, and to draw conclusions" rather than merely the ability to recall facts. ("Report on the B.C.S.C. Schools of the Interior," July 1945.)

60. Booth, "Education, British Columbia, November-December 1943." British Columbia students as a whole traditionally scored well on such American tests. George S. Tomkins, A Common Contenance: Stability and Change in the Canadian Curriculum (Scarborough: Prentice-Hall, 1986), 242.

61. MacNamara to Collins, 31 August 1943 and Anstey to Collins, 29 October 1943, BCSC, vol. 13: 503; Booth, "Education: British Columbia," July 1944 and "September-December 1944," BCSC, vol. 13: 514; Booth to Hyodo, 9 November 1943, BCSC, vol. 12: 501; *The New Canadian*, 22 January and 29 April 1944.

62. Booth, "Education," 15 April 1943; *Summer School Echoes*, 4 August 1943 (copy in BCSC, vol. 28: 1316).

63. *Annual Report*, 1943-44, copy in BCSC, vol. 13: 514; *Rosebery, Principal's Report*, January and February 1945, BCSC, vol. 13: 513; Pammett to Booth, 6 February 1945, NAC, Department of Labour Records, vol. 657; MacNamara to Collins, 8 November and 13 December 1943, BCSC, vol. 13: 503.

64. Booth, *September-December 1944*, BCSC, vol. 13/514.

65. *Popoff School Report*, March 1945; Sugiura to Booth, 2 May 1945, BCSC, vol. 13: 513; Booth, "September-December 1944," and "January to June, 1945," BCSC, vol. 13: 514; Yoshiko Tanabe to Booth, 2 May 1945 and M. Uyeda to Booth, 3 May 1945, BCSC, vol. 13: 513; H.T. Pammett, "Report on Inspection Trip to Vancouver and through Japanese Projects – June 15-30, 1945," BCSC, vol. 17: 630.

66. T.B. Pickersgill to MacNamara, 17 September 1945, BCSC, vol. 13: 514.

67. H.T. Pammett, "Report on Inspection Trip to Vancouver and through Japanese Projects – June 15-30, 1945," BCSC, vol. 17: 630.

68. MacNamara to T.B. Pickersgill, 18 August 1945, BCSC, vol. 14: 514.

392 Organizing and Reorganizing Schools

69. This complex matter is discussed in greater detail in Roy et al., *Mutual Hostages*, ch. 6. Sugiura to Booth, 2 October 1945, and *Report*, November 1945, BCSC, vol. 13: 513.

70. A total of 3 964 individuals were "repatriated" to Japan in 1946. Of these, a third were children under the age of sixteen. Canada, Department of Labour, Report on the Re-Establishment of Japanese in Canada, 1944-1946 (Ottawa, 1947), 15.

71. Pammett, "Report on Inspection Trip to Vancouver and through Japanese Projects – June 15-30, 1945," BCSC, vol. 17: 630; Macnamara to Pickersgill, 8 June 1946 and Booth to Pammett, 19 February 1947, BCSC, vol. 12: 500.

72. Booth to Pammett, 19 February 1947, BCSC, vol. 12: 500; Public Schools, *Annual Reports*, 1945-48, *passim.*

73. Anstey to Booth, 29 October 1943, BCSC, vol. 13: 513. [Italics in the original.]

74. Suzuki, *Metamorphosis*, 68; Broadfoot, *Years of Sorrow*, 252-3; W. McBride, "Tashme," BCARS, Mrs. J.W. Awmack Collection; Kogawa, *Obasan*, 157.

75. Arthur Anstey, "Report on B.C.S.C. Schools of the Interior," July 1945, BCSC, vol. 13: 514.

76. *Bay Farm School Report*, 16 June 1945, BCSC, vol. 13: 513.

20

Deprivatizing Private Education: The British Columbia Experience[1]

Jean Barman

In 1977 British Columbia embarked on an educational policy virtually unique in North America.[2] Until then the province's private schools were unregulated, subject to no external requirements apart from basic health and safety standards applicable generally across the society. Then came provincial legislation. Today, not only do the overwhelming majority of non-public schools receive 50 percent of the funding accorded local public schools, but all educational institutions must register with provincial authorities whether or not they desire financial assistance. Private education has been deprivatized.

Although the British Columbia experience generated initial scholarly interest, effects over the long term have not been analyzed.[3] My argument is that family choice and state control have grown dialectically. Government funding, intended to expand the boundaries of choice for parents, did bring higher enrolments and new schools. This in turn encouraged greater public oversight, which has then constrained the boundaries of choice. I do not enter the debate over the comparative merits of public and non-public education.[4]

Background

Until 1977, private schooling in British Columbia was limited in its influence to small minorities centred in specific social settings and geographical areas. Over 95 percent of children attended local public non-denominational schools. The provincial government concerned itself only with the public sector. Private schools were not mentioned in the Ministry of Education's annual reports, much less monitored. There were three distinctive groups of private schools, each of which for its own reasons helped form the lobby that from the 1960s sought to persuade the provincial government to enact the crucial legislation.

The oldest group were Catholic schools whose beginnings went back as far as did European settlement itself to the mid-nineteenth century.[5] Because the Catholic church failed to secure legal recognition for its schools prior to British Columbia's entry into Confederation in 1871, the schools acquired no claim under the terms of the British North America Act to be financially supported as alternatives within the public system, as occurred with Catholic schools in some other areas of Canada. British Columbia's handful of Catholic schools limped along as private institutions, continuing to believe, however, that they were legitimately entitled to official recognition and public funding. After the Second World War an increasingly assertive Catholic hierarchy took direct action. Not only were dozens of new schools constructed across the province to serve the one in seven British Columbians who was Catholic, but a very public war of words was waged through repeated briefs and appeals to the provincial government.[6] The number of Catholic schools quadrupled between the early 1950s and mid-1960s to well over sixty, but, despite its higher profile, the Catholic church was unable on its own to obtain any concessions or assistance from the province.

A second group of non-public schools had origins going back almost as far in time, to British Columbia's origins as a British colony.[7] As around the world, so in colonial British Columbia the Church of England established its own private, elite schools which on Confederation also remained outside the provincial system. The Anglican tradition was buttressed early in the twentieth century as a consequence of extensive upper-middle-class British immigration into British Columbia, which many newcomers perceived as still a British outpost where they could educate their children in the same class-based fashion as in Britain itself. Over a hundred private boys' and girls' schools on the British model were established in areas of extensive British settlement, many soon also acquiring students from among families of other backgrounds who sought similar, supposedly superior status for their children. By mid-century many of the three dozen or so schools still in operation had fallen on hard times, unable to provide the costly physical amenities of the postwar public system. At the same time schools continued to attract many offspring of influential families, including those whose fathers were willing to use political connections to ensure the schools' survival. This was particularly the case once attention turned to the securing of financial support from the provincial government.

It was the third principal group of private schools that spearheaded the joint lobbying effort to obtain government support. The Netherland's devastation in the Second World War brought many young people to areas of the world with similar geography. Upwards of 20 000 settled in British Columbia's fertile river valleys.[8] Like their British predecessors, the Dutch brought with them a strong commitment to private education. The unquestioned assumption in the Netherlands was that each child would be schooled according to the family's religious beliefs in a government-supported but denominationally based institution. Many Dutch immigrants to British Columbia were Calvinists committed to what they termed "Christian" schooling. Assisted by missionaries from older settlements in the United States, they soon established some two dozen Christian schools.[9] These new British Columbians firmly believed that government, be it in the old world or the new, had a responsibility to fund their offsprings' schooling just as it did that of most other children in the society.

By the early 1960s each of the three groups of schools realized that, on their own, they were unable to change a provincial policy that had never acknowledged, much less funded, educational alternatives to the public system. In 1966 the associations representing the three groups, totalling 121 schools, came together to form a joint lobby, the Federation of Independent School Associations. FISA, as it is usually known, was not an organization of schools but rather of their separate associations, whose continued existence showed the great extent to which the separate strands in private education stood apart from each other. The word "independent" in the name of the federation denoted these schools' conscious change in orientation from being "private," in the sense of private profitmaking, to independent, in the sense of distinct from the public system.[10]

FISA's sole mandate was to secure provincial recognition and funding. Its executive director, Gerry Ensing, came out of the very vigorous Dutch Calvinist tradition and was determined that the provincial government must acknowledge the private sector's contribution to education and accord it its financial due. Ensing was extraordinarily capable and effective in promoting grass-roots activism among private-school supporters. "Think carefully! YOU have supported your private school, financially, YOU have read and heard all about this subject and presumably, agree. BUT, HAVE YOU WRITTEN YOUR LETTER? Male or female, youth or adult the testing time is NOW! The wedge is inserted! DRIVE IT HOME, WITH A GENTLE BUT FIRM BLOW WITH YOUR PEN!"[11] Key provincial legislators of diverse political orientations soon saw the practical advantages in supporting the cause. As L.W. Downey has analyzed in detail, the passage of legislation in September 1977 underlined the extent to which a small but determined vested-interest group could set public policy.[12]

Legislation

The School Support (Independent) Act of 1977 provided for two levels of per-pupil funding to schools in operation for at least five years. To qualify for assistance at 10 percent of what it cost to educate the same child in a public school in the same district, a school had only to satisfy a school inspector that it did not promote racial or religious intolerance or social change through violent means, and that it had adequate facilities. Funding at the higher rate of 30 percent of comparable costs required adherence to the same basic educational program being offered in the public system, subsequent employment of qualified teachers, participation in provincial student assessment and examination programs, and operation as a non-profit enterprise. Most established schools requested funding at the higher level even though the legislation did not, it must be stressed, compel schools to seek recognition and funding. Only a small minority then or later sought assistance at the lower level. Schools that for religious or other reasons rejected the principle of government control over education remained free to operate unhindered by any outside authority, be it the provincial government or FISA. Official terminology thereafter tended to refer to schools receiving funds as independent, those opting to go their own way as private.

The original Act was subsequently amended and rewritten in ways more favorable to schools seeking funding. In 1982 the time a school had to operate before applying for assistance was cut from five to three years, in mid-1987 to just a single year, shifts that encouraged the foundation of new schools. Also in 1987 the date when a school would actually receive the first payment for a particular school year was advanced from November of the subsequent year to February of the year in question, a considerable boon for smaller schools operating on the economic margin.[13] Maximum funding was at the same time raised to 35 percent.

Responding to recommendations of the provincial Sullivan Royal Commission on Education, which reported in 1988, a new Independent School Act was passed in mid-1989. The funding level was raised to 50 percent for schools whose per-pupil operating expenses did not exceed those of public institutions in the same school district and which, as summed up by the Minister of Education during debate on the legislation, "meet all the requirements or parallel requirements of the public school system in terms of educational programs." For schools whose per-pupil costs were higher than in public schools in the same district, the same regulations held but funding remained at 35 percent. The lower rate continued at 10 percent. Although the latter schools did not have to follow the provincial curriculum, they were now, as the minister emphasized, "required to provide an educational program, as . . . in the public schools."[14] Schools' capital and other non-operating costs are not provincially supported, although schools have been and continue to be accorded a proportion of funds targeted from time to time for special purposes, such as Pacific Rim initiatives, computer education, and programs for children with learning disabilities.[15]

The 1989 Act also put private education as a whole under state control for the first time in British Columbia. All schools enrolling ten or more children and all home-schooling families, defined as school-aged groups of fewer than ten, were required to register with provincial authorities.[16] Upon registration, a school was officially inspected. Home-schooling families were subject to superintendents' inspection. As had been the case in funded schools, all schools were now explicitly prohibited from offering programs that fostered racial or ethnic superiority, religious intolerance, or social change through violent means.

Very importantly, the Independent School Act of 1989 began with the same preamble as did its companion School Act, for the first time committing all schools across the province to a common purpose developed by the ministry for the public system. "The purpose of the British Columbia school system is to enable learners to develop their individual potential and to acquire the knowledge, skills and attitudes needed to contribute to a healthy society and a prosperous and sustainable economy."[17] Although non-funded schools could still make a profit and hire unqualified teachers, the requirement clearly and unequivocally put the state's social and economic priorities up front. British Columbia's remaining "private" schools were in effect legislated out of existence.

Growing Numbers

Since 1978 both the number of pupils in non-public schools and the number of institutions have grown steadily, although, as Table 1 makes clear, two important shifts sometimes attributed to the legislation were already underway. Demographics were depressing public school enrolments even as those of non-public schools were rising, partly in reaction to what some British Columbians perceived to be public-school permissiveness. The number of children in the public system fell from a high of 549 00 in 1973/74 to under 530 000 by 1977/78, during which time enrolment in non-public schools grew from just over 21 000 to almost 24 000.

Funding accelerated the trend in favor of non-public school enrolments. Public school numbers troughed at 486 000 in 1986/87, moving slowly upwards thereafter, whereas the number of non-public pupils surpassed 41 000 by 1990/91. Overall, the proportion of British Columbia children being educated outside the public system rose by two thirds, from 4.3 percent in 1977/78 to 7.3 percent in 1990/91. The number of non-public institutions also grew by two thirds, from approximately 167 in 1977/78 to 279 by 1989/90. In addition, an estimated 2 000 to 3 000 children, or just over 0.5 percent of their cohort, were being home-schooled.

Overall figures are somewhat misleading, for growth in numbers and thereby in families' choice of school for their children has not been evenly dispersed between the principal groups of non-public schools. As Table 2 shows, Catholic enrolments have increased least. Yet the influence of funding for this, the largest group of schools, has probably been the most significant. The province's Catholic schools had by their own admission fallen on hard times, a situation worsened by a worldwide shortage of cheap, dedicated Catholic labor. Many schools so optimistically established across hinterland British Columbia during the postwar years were barely surviving. The church's willingness to countenance, never mind to champion, a joint funding campaign is perhaps the best evidence of the situation's gravity. Funding turned matters around. By 1980 enrolments were slowly but steadily moving upward. Fees could be kept down while individual schools were made more attractive through the improvement of deteriorating facilities and employment of paid teachers to replace aging nuns and lay brothers.

Of sixty-seven Catholic schools in operation on the eve of funding, 1977/78, just four subsequently closed, two at least for non-economic reasons. Overriding strenuous parental objections, an elderly order of nuns from Montreal shut down an exclusive Vancouver girls' school rather than see it fall into the hands of lay teachers. A few years later a popular girls' high school in nearby Burnaby was summarily closed by the local archdiocese rather than submit to unionizing teachers' demands.[18] Nine new Catholic schools were founded in the early to mid-1980s, primarily in rapidly expanding suburban communities.[19] Their appearance partially accounts for the rise in enrolments from just over 13 000 at the beginning of the decade to 17 000 by 1987. Totals thereafter levelled out. This is in part because, rather than reducing

TABLE 1
Comparison of British Columbia Public and Private School Enrolments,
1970/71 - 1990/91*

	Public school enrolment	% change over prev. year	Private school enrolment	% change over prev. year	Total enrolment	Private enrol. as % of total
1970/71	526,991	—	21,319	—	548,310	3.9
1971/72	524,305	-0.5	21,777	2.1	546,082	4.0
1972/73	537,067	2.4	22,061	1.3	559,128	4.0
1973/74	549,019	-2.2	21,421	-2.9	570,440	3.8
1974/75	541,575	-1.4	21,055	-1.7	562,630	3.7
1975/76	542,680	0.2	23,071	9.6	565,751	4.1
1976/77	536,237	-1.2	23,318	1.1	559,555	4.2
1977/78	527,769	-1.6	23,691	1.6	551,460	4.3
1978/79	517,786	-1.9	24,556	3.7	542,342	4.5
1979/80	511,671	-1.2	24,827	1.1	536,498	4.6
1980/81	509,805	-0.4	26,314	6.0	536,119	4.9
1981/82	503,371	-1.3	27,936	6.2	531,307	5.3
1982/83	500,336	-0.6	28,280	1.2	528,616	5.4
1983/84	497,312	-0.6	29,118	3.0	526,430	5.5
1984/85	491,264	-1.2	30,326	4.1	521,590	5.8
1985/86	486,777	-0.9	33,553	10.6	520,330	6.5
1986/87	486,299	-0.1	34,242	2.1	520,541	6.6
1987/88	491,309	1.0	36,724	7.3	528,033	7.0
1988/89	500,088	1.8	37,731	2.7	537,819	7.0
1989/90**	513,533	2.7	39,240	4.0	552,773	7.1
1990/91**	527,900	2.8	41,391	5.5	569,291	7.3
% change over 20 years		0.2		94.2		3.8
% change since funding		nil		74.7		3.2

*Federal schools for native Indian children and schools for blind and deaf students are excluded from the total.
**Figures shown are estimates.
Sources: Statistics Canada, *Elementary-Secondary School Enrolment* (81-210) and *Advanced Statistics of Education* (81-220), and FISA calculations.

fees and so encouraging additional families to consider attendance, institutions used provincial funds primarily to raise teachers' salaries toward provincial norms in the public system, hoping to counter threats of unionization. State funding has been critical to the renaissance of Catholic education in British Columbia.

In the case of the province's elite schools on the British model, their relatively small growth in enrolments has been largely self-imposed. The ten that survived into the late 1970s used funding primarily to retrieve lost exclusivity. Rather than moderating fees, they chose to upgrade facilities or even open new campuses in order to maximize appeal and thereby pupil selectivity. Their success was most visible in the foundation in the heavily populated Greater Vancouver area of several new schools quite contented to accept the older schools' rejects.[20] These institutions, old and new, have been especially concerned to maintain their image as distinct from and superior to the public system.[21] In 1989 they opposed any further rise in provincial funding beyond 35 percent and helped fashion the dual policy whereby only schools whose per-pupil cost was below that in local public schools received the higher rate of 50 percent.

Christian schools have expanded the most dramatically in numbers and enrolment. The general appeal of conservative Christian values has been evident in the parallel growth of funded Christian schools and of their non-funded counterparts.[22] Funded Christian schools have increased enrolments one and a half times over the past twelve years, while overall enrolments in non-funded private schools, the majority evangelical Christian in outlook, have doubled.

In practice the two kinds of Christian schools intertwine.[23] Those originating in Dutch immigration have gradually become more welcoming of families belonging to other Protestant churches.[24] State funding has been vital in legitimizing curricula and teachers and thereby achieving broadly based acceptability within the larger Christian community. Some non-funded Christian schools begun by particular evangelical or fundamentalist denominations have moved closer to their funded counterparts by joining the association encompassing funded Christian schools and applying for provincial recognition and financial assistance. Thus, enrolment in non-funded schools as a whole began to decline in the late 1980s even as, so Table 2 details, that in funded Christian schools continued to rise. Newer funded schools were mostly located in geographical areas without Dutch settlement, thereby increasing funded Christian schools' accessibility to families across the province. By the end of the 1980s, twenty-five to thirty different denominations were represented among pupils attending funded Christian schools.

Christian schools choosing to remain non-funded have often had relatively short life spans. Founded by an enterprising minister and operating in ad hoc quarters, likely a church basement, they have relied on individualized curricula such as Alpha-Omega or Accelerated Christian Education, the latter able to be overseen by non-professionals, often the minister and his wife or other volunteers from within the church. Thus, almost half the approximately sixty non-funded Christian schools in operation in the early 1980s had begun after 1977 but were closed by the end of the

1980s, by which time another thirty or so new non-funded Christian schools were in operation across British Columbia.[25]

Other non-public schools have fared variously. The stagnation of alternative school enrolments, even where such schools received funding, was likely a consequence of general conservatism in social values in the 1980s. Seventh Day Adventists, who at first rejected government funding, have had little success in opening new schools. Other religious schools, schools for very young children, and schools for children with special needs have each tripled in numbers, due largely to the increased ease of obtaining provincial funding. Among groups establishing schools in the 1980s in British Columbia were Mormons, Sikhs and Muslims.

Increased Oversight

The growth in numbers of pupils and schools has both encouraged and been encouraged by increased official and unofficial oversight of non-public education. The shift has gone beyond changes in legislation into attitudes. Non-public schools have come to be perceived as an integral component of a provincial system of education. Whereas once it was the Federation of Independent School Associations alone that spoke out for private education, three powerful groups now look out for their interests.

First, unlike some lobbies that fold their tent as soon as their goal is secured, FISA strengthened its presence in British Columbia as the principal liaison between, and advocate for, various groups or associations of schools that otherwise continued to have relatively little in common.[26] The federation communicates schools' concerns to the proper authorities, monitors government actions, and administers some provincial programs encompassing non-public schools, making FISA a direct agent of state control. FISA also functions as the principal advocate of independent education, in the press and elsewhere defending the principle of funding and making the case for family choice and diversity in education.[27] FISA's role should not be underestimated. FISA has had internally to maintain a delicate balancing act between school associations, some of which favor increased funding, even as high as 100 percent, whereas others oppose any change appearing to legitimize government intervention in their operations. FISA has been remarkably successful in quietly and effectively reconciling very different perspectives.

The provincial Ministry of Education officially oversees non-public education, ensuring that individual schools adhere to designated standards for curriculum and teachers' credentials. The presence of an Independent Schools Division within a government ministry traditionally responsible only for public education has played a major role in legitimizing private schools as integral to the provincial system. Although some individuals within the division, including Gerry Ensing, formerly of FISA, have been scrupulous in their public neutrality, others have sometimes sounded "more like an apologist for the private schools than their inspector."[28]

TABLE 2
British Columbia Private School Enrolment, 1977/78-1990/91

	Catholic	% incr. over prev. year	Elite	% incr. over prev. year	Funded Christian	% incr. over prev. year	Other funded	% incr. over prev. year	Non-funded	% incr. over prev. year	Total
1977/78	13,264	—	3,559	—	2,471	—	1,357	—	3,040	—	23,691
1978/79	13,395	1.0	3,556	-0.1	2,702	9.8	1,411	4.0	3,492	14.9	24,556
1979/80	13,226	-1.3	3,667	3.1	2,946	9.0	1,273	-9.8	3,715	6.4	24,827
1980/81	13,712	3.7	3,661	-0.2	3,239	10.0	1,498	17.7	4,204	13.2	26,314
1981/82	14,077	2.7	3,839	4.9	3,436	6.1	2,056	37.3	4,528	7.7	27,936
1982/83	14,620	3.9	3,872	0.9	3,592	4.5	2,002	-2.6	4,194	-7.4	28,280
1983/84	15,516	6.1	3,935	1.6	3,745	4.3	1,518	-24.2	4,404	5.0	29,118
1984/85	15,421	-0.6	3,886	-1.3	3,969	6.0	1,756	15.7	5,294	20.2	30,326
1985/86	16,592	7.6	4,331	11.5	4,149	4.5	2,047	16.6	6,434	21.5	33,553
1986/87	16,934	2.1	4,484	3.5	4,639	11.8	2,563	25.2	5,662	-28.2	34,242
1987/88	17,029	0.6	4,697	4.8	5,133	10.0	3,396	32.5	6,469	15.1	36,724
1988/89	16,734	-1.7	4,814	2.5	5,509	7.3	3,755	10.6	6,919	6.9	37,731
1989/90	16,845	0.7	5,196	7.9	6,281	14.0	4,570	21.7	6,348	8.3	39,240
1990/91	17,354	3.0	5,158	-0.7	7,476	19.0	5,344	16.9	6,059	-4.5	41,391
% increase since funding	30.8		44.9		202.6		293.8		99.3		

Enrolments in non-funded schools are estimates only.

Source: Enrolment statistics compiled by the Federation of Independent School Associations on behalf of Statistics Canada.

The third critical support group is the provincial government itself. The centre-right Social Credit coalition that raised the funding level to 50 percent actively encouraged non-public schooling as an option for British Columbian families. Some MLAs have been attracted by the elitism, others have been genuinely concerned to give parents the opportunity to opt for religiously-based schooling for their offspring. Over the past dozen years evangelical Christians have played a growing role in government as members of the legislature and as ministers. Overall, the vision of society held by some members of government has more closely approximated the non-public sector, or at the least the freedom to choose, than public education.[29]

The Dialectic

Growing oversight combined with the expansion in family choice has fundamentally altered the character of non-public education in British Columbia. Provincial funding revitalized non-public schools, but at a price. Whereas a dozen years ago these schools quietly went their own way, they are now accountable not just to the government but in the court of public opinion. Their every action is monitored by and discussed in the press, due in good part to their appeal.

The dominant image of private education depicted in the press is of a panacea inaccessible to ordinary British Columbians. An editorial in the province's major newspaper unequivocally asserted in 1987 that all private schools "are elitist."[30] Such an assessment gains credibility from the frequent advertisements in the daily and periodical press for the province's handful of truly elite schools, containing details like "fully 96% of last year's graduating seniors gain[ed] admission to universities such as Harvard, Princeton and MIT."[31] Newspaper headlines at first glance negative in tone "Hefty private school funding hike angers cash-strapped public schools" leave much the same message.[32] FISA's very success in holding together an independent school coalition has ironically heightened the perception of all non-public schools as fashioned in the image of the select few.

The press's tendency to obscure schools' differing goals and clientele is due in part to its distillation of expertise. Having polled British Columbians to determine their level of support for private education, Donald Erickson lumped his findings together as though they applied equally to all kinds of non-public schools.[33] The Ministry of Education has contributed to the same perception through such actions as highlighting in its annual report a public opinion survey indicating that, "if money was no object, more than half the population would choose to send their children to an independent school."[34] One consequence is that families believe they will obtain for their child at an economy-model Catholic or evangelical Christian school the attributes of exclusivity promised by one elite school with its public assertions that "the world steps aside for any man who knows where he is going."[35] To the extent that families do not experience anticipated satisfaction or cannot afford a non-public school in the first place, antagonisms grow and non-public schools become more accountable for their every action.

Non-public education's new visibility has meant that individual schools are monitored as never before. Efforts to get rezoning or other concessions result in extensive press coverage.[36] The revelation in spring 1989 that two of Vancouver's elite schools limited admissions of local students of Asian background in the interests of maintaining an "appropriate ethnic mix" unleashed a public furor. Whereas half the children entering the public system in Vancouver speak English as a second language, half of these a Chinese language, one of the two schools deliberately kept the proportions of Asians to 20 percent and of other ethnic groups to between 2 and 3 percent, despite half its applicants being of Asian descent.[37] Another outcry erupted a year later over the realization that some non-public schools issued tuition rebate slips for income tax purposes on the ground that the school offered at least one post-secondary course and therefore the fees of all students, whatever their academic level, were deductible for tax purposes, a position apparently upheld by Revenue Canada.[38] Also in 1990 came news that one of the province's best-known elite schools had decided to continue to restrict its enrolment to males, which some in the public considered reason for withdrawing public funds from the institution.[39]

Funded schools whose religious underpinnings have appeared to take precedence over their educational function have also come under public scrutiny.[40] The most extreme case was a conflict between the Catholic church and teachers at the province's only Catholic girls' high school. In the end the church got its way by simply shutting down the school, but the cost was much heavier than if the events had occurred a decade previous. The conflict began when teachers sought to unionize in order to raise their salaries and to secure better working conditions. The Catholic hierarchy was unwilling to discuss such issues as teachers' personal behaviour outside school hours. Many interpreted it as a warning to teachers in other Catholic schools considering unionization that the church closed the school over the protests of students, parents and teachers. Every scene and act in a lengthy drama of conflicting views was monitored by the daily press, and the church lost decisively in the court of public opinion.[41] The Catholic church was made accountable for its actions in so unfavorable a light as to make it highly unlikely that any school or religious group would ever again act in similar fashion. All non-public schools across British Columbia were put on guard that even in terms of their philosophical and religious underpinnings, there were public standards for acceptable behavior. As for the Catholic church, it not suprisingly used much of the 1989 funding increase to raise teachers' salaries.

Neither are funded schools any longer independent in terms of daily operations. Individual schools still embody very different philosophical, religious and even class-based perspectives. Yet each must now serve the same basic purposes as does the public system, summed up in the preamble to the 1989 legislation. Educational programs build on a core curriculum developed within the public system. Some long-standing teachers are qualified through experience, but more and more receive their training in the same post-secondary institutions serving the public system and are similarly certified, meaning that they can readily move between public and non-public schools.[42] All students take the same provincial graduation examinations and graduate equally qualified to enter institutions of higher learning. The provincial inspector of independent schools has the authority to appraise all school records as well as to "examine the achievement of students and examine and assess teachers, programs, operations and administration."[43]

Further, by accepting funding non-public schools have committed themselves in advance to whatever new regulations the Ministry of Education may implement for the system as a whole. Through FISA, schools have some voice in policy formation, but that voice is very small compared to that of the much larger public system. When during the early 1980s the provincial government repeatedly cut back public education in the name of economic restraint, independent schools were also cut back. Far-reaching policy changes consequent on the 1988 Sullivan Royal Commission look toward a fundamental restructuring of the entire system by the year 2000.[44] Although independent schools have some flexibility, the widespread assumption that their academic component equals or surpasses that in the public school creates tremendous pressures to conform. As one independent school head put the case, "it's our job to be up-to-date with what's happening educationally."[45] For non-public schools in British Columbia, the future is no longer theirs alone to determine.

The 1989 legislation paired the carrot of funding with the stick of mandatory registration and what the minister termed "stronger inspection."[46] The appeal of financial assistance had already brought into the regulated category the majority of schools, together enrolling about 85 percent of non-publicly educated children. Although the new Act does not force the remaining schools to accept provincial funding, it does stipulate that they as well as home-schooling families must, for the first time, acknowledge themselves before the state. When the legislation was passed, the provincial inspector of private schools commented that some non-funded schools deeply opposed the new Act. "They don't want us to know about them because they're afraid of government intervention."[47]

The new Act effectively puts children's right to a basic education, whatever school they attend, above their parents' and the school's philosophical or religious predilections.[48] As the Act's preamble affirms, children's rights take priority: "The purpose of the British Columbia school system is to enable learners to develop their individual potential and to acquire the knowledge, skills and attitudes needed to contribute to a healthy society and a prosperous and sustainable economy." The Minister of Education explained the preamble's purpose as ensuring that non-public schools "meet more stringent requirements relative to the public school act, so that if students had a choice, they also had equal opportunity to get an education that would prepare them for a healthy society."[49]

Most supporters of non-public education, by distinguishing between schools' didactic and moral functions, have had little difficulty accepting the state's greater role. They applauded the 1989 legislation as putting "into a legislative code a commitment to pluralism in education" with "room for parental choice."[50] They hold that their ability to teach from their own philosophical or religious perspective has been little, if at all, affected by the growth of state oversight. A minority, including some members of the evangelical Christian community, have expressed reservations based on their strong belief that the state has no role in schooling. Others worry over the appropriate percentage of financial support, with its implication of a comparable degree of state control. The greater the reliance on government funding, the more difficult it becomes to oppose government requests that might in the event of opposition become demands. Thus, during internal debate preceding the 1989 legislation, some voices within FISA argued that the proportion should not top the current 35 percent, others that it not exceed 49 percent, to ensure schools retain 51 percent control.

For the overwhelming majority, the security of financial support far outweighs apprehensions that a provincial government of a different political orientation might revise regulations. FISA's effective cooption of provincial political parties and of most major interest groups through ongoing liaison has ensured there will be no drastic reversal in policy.[51] Funding itself is no longer at issue. The government in power in 1995, the New Democrats, has since the early 1980s committed itself to maintaining financial support of non-public schooling. In debating the 1989 legislation, the NDP critic for education, Anita Hagen, emphasized that "we agree with the government that choice and alternatives should be the hallmark of an educational system," even though the preference would be for "that kind of choice and diversity to exist within the public school system as broadly as possible." She continued, "So I am passionately committed to the public school system, but I recognize too and certainly we have recognized and acknowledged that parents are seeking choices related to the educational needs of their children and also to the values that they feel are important."[52]

Thus, what began in 1977 as a single piece of legislation secured by a small interest group has become an integral component of public policy. Growing numbers of British Columbian families have come to consider non-public alternatives for their children. At the same time, family choice has been constrained, in part through non-public schools' very success. The didactic function of most such schools now differs little from that of their public counterparts. Even schools' philosophical and religious underpinnings, supposedly the reason for their existence in the first place, have increasingly come under public scrutiny. Individual schools may still run roughshod over teachers and families, but only at considerable cost in terms of public censure. Independent education's new visibility may not dictate but certainly tempers schools' behaviour in philosophical and religious as well as in didactic realms.

From the perspective of children's rights, events in British Columbia have further meaning. The distinctive philosophical and religious underpinnings of independent schools have been moderated by the right of all children, to quote once again from the preamable common to the School and Independent School Acts, to "acquire the knowledge, skills and attitudes needed to contribute to a healthy society." Children are protected, at least in theory, against the actions of willful schools even where those are selected by equally willful parents. Education in British Columbia may not conform to the traditional image of the local public school as the common meeting ground for the next generation, yet the system has since 1977 moved markedly in that direction.

Notes

1. I am grateful to the Social Sciences and Humanities Research Council for financial support of the Canadian Childhood History Project, under whose auspices this assessment was developed. It draws not only on written sources including the daily press but on conversations with numerous individuals more expert than myself, including Gerry Ensing, Fred Herfst, Harro Van Brummelen, and private-school teachers and principals in Vanderhoof, Vernon and Vancouver.

2. Only Alberta is comparable, although Saskatchewan, Manitoba and Quebec also fund private schools. Private education across Canada is discussed in an international context in John J. Bergen, "Canada: Private Schools," Geoffrey Walford, ed., *Private Schools in Ten Countries: Policy and Practice* (London: Routledge, 1989), 85, 104 and in Charles L. Glenn, *Choice of Schools in Six Nations* (Washington, DC: U.S. Department of Education, 1989), 145-85.

3. The largest was the multi-year COFIS ("A Study of the Consequences of Funding Independent Schools in British Columbia") study undertaken by Donald Erickson, whose published findings have been sparse. See Donald E. Erickson, Lloyd MacDonald and Michael E. Manley-Casimir, *Characteristics and Relationships in Public and Independent Schools* (San Francisco and Vancouver: Centre for Research on Private Education and Educational Research Institute of British Columbia, 1979); and Donald A. Erickson, "Should All the Nation's Schools Compete for Clients and Support?" *Phi Delta Kappan*, September 1979, 14 17, 77.

4. Some of these issues are discussed in Donald Fisher, "Family Choice and Education: Privatizing a Public Good," Manley-Casimir, ed., *Family Choice*, 199-206; Donald Fisher and Averlyn Gill, "Diversity in Society and Schools," *Pacific Group for Policy Alternatives* (paper no. P-85-03), (Vancouver, 1985); and Donald Fisher and Betty Gilgoff, "The Crisis in B.C. Public Education: The State and the Public Interest," Terry Wotherspoon, ed., *A Sociology of Education: Readings in the Political Economy of Canadian Schooling* (Toronto: Methuen, 1986), 68 93.

5 On the broader historical context, see chapter 1.

6. The official Catholic interpretation of events is summarized in "History of B.C.'s independent school struggle," *B.C. Catholic*, 18 September 1977, 3.

7. On these schools, see Jean Barman, *Growing Up British in British Columbia: Boys in Private School* (Vancouver: University of British Columbia Press, 1984), chapter 18.

8. On Dutch immigration to British Columbia, see Edith M. Ginn, "Rural Dutch Immigrants in the Lower Fraser Valley" (M.A. thesis, Department of Geography, UBC, 1967).

9. See Harro W. Van Brummelen, *Telling the Next Generation: Educational Development in North American Calvinist Christian Schools* (Lanham: University Press of America, 1986), 250-65.

10. The term "independent" began to be used by the elite schools in British Columbia after the Second World War, as it was in Britain, to set themselves apart as no longer private-profit-making. The British Columbia press still uses the two terms interchangeably.

11. Undated FISA bulletin from 1970. Capital letters in original.

12. L.W. Downey, "The Aid-to-Independent Schools Movement in British Columbia," Nancy M. Sheehan, J. Donald Wilson and David C. Jones, ed., *Schools in the West: Essays in Canadian*

Educational History (Calgary: Detselig, 1986), 305-23. More revealing of events from the perspective of proponents within the private schools are "FISA: Working against all the odds," *B.C. Catholic*, 18 September 1977, 3 and the minutes of the Independent Schools Association of British Columbia, available in the British Columbia Archives and Records Service [BCARS].

13. FISA Memo, 4 September 1987; *Sun*, 25 June and 5 September 1987; and FISA, "Commentary on the Independent School Act, 16 October 1989, 2. The 1989 legislation continued these provisions.

14. Anthony Brummet, 4 July 1989, in Legislative Assembly, *Debates*, vol. 14, no. 23, 8120.

15. For examples, see Ministry of Education, "News Release," 22 June 1987, and FISA, Monday Bulletin, 1 February and 13 June 1988.

16. More specifically, home-schooling families were required to register with a local public or non-public school of their choice or with the Ministry of Education's correspondence division. In exchange for providing access to evaluation and assessment services and loan of educational materials, the school receives for each home schooler registered one-quarter of its per-pupil provincial funding. Bill 67, School Act, 1989, part two, sections 12 13; Bill 68, Independent School Act, regulations, section 6; and Sun, 1 November 1989.

17. Ministry of Education, *Annual Report*, 1987/88, 3, amd School Act and Independent School Act, 1989, preamble.

18. Respectively, the Convent of the Sacred Heart and Marian Regional High School.

19. Data compiled from FISA's annual *Independent Schools Directory*.

20. Notably North Vancouver's Collingwood and Maple Ridge's Meadowridge, founded specifically to take rejects from Vancouver's St. George's School and Crofton House as well as students who might prefer an elite private school closer to home. *Sun*, 18 and 30 January, 9 June and 20 September 1984, 24 June 1985, and 9 June 1987, and *North Shore News*, 15 April 1984. Among the more eclectic newcomers have been Woburn Ladies College, established as a girls' finishing school, and Marlborough College, founded by a property developer "to create millionaires." *Sun*, 27 April and 3 and 14 September 1988.

21. This point underlies Elizabeth J. Thomas, "The Importance of School Culture in School Improvement: A Case Study" (M.Ed. paper, Department of Administrative, Adult, and Higher Education, University of British Columbia, 1988), a portrait of Crofton House from the perspective of a participant-observer.

22. For detail on these schools' operation, see Gordon C. Calvert, "Growth of Non-FISA Christian Schools in British Columbia: 1975-1985" (M.A. thesis, Department of Social and Educational Studies, UBC, 1987). For more general introductions with relevance to British Columbia, see Alan Peshkin, *God's Choice: The Total World of a Fundamentalist Christian School* (Chicago: University of Chicago Press, 1986), and Susan D. Rose, *Keeping Them Out of the Hands of Satan: Evangelical Schooling in America* (New York: Routledge, 1988).

23. This point is incisively elaborated in Harro Van Brummelen's comparative study of three Christian schools in a single Fraser Valley community. *Curriculum Implementation in Three Christian Schools* (Grand Rapids: Calvin College, 1989).

24. See Harro Van Brummelen, "Leadership without coercion," Canadian School Executive, January 1984, 14 15, and his *Telling the Next Generation*, esp. pp. 1, 253 54 and 265. Church membership is often a qualification for admission.

25. FISA, *Independent Schools Directory*, 1978/78, 1983/84, and 1990/91.

26. Visiting the different non-public schools in two small interior communities in the mid-1980s, I was repeatedly queried by school heads about the operation of other schools in the same community. It was clear they knew almost nothing about each other, their horizons extending

no further than maintaining day-to-day operations and satisfying parental expectations within the philosophical framework mandating their existence.

27. FISA's role is well summed up in its annual brochure.

28. *Vancouver Sun*, editorial of 6 October 1982, referring to E. Lester Bullen, who became provincial inspector of independent schools in 1980. Bullen's views are clear in his "Freedom of Choice in Education," *Education Canada* (Fall 1978): 24-30.

29. See Harold S. Drysdale, "The B.C. Independent School Debate: Cultural Diversity, Family Choice, and Privatization," *Policy Explorations* 2, 5 (n.d.), 1-4.

30. *Vancouver Sun*, 29 June 1987. Several days later (9 July) came the rebuttal from FISA's executive director. Similarly, an editorial by Walter Block in the weekly newsmagazine *British Columbia Report* in early 1991 characterized the province's private schools as "vastly superior" (25 February 1991, 4).

31. Advertisement for St. George's School, Vancouver, appearing in a wide variety of provincial daily and weekly newspapers and magazines, as well as in Toronto's *Globe and Mail* in January 1991.

32. *Vancouver Sun*, 25 March 1988. Due to continued enrolment growth, the budget of the province's 206 funded private schools had risen over the past year from $40.7 to $48 million, or by 18 percent, at the same time as total public school funding only increased from $1.73 to $1.85 billion, or by 7.4 percent.

33. Donald Erickson quoted in *Toronto Star*, 6 July 1982, as well as the other findings from the COFIS study. The tendency by scholars to generalize across non-public education is not limited to British Columbia, as evidenced by the aggregate approach of James Coleman and others in analyzing non-public education in the United States. James Coleman, Thomas Hoffer and Sally Kilgore, *Public and Private Schools* (Washington, DC: National Center for Education Statistics, 1981); James Coleman and Thomas Hoffer, *Public and Private High Schools: the Impact of Communities* (New York: Basic Books, 1987); Daniel C. Levy, *Private Education: Studies in Choice and Public Policy* (New York: Oxford University Press, 1986); and Neil E. Devins, ed., *Public Values, Private Schools* (London: Falmer, 1989), among other studies.

34. Ministry of Education, *Annual Report*, 1987-88, 49.

35. *Vancouver Sun*, 5 February 1988, ad for St. George's School, Vancouver.

36. Exemplary was Collingwood's rezoning application, detailed in the *Vancouver Sun* [hereafter *Sun*] through May and June 1988. The press can also compliment schools, as in its recognition of the efforts by Vancouver's Sikh school to rectify health and other problems. *Sun*, 19 February 1990.

37. *Sun*, 25 April and 2 and 12 May 1989.

38. *Ibid.*, 28 April and 1 May 1990. Other tax benefits include property tax relief for schools, and deductions allowable to individuals for charitable donations made to school building programs and to the religious group operating a school.

39. *Sun*, 27 April and 16 May 1990, and *Western News*, 26 April and 24 May 1990.

40. See, for instance, the charges made in the press in September 1990 against a funded Mormon school that it favored the children of prominent sect members, used excessive discipline, and had included in a grade 11 biology examination questions on the sect's polygamous marriage practices. *Sun*, 15 September 1990.

41. *Sun*, 13 and 25 August 1987 and 24 27 May, 1 3, 6 7, 9 11, 15 16, 21 25 and 29 June, 6 July and 10 August 1988.

42. With the 1989 legislation, teachers are encouraged to be certified by the province's College of Teachers. This point is underlined in FISA, "Commentary on the Independent School Act," issued 16 October 1989, 2.

43. Bill 68, Independent School Act, 1989, section 2.

44. Royal Commission on Education, *A Legacy for Learners*, 1988, and Commissioned Papers, vol. 1-7, 1988.

45. John Parry, headmaster of St. George's School, Vancouver, quoted in the *Sun*, 25 September 1989.

46. Brummet, 4 July 1989, in Legislative Assembly, *Debates*, vol. 14, no. 23, 8119.

47. Glenn Wall, in *Globe and Mail*, 8 July 1989.

48. On this issue, see Eamonn Callan, "Justice and Denominational Schooling," *Canadian Journal of Education* 13 (1988), 367-83.

49.. Brummet, 4 July 1989, in Legislative Assembly, *Debates*, vol. 14, no. 23, 8119.

50. Leo Hollaar, educational coordinator for the Society of Christian Schools (funded Christian schools) in British Columbia, quoted in *Globe and Mail*, 8 July 1989.

51. For example, FISA, *Monday Bulletin*, 7 November 1988, 2, and 5 December 1988, 2.

52. Anita Hagen, 4 July 1989, in Legislative Assembly, *Debates*, vol. 14, no. 23, 8121.

21

Royal Commission Retrospective

Jean Barman and Neil Sutherland*

Canadians have traditionally employed royal and other commissions of enquiry to investigate complex or critical situations. Since they usually involve systematic, informed, and public discussion, commissions on education provide us with focal points for a series of snapshots of education in British Columbia. Almost fifty official inquiries have examined aspects of education in the years since 1872, when the province's school act was put in place shortly after British Columbia entered Confederation. Most of these investigations had fairly narrow mandates ranging from the activities of specific school boards to the education of Doukhobor children to aspects of higher education.[1]

Eight of the educational inquiries have had broader terms of reference. If not royal commissions, they functioned very similarly and can be directly compared. Two were largely successful as measured by implementation of their recommendations, two were quite influential and three were relative failures. The verdict on the eighth, the *Royal Commission on Education*, or Sullivan Commission, which reported in 1988, is still coming in. As has been the case with this most recent educational commission, and its subsequent "Year 2000" followup material, the degree of success has related closely to several key factors, including the social, economic and political contexts out of which they emerged, the stature of their leadership, extent of public input, and how well they read the public mood.

Just as the 1988 Royal Commission will very likely go down in history under the name of its commissioner, Barry M. Sullivan, so past inquiries have become identified with the individuals most prominently associated with them. What was officially designated on its establishment in spring 1924 as a *Survey of the School System* is known generally as the Putman-Weir Commission after its two commissioners, J. Harold Putman and George M. Weir. A 1932 *Committee Appointed to Investigate the Finances of British Columbia* has become equated with its chairman, George Kidd, and a 1935 *Commission of School Finance in British Columbia* with its technical advisor, H.B. King. The 1944-45 *Commission of Inquiry into Educational Finance* is most often named after its commissioner, Maxwell Cameron. The *Royal Commission on Education* of 1958-60 is known by its chairman, S.N.F. Chant, as is the Bremer Commission of the 1970s. The sole exception is the 1967-68 non-governmental inquiry, more often identified with its sponsoring organization, the British Columbia Teachers Federation (BCTF), than with its chairman, D.B. MacKenzie.

Of the seven earlier investigations, only the Putman-Weir and Chant Commissions had mandates as broad as the Sullivan Commission. The purpose of the first was no more and no less than "to enquire into all matters pertaining to state education," appended to which was a list of nineteen specific issues to be addressed. The Putman-Weir Survey's terms of reference followed logically from the larger context out of which it emerged. Two sets of circumstances intertwined. In 1924 British Columbia was finally heading into good times following difficult economic circumstances. Mass immigration preceding the First World War more than tripled the number of children in school to about 60 000. Urban areas had witnessed a spate of school construction, bringing into existence many of the imposing brick structures still with us at the end of the twentieth century. The outbreak of hostilities then curtailed all unnecessary expenditure. In Vancouver, for instance, the bylaws necessary for capital expenditure were systematically rejected by voters not only through the war but during the subsequent economic downturn.[2] By 1923, when the recession finally began to lift, almost 100 000 children were in school across British Columbia in settings virtually unchanged from a decade previous. Overcrowding was the order of the day in urban areas while rural schooling remained little altered from its spartan nineteenth-century origins.

Also impinging on British Columbia was the whole cluster of notions that came together in Canada as the "new education." The "progressive" ideas of John Dewey urged attention to the ways that children actually learned as opposed to imparting knowledge in traditional "full pitcher-empty cup" fashion. The more general concept of scientific efficiency was also being applied to children, who were perceived as best fitted into appropriate adult niches through being tested and measured and then offered the sequence of courses deemed most suitable. The utility of the educational survey as a vehicle through which middle-class reformers could direct attention to the necessity for change was already well established across North America. To quote a contemporary observer of the Putman-Weir survey, "one of [its] chief benefits will be to give the quietus for years to come to the grumblers against our education system."[3]

Public pressure grew within British Columbia to review the state of public schooling. The first initiative is generally conceded to have been taken by the recently-established voluntary organization for teachers known as the British Columbia Teachers' Federation at its 1922 convention. Over the next two years a wide variety of groups from business to organized labour pressed for an inquiry, although not necessarily with the same goals in mind. Despite the economy's upturn, by the spring of 1924 the Liberal government, originally elected in 1916, was running out of steam. Faced with growing political dissension combined with a continuing mandate for social reform, Premier John Oliver realized the utility of turning over to an external commission what had become a difficult issue. At the same time, the government largely predetermined the commission's outcome by opting for credentialled middle-class reformers as opposed to, for instance, representatives of provincial pressure groups. The two commissioners possessed doctorates in pedagogy and were already publicly acknowledged to be in the reform camp. J.H. Putman was senior inspector of schools for the city of Ottawa and a leader in the child study movement. G. M. Weir had been principal of the Saskatoon normal school until his recent appointment as the first Professor of Education at the University of British Columbia (UBC), the new position itself a mark of the growing importance of issues dealing with schooling.

The Putman-Weir Commission, which has been described by a leading educational historian as "the most thorough examination of any school system in Canada" to that time, adopted the two-fold process common to most wide-ranging commissions of the day.[4] Under their terms of appointment, Putman and Weir were authorized to employ technically trained experts, the most notable of whom was probably Professor Peter Sandiford of the University of Toronto, an international expert in educational psychology who undertook a massive testing program of British Columbia students. As well, the two commissioners travelled extensively around the province with both big-city and local newspapers closely following their itinerary. In the course of almost 16 000 kilometres, they held more than 200 hearings and visited over 150 individual schools. While the immediate consequence was a necessary increase in the commission's time frame and budget, the more significant result was that no geographical or interest group could argue that it had been excluded from the process. All who so chose had the opportunity to participate.

Putman and Weir's recommendations should have surprised no one. The economy could afford change and the commissioners were committed to change in the direction being taken across North America: the individual child was to be kept in school longer so as to play a more useful role in the larger society. This is not to say that all the briefs or the whole population supported such a position. Moreover, whatever consensus did emerge about childhood and education at this time, it worked itself out in inequitable ways in the lives of those who did not belong to the white racial majority.[5]

Within the majority population, Putman and Weir "scientifically" managed the various groupings, labelling one minority "reactionary" or "conservative," another "progressive" or "radical." This left about half to be termed "moderate," which direction the report then took.[6] The emphasis was on greater sorting of children by ability into distinctive programs offering more curriculum diversity with less attention to standardized government exams. The report proposed urban re-organization of grades from an 8-3 (8 elementary and 3 high school) to a 6-3-3 sequence with the aim of keeping all children in school through nine grades, at the end of which they would either be prepared for the work force or continue in a specialized senior high school. All of this would take money. As a more equitable alternative to the existing system of property taxation for schools, Putman and Weir proposed a universal income tax for education and greater ministerial authority to distribute moneys. Overall, Putman and Weir reaffirmed the urban, Lower Mainland and southern Vancouver Island perspective on schools and schooling.

There were, however, other British Columbias. One consisted of a social and economic elite that established its own class-based private schools.[7] Another, more important British Columbia consisted of its hinterland, that vast area of the province that lay outside of the Lower Mainland and southern Vancouver Island. In each, notions promulgated through the Putman-Weir Report interacted with local conditions.[8] Hinterland British Columbians in particular would have to wait until after the Second World War for their very real educational concerns to be met.

It has been generally accepted by educational historians such as F. Henry Johnson that the Putman-Weir recommendations played a major role – if not *the* major role – in shaping the British Columbia school system until mid-century. Implementation did not come immediately, nor was the report unanimously supported. Not unexpectedly, Vancouver and its adjacent middle-class suburb of Point Grey led the way to establishment of junior high schools for grades 7-9. Even then, significant objections were raised by the business community with its traditional cry of why tax us for other people's children? Rapid enaction at both the school board and bylaw levels was due in good part to the breadth of joint support ranging from the University Women's Club to the Vancouver Trades and Labor Council.

The widespread support which existed both in Vancouver and about the province could not withstand, first, the cost cutting measures of the new Conservative government that came to power in 1928 under Simon Fraser Tolmie and then the depression, which not only curtailed expenditures but, perhaps more importantly, turned attention to more immediate survival priorities. However, the Putman-Weir recommendations got a second wind when Weir became Liberal MLA for Point Grey in 1933 to be immediately named Minister of Education, a position he held until 1941, and again between 1945 and his death in 1947. Weir's personal dynamism assisted implementation of much of the report, including extensive curricular revision.

Weir's ability to realize the moderate recommendations of the Putman–Weir Commission was facilitated by two intervening inquiries whose extremism enhanced the earlier report's acceptability. Just as the Putman-Weir Commission was a creature of good times, so the first of these, the Kidd Committee, was a direct response to the depression and perhaps indirectly to the Vancouver business community's dissatisfaction with levels of educational expenditure in the second half of the 1920s. The depression hit Vancouver particularly hard, economic adversity being compounded by prairie transients hoping at least to keep warm while trying not to starve to death. Unable to maintain control and fearful of losing the next election, the Conservative government acceded to demands by leading business groups, centred in Vancouver, to appoint a committee to find financial solutions. A hint of a political tradeoff existed in the business groups' declared willingness to back politically whoever supported their proposals.

Although the Kidd Committee's mandate was "to investigate the finances of British Columbia" generally, its recommendations had special impact for education.[9] The pressure on the government to set up the inquiry extended to its membership, which comprised five leading business figures under the chairmanship of the past head of the private B.C. Electric Railway Company, George Kidd. To the extent that the committee was guided by larger principles, it was the conviction that application of business principles would lead to more effective governance. External influences were apparently limited to the 1931 May Commission in England which had recommended major economic retrenchment centering on massive educational cutbacks. The appeal of such a proposal is hardly surprising given that at least four of the five committee members were not personally committed to the public system as evidenced by their offspring's private education or their own participation on governing boards of elite private schools.

Just as the Putman-Weir recommendations reflected that commission's membership, so did those of the Kidd Committee, except that they went much further than anyone anticipated. The report proposed a balanced budget without increased taxation through drastic cutbacks in a number of areas including the civil service, size of the provincial legislature, capital expenditures, and highway construction – but particularly in education. As well as closing the province's sole university, UBC, the Kidd Committee urged that free schooling be limited to age fourteen. Both recommendations were premised on the assumption that those whose families could afford to pay for their schooling were also those who should in any case assume positions of leadership within the society.

While all the recommendations met with vigorous opposition, the education proposals were among the most hotly debated. Even business people were divided. Very importantly, as David Jones and Tim Dunn have demonstrated in their analysis of the Kidd recommendations, "tremendous popular antagonism" was buttressed by an outspoken academic community which perceived itself under direct attack. UBC Professor Henry Angus, who had served as an advisor to the Putman-Weir Commission, labelled the Kidd Report a "fascist" document. Angus added that for the report to be legitimate it would have had to be undertaken by a more broadly based group as opposed to one "which represented employers but not labour, rich but not poor, men but not women."[10] In the end the Kidd Report may have had exactly the opposite function intended. By further tarnishing Tolmie's government, it helped Duff Pattullo's Liberals gain power and so gave the Putman-Weir proposals their second chance at implementation.

Weir's appointment as education minister also set the scene for the King Commission. However much Kidd's recommendations might have been discredited, school finance remained, to quote F. Henry Johnson, a "very hot potato."[11] Although the largest item in the provincial budget, education was still no more equitably funded than had been the case a decade and more previous. Rural school districts, which very often lacked an adequate property base, were going bankrupt and simply handing over their affairs to official trustees. The depression had greatly exacerbated their problems. The government's not unexpected response was to turn the matter over to a commission that was especially mandated to survey educational financing.[12]

The commission established in June 1934 consisted officially of Weir as Minister of Education and John Hart as Minister of Finance, along with the principal of one of Vancouver's new junior high schools, H.B. King, who was appointed technical advisor. Assisting the commission was a thirty-member committee representing public organizations concerned with education and headed by BCTF general secretary Henry Charlesworth. That large committee's findings were then to be interpreted for the commission by a five-member revision committee. It is, however, generally concluded that process was subordinated to King's powerful personality and controlling position. The revision committee's report was relegated to a thirteen-page appendix of the final document whose 230 pages of text were written by King himself.

In its own way, the King Report was as dramatic as its predecessor. Its recommendations centred on achieving financial efficiency through centralization. Costs of education were to be met directly by the provincial government. British Columbia's over 800 school districts were to be administratively centralized with local boards eliminated so as to effect additional economies. Just as the British Columbia public could not accept the reactionary direction of the Kidd recommendations, so it spoke out against the revolutionary thrust of King's proposals. While the opposition of some groups, such as the BC School Trustees Association and rural MLAs, was to be expected, a more general feeling emerged that the King Report was essentially anti-democratic in its elimination of local control in the name of efficiency. The government's ability to ignore the report – which it did – was, of course, facilitated by the Putman-Weir recommendations being on hand as an agenda for action. Indeed, they were quickly transformed into 2 700 pages of detailed curriculum covering all the twelve grades.[13]

The emphasis during the 1930s on curricular revision left unresolved the thorny matter of school finance and related issue of rural education. While the number of districts slowly declined to below 700 through consolidation of schools in the Peace River, Okanagan, Fraser Valley and greater Nanaimo areas, disparities between urban and rural British Columbia remained overwhelming in terms of physical conditions and overall quality. Rural areas simply could not afford more. Even the argument for local control lost its impact as more and more districts succumbed to official trusteeships. Then came the Second World War, which put educational matters on hold, but at the same time helped create material conditions conducive to mass school consolidation in the form of better physical infrastructure across the province.[14] As well, the principle of school consolidation, first introduced in Canada early in the century, was gaining favor not only in Ontario but closer to home in Alberta.

By late 1944 wartime conditions had improved the financial situation sufficiently for John Hart's Coalition government to counter growing dissatisfaction over educational conditions, spearheaded by the BCTF, by appointing a one-man commission "to inquire into the existing distribution of powers and responsibilities between the Provincial Government and the school districts and to appraise the present fiscal position of the school districts in British Columbia."[15] The commissioner was Maxwell Cameron, UBC Professor of Education who through his experience as a teacher was personally acquainted with conditions in rural British Columbia. Like Putman and Weir, Cameron was a known quantity who had already authored a study on school finance in Ontario and spoken out publicly in favor of provincial equalization grants to local authorities. Once again the government knew in advance what it was going to get. Cameron both toured the province and encouraged briefs, holding twenty-seven hearings and receiving seventy-five briefs. The public process built local support for consolidation. In an atmosphere of optimism about the new, post-war world, parents increasingly saw modern schooling as central to the future in terms of their own youngsters, wherever in the province they might live.

Sports day has been a regular and very popular feature in British Columbia Schools througout their history. (Vancouver Public Library, 68953)

While the Cameron Report was, like its two immediate predecessors, principally concerned with controlling the cost of education, its emphasis was not on economy per se or on centralization as an end in itself but rather on systematization of costs through marginal sacrifice of local control. Cameron urged the province's division into seventy-four locally–controlled school districts, so far as possible reflecting existing geographical, social and economic units. While localities should be consulted, their approval was not requisite to implementation. Also recommended was a system of finance buttressing local property taxation with the provincial assistance necessary for equitable standards of schooling across British Columbia. Responding to largely favorable public opinion, the government promised that if re-elected in October 1945 immediate and complete implementation would follow. It was and it did. The seventy-five school districts with us today essentially came into existence. The financial changes equalizing the costs of education necessitated over a hundred amendments to the province's public school act. For the first time, all British Columbia public-school pupils and teachers were brought within a single system characterized by graded classrooms, centralized curriculum, and hierarchical and patriarchal order. The Cameron Report was an exemplar as to how a government commission could be an effective instrument to consolidate an educational consensus and then expeditiously implement recommendations flowing from that consensus.

In the years following the Second World War, the "new education" appeared triumphant in British Columbia. The curricular revisions of the 1930s made progressivism the policy of the provincial educational system. In turn, the consolidations that grew out of the implementation of the Cameron Report made it possible for progressive practices to spread from the major cities to all areas of the province.[16] Nonetheless, in the 1950s socially-conservative Canadians began to express strong concerns about the malign influence of American progressivism on their schools. Critics obtained considerable ammunition for their attack from Hilda Neatby's widely-read *So Little for the Mind: An Indictment of Canadian Education.*[17] A University of Saskatchewan history professor, Neatby had been a member of the federal *Royal Commission on the Arts, Letters, and Sciences* (Massey Commission). Using as her basis a careful reading of "publications of various Departments of Education, courses of study, bulletins, handbooks, reading lists, and other material intended for the direction and information of school boards and teachers," Neatby telegraphed her conclusions through her title. She demanded that Canadian schools return to a tradition that would "convey to all, in so far as they are capable of receiving it, the intellectual, cultural, and moral training which represents the best in a long and honourable tradition of Western civilization."[18]

In 1957 the Soviet Union's world-circling Sputnik supposedly demonstrated the failure of American science, and especially the teaching of science in American schools. Since Canadian curricular rhetoric was so similar to its neighbor to the south, its science and other teaching shared in this condemnation. Clearly that part of the twentieth century consensus on childhood that dealt with their appropriate schooling had collapsed. In 1959 and 1960 alone, no less than half of the ten Canadian provinces – Manitoba, Saskatchewan, Alberta, Prince Edward Island, and British Columbia – had commissions that reported on elementary and secondary education in their provinces. British Columbia's Royal Commission on Education was one of this number. S.N.F. Chant, Dean of Arts and Science at UBC, was a psychologist who had at one time conducted child study research at the University of Toronto with its famous Dr. W.E. Blatz. His fellow commissioners were John E. Liersch, formerly Head of the Forestry Department at UBC and now Executive Vice President of the Powell River Company, and Riley Paul Walrod, General Manager of British Columbia Tree Fruits Limited. Academic expertise was partnered by members of the business community.

Chant and his colleagues conducted an extensive investigation. The commission initiated its own research, held public hearings throughout the province, made 116 school visits, examined a wide range of educational literature and received 366 briefs, some of which were very extensive. Briefs from long-settled parts of British Columbia concerned themselves with educational theory and practice. Those from fast-growing areas of the hinterland emphasized the need for more school buildings and the problems posed by a severe shortage of teachers. In keeping with the temper of the time the Chant Report was a conservative document. While the critic who said that the report "exuded an air of Dustbin and oiled floors" perhaps exaggerated its backward-looking qualities, the Commission did recommend that "the primary or general aim of the educational system of British Columbia should be that of promoting the intellectual development of the pupils."[19]

While the provincial government moved quickly to carry out many of the recommendations of the Chant Commission, its long-term effects on the educational system of British Columbia were very different from those intended by the commissioners. Using the Chant Report as their rationale, a host of curricular reformers quickly began to dismember what was still very much an integrated, hierarchical organization characterized by formalism in teaching as well as other aspects of educational administration. Initially, reforms inspired by the American psychologist Jerome Bruner had the greatest influence on curricular change in the province.[20] Academics and teachers looked for the "structures" inherent in the disciplines and for ways by which pupils could be brought to discover them. Much of the revised provincial curricula of the mid and late 1960s were characterized by their Brunerian quality. Just as the province began to put its new, academic-centred curricula into place, a second wave of change, characterized as neo-progressivism, became highly popular among many teachers and pupils in British Columbia. Neo–progressivism was in part a reaction to the heavily academic quality of the "structural" curriculum and in part a reflection of the social excitement and experimentation that came to characterize the late 1960s in many parts of the Western world.

Together, discovery-based curricula and neo-progressivism brought about the fragmentation of what had once been a highly prescriptive provincial curriculum. School districts, schools, and even individual teachers embarked on a host of innovations. Some of these new curricula were carefully crafted efforts that in some way combined theory and practice, while others reflected personal and sometimes highly idiosyncratic beliefs about teaching and learning.

The next major investigation of education in the province was appropriately conducted, not by an official agency, but by the British Columbia Teachers Federation. The BCTF's Commission on Education chaired by D.B. MacKenzie, a retired Assistant Superintendant of Vancouver schools, was made up entirely of professional educators, reflecting the growing belief amongst teachers that their profession, like those of doctors and lawyers, should have exclusive control over the practices that they carried out.[21] Like its predecessors, the BCTF Commission read widely in the educational literature, talked to educational experts, students and teachers, and considered the 266 briefs submitted to it. The commission's report in a sense legitimated the profusion of curricular and other changes characterizing British Columbia's education. Though not nearly as extensive as the report of the Hall-Dennis Commission in Ontario at about the same time, it was very much in the Hall-Dennis tradition. "We hope," concluded the Commissioners, "that our recommendations will free teachers from . . . inhibiting factors. . . . We expect that teachers and principals, in consultation with others concerned, will then change the curriculum to meet the needs of children. In other words it will become possible for principals and teachers to solve their own curriculum problems."[22] The commission listed the factors that it found inhibiting and this list included external examinations, prescribed textbooks, supervisory personnel, some administrative forms and procedures, and teachers' hesitation to depart from subject content with which they felt secure.

The general dissatisfaction of the 1950s and the cultural diversity of the 1960s, represented in British Columbia education by the Chant and BCTF commissions, had real effects on classroom practice. Elementary classrooms became more humane and effective centres of children's learning. An increasing band of better educated, better trained and thus more confident teachers began to make curricular and other choices as to how they would conduct the learning in their own classrooms. In this endeavor they were greatly assisted by a gradual decline in class size which enabled them to see their charges more clearly than had been possible for their predecessors. What they shared with the best of the formalist teachers of earlier years was a real sense of knowing where they were going and why they were heading in that particular direction. They differed from their predecessors in having a variety of theoretical positions and a variety of goals derived from them.[23]

At the secondary level change was even more complex. A wider, more humane curriculum permitted, even encouraged, a larger proportion of the population to complete secondary schooling and even go further. The Chant Commission had reported that just over one half of those who were together in grade 2 were still together in grade 12.[24] Able pupils who had previously been selected out of school by all sorts of factors stayed in school and came closer to realizing their full intellectual potential. Other youngsters stayed in school because there was little for them to do in the work force, and to meet the general rise in social expectations that had gradually moved a minimum education from passing the high-school "entrance" examination to completing junior high school to staying in school until age sixteen to graduating from high school. For a time, some teachers tried to entice the less able or the less willing students by employing a lot of trendy nonsense in their classrooms. In the long run probably the most important effect of the general increase in the secondary school population was the increasingly widespread prevalence of what the American literature calls "classroom bargains." "You give me order and attendance and I'll give you passing grades and no home work."[25]

In the 1970s education in British Columbia became pulled in two directions at the same time. On the one hand the social climate became more conservative with a concomitant demand on the part of parents that the school system reduce its diversity and increase its accountability. On the other, in 1972 British Columbians elected their first New Democratic government. Premier David Barrett appointed a former teacher, Eileen Dailly, as Minister of Education. While in opposition Dailly had been a vigorous critic of the system. Her background and her record perhaps led those who felt that, despite the changes of the 1960s, the educational system in the province was at best only half-transformed to develop unrealistic expectations of what the NDP in general and Dailly in particular could do. In any case, she recruited John Bremer to conduct no less than three tasks: as well as heading a commission on elementary and secondary education, he chaired a commission on post-secondary education and a committee on teacher education. An Englishman who described himself as an "egalitarian progressive," Bremer was most noted in North American for his creation of Parkway, a "schools without walls" project in Philadelphia.

These efforts were unsuccessful, and it is useful to speculate why such a major initiative eventually led nowhere. Certainly an increasingly conservative social climate heightened public skepticism regarding any more educational innovation. As Minister, Dailly seemed incapable of decisive action, and her tenure was more characterized by preparing for change than its implementation. Bremer's style heightened the suspicions of skeptics. He toured British Columbia trying to promote discussion on educational issues, sometimes even suggesting that the public schools might disappear. His style – that of a discussion leader, a provoker of debate, a "change agent" – irritated both the public and the educational communities.

Premier Barrett's frustration at what he perceived to be the joint inaction of Dailly and Bremer drew him to remark on television concerning the latter that "his programs are a bit of a flop . . . he's . . . a bit of a failure." Bremer's dismissal was followed by that of Dr. Stanley Knight, director of Dailly's department's Research Division, and five of his staff.[26] In the aftermath of this turmoil Dailly produced a White Paper on Education, the main thrust of which was the need for even more discussion.[27] Soon afterwards, in 1975, the NDP lost the election and Dr. Patrick McGeer succeeded her as Minister of Education. Eileen Dailly, however, passed one important legacy on to Dr. McGeer. In her White Paper she stated that "each student will be offered a core program, the intent of which will be to ensure the development of functional literacy."[28]

McGeer's tenure as Minister of Education opened an era of ever-increasing acrimony in the history of British Columbia education that critic Crawford Killan came to characterize as the "great school wars."[29] Both public and professionals were increasingly divided as to what knowledge was of most worth, and how the young should acquire it. All levels of government became concerned by what they saw as the escalating cost of education. Vigorously competing theories and practices pervaded literature, and each found its proponents and practitioners amongst teachers. How reading should be taught, for example, took on many of the characteristics of a theological debate: "I believe in ITA!" "I believe in phonics!" "I believe in whole language!" Teachers increasingly demanded greater control over school and classroom practice. What had been a non-denominational but basically Protestant system had been secularized, and those parents who believed that education must be rooted in religion extended greatly the number and range of private schools in the province.[30] Parents, teachers, local school boards, and the provincial government quarrelled with increasing bitterness over the financing of education. By 1987, essentially a generation after the Chant Commission, the time seem ripe for another major review of education.

The Social Credit government selected Barry M. Sullivan as sole commissioner. Again, the government likely had a broad sense what it was getting. A lawyer, and clearly a moderate in his views, Sullivan had already satisfactorily conducted one investigation for the Ministry of Education.[31] The terms of reference given Sullivan in this new enterprise emphasized that "education is a lifelong process . . . not limited to an institutional setting."[32] The government's objective was "a population well prepared to meet the rapidly changing challenges of everyday life in the 21st century." As had his predecessors, Sullivan commissioned studies and conducted hearings all over the province. There were 66 public hearings, 54 meetings with teachers, visits to 139 schools in 89 communities, and almost 2 350 written and oral submissions. In a new departure, Sullivan encouraged students to appear before him and had his staff conduct extensive interviews with a representative sample of young people.

"The more things change. . . ." Children hard at work in a primary classroom in the 1990s. (Courtesy of Emily Sutherland)

Sullivan's report, in fact mostly written by the Commission's professional staff, was less sharply focussed than some of its predecessors, at some points appearing to have a progressive agenda, at others a conservative one. The report recommended "that developmental criteria, rather than chronological age, be used in selecting the educational placement of children entering school" and that the primary level (Kindergarten-Grade 3) be ungraded so that children could advance at their own pace.[33] Sorting and grading were in general de-emphasized. 80 percent of instructional time in grades 1-10 was to be occupied by four curricular strands (humanities, fine arts, sciences, practical arts), the remainder by locally developed programs. At the end of Grade 10 students would be given an "official certificate of entitlement" to two more years of secondary schooling to be focussed on their particular career objectives and possibly including upwards to a year of work experience. If some recommendations presaged major shifts, others seemed only to consolidate familiar turf. The province's seventy-five school districts were not touched. There were no major changes in the way educational expenses were to be met. Provincial Grade 12 examinations, made compulsory again earlier in the decade, were to be extended to all subject areas. The report urged greater governmental control over children being home schooled or otherwise privately educated. Although not much addressed in terms of specific recommendations, the report's unifying theme – to the extent it had one – was the concept of "lifelong learning" as set out in the commission's mandate.

Lifelong learning did not capture the public imagination, and initial reaction to the Sullivan recommendations was muted, neither highly favorable nor unfavorable. Minister of Education Tony Brumett, a former teacher and school administrator, nonetheless pledged the government's support for the report. The ministry set up, under a "Year 2000" rubric, various groups both within its staff and amongst teachers and other interested groups to move Sullivan's recommendations into practical policies and practices. Brummet's commitment to the Year 2000 transformation of education was accepted by his New Democratic successors on their accession to provincial power at the beginning of the 1990s. The consequence was that, although very vigorous debates and revisions characterized the Year 2000 process, disagreements were remarkably free of the partisan political rhetoric that pervaded the 1970s and 1980s. In turn, the various manifestations of the Year 2000 proposals soon moved away from the more radical of the Sullivan recommendations. Twice-annual "dual entry" into kindergarten and the year at work quickly disappeared, for example.

Increasingly the Sullivan recommendations were overtaken by public opinion. Rising government costs and economic recession characterized the early 1990s across North America. A perception of growing violence in schools were interpreted by some as evidence that teachers and governments were not doing their jobs. On leaving school many young people found themselves unable to secure employment. Accountability, higher standards, curricular relevance and "back to the basics" became buzz words in the media and among a vocal portion of the general public. Traditional notions of schooling that had for a generation been viewed as "old-fashioned" once again found favor.

In British Columbia aspects of the Sullivan Report implemented through the Year 2000 initiatives came under hard scrutiny. A growing "back to the basics" movement found much to criticize in non-graded integrated primary classrooms. The supposed advantages of private schools encouraged some parents so to seek to refashion local public schools in their generally more conservative image. The NDP provincial government was forced to redraw its educational priorities. In 1994, in the interests of accountability and cost savings, it stripped local school boards of most of their financial independence by centralizing budgeting and, especially, by making salary bargaining for teachers a province-wide process. Although opposed by the BCTF, the teachers' response was, perhaps not unexpectedly, subdued. The new conservatism soon extended into the classroom. While not publicly disavowing Year 2000 or the Sullivan Report, Premier Michael Harcourt committed the Ministry of Education to putting greater emphasis on "the basics" and job-related curriculum, giving parents a set of standards against which to measure their children's performance and progress in school, providing detailed written report cards from kindergarten through grade 12, and accrediting elementary as well as high schools every six years with the results being made public. If fast approaching, Year 2000 was also receding from view.

Viewed as a group, British Columbia's eight major educational inquiries suggest some patterns worth noting. Several inter-related circumstances have correlated with probability of implementation. When the Putman-Weir, Cameron, Chant and BCTF commissions are compared to the Kidd, King and Bremer inquiries, factors critical to the former's success become apparent. Economic and social conditions were conducive to change. Both the public and the government supported the commissions' establishments. Individuals in charge were credentialled with expert status, and the process ensured broadly-based public input. Commissions' recommendations caught the popular imagination. In each case, as also with the Sullivan commission, British Columbians made known their support or disapproval for the eventual recommendations in such clear terms that the government was forced into action. Only in the case of the Chant Report was the professional educational establishment able to subvert the popular mandate, replacing the desire for a return to an old-fashioned school system with the latest in educational nostrums.

Overall, public opinion in British Columbia has played a major role in either legitimizing or discrediting educational inquiries. What most view as sensible suggestions are put into place. Those viewed as extremes tend to be ignored. Practice, if not theory, has had a strong tendency to revert to the mean. The gradual narrowing of the Year 2000 proposals growing out of the Sullivan Commission suggests that today, no less than in the past, the pendulum of public opinion cannot be ignored.

Notes

* We are grateful to the Social Sciences and Humanities Research Council of Canada for funding the Canadian Childhood History Project, under whose auspices an earlier version appearing in *Policy Perspectives* 3, 1 (Winter 1988): 6-16, was conceived and written.

1. Cary F. Goulson, *A Source Book of Royal Commissions and Other Major Governmental Inquiries in Canadian Education, 1787-1978* (Toronto: University of Toronto Press, 1981), esp. 294-338 on British Columbia.

2. See Jean Barman, "'Knowledge is Essential for Universal Progress but Fatal to Class Privilege': Working People and The Schools in Vancouver During The 1920s," *Labour/Le Travail* 22 (Fall 1988): 9-66.

3. A Vancouver municipal school inspector quoted in B. Anne Wood, *Idealism Transformed: The Making of a Progressive Educator* (Kingston: McGill-Queen's University Press, 1985), 151.

4. C.E. Phillips, *The Development of Education in Canada* (Toronto: Gage, 1957), 263.

5. In this volume Timothy Stanley's "White Supremacy" and Jean Barman's "Schooled for Inequality" [ch. 3] and "Separate and Unequal" [ch. 17] uncover the ideology that underlay both the discussion and Putman-Weir Report.

6. *Survey of the School System* (Victoria, 1925), 24-29.

7. In "Growing Up British" Jean Barman introduces us to the schooling of a privileged elite.

8. Jean Barman's article "Reflections" [ch. 16] shows the complex ways in which urban notions interacted with a particular community. J. Donald Wilson and Paul Stortz's "'May the Lord,'" [ch. 11] Thomas Fleming and Carolyn Smyley's "Diary of Mary Williams," (ch. 13) and Penelope Stephenson's "'Mrs Gibson looked'" [ch. 12] show the difficulties faced by teachers sent from British Columbia's urban centre to bring the message of civilization to the hinterland. Sutherland "'I can't recall'" [ch. 6] demonstrates how the lives of rural youngsters had a dynamic which was very remote from the ideas emanating from the centre.

9. *Report of the Committee Appointed by the Government to Investigate the Finances of British Columbia* (Victoria, 1932).

10. David C. Jones and Timothy A. Dunn, "'All of Us Common People' and Education in the Depression," *Canadian Journal of Education* 5, 4 (1980): 41-57. Rural British Columbia was also ignored. Although the Kidd commission grew out of and expressed urban concerns about the depression, the depression had more far-reaching effects on the lives of rural teachers. J. Donald Wilson's "'I am ready'" [ch. 14] shows what little real comfort came to them from Victoria.

11. F. Henry Johnson, *A History of Public Education in British Columbia* (Vancouver: UBC Publications Centre, 1964), 116.

12. H.B. King, *School Finance in British Columbia* (Victoria, 1935).

13. George S. Tomkins, *A Common Countenance: Stability and Change in the Canadian Curriculum* (Scarborough: Prentice-Hall, 1986), 143.

14. While the start of the Second World War brought most general discussion of education to a halt, the movement of people to the war industries of Vancouver and other cities put considerable strains on the local school system. Emilie Montgomery's "'The war was a very vivid part'" (ch. 8) details the war's effect on children and how youngsters entered into the war effort.

15. Maxwell A. Cameron, *Report of the Commission of Inquiry into Educational Finance* (Victoria, 1945), 3.

16. In fact, as Neil Sutherland's "'Triumph of Formalism'" [ch. 5] clearly shows, a wide gap existed between the goals expressed in curricular documents and classroom practices, which overall remained as formal in the 1950s as they had been in the 1920s.

17. Toronto: Clark Irwin, 1953.

18. Neatby, *So Little for the Mind*, 374 and 14.

19. *Report of the Royal Commission on Education* (Victoria, 1960), 3-10 and 17-18.

20. The Canadian and international context for these changes are laid out in Tomkins, *A Common Countenance.*

21. Commissioners were W.V. Allester, former president and then Director of Professional Development in the BCTF; Mrs. L. Hanney, Intermediate Supervisor in Burnaby; and R.J. Carter, Vice Principal, Point Grey Secondary School in Vancouver.

22. *Involvement: The Key to Better Schools: The Report of the Commission on Education of the British Columbia Teachers' Federation* (n.p.).

23. In "From Normal School to the University" [ch. 15], Nancy Sheehan and J. Donald Wilson show how the gradual move towards a truly professional education of teachers in turn played a major role in transforming the system.

24. *Report of the Royal Commission*, 52.

25. Michael W. Sedlak et al, *Selling the Moderates Short: Classroom Bargains and Academic Reform in the American High School* (New York: Teachers College Press, 1986).

26. Loren J. Kavic and Garry Brian Nixon, *The 1200 Days: A Shattered Dream: Dave Barrett and the NDP in B.C. 1972-75* (Coquitlam: Kaen Publishers, 1978), 164-75. Barrett later made a public apology for his comments. Bremer eventually made his "report" on British Columbia in John Bremer, *A Matrix for Modern Education* (Toronto: McClelland and Stewart, 1975), chapter 15.

27. Eileen Dailly, "The Public School System: Directions for Change," tabled in the Legislature, 20 March 1974.

28. Dailly, 3.

29. Crawford Killiam, *School Wars: The Assault on B.C. Education* (Vancouver: New Star, 1985).

30. See Barman, "Deprivatizing" [ch. 20].

31. *A Legacy for Learners: The Report of the Royal Commission on Education* (Victoria, 1988).

32. Terms of reference set out in Order 446 of the Lieutenant Governor in Council, 14 March 1987, reproduced in *A Legacy for Learners*, 227.

33. *A Legacy for Learners*, 93.